SOCIAL SCIENCE UNDER DEBATE

MARIO BUNGE

Social Science under Debate:
A Philosophical Perspective

UNIVERSITY OF TORONTO PRESS
Toronto Buffalo London

© University of Toronto Press Incorporated 1998
Toronto Buffalo London
Printed in Canada

ISBN 0-8020-4298-8

Printed on acid-free paper

Canadian Cataloguing in Publication Data

Bunge, Mario, 1919–
    Social science under debate : a philosophical perspective

    ISBN 0-8020-4298-8

    1. Social sciences – Research.   I. Title.

    H62.B85 1998   300′.7′2   C97-931552-2

85.00

University of Toronto Press acknowledges the financial assistance to its publishing
program of the Canada Council for the Arts and the Ontario Arts Council.

Contents

Preface

This book deals with controversies that divide the students of society, social-policy makers, and philosophers of social studies. These scholars are indeed split over philosophical questions about the nature of society and the best way of getting to know it, as well as on the fairest way of solving social issues. Thus, for instance, if people are assumed to follow exclusively the laws of nature, then we may discover the social order but it is not for us to question it, let alone try and alter it. Again, if social facts cannot be understood the way any other facts can, namely by observation, conjecture, and argument, then the study of society can never become scientific and thus be a reliable guide to social policy and political action. And if rationality is nothing but self-interest, and the only serious social theories are of the rational-choice kind, then, given the social traps that self-seeking behaviour can lead us to, we must give up all hope of conducting our affairs in the light of social studies, or perhaps even in the light of reason. Are we really so badly off, or is there a way out?

A second telling example, among many, is this. Whom shall we follow in studying social facts: Marx, who held that we must always start from the social whole, for it shapes the individual in every particular, or Weber, who preached that to explain a social fact amounts to "interpreting" individual actions? Or neither, if only because Marx's holism explains conformism but not originality, initiative, or rebellion, whereas Weber's individualism overlooks the fact that every individual is born into a pre-existing social system? (Incidentally, this example shows that, if these scholars had been consistent, the former ought to have been a conservative and the latter a revolutionary.) Is there an alternative to both holism and individualism, that is, an approach that views individual action in a social context, and society as a system of individuals who, through their interactions, modify themselves and build, maintain, reform, or dismantle social systems such as families, schools, orchestras, soccer teams, car pools, clubs, business firms, governments, and entire nations?

These and many other questions that worry and divide the students of society are philosophical. Once this point is granted, it follows that philosophical assumption, analysis, and argument are relevant to important problems in social science and social policy. This, then, is a practical justification for doing philosophy of social science and technology: namely that, for better or for worse, philosophical ideas precede, accompany, and follow any deep social study and any radical social policy. Social science and sociotechnology certainly differ from from philosophy, but they cannot get rid of it. Philosophy can be repressed but not suppressed. Like Victorian children, philosophers are seldom seen and never heard in social studies, but they are always around – for better or for worse.

The curious and industrious philosopher is a jack of all conceptual trades. As such, he is expected to trespass interdisciplinary fences. (Incidentally, the present author is guilty of multiple trespassing: he is a physicist turned philosopher, and has made incursions into sociology, science policy, psychology, and biology.) The philosopher sharpens tools, digs up tacit assumptions, and criticizes fuzzy concepts; he spots, repairs, or discards invalid reasonings; he examines frameworks and questions old answers; he asks unsettling questions and patrols the borders of science. His is a necessary, fun, but thankless task that must be carried out in the interests of clarity, cogency, and sound (i.e., constructive) scepticism, as well as to protect the honest search for objective truth and its fair utilization.

This book is not an impartial description and dispassionate analysis of the current state of the social sciences and sociotechnologies. Far from gloating over accomplishments, it focuses on flaws likely to be rooted in either mistaken philosophies or ideological dogmas. This admittedly unbalanced selection should not give the impression that contemporary social science is all warts. I do believe that social science has been advancing and can continue to do so – provided it resists the bulldozing of "postmodern" irrationalism. But I have chosen to highlight some of the philosophical obstacles to further advancement. Other scholars are likely to note flaws of a different kind, such as neglect of theories of social changes and mechanisms (e.g., Sørensen 1997) and insufficient longitudinal data to test those theories (e.g., Smith and Boyle Torrey 1996).

Most scientists, being eager to get on with their work, are impatient with controversy and philosophy. But what if one has unwittingly adopted a wrong approach to the problem at hand? And what if such an approach has been prompted by an unexamined philosophy that hinders the exploration of reality – e.g., by holding that reality is a construction, or else self-existent but impregnable to the scientific method? In such cases philosophical debate is indispensable, not only to unearth and examine presuppositions, clarify ideas, and check inferences, but to make research at all possible.

I take a definite philosophical and methodological stand: I argue for objective and relevant fact-finding, rigorous theorizing, and empirical testing, as well as for morally sensitive and socially responsible policy design. Consequently, I argue against irrationalism and subjectivism—in particular constructivism-relativism – as well as against opaque rhetoric passed off as theory and partisan sloganeering passed off as serious social-policy making. (This stance distinguishes my critique from the "radical," "rhetoric," "feminist" and "environmentalist" attacks upon social science, all of which are obscurantist and counterproductive.) In particular, I argue that, if the burning social issues of our time are to be tackled effectively and fairly, they must be approached in the light of serious social research together with moral principles combining self-interest with the public good. There can be no effective and lasting social reform without serious social research. Rational action is guided by knowledge.

I also argue that social-science research ought to be guided by lucid and realistic philosophical ideas. Among these is the hypothesis that problems, whether conceptual or practical, are not isolable but come in packages, and must be addressed as such if they are to be solved. The reason for this is that the world itself, in particular the social world, is a system rather than an aggregate of mutually independent items – but, of course, it is a changeable system not a rigid one, and moreover it is analysable. To be sure, unlike basic social science, social technology is seldom if ever impartial: it is bound to side with or against certain interests. However, to be effective it must be just as objective as basic social science. Again, this distinction between objectivity (a philosophical category) and impartiality (a moral and political category) is of a philosophical nature.

Much of the following will be critical of certain fads in contemporary social and philosophical studies. This should come as no surprise to those who believe that there is some truth in the statement that, whereas modern society would have been impossible without natural science and engineering, it would have made little difference if social science had never been born (Lindblom 1990, 136). Nor should my criticisms of certain philosophical fashions shock those who fear that philosophy is passing through a slump, to the point that some philosophers have prematurely announced its death.

Prominent among the targets of my criticisms are certain radical views: holism (or collectivism) and individualism (or atomism); spiritualism (idealism) and physicalism; irrationalism and hyperrationalism (apriorism); positivism and obscurantist anti-positivism; social constructivism and relativism; zealotry and insensitivity to the moral aspect of social issues; bogus rigour and the cult of data; grand theory and ideology; moralizing ignorant of social science; and the compartmentalization of social studies. Spare the rod and spoil the tender-minded.

However, my criticisms should not be mistaken for the rash views that social studies are necessarily nonscientific and that all philosophy is rubbish. Even less for the paralysing dogmas that there can be no science of society because man is erratic and mysterious, or because beliefs and intentions cannot be studied objectively, or because reality is a construction, whence objective cross-cultural truth would be unattainable. These objections on the part of the literary or "humanistic" (armchair) camp, particularly in its "postmodern" phase, will be met by unearthing and refuting their philosophical presuppositions, which go back to Vico, Kant, the German Romantics (mainly Hegel), Nietzsche, Dilthey, and Husserl. They can easily be falsified by just listing some of the genuine accomplishments of social science scattered throughout the scholarly literature.

My own view is that the study of society, though still backward, can and should become fully scientific, particularly if it is to guide effective and responsible social action. This does not entail that human society is a chunk of nature, whence social scientists should ape in all respects their counterparts in the natural sciences. On the contrary, I will stress that human beings are highly artefactual; that their feelings and thoughts guide their social behaviour; that social conventions operate alongside laws; and that all social systems have non-natural properties. (Recall Maurice Ravel's *bon mot*: "I'm artificial by nature.") Since different research objects call for different hypotheses and research techniques, social science is not a part of natural science even when it utilizes some of it.

Still, no matter how different, electrons and societies are concrete albeit invisible things. And human brains, however different from one another, perceive and reason in similar ways, and are able to communicate their thoughts and discuss them – at least when minimally clear. Therefore, all of the sciences, whether natural, social, or biosocial, share a common nucleus: logic, mathematics, and certain philosophical hypotheses about the nature of the world and its scientific study. This common core allows one to speak of science in general, in contrast to ideology or art, as well as to discuss it rationally.

Similarly all the technologies, from civil engineering and biotechnology to management science and jurisprudence, share two features: they are expected to be rational and to utilize the best available relevant basic science; and they are tools that help alter reality in an efficient (though not necessarily beneficent) way. However, the social technologies will be examined in part B of this book. Part A is devoted to the social (and socionatural) sciences, semisciences, and pseudosciences. And most of the gory technicalities, whether genuine or bogus, have been shunted to the appendices.

The general philosophical concepts occurring in social research, such as those of system, process, emergence, theory, explanation, testability, and truth, are not treated in any detail in this volume. The same holds for the philosophical problematics common to all of the social sciences, such as the holism-individualism-systemism and the rationalism-empiricism-realism trilemmas. All that and more is discussed in my *Finding Philosophy in Social Science* (Bunge 1996a).

Finally, a word of encouragement to the prospective reader who may be put off by the large number of disciplines examined in this book. This diversity has turned out to be manageable for being unified with the help of only a dozen master ideas. These are the following. 1/ The real world contains only concrete (material) things: ideas, beliefs, intentions, decisions, and the like are brain processes. 2/ Every thing is in flux in some respect or other. 3/ All things and their changes fit patterns – natural or made. 4/ Concrete things come in five basic kinds: physical, chemical, biological, social, and technical. 5/ Every thing is either a system (a bundle of things held together by bonds of some kind) or a component of one. 6/ Some of the properties of a system are emergent: they originate along with the system and disappear if and when it breaks down. 7/ Although human beings are composed of physical and chemical parts, they have irreducibly biological and social properties. 8/ Every society is a supersystem composed of subsystems with properties that their individual components lack. 9/ Reality can be known, albeit partially and gradually, through experience and ideation. 10/ Scientific research yields the deepest, most general, and most accurate knowledge – yet seldom definitive. 11/ The most responsible and effective actions and social policies and plans are designed in the light of scientific findings. 12/ Science and technology advance not only through theoretical and empirical research but also through the elucidation, analysis, and systematization of their own presuppositions, generic constructs, and methods – a typically philosophical task. *Nec timeas, recte philosophando.*

Unless stated otherwise, all translations are my own. And masculine pronouns are used throughout this book to denote all sexes. Antisexism, which I endorse, should be a matter of ideas and deeds not just words.

Acknowledgments

I thank the Social Sciences and Humanities Research Council of Canada for supporting some of my research over many years. McGill University, my academic home for three decades, has granted me the academic freedom required for intellectual exploration and heterodoxy. And the Istituto di Economia of the Università degli Studi di Genova hosted me during a decisive phase in the writing of this book.

I am grateful to Joseph Agassi, Amedeo Amato, Alfons Barceló, Raymond Boudon, Charles Tilly, Camilo Dagum, Ernesto Garzón Valdés, Ernest Gellner, John A. Hall, Erwin Klein, Martin Mahner, Edmond Malinvaud, Andreas Pickel, Anatol Rapoport, Bruce G. Trigger, Axel van den Berg, and Ron Weber for their valuable comments on some parts of this book. I am equally grateful to my former students David Blitz, Moish Bronet, Marta C. Bunge, Martin Cloutier, Mike Dillinger, Martha Foschi, Andrés J. Kálnay, Joseph and Michael Kary, Jean-Pierre Marquis, Karim Rajani, and Dan A. Seni for many a stimulating discussion.

Richard N. Adams, Sidney Afriat, Evandro Agazzi, Hans Albert, Maurice Allais, Carlos Alurralde, Athanasios (Tom) Asimakopulos, Luca Beltrametti, Dalbir Bindra, Alberto Birlotta, Judith Buber Agassi, James S. Coleman, A. Claudio Cuello, Alberto Cupani, Georg Dorn, Torcuato S. Di Tella, Tito Drago, Bernard Dubrovsky, José M. Ferrater Mora, Frank Forman, Johan Galtung, Lucía Gálvez-Tiscornia, Máximo García-Sucre, Gino Germani, Johann Götschl, Jacques Herman, Irving Louis Horowitz, A. Pablo Iannone, Ian C. Jarvie, Raymond Klibansky, Jim Lambek, Werner Leinfellner, Richard C. Lewontin, Larissa Lomnitz, Michael Mackey, Antonio Martino, Alex Michalos, Hortense Michaud-Lalanne, Pierre Moessinger, Bertrand Munier, Jorge Niosi, Lillian O'Connell, Mario H. Otero, Sebastián Ovejero Sagarzazu, José-Luis Pardos, Francisco Parra-Luna, Jean Piaget, Karl R. Popper, Raúl Prebisch,

Miguel A. Quintanilla, Nicholas Rescher, Hernán Rodríguez-Campoamor, Gerhard Rosegger, J.C. (Robin) Rowley, Jorge A. Sábato, Manuel Sadosky, Fernando Salmerón, Viktor Sarris, Gerald Seniuk, William R. Shea, Georg Siebeck, David Sobrevilla, Herbert Spengler, Richard Swedberg, Bartolomé Tiscornia, Laurent-Michel Vacher, Paul Weingartner, Herman Wold, and René Zayan have contributed over the years valuable information or criticism, encouragement or friendship, advice or support. Last, but not least, I am particularly indebted to Bob Merton for his sustained encouragement.

Several generations of curious and critical students have raised interesting queries and drawn my attention to pertinent publications. A multitude of readers scattered worldwide have supplied information, asked questions, and offered criticisms. Finally, a number of universities and learned societies in two dozen countries have given me the chance of talking to uncounted researchers and students, in many different fields, with whom I have exchanged information and problems, hopes and fears.

Last, but not least, I am grateful to Virgil D. Duff and Margaret Williams, of the University of Toronto Press, for having shepherded this book along the editorial labyrinth, as well as to John St James, for his wise copy-editing.

I dedicate this book to the memory of my father
Augusto Bunge (1877–1943)
physician, sociologist, writer, and parliamentarian. He kindled very early in life my interest in social issues, studies, policies, and movements, and taught me by example that reason and passion, research and action, as well as morals and politics, can go and always ought to go hand in hand.

SOCIAL SCIENCE UNDER DEBATE

PART A

Basic Social Science

Scientists are expected to explore the world in order to understand it. They ask, answer, and argue. They observe facts – natural, social, or mixed – and invent hypotheses to explain or forecast them. They classify and construct systems of hypotheses, that is, theories, of various degrees of depth and breadth. They check data and guesses to find out whether these hypotheses are at least roughly true. They invent techniques to collect, check, or process data. And they argue over projects and findings broad and narrow.

Scientific researchers are expected to abide by the scientific method, which boils down to the following sequence of steps: background knowledge → problem → solution candidate (hypothesis, experimental design, or technique) → test → evaluation of candidate → eventual revision of either solution candidate, checking the procedure, background knowledge, or even problem.

The checking of propositions consists in testing for both consistency and truth – which often proves to be only approximate. This test may be conceptual, empirical, or both. No item, except for conventions and mathematical formulas, is deemed to be exempt from empirical tests. Nor is any science without tests – or any science without search for or utilization of pattern either.

I submit that the above summary description holds for all sciences, regardless of differences in objects, special techniques, or degrees of advancement. It fits the social sciences, like sociology, as well as the biosocial ones like psychology, and the natural ones like biology. If a discipline does not employ the scientific method, or if it does not look for or employ regularities, it is either protoscientific, nonscientific, or pseudoscientific. Technology is different: it uses knowledge to design artefacts and plans that help alter reality (natural or social) rather than map it or understand it.

Science, which enjoyed an enormous prestige during the two centuries between the Industrial Revolution and about 1970, has become the target of attacks from left and right, and from outside and inside academia. Not only the popular counter-culture movement but also a number of academics are voicing nowadays plenty of grievances against science. For instance, it is claimed that science ignores subjective experience and does not seek understanding; that it is reductionist and positivist; that it is androcentric and anti-environmental; and that scientists are obsessed with gaining power, or else are mere tools of the powers that be. I shall examine these claims and shall find them unwarranted, whence the philosophies underlying them will be judged to be equally unjustified. I shall defend instead the scientific approach as the most successful of all the known strategies for getting to know and control the world, not least the social world. In other words, I shall unabashedly espouse the scientism inherent in the Enlightenment.

However, scientism should not be mistaken for either naturalism or positivism. Naturalism – in particular sociobiology – is inadequate to tackle social facts for four reasons. Social facts are made, social relations pass through the heads of people, we react to the world as we perceive it rather than to the world itself, and such perception is largely shaped by both personal experience and society. (For example, painful memories of inflation may induce exaggerated fear of inflation, which in turn may lead to recession.)

As for positivism, it too fails, for discarding mental life (although it is subject-centred) and for being theoretically shy. Positivism is empiricist, whereas I argue for a synthesis of empiricism and rationalism. Positivism is anti-metaphysical, whereas I claim that science cannot dispense with some metaphysics (or ontology) – of the intelligible and relevant kind, though. And positivism denies the difference between social science and natural science, whereas I stress it. However, if critical thinking, concern for empirical evidence, and love of the scientific approach be (mistakenly) deemed to be the trademarks of positivism, then I do not mind being branded a positivist. I have been called worse.

This volume tackles a number of methodological and philosophical controversies in social studies, such as the differences between these and the socio-technologies, the natural science / social science dichotomy, the lawfulness of social events, the role of rationality, the testability of social theories, the individualism-holism-systemism trilemma, the reliability of mainstream economics, the moral ingredient of socio-economic policies, and the theoretical and ideological vacuum left by the demise of Marxism-Leninism.

A controversy over a particular problem, datum, method, experimental design, or theory can be circumscribed and it can usually be settled without resorting to philosophical considerations or ideological controversies. Thus, at least in principle a datum can be checked, an experimental design can be examined and compared with rival procedures, and a theory can be evaluated in the light of the relevant information. Not so a controversy involving broad and fundamental issues, because these are born and discussed within or among philosophical or even ideological schools. This is the case with the debates over objectivity and subjectivity, lawfulness and disorder, explanation and *Verstehen* ("interpretation"), individualism and holism, spiritualism and materialism, intuitionism and pragmatism, rationalism and empiricism. These broad issues in the field of social studies are discussed in general terms elsewhere (Bunge 1996a). Here I will only discuss the particular form they acquire in the various special social and biosocial sciences and sociotechnologies.

I submit that the above-mentioned philosophico-scientific controversies, though conceptual, cannot be settled in an empirical void. If we want to know whether a given social view is true, we must subject it to a "reality check." Thus, in discussing mainstream economic theory we must check whether it is supported by the available empirical knowledge about real people and real business firms and markets. Whence a feature of this book that is unusual in philosophical works, namely, recourse to some empirical data when evaluating the truth claims of certain popular views.

Let us start by examining the commonalities and differences between the natural and the social, as well as their respective studies.

1

From Natural Science to Social Science

One of the most fundamental, interesting, and persistent of all the philosophical controversies in the metatheory of social science concerns the distinction between nature and society, and the concomitant natural science / social science divide. This controversy is philosophical because it concerns broad categories and thus affects all the social sciences. And it is fundamental because the very social-research strategy depends upon the stand one takes in the controversy.

The traditional answers to the question of the nature of society and social science are social naturalism and idealism. According to the former society is part of nature, whereas idealism contends that society hovers above nature in being spiritual rather than material. The first answer implies that social studies are included in natural science, whereas the second implies that they belong in the humanities. I shall argue that there is a grain of truth in each of these traditional views, and will advance a third view expected to encompass these grains of truth.

I submit the platitude that, although newly born humans are animals, they turn gradually into live social artefacts (persons) as they grow up, become encultured, learn skills and norms, and engage in activities that trespass on the biological. Likewise, the band and the family originate to meet biological and psychological needs, whence they may be called supra-individual biological systems. But they also constitute social systems for being endowed with non-natural or made properties. Such artificiality is particularly evident in the cases of the economy (E), the polity (P), and the culture (C). Joining these three to the biological system (B) we form the *BEPC* sketch of society. Only the B(iological) subsystem is natural and, even so, it is strongly influenced by the three artificial subsystems E, P, and C. Moreover, every one of the four subsystems encroaches partially on the others, because every individual is a part of at least two of them.

The consequence of the preceding for the study of people and society is obvious: the sciences of man are rooted in natural science without being included in it. Furthermore, although there are distinctly *social* sciences, such as economics and history, the natural and social sciences have a non-empty overlap composed of such hybrids as social psychology, anthropology, linguistics, geography, demography, and epidemiology. The mere existence of these hybrids, which may be called *biosocial* (or *socionatural*) sciences, refutes the idealist thesis that the social sciences are disjoint from the natural sciences.

Admittedly there are several clear differences among the natural, socionatural, and social sciences – particularly differences in objects and techniques. But they also have important commonalities, among them the scientific approach. Otherwise we would not regard them all as sciences – albeit, in different stages of evolution.

1 Nature and Society

Nothing seems more obvious than that, whereas individual humans are animals, societies are not. The first conjunct is evident but, like many other self-evident propositions, is only partially true. In fact, the newly born human being is indeed an animal, but one born into a society that will help or hinder the actualization of his genetic potentialities. In other words, people are artefacts. Like all artefacts, we are fashioned from natural entities; but, unlike other artefacts, we are largely self-made and sometimes even self-designed. Thus, we train ourselves and perhaps others as farmers, historians, or what have you. As we do so we sculpt our own brains. The successful apprentice has become what he set out to be. He is the product not only of his genes but also of his society and of his own decisions and actions. In sum, human nature is quite unnatural: this is what sets us apart from other animals. Hence, it is not true that man is of a piece with nature and that human nature is as unchanging as the laws of physics. (For the roots of this view, particularly among economists, see Clark 1992. For criticisms see Popper 1961; Geertz 1973; and Bunge 1996a.)

The view that human nature is partly artefactual, and therefore variable and in our hands rather than unchanging, overcomes the obsolete nature/nurture and body/soul dualisms, which are incompatible with scientific psychology anyway. Indeed, developmental and social psychology teach that we are as much products of our environment and of our own actions as of our genetic endowment (see, for instance, Lewontin 1992). And the main philosophical input and output of physiological psychology is the psychoneural identity hypothesis, according to which all mental processes, whether emotional, cognitive, or conative, are brain processes. (See, for instance, Hebb 1966; Bindra 1978; Bunge

1980; Bunge and Ardila 1987; Kosslyn and Koenig 1995; and Beaumont et al. 1996.)

As for the nature of society, there are two extreme views: that it is natural, and that it owes nothing to nature. The first view is usually called (social) *naturalist*, and the second *historicist* or *historico-cultural*. (What is here called social naturalism must not be mistaken for ontological naturalism, or anti-supernaturalism.) Social naturalism is a naive or primitive form of materialism, which equates reality with nature: it declares that humans are nothing but sophisticated apes, and that human societies differ from anthills only in complexity. These naturalist theses have the methodological consequence that social matters are to be studied exclusively with the ideas and techniques of natural science, so that science is basically one with regard to subject matter as well as method.

In the metascientific literature on social science 'naturalism' is often understood as the thesis that society can be studied scientifically (see Bhaskar 1979, and Wallace 1984). This is a confusion, for one may advocate the scientific study of social facts while at the same time admitting that social systems have non-natural properties. In other words, one may be at the same time scientistic and non-naturalistic (yet non-supernaturalistic), as Marx and Dukheim were.

Social naturalism has an interesting pedigree. Aristotle's *Politics* was naturalistic in asserting the existence of "natural masters" and "natural slaves," as well as in holding that the household, the village, and even the state "have a natural existence," in developing naturally rather than emerging by deliberate action. The Stoics too were naturalists, and so were the members of the natural-law school, from Cicero to Aquinas to Grotius to Spinoza to Kant – each in his own way. All of them believed that there is a natural social order involving natural law and natural justice, which is universal or cross-cultural. Theirs was obviously an ahistorical view. But of course there was good reason for this: the serious historical investigation of institutions only began in the nineteenth century.

Contemporary social naturalism comes in two main varieties: geographical determinism and biologism. The former states that social organization is an adaptation to the physical environment. There is a grain of truth in this, for the actions people can perform depend to a large extent on the natural resources they have access to. Thus, the coast is suitable for fishing, the prairie for agriculture and cattle breeding, the mountain for mining, and so on. In turn, differences in activity mould different lifestyles and personalities. However, the environment can explain only so much, as may be seen from the huge differences in social organization among the societies that have occupied successively a given territory in the course of history: think of Greece or of America.

The environment offers and constrains but does not construct society: only people-in-their-environment do this. (By contrast, environmental catastrophes can wipe out entire communities.) Moreover, people can alter their natural environment, sometimes to the point of making it uninhabitable.

In short, geographical determinism contains only a grain of truth, albeit an important one. (Durkheim denied it tacitly when stating that the cause of every social fact is another social fact.) After all, the survival of every biopopulation depends on its resource base and, in particular, on the latter's carrying capacity (see, for example, Catton et al. 1986). If the Sumerians and Mayas had known this they might have saved their respective civilizations. And if all of us realized this we would not be suffering from overpopulation and its sequels, such as famine and war. Forget the environment and it won't forgive you.

The second main variant of social naturalism is biological determinism, or the view that people are fully products of heredity and society is a biological outgrowth, and only a device for meeting biological needs. Biologism is a bastard of evolutionary biology. It is manifest in social Darwinism – particularly in Spencer, Nietzsche, and Sumner – as well as in the tenet of the born criminal. It is also obvious in the Nazi *Rassenkunde* and *Soziobiologie*, as well as in the racist interpretation of differences in IQ and contemporary human sociobiology. (By contrast, the psychoanalytic myth that human conflicts are results of "constitutional aggressiveness" and manifestations of the male's revolt against his father or "father figure" is a sad case of psychologism not of biologism. Indeed, Freud, Jung, and Lacan stressed the autonomy of psychoanalysis *vis-à-vis* biology.)

No doubt, there is some truth to biologism, but not much. We are indeed animals, but economic, political, and cultural ones. We do differ somewhat from one another by our genetic endowment, but social standing depends more on a combination of accident with initial economic and educational endowment than on genes. Personality is not uniquely determined by the genome, as shown by the cases of identical twins who adopt different occupations, and consequently end up by acquiring different personalities and social status. And every modern social group is genetically inhomogeneous.

The behaviour of eusocial insects, such as ants and bees, is rigid or genetically "programmed," hence neurally "wired in." In stark contrast, that of mammals and birds is plastic and adaptive, because their brains contain plastic subsystems, that is, systems of neurons capable of "rewiring." (In the case of humans such changes in neuronal connectivity are sometimes spontaneous, that is, not due to environmental stimuli.) Thus, in the course of its life, a coyote may adopt different types of social behaviour, from pack to monogamous couple to solitariness, depending on the kind and distribution of the means of livelihood (Bekoff 1978). Hence, sociobiologists are quite right in emphasizing the biological roots of sociality. But they go wrong when they chop to stump the great tree of human life, trying to explain everything social, even morality, as a product of evolution. Man is in part a self-made animal, the artificer and destroyer of all social norms. In particular, we are born neither good nor bad, but can turn either or a combination of both.

As for Social Darwinism, it can instantly be disposed of by noting that its key notions, namely those of competition and fitness, lack biological counterparts. Indeed, *Darwinian* fitness is defined as the average number of offspring per parent. And the intensity of *biological* competition equals the ratio of those who die to those who survive to sexual maturity. Neither of these technical concepts is of great interest to social science.

In short, biological determinism contains only a grain of truth. For example, while it rightly emphasizes the biological roots of some social institutions, such as marriage, it does not account for the differences between endogamy and exogamy, secular and religious wedding ceremonies, or arranged marriage and marriage for love. Worse, because it claims that social differences are due exclusively to inborn biological differences, biologism has been used to justify social inequality, racism, and colonialism.

However, the rejection of biologism does not entail that we may safely ignore biological constraints. One cannot understand society without keeping in mind that it is composed of organisms intent on surviving. Imagine an anthropologist uninterested in food, sexual mores, or child care; or a sociologist, politologist, or historian who overlooks biological urges. Social science *sur*passes natural science because it studies suprabiological systems, but it cannot *by*pass biology without becoming unrealistic. Moreover, the social scientist can learn something from studying other primates. For instance, it has been found that apes refer to themselves and "interpret" actions of conspecifics (i.e., they conjecture what others are up to from observing their behavior). It is also known that chimpanzees make tools (e.g., McGrew 1992) and are smart politicians (de Waal 1989).

In short, naturalists are right in stressing the continuity of society and nature, as well as in regarding societies as concrete entities rather than as spiritual ones – for instance, as sets of values, beliefs, and norms. But they err in overlooking the artificial components of every society, however primitive – namely its economy, polity, and culture. They are also wrong in refusing to acknowledge that beliefs, interests, and intentions contribute to determining actions and thus to building, maintaining, or altering the social order. Because of its crude reductionism, naturalism fails to account for the amazing variety and mutability of social systems; and it masks the economic, political, and cultural sources of social inequalities and the resulting conflicts. Nothing social can "take its natural course," because everything social is at least partly artefactual. (Corollary: Every social process can be altered by deliberate – in part, rationally planned – human intervention, in particular coordinated collective action.) In short, the term 'social naturalism' is an oxymoron.

The inadequacies of social naturalism have encouraged the idealist exaggeration of the differences between humans and nonhuman animals, as well as the concomitant separation between social and natural science. This is notably the case with the historicist or historico-cultural view of society fathered by Vico and Kant, nursed by Dilthey, and endorsed by Weber. This view is correct in emphasizing the non-natural character of social institutions and the differences between cultural and natural evolution. But it is wrong in opposing society to nature and in upholding the ancient theological opposition of nature and spirit, as well as in asserting the self-sufficiency and absolute primacy of the latter. To be sure we cannot account for anything social unless we take experiences, beliefs, aspirations, and intentions into account. But it is self-defeating to ignore our biological needs – e.g., for food, shelter, parental care, and sex – and the so-called material conditions of social existence, that is, environmental and economic factors. We are not only what we perceive, think, and dream, but also what we eat, feel, and do.

The opposition between history and nature, stressed by the historicist school, became obsolete at the birth of the historical sciences of nature – cosmology, geology, and evolutionary biology. Even certain physical systems, such as steel swords and magnets, are known to possess hereditary properties, such as elastic and magnetic hysteresis. That is, unlike such simple things as electrons and photons, the behaviour of a macrophysical system such as a chunk of steel or plastic depends upon its history. (In mathematical parlance, the current state of a system of this kind is a functional of its past.) The same holds, a fortiori, for organisms and social systems: their behaviour depends not only upon their current state but also upon their past. In the case of organisms their evolutionary past is encoded in their genome; in that of higher animals, part of their developmental past is recorded in their brains; and in that of social systems, part of their past is recorded in their institutions. In short, the history/nature opposition is untenable.

Thus, naturalism and historicism each hold a grain of truth. An alternative to both is the *systemic* view, according to which only the living components of human society are animals – and even so largely artefactual, for they are shaped by society and in turn they create, modify, or utilize objects that are not found in nature, such as tools, machines, ideas, symbols, norms, and institutions. Being made, human social systems are artefacts just like tools, houses, books, and norms. However, unlike the latter, social systems have often emerged – as naturalism holds – in a spontaneous way rather than as a result of deliberation and design. Still, from the birth of civilization, about five millennia ago, the ratio of the number of spontaneous to designed social systems has been decreasing. All bureaucracies, health-care, educational, and defence systems, manufacturing and trade consortiums, as well as transportation and communications networks, have been designed, although they have often evolved in unintended or even perverse ways.

Moreover, because all sociosystems are made, and in modern times they are increasingly organized according to explicit rules, they can be altered or even dismantled by deliberate human action (or just neglect). All this is unpalatable to holists, for whom social systems are givens, as well as to individualists, who deny the very existence of social wholes, or believe them to be the result of spontaneous aggregation. Still, it is true. Moreover, it is scientifically and politically relevant, for, if society is artificial rather than natural, then we may redesign it to suit our ideas of a good society. And, if society is concrete rather than spiritual, then social action may succeed in reconstructing it, whereas mere contemplation, intuitive *Verstehen* ("understanding") and hermeneutic "interpretation" (attribution of purpose) will only conserve the bad along with the good.

In sum, radical naturalism views society as part of nature and consequently it fails to account for the specific or non-natural features of society, as well as for the diversity of social organizations. Its opposite, radical anti-naturalism, places society above nature and thus ignores the fact that people happen to be organisms, in particular primates, and that social systems are concrete entities. By contrast to both naturalism and antinaturalism, I view persons as artefacts with both biological and social traits, and social systems as *sui generis* concrete systems embedded in nature but different from it for being impersonal. (For details see Bunge 1979a, 1981a, and 1996a.) This materialist, emergentist, and systemic viewpoint has important methodological consequences, to which we now turn.

2 The Natural Science / Social Science Divide

The Enlightenment proclaimed the unity of society and nature, and consequently the unity of knowledge about natural, social, and artificial objects. Thus, in his 1782 reception speech at the Académie Française, the founder of modern political science declared that the moral (social) sciences, based like the physical ones upon the observation of facts, "must follow the same methods, acquire an equally exact and precise language, [and] attain the same degree of certainty" (Condorcet 1976, 6). And he noted that "[t]his opinion is generally contrary to received ideas, and necessarily so. Two very powerful classes have an interest in combating it: the priests and those who exercise authority" (p. 17).

In the euphoria of the Enlightenment, Condorcet could not dream that those received ideas that he was fighting would soon be revived by the counter-Enlightenment movement, first in Romanticism and later on by the neo-Kantian school, which exalted the spiritual, despised the material, detached society from nature, placed intuition above reason, and denigrated science. If humans are spiritual beings, and society hovers way above nature, then the social sciences are autonomous *Geisteswissenschaften* (sciences of the spirit, or humanities). This is the historico-cultural, anti-naturalist, and idealist view of the neo-Kantians Dilthey, Windelband, and Rickert. The imprint of this school on Menger, Simmel, Weber, von Mises, Kelsen, and Hayek, as well as on herme-neuticians, phenomenologists, existentialists, critical theorists, Wittgenstein-ians, "postmoderns," and even Popper, is manifest. (See, for instance, von Schelting 1934; Outhwaite 1986; and Oakes 1988.) The roots of this school in Christian theodicy, Vico, the counter-Enlightenment, and idealism – particu-larly that of the Kantian type – are just as obvious as its hostility to positivism and materialism.

According to this school, the *Geisteswissenschaften* include theology, philos-ophy, psychology, linguistics, philology, art history, and all the social studies proper – in short, the usual menu of a traditional faculty of arts or *faculté des lettres*. These disciplines are said to be exclusively concerned with disembodied beliefs, intentions, and choices, never with material things such as natural resources and tools, or processes such as manual work. All these studies would be non-empirical and non-quantitative. Thus, Geertz (1973, 5) states that, because "man is an animal suspended in webs of significance he himself has spun," the analysis of culture is "not an empirical science in search of law but an interpretive one in search of meaning." (But he does not tell us what 'mean-ing' means.) Further, those disciplines that, like sociology, economics, political science, and history, do deal with brute facts, are to restrict themselves to describing them in qualitative terms, abstaining from seeking any regularities other than the norms of social life: they must be idiographic or particularistic, not nomothetic or generalizing. And, because they have no laws of their own – except for the "law" of maximizing utility – they must abstain from framing explanations and predictions of social facts. So far, the idealist view.

The forte of this school is, of course, its emphasis on the relevance of subjec-tivity – beliefs, evaluations, intentions, expectations, and choices – to social action. It is true that, because people have a mental life, and because they nor-mally abide by certain norms and social conventions, they ought not to be stud-ied the way physicists study atoms or stars, or even the way ethologists study the behaviour of animals other than primates. However, social scientists –

unlike psychologists – have no direct access to intentions: they can only observe the objective outcomes of purposeful actions. To be sure, they may impute individuals' intentions, expectations, and the like. But these attributions are dicey, even when testable in principle and compatible with experimental psychology.

Furthermore, it is mistaken to detach society from nature, for even spiritualists have been known to feel animal urges, and they might not survive in a hostile natural milieu or without someone doing some manual labour for them. Second, the claim that spiritual activities can be uncoupled from bodily processes, and thus studied separately from the latter, is a remnant of theology unjustifiable in the light of physiological psychology. Since according to the latter there are no ideas in themselves, but only ideating animals, the so-called sciences of the pure spirit are impossible.

In particular, scientific psychology is not a branch of the humanities if only because, from its birth in the mid-nineteenth century, it has been an experimental and mathematical science. To regard psychology as a *Geisteswissenschaft* on a par with biography or literary criticism – as Dilthey did – is to condemn it to the status of lay (or folk) psychology (Kraft 1957). This is fine only with psychoanalysts. (Thus, for Lacan [1966] psychoanalysis is "the practice of the symbolic function" – a kind of rhetoric, not a branch of science.) Of course, psychology proper tackles the mind-body problem, which is philosophical as well as scientific; but it does so in a scientific way (see, for example, Hebb 1980; Bunge 1980; Kosslyn and Koenig 1995). To treat psychology as an autonomous discipline concerned with the immaterial soul is to turn the clock back and to deprive mental patients of the benefits of behaviour therapy, psychopharmacology, and neurosurgery. (For the status of psychology as a multidiscipline see Bunge 1990b.)

There is no reasonable objection to studying ideas in themselves, that is, regardless of the people who think them and, a fortiori, regardless of their social circumstances. We do this when examining the logical structure, meaning, or truth value of a proposition – though not when examining the social impact of belief in the proposition. However, when studying ideas in themselves we do not engage in *social* studies: these are about human groups not pure ideas. This is one of the reasons that philosophy is not a social science although it is often classified as such. To wrestle with abstract ideas one must *pretend* that they exist by themselves (Bunge 1997a). It is only when placing them in the scheme of things that we must remember that ideas are processes in live brains.

The same holds, *mutatis mutandis*, for the study of language in itself (that is, general linguistics) rather than either as a brain process or as a means of social intercourse. This part of linguistics does belong in the humanities. But because of this it cannot tackle such problems as why certain brain lesions cause semantic aphasia and others syntactic aphasia, why the Norman conquest of England wiped out genders, or why the subjunctive is all but gone from American English. By contrast, neurolinguists and psycholinguistis deal with live speakers, and sociolinguistis with linguistic communities, not with linguistic expressions in themselves. Hence, these branches of linguistics belong in the socionatural sciences, along with social psychology, geography, and palaeopathology, not in the humanities. The upshot is that linguistics as a whole has one foot in natural science, another in social science, and a third in the humanities. (More in section 8.)

The historico-cultural school, particularly in its hermeneutic version, emphasizes the need to "interpret" human actions, that is, to figure out their "meaning" (purpose). Furthermore, it claims that this feature sets social science apart from natural science (e.g., Dilthey 1959, Weber 1988a, Geertz 1973). However, on inspection "interpretation" turns out to be no other than untested hunch, conjecture, or hypothesis (Bunge 1996a). For example, "interpreting" someone's gestures as friendly or hostile is nothing but conjecturing. Besides, not all social actions are purposive: some are performed automatically. Nor are all of them carried out in self-interest: many are performed under compulsion or out of benevolence. Nor do all deliberate actions attain their goals: some have undesirable consequences.

Moreover, whether or not a social fact is the result of intentional behaviour, the social scientist is seldom in a position to find out, for almost all of his data concern either individuals with whom he is not personally acquainted or macrosocial facts. Furthermore, even if he did have access to the intentions of his characters, they would hardly explain such macrosocial facts as economic recessions and the decay of inner cities, not to mention the social consequences of such natural disasters as droughts, floods, blights, or epidemics. Since intentions are ensconced in brains, the followers of the "interpretive" (or "understanding") school are guilty of arrogance in claiming to be able to read the intentions of social agents off their overt behaviour or off written texts referring to them.

The above-mentioned philosophical and methodological flaws of the "humanistic" (in particular, the hermeneutic) school explain its barrenness. Indeed, it has not yielded any important findings. In particular, this school "seriously impoverished historical scholarship when it dismissed the great theoretical questions facing humanity as legitimate objects of historical study. The cult of the particular atomized history; the cult of the past 'for its own sake' cut the thread between history and life; the denial of the possibility of generalization from past experience and the emphasis on the uniqueness of individual events broke the link not only with science but also with philosophy" (Barraclough 1979, 14).

Another claim of the "humanistic" school of social studies is that social experiments are impossible. This is false: archaeologists, sociologists, economists, management scientists, and other social scientists have conducted experiments, though admittedly not as often or perhaps as carefully as they should. (See, for instance, Roethslisberger and Dickson 1943; Greenwood 1948; Laponce and Smoker 1972; Coles 1973; Riecken and Boruch 1978; Bonacich and Light 1978; Hausman and Wise 1985; and Davis and Holt 1993.) Thus, archaeologists replicate ancient artefacts and try them out to find out how they may have been fashioned and what might have been achieved with them. Anthropologists and sociologists have studied, under controlled conditions, the effects of introducing modern technologies, sanitation, inoculation, birth control, education, and so on, in traditional societies. Moreover, some social scientists have realized that proposing important social programs on a nation-wide scale, without first trying them out on a small scale, is intellectually and socially irresponsible. This is why during the 1970s the United States government alone spent over $500 million on social macro-experiments designed to test the effects of certain social policies, such as the well-known New Jersey guaranteed-minimum-income experiment. For the same reason, since the mid-twentieth century businesses have spent billions of dollars paying consultants to do experimental consumer-behaviour research.

What is true is that large-scale social experiments are scarce. This is partly because most social scientists and funding agencies do not realize the feasibility and importance of macrosocial experiments. If they did, they would invest as much in them as in mindless Wars on Crime or Drugs. In short, the scarcity of experiments *is* a serious drawback of current social science. But it is a practical matter not one of principle.

It is equally true that social experiments differ from most physical and chemical experiments in at least three important respects. One is that nearly every contemporary experiment in natural science is designed in the light of sophisticated theories that tell the experimenter which are the relevant variables and, therefore, which of them should be "frozen" and which ones "tuned." Another difference is that, whereas in natural science most variables can be monitored continuously, in social science they are usually measured at long intervals, often only before and after the stimulus has been applied. A third difference is that human subjects are likely to alter their behaviour not just in response to experimental stimuli but also spontaneously, as well as in response to changes in their social environment that are beyond the experimenter's control. For example, they can learn, change jobs, get married or divorced, cheat on the experimenter, and even drop out of the experiment. (For example, the original interpretation of the famous Hawthorn experiment [1924–32] on the relation between productivity and job satisfaction overlooked the fact that the intervening Great Depression made workers work harder for fear of losing their jobs: see Franke and Kaul 1978.) However, the experimental biologist faces similar problems: his mice can acquire or lose immunity, mature sexually, escape, or die.

In short, there are important differences between social experiments and experiments in the natural sciences. These differences combine to make the former much harder than the latter. As a consequence, it is far more difficult to test hypotheses and theories in the social sciences than in the natural ones. But the philosophically relevant point is that social experiments are feasible. Moreover, the philosophical and budgetary barriers to social experiments should be lifted, because no amount of observation can substitute for a well-designed experiment. Let us see why.

Macrosocial experiments – that is, experiments performed on social groups rather than individuals – have two sets of advantages over social surveys and econometric analyses: conceptual and practical. The former are that experiment involves (a) randomization, and thus minimizes the risk of biased selection; and (b) the controlled alteration of certain variables, which alone allows one to find causal relations (Bernard 1865). The main practical advantage of social experiment is that it enables us to try out new policies and check how they fare before enshrining them in laws and building a bureaucratic apparatus that may turn out to be needless or worse. (More in Bunge 1996a.)

Experience has shown that the costs of sociotechnical improvisation, often engaged in for purely electoral purposes, can be staggering (see, for example, Mosteller 1981). The armchair student of society is likely to rejoin that this only confirms his view that society should not be tampered with – but this is just a tacit confession of conservatism. We are not forced to choose between social insensitivity and improvisation; we can opt for responsible planning based on sound theory and experiment. (More in chap. 11, sect. 5.)

Anti-naturalists, in particular the partisans of the *Verstehen* (or meaning, interpretation, understanding, comprehension, or "thick description") approach, as well as ordinary-language philosophers, have made much of the difference between explaining by causes and explaining by motives and reasons (see Bunge 1996a). However, they have not bothered to elucidate the very meaning of the expression 'meaning of human action.' Thus, some members of this school equate *Verstehen* with empathy, others with insight or intuition, and still others with the disclosure (or rather guessing) of intention or purpose (Dallmayr and McCarthy 1977a). Such chaos is an indicator of muddled thinking.

The partisans of *Verstehen* have assumed, explicitly or tacitly, that, whereas causation is lawful, intention and reason are not – so that, while the former is within the reach of science, the latter are not. These beliefs betray simplistic views of both mentation and science. To be sure, neither intentions nor reasons for acting are within the purview of behaviourism and other "empty organism" psychological schools; nor are emotion and valuation. But they are within the reach of neuropsychology, which is slowly succeeding in explaining them in terms of neural processes (see, for instance, Damasio et al. 1996). By contrast, an ordinary-knowledge account of actions, reasons, and causes (for instance, by Kenny 1964 and Davidson 1980) is bound to be prescientific, shallow, and therefore just as unilluminating as an ordinary-knowledge description of the movements of celestial bodies.

Science is not just a continuation of common sense, as the empiricist and linguistic philosophers claim. Science starts where ordinary knowledge stops, and it subverts many commonsensical intuitions. This holds particularly for social systems because – unlike their individual components – such systems have counterintuitive properties, most of them imperceptible, so that sometimes they behave in unintended and even perverse ways. Therefore, the claim that we have an immediate or intuitive knowledge of other people (Schütz 1967) and the demand that the models in social science should be generally understandable (Schütz 1953) are guaranteed to produce truisms and falsities in industrial quantities. By the same token such dogmatic pronouncements rule out technical concepts and hypotheses representing deep features of social reality, and block the construction of mathematical models. We are asked to opt between common sense – inclusive of slippery and uncontrolled *Verstehen* – and science. If we opt for the latter, research and praxis will educate our intuition to the point of finding intuitive or nearly so what the beginner finds counterintuitive (Bunge 1962).

Another received belief is that social science is inherently more difficult than natural science for dealing with far more complex objects, hence with many more variables. The tacit premise here is that the more complex an object the harder the problems it poses. But this premise is false. Thus, the three-body problem in mechanics is far tougher than any problem involving zillions of bodies, for the latter can be treated in some respects as a single system. (Recall the gas laws.) Likewise, it is far easier for a demographer to make projections involving millions of people than to predict whether a given couple will have a preassigned number of children; or for a pollster to forecast the results of an election than to predict how a given citizen will vote. In a sense, a person is more complex than any social system because he performs many more functions than the latter, and because he is the product of an enormously complex biological and social process: just think of the complexities of morphogenesis, mental development, enculturation, and daily life.

The moral is straightforward if paradoxical: social science is hard not because it deals with too many people but because it concerns too few. (For one thing, when dealing with small systems we must expect large fluctuations.) As for the number of variables occurring in a typical social-science problem, it is actually seldom larger than in such fields as solid state-physics, physical chemistry, or neuropsychology. What is true is that either or both of the following situations prevails: the variables are untamed by theory, or the theory is simplistic, that is, it involves too few relevant variables or it links them in too simple a fashion (usually linear). For example, the key variables in all rational-choice models are utility and probability, and the quantity to be maximized is a linear combination of these.

It is sometimes claimed that a peculiarity of the social sciences, in particular economics, is that it contains *ceteris paribus* (all else equal) clauses, which render empirical tests hard. Indeed, if a hypothesis and a *ceteris paribus* condition jointly imply a prediction, and the latter is not borne out, then either the hypothesis, the said condition, or both may be at fault. However, such clauses occur in all sciences. (The concept was born in eighteenth-century mathematics: a partial derivative with respect to a given variable is a derivative taken while holding all other variables constant.) The difference between such clauses in the more advanced sciences and the less advanced ones is this: in the former the variables assumed to remain constant (e.g., temperature) are explicitly identified and controlled, whereas in social studies they are usually left unidentified and uncontrolled; in these the expression *ceteris paribus* is commonly used to denote whatever the theorist overlooks.

But in all disciplines the expression in question points to deliberate streamlining or "stylizing," such as the simplifying assumption that the system of interest is closed or isolated, hence protected from exogenous shocks. Normally the clause points to an honest admission of limitation. But occasionally, particularly in social studies, the clause in question discharges the dishonest task of protecting a theory from refutation, by blaming its empirical failures on extra variables, such as unexpected external shocks (Hollis and Nell 1975, 27ff.).

Another alleged difference between social science and natural science is that the former is anarchic, argumentative, and inconclusive, whereas natural science is orderly, authoritative (even authoritarian), and conclusive. In Kuhn's (1962) words, the natural scientist works – until the next revolution – within a single, well-defined, and firmly established paradigm, whereas the student of society does not. The truth is more complex than this. First, there is a sharp contrast only between natural *science* and *prescientific* (as well as *protoscientific*) social studies. That is, the fundamental divide is between science and nonscience. (Kuhn and Popper failed to understand this point as a consequence of their inability to demarcate correctly science from nonscience; Gellner 1974, chap. 9.)

Second, there are controversies in all sciences – formal, natural, social, and biosocial – regardless of their degree of advancement. Such controversies concern not only theories but also techniques and philosophical principles, as exemplified by the strife over the interpretation of quantum mechanics, cosmological models, genetic determinism, and the cradle of humankind.

Third, all fields of study are multiparadigmatic, not monoparadigmatic. For instance, "classical" physics, chemistry, and biology are still being successfully cultivated and enriched alongside their "modern" counterparts.

To sum up, the anti-naturalists (or intentionalists or interpretivists) are right in (a) stressing the differences between society and nature, and the concomitant differences between the corresponding sciences; (b) emphasizing the importance of belief, intention, and deliberate action, and consequently in stressing the need to try and reconstruct the purposes of people's actions instead of regarding the latter as automatic consequences of environmental stimuli; (c) holding that the students of society must "interpret" what their informants "are up to, or think they are up to" (Geertz 1973, 15); and (d) stating that (so far) qualities (or imponderabilia) have played a much greater role in social studies that in natural science. However, the failure of naturalism is no excuse for fleeing from science.

Moreover, the virtues of anti-naturalism are as nothing compared with its sins. Indeed, the school is wrong in (a) denying the continuity between nature and society and the corresponding commonalities between the social and the natural sciences; (b) ignoring the very existence of mixed or socionatural sciences such as demography, human geography, psychology, and linguistics; (c) denying that beliefs and intentions can be studied by natural science as brain processes; (d) ignoring that imputing intentions to agents is both dicey – for such attributions are purely conjectural – and insufficient, for the unintended consequences or side effects of human action can be just as important as the intended ones; (e) underrating the importance of "material" (environmental and economic) factors; (f) regarding *Verstehen* ("interpretation," "comprehension") as the alternative to causal (and probabilistic) explanation rather than as its complement; (g) exaggerating the possibility of reconstructing the experiences of others; (h) failing to check the hypotheses ("interpretations") concerning intentions, when not claiming that they are intuitive and infallible; (i) evading macroproblems, such as those concerning the emergence and breakdown mechanisms of social systems, or attempting to reduce them to individual actions; (j) denying the existence of social regularities other than enforced conventions; (k) rejecting the positive features of positivism and naturalism along with the negative ones; (l) opposing scientism and its claim of the possibility of building an objective social science; and (m) believing that scientism results in "great damage to human dignity" (Schumacher 1973) – while actually the intuitive approach is the one that blocks understanding and paralyses rational action, rendering people easy preys of dictators, demagogues, and utopians. In sum: non-naturalism, sí, anti-naturalism, no.

Finally, what about the ranking of the sciences? There are two standard views on this matter: the positivist and the idealist. The former is that the social sciences are based on the natural ones, and moreover cannot help being far "softer" (less rigorous) than the latter. However – so goes this view – all of the sciences share the same logic and method, and can (at least in principle) be couched in the same language, or even be reduced to a single science (such as psychology or physics). By contrast, the idealist view is that the natural and the social sciences are on the same footing, but have totally disjoint subject matters, logics, and methods, so that they are incomparable as to rigour. Otherwise, both parties are subjectivist: both attempt to build knowledge, and even the world, out of subjective elements – experiences in the case of positivism, ideas in that of idealism.

In my view there is some truth to each of these rival views. The neopositivists were right in stressing the logical and methodological unity of all the sciences. But they were wrong in espousing either psychologism (Mach and Carnap) or physicalism (Neurath), which are radical versions of reductionism. And the idealists are right in emphasizing the differences in subject matter. But they are wrong in overlooking the fact that in all disciplines we use the same organ (the brain), and in denying that we need the same organon of rational discourse (logic), as well as of rigorous checking. Finally, both parties are wrong in assuming that there is a clear natural/social divide, for actually there are mixed facts, such as marriage and war, comunicating and child rearing, and consequently hybrid sciences such as demography and linguistics. Since neither positivism nor idealism has succeeded in ranking the sciences correctly, we must look for an alternative.

Regardless of their subject matters, the sciences can be ordered in at least two different though mutually compatible ways: by cognitive precedence or by maturity. Of two sciences, A and B, A may be said to be *epistemically prior* to B if B makes use of A but A makes no use of B. Examples: physics and chemistry are epistemically prior to biology; geography, demography, sociology, economics, and political science are epistemically prior to history. (By contrast, it will be argued below that sociology, economics, and political science overlap partially, so that they cannot be ordered epistemically.) According to this view, a science (such as sociology) may draw on another (such as psychology) without being reduced to (or included in) the latter. Thus, social science is based on natural science without being included in the latter. Nor does the converse inclusion relation hold. Indeed, it is false that, as a "feminist philosopher" puts it, "the natural sciences should be considered to be embedded in the social ones because everything scientists do or think is part of the social world" (Harding 1991, 99). The fact that scientific research is socially embedded does not prove that it is always about social facts, just as the fact that fish live in water does not imply that they are watery.

As for the degree of maturity of a science, it concerns the number, accuracy, and above all the depth of its findings (Bunge 1968). For example, history is arguably more mature than any other social science, and even more so than a number of natural sciences, such as cosmology, the study of protein synthesis, and the physiology of mental processes.

In summary, there are important differences between the natural and the social sciences, as well as between the mature and the emergent sciences. But such differences pale by comparison with the sharp contrast between science and nonscience, in particular pseudoscience and antiscience. Hence, we shall assume that, beneath their specific differences and stages of evolution, all the modern research fields concerned with the real world constitute a system. This system may be characterized as follows (Bunge 1983b, 1996a).

The system of the *factual sciences* is a variable collection, every member $\mathcal{R}$ of which is representable by a list

$$\mathcal{R} = < C, S, D, G, F, B, P, K, A, M >,$$

where, at any given time,

1/ C, the *research community* of $\mathcal{R}$, is a social system composed of persons who have received a specialized training, hold strong communication links amongst themselves, share their knowledge with anyone who wishes to learn, and initiate or continue a tradition of inquiry (not just of belief) involving the search for objective truths;

2/ S is the *society* (complete with its culture, economy, and polity) that hosts C and encourages or at least tolerates the specific activities of the components of C;

3/ D, the *domain* or *universe of discourse* of $\mathcal{R}$, is composed exclusively of (actual or possible) real entities (rather than, say, freely floating ideas) past, present, or future;

4/ G, the *general outlook* or *philosophical background* of $\mathcal{R}$, consists of (a) the ontological principle that the world is material and its components change lawfully and exist independently of the researcher (rather than, say, ghostly, miraculous, unchanging, or invented entities); (b) the epistemological principle that the world can be known objectively, at least partially and gradually; and (c) the ethos of the free search for truth, depth, understanding, and system (rather than, say, the ethos of faith or that of the quest for sheer information, utility, profit, power, consensus, or good);

5/ *F*, the *formal background* of $\mathcal{R}$, is the collection of up-to-date logical and mathematical theories (rather than being empty or including obsolete formal theories);

6/ *B*, the *specific background* of $\mathcal{R}$, is a collection of up-to-date and reasonably well confirmed (yet corrigible) data, hypotheses, and theories, and of reasonably effective research methods, obtained in other fields relevant to $\mathcal{R}$;

7/ *P*, the *problematics* of $\mathcal{R}$, consists exclusively of cognitive problems concerning the nature (in particular the regularities) of the members of *D*, as well as problems concerning other components of $\mathcal{R}$;

8/ *K*, the *fund of knowledge* of $\mathcal{R}$, is a collection of up-to-date and testable (though rarely final) theories, hypotheses, and data compatible with those in *B*, and obtained by members of *C* at previous times;

9/ the *aims A* of the members of *C* include discovering the patterns (in particular, laws and norms) and circumstances of the *D*s, or using them to explain or predict, putting together (into theories) hypotheses about *D*s, and refining methods in *M*;

10/ the *methodics M* of $\mathcal{R}$ is a collection of explicit, uniform, scrutable (checkable, analysable, criticizable), and justifiable (explainable) procedures, in the first place the general scientific method (see introduction to part A).

Besides, every science must satisfy two conditions. The first is that there be at least one other *contiguous* scientific research field, in the same system of factual research fields, such that (a) both fields share some items in their general outlooks, formal backgrounds, specific backgrounds, funds of knowledge, aims, and methodics; and (b) either the domain of one of the two fields is included in that of the other, or each member of the domain of one of the fields is a component of a concrete system in the domain of the other. The second condition is that the membership of every one of the last eight components of $\mathcal{R}$ *changes*, however slowly at times, *as a result of inquiry* in the same field (rather than as a result of ideological or political pressures, or of "negotiations" among researchers), as well as in related (formal or factual) fields of scientific inquiry.

Let us glimpse next at condition 9 above, which stipulates that scientific research aims at discovering patterns or applying knowledge of them.

3 The Nomothetic/Idiographic Dichotomy

Positivists and Marxists, as well as many scholars who are neither, hold that social matter, however messy, is lawful, and that the explanation of social facts does not differ fundamentally from explanation in natural science (see, for instance, Gardiner 1959; Hempel 1965). Moreover, the logical form of any valid explanation would be: "Law(s) & Data ⇒ Explanandum [that is, the proposition describing the fact(s) to be explained]." Example: "Any technological innovation that affects the mode of production favours social mobility. Automation is affecting the mode of production. Ergo, automation is enhancing social mobility."

So far so good. But this is just an example, and one where values and norms, typical of social action, play no ostensive role. For example, no known laws explain either stagflation (unemployment with inflation) – which has been endemic in the so-called West from 1970 to 1990 – or the collapse of the Soviet Union in 1991. If one stresses the paucity of laws found so far by the social sciences, and combines this poverty with the idealist dogmas that only mind matters, and that mind is utterly free and anomalous, then one is likely to embrace *antinomianism*, or the utter denial of the lawfulness of social matter.

Antinomianism is precisely a major thesis of the hermeneutic or *Verstehen* school championed by Dilthey. It denies the existence of behavioural and social regularities, and consequently the possibility of using them to construct scientific explanations and forecasts. Thus, this school holds that the only task of the social scientist is to describe past and present particulars, and moreover as outcomes of purposive and idiosyncratic individual actions. In accordance with this view, the neo-Kantian philosopher Windelband and his disciple Rickert split the sciences into *nomothetic* (universalizing or law-seeking) and *idiographic* (concerned with the individual and unrepeatable). And they added that, whereas the natural sciences are nomothetic, the *Geisteswissenschaften* are idiographic and historical. This view has influenced Weber, Popper, Collingwood, Winch, Habermas, and others, and it underlies the title of the journal *History and Theory*. It also underpins the division of the sciences adopted by Harvard University, namely into "experimental-predictive" and "historical" – which, if carried out consistently, would group cosmologists, geologists, evolutionary biologists, and historians into a single faculty.

In his methodological writings Weber emphasized the nomothetic/idiographic dichotomy he had learned from Rickert (see Oakes 1988). However, in his substantive works Weber used idiographic documents, such as biographies, only as raw materials to formulate "nomothetic hypotheses about such abstract sociological problems as the relations between institutionalized ideas and social organization as well as the modes and dynamics of structural interdependence of seemingly unconnected social institutions" (Merton 1987, 15). Moreover, Weber used the concept of an ideal type – as exemplified by capitalism and bureaucracy – as a methodological device "to permit statements of sociological relationships of a fairly general order" (Martinelli and Smelser 1990, 13). In other words, ideal types bridge the idiographic and the nomothetic. Thus, Weber hardly practised what he preached (see also von Schelting 1934 and Andreski 1984). This is why he counts as a scientist. Regrettably, when studying Weber, most philosophers rely exclusively on his muddled methodological sermons. (More in Bunge 1996a.)

The nomothetic/idiographic dichotomy is untenable because *all* sciences are nomothetic *as well as* idiographic. In fact, all of them seek patterns underneath data, and all of them account for individuals in terms of universals, and employ particulars to guess at and check generalities (see Nagel 1961; Harris 1968; Trigger 1978; and Tilly 1984). Thus, in his path-breaking *The Sources of Social Power*, the historical sociologist Michael Mann (1986, 1993) proposes many generalizations, most of them peculiar to a given region and period. They suggest to him that, far from being chaotic, human society is "a patterned mess," that is, a combination of law and accident – just what one would have suspected from its analogue, biological evolution. As Levins and Lewontin (1985, 141) state, "[t]hings are similar: this makes science possible. Things are different: this makes science necessary." Facts and stories can be local; science never is.

The source of social regularities is this. When all the members of a social group have roughly the same needs and desires, and are subjected to similar constraints and social forces, individual idiosyncrasies cancel out, so that group properties and patterns emerge. Stinchcombe (1968, 67–8) has drawn a correct analogy between such a group and a run of measurements of a magnitude: the random measurement error (idiosyncrasies) is inversely proportional to the square root of the number of observations (group membership). Even such a staunch "localist" as Geertz (1988, 217) has ventured the odd universal hypothesis – for instance, that "the legal mind, in whatever sort of society, seems to feed as much on muddle as it does on order."

The differences among the sciences with regard to their use of general concepts and propositions is one of degree not kind. What is true is that, in any science, the student focuses now on the general or law-like, now on the particular. He does the former when seeking patterns, the latter when accounting for (describing, explaining, or predicting) individual facts in terms of patterns. (See also Wallerstein 1991, chap. 18.) It is also true that some sciences use more laws than they generate. This holds particularly for the historical sciences, both the natural and the social ones. For example, cosmologists, geologists, palaeontologists, and evolutionary biologists – all of them historians of nature – have not come up with many laws, but they do make use of a number of physical or chemical laws – for instance, when explaining continental drift and the extinction of certain species. (Incidentally, the very existence of natural-historical sciences ruins Rickert's equation "Historical = Social.") Likewise, historians may not discover any universal laws, but they certainly find spatio-temporally bounded regularities, and use a number of universal generalizations borrowed from psychology, sociology, and economics (Nagel 1952; Joynt and Rescher 1961; Stone 1972; McClelland 1975; Fogel 1982a).

The idiographic/nomothetic distinction involves the difference between individuals (or particulars) and universals (or general properties). According to nominalism – a variety of naive or vulgar materialism – there are only individuals, and universals are just words or, in the best of cases, artificial constructions out of individuals. (E.g., the chemical and biological species would be just conventional groupings.) By contrast, Platonism – a variety of idealism – holds that universals (or properties) are supremely real, whereas individuals are only instantiations or copies of the former. (E.g., a just person would be a particular incarnation of the idea of Justice.)

Mathematics, factual science, and technology espouse neither nominalism nor Platonism: they use side by side the categories of individual and universal. The reason is that every individual has some properties, and every property (though not every attribute or predicate we may fancy) is a property of at least one individual. Thus, we attribute a property to some individuals, and collect all the individuals possessing a given property into a class or species. Moreover, we individuate things by their properties, in particular the regularities they satisfy. In short, whenever we attribute, collect, or individuate we combine individuals with universals.

Consider the following examples. Our planet is unique, but it is just one of several; and it has a unique trajectory, but one that falls under the general laws of celestial mechanics. Likewise the French economy is unique, but it is a member of the class of mixed economies; and every capitalist crisis is like no other recession – except that it is one more downturn in the general capitalist cyclic movement. And all the important events in a person's life – such as being born, learning to walk, getting the first job, and dying – occur only once. But events of all of these kinds occur over and over in any society, and they fit statistical regularities that enable government departments and insurance companies to make statistical forecasts. Accident and randomness on one level may be respectively law and causation on the next (Bunge 1951).

The well-balanced anthropologist, archaeologist, or historian will consequently be just as interested in the similarities as in the differences among societies ("cultures"). For example, he will be drawn to the similarities between all the early civilizations (e.g., regarding kingship, public works, taxation, bureaucracy, and state ideology) as well as to the unique Egyptian cult of the dead, hieroglyphic writing, or king-god. Particulars will suggest, circumscribe, and test generalizations, and in turn the latter will help find and shed light on the former (see Gallay 1983; Trigger 1993). In this regard the student of society behaves just like the evolutionary biologist, who studies differences among bio-species as well as the features common to all life kinds – e.g., metabolism, mutation, cell division, and selection. Both students are scientists, and both seek the nomothetic as well as the idiographic. Consequently, neither of them abides by the historico-cultural methodology.

What about human idiosyncrasies and imperfections? Do not they condemn the search for social laws to failure? This question presupposes that natural things are uniform and perfect, as celestial bodies were supposed to be before Galileo discovered the solar spots. If all the members of a natural kind were identical, they would be indistinguishable, hence they would be one. Actually, the members of any given natural kind are not identical but similar or equivalent in a number of respects. Hence, individual differences do not prevent them from satisfying the same laws.

Much the same holds for imperfection, or departure from ideal type. An object is perfect if and only if it possesses all the properties that characterize its kind, imperfect if it lacks some of them. For example, a perfect atom is one with as many electrons as protons. But many atoms are ionized, that is, do not have the "right" number of electrons: they are imperfect. Likewise, most of the valuable gems are imperfect crystals, in that they contain "impurities." Again, every organism has certain abnormalities, such as an excess or defect of some chemicals. And every artefact is somewhat short of its blueprint – and so on.

As we climb up the levels of organization, the deviances, irregularities, "imperfections," and "impurities" increase in number: idiosyncrasies become more pronounced, and atypical cases more numerous. (There are not the likes of Newton or Mozart among molecules.) However, this does not entail that we lose lawfulness altogether: the world is at least roughly lawful though not uniform, and the very concept of deviance makes sense only in relation to that of normality. For example, all social artefacts, from languages to business firms, are imperfect, yet they all abide by certain norms; otherwise they would not discharge their functions. Moreover, all collections of individuals, whether natural or artificial, fit objective statistical patterns. This is why statistics are collected and analysed.

It is precisely the differences among individuals that have suggested the search for statistical regularities. Insurance firms rely on such patterns. Thus, the differences in individual lifespans does not prevent actuarial mathematicians from computing rather accurate premiums, thus ensuring the profitability of life insurance companies. In general, a mass of independent random events exhibits certain constancies such as averages and variances. This was a great discovery of J. Bernouilli (eighteenth century) in reference to physical events, and of Quetelet (nineteenth century) in reference to social events. (See Porter 1986 for a history of social statistics.)

Quetelet found that even the frequencies of such acts of free will as marriage, crime, and suicide are roughly constant within each social group, hence statistically predictable from one year to the next. Because social scientists do not study individuals but social groups and social systems, they can be expected to find mass regularities if only they search for them. For instance, it has been found that in all societies crime is roughly thirty times more frequent among males than among females, and that the crime rate is about thirty times greater in the United States than in the United Kingdom. (Whether these ratios will hold up over time is unknown.)

Some social scientists disbelieve in social regularities because the patterns of human organization are changeable. Thus, Giddens (1984) recommends that social scientists propose certain "sensitizing concepts" – e.g, those of resource, social system, and rule – instead of attempting to formulate law-like statements. However, change is consistent with lawfulness; so much so that the equations of motion constitute the nucleus of dynamics. What is true is that most social regularities are society-specific and time-bound. But then something similar holds for all chemical and biological regularities: they hold only within narrow temperature and pressure intervals.

Yet there *are* some universal social regularities. For example, all normal humans seek stimulation, company, and recognition; all people enjoy some activity, practise reciprocity, and are more sensitive to loss than to gain; all societies change and adopt norms of social behaviour; all social systems deteriorate unless repaired; and crime increases with anomie. If there were no such universals we would not be justified in talking about human nature and society in general. Moreover, Giddens's "sensitizing concepts" are precisely those that occur in social generalizations, such as "All societies depend on their resource base" and "Every social system has its own system of values and norms." In conclusion, there are social regularities; otherwise we would have no use for general social concepts. (More on this below.)

Is not freedom incompatible with lawfulness, and hence a major reason that laws are so hard to come by in social science? This complex question invites a complex answer. First, freedom does not equal lawlessness but either the ability to elude or overcome external constraint or coercion, or the power to act according to one's will. In other words, there are two kinds of freedom: passive or negative, and active or positive – or freedom *from* and freedom *to* (see Berlin

1957). One attains freedom *from* X by escaping from or subduing X, and freedom *to* do X by securing the means to carry out X. And freedom comes in degrees: we may choose from a menu, choose a menu, or design our own menu. Second, all freedom is restricted. Even the individualist Weber (1920a, 203) admitted that in industrialized societies we live in "steel cages": that is, our lives are rather severely regimented. Not even tyrants and tycoons are omnipotent and above all norms.

None of this is to deny that social patterns differ from natural ones because of our ability to invent and to make decisions, in particular, decisions based on long-term expectations. Whereas all organisms live in the shadow of the past, humans are unique in living also in the shadow of the future, about which they worry, and to face which they make plans and sacrifices. (Of course, it is not that the future affects the present, but that our current imagining of the future casts a shadow on our current actions.)

Human life is certainly full of accidents, but it is not a gamble. If it were totally lawless, we could not count on anything or anyone to get anything done. But in fact we learn certain regularities that allow us to form the expectations we live by. So much so that every case of unforeseen behaviour catches us by surprise; it either baffles, outrages, or amuses us. Moreover, we disbelieve certain reports of unusual behaviour in judging them to be "out of character." In short, we expect human behaviour to fit certain patterns even while admitting that we are largely ignorant of them.

Expectations guide actions, but some of these have unexpected and undesired consequences. Thus, if we expect the price of a commmodity to rise, we may attempt to stock on it – with the "perverse" effect of contributing to a price increase. It is not that today's prices are influenced by tomorrow's: the future, being non-existent, cannot influence the present. What happens is that the going prices depend partly on our expectations concerning future prices. The same holds, *mutatis mutandis*, for quantities, interest rates, and many other variables. All of them fit definite patterns.

The occurrence of knowledge, conjecture, expectation, and decision in human affairs accounts for a well-known difference between the forecasts made in natural science and those made in social science. Thus, an omniscient astronomer would expect exactly what actually happens, whereas an omniscient and omnipotent businessman or statesman would try to make happen what he desires. The former performs what may be called *passive* forecasts, the latter *active* ones. This difference, which is involved in social and economic planning, is of particular importance to sociotechnology (see part B).

Of course there are no omniscient and omnipotent people; there are only some individuals with more knowledge or clout than others. Moreover, different persons are likely to have somewhat different expectations; hence, they must be expected to act in different ways, particularly if their expectations are intuitive rather than computed on the strength of laws and data. For example, no two bakers and no two economists are likely to agree on the price that a loaf of bread will fetch in a year's time. What holds for bread holds, a fortiori, for securities: transactions in these commodities occur largely because the expectations of buyers differ from those of sellers (see Tobin 1980, 26). And this *is* a social constancy, and one that makes for statistical predictability.

So far we seem to have been beating around the bush. The time has come to try to answer the two key questions: *Are* there social laws and, if so, are they (jointly with the relevant data) *sufficient* to explain social facts? There is only one straight answer to this question: namely, to admit that social science is a land with many prophets but few laws, and yet to propose a few candidates to the law status. I nominate the following score.

1/ Population size is limited by the volume of economic production, which in turn is limited by the natural resources and the technology. 2/ Population deficits give rise to fertility rites, whereas population surpluses motivate birth-control practices, from contraception to abortion to infanticide. 3/ Rapid population growth causes overcultivation and deforestation, which cause erosion and loss of soil fertility, which eventually decrease food production, which eventually causes food shortages. 4/ Societies with subsistence economies are more egalitarian than societies with production surpluses. 5/ Social change is more frequent in heterogeneous than in homogeneous societies; and the more pronounced the stratification, the deeper the change. 6/ Similar issues prompt parallel solutions in different situations. 7/ The cohesiveness of a community results from the involvement of its members in various groups or activities, and it decreases with segregation. 8/ In market economies, productivity decreases with income inequality. 9/ Unprofitable lines of production or trade end up by disappearing. 10/ Manpower shortages (surplus) favour (discourage) technical innovation. 11/ War stimulates technical invention but inhibits scientific and humanistic creation. 12/ Superstition thrives on calamity, uncertainty, and oppression, and withers with peace, prosperity, and liberty. 13/ Misery, oppression, and greed breed corruption. 14/ Corruption erodes institutions. 15/ Political allegiance lasts as long as it is seen as beneficial. 16/ Oppression and exploitation can be increased only so much without breeding passive resistance, discontent, or revolt. 17/ Concentration of economic power facilitates concentration of political and cultural power. 18/ Economic growth alone, without concomitant cultural and political advances, results in a lopsided and unstable social order. 19/ Only integral (economic, political, and cultural) social reforms are effective and lasting. 20/ All social systems suffer from dysfunctionalities and risk decline; but, given some cultural and political freedom, we can always correct the former and arrest the latter.

There are literally hundreds of further generalizations of the same kind. (For more of them, both plausible and dubious, see Adams 1975; Harris 1979; Collins 1989; Deutsch et al. 1986; Luce et al. 1989; and Mann 1993.) True, few social regularities are universal or cross-cultural; most of them are local, that is, space- and time-bounded. But so are the laws of chemistry and biology. Only physics contains cosmic laws, such as those of gravitation and quantum theory. And even physics contains laws, such as those concerning liquids and solids, that hold only on planets and asteroids.

The transformation of the above and similar empirical generalizations into rigorous law statements requires rendering them more precise as well as incorporating them into hypothetico-deductive systems, that is, theories proper (see Bunge1967a, 1996a). Both tasks are greatly facilitated by the use of mathematics, not as a data-processing device but as a tool for constructing exact concepts and well-organized sets of assumptions.

Regrettably, two influential philosophies have actively opposed the search for laws and the construction of precise mathematical models of social facts. One of them is classical positivism, which, in reaction to groundless speculation ("grand theories"), demanded focusing on what Comte called *les petites choses vraies*. This has led most social students in our time either to cast off every *vue d'ensemble* and to accumulate more or less haphazard data (*dataism*), or to the endless honing of techniques (*methodism*). Even today hard-nosed social scientists distinguish theory from research and often contrast them. Yet, a careful analysis of advances over the first seven decades of the twentieth century shows that they "typically combine theory, methods, and results [data], rather than choosing one of these elements as a focus of interest ... In the light of these findings the long-standing quarrel about whether to emphasize theory, methodology, or empirical results seems ill-conceived and obsolete. All three seem to form part of one production cycle of knowledge" (Deutsch et al. 1971, 456).

The other extreme is of course idealism, which disdains empirical research as well as mathematical modelling, arguing that social science deals only with subjective intangibles such as intention, belief, and knowledge – not to mention such holistic fantasies as the universal spirit, collective consciousness, and national destiny. In this way idealism since Kant and Hegel has encouraged the proliferation of programmatic conjectures (Homan's "orienting statements") of the form "A determines B," as well as the construction of purely verbal "grand theories." By the same token it has discouraged the construction of what Merton (1957a) called "middle-range theories," that is, precise theoretical models representing circumscribed domains of facts, such as deviant behaviour and inflation.

Back to the question of social laws. Assume, for the sake of argument, that we know some reliable social generalizations, and let us ask whether they (jointly with the pertinent data concerning circumstances) suffice to explain and predict every possible social fact. Our answer is in the negative, because people are inventive and they hold values, and social systems satisfy man-made rules of various kinds – legal and moral norms among them – in addition to laws. Hence, the explanation or the forecast of a social fact may require four rather than two sets of premises: law statements, valuations, rules, and empirical data. Thus, explaining or predicting the observable fact that an individual or group of kind K engages in actions of type A may require the following premises:

Law: In social systems of kind K, fact (state or event) B follows state or event A, always or with a certain frequency (constant or lawfully changeable over time).

Valuation: Individuals in social systems of kind K perceive fact B as optimally valuable (or just satisfactory).

Rule: Try to attain whatever seems to be optimally valuable (or just satisfactory).

Datum: The individual or group in question, belonging to a social system of kind K, attempts to make fact A happen.

If this kind of explanans (explaining) premises is accepted, then the no-law view (antinomianism), in particular voluntarism, cannot be upheld. I submit that social facts can be explained by analogy with natural facts, namely in terms of patterns – preferably including mechanisms – and circumstances; but that in the case of social science the laws and norms are made, and the patterns include valuations and norms in addition to laws. The upshot is that there is no justification for the hermeneutic claim that in social science hypothesis and explanation must be replaced with "interpretation" (see Bunge 1996a).

What holds for explanation also holds, *mutatis mutandis*, for forecast. According to popular opinion human behaviour is totally unpredictable. The distinguished psychologist Neal E. Miller (1964, 948) objected: "This is not true. Under appropriate cultural conditions there is a high degree of predictability. Without such predictability civilization would be impossible. Look around you. It is safe to predict that no one will be sitting there naked. You might stop for a moment to think how much someone would have to pay you to make you undress at this meeting. This will give you some idea of the power of culture."

The reason for the (partial) predictability of individual human behaviour is that we all learn, and learning is acquiring behaviour (and mentation) patterns, that is, regularities. This holds, in particular, for enculturation and acculturation, that is, adaptation to the social environment. However, individual (quasi)predictability does not entail social forecasting, because social systems have emergent (systemic) properties, and they are composed of individuals with somewhat different experiences, skills, goals, and expectations, as well as creative potentials. It is one thing to predict the behaviour of an unknown individual in a known system, and another to forecast the latter's behaviour.

The most common argument against the possibility of social forecasting is that it would require detailed knowledge of the characteristics and circumstances of a myriad of individuals. This objection is invalid for, even if every component of a very complex system were to go its own way, the system as a whole would still follow a regular course, at least between large-scale catastrophes. Witness statistical physics, demography, actuarial statistics, and tax-revenue forecasts.

Another common objection to the possibility of social forecasts is that, even if they were made, they could not be put to the test because each social event is unique and unrepeatable (Machlup 1955). This objection ignores the fact that, although no two (social or natural) facts are identical, there are kinds of *similar* facts – e.g., being born, learning, working, raising a family, cooperating, and competing. Furthermore, as Russell (1914, 219ff.) noted, when asserting that variable Y is a certain function of variable X, we affirm that the *relation* between X and Y is invariant, not that any particular values of them will recur and become observable as often as desired.

In any event, since there *are* patterns (laws, trends, and norms) of social behaviour, by getting to know them we can forecast some social facts, at least in outline and in the short term. To be sure, such patterns are mostly confined to special kinds of society – that is, they are spatio-temporally bounded – but so are the chemical and biological laws. It is also true that economic and politological forecasting has not been very successful – but this may only suggest that the corresponding disciplines are still backward.

However, there *are* important differences between forecasts in social and in natural science. The best known of them is that a social forecast may affect human behaviour to the point of either forcing the forecast to become true or preventing it from being borne out. These are the well-known phenomena of the *self-fulfilling* and *self-defeating* prophecies (Merton 1957a, 128ff. and chap. 11; Bunge 1967b, 141ff.). For example, the publication of a political opinion poll may sway vote intentions ("bandwagon effect"). Consequently, we cannot know whether success confirmed our theory (or failed to refute it), or whether it was a psychological effect of the forecast having become known to some people and thus having affected their behaviour. This handicap of social science may eventually be corrected by including in the forecast the possible effect of its being made public. (A mechanism with a feedback loop comes to mind.)

By contrast, the social scientist is in the enviable position that, rather than being a helpless spectator, like the astronomer or the geologist, he can often meddle effectively, if not always beneficially, in human affairs. In fact, by designing social (economic, political, or cultural) programs, and having them adopted by a government or a business concern, the sociotechnologist can help alter the course of society: he can force his own forecasts to come to pass. In brief, whereas passive social forecasting is dicey, the active forecasting involved in business and social plans can be quite effective. (More in part B.)

Another difference is that changes in the type of social organization – for instance, from rural to urban, or from privately to publicly owned or conversely – are accompanied by changes in social patterns. And, since humans keep reforming and even creating and destroying social systems, *precise long-term* social forecasts are well-nigh impossible. However, this situation is not unheard-of in natural science. For example, even knowing the laws of genetics and embryology, we cannot forecast accurately the development of an individual organism, subject as it is to both endogenous and exogenous accidents.

Lastly, let us address the question whether valuations and rules are themselves arbitrary or conventional rather than being made and unmade in accordance with laws and circumstances. There are two classical views on this question: holism (organicism or collectivism) and individualism (see Tönnies 1979 and Dumont 1966). Most holists believe in impersonal forces, timeless norms, and historical laws, all of which they hold to be unbendable like fate. But they offer neither clear definition nor hard evidence. And invoking such forces, norms, and laws explains as much as invoking divine providence or fate. Moreover, some holists – in particular Hegel and Marx – mistake histories or trajectories for laws. This is a mistake because histories, whether biological or social, individual or collective, are determined not only by laws (or rules), but also by constraints and circumstances. Hence, one and the same law (or rule as the case may be) subsumes ("covers") an entire sheaf of possible histories – trajectories, life histories, or phylogenies. (For the biological case see Mahner and Bunge 1997.)

By contrast, individualists believe in rules or norms but not in social laws, and they hold that social rules appear or disappear by acts of will of "great men," by collective agreement (social contract), or as a spontaneous result of self-interested behaviour. No doubt, this view explains some events in the history of civilized societies. But it does not explain such sea changes as the beginnings of agriculture and civilization, or the birth of capitalism and the collapse of empires; neither of these processes is likely to have been the outcome of free rational choices. Nor does individualism explain some of the basic customs and regulations, such as those concerning kinship and incest, attitudes towards foreigners or technical innovation, or the adoption and rejection of new beliefs.

The alternative to both holism and individualism is *systemism*. According to this view all patterns of social behaviour – whether laws, rules, or trends – are artificial, that is, made; but they are rarely adopted or dropped as a result of deliberation and rational choice. Social patterns emerge along with new social systems, much as chemical laws emerge along with new chemical compounds; they are constrained by natural laws, environmental circumstances, and tradition; and they weaken when the system they inhere in declines or breaks down – although they may become so ingrained in the culture that they may be ritually observed long after they have ceased to be functional. In sum, the rules of social behaviour are made and unmade by humans, though often unintentionally, and they are constrained by laws and circumstances.

To sum up, the nomothetic/idiographic dichotomy is a philosophical artefact, for every science is both nomothetic and idiographic. Likewise, the opposition between natural and historical sciences is untenable because there are a number of natural sciences that are historical. And the claim that the social sciences do not find or even use regularities is falsified by the existence of a number of social (in particular statistical) regularities. (Social scientists have found more patterns than earth scientists and evolutionary biologists, whose scientific credentials nobody dares question.) Any of these results suffices to demolish the core of the historico-cultural school from Dilthey to present-day hermeneutics. If any doubt were to remain, the following sections should put it to rest, for they will examine a handful of socionatural sciences, whose very existence refutes the social science / natural science (or idiographic/nomothetic) dichotomy invented by that school.

4 Biosociology and Sociobiology

Since humans are animals, some kinds of social behaviour can and must be studied from a biological viewpoint. Think of eating, drinking, or sexual habits. Or take alcoholism, a social plague in so many countries: Are some people genetically prone to alcoholism and others congenitally intolerant to alcohol? Or consider violence: Is it innate, learned, or both? And how does poverty affect biological and mental development?

The biological study of social behaviour may be called *biosociology* – not to be confused with sociobiology. Typically, the biosociologist studies the social behaviour that animals, among them humans, engage in when seeking (whether automatically or deliberately) to meet their needs or wants. Whether zoologist, ethologist, behavioural geneticist, or biologically oriented social psychologist, a scientist will do biosociological work when studying the biological roots of pair bonding, cooperation, flocking (or ganging up), territoriality, aggression, dominance, or division of labour. He cultivates the same discipline when studying the dependence of such biological features as height, weight, longevity, morbidity, fertility, and scholastic performance upon socio-economic status via income, nutrition, and health care (see, for instance, the journal *Social Science and Medicine*).

Biosociologists investigate the correlations and functional relations between social and biological (or psychological) development, for instance, between nutrition, on the one hand, and thickness of the cerebral cortex as well as scholastic achievement, on the other. They do not hold dogmatically that all human behaviour is genetically programmed; consequently, they do not claim that social science is reducible to biology or even to psychology. For example, they admit that most murderers are men, but do not conclude that murder is an inborn male characteristic, for murder rates vary considerably across societies. Rather, they may hypothesize that small-scale murder is one way of wielding power, as well as getting excitement and notoriety, in a poverty-stricken and culturally depressed social environment. In short, they attempt to account for murder and social behaviour of other kinds in terms of biological, psychological, and social variables.

Likewise, *biopolitology* is the emerging interstitial science that studies the biological factors in the genesis, maintenance, and dissolution of power structures in primate societies, particularly human groups. Though young, it has a few findings to its credit. For instance, it has been found that dominance need not be based on aggression; that chimpanzees spend much of their time politicking – e.g., forming coalitions or breaking them up (de Waal 1989); that power relations in groups of children get stronger with age; and that in most cases ethnicity is more economic or political than biological.

The complement of biopolitology, which may be called *politobiology*, is another fledgling socionatural science. It studies the impact of politics upon longevity, morbidity, fertility, and other biological features. For example, epidemiological studies have shown that in Great Britain the increase in social inequality resulting from the conservative social policies of the 1980s caused a dramatic rise in morbidity and mortality among the poor (Wilkinson 1994). The moral is clear: Thatcherism is hazardous to health.

Neither politobiology nor biopolitology must be confused with the attempt to reduce political science to biology, that is, to explain all of politics in terms of genes, race, sex, or innate aggressiveness – as when Tiger and Fox (1971) characterized the political system as a breeding system centred in the male hunter. Much the same holds for psychopolitics, which attempts to explain politics in terms of the (largely invented) personalities of political leaders. For example, at the time of the Persian Gulf War an American professor of psychiatry and politics explained the Iraqi aggression against Kuweit saying that Saddam Hussein suffers from "malignant narcissism." Apparently, oil and geopolitics were not relevant – and psychiatric diagnosis at a distance is valid.

To return to biosociology. This discipline is not to be confused with *sociobiology*, which attempts to reduce the entire field of social behaviour to biology and, in particular, to neo-Darwinian evolutionary theory (the so-called Modern Synthesis). Thus, Wilson (1975, 4): "sociology and the other social sciences, as well as the humanities, are the last branches of biology waiting to be included in the Modern Synthesis. One of the functions of sociobiology, then, is to reformulate the foundations of the social sciences in a way that draws these subjects into the Modern Synthesis." (See also Tiger and Fox 1971; Rosenberg 1980; and Fox 1989.)

Sociobiology was instantly denounced as a piece of reactionary ideology on a par with Social Darwinism. This charge is unfair, because sociobiology started as an earnest attempt to explain sociality in terms of modern biology. That the attempt has failed with reference to humans is another story. The trouble with human sociobiologists is that, like psychoanalysts and religious fundamentalists, they are obsessed with sex and reproduction. Although these are undeniably important, the overriding concern of higher animals is with individual survival, hence with feeding and defence – not with spreading their genes. Nor do all men attempt to impregnate as many women as possible, and as often as possible, to maximize the diffusion of their own genes. In fact, anthropologists and family sociologists have found that most men are monogamous; that most families are planned even where no contraceptives are available; and that birth control has been practised since antiquity. Even more to the point: in modern human societies dominance and status are inversely correlated with fertility (Vining 1986).

However, the centrepiece of sociobiology is its alleged explanation of altruism in terms of kin selection or nepotism. Certainly, there are some examples of altruistic behaviour or what appears to be such. For example, on sighting a predator, the ground squirrel (or prairie dog) gives an alarm call that may save the lives of the inhabitants of its burrow while endangering its own life. The sociobiological explanation is that such behaviour is encoded in the animal's genes because it maximizes the "survival" of the genes distinctive of the individual's kin. This is the hypothesis of kin selection, proposed by W.D. Hamilton (1964). According to it altruism, though bad individual business, is an excellent genetic investment. Thus, prairie dogs would be selected not only on the strength of their individual fitness, but also on that of their ability to protect their kin: what matters would be total or inclusive fitness. For example, it would be good kin business for a prairie dog, or even for a sociobiologist, to lay down his life in defence of three or more siblings.

However, alternative explanations of apparent altruism are possible. For example, when a prairie dog gives an alarm call, it alerts not just its relatives but the entire neighbourhood (Sherman 1977). So, if it invests anything, it does so in the community rather than in its own kin. Besides, it is just possible that the animal cries out of fear rather than to defend its neighbours. The empirical evidence produced by the observation of animals of other species is likewise inconclusive. And in all cases it is weak for being observational rather than experimental. In sum, the ingenious hypothesis of kin selection is still in limbo for nonhuman animals.

Why should this hypothesis be true of people, whose actions are even less bound by their genomes, are often bound by relations of love, partnership, or authority, sometimes stronger than kinship relations, and are directly rewarded for altruistic actions? Cooperation and reciprocal altruism among invertebrates and lower vertebrates may be explained in strictly biological terms. But to account for the social behaviour of higher vertebrates we need something more than biology, namely social (animal or human) psychology. The reason is that here we are dealing with animals endowed with partially plastic brains, capable of feeling more than just hunger or fear, and above all capable of learning new tricks, and consequently of altering their own behaviour patterns. Social inventions are not products of biological evolution; if they were, they would be neither imitated nor resisted. To sum up, human sociobiology is a failed science. It failed in skipping levels, just as atomic physics would fail if it attempted to explain earthquakes. (For further criticisms see Sahlins 1977; Kitcher 1985; Schwartz 1986; Hernegger 1989; Lewontin 1991; and Maynard Smith 1992.)

Dawkins (1976, 21) has formulated an even more radical program: that of reducing psychology and social science to genetics, on the assumption that our genes "created us, body and mind." Developmental biology and psychology deny this opinion. Thus, caterpillar and butterfly have the same DNA. And presumably Mussolini did not turn from anarchist to socialist to fascist as a result of mutations. Ethologists and psychologists have always known the importance of the environment. So have the social psychologists and sociologists interested in life-course processes. They realize that human development is unpredictable from information about genes and childhood experiences alone, because both position in social structure (for instance, in a job ladder) and social change are critical for achievement (see, for instance, Sørensen 1986). And there is reason to suspect that the human genome records major social upheavals, such as genocides, mass migrations, and miscegenations, as well as biological evolution. In sum, DNA proposes: environment disposes. (See Diamond 1997.)

There have been several other attempts to ape biology. One of them is the application of the ideas of population ecology to "populations" of organizations (e.g., Hannan and Freeman 1977 and Carroll 1984). These authors write about "natural" selection, organization "life" cycles, progeny, niche, and the like, with reference to business firms and other formal organizations. Such analogies have at best heuristic value, because organizations have no genes, whence they suffer no genic changes that may confer them advantages or disadvantages in competition; and they are subjected to social (economic, political, or cultural) selection, not natural selection.

In sum, human biosociology is legitimate because people are animals. By contrast, neither human sociobiology nor genetic determinism nor human population ecology can explain society, because (a) people are largely artefactual and join in social systems that allow them to overcome their individual biological and psychological limitations; and (b) such systems have systemic properties (economic, political, and cultural) that no person could possibly possess, and some of which have no obvious biological roots. For example, whereas individual aggressivenes can be controlled by threat or love, drugs or surgical means, organized violence can be handled efficiently only with legal or political means.

5 Demography and Geography

The very first problem a sociologist, economist, politologist, or historian should ask and answer is: How many people are involved in the social system or fact of interest? The priority of this question derives from the well-known fact that small-, medium-, and large-size systems have different properties, and accordingly must be studied by somewhat different methods. For example, Aristotle held that democracy works only for small city-states; economists know that mass production requires a type of technology and management different from artisanal production; and historians know that population increase leads to an increse in production, which in turn may cause environmental depletion, which induces either territorial expansion or migration. In short, demography should precede all the social sciences.

Here is a sample of the technical vocabulary of demography: population and population density, birth and death rates, lifespan, average puberty and menopause ages, marriage rate, average number of children per mother, percentage of unwed mothers, morbidity rate, ratio of urban to total population, external and internal migration rate, and genetic effects of migrations and plagues. All of these concepts are biosocial. For example, individual births and deaths are biological events, but the norms and ceremonies associated with them are social facts. The other key concepts of demography are parallel. Consequently, all the propositions of demography are biosocial. Hence demography – traditionally included in sociology – is a *biosocial* science. Its mere existence disproves the idealist thesis that there is chasm between the social and the natural sciences.

Demography and its sister, epidemiology, pose a number of interesting methodological problems, of which only a few will be mentioned. The first and oldest is the status of the concept of an average person. For Quetelet, the father of modern social statistics, the *homme moyen* was not a statistical artefact. He claimed that the average person should be treated as the representative of society, much as the centre of mass can be taken to represent a body. The average man of a given society has not only biological traits, such as age, height, and weight, but also "moral" ones such as propensity to crime. We know now that the mode, or most comon value, is a better representative of the whole than the average. But sometimes we forget that both parameters are artefacts; and we still tend to think in terms of ethnic or national stereotypes, all of which are, at best, statistical modes or ideal types.

A tougher problem is whether the observed rates and trends could be explained and, if so, how. The foes of explanation, whether irrationalists or positivists, choose the easy path and prescribe that demographers should confine themselves to description. But some demographers wish to understand what they "observe." For example, knowing that the birth, death, and morbidity rates are variable, they investigate how they may depend on such variables as natural resources, income, and educational level. Their ambition is to do demography as human ecology (Keyfitz 1984).

Another example: It has been known for a long time that there is a high positive correlation between longevity and the married state. How may this statistical association be explained? More than a century ago, J. Bertillon surmised that marriage is healthy, whereas H. Spencer suspected that marriage selects the healthier. Probably both were right, and the conundrum is yet to be satisfactorily solved. A similar causation-selection controversy concerns the inverse correlation between mental health and socio-economic status found by E. Jarvis in 1855. According to one hypothesis, low socio-economic status causes mental disorder; according to the rival hypothesis, genetically predisposed persons tend to slide down the social scale or not to rise in socio-economic status. A recent ingenious and massive epidemiological study proposes a Solomonic solution: social factors may explain the inverse correlation in the case of depression in women as well as antisocial behaviour and drug addiction in men; by contrast, social selection may explain the correlation in the case of schizophrenia (Dohrenwend et al. 1992).

A third interesting problem is that of demographic forecasts and hindcasts. Both are computed with the help of a well-known equation and data concerning the current level of population, as well as birth and death rates. (If migration is disregarded, the law in question is: $P_t = (1 + b - d) P_{t-1}$. Although so obvious that it is usually called an identity, this is a typical conservation law: in fact, it states that people do not just appear out of the blue but are born, and do not disappear in thin air but die.)

Once the data are in, computation is trivial. But the birth and death rates are likely to be affected by unforeseen environmental, biological, economic, cultural, and political factors, such as droughts and wars. Hence, any demographic projection is bound to be uncertain. This is why demographers usually make at least three different projections: assuming the current fertility, mortality, and migration rates, as well as somewhat higher and somewhat lower values of the same parameters. In this way at least three "scenarios" result. (In other words, different values of the parameters are plugged into a single law statement.) Surprisingly, some trends – for instance, those concerning age composition – are "robust," that is, they are largely insensitive to birth and death rates.

Reasonably accurate demographic projections (alas, somewhat on the short side) have been available for a few decades. Increasing accuracy is likely to result not from more data but from smarter theoretical research into the functional dependence of the key demographic parameters upon environmental and social variables. Whether such research will be encouraged depends critically on the philosophy of science of demographers and their employers.

Demographic hindcasts are more conjectural. Yet we now have, among others, fairly reliable estimates of the population levels of the ancient civilizations of Sumer and Egypt, as well as lower and upper bounds of the Amerindian population level at the time of the "discovery" of America. One of the most daring demographic retrodictions is the estimate that the maximum lifespan of our hominid ancestors, who lived about three million years ago, was roughly half ours. This projection was performed on the basis of the strong correlation – found by R.G. Cutler in 1959 for primates and other mammalian species – between maximum lifespan on the one hand, and body weight and brain weight, on the other (see Matessi 1984). However, like all other long-term demographic hindcasts, this one is likely to remain somewhat speculative.

Another speculative yet well-grounded and useful kind of demographic retrodiction is the "what if" or alternative historical scenario – an exercise in counterfactual history. It consists in recalculating past demographic histories, pretending that certain events did not happen – for instance, that either of the two world wars did not occur or that certain migratory waves failed to happen. Comparing an imaginary demographic history with the real one helps understand what really happened. Moreover, it helps design demographic (in particular, migratory) policies (see Foot 1982, 81–5). This excercise shows once again that, contrary to empiricism, scientific research is not just data collection but also disciplined imagination.

In short, demography and epidemiology are socionatural sciences, and they hazard explanations, predictions, and retrodictions, though admittedly somewhat inaccurate ones, on the strength of laws and trends. Moreover, certain demographic forecasts, for instance, that the world population is likely to double by the mid-twenty-first century, are already affecting global policy making. Previous demographic forecasts should have been listened to by national policy makers, but they were not for ideological motives – to everyone's loss.

The next-door neighbour of demography is human geography, the social branch of biogeography. Unlike the latter, which studies the dispersal of plants and animals, human geography studies human setlements. (However, the two disciplines have a partial overlap, for many plant and animal species have been propagated by human migrations: remember potatoes and tomatoes. See Solbrig 1994.) In particular, human geography studies the concentration of humans in towns and their rural hinterland, and it attempts to explain "spatial dynamics" in terms of environmental resources and political constraints as well as trade, occupation, and cultural opportunities and choices. Animal dispersal can be accounted for, to a first approximation, as a result of the combination of natural selection with random walk (or swimming, slithering, or flight) in response to resource scarcity and predation. By contrast, in human migration and settlement, economic and political conditions, knowledge, curiosity, expectation, membership in a network, and deliberate choice and planning weigh more than randomness and natural selection. That this is so can be documented in recent times, but must be conjectured for the remote past.

Up until recently, human (or socio-economic or cultural) geography was purely descriptive. Since 1954 a number of mathematical models endowed with some explanatory and normative power have emerged, mainly localization models such as central place theory with its nested hexagons (see, for instance, W. Bunge 1962 and Krugman 1996). Another interesting development is the emergence of mathematical models of environments utilizable in resource management, town planning, and generally social-policy design (see, for example, Bennett and Chorley 1978).

The emergence of geographical theories has stimulated the birth of a ratio-empiricist philosophy of geography (see, for instance, Alvarez 1991). By the same token it has weakened the hold of the "humanistic" approach. Still, there are some self-styled phenomenological geographers who write obscurely about the "meaning of space"; and there are Marxist geographers who scold their scientific colleagues for describing the world instead of changing it. (See, for example, Gale and Olsson 1979.) Luckily for the explorers of the New World, their cartographers were realists intent on mapping the world in the truest possible way.

To conclude. One of the philosophically more interesting and least noticed features of demography and human geography is that they do not fit the idiographic ideal. Indeed, they use particulars or "accidents" as raw materials for unveiling systems, such as market areas, the American prairies, or the Pacific Rim; for extracting emergent properties, such as critical town sizes; for unveiling trends, such as increasing (or decreasing) regional economic integration, and changes in lifespan, marriage age, and family size; and even for hazarding laws, such as "The number of cities with populations larger than P is inversely proportional to P." As with every other basic science, in geography the individual or particular is only the starting point; the ultimate goal is to ferret out system and pattern.

6 Social Psychology

Social psychology is the socionatural (or biosocial) science that studies the impact of social relations on the individual, and the reaction of individual behaviour to society (for example: enculturation and deviance respectively). In the former case one speaks of *psychological* social psychology, in the latter of *sociological* social psychology; or of sociopsychology and psychosociology respectively. Usually the former discipline is cultivated by psychologists and the latter by sociologists.

This separation is unfortunate because it amounts to artificially splitting the study of interactions into the study of actions and that of reactions. Thus, when studying roles, a scientist may investigate the way his subjects perform them, or the manner in which such actions alter the behaviour of other individuals – and preferably both. When studying enculturation (or socialization), he may focus on the individual who becomes socialized or on the agents of his enculturation (parents, peers, teachers) – or, preferably, both. Any serious study of a social-psychological fact will involve both agent and patient, and this for a mere *logical* reason: to understand a relation we must examine all its relata.

There is also a *methodological* reason for favouring a closer contact between the two halves of social psychology; namely, that one can now make use of objective quantitative physiological indicators of the effects of some social stimuli (e.g., words) on a subject. In fact, there is such a thing as physiological social psychology, a field that the sociological social psychologist can only ignore at his peril (see, for instance, Cacioppo and Petty 1983). For example, it is well known that social stressors weaken immunity, by increasing the concentration of corticosterone in the blood plasma, which in turn damages lymphocytes and thymus elements. Another example: The two kinds of social learning – in the classroom, and in the playground or the workplace – are so different that they are likely to involve different neural systems (Lamendella 1977).

Still, the social psychologist need not dip on every occasion into neurophysiological detail, any more than the physicist need analyse every extended body into its elementary constituents. In fact, the social psychologist can group brain processes into large categories, such as affect, cognition, and volition, taking his research from there and trusting that the biopsychologist will eventually delve into them. Likewise, when studying, say, the interactions between personality and social structure, he may take the latter for granted, trusting that the sociologist will account for it. He is even forced to do so when the psychological feature in question has hardly been studied from a biopsychological viewpoint, as is the case with moral judgment, artistic appreciation, and religious worship. (Berlyne 1974 is an exception.)

Whether he emphasizes the subjective or the social aspect, the social psychologist deals all the time with both micro and macro levels. The psychological social psychologist tends to be an upward (or top-down) reductionist, whereas the sociological social psychologist tends to be a downward (or bottom-up) reductionist. In other words, the former tends to favour holism and the latter individualism. The individualist will credit (or blame) the subject concerned for all he or she does or fails to do, while absolving the social order. By contrast, the holist will credit (or blame) society as a whole, or at least some institutions, for every feature of personal development, lifestyle, and job performance. Where the former sees moral failure, the latter sees social failure.

But surely whoever pays exclusive attention to either individual experience (the approach of classical rationalists and empiricists) or social circumstances (the approach of Marx, Durkheim, Vygotsky, and the antipsychiatry movement) is bound to fail. Social psychology is still excessively concerned with internal states and processes, such as attribution, attitudes, choice of breakfast cereal, career, or mate, with neglect of the group, the system, and history (Steiner 1974; Sherif 1977). But of course the opposite strategy would be just as mistaken. Balance is essential in any hybrid science.

Exclusive use of either strategy is mistaken because every human is embedded in several social systems, and the latter happen to be formed, kept, and altered by individual action. The correct strategy combines bottom-up and top-down analyses: one must attempt to explain macrofacts in terms of microfacts and conversely. For example, when studying a religious or political movement, one should try to explain conversion (or its opposite, disillusion) not only in terms of personal background and experience, but also in terms of social circumstances, in particular peer pressure, coercion, and propaganda. Thus, when studying the rise and fall of a social movement one should try to find out what "perceived" virtues or shortcomings of the movement makes individuals join or leave it.

Incidentally, it may be remembered that social psychology started out as crowd psychology – a pseudoscience. Its creators, H. Taine and G. Le Bon, had a correct insight, namely, that an individual's behaviour is altered when becoming part of a crowd. But, being conservatives, they held mass behaviour to be always intellectually and morally inferior to that of the isolated individual; they overlooked the unselfish actions that people are capable of when joining a social movement. Not surprisingly, Le Bon's best-seller became a manual for the manipulation of the masses; Mussolini and Hitler used it.

Nor is this the only case of ideological contamination of social-psychological studies. An earlier instance is Marx's thesis that alienation (*Entfremdung*) is a product of capitalism, which robs the worker of most of the product of his work. But in the 1970s some Russian sociologists found to their surprise that alienation was just as common among workers under "real socialism" as under capitalism. (Moreover, maybe the potters in ancient Greece, who fashioned hundreds of nearly identical amphoras, felt alienated too.) The problem seems only to have been compounded by the extreme division of labour and the authoritarian management characteristic of modern industry. In short, alienation is likely to be independent of property rights; it may be a side effect of mass production. (See Miller 1977.) This hypothesis could be tested by studying self-managed (cooperative) industrial firms without assembly lines. In short, beware of ideology.

A third and far worse case of ideological contamination is Hobbes's hypothesis, revived by Freud and Lorenz, that aggression is innate and the unavoidable cause of all wars. The following objections must be raised against it. First, mice, dogs, and other animals can be bred selectively for aggressiveness, whereas no such inborn traits have been shown for people: in the latter, deprivation, learning, and the cognitive appraisal of social situations are critical. Second, the occurrence of hostile feelings and actions in people and other animals can be experimentally induced or inhibited (e.g., by electric stimulation of the appropriate region of the limbic system). Third, aggression is not the same as belligerence, that is, organized collective armed aggression. Whereas the former occurs sometimes naturally, belligerence is unrelated to aggressive feelings: it is organized and waged in cold blood for economic, political, or cultural goals (Lagerspetz 1981). The French fascist Count Jacques de Bernonville told the executioners under his orders: "Do not shoot these *maquisards* in anger, for they are our brethren."

To get a "feel" for the state of the field and the methodological issues it raises, let us take a quick look at a couple of interesting topical issues. The first is reference-group "theory," which asserts that we form many beliefs and attitudes by taking certain individuals or groups as standards against which we compare our own circumstances and aspirations. This hypothesis explains why conformism prevails in a homogeneously poor group, and why discontent or even rebellion flares up in the face of obvious inequity, as when one social group advances much more rapidly than others. This view has been satisfactorily confirmed. But is it a *theory* and, in particular, a middle-range theory, as Merton (1957a, 280) called it? I submit that it is not a theory (hypothetico-deductive system), for it boils down to a single proposition, namely: "The perception of deprivation is relative to the [reference] social group the subject chooses." It is a middle-range (neither sweeping nor narrow) *hypothesis*. But it is general enough to subsume such special hypotheses as Boudon's discovery that the youngsters of well-off families do better at school than those of poorer families, not only because they have a head start but also because they are more strongly motivated: they expect and are expected to do well in their studies. (Being more specific, this proposition is more complex than the reference-group hypothesis.)

Our second example is the proposed mechanisms of belief acquisition. Empiricists claim that people will hold a certain belief if it fits their own experience. This may be an adequate account for beliefs involved in day-to-day survival actions, such as that water quenches thirst, but it fails to account for ideological (in particular religious) beliefs. (Recall Festinger's [1957] finding concerning the way fanatics cope with failed prophecies.) Feuerbach, Marx, and others believed in interests: people would tend to believe what is convenient for them to believe. Although this is indeed so in many cases, it does not hold for well-grounded (e.g., mathematical and scientific) beliefs. Finally, Pareto claimed that, in nonscientific matters, belief is only a matter of sentiment. Again, this view fits some cases – particularly ordinary beliefs concerning other people – but not others.

The primitive cosmogonies are not accounted for by any of the previous views. For example, the Haida of British Columbia believed that in the beginning humans were trapped inside a clam, and that a crow set them free. What does this have to do with either feelings, interests, experience, or reason? It seems to be just a yarn invented to entertain as well as to answer the age-old question 'Where do we come from?' A moral of this example is that there may be at least as many kinds of belief-acquisition mechanisms as types of belief – and that we do not know much about any of them anyway.

What can we make of the expression 'public opinion'? Non-holists must interpret this phrase as shorthand for the collection of the most commonly held beliefs in a social group. For example, the so-called West (which of course includes Japan and Israel) is supposed to believe in individualism, free enterprise, political liberty, civil rights, the force of arms, high levels of consumption, and a measure of social welfare. But how strong is this belief? A simple way to measure the strength of the beliefs in a given social group is to make a list of ideas and count the number of people who believe in each of them. Calling n_i the number of people who believe item i in the list, the degree of belief in i in the group may be defined as $b_i = n_i/n$, where n is the group size. And the degree of belief of the group in the given set of ideas may be defined as the sum of all the b_i divided by the number m of ideas concerned, that is, $b = (1/mn) \Sigma_i n_i$. This measure can be refined by assigning a weight to every person's belief – for instance, strong, medium, and weak.

Another notion central to social psychology is that of anomie or normlessness. Merton (1957a, 134) explained it as an effect of the mismatch between social norm (or aspiration) and opportunity: a discrepancy between what is socially acceptable and desirable and what an individual can actually achieve. The concept of anomie is important enough to deserve being quantitated, and thus be readied for measurement and incorporation into some mathematical model. Let us do this. Call D the set of a person's desiderata, and C the set of his consummata, or wants and needs that he has been able to met. We stipulate that his anomie is the set equal to the difference between his desiderata and his consummata, that is, $A = D \setminus C$. (A contains the elements in D but not in C.) Calling $|S|$ the numerosity of an arbitrary set S, the *degree of anomie* may now be defined as $\alpha = |D \setminus C|/|D|$. This is a number between 0 (when D = C, or full contentment) and 1 (when $D \setminus C = D$, or total frustration). When half of the desiderata are met, $\alpha = \frac{1}{2}$. Finally, the degree of anomie of a group can be defined as the average of the sum of the anomies of the group members. Presumably, necessary conditions for group rebellion are that group anomie exceeds a certain threshold but, at the same time, is on the decline – that is, when people start to see light at the end of the tunnel.

To conclude. It is no secret that social psychology has to its credit but a few robust findings, and that it is in a permanent state of crisis. I venture to suggest what is often wrong with research in this field:

1. Few social psychologists adopt the systemic approach: whereas some of them overlook social structure, others underrate the inner springs of behaviour.

2. Too much time is wasted debating whether investigators should choose problems for their theoretical interest or for their practical relevance, as if the discipline could not afford to have both basic and applied components.

3. The literature, particularly on the sociological side, is plagued by an obscure and pretentious jargon whose only function is to pass off platitudes as scientific advances.

4. There is a tendency to skirt serious issues, such as the devastating psychological effects of unemployment, discrimination, torture, war, and forced migration. Consequently, there is a glut of trivial hypotheses, such as "Rapid social change widens the generation gap," "The more technically qualified individuals tend to adopt a more modern outlook," and "As people get older they become less receptive to changes in ideas and values."

5. Many of the measures and tests are not well validated, so that they can be interpreted in alternative ways. For example, Adorno's widely used F scale was supposed to measure authoritarianism. Recent work suggests that it does this only for the well educated: at lower educational levels it measures acquiescence, not authoritarianism (Schuman et al. 1992). As well, there is excessive tolerance for untested or even untestable hypotheses borrowed from other fields, particularly psychoanalysis – which attracts so many people because it purports to explain everything, whether personal or social, in simple but, alas, fantastic psychological terms (see, for instance, Gellner 1993).

6. Most of the hypotheses are stated verbally: there are too few mathematical models both nontrivial and realistic. Worse yet, some of them are pseudomathematical. (For instance, certain well-known researchers add statements, as in "a likes b + b likes c .")

7. Most observations and experiments have only a remote bearing on real life, because they are performed mostly on college students (Amir and Sharon 1988, 385). Moreover, the subjects are gathered in artificial small groups, that is, groups formed occasionally by the experimenter, so that they do not constitute social systems.

8. Far too many experiments are performed "not to test our hypotheses but to demonstrate their obvious truth"; hence, when they fail to do so, "better" subjects, not better hypotheses, are selected (McGuire 1973).

9. Too many experimental results are accepted uncritically and, as a consequence, the field grows too slowly and, worse, the experimental method falls into disrepute. For example, it took seventeen years to replicate the sensational findings of Schachter and Singer (1962) on the influence of cognition upon mood. Worse, the attempts failed (Maslach 1979; Marshall and Zimbardo 1979).

10. Experimental findings concerning subhuman animals observed in cages (for example, concerning the negative effects of crowding on dendritic spine density and the positive effect on aggressiveness) are too often extrapolated uncritically to humans. This disregards the fact that some institutions and norms have been introduced precisely to keep under control the destructive effects of social interaction and deprivation.

In sum, social psychology is in a state of crisis, which is due in part to insufficient philosophical self-examination.

7 Anthropology

Anthropology too is a biosocial science, by dealing with "cultural" (social) as well as "physical" (biological) aspects of the human condition. It is also the most basic and comprehensive of all the social sciences, in studying all aspects of social behaviour, from kinship systems, child rearing, tool making, and food production to social organization, political action, and "symbolic" activity, such as speech and prayer. It combines the search for universals (cross-cultural patterns) with that for particulars: the nomothetic with the idiographic. It studies humans from their hominid beginnings about three million years ago to our days, and from pristine gatherer-scavenger-hunters to advanced societies. Nothing human is alien to anthropology: it is the science of man in the broadest possible sense. Every other synchronic social science may be viewed as a branch of anthropology.

The broad scope of anthropology may be a major reason for the uncertainty of many of its practitioners concerning the very nature of their own discipline. Thus, whereas some of them believe anthropology to be about real people mainly interested in survival, others claim it is only about rules, values, and symbols. Some researchers hold that anthropology should study only primitives, whereas others take all societies for their domain. And whereas some advocate ascetic description, others claim to practise *Verstehen* (or interpretion, or "thick description"), and still others embrace the scientific approach. Yet, regardless of their differences, nearly all anthropologists are diffident regarding theory. But, of course, they cannot help making hypotheses, which they often dignify with the name of 'theories' (see Harris 1968 and Trigger 1989). Actually, aside from vague "grand theories," such as evolutionism, diffusionism, functionalism, conflict theory, and cultural materialism – all of them largely programmatic hypotheses that have inspired fruitful research projects – anthropology contains hardly any *theories*, that is, hypothetico-deductive systems.

The typical research project in anthropology is a fact-finding mission to study some social group, be it the natives of a distant land, the gang around the corner, or the team working in a laboratory. The normal outcome of such fieldwork is a descriptive report. Most anthropologists stop here, and some claim that this is all there should be. (For a critique see Coser 1975.) However, many anthropologists wish to understand what they record. And this calls for a clear idea of the very nature of both explanation and anthropology.

Anthropology is commonly characterized as "the science of culture." This is unhelpful given the vagueness of the term 'culture,' which has been defined in about two hundred different ways (Kroeber and Kluckhohn 1952). Worse, many anthropologists equate 'culture' with 'society.' This equation has two flaws. The first is that it condones the idealist tradition of disregarding matters of reproduction and means of earning a livelihood, focusing instead on disembodied norms, values, and symbolic forms, and regarding people as being actuated by them, and institutions as "embodying" them – an idea as old as Plato and one central to the symbolatry and glossocentrism of "postmodern discourse."

Thus Geertz, a champion of the hermeneutic, or "interpretive," school (1966, 643) has proposed the following oft-quoted definition of religion: Religion "is (1) a system of symbols which acts to (2) establish powerful, pervasive, and long lasting moods and motivations in men by (3) formulating conceptions of a general order of existence and (4) clothing these conceptions with such an aura of factuality that (5) the moods and motivations seem uniquely realistic." Such attribution of causal efficacy to symbols is a piece of magical thinking. Symbols are not self-existing: they stand for something or other, and they are created or transformed, used or discarded, by people. In particular, religionists create symbols in the process of inventing or teaching religious ideas, worshipping, communicating with coreligionists, and so on. Moreover, the faithful are not expected to mistake ritual for religion. If they do, good Christians call them 'Pharisees.'

A second defect of the equation "Culture = Society" is that it prevents one from speaking of the culture of a society (or a firm or an army), as well as of the economy and the politics of a culture and, in particular, of the cultural policy of a government. In order for these expressions to make sense we must adopt a narrower concept of culture. We should view the culture of a society as that concrete subsystem of it whose members perform mainly cognitive, technical, artistic, moral, or religious activities (Bunge 1981a). Thus, keeping track of the seasons, healing, making music, studying nature, society, or ideas, designing tools or plans, and participating in religious ceremonies are cultural activities, whereas scavenging, gathering fruits, digging holes, feeding children, nursing the sick, making tools, organizing people, and warring are not. Again, though cuisine, dress, play, love, and much more are strongly influenced by culture, they are not part of it.

This narrower concept of culture fits the actual scope of anthropology, which embraces all four subsystems of every human society: the biological, economic, political, and cultural. Thus, anthropology can be redefined as the study of all the features of human groups (in particular social systems). All the other social sciences are specializations of anthropology. In particular, sociology, economics, and political science are the branches of anthropology that study contemporary societies.

The very first problem that anthropologists face is one they share with philosophers; namely, What is man? – or, equivalently, What is human nature? Since humans are studied by a large number of disciplines, it should not come as a surprise to learn that every one of them yields its own partial view of man. The biologist sees the animal where the theologian sees a hybrid of beast and angel. And other specialists adopt the models encapsulated in the expressions *homo faber, homo œconomicus, homo ethicus, zoon politikon* (social animal), *homo sapiens, homo loquens, homo symbolicus* (Cassirer), *homo ludens* (Huizinga), *homo aleator* (gambler), *self-interpreting animal* (C. Taylor), *structure-making animal* (Lévi-Strauss), *homo machina* (La Mettrie and computationalist cognitive psychology), and a few others. Let us take a quick look at some of these views.

According to the *religious model*, man is a spiritual being who uses his body as a tool during his brief stopover on earth, and who is distinguished by the worship of supernatural powers. This spiritualist (hence idealist) model is incompatible with biology and physiological psychology, and it overlooks reproduction, sociality, work, and social conflict. Therefore, anthropologists find no use for it except as a subject of research.

The *biological model* of man, inherent in Social Darwinism and sociobiology, stresses our animal nature to the point of regarding economic, political, and cultural activities as mere means for meeting biological needs and wants (see, for instance, Fox 1989). It has the great merits of directing attention to the biological roots of some such activities, as well as of stressing the evolutionary continuity between hominid and man, thereby discrediting the spiritualist conception of man. But biologism does not account for boundless economic and political greed any more than for disinterested curiosity, aesthetic pleasure, or religious devotion. And it has misled many anthropologists into believing that their goal in studying gatherer-scavenger-hunters is to discover man "in the state of nature" – as if humans, however primitive, were not largely artefactual. What gatherer-scavenger-hunter studies do provide is "a vision of human life and human possibilities without the pomp and glory, but also without the misery and inequity of state and class society" (Lee 1992, 43).

The *psychological model* of man stresses emotion, cognition, valuation, volition, and language. It has become the dominant view of human nature in what Gross (1978) has called the Psychological Society. Obviously, it accounts for some features of human nature; but it neglects others. In particular, it overlooks the facts that all of us are born into a society that shapes our mental development, and that every structural social change is likely to alter the mode of enculturation. The psychological model of man is inherent in all the attempts to reduce social science to psychology, whether it be folk psychology, psychoanalysis, or behaviourism. All rational-choice theories adopt it, as is obvious from the fact that their basic concepts are those of subjective value and subjective probability. But this is of no help to the anthropologist intent on understanding not only the cross-cultural invariants but also the peculiarities of a particular society.

The *sociological model* of man is correct in stressing sociality. But it leaves the biological and psychological aspects aside. This has the undesirable consequence that it promotes "sociologism" (a variety of holism), and consequently underrates the importance of curiosity, creativity, and initiative, without which there would be neither economic and political entrepreneurship, nor art, science, technology, or ideology.

We shall leave aside the views that man is essentially a symbolic animal, a player, a gambler, or a machine (in particular a computer), for being far too narrow. Of course we all use symbols, play, gamble (or rather take risks), and try to mechanize routine tasks. But we do many more things besides, such as working, fighting, loving, educating, and caring for others.

Collecting the positive features of biologism, psychologism, and sociologism, and discarding their negative components, we arrive at the *systemic model*, which views a human being as a highly evolved animal who is a member of partially intersecting biological, economic, political, and cultural systems. Adopting this model implies rejecting both the idealist and the behaviourist research strategies, recommending instead that social scientists should study people who learn, think, and evaluate, as well as work, fight, play, have sex, and interact in a great many ways in the midst of systems of various kinds. In short, man is the gregarious, largely artefactual, and encyclopaedic animal.

Systemists do not oppose the mental (or *emic*) to the behavioural (or *etic*). Instead, they regard each of these as being sometimes the source or cause (or independent variable) and at other times the sink or effect (or dependent variable). Accordingly, systemists use constructs of both kinds, provided they can find objective indicators of the ideational and valuational processes – that is, provided they manage to "get inside people's heads" in a testable manner, at least by questioning and at best by brain imaging. (For the emic/etic controversy see Harris 1968, 1976.) Much the same holds for the Marxist material infrastructure / ideal superstructure duality: this one too is subsumed under the systemic model. So are the individual/collective, micro/macro, and agency/ structure pairs. Though mutually opposite, these concepts are not mutually exclusive.

I submit that the systemic model is the one tacitly employed by field anthropologists – except of course when they embark on a crusade to promote some alternative view. In fact, when doing fieldwork, the anthropologist studies sexual habits and kinship relations, food production and tool making, social organization and warfare (if any), language and folklore, modes of thought and value systems, skills and beliefs, norms and ceremonies, and much more. He studies individual behaviour to discover social structure, and the latter to understand the former. He goes back and forth between micro and macro, agency and structure. In fact, the anthropologist is the most thorough and consistent if spontaneous systemist of all social scientists. (However, in anthropology as in other sciences, when engaging in metatheoretical discussions many students confuse systemism with holism. This holds, in particular, for functionalist anthropologists.)

The problem of the proper view of man – or of the adequate definition of the concept of man – is not only of theoretical interest to science and philosophy. It is also practically important, for it comes up in the daily work of the palaeoanthropologist. Indeed, the latter needs a fairly clear concept of human nature and a set of fairly reliable indicators of the presence of humans at a site. He works on two sets of data: direct evidence constituted by fossil bones, tools, hearths, footprints, and remains of other animals, and of seeds and pollen grains, as well as indirect evidence provided by comparative anatomy, the study of DNA and protein evolution, and the study of the social organization of modern primitive societies, and even modern primates.

Exclusive attention to either set of data is bound to lead to serious error. Example 1: Neglect of small stature and dentition bolstered the myth that our remote ancestors were mainly hunters, whereas exclusive attention to teeth will not tell us whether their owners were bipedal. Only an examination of the pelvis and the cervical vertebrae can help to solve the latter problem. Example 2: Exclusive attention to either fossils, tools, or DNA (in particular mitochondrial DNA) evolution results in so many mutually incompatible hypotheses concerning the origin of modern humans between 100,000 and 200,000 years ago. The most popular among these speculations are the African "Eve" hypothesis (our most remote common ancestor) versus the multiregional-origin hypothesis. But neither of these rivals nor any other known contender accounts for the full extant evidence. To solve the problem we need more data of all three kinds, as well as anatomically plausible conjectures about bipedalism and the coevolution of brain, hand, and group size. Here again, only a systemic view is plausible. (See Aiello 1993 and the accompanying papers.)

The same holds for other indicators of humanity: every one of them is partial and even ambiguous, so a whole battery of them is needed. But no investigator who holds a one-sided model of man will strive to construct such a battery. By contrast, if he upholds a systemic model, he will find it easier to reconstruct the lifestyle of the group of hominids or of humans who used to inhabit the site he is studying. In turn, this hypothesis will suggest looking for further items, and their finding will correct or enrich the previous reconstruction.

Once we have formed a fairly clear concept of human nature we may ask the question of anthropogenesis or hominization. It is remarkable the extent to which myth – in particular, the myth of the Golden Age and subsequent Fall – has influenced the investigation of this problem (Stoczkowski 1991). This is apparent, for instance, in the hypothesis that hominization was elicited by the desiccation of Eastern Africa at the end of the Tertiary period, which would have forced hominids to behave more cleverly in their search for food and their defence against the great carnivores. However, there is evidence that the tropical forest and the savannah coexisted at that time. A rival hypothesis is that of optimal-foraging theory, inspired in the modern myth that all humans are profit maximizers (see Bettinger 1991 and Smith and Winterhalder 1992). According to this view, in the beginning there was plenty (as in the garden of Eden), which forced hominids to optimize their choice. The trouble with this hypothesis is triple: (a) it assumes what it wishes to explain, namely the emergence of intelligent behaviour; (b) scarcity might have had the same effect; and (c) maximizing behaviour is inconsistent with the law of diminishing returns.

Biologists are naturally tempted to answer the question of human origins in strictly biological terms, such as mutations (even macromutations) leading to larger brains and bipedalism – or perhaps in terms of adaptations of arboreal primates to the plains. By contrast, sociologically oriented palaeoanthropologists tend to give all credit to tool making and social organization, including communication. Presumably, each of these answers contains a grain of truth, and the whole truth is biopsychosociological – not sociobiological, though. The first such synthesis was hazarded by Engels (1876, chap. 9), according to whom hand, labour, and speech coevolved. In fact, it looks now quite likely that small accidental and cumulative increases in brain size, complexity, and plasticity made small advances in mental and social behaviour possible, which in turn gave further biological changes of the same kind an edge. This is suggested by the finding that, although the brain size of primitive humans increased relentlessly, their tool-making techniques remained stagnant for over one million years. Be that as it may, it is clear that brain and hand, tool and language, parenting and socializing coevolved through positive-feedback mechanisms (Dunbar 1993). Shorter: Biosociology, sí, sociobiology, no (sect. 4).

This conjecture helps to unveil the "mystery" of the human mind. This, too – or rather the minding brain – must have evolved by biosocial mutation and selection. And such process occurred without need for an intelligent designer – other than man himself, who transforms his own brain as he learns and acts. The same hypothesis of the coevolution of the social and the natural also throws light on the question of social universals, such as speech and spatial orientation. All such universals seem to be "natural," that is, anchored in the human genome – or so they are *now*, after hundreds of thousands of years of biological and "cultural" (social) mutation and selection. Interestingly, the progress of anthropology has brought about a shrinking of the collection of social universals, that is, cross-cultural ideas and habits. A recent casualty is the left/right discrimination, once thought to be basic and natural: it is absent among the Tenejapans in Mexico (Levinson and Brown 1994).

The intertwining of nature, nurture, and invention in human evolution is highlighted by the fact that not even the kinship structure of every society is exclusively determined by "blood" or genetic relations. To be sure, the basic social relationships – sex and child rearing – are biological. But the ways they are regulated, in particular the sexual permissions and prohibitions, as well as the determination of kinship relations, are made. The fact that they may vary from one society to the next, and that they are occasionally altered or even broken – though usually at a price – only shows that they are social conventions, not natural laws.

However, kinship conventions are not on the same footing with such arbitrary conventions as meaning-sound correspondences. In fact, the former are correlated with social organization. For instance, it is unlikely that the incest and dietary taboos were adopted arbitrarily. Instead, the former may have been adopted to prevent the disintegration of the family, and the latter to protect natural resources. In any event, these particular social conventions were presumably adopted for being believed to enhance either survival or social cohesiveness. Much the same seems to apply to such basic universal moral norms as that of reciprocity or mutual help. Particularly, the latter promotes the stability of the social system and it is a "starting mechanism," that is, it helps to initiate social relations (Gouldner 1960).

Any discussion of social norms is bound to evoke functionalism and relativism, which often coalesce. Actually, there are two kinds of functionalism: *ontological* and *methodological*. The former is teleological: it holds that, in all societies, every material object, custom, rule, and belief "fulfills some vital function, has some task to accomplish, represents an indispensable part within a working whole" (Malinowski 1926, 133). By contrast, methodological functionalism "does not require the dogmatic assertion that everything in the life of every community has a function. It only requires that it *may* have one, and that we are justified in seeking to discover it" (Radcliffe-Brown 1935).

A further difference between the two varieties is that the former, championed by Malinowski and inspired by psychoanalysis, holds that everything social exists or happens for the greater happiness of the individual, in particular to relieve his anxiety and help him cope with maladjustment. By contrast, methodological functionalism, inspired by Durkheim – upheld in anthropology by Radcliffe-Brown and in sociology by Parsons – asserts that the positive or eunomic social items exist or happen for the good of the community. Which is one more instance of the individualism-collectivism conflict.

The only evidence for ontological functionalism is the general usefulness of *some* norms and institutions. The contrary evidence is constituted by social dysfunctions, such as overpopulation, large investments in religious ceremonies, and militarism, as well as by "social survivals" or vestiges – that is, institutions, ideas, and behaviour patterns that no longer discharge any useful function, such as fertility rites and religious fundamentalism.

Both forms of anthropological functionalism have positive as well as negative features. Their virtue is that they stress the systemic character of every community, and thus warn (a) the researcher not to detach any one feature from the others and (b) the social reformer not to tamper with components one at a time, for a change in one may affect all. Their main defects are that (a) they ignore counterexamples, and (b) they are inconsistent in holding that we know nothing about the past of the preliterate tribal societies, while claiming at the same time that primitive societies are static (Gellner 1973, 115).

Further negative features of ontological functionalism are the dogmatism noted earlier, and the concomitant exaggeration of synergy, and the resulting conservatism, or reluctance to introduce social reforms. (It is no coincidence that ontological functionalism was used by colonial administrators to check any temptations to introduce social reforms in the territories under their control.) Finally, both functionalist schools hold that functional analysis – the uncovering of the function of each social item – is different from the standard scientific account in terms and laws and data. This is doubtful, for functional analysis itself involves the search for pattern (see also Gouldner 1970 and Martindale 1975).

The current controversy in social studies between functionalism and conflict theory is a replay of the century-old debate between Durkheim's solidarism and Marxist dialectics. And on the theoretical level it parallels the ideological struggle between political conservatism and socialism. From a systemic viewpoint there is no reason for this controversy to persist, because social conflict (in particular economic competition and class warfare) is just as real as social cooperation (and the corresponding cohesion). Far from being incompatible, competition and cooperation are two sides of the same coin. Cooperation in some respects holds social systems together, and conflict (internal or external) may rearrange them – that is, it may cause structural changes. (See appendix 2.)

As for anthropological relativism, it holds that there are no anthropological universals or cross-cultural features, and that all "cultures" are equivalent (see, for instance, Geertz 1984). In particular, it denies the primitive/advanced distinction stressed by evolutionism. (The "postmodernist" relativists hold that the anthropologists themselves have constructed all the differences among societies.) Relativism is confirmed by all the patterns and institutions peculiar to particular societies or periods. But it is refuted by any universal norm, such as that of reciprocity, as well as by every step forward, such as the emergence of agriculture, numeracy, literacy, critical thinking, science, vaccination, scientific birth control, sanitation, refrigeration, and telecommunication. Moreover, relativism is refuted by the very practice of the scientific anthropologist, for he studies and understands alien societies not in terms of the latter but in those of contemporary "Western" science (Gellner 1973). Consequently, relativism is false. But this objection does not bother the consistent relativists, for they have no use for the concept of objective truth.

As for method, since Malinowski's time anthropologists have preferred participant to passive observation. (These methods are also called, incorrectly, "subjective" and "objective" respectively.) The advocates of participant observation argue that the anthropologist must "come off the verandah," learn the natives' language, mix with them, follow them around in their daily chores, and become their confidants, instead of studying them at arm's length as if they were subhuman animals. Actually, both methods have their virtues and flaws. Indeed, the passive or "naturalistic" procedure can yield only limited and even distorted results, because one cannot get to know what other people think and want and do unless one succeeds in communicating directly with them and even tries to share in some of their activities. But the participant-observer method may lead to dogmatism: "appeals to the authority of personal experience and to unique insights become uncomfortably prominent" (Kuper 1989).

Participant observation by different investigators in quick succession might have corrected this defect. After all, in no other science are the observations of a single worker lent so much credence. However, the succession should be quick, because the group under study may undergo important changes between observations. A case in point may be the divergent results on adolescence in Samoa obtained by Margaret Mead (1928) and much later by Derek Freeman (1983). Where Mead saw gentle, happy, and sexually uninhibited adolescents, Freeman saw violence and youngsters oppressed by the virginity taboo. Perhaps both observers were influenced by their respective psychological and anthropological tenets, or else misled by their native informants, who seem to have been fond of teasing ethnographers. But it is also likely that Mead and Freeman saw really different things, because Samoa experienced enormous sea changes between the 1920s and the 1960s: Mead saw "savages," whereas Freeman studied their accultured offspring. (Besides, Freeman's report seems to be seriously flawed: see Shankman 1996.)

Another controversy, which threatens to be just as acrimonious as the preceding, was sparked by Chagnon's best-seller *Yanomano: The Fierce People* (1977). He painted these natives of the Amazon forest as engaging in perpetual war with neighbouring peoples and even among themselves. Chagnon explained this in Hobbesian terms: The Yanomama, like everyone else, are naturally ferocious but, unlike others, they act violently because they lack social controls. Kenneth Good, a doctoral student of Chagnon's, went to live for a decade with the Yanomama, adopted their lifestyle, and married a Yanomama girl by whom he had two children. His findings refute Gagnon's thesis and confirm Marvin Harris's (1977): "War among the Yanomama was a way of keeping communities dispersed to ensure that the population density in a given area would not outgrow the availability of game" (Good and Chanoff 1991, 49). Moreover, according to Good, the Yanomama make war only in case of need, and on the whole their life is harmonious: in short, they are not fierce. Who is telling the truth and, accordingly, whom are we to believe: Professor Chagnon or his former student? Obviously, this case merits further investigation. However, few contemporary scientists agree with Hobbes's (and Freud's and Lorenz's and Mussolini's) thesis that humans are naturally violent. Hence, few are likely to agree with Chagnon's (1988, 985) view that violence "may be the principal driving force behind the evolution of culture."

Nevertheless we are left with the suspicion that some anthropological writings, in being hard to test, are more similar to stories than to reports. Consider, for instance, the symbolic sexual violence among the Tukanoan in the Northwest Amazon. According to Jean Jackson (1992), women wield much actual power among the Tukanoan. Men compensate for this by performing rituals in which women are represented as defective and powerless – the way psychoanalysts see them. This is, of course, the anthropologist's own interpretation – one that "probably no Tukanoan would accept" (jackson 1992, 2). Whether there is a way of settling this matter – e.g., by experiment – seems to be an open problem. As long as no alternative is found, the study in question remains inconclusive.

Let us finally deal briefly with a rather fashionable trend in anthropology, namely hermeneutics, born and reared in the occult "sciences," theology, and philology (see, for instance, Mueller-Vollmer 1989). In fact, it can be traced back to the Bible: "In the beginning was the Word, and the Word was with God, and the Word was God" (John 1:1). Anthropological hermeneutics adopts the principle that everything social is a text, hence a symbol for something else. In particular, "the culture of a people is an ensemble of texts, themselves ensembles, which the anthropologist strains to read over the shoulders of those to whom they properly belong" (Geertz 1973, 452). For example, cockfighting – or for that matter any other social activity – would be "a collectively sustained symbolic structure" (ibid., 448). Moreover "societies, like lives, contain their own interpretation. One has only to learn how to get access to them" (453). That is, the anthropologist's task is to unearth the "interpretation" (or "meaning") hidden in social facts, "reading" them like texts.

Regrettably, we are never told clearly how to interpret 'interpretation.' From the examples used one gathers that it is just conjecturing either meaning or purpose – what scientists call 'hypothesis about function or goal.' Worse, hermeneuticians do not propose any objective tests of their "interpretations" or "thick descriptions," for they do not worry over possible misinterpretations. This is a dogmatic and risky stand, for misunderstanding is a very common occurrence in social life, even in happy families. But then hermeneuticians dismiss any concern over tests for truth as "positivist bias": they are subjectivists and relativists, hence they have no use for the concept of truth. (If truth is out of the question, "reality checks" are pointless.) To facilitate their task even further, hermeneuticians avoid serious social issues, concentrating instead on banalities such as greeting, small talk, and cockfighting – the subject of Geertz's most popular article. (More in Bunge 1996a.)

To sum up, anthropology is as exciting, theoretically underdeveloped, and rife with philosophical controversy as ever. Hence, it should be a very rewarding subject of discussion for any rigorous philosopher.

8 Linguistics

Since speech is both a mental (or brain) process and a medium of social contact, its scientific study – linguistics – is a socionatural science. In fact, linguistics is composed of pure (or general) linguistics, neurolinguistics, psycholinguistics, sociolinguistics, historical linguistics, and applied linguistics. (Philosophical linguistics à la Wittgenstein is not included because it ignores scientific linguistics and is philosophically shallow.)

Neurolinguistics is a strictly natural science, and aphasiology, a chapter of it, is half science and half medicine. By contrast, psycholinguistics, like psychology in general, is a socionatural science, for language acquisition and use occur in a social matrix. In particular, language learning is a brain process that happens to be an aspect of the socialization (or enculturation) process as well as that of mental development. Hence, it is of interest to social psychology as well as to psycholinguistics and neurolinguistics.

Sociolinguistics and historical linguistics are properly social sciences, for they study human communication as a social relation and as a component of the mortar that holds human social systems together and coevolves with them. Their units of analysis (referents) are neither linguistic expressions nor individual speakers but speech communities. They ask such questions as "What motivates some social groups to welcome and others to resist speech innovation?" and "How do conquerors and conquered influence one another in speech?" And they search for patterns such as "Social barriers generate speech barriers," "Urbanization and mass communication increase linguistic standardization," and "Nationalism favours linguistic isolation."

However, neither sociolinguistics nor historical linguistics can be cultivated in detachment from pure or general linguistics, for only this study tells us what language is and what distinguishes speech from other mental and social processes. (Thus, before asking how a given language acquired articles or lost genders we must know what these are.) Nor should sociolinguistics and historical linguistics be detached from psycholinguistics, whose task is to unveil the mechanisms of speech production and understanding (and misunderstanding). In sum, since speech is a bio-psycho-social process, it should be studied from all three angles, and specialization in any one aspect should be only a matter of emphasis. (For systemic approaches to linguistics see Givón 1979; Bain 1983; and Bunge 1984.)

Both the idealism/materialism and the rationalism/empiricism cleavages – the former ontological and the latter epistemological – emerge in all the major controversies about language and linguistics. They appear, in particular, in the controversies over the nature of language, the mechanisms of language acquisition, the evolution of language, and the proper methods of linguistic research. Idealists regard language as a self-existing ideal (or abstract) object, either as a Platonic idea (Katz 1981) or as a human creation that has attained autonomy (Dilthey's "objective mind" and Popper's "world 3"). They focus on grammars and disregard the biological and social features of speech. Chomsky (1972) used to be the most eminent contemporary representative of this idealist approach. (He now [1995] favours a naturalistic view.) By contrast, materialists hold that the primary linguistic facts are not grammars but the brain processes of speech production and understanding, and the dual use of language as a thinking tool and a means of social intercourse. Everything else about speech is construct not fact. (See Bunge 1984 and Müller 1996.)

For analytic purposes one may *feign* that languages, and even language in general, exist by themselves, in abstraction from brains and speech communities: this is what syntax and semantics do. This approach is legitimate as long as one regards such an abstraction as only a methodological device. That was clearly seen by de Saussure (1916), who contrasted *langue*, "a system of signs," to *parole*, "a social fact." This distinction is usually overlooked by those who – following the tradition of classical philology – regard linguistics as a branch of the humanities, and believe they can afford to ignore psycholinguistics, neurolinguistics, sociolinguistics, and historical linguistics, all of which deal with real speakers and linguistic communities. The result is that they usually study exclusively the standard dialects – e.g., the Queen's English – which sociolinguists tend to regard as the dialect of the uppermost class. (See, for instance, Newmeyer 1988.)

Idealists do not have a theory of language acquisition and do not feel the need for one. Thus, Chomsky (1981) only christened the mechanism of language learning when he wrote about the inborn "language acquisition device" without specifying it, or when he said that "language grows in the [immaterial] mind." By contrast, since about 1850 neurolinguists have been identifying a number of brain subsystems or "areas" – such as Broca's and Wernicke's – each in charge of a special linguistic function. And developmental psychologists have found that "[s]igns and words serve children first and foremost as a means of social contact with other people" (Vygotsky 1978, 28). Thus, language learning is both a process of brain maturation and an aspect of enculturation or acculturation: there is no learning of any kind without a brain or in a social vacuum.

A similar controversy is induced by the old question of the origin and evolution of language. Idealists are anti-evolutionists: they define "language" in such a manner that only modern languages, endowed with complex grammars, will qualify. Moreover, they deny emphatically that human speech has evolved from more primitive forms of animal communication (see Chomsky 1972). Hardnosed scientists approach this problem in five convergent ways: biologically, comparatively, palaeoanthropologically, historically, and sociologically. The first consists in tracing back the concomitant anatomical changes in both the brain and the vocal tract that made the emergence of new mental functions possible (see Lieberman 1984). The second approach looks at animal communication systems. In particular, it compares the language-comprehension skills of pigmy chimpanzees (bonobos) and two-year-old children, which seem to be roughly equivalent (Savage-Rumbaugh and Rubert 1992.) The palaeoanthropological approach consists in hypothesizing the kind of minimal system of calls required by the production of tools and the primitive social organization suggested by archaeological remains. Admittedly, this line of study is rather speculative, yet no more so than other evolutionary studies; and in any case it is more plausible than the idealist myth that languages have not evolved at all. The fourth or historical approach consists in reconstructing lost languages, such as proto-Indo-European, and it has proved successful. The fifth or sociological approach consists in studying the formation of creoles (hybrids with full-fledged grammars) out of pidgins, which are extremely simple amalgams of two languages (see Bickerton 1984). The upshot of these five converging lines of inquiry is that modern languages have indeed evolved from more primitive communication systems. It has even been suggested that the first fully modern-type languages emerged as recently as about 30,000 BP (Noble and Davidson 1991).

As for the empiricism/rationalism cleavage, it shows clearly in the frequent disjunction between empirical and theoretical linguistic research. Whereas empiricists deal with flesh-and-blood people immersed in speech communities, rationalists focus on the ideal speaker-listener – the tape recorder versus the ear-plugged thinker. As a result, many data are of little interest and, when interesting, leave the theorist cold, whereas armchair work is often far removed from reality and thus of little help to empirical research. Here as elsewhere the ticket is a wise blending of observation and theory, that is, ratio-empiricism.

Though radically different in many ways, society and nature are continuous. We descend from hominids that possessed only rudimentary forms of social organization (see Bonner 1980). And we are born animals, though into artificial social systems that transform us quickly into live artefacts. The natural/social dichotomy is not fact but, like the concomitant body/mind dichotomy, an artefact of idealist philosophy, whose main function is to block the scientific study of reality. The dichotomy is at variance with the methodological unity of the sciences, as well as with the existence of a number of disciplines that are both natural and social, such as psychology and anthropology.

True, unlike most natural sciences, social science must reckon with cognition, emotion, creativity, intention, deliberate action, and convention, as well as with the way people "perceive" themselves and others. But this does not entail that the social sciences are only "concerned with man's conscious or reflected action, actions where a person can be said to choose between various courses open to him" (Hayek 1955, 26). Indeed, we are not free from physical constraints and biological drives, but animals acting in or on social systems; our actions are stimulated or inhibited by emotion and fantasy; and we change as we alter our physical and social environment. Besides, whereas biology and psychology focus on individuals, the social sciences study social systems and the links between individual action and social relations. Which brings us to sociology.

2

Sociology

Sociology may be defined as the scientific synchronic study of society. Now, society is a system of systems – families, firms, schools, states, and so on. Hence, sociology may also be characterized as the scientific and synchronic study of social systems of all kinds and sizes and, in particular, of their structure and its changes. Here "structure" is interpreted as a set of relations, in particular bonds or forces, among the system components and among these and items in the system's environment. ('Structure' is thus synonymous with 'organization' and 'architecture.') I submit that, like any other system, a social system is analysable into its *composition* or membership, *environment* or context, *structure* or relationships, and *mechanism* or the processes that make it tick. Let us call this the *CESM* view of a system.

Sociologists study social relations of all kinds. To be sure, they may also be interested in uncovering biological and psychological features, but only insofar as these contribute to the emergence, maintenance, change, or breakdown of social systems. They study economic relations too, but only to the extent that they affect social groups: the effects on individuals are studied by social psychology. Sociologists also study political relations, in particular those of power and management, but only insofar as they contribute to determining the state of social groups. And they study cultural relations, particularly those of communication and social learning, but only as long as they affect social structure.

There are two main kinds of relation: those that make some difference to the relata and those that do not. Thus, when people enter into a subordination relation they alter in the process. By contrast, spatial relations do not modify the relata: at most they make certain ties or bonds possible and others impossible. (More on bonding and non-bonding relations in Bunge 1979a and 1996a.) In principle, all the social relations of the first type can be represented as edges in a graph whose nodes are individuals or social systems such as families or schools. In fact, network theory and analysis are typically systemic, in that they analyse systems constituted by individuals connected to one another directly or indirectly (see Sørensen 1979; Burt 1980; Marsden and Lin 1982; and Wellman 1983).

Radical individualists object to all talk of social system, and they even mistrust the word 'society.' But, since every individual belongs to at least one social system (or network or circle), a strictly individualistic account is at best shallow, at worst impossible. Take for instance the statement that Jane's business prospered because she was smart and hard-working, borrowed money when interest rates were low, and traded in scarce commodities. Whereas being smart and hard-working are properties of individuals, the concepts of commodity, exchange, business, lending, interest rate, plenty, and scarcity only make sense with reference to an economic system. In other words, Jane's good fortune cannot be explained exclusively in terms of her personal characteristics: explicit mention of her place in some social network or other must be included. (More in Mandelbaum 1955; Goldstein 1958; Burt 1982; and Bunge 1996a.)

In other words, the sociologist explains social wholes in terms of individual actions, and at the same time he accounts for the latter in terms of social structure and impersonal "social forces." (The expression 'social force' is ambiguous, for sometimes it denotes social systems, such as the state, whereas at other times it stands for social processes, such as urbanization.) That is, the sociologist explains the whole by its parts, and the latter by their being immersed in the whole. This is the same approach adopted in all of the sciences, from physics to history: it is the systemic approach, an alternative to both individualism and holism (see Bunge 1979a, 1996a).

It is arguable that sociology has made great strides in the course of this century: it has studied groups, systems, and activities that had been all but ignored in earlier times, such as the family, the street-corner gang, the informal network, the business firm, and the state (see Smelser 1988). As a consequence, a number of new special fields have emerged, notably those of economic, political, historical, legal, and medical sociology. There has also been a start in quantitation and mathematical modelling. Last, but not least, the social-indicators movement born in the 1960s has yielded a variety of revealing statistics on many aspects of human life (see Sheldon and Moore 1968 and the journal *Social Indicators Research*).

Sociology has been flourishing, but it is also generally admitted that, as Merton once said, it has "more approaches than arrivals." Worse yet, it is in a state of permanent crisis accentuated since about 1970. Indeed, one often reads complaints that sociology is excessively fragmented; that an increasing number of young sociologists are seduced by literature; that serious social issues are being ignored; and that rigorous theorizing is being neglected or even scoffed at. Let us address quickly these various charges, to see whether they are justified and, if so, whether they call for philosophical analysis, as Stinchcombe (1968), Boudon (1980), and a few others have demanded.

The fragmentation of sociology is to be celebrated as well as deplored, for it is a sign of diversity. Even strategic differences are welcome as long as they remain within the general scientific approach and are only differences in emphasis or technique. By contrast, the increasing popularity of nonscientific approaches, manifest in subjectivism and relativism, as well as in the cult of obscurity and the contempt for statistics, is definitely a step backwards. But of course this fashion is understandable. Why should students in permissive universities bother with painstaking observation, data collection, statistical processing, and hypothesis testing, when they can get by writing literary essays?

The charge of irrelevance to serious social issues does not touch mainstream sociology; it is true only of marginal schools such as phenomenological sociology and ethnomethodology (see sect. 8). Main-line sociology has become much more relevant since the time when it had to wait until a foreign scientist (Myrdal 1942) pointed to the most grievous of all American social sores. Still, mainstream sociology has overlooked such pressing social issues as those of income distribution and the social distortions caused by the arms race and the Cold War (see, e.g., Caplow 1986).

As for rigorous (mathematical) theorizing, at the time of writing it seems to be at a standstill or even in decline, after having made a promising start immediately after the Second World War. In fact, over the last two decades very few new mathematical theories about social facts have been proposed. Worse, on examination many supposedly mathematical models have proved to be pseudomathematical games, for involving undefined or unmeasured subjective utilities and probabilities (Bunge 1996a). Blalock (1989) blamed this decline on the fact that the new cohorts of sociologists received a far poorer training in methodology and mathematics than their predecessors. No doubt, but in turn why has this training been neglected? In my view there are two main culprits: the failure of most mathematical sociologists to address important social issues and the antiscientific wave that has swept the academic world since about 1970. This denigration of rationality dulls critical thinking and induces sloth. Indeed, why make the effort of crafting or testing mathematical models if one can get by videotaping banal incidents, writing comments on the classics of sociology, or even denouncing the scientific approach?

There are plenty of prophets in sociology. When solicited by a multitude of prophets, one should resort to a practical indicator. Matthew (7:16) proposed one: "Thou will know them by their fruits." In the following we shall confine ourselves to examining the fruits of three approaches: the systemic, the rational-choice, and the irrationalist ones. We shall hardly touch on Marxist sociology, for it has not advanced much beyond some insightful but sketchy essays; it is more interested in controversy and social criticism than in either rigorous theorizing or painstaking empirical research; and it has been blind to the ills of so-called real socialism, and therefore has failed to foresee its downfall.

1 Agency and Structure

Individualists focus on individual action against a hazy social background. Thus, Weber (1988a [1913], 439) stipulated that "interpretive" or "comprehensive" (*verstehende*) sociology should handle "the individual and his action" as the basic unit or "atom," seeking to reduce all the supra-individual categories, such as "state" and "feudalism," to the actions of the individuals concerned. But as a matter of fact neither Weber nor anyone else carried through the individualist project. This project faces three insurmountable obstacles: two theoretical, the third practical. The former are that (a) the social behaviour of an individual can be characterized only with reference to the systems (e.g., organizations) where the individual is active: think of role, status, and group effect; and (b) social wholes, such as schools and firms, possess properties that their components lack, much as a triangle has properties that its sides do not have. The practical obstacle is that nobody, except for an omniscient being, could possibly observe, let alone explain, the myriad actions of every single individual member of any large social system. In sort, individualism is impotent except as a useful critique of holism (more in Bunge 1996a).

Holism, which focuses on social wholes hovering above agency and even guiding it, is no more viable than individualism. Thus, in rightly criticizing Adam Smith's atomism, Marx (1973 [1857–8], 84) proposed defining the individual as "the ensemble of social relations." But this is logically untenable, for a person is a concrete thing, whereas an ensemble – set, collection, class, kind – is a concept. Individuals are the relata of relations; and the set of all the social relations in a given society is the structure of the latter – by definition. Furthermore, Marx postulated that people are swept by economic forces and are the "tools of history." By and large Marx minimized the importance of the natural environment, bypassed the biological and psychological features of human beings (except for the feeling of alienation), laughed at the very notion of human nature, and was not interested in human rights. By overemphasizing the social matrix of individual action, Marx lost sight of the individual. This is one of the clues to the failure of Marxism in the fields of political science and management (Heilbroner 1980, 163). But why are holism and individualism still popular despite being basically flawed? Perhaps mainly because of ideological blinkers and the seeming paucity of alternatives.

Fortunately there is a viable alternative to both holism and individualism: systemism (Bunge 1979a, b; 1996a). In a systemic perspective there are impersonal constraints – e.g., political, economic, and environmental – but there are no autonomous social forces. In this view all social forces are collective actions – whether concerted (as in a factory) or unconcerted (as in a free election) – or results of actions. Examples: overpopulation, imbalance between supply and demand, technological innovation (invention plus diffusion), and political or cultural intimidation. Hence, every social force, far from acting upon individuals like an ocean current on a shrimp, is the resultant of individual actions. But of course the latter are never fully free: they are constrained by social norms (tradition) as well as by natural and social circumstances. Moreover, every rational agent, however potent, must always take into account the actual and potential actions or inactions of other people. In sum, individual actions are not mutually independent but interdependent.

In other words, structure and agency – that is, system and component – go hand in hand. Social action is the ultimate source of social structure, and it occurs in some system or other endowed with a definite if changing structure. Take social behaviour away, and no structure remains, because social systems emerge and are held together by social actions; conversely, take the whole away, and no part remains. So, agency and structure – or individual and system – are mutually complementary and they coevolve. Action A_1, taken at time 1 and constrained or stimulated by structure S_1, results in a somewhat different structure S_2, which in turn conditions further action A_2 – and so on.

If structure influences agency, then it must be real, though not independently so; it is a property of a real system. This may seem obvious, but it has been denied by the structuralists. Thus, Lévi-Strauss (1953, 525) held that "social structure has nothing to do with empirical reality but with models built after it." Moreover, such models must be such that "they make immediately intelligible all the observed facts." In other words, social scientists would build their models a priori. The trouble with apriorism is of course that, while it holds sway in pure mathematics, it has no rightful place in factual science. In the latter one is expected to study facts and build models to accommodate or foresee them; hence, any model that fails to match the relevant data must be either recast or given up (see Merton 1957a, 108ff; Nadel 1957, 150).

The concept of social structure makes full sense only in a systemic perspective, because every structure happens to be a property of a system, that is, an object composed of interconnected parts. But, like all properties, social structure can be conceptualized in alternative ways. (This is just an instance of the difference between an objective property and the predicates representing it; see Bunge 1977a.) In particular, the structure of a hierarchical system may be represented either as a directed graph, whose nodes represent the system components or, less perspicuously, as a matrix (called the adjacing matrix). Example:

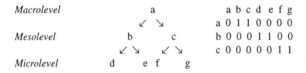

		a				a b c d e f g
Macrolevel		a				a 0 1 1 0 0 0 0
		↙ ↘				a 0 1 1 0 0 0 0
Mesolevel	b		c			b 0 0 0 1 1 0 0
	↙ ↘	↙ ↘				c 0 0 0 0 0 1 1
Microlevel	d	e f	g			

Figure 2.1 Two equivalent representations of a three-tiered social system

This is a sketch of a three-tiered hierarchical social network, such as a school, an army, or a business conglomerate. It relates three levels: micro (individual), meso (subsystem), and macro (whole). And it exhibits graphically the impossibility of detaching relations from relata: indeed, the system components (nodes) are shown as related (edges). True, such a model is primarily descriptive: it displays data about agents and their mutual relations. However, occasionally it is also explanatory. For example, it can explain the clout (or lack of it) of an individual (or subsystem) by the position he (or it) holds in the network. It is also true that every such model is static. However, nothing prevents one from modelling structural social change as a sequence of graphs (or their adjacing matrices).

In line with the distinction between the biological, economic, political, and cultural subsystems of society – joined in the *BEPC* sketch – the *total* social structure of a society can be defined as the union of its biological, economic, political, and cultural structures. (Since each structure is a set of relations, the union of two or more structures is to be understood as their set-theoretic union.) In particular, if the ties in a social network are of two or more kinds (e.g., economic and political), the network must be represented by two or more graphs or their associated matrices (for details see Bunge 1974c, 1981a).

2 Class and Status, Role and Norm

Up until the mid-twentieth century most Americans avoided the expression 'social class.' This may be due to the vagueness of the concept, reluctance to challenging the myth that the United States is a classless society, or fear of being taken for Marxists – a possible instance of the inhibiting effect of politics upon science. Warner's (1949) pioneering and influential empirical investigation of social stratification in the US changed all this. However, it was marred by conceptual imprecision – for instance, confusion between class and status. Parsons (1940a) perpetrated the same confusion, as did Lasswell and Kaplan (1952). Moreover, Parsons's idealist definition of a social class as a group of people who share certain values, in particular moral ones, is inadequate because the value consensus in every social class is weak (Mann 1970). To be sure, membership in a class involves sharing some values, but the converse is false. Indeed, any social group, from family to nation, is characterized by certain shared values. This is what group "identity" and "identity crisis" are all about.

Nowadays nearly everyone uses the concept of a social class (see, for instance, Dahrendorf 1959; Bendix and Lipset 1966; Giddens 1973; and Giddens and Held 1982). But nobody – certainly not Marx – seems to have defined it in exact terms. In particular, nobody tells us exactly what the middle class(es) and the underclass are. In any event, we shall deal only with two of the philosophical problems raised by the concept in question. One is the choice of defining predicate: shall it be biological, psychological, economic, political, legal, or cultural? The other is the ontological status of a social class: is it entity or idea?

Marx and Engels were perhaps the first to realize the centrality of the concept of a social class in social studies (see, for example, Engels 1845). However, they conceived of social classes exclusively in economic terms, namely according to the place or role of their members in the economy – and even so this concept was far from clear. (Weber 1922 2: 538–9 followed suit.) Their quasi-definition allowed Marx and Engels to characterize the classes of wage earners, capitalists, and rentiers. This classification made no clear room for the petty bourgeosie, the farmers, and the *Lumpenproletariat* – much less for the political, military, bureaucratic, managerial, and priestly classes and castes. These exclusions show that the quasi-definition in question is inadequate. Hence the need for a broader definition.

I suggest defining a social class as a social group that dominates another, or is dominated by it, in some respect – economic, political (in particular military), cultural (in particular religious), or other. Thus, the workers form a class, and the capitalists another. By contrast, the intellectuals do not constitute a class for, whereas some of them belong to the economic or political upper class(es), others do not, and still others are or believe themselves to stand above the fray. And every social class, far from being homogeneous, is fractured along ethnic, political, or religious lines (see Mann 1993).

Since our definition involves the concepts of group and domination, we must start by characterizing them. We shall work from the bottom up. A *social group* is a collection of individuals sharing certain features – biological, economic, political, or cultural. Think of sex, occupation, income, political, or religious groups. The social group characterized by the feature(s) F is the set of people sharing F. (In obvious symbols, $S_F = \{x \in P \mid Fx\}$.) Any two members of such a group are F-alike, or equivalent (not identical) in the respect F, no matter how much they may differ in other respects. (In symbols, $x \sim_F y =_{df} x \in S_F \ \& \ y \in S_F$, which amounts to $x \sim_F y =_{df} Fx \ \& \ Fy$, where $\sim_F$ is reflexive, symmetric, and transitive.)

We stipulate next that, if x and y are individuals, and F is a feature of someone or something, then x *F-dominates* y if and only if the action of x upon y is necessary for y to act on any items z of kind F. Note that, since the dominance relation is relative to some feature F, an individual may dominate another in one respect (e.g., economically) while being dominated by the latter in a diferent respect (e.g., politically). Examples: a manager intimidated by the local union leader; a political boss under the thumb of his confessor.

Let us move next from individuals to social groups. We stipulate that one group dominates another if and only if all of the members of the latter are dominated by some members of the former in the same society. More precisely, a human group C is a *social class* in a given society if and only if (a) there is another social group C', in the same society, that either dominates C or is dominated by C in some respect (biological, economic, political, or cultural); and (b) the members of the dominant group benefit from their membership in it more than those of the dominated group in theirs. Since this definition concerns an arbitrary pair of classes, it makes room for any number of classes between the lowest and the uppermost.

The relativization of class to a given society, indicated in clause (a), is a reminder that social stratification, when it exists, is internal to a society. And clause (b) is intended to prevent us from regarding parents (relative to children), teachers (relative to pupils), and physicians (relative to patients) as social classes. Our concept subsumes the Marxian one, because the predicate variable F occurring in our definition (via that of domination) may, in particular, take on the value "ownership." But F may also take on alternative values, for instance, biological, political, or cultural. Hence, it allows one to define sex, age, political, cultural, and other classes. Thus, in a strongly male-oriented society, men constitute a ruling class; and, under a military rule, the civilians are a lower class.

Given that there are as many class divisions as values of the relevant respect F, one and the same society can be stratified in several ways: that is, a society may have different class structures. A modern society may thus be likened to four superposed pyramids: biological, economic, political, and cultural. (In obvious notation, $S_F = \ <C_F, >_F >$, where C_F is the family of F-classes, and $>_F$ the relation of F-dominance. The set of all these partial class structures is the society's total class structure.) Equivalently: this concept of a social class allows for more than one class in each rank (or rung in the power ladder). Thus, bankers, corporation managers, big landowners, rentiers, church dignitaries, senior government officials, warlords, and opinion makers are included in the "power elite" (Mills 1959). Similarly with the various middle and working classes. Ditto the underclass: it is a class because it benefits people in the other classes, by staffing the reserve army of labour and supplying illegal goods, scapegoats, and moral legitimation (Gans 1995, 91–102).

Our second problem is whether social classes are real. This question has kindled endless debate. The reason is that is just as ambiguous as the question whether chemical or biological classes are real or conventional. No wonder that it elicits a sybilline answer: Social classes are objective yet not concrete. Let me explain. From the above definition it is clear that a social class is a collection, and as such a concept, not a concrete thing. This is because the members of a class, unlike those of an organization, are not necessarily bonded together by any social ties. (Marx [1847] expressed this distinction in the jargon of Kant and Hegel: he called the unorganized group a class *in itself*, and the organized one a class *for itself*.) For example, the wage-earning class is the collection of people who work for others in exchange for a wage, and do not participate significantly in the decisions or the benefits of their employers. By contrast, a labour union is a social system and therefore just as concrete and real as its members. Hence, whereas the labour movement is an (impersonal) actor, the working class as such ("in itself") is not.

Still, a partition of a human population into social classes need not be arbitrary or subjective. Likewise, although the chemical and biological species are collections, not things, the similarities among their members, as well as the differences among different species, are real. In other words, social classes, biospecies, chemical species, and other natural kinds are concepts that represent real commonalities among concrete individuals. In short, classes are concepts, not things, but classes may or may not match facts. Yet, like everything social, class perceptions are likely to be distorted. Thus, most people in the "West" think they are middle class (Kelley and Evans 1995). But take heart: this is only an instance of the fallibility of everyday judgment (see Gilovich 1991).

If classes are not concrete things, how are class conflicts possible? Answer: The expression 'class struggle' must be interpreted elliptically, as denoting a conflict that may occur on two different levels. There is first the pairwise conflict among members of different classes. Then, there is the conflict among organizations, such as unions and political parties, that assume the defence of certain class interests – or rather the interests of members of certain classes. That such class interests are sometimes ill served by officers who trust more ideology than fact, or who put personal advancement before service, is true but beside the point. The point is that there are class conflicts. These are likely to be the more intense, the larger the perceived gaps among the contending classes. Moreover, a social class (just like an ethnic group) is likely to be the more cohesive, the stronger its enemies. Consequently, the victor in a class struggle is likely to become fragmented, thus increasingly vulnerable, unless it coopts some of the defeated. Here as elsewhere success is its own worse enemy.

The admission that there are social classes with conflicting interests does not entail that they lack any common interests. In fact everyone, regardless of social class is, or ought to be, equally interested in environmental protection, checking population growth, and avoiding nuclear war, plagues, famines, runaway inflation, economic recession, mass migration, and similar disasters. Nor does the recognition of the existence of social classes imply that in stratified societies class warfare is the main conflict and the main source of social change. There are many additional conflicts in modern society: sexual, ethnic, skilled labour-unskilled labour, management-shareholder, bank-borrower, North-South (or centre-periphery), and so forth. Whereas some momentous social changes in the twentieth century have resulted from class conflicts, others have not – for example, the two world wars, the national independence movements, and advances in sanitation, vaccination, education, agriculture, manufacture, transportation, communication, science, and technology.

This brings us to another fundamental obscurity in Marxist sociology. On the one hand, it tells us that every society is divided into two layers: the (material) infrastructure and the (ideal) superstructure, and that the former "determines" the latter (or the latter "reflects" the former). On the other hand, we are told that every post-primitive society is divided into rival classes, and that this division is determined by the material or economic infrastructure. However, the classes themselves are neither in the base nor in the superstructure: these seem to be uninhabited. We are thus confronted with two distinct and mutually incompatible schemata. According to schema A, ideas and norms somehow emanate from the material infrastructure. In schema B the economic infrastructure determines the classes, which in turn create the superstructure:

	Superstructure	$\leftarrow$	Ruling class(es)	
Schema A	$\uparrow$		$\downarrow$	*Schema B*
	Infrastructure	$\rightarrow$	Working class(es)	

Furthermore, neither of the two schemata hints at the possible mechanisms whereby the economy induces class divisions, or each class creates its own culture. We conclude that Marxist sociology is inconsistent and simplistic. However, it would be niggardly to deny that it does contain some powerful insights that should be refined, systematized, and purged from all vestiges of Hegelian-ism – for instance, the ideas that culture is ideal, that all change is the outcome of some struggle or other, and that individuals are but the tools of History.

Let us now turn from class to status – a category absent from Marxism, per-haps for being psychosociological rather than sociological. Indeed, the *status* an individual enjoys (or suffers) in a social system is the rank he is generally *per-ceived* to hold in the system. White-collar workers enjoy a higher status than blue-collar workers even if they earn less and have less clout. An impoverished aristocrat or brahmin enjoys a higher status than a rich merchant. Presumably even in a classless society some individuals would enjoy a higher status than others. Status is a matter of birth, honour, prestige, opportunity, and influence rather than wealth or actual power. High-status people are more often imitated than obeyed. And they are more likely to conform to the group norms (Homans 1950).

Finally, the *roles* of an individual (or of a subsystem of a social system) may be defined as his functions (or tasks) in the given system. The relation between status and role is not one-to-one but one-to-many: that is, every status is associ-ated with a whole set of roles (Merton 1957b). However, two or more role-sets in a given social system may intersect. Thus, all university professors are expected to investigate and teach; however, some of them occupy a higher rank (status) than others, and are thus eligible for positions closed to their lower-rank colleagues. Moreover, since people belong simultaneously to different social systems (or "move in different circles"), they assume different roles and occupy different statuses in different systems – for example, humble clerk at work and elder in church.

The concepts of status and role highlight the inability of individualism to characterize individuals. Indeed, the status and role (or rather role-set) of an individual in a social system can be characterized only by reference to the latter. For example, "X is a soldier" contains the sociopolitical concept of an army. To be sure, all soldiers are individuals, but they can enact their specific role only in a social system of a special kind: no army, no soldier. Moreover, soldiers are expendable, particularly in wartime, whereas armies are, alas, hard to disband even when useless or worse.

The collection of roles in a society is a system rather than a formless set (Par-sons 1951). Indeed, the enactment of every role is possible only if other roles are performed at the same time. Thus, there are no teachers without pupils, no judges without litigants, and no managers without employees. Given any two related roles, one of them may depend upon the other, or they may be mutually complementary.

Moreover, roles are ruled by norms. (The converse is false. Thus, the norms of polite behaviour do not guide any roles.) When role norms change, so do the corresponding roles, and conversely. However, changes in role following alterations in role norms are usually time-lagged rather than synchronic; the same holds for changes prompted by alterations in roles. Occasionally some roles disappear altogether, and the corresponding norms become obsolete and are eventually forgotten.

According to idealism, norms are self-existing ideas. This hypothesis has no empirical support: on the contrary, history shows that only real people set up, observe, break, or repeal norms. A materialist must distinguish two concepts of a norm: an objective behaviour pattern, which may be followed unwittingly, and a proposition (or an imperative), which may or may not represent truly an actual or desirable behaviour pattern. A behaviour pattern may emerge spontaneously, perhaps initiated by an individual and imitated by others. If adopted by most of the members of a social group, it becomes a rule or norm in the group, and any behaviour that breaks the rule is branded as deviant. From this moment on normal behaviour becomes rule-governed – until further notice. Large changes may cause the decay and final disappearance of behaviour rules. However, with the advancement of technology, law, and statecraft, some social norms start as ideas and end up as behaviour patterns. That is, they are first designed and then imposed or adopted – again, until further notice. In either case, far from being self-existing, norms are either patterns of actual or desirable social behaviour, or their conceptualizations.

The existence of roles and social groups (in particular classes) does not preclude social mobility. (Only the division into castes blocks mobility.) On the contrary, the idea of mobility makes sense only when there are different social groups and roles. Indeed, by definition social mobility is either the passage of individuals from one group or role to another, or the emergence or disappearance of groups or roles. And of course mobility can be horizontal, as in a change of jobs with similar status, or vertical (upward or downward), as in the cases of promotion and demotion.

Note that, in defining certain concepts, we have proceeded from the bottom up, whereas in other cases we have proceeded from the top down. We have thus tacitly distinguished different social levels and have admitted that both strategies are required for different purposes. More on this in a moment.

3 Micro-Macro Relations

We are justified in talking of *levels* of some type whenever we deal with things ordered by the part-whole relation, where the whole possesses (emergent) properties that their parts lack. The distinction between levels of organization or complexity is cross-disciplinary. For example, in social science individuals constitute the lowest level, followed by families and other social systems of various sizes. In the simplest case the various levels are similar to rungs in a ladder. Since one and the same individual is likely to belong to several social systems at the same time, we are faced with parallel arrays of levels. In every case the level order is determined by the composition of the things concerned. Thus, the person-band-clan order follows from the fact that clans are composed of bands, which in turn are composed of persons. In general, level L_n *precedes* level L_{n+1} if and only if every member of L_n is a part (belongs to the composition) of at least one member of L_{n+1}. (In obvious symbols, $L_n \leq L_{n+1} =_{df} (\forall x)(\exists y)[x \in L_n \ \& \ y \in L_{n+1} \Rightarrow x \in C(y)]$.)

In social science it is frequent to distinguish just two levels, micro and macro. But of course one often needs to distinguish several additional levels of organization – for example, pico, nano, meso, mega, and giga. For instance, a megacorporation or a big government is likely to be composed of several branches, every one of which is in turn composed of various departments, which are ultimately composed of individuals. Such level distinctions are objective and they help characterize and explain social facts in what are usually called bottom-up and top-down fashions. Let us take a glimpse at these operations and their combinations. We will do so from a systemic viewpoint, that is, assuming that individuals belong to systems, and that the latter are analysable into their components together with the bonds that hold them together. In this perspective every ladder of levels of organization can be climbed up or down. The former process uncovers mass regularities and the latter reveals increasing amounts of detail: Marx's telescope and Weber's microscope. The former places individuals in context, and the latter points to the sources of structural features. Both moves are parallel and mutually complementary; neither is ultimate. Consequently, we substitute the systemic strategy, bottom-up *and* top-down, for the traditional strategies: bottom-up or individualist and top-down or holist. (More on the individualism-holism-systemism trilemma in Bunge 1979a, 1979b, and 1996a.)

The foregoing will be used to distinguish two kinds of definition. But before doing so let us recall two points in the theory of definition, a part of logic. The first is that not every concept is definable in a given context: some concepts, the basic (or primitive) ones, perform the job of defining others. Second, every correct definition (a) bears on concepts (or the words designing them), not on things; and (b) is an identity of the form "$A =_{df} B$." The left-hand side of this identity is called the 'definiendum,' and the right-hand side the 'definiens' – which, to avoid circularity, must not include the former. We also warn that the word 'component' occurring below may denote either a person or a subsystem.

Call D a definition of a concept C. We stipulate that

1. D is a *bottom-up definition* of C if and only if (a) C denotes a social group, a social system, or a collection of either; and (b) D characterizes the denotatum (referent) of C in terms of its individual components and their features, or their actions and interactions;

2. D is a *top-down definition* of C if and only if (a) C denotes a component of a system S, or an item in the environment of S, or a link in the structure of S; and (b) D characterizes the denotatum (referent) of C by its place or function, status or role in S.

Any definition of a social group (e.g., in terms of a feature shared by all its members) is of the bottom-up type, whereas any definition of a role or function (of a part in a whole) is of the top-down kind. We place no restrictions, other than non-circularity, on definitions of the first type. By contrast, we lay down the following restriction on every top-down definition: (a) the only collective concept(s) that may occur in its definiens are those of system, supersystem, or family of systems; and (b) these collective concepts must have been previously defined in a bottom-up fashion. The function of clause (a) is to avoid circularities such as "A worker is a member of the working class"; that of clause (b) is to block any recourse to the unanalysed totalities dear to holists.

In addition, we need another two kinds of definition: those referring only to individuals (or subsystems) and those referring only to systems (or supersystems). "An orphan is a person without living parents" is of the first type; "An international conflict is one that involves at least two countries" is of the second. We call the former *interpersonal* and the latter *intersystemic*. Given the current irrationalist wave in social studies, we stipulate the following restrictions. First, interpersonal definitions should refrain from attributing to individuals superhuman or supra-individual features. Second, intersystemic definitions should not attribute social systems any properties of persons.

Let us now look into explanation. Sociologists are likely to tell us that objects of two kinds can be explained: variables (designating properties) and facts (such as events and processes). A *variable* is said to be explained when shown to be a function of other variables – which is actually a case of analysis, not explanation. By contrast, a *fact* is explained when the proposition representing it is shown to follow logically from one or more generalizations concerning some mechanism(s) jointly with one or more data. This account of scientific explanation differs from the received one, the "covering law model": Law(s) & circumstances ∴ Fact(s) to be explained. The latter only *subsumes* the particular under the general: it involves no reference to mechanism. But in science and technology one explains something only when uncovering how it works, that is, in terms of mechanisms. That is, one seeks *mechanismic* explanations (Bunge

1983b, 1997b). Let us now apply these notions to the explanation of social variables and social facts.

We shall define three kinds of "explanation" – actually analysis – of a social variable. A social variable v is given (a) a *bottom-up analysis* if and only if v represents a property of a whole and is interpreted as a function of independent variables, some of which represent features of parts of the whole and none of them represents features of a whole; (b) a *top-down analysis* if and only if v represents a property of a part of a whole and is analysed as a function of independent variables, some of which represent features of the whole and none of which represents features of any parts; (c) a *mixed* (or *micro-macrosociological*) *analysis* if and only if v is analysed as a function of independent variables, some of which represent features of individuals, others of systems, and still others possibly of environmental items.

Here is an example of each of the above types of analysis. Bottom-up: The cohesion of a social group is a function of the extent to which its individual components participate in group activities and share beliefs, interests, goals, and expectations (Bunge and García-Sucre 1976). Top-down: The US fiscal budget deficit during the 1980s grew in proportion to the military expenditures and tax cuts. Mixed: The volume of the construction industry declined in the Western world during the 1980s, as the population of potential home buyers decreased (passing of the baby boom peak), and because most prospective home owners could not afford the high mortgage rates intended to fight inflation.

Let us now tackle the explanation of facts, or explanation proper, in social-science. To begin with, we stipulate that a social fact is one involving at least one social system, such as an event happening in it. We also stipulate that a genuine explanation of a fact is more than a deduction of a particular from generalizations and circumstances. Indeed, a generalization has explanatory power just in case it describes some mechanism – causal or stochastic, biological or social, or a combination of any pure types. (The mechanism may be physical, chemical, biological, social, or a combination of these types.) Moreover, social science explanations may involve norms in addition to laws. For example, the very concept of deviant behaviour presupposes that of social norm, whether legal or moral.

To the extent that they admit the existence of social facts, individualists (like Tarde and Weber) demand that these be explained exclusively in terms of individual actions. By contrast, holists (like Marx and Durkheim) require that social facts be explained exclusively in terms of social wholes. For instance, an individualist is likely to attempt to explain everything social as the outcome of the efforts of individuals to maximize their expected utilities – a case of bottom-up explanation. By contrast, a holist may attempt to explain every piece of an individual's behaviour in terms of the social group(s) or system(s) to which he belongs – a case of top-down explanation. In line with the systemic viewpoint, and in agreement with Piaget (1965), I admit both kinds of explanation as well as their combination. Let us define them.

Let us stipulate that a social fact involving a social system, and represented by a proposition p , is given (a) a *bottom-up* (or *microsociological*) *explanation* if and only if p follows from one or more generalizations and data referring exclusively to individual components of the system; (b) a *top-down* (or *macrosociological*) explanation if and only if p follows from one or more generalizations and data referring exclusively to wholes (social, natural, or mixed) including the system; and (c) a *mixed* (or *micro-macrosociological*) *explanation* if and only if p follows from some generalizations and data referring to individual components of the system, and others to wholes including the system. In all these cases the generalization in question must describe some mechanism, such as a modus operandi.

An example of each of these kinds of explanation follows. Bottom-up: The local labour union went on strike because its members were dissatisfied with their working conditions. (Tacit generalization: People engage in collective action to defend what they believe to be their best interests.) Top down: Unemployment inhibits workers from demanding wage hikes. (Tacit generalization: People abstain from engaging in collective action when they expect to lose their cause.) Mixed: The populist candidate won the election because the voters were disillusioned with the traditional parties (bottom-up), and because he earned the support of powerful groups that influenced the attitude of the voters (top-down). (Tacit generalization: Political attitudes are shaped by personal interests – real or apparent – as well as by macrosocial events in the social systems to which the individuals belong.)

Pure bottom-up and top-down explanations, favoured by individualists and holists respectively, have the charm of simplicity. But the former overlook the social constraints on agency, whereas the latter underrate individual interest and initiative. Given the complexity of the world, simple explanations are suspect (Bunge 1963). This holds not only for social facts but also for physical and chemical ones. Indeed, full microreduction (bottom-up explanation) fails even in atomic physics, where the state of an atom depends not only upon its composition and structure but also upon its environment (often represented schematically by the boundary conditions). As for macroreduction (top-down explanation), it never works fully in physics, because every thing has intrinsic properties – such as number of components, entropy, electric charge, and spin – in addition to relational ones such as position, velocity, force, energy, and temperature (Bunge 1991b).

For the above reasons I propose the following *Analyse-and-synthesize rule*: When attempting to explain a social fact (a) avoid explanations of the pure bottom-up type – unless they make explicit reference to the social context; (b) admit only provisionally explanations of the top-down kind – as long as they do not assume that individuals are passively swept by obscure and irresistible social forces; and (c) always prefer explanations of the mixed type – provided they involve (sufficiently) true or at least plausible premises describing mechanisms of some kind.

Sociologists at their best practise this maxim regardless of their methodological allegiance. Let us review three examples. Sørensen (1977a) explains social mobility as a result of an interaction between individual skills (human-capital theory) and the emergence or submergence of vacancies (chains-of-opportunity theory). Boudon (1981,100ff.) notes that semi-feudal systems are technologically stagnant, and proceeds to explain this fact as follows. Landowners resist social change, in particular technological innovation, because any change would increase the income of their tenants, and thus limit their dependence upon the owner, the eventual aggregate effect of which would be the breakdown of the semi-feudal system. And Coleman (1990, 7ff.) starts from a macrosocial situation, "dips to the level of the individual," and then resurfaces.

The three preceding cases exemplify what I call a *Boudon-Coleman diagram*. Boudon's example can be diagrammed thus:

Macrolevel	Technological innovation	$\rightarrow$	Weakening of semi-feudal order
	$\downarrow$		$\uparrow$
Microlevel	Rise in tenant's income	$\rightarrow$	Drop in individual dependence

When numerical variables are available, the simplest Boudon-Coleman diagram looks like this:

$$M \qquad F$$
$$X \longrightarrow Y \quad \textit{Macrovariables (e.g., interest rate and demand inflation)}$$
$$g \downarrow \qquad \uparrow h$$
$$m \qquad x \xrightarrow{f} y \quad \textit{Microvariables (e.g., borrowing and spending)}$$

That is, the M-M link is analysed into three successive links: $M \rightarrow m \rightarrow m \rightarrow M$. (In symbols, $Y = h(y)$, $y = f(x)$, and $x = g(X)$, whence $Y = h(f(g(X)))$.) Shorter: $F = h \circ f \circ g$.) Any such explanation exemplifies the systemic approach. Obviously, holists have no use for Boudon-Coleman diagrams, and consistent individualists should regard them as purely analytical devices. I submit that a diagram of this kind is useful to the extent that it is both truthful – that is, it matches actual micro-macro links – and insightful, that is, it suggests mechanisms. For example, it is common knowledge that, in the less-developed countries, the absence of adequate public health care and social-security systems (macrosocial condition) induces peasants to procreate too many children (microsocial fact), the aggregate effect of which is overpopulation (macrosocial fact) and its sequel: poverty.

Given the limited success of microreduction and macroreduction, they should be combined into a mixed strategy, not only in the case of explanation but in that of scientific research in general. This strategy has proved fertile in all research fields. For example, the students of condensed matter also analyse it into its constituents; biologists, though basing themselves on physics and chemistry, go beyond these and study cells, organisms, and populations on their own levels; likewise, psychologists employ specific concepts, such as those of cognition and mood, and at the same time attempt to anchor them to neurophysiological variables (bottom-up procedure) as well as to sociological ones (top-down procedure); and social-network theorists locate agents in a network and in turn attempt to explain "the emergence of social structure as the product of the interdependent choices of structurally constrained actors" (Macy and Flache 1995). In all these disciplines radical reduction is rare; whereas moderate reduction, which acknowledges the existence of systems and supersystems with emergent properties, is fertile and rather common. In sum, the idea is to join partial microreduction with partial macroreduction. Once again, moderation is the ticket.

However, moderate reduction is insufficient, because the partition of human knowledge into disciplines is rather arbitrary. Therefore, when dealing with many-sided things, particularly things that, like human beings, cross several levels of organization, we are forced to adopt multidisciplinary and cross-disciplinary approaches. Sometimes we must even integrate two or more theories or research fields: think of any hybrid science, such as physiological and social psychology, or economic and historical sociology.

In sum, the best overall research strategy combines moderate reduction with integration (or merger), as proposed by the following *Reduce-and-integrate rule*: When studying systems of any kind (a) reduce them to their components (at some level) and the interactions among these, as well as among them and environmental items – but acknowledge and explain emergence whenever it occurs; and (b) approach systems from all pertinent sides and on all relevant levels, integrating theories or even research fields whenever unidisciplinarity proves to be insufficient.

Compliance with this rule should result in ever fuller and deeper accounts of the behaviour of systems of any kind. Now, the word 'fuller' in the preceding sentence is hardly problematic (unlike its cognate 'complete'), but 'deeper' may be. Therefore we must agree on what it signifies. Let us agree on this convention: If A and B are two accounts (descriptions, explanations, predictions, or theories) of the same factual items (things, their properties, or changes thereof), then A is *deeper* than B if and only if A makes reference to entities or processes (in particular, mechanisms) on more levels than B does. (Shorter: Depth of an account A = Number of levels referred to by A.) Accordingly, the combination of bottom-up and top-down accounts, as well as of reductive with integrative strategies, is deeper than either of the same-level procedures.

So much for sociological analysis and synthesis in the light of reason and experience. Let us now move to a fashionable if insecure terrain: sociological rational-choice theory.

4 Coleman's Linear System of Action

A rational-choice model of social facts of some kind is one that treats the social system concerned as if it were a market populated exclusively by free agents intent on maximizing their expected utilities in the course of their exchanges. One of the most precise and elegant of all rational-choice models is Coleman's "linear system of action," included in his monumental *Foundations of Social Theory* of 1990. This model belongs to the sociological tradition of exchange theory, and it is based on neoclassical microeconomics. Coleman attains precision by fully specifying the utility function of every agent, a function that is usually characterized in the vaguest of terms. This allows him to rigorously derive a large number of consequences from a small number of postulates. We shall restrict our examination to the latter, which we reconstruct axiomatically as follows.

P1 Every agent exerts control over some surplus divisible (non-public) goods.

P2 All an agent does is to exchange divisible goods – that is, every agent is a trader, and every social system is a market.

P3 The market pre-exists the agents and is not modified by them: the values of the goods and their exchange rates are given once and for all.

P4 The agents are not confronted with one another but with the market [the "structural interdependence" hypothesis].

P5 Every agent has a definite and "stable" (unchanging) utility function, whose values depend only upon the quantity of resources he controls and on his interest in them, and is independent of the utilities of any other agents.

P6 The utility function of every agent is of the Cobb-Douglas type. (That is, for any two goods, such as Pareto's proverbial bread and wine, the utility function of every agent is $U = A^a B^b$, with $a + b = 1$, where A and B denote the quantities of the goods in question, and every exponent represents the agent's objective "interest" in the good.)

P7 Every agent acts so as to maximize his own raw (not expected or average) utility.

Let us examine these assumptions.

P1 excludes anyone who has no surplusses to exchange: it hardly applies to poor children or housewives, the unemployed, or any other economically or politically powerless individuals. This restriction, though reasonable in economics and political science, is unreasonable in sociology, particularly with reference to a world plagued by social issues deriving from economic or political powerlessness.

P2 reduces society to an aggregate of traders – which is how the eighteenth-century mercantilists and the nineteenth century marginalist economists saw it. It overlooks production, without which there can be neither goods nor (honest) trade. And it excludes all actions other than the exchange of commodities; in particular, it excludes such actions as child bearing and rearing, cooking, helping strangers, playing, engaging in conversation, or cheerleading. Moreover, it makes no room for public goods, for these are not traded. It is typical of "economic imperialism," a school which we shall meet in the next section.

P3 violates the postulate of methodological individualism, which Coleman defends but does not abide by in a consistent manner. Indeed, the values of the goods and their exchange rates are assumed to be given, instead of resulting from individual actions. Worse, P3 is contrary to fact. Indeed, we know that values in exchange and exchange rates result from such processes as competition and collusion, bargaining and striking, advertising and dumping, politics and war, not to mention floods, droughts, and famines.

P4 plays the part that the social order plays in other social theories. Here the social structure is revealed only through certain features of the market. Like P3, P4 too goes against the grain of methodological individualism. In fact, it is typical of what may be called *individholism*, or individualism with a hidden holistic component (Bunge 1996a). Worse, P4 involves overlooking the very marrow of sociality: face-to-face interactions.

P5 is unrealistic. Indeed learning, expectation, and changing circumstances alter one's evaluations – unless one happens to be mentally retarded, a maniac, or a fanatic rather than a rational agent.

P6, the particular choice of the utility function, is not satisfactorily justified other than by analogy with the Fechner-Weber psychophysical law, often assumed to hold for perception – a far cry from ownership and exchange. More on this in a moment.

P7, the "rationality" assumption, has been known since the early 1950s to be descriptively (that is, psychologically) false (see Allais and Hagen 1979; Bunge 1996a; and Moessinger 1996). It is also known to be normatively inadequate, for involving staggering information and opportunity costs: a bird in hand is worth ten in the bush. The so-called bounded rationality rule – "Do not maximize but satisfice" – is better suited to practical affairs, particularly business deals (March and Simon 1958; Simon 1979).

Let us take a closer look at P6, the utility function with a Cobb-Douglas shape. There are several problems with it. One of them originates in Coleman's wish to construct an analogy with the classical Fechner-Weber psychophysical law, according to which the felt intensity of a stimulus is proportional to the logarithm of the physical intensity of the latter. Coleman stipulates that the satisfaction of an individual equals the logarithm of his utility rather than the utility itself. But this stipulation does not square with the accepted sense of "utility," according to which it is synonymous with "satisfaction," "pleasure," or "gain."

A second problem with P6 is that it entails that satisfaction (in Coleman's Pickwickian sense) is additive. That is, the satisfaction derived from controlling two or more goods would equal the weighted sum of the partial satisfactions they procure. (In fact, for two goods, 1 and 2, $ln\ U = ln\ A^a + ln\ B^b = a\ ln\ A + b\ ln\ B = s_1 + s_2$.) But, because of budget constraints, goods' ownership interferes with one another, so that satisfaction should be strongly subadditive or superadditive, depending on the nature of the goods.

A third problem is that in real life not all goods are subject to decreasing returns, as they should according to the Cobb-Douglas function. For example, the utility and the marginal utility derived from both knowledge and money are usually assumed to increase exponentially, whence the restriction "$a + b = 1$" does not hold in these cases.

A fourth problem with Coleman's formula is that it is not dimensionally homogeneous – unless it be explicitly demanded that the quantities of goods be reckoned in a dimensionless manner – an exceptional condition. (Think, for instance, of control over income and leisure time.)

A fifth problem is that, by Coleman's own admission (1990, 689), normally the interest of an actor in a good is unknown, whence it must be either left indeterminate or assigned arbitrarily. In either case empirical tests become pointless. Therefore, strictly speaking, the formula can be assigned no truth value; hence, it can be no part of science.

A sixth problem is that a production function, such as Cobb-Douglas's, may make sense for a manufacturing firm, since in this case the inputs and outputs are rather clearly definable and measurable. But, if a single production function could be found for service units – such as schools, hospitals, plumbing firms, consultant firms, or government departments – it might turn out not be of the Cobb-Douglas form. For example, the standard if tacit formula for the productivity, value, or merit of a university professor is: $M = rR + tT + aA$. Here R, T, and A represent the individual's contributions to research, teaching, and administration respectively, whereas the values of the corresponding weights r, t, and a – which must add up to unity – depend on the university department. (In a research-oriented department $r > t > a$.) If a university were to use a Cobb-Douglas function, such as $M = kR^r T^t A^a$, with k a dimensional constant, and $r + t + a = 1$, it would face the following difficulties. First, the function involves diminishing returns in all three variables, while as a matter of fact the productivity of a professor in a research-oriented university increases at least linearly with his research output, whereas in a good undergraduate college it increases at least linearly with his teaching output. A second problem is that nobody would be regarded as a *good* professor unless he were equally good (hence mediocre), at research, teaching, and administration (that is, $r = t = a = \frac{1}{3}$.) By contrast, the usual additive formula allows for the standard (and reasonable) trade-offs between the three activities.

In sum, the seven postulates of Coleman's model are at least dubious. Hence, it is small wonder that some of their consequences are puzzling to say the least. One of them is that an individual will devote the same fraction of his income to obtaining a good regardless of income and price (1990, 694). But, according to Engels's law, known for over a century, the poorer a person, the larger the fraction of his income he devotes to food and rent; besides, most people simply won't buy goods priced above a certain upper bound.

Finally, Coleman's model falls short of its inventor's own requirement – fitting in with methodological individualism – that macroentities and their properties should emerge from the interplay of individuals. True, the model does contain certain relations between microvariables and macrovariables. For example, the total value of an agent's resources is defined as the sum of the values of each of the goods he holds (Equation 25.6 in Coleman 1990). But (a) such individual values are assumed to be determined by "the market," that is treated as an unanalysed social whole; and (b) such relation does not describe any "transition" between the micro and the macro levels: the whole thing is static.

Furthermore, the model actually involves an assumption that Coleman himself (1990, 300) rightly regards as a fiction, namely that "society consists of a set of independent individuals, each of whom acts to achieve goals that are independently arrived at, and that the functioning of the social system consists of the combination of these actions of independent individuals." Such fictitious independence, that is, lack of interaction, inheres in Coleman's model just as it does in both classical and neoclassical economics. A further flaw is that it is static: it does not contain the time variable and consequently it does not account for social change. Such is the high price of conformity with economic orthodoxy.

Nowadays there is little exact sociological theorizing. And most of what there is, like Coleman's, is constrained by the straitjacket of rational-choice theory (see Bunge1995a, 1995b, and 1996a for detailed criticisms). Much of what passes for sociological theory in the "humanist" camp is irrationalist handwaving or vague "theorizing about theorizing, not attempting to formulate coherent accounts of things happening 'out there'" (van den Berg 1997). Neither of the two schools is producing realistic accounts of social life. For these we must fall back, for the time being, on either purely descriptive studies, or "middle range theories" (hypotheses or models) with no underlying "grand theory."

Does this entail that one should avoid theory altogether? Certainly not. Since only theory can colligate, and since only true theory can guide effective social policy-making, serious theorizing should be strongly supported. But it should be clear that serious sociological theorizing involves concern for empirical fit and avoidance of received dogmas. We shall next examine a school that meets neither condition.

5 Economic Imperialism

"Economic imperialism," or economicism, is the attempt to reduce and thus subordinate anthropology, sociology, political science, culturology, and history to economics. The central hypothesis of economicism is that everything social is, either directly or indirectly, of an economic nature. The reasons look obvious at first sight: (a) humans must work in order to eat, and eat to survive; (b) all social transactions involve exchanges of some kind, if only of smiles; and (c) in modern society everything seems to carry a price tag.

The impact of economicism is obvious in all the social sciences and sociotechnologies. Thus, we are told that income is a faithful indicator of welfare – regardless of the extent to which the individual enjoys his work and is integrated in his social environment. We are also told that, once the economy gets going, everything else follows – as if the modern economy could move without a skilled workforce and without some state regulation, and as if it did not matter whether economic growth is due to an increase in the output of guns or of means of livelihood. Sometimes we are even told that the main motivation for mathematical, scientific, and humanistic research is profit; and, moreover, that every finding in these fields is a commodity and moreover has an economic content. And occasionally we are told that all history – even demographic, political, and cultural history – must be reduced to economic history.

The earliest influential version of economic imperialism was the historical materialism of Marx and Engels (Marx 1859). The "new wave" of economic determinism, which emerged one century later, is the conservative counterpart of Marxist economicism (see Swedberg 1990). Marx and his followers believed that, though man has an unlimited potential and is capable of altruism, "in the last analysis" the "relations of production" dominate not only all the other social relations, but also individual behaviour. By contrast, the new economic imperialists claim that (a) people are "bundles of desires chasing bundles of commodities"; (b) individuals are propelled solely by self-interest; (c) all social relations are of the exchange (or trade) kind; and (d) neoclassical economics – which postulates that humans are utility maximizers – has been successful in explaining and predicting economic processes, whence it should be aped by all social scientists. As a well-known social scientist put it optimistically, "neoclassical economics is a powerful calculus for predicting individual behaviour and explaining the workings of social groups."

However, economics cannot encompass all social life, because there are plenty of key goods that can be neither purchased nor exchanged: think of love, friendship, goodwill, trust, solidarity, loyalty, curiosity, or peace. And some of these goods, such as trust and peace, make market transactions possible. Moreover, as will be seen in the next chapter, mainstream economics does not fit real-world economies. Indeed, it largely ignores work and is unable to explain, much less forecast, the actual behaviour of consumers and businessmen, price formation, the emergence and domination of oligopolies, business cycles, market disequilibria, "externalities," stagflation, and much more. In short, the so-called economic approach to human behaviour does not even explain economic behaviour. What then is the orthodox economist to do after having failed to conquer his own turf? He can try to conquer some foreign territory, preferably one whose natives are in awe or fright of the mathematical rigour allegedly characteristic of mainstream economic theory.

Professor Gary S. Becker, a Nobel laureate in economics, is one of the boldest and most lucid and consistent champions of this approach, which he has applied to the family, politics, crime, and more. He describes it thus: "The combined assumptions of maximizing behaviour, market equilibrium, and stable preferences, used relentlessly and unflinchingly, form the heart of the economic approach as I see it" (Becker 1976, 5). Regrettably, Becker does not examine critically any of these assumptions; he overlooks the many objections that have been raised against every one of them in the literature (see chap. 3); and he does not soil his hands with empirical data. Moreover, he takes it for granted that those assumptions hold for all human behaviour: "the economic approach is a comprehensive one that is applicable to all human behaviour, be it behaviour involving money prices or imputed shadow prices, repeated or infrequent decisions, large or minor decisions, emotional or mechanical ends, rich or poor persons, men or women, adults or children, brilliant or stupid persons, patients or therapists, businessmen or politicians, teachers or students" (ibid., 8). In short, economic imperialism is a clear instance of both dogmatism and radical reductionism or nothing-but-ism. (Caution: Reduction is admirable when it works, as in the cases of the reduction of statics and kinematics to dynamics, and of optics to electromagnetic theory; but it is pathetic when it fails, as in the cases of genetic determinism, human sociobiology, and economicism.)

Becker's is also a clear instance of mercantilism and even market worship. Indeed, not only would every human action be either market-aimed or market-driven but, thanks to the market, ours is the best of all possible worlds. So much so that, even when – contrary to the basic hypothesis – individuals behave irrationally, the market as a whole is said to remain rational. Indeed, "market rationality is consistent with household irrationality" (Becker 1976,161). But the attribution of rationality to the market is triply flawed. First, by definition rationality is a property that can literally (not metaphorically) be predicated of individuals, not aggregates. (After all, social groups are brainless, hence neither selfish nor altruistic, neither smart nor dumb.) Second, markets that fail to clear, or go unpredictably into recession, or panic and crash without warning, cannot be said to behave "rationally" – not even metaphorically. Third, let us recall that in many cases economic growth is achieved at the price of inflation, increased income inequality, depletion of natural resources, or irreversible deterioration of the environment. These are clear instances of the "collective irrationality" brought about by individual economic "rationality," which leads to "social traps" (see, for instance, Cross and Guyer 1980). The best-known example of such a trap is the so-called tragedy of the commons (Hardin 1968, 1985). It consists in the unregulated exploitation of a common good, such as public land, or a fish bank, for private profit. The result is that the good is ultimately destroyed. Nonetheless, let us take a look at some of Becker's results (see Becker 1976, 1981).

One of Becker's most striking contributions is his study of marriage. He conceives of marriage as a device for producing certain commodities, and assumes that potential spouses shop for mates in the "marriage market" much as they might shop for cars: they would be rational consumers attempting to maximize gains and minimize costs. Love, chance, informal social networks, moral considerations, and compulsion (as in arranged and in shotgun marriages) would play no role at all. Yet we all know that such non-rational factors do play significant roles even in economic behaviour (see Frank 1988). In particular, only a network model, rather than an open market one, seems to account for the strong correlation between the levels of education of the spouses as well as between their levels of physical attractiveness (Stevens et al. 1990).

Becker's much-quoted 1960 paper on fertility contains certain shockers, such as treating children as "consumer durables" with "shadow price" tags. It also suggests that the quantity of children is a close substitute for their "quality" (as measured by investment in their upbringing). Aside from such ghostly notions, the model contains the reasonable assumption that family size, far from being a random variable, depends on income, child-rearing costs, and cultural level. It is true that fertility depends on economic variables. (See, for instance, Harris and Ross 1987 for a cost-benefit analysis of fertility regulation.)

The fly in the ointment is the computation of the expected utility from having a child. This computation of Becker's shows no awareness that the utility "function" he handles is not mathematically defined, and that its values are assigned arbitrarily so as to get the desired results (see Bunge 1996a). Such pseudofunctions occur throughout Becker's work. As a result, his symbolism is purely ornamental. The phony exactness of Becker's work is particularly obvious in his treatment of social interaction (Becker 1976, chap. 12). Thus, he postulates that the opinion R of an actor held by other persons in the same occupation is decomposable into the effect h of the actor's effort, and the opinion D he deserves when making no effort: that is, $R = h + D$. But Becker says nothing about the forms of h and D, let alone about ways of measuring them. Hence the value of R is indeterminate. Becker has "added" words, not functions: his economic model of social action is pseudomathematical. It is also pseudosociological, for he only considers one individual, whose social environment he lumps into a single variable, namely the opinion that other people hold of the individual. In this model there are neither social systems nor actions. It is an example of the individholism we met in the preceding section.

Economic imperialism treats crime as an industry, and law and order as another. Becker's 1968 paper on this subject deals with crime supply, though not, dissapointingly, with crime demand. How can the crime "market" ever reach equilibrium if there is so much supply and so little demand? And given the glut, why don't criminals offer irresistible bargains? In any event, economic imperialism regards the choice of crime as a career, as if it were purely a matter of expected utility (see Becker and Landes 1974 and Becker 1976). The key variable here is the subjective probability (that is, strength of belief) of apprehension: crime supply would decrease with the increase in the subjective probability of getting caught. Since there is no way of measuring this "probability" (or rather likelihood), empirical data are irrelevant to the evaluation of the model.

In Becker's study of crime there is no hint of the social circumstances, such as poverty, unemployment, ignorance, boredom, moral blindness, selfishness, and anomie, that draw some people to crime. Moreover, Becker explicitly refuses to take these variables into account: being psychological or sociological, not economic, they would seem to be beneath the economist's contempt. Hence, his only concern is hitting on a cheap punishment policy. The very ideas of preventing crime by attacking its sources, and of rehabilitating criminals, hardly cross Becker's mind; he only suggests punishment, particularly in the form of fines. Beccaria, writing in 1764, was far more enlightened.

For better or for worse, given one rational-choice model of criminality (or of anything else), there is at least one alternative model of the same kind. For example, Tsebelis (1990) proposed an elabourate game-theoretic model purporting to prove a priori that punishment does not pay. Characteristically, Tsebelis cares no more than Becker for statistical data concerning the effectiveness of punishment in deterring crime. But apriorism, legitimate in pure mathematics, reeks of premodern and, particularly, medieval scholarship when practised in reference to matters of fact.

Our next example is the economic approach to politics pioneered by Anthony Downs (1957). According to it, politics is an economic activity and, more particularly, an exchange of commodities: votes are traded for expected services or privileges. Downs's theory has the merit that it contains a testable hypothesis: Hotelling's "law." This is the hypothesis that, in a two-party system, competition for votes will draw both parties to the centre. To be sure, this prediction has often been confirmed. But it has been refuted just as often: indeed, many elections end up either in convergence or in left-right polarization. The mechanisms at play are not hard to guess. Convergence occurs when the incumbents are perceived favourably by the majority; in this case the opposition's tactics is, "We'll deliver that and more." If, by contrast, the incumbents are unpopular, their opponents will promise, "We'll do just the opposite." Thus, divergence will emerge. In short, Downs's theory is testable though, alas, true only sometimes.

Becker's voting theory has a far narrower scope: it only attempts to account for political apathy. And, unlike Downs's, it makes no forecasts other than that there is no rational hope for democracy. Indeed, Becker's "rational" citizen is essentially a selfish individual – a "free rider." This individual figures that, since he has only one vote, it does not "pay" him to bother with politics: he has more profitable things to do. This assumption is at variance with the finding of most political analysts, that voter apathy – where it does exist, as in the United States – is mainly due to dissatisfaction with all the options offered the electorate. In short, Becker's theory of democracy has no empirical basis. The same holds for Olson's (1971), which we shall meet in chapter 7. In short, the "rational" citizen is either politically indifferent or corrupt. In either case he is an enemy, passive or active, of political democracy and, a fortiori, of economic democracy. The economic approach to politics can shed some light on the dark side of politics, but it does not account for its sunny side – voluntary popular participation, concern for the public good, solidarity, and the struggle for progressive social reform. This other side is studied by political sociology (see, for instance, Horowitz 1972).

Our last example will be the economic approach to racial segregation. In his 1955 doctoral dissertation on this subject, Becker concluded that discrimination by whites against blacks reduces the incomes of both groups – a result that went against conventional wisdom. But, if Becker's conclusion is true – as it seems to be – it refutes the "rationality" assumption. Indeed, if racial discrimination does go against the self-interest of the whites, why have so many of these practised it systematically and for so long in the US, Brazil, the Caribbean, Africa, and elsewhere? Is it not because it was highly profitable?

Whereas Becker inquired into the economic consequence of racial segregation, Schelling, a fellow crusader for economic imperialism, wants to know its causes. To this end he "examines some of the *individual* incentives and individual perceptions of differences that can lead *collectively* to segregation" (Schelling 1978, 138). For instance, black neighbourhoods, churches, and schools in American cities would emerge because blacks "feel more comfortable among their own color," and because black landlords advertise vacancies on black church bulletin boards. Moreover, the choice of neighbourhood is largely voluntary: "To pick a neighbourhood with good schools, for example, is to pick a neighbourhood of *people* who want good schools" (ibid., 139). Presumably, those who do not *want* good schools (or leafy streets or gardens with swimming pools) choose, of their own free will, inner-city ghettos. The Free Market giveth, and the Free Market taketh away.

In short, racial *seg*regation would result mainly from *cong*regation stemming from natural affinity and free rational choice: it would be just a matter of taste. True, Schelling admits that his analysis overlooks the economic and political segregation mechanisms – presumably the strongest and the ones that prompt blacks to flock together. But, if so, the approach under consideration is at best shallow, and at its worst a smoke-screen concealing a serious social issue. What a comedown from Myrdal's 1942 epochal study!

6 Economicism Does Not Pay

The account of all human behaviour as utility maximizing, and of all social systems as competitive markets, has the virtues of simplicity and uniformity; furthermore, it facilitates mathematical modelling. But these are advantages only on the assumptions that the economy is everything, and that mainstream economic theory is true – which, alas, is not the case, as will be argued in chapter 3. Besides, the market model overlooks direct (face-to-face) social interaction as well as social structure, whence it is bound to produce only trivial results. Indeed, if a social system is regarded as a "system of (individual) actions" (the way Parsons saw it), and moreover as a bunch of exchanges, rather than as a system composed of people linked by social relations of various kinds, then the very existence of social systems and their changes remains unexplained. Last, but not least, the market models of social systems are just as static as the neoclassical economics they rely on.

The economic approach to everything social homogenizes and flattens social science by reducing all social relations to exchanges, and all goods and bads to commodities, without regard to their specific functions. The approach does not and cannot work for families or clubs, schools or hospitals, scientific laboratories or artist's ateliers, churches or charities, political parties or government departments, police stations or court rooms, if only because in all these cases much more than trade is involved. The approach does not and cannot work for all social systems, because markets are very peculiar social systems: their structure only involves one kind of connection, namely trade, which is neither a strong nor a lasting bond – not even in the business world.

A second reason for the failure of economicism is that equilibrium, which is indeed a legitimate desideratum for markets, is not always desirable for society as a whole. For example, social mobility – a kind of disequilibrium – is desirable for offering opportunities for personal advancement and thus, paradoxically, facilitating equality (Gellner 1984). Political instability is desirable in an unjust social order. And cultural disequilibria may be desirable for promoting the trial and diffusion of unorthodox ideas and practices. In sum, social equilibrium is not an absolute desideratum. And even if it were, the sociologist should not fix his gaze on equilibrium, for it is exceptional in modern societies.

As mentioned earlier, the economicist approach fails even with respect to the economy. One reason for this failure is that, far from being a closed system, hence one describable in purely economic terms, the economy is open to the environment as well as to the political and cultural systems. (See, for instance, Polanyi 1944; Akerlof 1984; Frank 1985; Granovetter 1985; and Sen 1987.) A second reason is that usually, whether in formal or informal systems, people make a point of becoming acquainted with their fellow players in order to guess intentions, inspire trust, secure reciprocity and loyalty, exploit patron-client relations, increase the number of deals, or find out about business or job opportunities (see Ben-Porath 1980; Lomnitz 1988; and Burt 1992). A third reason is that business firms are organizations, and these are social systems that should be studied primarily from a sociological viewpoint, the way behavioural economists, socioeconomists, and industrial sociologists do. Moreover, the departments of large business firms engage in internal political wrangles, so that they should draw the attention of the politologist as well as of the sociologist. By contrast, mainstream economics treats firms as black boxes, social relations as being all of the same kind, and individuals as faceless.

Having pronounced such harsh judgment on the economic approach to everything social, let me hasten to admit that every social problem does have an economic *aspect* – along with physical, biological, political, and cultural aspects. Whenever one of these five aspects predominates (for a while) one may, to a first approximation, confine one's study to it, tackling the remaining aspects as higher-order approximations are required. But in many cases at least two of the five aspects are essential, so that an exclusively economic approach will result in a caricature rather than a model. The same holds of course for the purely biological, environmental, political, and cultural approaches. In particular, all five aspects are important in modern industry, government, and warfare. Or think of the biological, environmental, economic, political, and cultural aspects of the health-care system. If we overlook any of them we won't understand how it works, and consequently we won't be able to improve on it. A pentagon is not reducible to one of its sides.

Admitting the need to take the economic aspect of every social system into account does not entail that all social systems can be treated as markets, and all social facts as commodity exchanges, for most of them are not. For instance, it would be ludicrous to treat learning and friendship, or life and death, as commodities – and yet this has been done. It would be equally preposterous to treat the judicial system as a market wherein crimes are traded for fines or prison terms, or churches as posts for trading sin for atonement, if only because the profit motive is absent in both cases. (More in chapter 5.)

In conclusion, economic imperialism is just as inadequate as political, cultural, environmental, or biological imperialism: these emperors have no clothes. The adequate approach to the study of any multifaceted system is an integrative approach tackling all the relevant aspects of a system – that is, the systemic approach. This approach fosters the merger of the various social sciences and resists the misleading attempts to reduce or subordinate them to a single discipline – let alone to a highly controversial theory like neoclassical microeconomics, to be examined in the next chapter.

7 Economic Sociology and Socio-Economics

Bridge building, rather than reduction, is the ticket in social studies. The reason is that the borders between disciplines in this field are largely artificial: they derive from sectoral vision, division of labour, or turf protection. Indeed, consider the classical findings that in the capitalist societies the marriage rate, emigration, morbidity, drunkenness, suicide, and crime rise and fall with the employment rate, which in turn rises and falls with the GDP, the volume of foreign trade, and the bank rate (see, for example, Thomas 1925).

Three of the bridges or interdisciplines in social studies are historical, political, and economic sociology. The latter may be defined as the sociological study of economic systems, such as manufacturing plants and banks, as well as their interrelations and the impact of their operations upon the rest of society. Economic sociology is flourishing nowadays (see Smelser and Swedberg 1994). It tackles, for example, the following questions: What is a farm? (Agricultural economists are not sure what it is: see Barkley 1984.) Who controls corporations: the shareholders, managers, or boards? How does organization, in particular management, affect productivity? What are markets and how do they emerge? How is customer satisfaction to be measured? Why does mainstream economics – obsessed with equilibrium – fail so dismally for the labour and financial markets? Is wage-push an important source of inflation? What is the economic impact of the decline in the power of labour unions? What affects workers' morale? Why have cooperatives thrived in some countries while failing in others? Do moral norms – such as reciprocity – and ideals – such as free trade and full employment – play any role in the economy?

One of the most powerful ideas introduced by economic sociology is that, far from being stray, individuals and social systems are firmly embedded in social networks of various kinds, from rather formless social "circles" to families and business conglomerates (Polanyi 1944). Granovetter (1974, 1983) has made a brilliant application of this systemic idea to the labour market and, in particular, to the process of getting a job. He splits a person's ties to other people into strong (relatives and close friends) and weak (acquaintances). And he argues that the latter are the more effective in helping to get a job. The mechanism is this: one's acquaintances are more likely to move in circles other than one's own, whence they tend to have access to job information that one lacks.

Granovetter's plausible hypothesis is philosophically interesting for being systemic rather than either individualist or holist. Indeed, it places individuals in dynamic systems. Moreover, the job information in question is of the micro-macro kind, for it concerns an opening in a social system – for instance, a firm – that may be of interest to certain members of the network. Finally, the hypothesis suggests the generalization that all markets operate through formal and informal social networks, so that the "market forces" do not suffice to explain market dynamics. If anything, informal social networks are even more important among the marginal groups living in shanty towns (Lomnitz 1977).

Socio-economics, the fusion of two disciplines, is somewhat different from economic sociology, an interdiscipline. Whereas the latter is the sociological study of economic systems, socio-economics is the merger of sociology with economics. The need for this fusion is realized upon thinking, for instance, of wealth and income distributions and the social causes and effects of macroeconomic policies; of the social effects of "downsizing" and "re-engineering"; of the social costs of both wealth concentration and government intervention; of the differences between "savage" and welfare capitalism, or between fascist and communist command economies. These questions are social (in particular, political and cultural) as well as economic, so they ought to be tackled simultaneously from (at least) the two sides. For example, the social and economic features of the "lean production" and "re-engineering" processes accentuated in the 1990s are combined in the following Boudon-Coleman diagram:

Macrolevel   Lean production & re-engineering   →   Increased income inequality
                              ↓   ↑
Microlevel   Loss of well-paid skilled jobs   →   Decline in workers' earnings.

Another typically socio-economic concept is that of social cost (Kapp 1950). It extends Marshall's "externality," to cover not only the undesirable economic effects of industry and commerce, such as mass unemployment, but also their negative environmental and health impacts – to which we should add adverse political effects, such as international conflicts motivated by competition for natural resources, markets, or trade routes. Typical socio-economic issues are those of reducing unemployment and homelessness, funding social security without suffocating business, and converting military industries into civilian ones. (For the potential of socio-economics see, for instance, Etzioni and Lawrence 1991.)

The neoclassicals, as well as the neo-Austrians and the contemporary "economic imperialists," are hostile to economic sociology and even more so to socio-economics. They believe that the economy is an autonomous self-regulating system, and moreover that all social actions are ultimately economic, so that sociology should be either disregarded or absorbed by (neoclassical) economics. (Recall sects. 5 and 6.) Though perhaps accepting economic sociology, all of them would have vehemently rejected the attempt to fuse sociology with economics, believing – in Pareto's words – that economics deals with "rational" (maximizing) behaviour, whereas sociology focuses on "irrational" behaviour. By contrast, Aristotle and Aquinas, Smith and Mill, Marx and Engels, and, closer to us, Weber, Veblen, Schumpeter, and Beveridge, as well as Gini, K. Polanyi, Perroux, W.A. Lewis, G. Myrdal, and K.E. Boulding were socio-economists – actually socio-econo-politologists. They might have welcomed the efforts of the Society for the Advancement of Socio-Economics. M. Allais, A. Etzioni, J.K. Galbraith, A.O. Hirschman, A. Sen, H.A. Simon, R. Burt, and others are in the same growing camp. (We shall return to this theme in chap. 11.)

8 Barbarians inside the Gates

A sociologist may do exclusively either theoretical or empirical research. But, if scientifically minded, he will attempt to fit theories to facts, or he will design and interpret empirical operations in the light of theories. In either case he will seek objective truths. That is, his speculations, however eccentric, will not be wild; and his data collecting and processing will not be blind. Shorter: like every other science of facts, scientific sociology is both theoretical and empirical.

This point was well understood and practised by Durkheim, Weber, Pareto, Merton, and their followers. But it has been resisted to this day by two groups of students of society: the data hunters and scavengers and the armchair theorists, or humanistic sociologists, who dispense with data altogether – and yet do not build theories proper either. Moreover, both groups are hostile to scientific sociology. Needless to say, they are aided and abetted by many influential philosophers. (Thus, for instance, Putnam [1978, 76] stated that "scientizing" the social studies is "a barbarous idea.") Let us take a quick look at two representatives of the humanistic camp – critical theory and phenomenological sociology – and one of the empiricist group – ethnomethodology. All of them reject the scientific approach and are characterized by uncritical thinking and hermetic language.

Critical theory, the successor to the Frankfurt school, is a variety of humanistic (or philosophical or armchair) sociology. It is characterized by a mixture of Hegel, Marx, and Freud; the thesis that all knowledge is born from, as well as serves, material interests; the denial of the distinction between science and ideology; the denunciation of science and technology as handmaidens of late capitalism; the rejection of rationalism and scientism; the demand that social science become a tool for social change; and long-winded, heavy, and semiopaque prose devoid of numbers and formulas. (See Adorno et al. 1976; Arato and Gebhard 1978; Habermas 1968, 1981; Horkheimer 1972; Marcuse 1964; and Seidman 1989.) Much the same holds for French structuralist Marxism (Althusser 1965; Foucault 1969; Godelier 1984), as well as for much of the American New Left. Obscurantism, once a preserve of the Right, now often sports leftist clothes and has become popular and entrenched in academe (see Gross and Levitt 1994).

We will concentrate on the philosophical components of this school. First, like Marxism, critical theory adopts uncritically Hegel's dialectics, a primitive and muddled metaphysics as well as a cloak for high-sounding sophistry: witness the thesis that every thing is a "unity of opposites." Dialecticians do not elucidate the vague terms 'opposite' and 'struggle,' and they overlook all the exceptions to the "law" that "contradiction" (opposition) is the only engine of change. In particular, they cannot account for reciprocity, cooperation, demographic change, invention, diffusion, or environmental catastrophes, none of which can be viewed as a struggle of opposites. (More on dialectics in Bunge 1981a.)

Second, critical theorists embrace uncritically psychoanalysis, with all its wild fantasies, thus exhibiting gullibility and inability to distinguish pseudoscience from science. Third, the self-styled critical theorists regard rationality as the supreme tool for the domination of man. Fourth, they endorse Engels's false thesis that "we *know* an object insofar as we can *make* it" (Habermas 1973, 61). (Obvious counter-examples: although we do not yet make cells, we know a lot about them, and we make many things without knowing how they work.) Fifth and consequently, they mistake science for technology, and are therefore unable to understand that basic science is neutral and innocent, hence useless as an agent of social change; that it is valuable not only as an input to technology but also for helping us understand the world. Sixth, they reject the distinction between science and ideology. Indeed, two central tenets of critical theory are (a) science = technology = capitalist ideology; and (b) sociologists are necessarily committed to either the conservation or the criticism and alteration of society – hence the adjective 'critical.' Seventh, they hold that science is neither epistemically objective nor morally neutral. Eighth, they brand as a positivist whoever believes it possible to gain objective knowledge of social facts – thus rendering positivism an undeserved favour. Ninth, their prose is opaque and pompous. Example: Habermas (1988, xiii) on one of his books: it "consisted chiefly in uncovering the dimension in which the symbolically prestructured object domain of social science could be approached through interpreting meaning."

Between the two world wars, the Frankfurt school tackled some real social issues, such as authoritarianism, the evils of capitalism and totalitarianism, and the impotence of liberalism. It performed a modest but useful ideological function even while disparaging the scientific study of those social facts. Since then critical theorists have continued to criticize the powers that be in imprecise general terms, but they have kept silent over the most pressing social issues in the post-war period, such as overpopulation, environmental degradation, the arms race, the North-South chasm, stagflation, ethnic conflicts, and the counter-culture. At the same time, they have turned increasingly to idealist philosophy. In particular, Habermas (1981) has shifted his focus from the important Marxist problematics to "communicative action" – the kind of action that intellectuals know best. Moreover, by rejecting the scientific approach to social issues, they have blocked their understanding, as well as any attempts to tackle them rationally and therefore effectively. In this way, despite its revolutionary rhetoric, critical theory has become an academically respectable safety valve for nonconformists. To top it all, despite their numerous publications over seven decades, critical theorists have not elucidated any key sociological concepts, designed any reliable social indicators, or proposed any theory proper. In sum, critical theory is neither.

Phenomenological sociology (Schütz 1932, 1974; Berger and Luckmann 1967) is the conservative counterpart of critical theory. It is characterized by idealism and subjectivism, as well as by individualism (both ontological and methodological) and conservatism – ethical and political. The first two features are obvious: According to phenomenology, social reality is a construction, not a given, for all social facts are "meaningful" (have a purpose) and thus subject to "interpretation" (attribution of purpose). Hence, everything social is spiritual and subjective, or at most intersubjective, rather than material and observer-independent. This thesis is neither true nor original. It is false because societies have preceded social scientists. And it is not novel because it stems from Dilthey and Weber. So does their ontological individualism.

The ontological individualism of phenomenology derives from its subjectivism. Because individuals are said to "interpret" themselves and others, without ever facing any brute social facts, the task of the sociologist is to grasp "subjective meaning structures" rather than to construct or test sociological models of social systems. In particular, he must study the *Lebenswelt* (everyday life) of individuals, staying away from large issues such as discrimination, poverty, unemployment, social conflict, and war. The phenomenologist claims to capture directly the objects of his study because they are ordinary. Moreover, he is graced with the "vision of essences" (*Wesensschau*), which allows him instant insight. Hence, he can dispense with statistics, mathematical modelling, and empirical tests. In short, phenomenological sociology is avowedly nonscientific and an invitation to sloth.

The ethics and politics of phenomenology are clear: far from being subjected to social constraints, the individual is autonomous because he constructs social reality. Hence there is no reason to bother about emancipation. The sociologist ought to be interested only in social order, because all men crave "meaning" (purpose) and order. He ought to shun conflict and, in general, social issues. The social *summum bonum* would be stability, with its accompanying order and certainty – not social progress, with the concomitant disorder and uncertainty. In short, phenomenology is ethically and politically conformist. (True, it attracts a number of socially concerned people, but only because it is unconventional – much as anarchists used to admire Nietzsche's unorthodoxies.) Hence, phenomenology is not a guide for any social policy other than that of "law and order."

Our third example of the reaction against scientific sociology is *ethnomethodology*, an offspring of the union of phenomenology with symbolic interactionism (see, for instance, Goffman 1963 and Garfinkel 1967). Ethnomethodologists practise what phenomenological sociologists preach: They record at first hand trivial events in the *Lebenswelt* (everyday life), focusing on symbols and ritual, and staying clear of any important social activities and issues. They engage in participant observation but shun statistics and experiment, which they disapprove of on philosophical grounds. They are storytellers, not scientists.

Lacking theories of their own, some ethnomethodologists invoke the murky pronouncements of hermeneutic, phenomenological, and even existentialist writers – all of them enemies of science. (See, for example, Husserl 1931, sects. 3 to 5, on the opposition between "genuine science," that is, phenomenology, and science; and Heidegger 1953, chap. 1, on the subordinate position of science *vis-à-vis* philosophy and poetry.) Obviously an antiscientific philosophy, opposed to the search for objective truth, could hardly inspire scientific research. Mercifully, ethnomethodologists make no use of these doctrines in their empirical work. In fact, in fieldwork they behave as pedestrian positivists – even while vehemently denouncing them – inasmuch as they spend most of their time collecting data that they cannot interpret at all for want of theory.

In fact, ethnomethodologists audiotape and videotape "the detailed and observable practices which make the incarnate production of ordinary social facts, for example, order of service in a queue, sequential order in a conversation, and the order of skillfully embodied improvised conduct" (Lynch et al. 1983, 206). Possible English translation: "The ethnomethodologists record observable everyday events."

The data thus collected are audible or visible traces left by people who presumably behave purposefully and intelligently. This is the only clue the ethnomethodologists can go by, for, lacking a theory, they cannot explain what makes people tick. Their practice does not differ from that of the empiricist and, in particular, the behaviourist – as even Atkinson (1988), a sympathizer of the school, has admitted. In short, they behave like positivists even while engaging in positivism bashing – a favourite among antiscientists.

Only the ethnomethodologists' barbarous prose suggests intimate contact with their philosophical mentors. For example, Garfinkel (1967, 1) states that ethnomethodology "recommends" that "the activities whereby members [of a group?] produce and manage settings [?] of organized everyday affairs are identical with members' procedures for making those settings 'account-able'[?]. The 'reflexive'[?] or 'incarnate'[?] character of accounting [?] practices and accounts makes up the crux of that recommendation." Or consider the same author's (ibid, 11) definition of ethnomethodology: it is "the investigation of the rational [intelligible?] properties of indexical [context-dependent] expressions and other practical actions as contingent [?] ongoing accomplishments [outcomes?] of organized artful [purposive?] practices of everyday life." Why use fuzzy and ponderous prose to give ordinary accounts of everyday life? To suggest profundity?

This is not to deny the merit of recording everyday-life occurrences, such as casual encounters and conversations – the favourite material of ethnomethodologists. Such observation, a common practice of anthropologists and social psychologists, yields raw material for the scientist to process in the light of hypotheses and with a view to coming up with new hypotheses – much as naturalists may collect useful material for biologists. But this material is of limited use unless accompanied by reliable information concerning the role that the observed subject enacts, for instance, boss and employee. The reason is that such roles – in other words, the system in which the protagonists are embedded – determine largely the "meaning" (purpose) of everyday actions and the content of conversations (R. Collins 1987). But ethnomethodologists overlook the macrosocial context and are not interested in any large social issues, such as poverty or marginality. This, combined with lack of theory and absence of tests of the proposed "interpretations" (hypotheses), explains the paucity of interesting findings of ethnomethodology.

Let us see now how ethnomethodologists view scientific research (Lynch et al. 1983). Their findings are essentially two. One is that "something more" is involved in scientific research than what can be formulated in even the most detailed of instruction manuals. This "something more" is the set of tacit assumptions and bits and pieces of know-how (procedural knowledge), both of them well known to psychologists, craftsmen, engineers, and philosophers. The other "finding" is that, no matter how elementary, a scientific experiment cannot be carried out without a modicum of theory – this being the reason that a partially paralysed chemistry student was able to do his lab exercises with the help of an able-bodied ethnomethodology student, largely ignorant of chemistry, who acted as the former's hand. But did we not know this all along, at least those of us who have had a scientific training and did not fall for crass empiricism? And if ethnomethodologists understand that there is no genuine science without theory, why don't they produce one?

Being radical individualists, and focusing on such everyday-life practices as conversation, ritual, and entertainment, the ethnomethodologists openly admit their indifference to the problems of social structure and, indeed, to all social issues (Garfinkel 1988; Hilbert 1990). By concentrating on individuals (or at most pairs of individuals), and overlooking all the important social activities and social systems, they skirt social reality. Why should people who only record trivial facts, have no theory proper, and write badly, be counted as social scientists? (For further criticisms see Blau 1968 and Mayrl 1977.)

Our fourth and last example is constituted by academic feminism, in particular *feminist theory* – not to be mistaken for serious political feminism. Feminist theorists hold that the scientific method is part of the "male-stream": they denounce precision (in particular quantitation), rational argument, "the myth of objectivity," the search for data, and the testing of hypotheses, as so many tools of male domination (see, for example, Harding 1986). Their goal is to undermine science, not to advance it. What they have actually achieved is to alienate women from science and technology, and thus further weaken their position in modern society (Patai and Koertge 1994, 157).

So much for the barbarians within the gates of academe. They have produced no noteworthy knowledge about society. But they have misled countless students, incapacitating them from thinking straight, getting facts right, and writing intelligibly.

Like other fields of social studies, contemporary sociology is split into four main currents: mainstream, rational-choice theory, humanistic (in particular "postmodern"), and Marxism. Mainstream sociology is the most rigorous of all, and it has produced some genuine findings. Rational-choice theory is so far removed from social reality that it does not even account for such everyday facts and occurrences as irrational attitudes and disinterested conduct. The "humanistic" school is hermetic and barren, and either contemptuous of empirical research or engaged in a positivist-like recording of events – mostly trivial to boot. Finally, Marxist sociology suggests a rich problematics; but, while strong on social criticism, it is weak on rigorous empirical research and even weaker on original and exact theorizing. Besides, none of these schools foresaw some of the most momentous social changes in the last hundred years.

Philosophically speaking, mainstream sociology is tacitly systemist but predominantly empiricist, and therefore short on theory. Rational-choice theory is individualist and rationalist, and therefore short on empirical research. Humanistic (or armchair) sociology is predominantly irrationalist and divided into two currents: one holist and the other individualist. And Marxist sociology is holistic and insufficiently rationalist and empiricist.

One can only hope for the emergence of a fifth current in sociology: one wrestling with social relations of all kinds, and approaching them in a rigorous fashion – that is, joining theoretical imagination with concern for empirical fit – as well as in sync with a scientific philosophy. In being realistic, this philosophy will encourage trespassing on the frontiers among the social sciences, by showing that they are artificial. In particular, it will favour merging sociology with economics. However, the latter deserves a new chapter.

3

Positive Economics

Economics has always been the most awe-inspiring of all the social sciences. So much so that, until about 1930, most economists were complacent and arrogant. This situation changed with the Great Depression, and then again forty years later with the end of the post-war growth process and the onset of stagflation. On both occasions it became obvious that mainstream economic theory hardly fits the real world, and thus it provides no reliable basis for economic policy. Substantive as well as methodological criticisms began to be heard, and not only from the predictable quarters – institutionalism and Marxism. First came the Swedish heretics (e.g., Myrdal 1930), then the great Keynes (1936) and his Cambridge (U.K.) school (e.g., Robinson 1962). More recently, many scholars have voiced stinging criticisms of all sorts (see Phelps Brown 1972; Bell and Kristol 1981; Leontief 1982; Eichner 1983; Thurow 1983; Kuttner 1984; Wiles and Routh 1984; Akerlof 1984; Schotter 1985; Etzioni 1988; and Ormerod 1994).

True, some recent work – for instance, a few chapters in the standard *Handbooks of Economics* edited by K.J. Arrow and M.D. Intriligator – deviates in some way or other from that tradition. But this work is not above criticism, for nearly all of it contains some or all of the foundation stones of orthodoxy, such as undefined or arbitrary utility functions; the postulate of utility maximization at all costs; the fiction that all agents are identical and all markets are in equilibrium or near it; the bottom-up strategy that ignores the macroeconomic, political, and cultural constraints upon individual action; and an almost total lack of concern with empirical tests. Altogether, deviations from orthodox theorizing are few, particularly compared with the frequent breakthroughs in other sciences. This is why Milton Friedman (1991, 33) could boast that, for all its formal sophistication, mainstream economics is just "old wine in new bottles." By contrast, authentic science renews itself incessantly.

It is no longer a secret that textbook economics is in deep crisis, to the point that it looks more like an antiques shop than a workshop. (Ormerod [1994] has gone as far as to announce the death of economics.) All the major economic theories, whether classical, Marxian, or neoclassical, are dead – and institutional economics never reached adulthood. So are all the major macroeconomic policies, in particular, monetarism and Keynesianism. Only a small though increasing band of scholars believe that this crisis is largely due to certain deep methodological and even philosophical flaws. This is all the more surprising given that no other research field has been cultivated by so many philosophically minded scholars – such as Smith, Mill, Cournot, Marx, Engels, Jevons, Menger, Pareto, Marshall, Schumpeter, Keynes, Robbins, von Mises, Hayek, Hicks, Hutchison, Morgenstern, Robinson, Myrdal, Friedman, Samuelson, Perroux, Allais, Wold, and Malinvaud.

The problematics of the philosophy and methodology of economics is vast and intriguing, and it has practical importance because economic theories and policies affect us all (see, for instance, Hollis and Nell 1975; Blaug 1980; Hausman 1984; and the journal *Economics and Philosophy*). Here is a random sample of this problematics. What is economics about?: goods and services, quantities and prices, scarce resources, individuals, or economic systems such as business firms and markets? What are the peculiarities of economic concepts, hypotheses, and theories? Are there any economic laws, or just economic trends and rules (that is, prescriptions)? Is it safe to make economic forecasts on the basis of trends? Is economics at all possible given that the economy interacts so strongly with the polity and the culture? Is microeconomics a chapter of psychology? And is it reducible to decision theory or game theory, two typically individualist theories? Is macroeconomics deducible from microeconomics? Is statistics a separate science or an auxiliary one? Is econometrics an inductive discipline, and can it suggest law statements or only test hypotheses? Should economic models be validated, and if so how? How are economic policies related to economic models, and how are they validated? Is normative economics value-free and morally neutral? Is all of economics – micro and macro, positive and normative – unavoidably contaminated by ideology? What is the scientific status of economics? And given that classical, Marxist, neoclassical, and institutionalist economic theories fail to match current economic reality, why are they still being taught at universities and discussed intensively in the economic literature?

Some of these problems will be tackled here. However, the present chapter deals only with "positive" (descriptive) economics; normative economics will be analysed in chapter 10. (Warning: positive ≠ positivist.) Moreover, the analysis of positive economics will focus on neoclassical microeconomics, being the most elabourate and popular of all economic theories. The neo-Austrian school of economics will be tackled in chapter 7, section 3, for its members – notably L. von Mises – regard it as a general theory of action.

The outcome of this analysis will justify the popular mistrust concerning the scientific status of mainstream economics. Indeed, it will be concluded that the discipline is neither conceptually rigorous nor empirically confirmed: that it is only a semi-science (sect. 10). However, I shall argue that the unhealthy state of mainstream economics is not irreparable, for the roots of the trouble are philosophical and ideological. Two of them are individualism (ontological, methodological, and ethical) and "swings between compulsive empiricism and footloose theoretical speculation" (Leontief 1983, 902). Exposing such roots should help explain failure and prepare the way for more solid work.

1 What Is Economics About?

Several decades ago Robbins (1935, 1) wrote this about economics: "We all talk about the same thing, but we have not yet agreed what it is we are talking about." This shocking uncertainty about the very referents or units of analysis of economics has not decreased in the meantime. Microeconomists claim to deal with consumers and individual firms, and macroeconomists with entire economies; labour economists and economic sociologists study economic organizations; economic politologists study politico-economic supersystems (such as military-industrial complexes); and the engineers who double as economists see only production and transportation, hence energy flows and conversions, and the associated technologies. In either case people are hardly in sight.

At first sight the problem of reference has a simple answer: Economics is about the production and exchange of commodities – or even about quantities and prices. This answer is cryptic and sketchy if only because it fails to specify what a commodity is. (Is labour just a commodity, a means of livelihood, or both? Is garbage a "dead" or a potential good?) Besides, the answer is ambiguous, for it can be understood either in the sense that economics is about *people* engaged in producing or exchanging commodities, about the *commodities* themselves – or both. Worse, the answer in question is basically flawed, for extruding the economy from society at large (see Granovetter 1991). It is also incomplete for omitting two important modes of economic transaction: reciprocity (or give and take among relatives, friends, and acquaintances) and redistribution through taxation or tribute (Polanyi 1944). Unlike market exchanges, which are optional, reciprocity and redistribution are mandatory. And all three economic transactions are firmly embedded in social networks. This alone suffices to indict the study of any economy as an autonomous system and, in particular, one free from political and cultural constraints and inputs.

It might seem helpful to add that economics can be divided into microeconomics, which deals "ultimately" with individual attitudes and behaviour, and macroeconomics, which handles entire economic sectors and even national and regional economies. Moreover, since economic systems, such as business firms, are composed of individuals, "in principle" – so a popular argument goes – macroeconomics would be reducible to microeconomics; thus, "at bottom" the whole of economics would concern only individuals in some economic capacity or other, that is, as entrepreneurs, managers, workers, or consumers (see, for example, Rosenberg 1976, Sargent 1987).

Now, since the science of individual behaviour is psychology, if the individualist view is adopted consistently it follows that economics is really (or "in the last analysis") a branch of psychology or, perhaps, of decision theory or game theory. To be sure, not all students share the latter assertion. In particular, Pareto, Weber, and Popper rejected any such reduction, and asserted the autonomy of social science. However, they were inconsistent, for the possibility of reduction follows logically from the neoclassical premise that economics is in the last analysis about the gains and pains of individual economic agents.

Still, a number of valid objections can be raised against the view that economics is reducible to psychology. First, if it were true, genetics should be directly relevant to economics, for behaviour and ideation are partly determined by the genome. In particular, the distribution of wealth should correlate with that of genes: on the whole the smartest people should be the wealthiest, and the dumbest the poorest. This hypothesis, popular among Social Darwinists since Spencer and Sumner, has been subjected to statistical tests and proved false: income is not genetically determined (Goldberger 1978). It is well known that initial economic endowment and membership in the "right" social network are strong predictors of business success.

Second, if economics were about individual behaviour, economists would be busy observing economic agents. In fact, economists seldom observe directly anything other than printed matter, such as statistics, business and government reports, and publications by fellow economists. In particular, the economists who write about individual economic agents seldom study them in the flesh – much as theologians pontificate about their God.

Third, if economics dealt only, or even primarily, with individual beliefs and behaviour, it might be interpreted as "the logic of rational choice," where choice would be determined jointly by preference, circumstance, and calculation. And if this were true, economics would be a decision technique rather than a social science intimately related to sociology, political science, and history.

However, (a) the problem of choice arises even where there is embarrassment of riches; (b) whereas the tycoon can often choose among several alternative courses of action, the rest of us have little if any genuine choice: we are forced to buy mostly from oligopolies, cartels, or state corporations, and are tied to our jobs – if lucky enough to have any; (c) focusing on choice among given commodities is a shallow approach, typical of the retailer who can afford to overlook raw materials, energy, production, technology, investment, employment, inflation, fiscal policy, government regulations, labour power, and other factors that precede and constrain business choices.

Macroeconomics has not yet been reduced to (that is, deduced from) microeconomics. In particular, the notions of GDP, balance of payments, discount rate, foreign exchange rate, state budget, and unemployment rate are not reducible to those of expectation, utility, or decision making. Nor is there any reason to expect that the reduction will ever be effected, and this for the following reasons: (a) every agent enters or leaves a pre-existing market – provided he surmounts the barriers to entry – so that his actions are constrained by the socioeconomic structure; (b) whereas microeconomics is concerned with households and firms, macroeconomics is about large-scale economic systems, so that it cannot help abound in systemic concepts such as those of national interest, institutional framework, inflation, foreign debt, and political stability. Moreover, any realistic microeconomic analysis will include macroeconomic parameters, because households and firms are embedded in, hence constrained by, the total economy. (More in sect. 8.)

Which are then the referents or units of analysis of economics? The best way to discover them is to identify typical economic activities and analyse the corresponding constructs – concepts, propositions, theories, policies, strategies, and plans. Even a cursory examination suggests that the referents of the key constructs of economics can be grouped into the following seven categories:

A: *natural resources* such as virgin land, forests, mineral deposits, water, and fisheries;

B: *nonhuman items under current human control*, such as cultivated land, machines, industrial plants, domestic animals, and cultivars;

C: *economic agents* such as households, business firms, cartels, trade unions, or regulatory agencies (national or international);

D: *economic sectors* (or industries) such as mining, textiles, and banking;

E: *markets* such as the labour and capital markets;

F: entire *economies*, whether regional, national, or international;

G: *mixed*, or composed of items in two or more of the above categories.

What all these categories share is that they have to do with *people* and the *work* they do to get the wherewithal required to meet their needs and wants.

Type A items occur in economics as possible inputs into economic activities. In other words, the corresponding constructs occur in economics only insofar as their referents are potentially exploitable – that is, as long as these are judged to have a potential as referents of constructs of type B. The constructs of the six remaining types refer, directly or indirectly, to people producing, trading, managing, or enjoying the fruits of work, in some social system or other. The system may be the household, the cottage industry, the firm, the cartel, the region, the European Union, or even the global economy. In other words, the central constructs of economics are about economic activities – such as production and trade, as well as the regulation of both – performed by people in some social system or other. All such activities sustain, alter, or undermine economic systems.

Note the shift in emphasis from individuals to systems: the former are no more and no less than components of the latter. Economic activity and, in general, social behaviour, is unintelligible separately from the system in which the activity occurs, just as the system cannot be understood except in terms of that activity. For example, the production of any commodity requires the production of several others; the exchange of any commodities requires at least a two-person system, however ephemeral; and economic equilibria (and disequilibria) are systemic properties. So are scarcity, income distribution, and many others.

Unsurprisingly, whenever an economist thinks of an economy as a whole he models it, more or less explicitly, as a *system*. Thus, setting up an input-output matrix for the American economy presupposes conceiving of it as a system made up of at least a thousand interacting sectors or industries. And talk of general equilibrium presupposes that the economy – often interpreted narrowly as "the market" – is a system. One may feel that in both cases the units of analysis – sectors and markets respectively – are too bulky. Still, thinking about the economy as a whole is systemic rather than individualist.

I submit that, whatever its degree of complexity, an economic system, such as a corporation, may be characterized qualitatively as the quadruple composition-environment-structure-mechanism (or *CESM*), where

Composition = the collection of persons (economic agents) and nonhuman things of certain kinds (in particular energy sources, tools, machines, and domestic living beings) in the system;

Environment = the collection of natural, social, and artificial items linked with members of the system;

Structure = the collection of relations of production, trade, consumption, management, supervision, regulation, and taxation involving goods and services, including the relations with sociosystems of other kinds (political and cultural); and

Mechanism = the collection of processes (e.g., work, trading, borrowing, and marketing) that determine (maintain or alter) the system's structure.

This broad definition of the concept of an economic system includes everything economists are interested in. In particular, the psychoeconomist is expected to study the behaviour of the human components of the first coordinate of the above triple – though not as isolated individuals but in relation to one another and as economic agents. The entities that interact with the economic system – resources, governments, trade unions, and so on – are included in the second coordinate, which represents the environment. The dealings of the economic system with other things, natural or social, are included in the third coordinate – the structure. (Thus, manufacturing and trading can be analysed as quaternary relations: "*a* manufactures *b* from *c* for *d*," and "*a* trades *b* for *c* with *d*.") The fourth coordinate represents what makes the system tick; hence, its study is that of both stasis and change. In turn, only such study explains in depth, for we know a thing only if we know how it works.

For example, the composition of a particular market is the collection of sellers, buyers, and commodities, plus the bankers, lawyers, and bureaucrats behind market transactions. Its environment is the society or societies to which the traders, bankers, and regulators belong. Its structure is constituted by the relation of selling and its converse, that of buying, plus the relations of financing and regulating. And its mechanisms are those of value-adding processes, technological innovation, price formation, financing, merging, and so forth.

Contrary to mainstream economists, I do not equate the economy with the market, but regard the latter as a subsystem of the former. The main reasons for this distinction are that (a) economies involve not only trade but also natural resources and labour; and (b) economic activities, though distinguishable from other social actions, are inseparable from some of them, and are moreover subject to institutional constraints. (For further reasons see Polanyi et al. 1957; Granovetter 1985; and Swedberg 1994.) Shorter: The market is a subsystem of the economy. Consequently, sound economics is not confined to studying the market: it also requires the consideration of political and cultural inputs. This, incidentally, was the view of the classical economists (Weldon 1988, 18).

We have defined the concept of a market in a bottom-up fashion, that is, starting with individuals and their actions. This does not entail that the features of a market derive exclusively from those of its components, and that the latter are not influenced by their entering the market. Far from it, the behaviour of sellers and buyers depends critically upon the state of the market as a whole – a state which, like that of an elastic body, is a macrovariable. For example, a worker's decision to change jobs at a particular time may be due to a favourable labour market or to his having the correct information and the right connections. Likewise, a businessman's success in a new venture depends not only on his talent, capital, and connections, but also on the market's barriers to entry, the current credit facilities, and the international situation. In short, the macro-micro (or top-down) arrows are just as important as the micro-macro (or bottom-up) and the horizontal (micro-micro and macro-macro) ones. (Recall chap. 2, sect. 3.)

We conclude that economists study economic systems, that is, social systems whose specific function is to meet the basic needs and the wants of people. Shorter: Economics is about *people* organized into economic *systems* – systems whose specific function is the production or trade of commodities. Consequently, the right approach to the study of the economy is the systemic one (see also Boulding 1985; Eichner 1991,18ff. and Malinvaud 1991, 41ff.). This platitude has been denied by all those who, from Adam Smith onwards, have conceived of the economy as an aggregate of free and self-seeking agents.

Economists study economic systems of different levels of complexity. In fact, one may distinguish at least the following economic levels and the corresponding branches of economics: *microeconomic* (small and medium-size firms), *mesoeconomic* (giant corporations and conglomerates), *macroeconomic* (national economies), and *megaeconomic* (regional economies and the world economy). The systems on each level have their peculiar features, and the corresponding discipline crafts its own concepts. And all these studies should be preceded by a study of the economic behaviour of individuals – which may be called *nanoeconomics*, which includes psychoeconomics.

Moreover, economic systems are not closed or self-contained, hence self-regulated and in no need of regulation by external agents. Actually they have environmental, political, and cultural inputs and outputs. In other words, every economic system is firmly embedded in both nature and society. Admittedly, some components or features of certain production processes – particularly the self-reproducing ones – are (nearly) natural in the sense that they are independent of the social structure and therefore universal or cross-cultural (Pasinetti 1981; Barceló 1992). Still, every social item is artefactual, and no component or feature of a system exists apart from the latter.

In sum, economics is about economic systems. Consequently, irreducibly social (in particular economic) variables are essential in describing such systems – as even Arrow (1994), a lifelong methodological individualist, has recently acknowledged.

2 Economic Concepts

We have just concluded that economics is about economic systems rather than about either their individual components or the quantities and prices of goods.

This does not entail that economists can overlook individuals and such mental states or processes as desire, intention, goal, learning, knowledge, uncertainty, fear, hope, expectation, decision, risk perception, trust, goodwill, or prestige. Economists must take them all into account, but only in reference to individuals *qua* members of economic systems – unless they incur the fallacy of ascribing such individual properties to systems like firms. Thus, to account for the economic behaviour of an individual it is not enough to know what his skills, wants, and aims are. One also needs to know something about the individual's means, his place in certain social networks, the role he plays in the economic system(s) he is or wants to become a member of, and the state of the system. In short, the economist is interested in individuals only as (actual or potential) components of economic systems.

Psychological variables, though by no means irrelevant to economics, are less important in economics than certain environmental, demographic, social, and political variables – not to mention the specifically economic ones. Thus, even the most talented and boldest of entrepreneurs won't achieve much in the midst of a desert or in the depths of a civil war. And the forecasts of a demographically blind economist are likely to fail, for every economy moves along with the population it services. In any event, the economist may use psychological constructs, but it is not his business to build or check them: his main task is to introduce and interrelate economic concepts. However, he cannot help using hybrid (psychoeconomic) concepts, such as those of work, risk aversion, and sales expectation; politological ones such as those of political instability and international crisis; and legal ones such as those of contract and liability.

Still, unlike the physical scientist, who leaves to the psychologist the secondary or apparent properties – that is, properties of things as perceived – the economist must reckon with them. For instance, although product quality, price, and quantity are perfectly objective, different people will "perceive" (evaluate) them in accordance with their own needs, wants, means, and goals. Consequently, they will decide and act differently. (Remember the dime illusion: A dime looks larger to a poor child than to a rich one.) Such differences in "perception" account for the existence of ordinary goods that sell at outrageous prices just because they carry prestige labels. Likewise savings, investment, insurance, and loans depend largely on expectations about one's own future and that of the economy. This is what investor and consumer confidence is all about: more or less well-informed though always somewhat subjective expectations.

(Caution: Given the present state of the discipline, most economic expectations are intuitive. There is no realistic system of equations enabling one to forecast correctly the state of an economy. To be sure, the rational-expectations school in macroeconomics claims that "the public" is omniscient, in that it possesses both the theory and the data necessary to form unbiased or "rational" expectations: see Lucas and Sargent 1981. But this assumption, and indeed the entire theory, is at variance with the facts: see, for instance, Ericsson and Irons 1995. Suffice it to recall that there is no generally accepted economic theory; that all empirical information about any complex system is incomplete; that only a few firms muster the resources required to find out the state and trend of the market, as well as to make minimally reasonable forecasts – and that the leaders among them make the future happen rather than forecasting it passively. At the time of this writing, talk of *rational* expectation is just hand-waving. We do form expectations all the time and act accordingly, but they are all more or less intuitive and fallible. Were they not, we would run no risks, would not stand to gain much, and the insurance industry, which thrives on risk taking and averting, would go bankrupt.)

In short, even though the features of an economic item are real, they may be "perceived" or "interpreted" differently by different agents, and they may raise different expectations – or none – in different people. In other words, every objective economic concept is likely to have a subjective counterpart. Yet the gap between the two can sometimes be bridged. For example, the real growth and interest rates – that is, the rates corrected for inflation – are rather subjective when forecast or prophesied. But they become objective once the period in question has elapsed and the statistics are in.

The dual nature of economic concepts is a real obstacle to rigorous economic concept formation and modelling, and it accounts in part for the fact that some of the key technical concepts of economics are nearly as obscure today as they were centuries ago. Take for instance that of money: it has been variously explicated as "the universal medium of exchange" and "the merchandise of merchandises"; "the unit of accounting" and "the link between present and future" (Keynes); as being "like a language" (Turgot); as "what money does" (Hicks); and even as "the source of every wickedness" (Sophocles). And, whereas shopkeepers, thieves, and monetarists assign money self-existence and causal efficacy, others regard it as an epiphenomenon and, moreover, a dispensable one, as shown by barter.

Such semantic vagaries will persist as long as no adequate *theory* of money is built. In particular, the most sophisticated model of a capitalist economy, namely the neoclassical theory of general equilibrium, makes no room for something that, like paper money, is intrinsically worthless (Hahn 1983) – which says something about the adequacy of the model. Ironically, monetarism does not include an adequate theory of money either: it does not even define the concept of money. And yet its central thesis is that all inflation is caused by "too much money chasing too few goods"; whence the prescription that tight control of the quantity of money suffices to guarantee economic health – at the price of the patient's life if necessary. (We shall not analyse monetarism because it has been shown to be both false and practically ineffective or worse. For the first feature see Brown 1983 and Hendry and Ericsson 1983; for the second, Dow and Saville 1988.)

What holds for the concept of money holds, *mutatis mutandis*, for that of capital – "the most elusive concept of economics" (Morgenstern 1963, 70). Indeed, no generally accepted theory seems to define it clearly, aside from stating that it is a factor of production (see, for example, Harcourt 1972). Something similar holds for the concept of labour, particularly in the case of knowledge-intensive industries. This would not be a serious flaw if there were a consensus on the correct formula for production in terms of capital, labour, and technology – but this is not the case. (More on this in sect. 3.) Not even the concept of a commodity is quite clear. For example, labour and public goods are not commodities on a par with consumer goods or capital goods. Indeed, labour is a means of both livelihood and self-realization (Marx 1867). As for public goods, there is no (lawful) market for them; for example, air, public parks, and armies are not (yet) traded in the stock market.

The notion of objective value, though central in classical economics, has fared no better. Smith, Ricardo, and Marx defined it as the social labour required to produce the commodity concerned. But, as we saw a moment ago, labour is neither well defined nor readily measurable. Besides, why should a commodity be assigned the same value in countries where labour costs are very different? Furthermore, the labour "theory" (actually definition) of value overlooks the contribution of managers, bankers, transporters, and retailers. Whence the devaluation of the concept of objective value in contemporary economics, where – for better or for worse – it has become "just a word" (Robinson 1962).

If anything, the concept of subjective value or utility, central to neoclassical economics, is even fuzzier than that of objective value. Indeed, it is seldom mathematically well defined. And, when defined at all (for instance, as either the logarithm or the square root of the quantity of the good concerned), it is not firmly anchored in observation (see Bunge 1996a). Fortunately nearly all a hard-nosed economist wishes to say about value can be said about price or value in exchange. In particular, the notion of surplus value can be replaced with that of surplus price or some more refined concept (Weizsäcker 1973).

Finally, other important economic concepts are not just fuzzy but simply do not occur in standard economic theory. One of them is that of the intrinsic property of a good – whence wood, for example, is treated as a close substitute for bread (Lancaster 1966). Another missing concept is that of product quality. This concept is important because quality is one of the determinants of price and market share, and because its deterioration may lead to a firm's decline, as Mr Quality Control (Deming 1982) emphasized. The reason for its omission in mathematical economics is obvious: the concept of quality is hard to quantitate in a general and uniform way. Thus, whereas in some cases it consists in performance (or efficiency), in others it equals durability, precision, reliability, aesthetic appeal – or a combination of some of these features. And, whereas some of these properties are quantitative, others are intangible. Several other key concepts occurring in business reasonings, such as those of trust, goodwill, and uncertainty, are vague too.

To be sure, one can avoid conceptual obscurity by sticking to easily observable variables, such as quantities and prices of goods and services, and abstaining from unveiling the mechanisms of their production and circulation. But the point of economic theory is to unveil such mechanisms in order to explain what turns a thing or activity into a commodity – that is, something exchangeable for something else and therefore fetching a price in a market – and what causes price changes. The economist who wishes to achieve these goals heeds the advice of Ricardo and Marx: Dip underneath appearances. That is, uncover work and capital, technology and management, competition and cooperation, conflict and bargaining, planning and government intervention, political and cultural factors, and so on. But as soon as one relates economic concepts to sociological and politological ones, he trespasses the borders of economics, to become a socio-politico-economist ready to be tarred and feathered by the guardians of economic monasticism.

From a methodological viewpoint the set of economic variables can be split into three classes, which we list in order of increasing abstraction or remoteness from experience:

1. *Observable*, such as quantities, times, prices, and market demand;

2. *Inferred* or *calculated* from observable variables, such as productivity (output/input) and gross benefit (gross receipts minus direct costs);

3. *Hypothesized* or *latent*, such as risk and consumer demand ($\neq$ market demand).

Some of the variables of interest to the economist are unobservable ("latent"), representing psychological propensities – for instance, to work, consume, save, or take risks. Others, such as global supply and demand, have no observable counterparts because they concern large economic systems, such as markets and industry sectors, which are not perceptible either. (Actual consumption can be measured; so can market demand, which equals consumption minus output. Not so consumer demand, for it equals need or want.) One can see the buildings of an industrial plant as well as its innards, but no one can see the company, for this is a sociotechnical system run not only by energy but also by brains, and subject to the actions of further invisible entities such as markets, legal codes, governments, unions, and foreign nations. Note that some hypothesized or latent variables, far from being ghostly, represent properties actually possessed by economic systems. (Natural science analogues: entropy, field intensity, valence, dissociation energy, genetic "information.") They are removed from everyday experience. They look suspicious to positivists but not to realists, who know that most of reality is hidden to the senses.

Still, one can get a "feel" for some economic variables because all economic systems, however large, share some of the properties of small familiar systems such as the household, the cottage industry, the small farm, and the retail shop. In this regard economists are much better off than nuclear physicists, astrophysicists, molecular biologists, or evolutionary biologists, all of whom deal with utterly unfamiliar items inaccessible to direct experience and intuition.

Latent (unobservable) variables should not be mistaken for ghostly concepts, that is, concepts lacking real counterparts. Observability is a methodological condition, whereas lack of real reference is a semantic one. Latent variables are admissible provided they are well defined and can be related to observable variables (or indicators) via indicator hypotheses (see Bunge 1996a). By contrast, ghostly variables are unjustifiable in science. Regrettably, there is no shortage of ghostly concepts in economics: think of the hidden hand, perfect competition, Walras's auctioneer, perfect knowledge, subjective probability, rational expectation, or the natural unemployment rate.

Should one always require the measurability of the properties denoted by economic concepts? No, because one might stifle theorizing and overlook important intangibles such as morale, trust, and loyalty. Besides, some clear and useful variables are hard to measure. Economic elasticities are a case in point. Marshall's (1890) definition is formally unobjectionable; thus, elasticity of supply (or production) is defined as the ratio of the relative increase in supply to the relative increase in price. Conceptually it is a good measure of the reactivity or sensitivity of producers (or consumers, as the case may be) to changes in price. However, elasticities are hard to measure. Shall we therefore give them up? Not if they occur in important generalizations (e.g., that the prices of essential foodstuffs are far less elastic than those of durable goods.) If they do, we should attempt to devise better measurements, whether direct or indirect (via indicator hypotheses).

The viability of any variable depends ultimately on its potential to occur in interesting and testable generalizations. Take, for instance, Keynes's marginal propensity to consume, defined as the derivative of consumption with respect to income. A consequence of this definition and other formulas is that the investment multiplier λ, occurring in the formula "$\lambda Y = \lambda \Delta I$," where ΔY is interpreted as increment in income, and ΔI as increment in investment, equals $1/(1 - p)$, where p is the marginal propensity to consume (Keynes 1936, 115). So, income and investment, two strictly economic concepts, are related to the psychoeconomic parameter p, which can be computed from the measured values of Y and I. The same parameter p occurs also in Keynes's theory of employment, according to which the volume of employment at equilibrium depends on supply, the propensity to consume, and the volume of investment. Whether these formulas are accurate is beside the point. The point is that in economics, just as in physics, unobservables can be accessed from observables via indicator hypotheses. (In the simplest case, $U = f(O)$.)

Lest the foregoing suggest that only quantitative variables are respectable, let me repeat that certain qualitative features of economic systems, such as organization, management style, job satisfaction, and product quality, are no less important than many a quantitative one. Mathematical economists tend to underrate qualitative variables. But economic sociologists and management experts know that some of them are critical. Thus, they will tell us that two firms in the same sector, with similar initial endowments, are likely to perform differently because of differences in organization, management-labour relations, technological sophistication, mode of financing, connections, morale, or opportunity. Not that such imponderables are intrinsically beyond reason: they can be spotted and conceptualized, albeit qualitatively. (For example, structural differences can be exhibited by different graphs or matrices: recall chap. 2, sect. 1.) Nor are all such features intrinsically qualitative: the only safe thing to say about them is that they have not *yet* been quantitated. (Only existence does not come in degrees.) Their occurrence should be regarded as a challenge to the theorist rather than as an excuse for sloppiness, let alone pessimism about the prospects of economics becoming an exact science.

Another common if lame excuse for either despair or sloppiness is the fact that economics fails to contain universal constants such as Planck's or the speed of light in a vacuum. This has suggested to Hicks and others that economic theories must be radically different from theories in the natural sciences. This objection ignores the fact that only physics and chemistry can boast of universal constants, and that these are overshadowed by "local" or species-specific constants, such as atomic numbers, and local parameters, such as chemical equilibrium constants, as one moves upwards from particle and field physics to the physics and chemistry of complex systems. As for biology, it has no universal constants of its own, and yet it is doing reasonably well. Every science teems with "local" (nonuniversal) generalizations containing only "local" constants.

Finally, a semantic caution. Mathematical economists sometimes fail to distinguish concepts from the things or properties they are supposed to represent. Thus, they are likely to say that a bundle of n commodities *is* (instead of *is representable by*) a vector in an n-dimensional Cartesian space – and similarly for the corresponding prices. This is a glaring mistake: one can eat some commodities, but not vectors. The conflation of identity with representation is harmless for most mathematical purposes, but it is a major obstacle to the correct interpretation of mathematical formulas in economic terms, as well as to any attempt to try alternative mathematical representations of the same entities or properties – or, conversely, alternative factual interpretations of a mathematical formalism. Regrettably, the confusion in question is not accidental but the cornerstone of the so-called structuralist and semantic views of scientific theories held by P. Suppes, J. Sneed, W. Stegmüller, U. Moulines, and other philosophers (see Bunge 1978, 1983a; and Truesdell 1984).

To avoid the said confusion it is always desirable to indicate explicitly the *referents* of the functions representing properties or activities of economic agents or systems. (This is done by explicitly including such referents in the domains of the functions in question. For example, the input and the output of systems of kind S can be represented by real-valued functions on the Cartesian product of S by T, where T is a segment of the real line representing a time interval.) Which brings us back to the beginning of this section: the need to know what one is talking about lest one be taken for a charlatan or a madman. (For the concepts of reference and representation see Bunge 1974a.)

3 Economic Assumptions

An assumption is a premise occurring in a deductive reasoning. Unless adopted as axioms, assumptions need not be known to be true. In fact, one often makes assumptions for the sake of argument, that is, to check them through some of the conclusions they entail. Moreover, the postulates of any factual theory or model are idealizations and thus at best approximately true. Still, they should eventually be checked for truth.

Assumptions can be explicit or tacit. If the latter, they are called *presuppositions*. For example, many economists overlook overpopulation and presuppose that natural resources are infinite. Consequently, they do not care if such resources are depleted or even destroyed, and they do not question demographic and economic growth: for them, the more consumers and goods, the merrier. Another common tacit assumption is that economies are the same as markets, whereas in fact the latter are only subsystems of the former (recall sect. 2). Obviously, presuppositions are risky: being unexamined, they may turn out to be untested or even false. One of the tasks of the student of the foundations of a discipline is to ferret out and examine the presuppositions of the latter: to render explicit the implicit.

In the study of the real world every explicit assumption is a hypothesis to be tested by its compatibility with other assumptions as well as with empirical data. What is peculiar to economic hypotheses is of course that they contain economic concepts and thus refer to economic facts – real or imaginary. Besides, an economic assumption must be neither self-contradictory nor tautological (true regardless of the state of the world): the former because economists are expected to respect the truth, the latter because they are supposed to care for quality truths. Yet occasionally they do utter cheap truths, such as "Rational businessmen always try to maximize gains," a tautology if 'rational' is defined as 'utility maximizer.'

Like every other research field, economics assigns a pride of place to assumptions of a particular kind, namely generalizations: that is, statements of uniformity or regularity supposed to hold for whole classes of facts. And, like every other social study, economics attempts to discover and utilize generalizations of four kinds: rules of thumb, trends, laws, and norms. Here are illustrations of these categories. Rule of thumb: "In the industrialized countries the ratio of capital to output is roughly constant and equal to about 3 to 1." Trend: "Manufacturing employment has decreased steadily in all industrialized nations since 1970." Law: "Profits increase with productivity." As for the "law" of compound interest, it is a social convention, a rule embedded in activities subject to contracts of a certain type (so much so that it fails when a debtor defaults, and that it does not rule Islamic banks). By contrast, the going interest rate is not purely conventional.

Roughly, the features of the four types of generalization are as follows. *Rules of thumb* are empirical generalizations or quasi-laws relating two or more variables in a somewhat imprecise way. A *trend* is the overall drift of either stasis or change in some property over a limited period of time. More specifically, it is the overall increase, decline, constancy, or periodicity in the value of some feature over time. For example, the once-famous Phillips curve, according to which inflation is inversely related to unemployment, seems to have matched the facts during the 1954 to 1969 period, ceasing to do so since the emergence of stagflation. Trends are temporary characteristics of processes: they emerge and submerge, often without warning. Besides, trends can be modified, even reversed, by deliberate (concerted or unconcerted) human action. For example, industrialization eliminated gradually informal production and exchange – until the emergence of the underground economy after the Second World War.

A *law statement* is an empirically confirmed general hypothesis embedded in a theory, and representing an objective regularity. (Note that I avoid confusing laws with hypotheses and theories: see Bunge 1967a, 1996a.) Unlike trends, objective laws cannot be tampered with – except of course by radically altering the systems in which they inhere. (For the difference between laws and trends see Popper 1957; Bunge 1967a, 1996a; and Brown 1973.) For example, the law that costs decrease with increasing productivity is assumed to hold universally, that is, regardless of the type of economic organization and ownership. To be sure, one may improve productivity by upgrading the technology, streamlining the organization, or introducing incentives. However, any such measures will satisfy the law. Unlike trends, laws are essential, permanent, and defining features of the things possessing them. Hence, if a given law-like generalization ceases to hold, we may infer either that (a) it was not a genuine law to begin with but just a temporary trend, or (b) the corresponding thing (e.g., economic system) has metamorphosed – for example, from family concern into corporation.

Regrettably, the philosophical problem of the nature of economic laws (and their distinction from the corresponding law statements) has received even less attention than that of natural laws. This neglect seems to have three different philosophical roots. One is the "humanistic" myth that human behaviour is totally free and haphazard, hence utterly unpredictable. Another is the related thesis of rational-choice theorists that economics deals with free individual choices, which in turn would obey a single law: that of maximizing the expected utility. A third source is Hume's empiricist view that we can ascertain only the existence of empirical regularities, never of objective patterns, which would be metaphysical fictions. The law "$E = mc^2$" suffices to falsify this view, since neither of the three properties it involves is directly observable.

The neglect of the methodological status of economic laws has been paid for with confusion. A case in point is the formula "$E = O/P{\cdot}H$" relating the number E of persons employed to output O, labour productivity P, and average weekly work hours H. Upon solving for P, one realizes that this is a definition of labour productivity, not a law statement subject to empirical confirmation or refutation. Likewise, the macroeconomic equation relating national income Y_t to consumption C_t and investment I_t in a given year t: $Y_t = C_t + I_t$. This is just a definition of national income. Therefore, GDP cannot be "explained" as the "effect" of consumption and investment, the way some econometricians (e.g., Wolff 1967) have claimed. In other words, in the above equation consumption and investment cannot be treated as causal variables, anymore than 2 and 3 are causes of 5 in the identity "$2 + 3 = 5$." (More on tautology and testability in economics in Agassi 1971.)

Assuming that we would recognize an economic law if we met one, *are* there any such laws? The answer is that there are some, though few if any universal ones like the basic physical laws. (But then even the chemical and biological laws are space and time bound.) Given the comparative youth of economics, this should not be surprising. But it is certainly disappointing that the collection of economic laws fails to increase. Worse, writing in the authoritative *New Palgrave* (1987, 2:54), Zamagni concludes that "[t]he list of generally accepted economic laws seems to be shrinking." (For example, the "law" of diminishing returns was refuted by the "law" of economies of scale, which in turn was infirmed by the discovery of diseconomies of scale.) He goes on to state that "economists now prefer to present their most cherished general statements as theorems or propositions rather than laws." Moreover, Zamagni regards this tendency as a "healthy reaction" against the "nomological prejudice." But he omits to justify such a bill of health.

Is this really a healthy reaction or rather an indicator of failure of nerve, of surrender to the "humanistic" (or "interpretive") school, or that mathematical economics is becoming increasingly remote from economic reality? If not, why do economists insists in building, or rather embellishing, general theories? After all, a general theory about a domain of facts is supposed to contain general statements that, if empirically confirmed, deserve being called 'laws.' (Incidentally, whether these are axioms or theorems is only of a logical or mathematical interest. Any physical theory contains law statements of both kinds, for instance, basic laws of motion and conservation theorems.)

In the next section it will be argued that there *are* some economics laws proper, that is, well-confirmed and precise generalizations belonging to hypothetico-deductive systems. For the moment let us note that, even if this statement is rejected, it can hardly be denied that economics contains numerous well-confirmed empirical generalizations that, because they are neither very precise nor members of theories proper, may be called *quasilaws*. Examples: 1/ Income is the major determinant of spending. 2/ The fraction of income spent on goods of any kind declines as income increases (Engel's law). 3/ The marginal propensity to save is greater than the marginal propensity to invest. 4/ Increasing earnings (profits or wages) without concomitant increasing productivity cause cost inflation. 5/ Stock price movements are similar to Brownian motion.

Finally, *norms* are conventional behaviour rules invented or adopted in the belief that they are conducive to certain goals – for example, staying in business or improving social justice. Examples: to plan operations, to abide by budget constraints, to avoid large risks, and to shirk competition. The difference between norms and laws is made clear by Mill's (1924 [1873], 175) example: There are laws of wealth production, but only social conventions on the distribution of wealth.

These are some of the features of social rules or conventions. First, being made, rules can be modified or given up altogether, as shown by changes in legislation. Second, every rule is (rightly or wrongly) expected to benefit someone – even if in fact it hurts everybody. Third, even the most foolish rules must be compatible with certain laws: were they not, they could not be enforced. (For example, they must all obey the law that nothing comes out of nothing and nothing reduces to nothingness.) Fourth, even though all rules must be compatible with the relevant laws, some are more efficient than others. In particular, the most efficient of all rules are those explicitly based on law statements. For example, the best rules for the exploitation of forests and fisheries are those based on the ecological laws of such systems; for one thing the harvesting rate must not exceed the natural growth rate – unless the aim is the destruction of the resource. In sum, rules, or at least efficient rules, are not totally arbitrary. It would be nice to discover laws of the type "Whenever humans are in state S, they devise or observe rules of behaviour of type R." But we do not know whether there are any such laws about rules.

Of the four types of economic generalization, laws are the hardest to come by. Trends are often discovered through econometric analysis of time-series; and some rules can be spotted by studying at first hand human behaviour as well as the functioning of economic systems such as farms, factories, and shops. By contrast, the discovery of laws calls for more than data: it requires imagination and goes hand in hand with the building of theories. So much so that, at least in the hard sciences, the following definition (Bunge 1967a, 1983a) is tacitly employed: A hypothesis is called a *law statement* if and only if (a) it is general in some respect; (b) it has been satisfactorily confirmed in some domain; and (c) it belongs to a hypothetico-deductive system (theory). Social scientists use the word 'law' in a more lax way, which may account for their reluctance to giving up a number of hypotheses that are either untestable or have been refuted, as will be seen shortly.

Standard examples of allegedly robust economic laws are the axioms of conventional consumer behaviour theory – untested until recently. According to them, people trade goods "rationally": that is, they expect gain. But some experiments (e.g., Kahneman et al. 1990 and Knetsch 1995a) have falsified these axioms. They have shown that individuals commonly prefer to keep a good rather than trade it for another good of a greater value: they value losses more than foregone gains in the same amount. In other words, most of us are not basically traders eager to sell tomorrow, for a reasonable profit, what we bought today.

Further alleged economic laws are those of the market. The best known of these is Say's, according to which in a competitive market supply creates its own demand, so that the corresponding market clears instantly – a basis of rational-expectations economic theory and "supply side" economic policies. This hypothesis is assumed to refer to free markets in equilibrium, but in fact it only holds for barter economies. In the real modern world sometimes there are no takers, so surpluses accumulate, and the market is thrown off equilibrium. The best one can do with Say's "law" is to use it to define the concept of a free market in equilibrium; the worst is to use it to defend "supply side" or "trickle down" economic policies (Reaganomics). In any event, whether regarded as a false hypothesis or as a definition, Say's is not a law proper, for it hardly fits real modern markets.

Another such "law of the market" is the so-called law of demand, the negatively sloped curve on the price-quantity plane. This curve, a key tool of marginalist analysis, is largely fictitious. Even Marshall (1920 [1890], 110) admitted that it is "highly conjectural except in the neighbourhood of the customary price." And Baumol (1977, 227) notes that demand functions "are rather queer creatures, somewhat abstract, containing generous elements of the hypothetical and, in general, marked by an aura of unreality." In other words, there are seldom if ever enough data to draw or test a demand curve. This fuzziness imperils mainstream economics because the equilibrium price is, by definition, the price at which demand equals supply – and without equilibrium prices the entire edifice of general equilibrium theory crumbles. However, this has little practical import because the oligopolistic firms, which control most of the manufacture and trade in the industrialized world, make no use of demand curves, hence of equilibrium prices: they are price-setters, not price-takers. In fact, it has been well documented that as a rule the megacorporations employ the cost-plus (or mark-up) method of pricing regardless of actual or expected demand (Cyert and March 1963; Silberston 1970; Baumol and Stewart 1971).

Yet it may be argued that the "law" of supply and demand has been experimentally confirmed (V.L. Smith 1962, 1991; Plott 1986; Plott and George 1992). In fact the "law" has been found to hold in experimental *mock* markets made up of college students. These are motivated to engage in clever trading because they are allowed to keep their profits – but, unlike real-world businessmen, they do not incur any significant risks, whence they are not as risk averse as authentic businessmen. Moreover, the design of these experiments is such that all traders have the same power, and they meet neither barriers to entry nor government regulations, so that perfect competition holds. Nor do they face oligopolies, much less lobbies, labour unions, or corrupt officials. And, of course, in the experimental group no one pays attention to either natural resources or labour: The goods drop graciously from academic heaven. In short, after over a century, neoclassical microeconomics has been shown to hold in laboratory markets under extremely artificial conditions set up arbitrarily by experimenters. What is being tested is not the theory but the experimental subject, who is told to behave like the worshipper of a cargo cult.

Real markets do not satisfy the "laws of the market." But policy makers often do. Indeed, they often enjoin governments to let the "laws of the market" prevail without governmental interference – as if deregulations and tax cuts could do anything to curb oligopoly power, lower barriers to entry, create jobs, or protect public health and the environment. Since the laws in question are not such, the advice given is at best incompetent and at worst dishonest. It is just an injunction to dismantle social services and allow dishonest business to prey on the public. It is ideology passed off as science.

Another classical example of an economic law that on inspection turns out not to be such a thing is the Cobb-Douglas production function relating production to capital and labour inputs – which we met in chapter 2. Robinson (1953–4) noted two methodological problems with this formula. The first is that the concept of capital is not well defined, to the point that it is not specified over what period or even in which units it is to be reckoned. The second is that, in the contemporary economy, labour is hardly distinguishable from capital, for it is done with the assistance of tools or machines that are usually reckoned as capital stock. And even when both capital and labour are well defined and operationalized, the "law" is found to fail in the few cases where it has been put to the test, for example, that of farms (Upton 1979). And it fails utterly for entire economies. For this reason Saikh (1974) dubbed it "the humbug production function."

Contemporary economists tend to avoid using the word 'law,' yet they often claim universal truth for their assumptions and theorems – that is, they treat them as if they were law statements. The theorem that earned Ronald Coase a Nobel prize is a case in point. It concerns the "externalities" or socially harmful effects of economic activity, such as health hazards and pollution, that had been ignored by the classical and neoclassical economists. The theorem states that, when the perpetrators and the victims of such "externalities" (deficiencies) are clearly identifiable, they can reach spontaneously an agreement whereby the former compensate their victims for the damage done. In other words, in a world where everything has a price, property rights would suffice to guarantee social rationality. Corollary: Government intervention is unnecessary to tackle externalities.

This theorem rejoices the enemies of government control. But it holds only in simple cases, namely when the parties and their property rights are clearly identifiable and the damages can be priced, as when your neighbour's goat strays into your garden and eats a known number of heads of cabbage. But the theorem is inapplicable in the cases of massive industrial pollution with its concomitant but imperfectly known health costs, depletion of non-renewable resources, and technological unemployment. (Worse, the theorem justifies selling the right to pollute and damage any public goods as long as "the price is right" – which is a way of commoditizing and privatizing public goods and bads.) In such cases the concerned citizen may blow the whistle, but only government intervention can protect public goods and consequently the public interest.

In sum, Coase's deduction is valid but, since it fails in serious real-life situations, some of its premises (in particular, the universal-commoditization postulate) must be false. It has become famous for being generally believed to have proved that the antisocial consequences of private property can be avoided by expanding rather than shrinking the scope of property rights, and by limiting the role of government to protecting such rights. In other words, it is used as an ideological prop rather than a scientific law.

Yet there *are* some law statements in economics, even subtracting the definitions that pass for laws, the dubious behavioural "laws" underlying mainstream economics, and the theorems that hold only for ideal or perfect competition. Here are ten examples of genuine law statements: 1/ The law of diminishing returns – as long as the number of kinds of input is kept constant. (That is, more of the same results in decreasing returns. But increasing diversity may produce increasing returns: think of the effects of R & D inputs.) 2/ Consumption and income are positively correlated. 3/ Essential goods are roughly price-inelastic. 4/ Demand increases investment. 5/ Monopoly breeds complacency, which in turn breeds stagnation or decline. 6/ Capitalism is expansionary. 7/ Free trade favours only the strong. 8/ The informal (or underground) economy erodes the social security system. 9/ "[T]he prevalence of imperfect competition [that is, oligopoly] in the real world sets up a tendency to exploitation" (Robinson 1933, 313). (The last two are examples of socio-economic rather than purely economic law statements.) 10/ Barceló's (1990) bioeconomic law concerning self-reproducing goods such as farm plants and animals.

Note that neither of these law statements involves subjective concepts such as those of utility, subjective probability, or rational expectation. But note also that neither of them can compete in precision with the laws of physics, chemistry, or physiology. True, there are some precise law-like economic statements, such as Okun's, but they are empirical and they only hold approximately if at all. (Okun's "law": A 2 per cent fall in GDP relative to the potential GDP is followed by a 1 per cent raise in unemployment relative to the "natural" unemployment rate. Caution: the existence of such a rate is doubtful because of the large disparities across nations and epochs [Rowley 1995; Hahn and Solow 1995].)

The existence of economic (and socio-economic) laws or quasi-laws can hardly be disputed, even granting that they are rather few and somewhat vague. Most economists disagree only over the scope of such laws. Some scholars, particularly those who place great store in utility and decision theories, hold that all of the economic laws are universal, being rooted in basic traits of human nature, such as selfishness. Others submit that all economic laws are regional or time bounded (or historico-relative). The historical record suggests a Solomonic solution: whereas some economic patterns are universal, others are local. In other words, whereas some laws hold for all economic systems, others hold only for systems of certain kinds. Thus, the hypothesis that in the long run technological progress eliminates jobs is likely to be a universal law. By contrast, any laws concerning either perfect or imperfect competition, as well as any laws concerning mixed economies, are bounded. The spatio-temporal boundedness of most economic laws is similar to that of the biological laws: there were no such laws before the first organisms emerged, and none would be left if all living beings were to perish. Unlike rules, laws do not hover above things but are inherent in them. Laws are complex and essential properties of things (Bunge 1977a, 1996a). (Simple example: $\forall x \, (Ax \Rightarrow Bx) = \forall x \, Lx$, where the predicate $L = A \Rightarrow B$ represents a property, namely, that the possession of B is necessary for that of A.) Consequently, laws emerge and submerge along with the things satisfying them.

There is good reason for such limitation in scope, namely that economic (and in general social) laws are not given but result from human action. Human beings are the creators, reformers, and destroyers of all human social systems, and social laws and rules are nothing but the patterns of being and becoming of such systems. The making of new rules and the breaking of old ones are constrained by laws but not ruled by them.

Hicks (1979) held that a difference between the laws of economics and those of natural science lies in the fact that the former contain time lags. (Thus, this year's harvest depends on what was sown last year.) This is not true. Biology, the physics of materials with memory, and even electromagnetic theory contain laws involving time lags. The crucial difference between social and natural laws lies elsewhere: it is that the former are made – though of course constrained by natural laws. (For example, all economic laws and rules have to obey the principle of conservation of energy.) Humans can (indirectly) create, twist, suspend, or annihilate some economic laws by building, modifying, or destroying the corresponding economic systems. This is the point of every radical economic reform, whether technological or political.

The collection of economic laws and quasilaws is variable: whereas once in a while new ones enter it, others leave it. The latter can happen in either of two ways. First, the economic systems of a certain type become extinct. Thus, the objective economic patterns of the slave and feudal societies went the way of those societies. A second attrition mechanism is criticism and empirical testing, as a result of which some hypotheses are demoted to the ranks of either false conjecture or mere trend. We saw earlier that this happened to the "laws of the markets" and the Phillips curve.

There is nothing shameful about scientific hypotheses being falsified. Only the stubborn clinging to hypotheses in the absence of supporting evidence, and even more so in the presence of negative evidence, should be cause for shame. (A case in point is the "law" of comparative advantage, for which there is no empirical evidence, despite which it is a cornerstone of international trade theory: see, for example, Noussair et al. 1995.) And when notoriously false hypotheses are used to design policies hurting millions of people – as is the case with the pseudo-laws mentioned a moment ago, as well as with the central hypotheses of monetarism – shame turns into scandal.

4 Laws and Rules, Theories and Models

Roughly, determinism boils down to belief in laws, and voluntarism to belief in free will. According to determinism, the economy is subject to social laws that are just as unalterable as the natural laws: we may perhaps get to know some of these laws and use them to advantage, but we cannot escape them. By contrast, voluntarism holds that there are no social laws: everything happens in accordance with decisions made more or less freely by individuals. Most economists and philosophers of economics are in either of the two camps; nobody admits Robert Musil's "principle of insufficient reason." To find out which if any of these two schools is right, let us start by examining a couple of examples.

Consider first an everyday occurrence, such as voluntarily dropping a cup onto the floor to check whether it is in fact unbreakable as advertised. The decision is free or spontaneous, even though the decision-making process satisfies psychological laws. In fact, the subject might have decided otherwise: he acted freely, not under external compulsion. But once he made the decision, the law relating decision to voluntary movement took over; and once he dropped the cup, the law of gravity took over. Hence, the entire process, from the moment the idea was entertained to the moment the cup broke, satisfies psychological and physical laws.

Consider next the economic generalization that production increases with investment (in capital, labour, organization, or R&D). This is certainly true, but investors may abstain from investing in business during periods of uncertainty caused by social unrest or some other events, keeping the cash or buying treasury bonds. So, although the generalization in question is true, it involves a variable – investment – that depends on choice, which in turn depends partly on opportunity, perceived risk, and expected gain. In other words, once the decision makers have assigned values to the factors of production, the dependent variable (volume of production) will respond according to the law and regardless of any personality traits of those individuals. That is, the economic laws operate from the moment an economic decision has been taken and implemented.

Thus, there are social (in particular economic) laws, but people (usually in groups) set them up (mostly unwittingly). And, if they get to know such laws, they can use or suspend some of them to their own advantage. In other words, in social matters laws combine with rules, and facts with values. Consequently, determinism and voluntarism contain a grain of truth each. Systemism embraces both, for it regards social systems as having features (in particular, patterns) of their own, yet as being maintained or altered by the actions of their individual components.

If we admit rules alongside laws, and values alongside facts, we may attempt to explain some economic facts in terms of laws and circumstances, others in terms of rules and values, and still others in terms of a mixture of all four items. Presumably the correct explanation of any complex economic fact requires at once rules and laws, as well as value judgments and data concerning particular circumstances and antecedents. Thus, explaining the fact that an individual or a firm engages in actions of a certain type may require premises of all four kinds. Here is an example:

Law. Every action of type A is followed by an outcome of kind B (always or with a certain frequency) by virtue of a mechanism of kind M. [I.e., $\forall x$ $[(Ax \Rightarrow Mx) \& (Mx \Rightarrow Bx)].$]

Rule. Try to attain whatever is feasible and valuable to you (or your system).

Valuation. Outcomes of kind B are valuable to individuals (or systems) of kind K.

Datum. Individual (or system) b is of kind K.

Fact to be explained. Individual b performs an action of type A.

This schema generalizes the standard or positivist one, called "covering law model" (recall chap. 2, sect. 3). And it is at variance with the "humanistic" or Romantic school, according to which social facts can be "understood" empathically, or "interpreted," but never explained scientifically.

Let us now examine the nature of economic theories and models. In ordinary language, as well as in the less advanced sciences, the word "theory" is often used to designate a hypothesis, a programmatic statement, a description, or even an opinion. Thus, Harrod's "dynamic theory" boils down to the single statement that the natural rate of growth equals the rate of investment divided by the incremental capital-output ratio. Mandel's voluminous *Marxist Economic Theory* (1968) contains no theory: it is a purely descriptive and critical work. And Milton Friedman's celebrated "theoretical framework for monetary analysis" (1970) revolves around three indeterminate functional symbols (f, g, and l), whence the formulas containing them are vague open sentences of the form "Y is some function of X." No wonder that, being a program for a theory rather than a theory proper, Friedman's fails to account for financial markets, inflation, and stagflation – notwithstanding which it has been advocated to control them.

We adopt the meanings of 'theory' and 'model' prevailing in mathematics and in the more advanced natural sciences. A *scientific theory* is a system of propositions held together by the relation of deducibility (syntactic glue) and a common subject matter (semantic glue). In a well organized or *axiomatic theory* every proposition is either a premise (postulate, definition, or datum) or a consequence (theorem) of some premises taken together. And, whether well organized or untidy, a theory is expected to contain only reasonably precise concepts – not fuzzy ones such as those of utility and rational expectation.

Theoretical models too are hypothetico-deductive systems and, whether in science or in technology, they are concerned with parts or features of the world, whence they ought to be checked for truth. (The models occurring in model theory, a branch of logic, are altogether different and irrelevant to factual science: they are examples or interpretations of abstract theories. For example, the integers constitute a model of group theory. However, the "structuralist" philosophy of science rests on the confusion between the two concepts.)

Theoretical models differ from theories in two respects. First, models have a narrower range (or reference class) than theories; to use Merton's expression, models are "theories of the midle range." Thus, we speak of a *theory* of an entire economy or economic process, but of a *model* of a pin factory. Second, unlike theories, theoretical models need not contain explicitly any law statements. Thus, whereas a model of a farm must contain or at least presuppose some specific biological laws, such as "Pigs take one year to reach maturity," a model of a bank is unlikely to contain any law statements other than a few generalities about human behaviour and society, as well as a few social conventions such as the "law" of compound interests and penalties for failing to repay loans. (More on the theory/model distinction in Bunge 1996a and Mahner and Bunge 1997.)

The theory/model distinction is a clue to the meaning of the expression 'applied economics.' The latter is not analogous to the expressions 'applied physics' or 'applied biology.' Indeed, as used in the economic literature, the expression 'applied economics' denotes the treatment of real-world issues in contrast to the highly idealized situations studied in mainstream economic theory. In other words, economic models belong in what is usually called 'applied economics' – though much of it is empirical or descriptive rather than theoretical. (Much the same holds for applied sociology.)

Contemporary economics contains a few theories and many models. The most ambitious of all economic theories is perhaps the Arrow-Debreu general-equilibrium theory. Its gist is that every perfectly competitive economy (or free market) is in equilibrium. There are two problems with this theory, one conceptual and the other empirical. The first is that, being static, the theory has actually a narrow scope. In fact, it does not account for disequilibria caused by internal changes such as technological innovation and the entry or exit of firms, let alone for external causes such as depletion of natural resources and government controls. (Moreover, only a dynamical theory couched in mathematical terms can tell whether a given state of equilibrium is stable, unstable, or metastable.) The empirical flaw of the theory is that, for the same reason, it fails to fit the real economy, which is in flux like any other thing in the real world. In this regard, then, mainstream economic theory resembles pre-Galilean mechanics, which was confined to statics. (The difference is that mechanical statics, though narrow, is true.)

Obviously, an economic theory or model must be couched in mathematical terms if it is to be precise: after all, it will concern people handling items that come in definite quantities at definite prices. Let us analyse a precise and general, yet very simple, economic theory: the simple or static "Keynesian model" of the economy (see, for example, Ackley 1961; Samuelson et al. 1988; Eichner 1991.) This theory is of interest not only because of its well-known implications for economic policy but also for certain methodological features. We will axiomatize it as an exercise in conceptual tidying up.

We start by listing the seven undefined (basic, primitive, or defining) concepts:

c (consumption), d (depreciation), g (government expenditures),
i (investment), r (transfer payments), t (tax), and y (GDP).
The concepts defined in terms of the above are:

disposable income $y_D =_{df} y + r - d - t$ [1]
marginal propensity to consume $b =_{df} \partial c / \partial y_D$
marginal propensity to save $s =_{df} 1/b$
multiplier $\lambda =_{df} 1/(1-b)$.

The axioms (or postulates) are as follows:

Axiom 1 $c = a + b \, y_D$, where a is a positive real number.   [2]

Axiom 2 $y = c + i + g$.   [3]

Axiom 3 $0 < b < 1$.   [4]

(A corollary of the last premise is that $\lambda > 1$.) Axiom 1 is a theoretical justification of Keynesian macroeconomic policies: To stimulate demand, raise wages (instead of, say, lowering the discount rate). Substitution of [1] and [2] into [3] yields another justification:

Theorem $y = \lambda \, (a - bd - bt + br + i + g)$.   [5]

The methodological interest of this theory is twofold. First, all of its independent variables are objective and in principle "measurable": that is, their values can be obtained from economic statistics. Hence, the theory is fully testable (both confirmable and refutable). Second, unlike its classical and neoclassical predecessors and successors, this theory does not treat the economy as closed and self-regulating, but as intimately coupled with the political system, in particular the state. This is obvious from the occurrence of three basic (undefined) strategic variables, that is, parameters that the political authority can manipulate: t (tax), r (transfer payments), and g (government spending). One major implication of this theory for economic policy is obvious: an increase in government spending g increases output y and consequently disposable income (y_D) as well – which in turn stimulates demand for consumer goods c. This is, of course, the basis of Keynesian macroeconomic policy. (More in sect. 7 and chap. 10.)

So much for a somewhat crude and shallow yet quite realistic theory of macroeconomic reality. Let us now indulge for a while in sophisticated economic daydreaming.

5 Neoclassical Microeconomics: Rationality and Perfect Competition

Neoclassical or marginalist microeconomics has been around since about 1870, and it is by far the most elabourate and best known of all rational-choice theories. It is mainly an exchange theory (or rather family of theories and models) – that is, one focusing on trade. Moreover, it assumes that all markets are competitive (free). Hence, contrary to classical economics, it plays down productive work; in particular, it ignores technology as a factor of production

(Jewkes et al. 1956; Rosegger 1996). Moreover, the theory overlooks the most important kind of competition: that between the new, technology-intensive and innovating firms and the old ones (Schumpeter 1942). As well, neoclassical microeconomics overlooks oligopolies, governments, externalities, and the fact that every long-term contract – for instance, between a firm and its suppliers – suspends market freedom. Consequently, the theory is not a true model of the modern business firm, let alone of the modern market as a whole. No wonder then that the theory has exerted only a marginal influence on business practice (Faulhaber and Baumol 1988, 592).

In view of these severe limitations of neoclassical microeconomics, it might be thought that there is no need to analyse it. After all, we live in the age of the megacorporation (in particular the transnational firm), the interventionist state, and the mixed economy and, above all, in a period of deep and rapid changes in the mode of production (and the patterns of employment, consumption, and income distribution) induced by technological advances and the globalization of trade and financial capital. True, a few of the flaws of the original theory have been repaired in some of the recent work, such as the research reported in the *Handbooks of Economics* series. However, it would be mistaken to ignore the older theory, for (a) it is still often being taught as gospel; (b) it passes for being a model of exactness even among many of those who admit its irrelevance; (c) it is often being held up as a model to be aped in the remaining social sciences (recall chap. 2, sects. 3–6); and (d) it is a pillar of the conservative ("neoliberal") ideology.

Here we only need to recall that neoclassical microeconomics assumes the (ontological and methodological) principles of individualism and economic "rationality" (that is, self-interest); that the economic agents are expected to obtain all the knowledge they need; and that they are assumed to be mutually independent. It also asserts that the economy is a closed system, the market is free (that is, perfectly competitive), and always in or near equilibrium (demand = supply); and that this state determines the price of a commodity. (In the general theory equilibrium is proved, not assumed.) Let us probe quickly these seven additional assumptions. But first let us reformulate them more precisely, and restate the first three with special reference to the economy.

A1 *Rationality*: All economic agents act so as to maximize their utilities (either raw or expected).

A2 *Ontological individualism*: The economy is the aggregate of sellers and buyers.

A3 *Methodological individualism*: The features of any economic unit, from household to firm, and indeed the economy as a whole, are best understood by studying exclusively the behaviour of the individuals belonging to it, especially those at the top.

A4 *Perfect knowledge*: Every agent can obtain all the factual knowledge he needs to make optimal decisions, that is, to implement the postulate A1 of economic rationality.

A5 *Mutual independence or additivity*: The agents are mutually independent, whence aggregate supply and demand result from the simple addition of individual supplies and demands respectively.

A6 *Closure*: The economy is a closed system, in particular one unrelated to either the political and cultural systems or to the physical environment.

A7 *Freedom*: All economic agents are free to choose and act, and the market is free (that is, perfectly competitive) or nearly so.

A8 *Hidden hand*: The maximizing behaviour of every individual results in the self-regulation of the economy, everybody's maximal utility, and social harmony.

A9 *Equilibrium*: All perfectly competitive markets clear instantly or nearly so – that is, they are normally in or near equilibrium.

A10 *Price*: The price of a commodity (good or service) is determined by market equilibrium – that is, the state in which the market supply and demand curves intersect.

Let us begin with the economic-rationality postulate A1. First, as Keynes (1936) pointed out, investors are guided by fairly irrational expectations concerning the future. This is particularly obvious in the case of the stock market, subject as it is not only to external shocks independent of actual company performance, but also to two basic and conflicting emotions: fear and hope (see, for instance, Adler and Adler 1984). In sum, economic rationality is anything but constant: it may emerge after a period of frantic irrational activity.

Second, Morgenstern (1972b, 1166) noted that A1 is unrealistic because the maxima and minima of neoclassical economics "exist and are attainable only if the individual or firm (or whatever other entity) *controls all the variables* on which the maximum [or the minimum] depends. If some variables, on which the outcome depends, are under the *conscious control* of other entities which wish to maximize their utility or profit, and who may either be opposed to a given economic agent ... or, as it might be, sometime may wish to cooperate with it, then such complete control is lacking for the individual and it is not a maximum problem which is involved, but a curious mixture of maxima, minima, etc."

Third, one of the few robust findings of the famous Hawthorne experiment is that the 20,000 workers studied "were not acting strictly in accordance with their economic interests," but were largely controlled by sentiments of group solidarity (Roethslisberger and Dickson 1943, 534). Something similar holds for their employers. Indeed, the behavioural economist H.A. Simon earned a Nobel prize for having shown that competent managers are not utility maximizers either but rather "satisficers": they seize every opportunity to make a reasonable profit instead of waiting indefinitely to make a big kill (March and Simon 1958). Regrettably, these empirical findings are routinely shrugged off by the true believers in the century-old dogmas of neoclassical economics.

Fourth, even assuming that it is always rational to maximize benefits, it does not follow that this goal is achieved by merely buying low and selling high. In fact, this only holds in equilibrium situations, which, in a quickly changing business environment, are the exception rather than the rule. Frequently profit maximization (or even satisficing) involves expansion or switching from a declining industry to a promising one. And either move requires risky new investment, sometimes in retooling or in reorganization – which, particularly when involving advanced technology, can be financed only by either accumulated profits, the emission of new shares, or bank loans. Clearly, these strategies are inaccessible to small and medium-size business firms. In "developing" countries only transnational firms and the state are powerful enough to make such investments – which is one of the reasons for both dependency and government hypertrophy in such countries. Neoclassical economics fails to account for such processes, and thus lacks an adequate theory of economic growth, because it keeps silent on what it takes to implement "rational" behaviour: it sets the goal but does not specify the means.

In the fifth place, the search for profit maximization is incompatible with other desiderata, such as increased market share, consumer satisfaction, and employee loyalty – not to mention public welfare. Indeed, the first desideratum may occasionally require selling at cost; the second calls for maintaining or improving quality, even at the cost of new outlays of capital; and the third cannot be earned through exploitation. In short, profit maximization is practically short-sighted and morally suspect. Worse yet, it is incompatible with the law of diminishing returns. No wonder it is seldom practised by normal businessmen, never by innovating entrepreneurs. Apparently Columbus, for one, did not compute the expected utility of the most successful commercial enterprise in history.

There would be nothing wrong if an economist were to hypothesize initially that everyone is motivated by the lowest of intentions: by proceeding in this manner he would be in the company of the best detectives. The trouble is that, unlike detectives, mainstream economists believe that hypothesis to be an unassailable universal truth about human nature, or even "a law of logic itself"

(Samuelson 1976, 436). Hence, they seldom bother to put it to the test, much less to look for alternatives, such as a combination of self-interest with other-interest.

Finally, what is the experimental verdict on A1? Three decades of laboratory work on individual decision making, mock markets, and economic games have given inconclusive results. Some of these confirm and others refute A1 and other assumptions of textbook economics (see, for instance, Davis and Holt 1993). Typically, economists – notably Vernon L. Smith and Charles R. Plott – find positive results, whereas psychologists – notably Daniel Kahneman and Amos Tversky – obtain negative results. However, the former are open to the following criticisms. First, the experimental subjects do not run the risks businessmen face: all they can lose is the money (or some other good) the experimenter gives them at the start. Consequently, the experimental setting does not reflect real life (recall sect. 3). Second, the typical experimental subject is an economics student: he has been trained to respond the way neoclassical theory assumes, namely as an egoist – by contrast to non-economics students, who tend to be cooperative, honest, and reasonably altruistic (Frank et al. 1993). In short, experimental economics has not confirmed the "rationality" postulate A1; on the other hand, field studies and statistics have cast serious doubts on it.

As for A2 (Economy = Market = Aggregate of individuals), I submit that it is inadequate: first, because it leaves production in the dark. Indeed, according to A2 only traders and consumers (particularly households) matter. The commodity is already available in the market, ready to be exchanged for another commodity. Just as the classical economists underrated trade, so the neoclassical ones overrate it. In this regard the "marginalist revolution" was a return to eighteenth-century mercantilism and thus a counter-revolution.

A second reason for the falsity of A2 is that it overlooks the fact that by far the most important consumers in any advanced economy are firms not households. This is a significant point because the demand mechanism is not the same for firms as for consumers. Indeed, whereas a firm's demands are dictated by its sales, which in turn depend on the state of the market, a household's demands are determined by its needs, wants, and budget (Arndt 1984, 33–4). Hence, whereas biology and psychology may help explain household consumption, only economic, technological, and sometimes political considerations may account for a firm's consumption.

A third reason for the falsity of A2 is that every component of the economy, in particular each firm, interacts in several ways with other components, such as competitors, suppliers, and buyers. In fact, there is both competition and cooperation among these units. Competition can be mild – as in the offer of "specials" – or aggressive, as in dumping, raiding, and slanderous advertising. And cooperation can go from technological alliance to occasional collusion to oligopoly or even monopoly, not to speak of common fronts against organized labour or government. Because of such links, the economy is not an aggregate of individuals but a system of subsystems.

Being a system, the economy possesses systemic or emergent properties and processes that individualism cannot cope with. For example, plenty and scarcity, boom and slump, growth and stagflation, are not individual (biological or psychological) categories but economic ones. No wonder that neoclassical microeconomics, which ignores such macroprocesses, fails to account for the macroeconomic constraints on the firm, not to mention the political ones.

In sum, A2 is false. Hence, so is its methodological partner A3, or the bottom-up strategy. The methodological individualist may promise to derive every emergent property from features of individuals and their interactions. But he won't be able to fulfill this promise because individual actions are constrained by the natural and social environments, much as the behaviour of electrons is subject to boundary conditions that are not reducible to properties of microentities. In particular, modern industry and trade are regulated by policies, management techniques, and the law, all of which impose such constraints as budgets, schedules, safety devices, inventories, liquidity, reserves, and government regulations, none of which is reducible to individual actions even though they are designed and implemented or eluded by individuals.

So much for the first three postulates, which are of a philosophical nature. (More in Bunge 1996a.) Let us move on. The perfect-knowledge assumption A4 is so glaringly unrealistic that we need not dwell long on it. Anyone with any business experience knows that (a) the normal condition of the decision maker is one of incomplete knowledge; (b) the cost of acquiring knowledge is usually prohibitive for the small or medium-size firm; and (c) privileged information, reserved for the few, is invaluable. Hayek criticized the dogma throughout his career, and made it the subject of his Nobel lecture, "The pretence of knowledge" (Hayek 1989). Stigler, another Nobel laureate, built a whole new discipline at odds with A4: the economics of information. And Akerlof (1984) explained the existence of markets for "lemons" by denying A4: If the buyer had known that the good offered him was seriously defective, he would not have purchased it. In addition to information asymmetries, there is the impact of forecast on action, in particular the self-fulfilling and self-defeating prophecies (see Merton 1957a). Because of all this, perfect foresight – a component of perfect knowledge – is impossible in social science.

The mutual-independence or additivity postulate A5 is contrary to fact. First, every individual belongs to several social networks, so that his valuations, expectations, decisions, and actions depend on those of other people. In particular, my supply depends on yours; demand is parallel. Consequently, neither supply nor demand are additive. Second, the mutual-independence postulate ignores oligopolies, collusions, mergers, and take-overs, all of which concentrate economic power. This restricts free enterprise and consumer sovereignty, and it may also buy political power. In short, interdependence and unequal power are the norm in the economy. Since this is increasingly being recognized, the days of A5 are counted – not surprisingly, since it is two centuries old.

The closure postulate A6 entails the methodological consequence that economists may safely ignore environmental, biological, political, and cultural variables. But this assumption is "heroic." Not even a society run by rational-choice economists would be free from environmental shocks such as droughts, floods, and earthquakes, or political ones such as social reforms, revolutions, and wars. Nor do business firms move in an institutional vacuum. On the contrary, they must reckon with laws, taxes, and state regulations (of, for instance, sanitary and safety conditions). They also count on public schools to provide skilled workers and competent engineers and managers, as well as consumers capable of reading ads. Managers trust most of their suppliers, clients, and employees to observe the rules of common decency, rather than trying to maximize their own short-term gains by all means. In short, far from being closed, the economy is open to its physical, political, and cultural environment. Hence, a purely economic approach to the economy is bound to fail. Shorter: Economics alone cannot possibly explain the economy, because the latter is not a closed system. Only the merger of all the social sciences can account for complex social facts. (Recall chap. 2, sect. 7.)

Let us now turn to the postulate A7 of total freedom of all economic agents and of perfect competition. It is simply false that economic agents, in particular consumers and workers, can ever be fully free to choose whatever they want to be or do. We are all subject to constraints of several kinds: environmental, biological, economic, political, legal, and cultural – in particular moral. We are seldom free to enter into mutually advantageous contracts, for there are such things as prior commitment and power, in particular economic power, which is asymmetrical. Most of the important choices are made for us by those who wield power over us, in particular our employers and rulers.

However, the very concept of power is absent from neoclassical economics, which feigns that we are all free to choose and enter into mutually advantageous contracts. (And the ideal of freedom of choice is often used as a disguise for the privatization of public services. When sick, I am free to go to a private clinic; you, to a quack doctor.) Therefore, mainstream economics ignores both the internal power structure of the firm, controlled by its management, and the economic power of the firm, as measured by its market share. It pretends that employer and employee, creditor and debtor, corporation and small farmer, wholesaler and retailer, are all on an equal footing, and that the state is or ought to be a neutral and fair umpire. Mainstream economics must make these obviously false assumptions to keep the fictions that the economy is an "autonomous sphere" not to be tampered with, and that economics is an autonomous science that must avoid contamination with sociology, political science, and history. This is one of the reasons that mainstream economics is of little use to the entrepreneur or manager intent on enhancing his economic and political clout both within the firm and in the market.

As for free competition, if it starts it cannot last, for, as Bertrand Russell (1934, 142) noted, "competition tends to issue in someone's victory, with the result that it ceases and is replaced by monopoly." In fact, unfettered competition is destructive, for it forces prices down, possibly to the point of bankruptcy. (See Chamberlin 1933 and Olson 1971.) This is why smart businessmen are seldom keen on Mafia-style cut-throat competition: they can rarely afford it. They usually prefer alternative strategies, such as carving out their own niches on the strength of technological innovation, obtaining government contracts or subsidies, taking over their competitors, or even entering into strategic alliances with them – as the Japanese corporations have been doing with great success.

"Capitalists are interested in the expansion of the free market as long as one of them succeeds ... in attaining a monopoly and thus closing the market." This sentence, that might have been written by Lenin or Rosa Luxemburg, is in fact from Weber (1922, 384). Given the existence of monopolies, oligopolies, and monopsonies (sometimes exerted by the state), as well as barriers to entry, labour unions, government regulations, subsidies, and protective tariffs of many sorts, the perfect-competition assumption is at best an extreme idealization required for shallow theorizing, and at worst an ideological fig leaf.

Since perfect competition – supposedly the mechanism guaranteeing market equilibrium – is illusory, the modern economy is not an isolated and self-regulating system. This became obvious to everyone, except for the orthodox economists, during the Great Depression. This crisis forced many Western governments in the 1930s to design and implement packages of Keynesian policies – such as the New Deal – to correct for market disequilibria and some of their social costs. These stabilization measures eventually limited the amplitude of the business cycles. But at the same time they gave rise to new conflicts, for the goals of the modern state do not always coincide with those of business.

Contrary to the free-market assumption, in every one of the highly industrialized countries, transportation equipment, primary metals, chemicals, electrical machinery, and other heavy industries, as well as telecommunications and electronics, are in the hands of four or fewer firms. Think also of the subsidies and protectionist regulations enjoyed by the North American, European, and Japanese farmers, as well as of the privileges graciously extended defence contractors. Neither group is subject to the so-called market forces. Consequently, they face little risk and do not require marketing skills. In the Third World a few transnational corporations hold a buying monopoly on key cash crops, and most of the industries employing advanced technologies are owned by transnational corporations or must pay them stiff royalties for the use of patents.

Nor is capital concentration without historical precedent. In fact, economic historians tell us that the market has always, even during the nineteenth century, been distorted by tariffs and monopolies as well as constrained by legislation. Hence, the assumption that the market is a self-regulating machinery contains "an element of truth, an element of bad faith, and also some self-deception" (Braudel 1977, 44). And yet, not so long ago the sophisticated *Journal of Economic Theory* (1980,121–376) published the proceedings of a symposium on the theory of perfect competition. And Debreu won the 1983 Nobel prize in economics for proving rigorously that general equilibrium is possible in a free (perfectly competitive) economy – that is, for capping an irrelevant theory. (For market "imperfections" see Robinson 1933; Chamberlin 1933; Galbraith 1967; and Blair 1972. For barriers to entry, see Bain 1956. For the real price-fixing mechanism under oligopoly, see Baran and Sweezy 1966; Silberston 1970; and Baumol and Stewart 1971. For the effects of the activities of transnational firms on their host countries, see Kindleberger 1970 and Vaitsos 1974.)

Granted, there is nearly perfect competition in some economically backward places, as well as – ironically – in the underground economy. But the free-market assumption does not hold for the advanced nations, where the public sector is large and oligopolies dominate the private sector. Moreover, even governments that preach the free-market and free-trade gospels to others subsidize certain sectors of their own economy. Finally, the concentration of capital was highlighted in the 1980s by gigantic takeovers and "leveraged buyouts." In short, in the advanced industrialized countries axiom A7 has become a mere aspiration leading millions of would-be independent businessmen to adventures ending mostly in bankruptcy. Therefore, A7 is "an economic aberration" (Morgenstern 1972b, 1172).

Ironically, for a theory that extols the value of the individual, the perfect-competition postulate presupposes that the action of every agent is insignificant. Indeed, if some agents were to exert an important influence on the aggregate outcome of economic activity, they would concentrate a disproportionate fraction of the total economic power. That is, in such case competition, if any, would be imperfect – which, of course, is the rule in the modern economy, where small businesses are dominated by megacorporations.

6 Neoclassical Economics Continued: Equilibrium and Price

Axiom 8, on the hidden hand, is posited because it cannot be derived in the standard Arrow-Debreu theory, which only proves that there are price equilibria. Indeed, this theory does not prove that prices *do* tend to such equilibria. Nor could it prove such a thing, for it is not a *dynamical* theory of systems endowed with negative-feedback mechanisms. Worse, it has been proved that prices can move *away from* equilibrium – as they often do in real life (see, for example, Saari 1994). Anyway, as Chandler (1977) and others have amply documented, in every key sector of the economy oligopoly and the "visible hand" of management operate instead of the hidden hand of market forces.

Axiom 8 discharges primarily the apologetic function of justifying free-market worship. Indeed, it conceals the fact that unbridled competition can wipe out the less "fit," among which are not only the weak but also, increasingly, corporations – which, when in the red, beg the state to bail them out. Second, A8 covers up the perverse effects resulting from unregulated business, such as unsafety, resource depletion, environmental degradation, and war. Third, the axiom reassures statesmen that they need not intervene in the economy for, when left alone, it is a self-regulating and self-repairing mechanism. As the popular slogan has it, "The market always gets it right." But the market often gets it wrong: think of crashes, "bubbles," "corrections," "imperfections," and "externalities." Fourth, the hidden-hand fiction is a surrogate for interaction, the marrow of social life. It is an excuse for ignoring sociology. In short, though formulated by the usually perceptive and sometimes prophetic Adam Smith, postulate A8 is worthy of Voltaire's Dr Pangloss.

The general-equilibrium statement A9 has become a theorem (the so-called existence theorem) of microeconomic orthodoxy. However, it is open to the following objections. First, it is not quite general, as it does not apply to the global economy, plagued as it is by such disequilibria as the US-Japan trade imbalance and the crushing Third World debt. Second, it does not identify any market price-adjustment mechanism. In particular, it does not exhibit the individual actions that would bring about the equilibrium of the whole. Hence, it violates the principles of ontological and methodological individualism (DeVillé 1990). Third, A9 flies in the face of such chronic disequilibria as the oversupply of North American and European agricultural products. Fourth, the theorem ignores business cycles. Fifth, equilibrium should be a consequence of disequilibrium dynamics, if only because equilibrium, when attainable, is the (temporary) end point of a process (see Fisher 1983). Sixth, although equilibrium is certainly a macroeconomic desideratum, it is not a microeconomic one, for there are profits to be made from local disequilibria.

Mainline economic theory fails to account for the market that interests most people, namely the labour market. In particular, it fails spectacularly to account for chronic involuntary mass unemployment – which some economists have the effrontery to deny, claiming that the unemployed "at any time can always find *some* job at once" (Lucas 1978). This act of faith (and indicator of moral stand) will not reassure the billion-plus unemployed or underemployed in the world, and it will not help formulate sound economic policies. Nor does the theory account for either the real-estate or the stock market. Indeed, the former is considered sound only if the supply is about ten times greater than the demand. And share price and return vary randomly and do not approach equilibrium: rationality is invisible here.

In sum, since economic equilibrium (particularly when general) is exceptional, any theory that focuses on it rather than on disequilibrium is bound to be false. Worse, "the powerful attraction of the habits of thought engendered by 'equilibrium economics' has become a major obstacle to the development of economics as a *science*" (Kaldor 1972, 1237). Worse still, the conjunction of A9 with A8 inspires the doctrinaire view that every state intervention is destabilizing, whence the only sensible economic policy is the conservative *laissez-faire* one. As Nobel laureate James Tobin (1980, 46) comments, "[t]hat they [government policies] are the only source of shocks to an intrinsically stable mechanism is a proposition that could be seriously advanced only by persons with extravagant faith in their own abstract models and with historical amnesia."

Furthermore, A9 is conceptually fuzzy because, as we saw in section 3, the very existence of precise demand functions is yet to be established. In the absence of reliable information about the full demand curve, it is sometimes *assumed* that price and quantity are inversely related. (A standard example is "$pq = c$.") But this assumption is doubtful. An authentically rational consumer does not buy an item he does not need, or cannot afford, or hopes that its price will soon fall, or is saving for a rainy day. And one does not buy more of a merchandise just because its price has fallen: there are such things as satiety and budget constraints. The offshoot is that the actual demand points are unlikely to lie on a simple curve, but will zigzag in a manner that is only partly controlled by price. (Recent work on this problem involves stochastic demand functions. However, the empirical testing of such hypotheses has hardly begun.)

Finally, the price axiom A10 is not a law proper for two reasons. First, because – as noted above – market equilibrium cannot be taken for granted. Second, because actual prices are often determined by non-market "forces." For example, the minimum wage, where it exists, is determined by law, not by the market; actual wages are determined jointly by management and labour after a bargaining process and largely regardless of individual productivity and of the state of the economy; the discount rate is determined by the central monetary authority, sometimes against the wishes of the business community; the prices of mass-produced goods are set by oligopolies; the prices of agricultural products are largely set by the state; the arms manufacturers are the beneficiaries of generous government research contracts, and are not precisely cost minimizers; the state industries and "natural monopolies," such as most public utilities, face no competition, so they are above the "laws of the market"; the price of crude oil is determined by OPEC regardless of the oil reserves – as a consequence of which that price is artificially low; oil and other export products of Third World countries have hidden costs, such as those of maintaining occupying armies or propping up friendly dictatorships (see, for instance, Hubbard 1991); and, except during severe and sustained recessions, the prices of many commodities are adjusted by the "cost-plus" procedure, sometimes regardless of demand (Cyert and March 1963; Silberston 1970; Baumol and Stewart 1971). In other words, not the consumer but the producer, the trader, and the banker – often in cahoots with the politician – are sovereign in the modern economy. Consequently, ours is anything but a free and demand-driven market economy. In other words, real markets are quite different from the ideal market postulated by main-line economics.

Besides, A10 fails to address two big real problems: those of the real or objective value of a commodity, and of its fair price. The former occurs whenever we have reason to believe something to be either overpriced or underpriced. Thus, it is well known that weapons, drugs, and legal services are generally overpriced. It is equally notorious that during deep recessions some commodities fetch prices below cost ("fire sales") and that most prices do not cover the social costs – for example, those associated with pollution and the depletion of natural resources. As for the fair-price problem, which has been with us since Thomas Aquinas, it is related to the problems of fair profits and fair wages, both of which are moral as well as economic concepts. (Incidentally, it has been experimentally shown that ordinary people and real-life businessmen are willing to pay for fairness: see Kahneman et al. 1986.) In conclusion, A10 does not fit actual economic behaviour.

To sum up, all ten axioms A1 to A10 are flawed, some for being fuzzy and therefore untestable, and others for being plain false. These objections would not deter someone who, like Latsis (1972), regards Axioms 1, 4, 5, and 7 as the "hard core" of neoclassical economics and, following Lakatos, states that every such "hard core" is composed of irrefutable ("metaphysical") hypotheses. But, if our analysis is correct, then all four said axioms are false rather than irrefutable. If they were irrefutable they would not belong in science; being obviously false, they might qualify at best as bad science. And, being rather specific, they would not even count as bad metaphysics. More on this in section 8.

The basic assumptions of neoclassical microeconomics are so unrealistic that neither they nor their logical consequences account for the major features of a modern economy. At the risk of some repetition, let us list a few of its major failings. 1/ The theory is one of pure exchange: it underrates or even ignores production, and therefore technology – perhaps the most potent engine of economic change. 2/ It makes no room for monopolies, oligopolies, and monopsonies – which, in most industrialized countries, control the bulk of the economy. 3/ The theory does not care for externalities or social costs, such as the depletion of non-renewable natural resources, pollution, and its effects on health. 4/ It does not explain how the business firm works, conceiving of it as being led by a single individual or board acting as a free agent busy drawing supply and demand curves and bent on profit maximization. 5/ The theory fails to account for the standard pricing method, which – at the source and in normal times – is fixed mark-up regardless of time, product, and often even demand. (Thus, when demand falls, corporations usually cut back production and fire employees instead of lowering prices.) 6/ It includes neither information or transaction costs nor the effects of taxation. 7/ The theory overlooks the interests of any stakeholders other than the shareholders, as well as political and cultural constraints – either of which may frustrate the most "rational" business strategy. 8/ It ignores the fact that (a) most businessmen are risk-averse rather than maximizers (Allais 1979); and (b) career managers – who nowadays are in charge of the vast majority of corporations – prefer stability and growth to maximal profit (Chandler 1977). 9/ The theory ignores the fact that, far from acting on careful calculations, most businessmen act on rules of thumb such as "Follow the leader," "Buy cheap and sell dear," and "Charge as much as the market will bear." Now, some of these rules conflict with other equally popular ones, such as "Innovate," "The best is the enemy of the good," and "Cut your losses." Since the set of all such business rules is inconsistent, it cannot be rational (Etzioni 1987). 10/ It does not account for the high rate of bankruptcies – roughly the same as the rate of birth of firms – and it fails to explain macroeconomic trends such as growth, stagnation, and decline. How could it, if it ignores time, disequilibria, interaction – the source of all social harmony and strife – technology, management, organized labour, top-down causal arrows – such as state interventions – and asymmetries, such as information inequalities and the centre-periphery (or North-South) relation? For these reasons, far from being a powerful analytical tool, marginalist analysis is mainly an academic industry.

Mainstream microeconomics is so rudimentary and unrealistic that it cannot even prove the long-term profitability of capitalism. In fact, one of its paradoxes is that theoretically, in a perfectly competitive market, long-run equilibrium is the state wherein price equals minimum average cost. Hence, in the long run there should be no profit after a modest opportunity-cost return to shareholders' investment is allowed (Samuelson et al. 1983, 493). So, neoclassical microeconomics, usually invoked in defence of capitalism, supports Marx's and Schumpeter's thesis that capitalism is self-destructive. To be sure, at the time of writing capitalism happens to be flourishing in the industrialized countries, albeit with ups and downs and often at the cost of chronic mass unemployment. But this is beside the point. The point is that neoclassical microeconomics has failed both as the theory and the ideology of capitalism, just as dismally as Marxist economics has failed both as the theory and ideology of socialism. Whereas the latter has of late been buried in a hurry, the former still marches on through classrooms, textbooks, and journals, sporting top hat, spats, and walking cane, unaware of its own inadequacies, undaunted by sea changes in economic reality, and utterly insensitive to the plight of billions of people.

Why have theoretical microeconomists failed to describe, explain, predict, and even persuasively defend capitalism? I submit that they have failed for sticking to the centenarian assumptions A1 to A10, embroidering them endlessly instead of studying real people involved in real economies, and slighting or even overlooking such factors as technology, management, and government – not to speak of the environment. In short, my diagnosis is that mainstream economics is senile. Amazingly, some economists mistake senility for good health. Thus, Milton Friedman (1991, 33) states that "the substance of professional economic discussion has remained remarkably unchanged over the past century."

Fortunately, this smug evaluation is not quite correct, for there *have* been some innovations in economic theory since the marginalist counter-revolution. What is true is that all of these innovations have come in opposition to neoclassical economics (Pasinetti 1981, 17). Witness Keynes's macroeconomics, Leontief's input-output analysis, labour economics, some theories of the business cycle, the sociology of the firm, bioeconomics, behavioural economics, socioeconomics, and economic history.

In sum, on the whole mainstream economists – despite momentous changes in their subject matter – have been remarkably orthodox over the last century and more. Now, in every field of human endeavour orthodoxy kills the creative impulse. As well, excessive love of simplicity and of mathematics for its own sake smothers all concern for realism. No wonder then that neoclassical microeconomics has become largely irrelevant and therefore an object of historical curiosity despite being required of every economics and management student.

(See further criticisms by Akerlof 1984; Arndt 1984; Balogh 1982; Bunge 1985b; Dyke 1981; Eichner 1983; Frank 1985; Galbraith 1973, 1991; Gini 1952; Hahn 1981a, 1981b; Holland 1987a, 1987b; Hollis and Nell 1975; Katouzian 1980; Leontief 1982; Morgenstern 1972a, 1972b; Pasinetti 1981; Perroux 1975; Schotter 1985; Scitovsky 1976; Sen 1995; Thurow 1983; and Wiles and Routh 1984.)

Consequently, any attempt to model the economy in a realistic way will have to drop Axioms A1 to A10, and assume the following instead: (a) all economic units are interdependent, hence anything but entirely free to choose, rather than mutually independent; (b) the firm envisaged by classical and neoclassical economics has been largely replaced by the corporation (with its shareholders and managers), which in turn is often a branch or subsidiary of a transnational conglomerate; (c) most businessmen are survivors rather than maximizers, and only a few – the proverbial entrepreneurs – are willing to take "irrational" risks (as Thomas J. Watson, the founder of IBM, confessed, some of them crave power even more eagerly than profit); (d) every microeconomic activity is embedded in society at large; whence (e) every realistic microeconomic model must include macroeconomic parameters – such as tax, interest, and unemployment rates – and macropolitical concepts, such as those of government regulation, political stability, and international tension.

In conclusion, to put it mildly, neoclassical microeconomics – the paragon of rational-choice theory – is neither quite scientific nor very useful. What then is the neoclassical microeconomist to do after repeatedly failing to conquer his own turf? He has only two choices, one hard and the other easy. The former is to rethink principles and try to come up with a radically new theory. This is what a small band of game-theory enthusiasts have been doing over the past decade (see, for instance, Shubik 1984). However, their assumption that all individuals have the same utility function is not just unrealistic. It is also at variance with the individualism professed by game theorists, since persons with the same preferences are not exactly *individuals*. Moreover, as will be seen in the next section, applied game theory too is simplistic and aprioristic, hence unrealistic. Therefore, only the easy way out is viable. This is to emigrate, preferably to a land whose natives are in awe of what passes for mathematical rigour in economics. We met earlier some of these migrants (chap. 2). We shall meet others in the field of political science (chap. 4).

7 Positive Macroeconomics

Macroeconomics is of course the study of entire economies, such as those of the United States or the European Union. Such study can be either descriptive (positive) or prescriptive (normative). In the former case we have a basic or pure science – or rather semiscience. Normative macroeconomics is quite different: it is a sociotechnology that, ideally, is based on sound macroeconomics. Indeed, it is concerned with designing and evaluating economic policies, which in turn can make or break the economy, the polity, and the culture of an entire country. A distinctive feature of normative as opposed to descriptive macroeconomics is that the former involves strategic variables. These are variables that, like the discount rate and the slice of the public pie devoted to social expenditures, are subject to social (in particular political) control.

But, whether positive or normative, macroeconomics is characterized by such systemic concepts as those of natural resource, scarcity, workforce, GDP (intensity of national economic activity), economic sector (e.g., manufacture), productivity, real growth rate, recession and contraction, savings and investment, monetary policy, interest and tax rates, tax evasion and informal economy, fiscal debt and balance of payments, tariffs and subsidies, and rates of inflation and unemployment.

Whereas all of these concepts refer to a macrosystem, namely a national or regional economy as a whole, a few of them result from mere addition. Thus, the national internal revenue is the sum of the taxes of all kinds paid by the taxpayers. But other concepts, such as those of natural resource, scarcity, productivity, recession, discount rate, rate of exchange, tax structure, budget, fiscal policy, wealth distribution, fiscal deficit, and national debt, are *irreducibly* systemic concepts. They represent properties of the economy as a whole. Consequently, such concepts defy any theories that adopt ontological or methodological individualism – that is, the bottom-up strategy – such as rational-choice theories (see Bunge 1996a). The same holds, of course, for some of the propositions of macroeconomics, such as that, over a certain period, the economy is booming. Moreover, a number of concepts occurring in microeconomics, such as those of quality, profit, work ethic, and management style, play no role in macroeconomics. If only for these reasons, there is a chasm between microeconomics and macroeconomics.

A mature macroeconomics would account for the development of a national economy – or, rather, that of a supersystem of national economies, since the state of each depends increasingly on that of others. Such a discipline should stand on its own regardless of changes in microeconomic theories, much as planetary astronomy has not been affected by atomic physics. However, many economists feel uncomfortable with the current gap between macroeconomics and microeconomics. This is understandable, since the economy as a whole is said to be "nothing but" a result of microeconomic activities. There should then be a bridge between macroeconomics and microeconomics. Although the search for such a bridge is hazardous given the dismal current state of micro-economics, it might inspire a much-needed renewal of both disciplines.

Some economists are more ambitious: they would like to see microeconomics entail macroeconomics. In particular, they would love to have Smith's "invisible hand" explained in terms of the pursuit of individual interests. More precisely, they would like to analyse every single macroeconomic variable into microeconomic variables. Some students hope for this reduction as a way of securing a solid foundation for macroeconomics, which so far has none. They would love to see economics follow the reduction path that, textbooks assure us, is standard in natural science – though actually it is exceptional (see Bunge 1983b, 1991b). Others wish the reduction to happen in order to minimize the conflicts between business practise and macroeconomic policy. Still other students would like to see this reduction because they have blind faith in neoclassical microeconomics and the accompanying "neoliberal" (that is, conservative) economic policies. But so far reduction remains a project, and not even a hopeful one, as will be argued in a while. Let us first look at three failed reduction attempts, and then at the reasons for the inevitable failure of *any* such reduction project.

The most straightforward of all reduction projects is the one centred on the idea of the single omniscient and immortal *representative individual* intent on maximizing his utility. This, like Quetelet's *homme moyen*, is an imaginary agent whose "rational" choices are supposed to match those of the heterogeneous individuals or firms in a whole sector of the economy. The basic idea goes back to Smith and the utilitarians: If everyone pursues his own interests and attempts to maximize his own utility without any regard for others, then the collectivity as a whole stands to gain. But this is false, as shown, for example, by the "tragedy of the commons" and other social traps (see, for instance, Cross and Guyer 1980).

In general, treating the components of a system as if they were mutually independent or isolated tells us next to nothing about the system as a whole. For example, simple individual behaviour may give rise to complex macrobehaviour and conversely (see, for example, Lippi 1988). To understand a system of any kind we must (a) start by describing the system on its own level; and (b) proceed to studying the systemic properties and processes resulting from the interactions among the various components, subject to the constraints imposed on the system of interest because it is embedded in a larger system.

Every system has emergent properties that its components lack. Thus, in the case of economics, the "representative individual" is likely to have preferences that differ from those of the individual components of the system. Or, if all the individuals have similar preferences, the economy may have a large number of unstable equilibria (see, for instance, Kirman 1992); but, of course, this is the last thing a neoclassical economist should wish for. In closing, the attempt to reduce macroeconomics to microeconomics by assuming the coalescence of all firms into a single "representative" firm shirks interaction, and it is about as reasonable as the attempt to reduce classical mechanics to atomic physics by assuming that a single "average" atom can represent an extended body in all respects.

The alternative *game-theoretic* approach is at first sight more realistic, in starting from a collection of interacting individuals with conflicting interests. But, since these agents are assumed to be maximizers, they are anything but bone-and-flesh individuals. Besides, the markets are assumed to be in or near equilibrium – a mathematical convenience but an economic chimera. Moreover, the utility functions and the entries of the payoff matrices occurring in the theory are posited rather than being empirically justified. For example, Shubik (1984, 75) postulates for all consumers a quadratic utility function, which entails a negatively sloped but linear demand function – at variance with the standard hypothesis. And he makes no effort to check the conclusions against any econometric models, let alone economic indicators. This theory represents no real economy, and is therefore unsuitable for effective policy making. In particular, since it focuses on non-cooperative games, it cannot tackle any of the global problems, all of which call for joint efforts. In conclusion, game-theoretic economics is just one more academic game.

The third and last reduction project to be examined is that of the *rational expectations* school around R. Lucas, T. Sargent, and R. Barro, popular in the 1980s (see, for instance, Sargent 1987). These economists "solve" the reduction problem by denying that it exists. Indeed, they reject the micro-macro distinction and, being methodological individualists, they approach the economy as an aggregate of atomic agents, whence every macrofeature must equal the aggregation of micro-actions. They assume, first, that all individuals have roughly the same needs and tastes (that is, utility functions), as well as skills and expectations – an unrealistic if mathematically convenient hypothesis. Their second axiom is that every agent can form "rational expectations" (precise unbiased forecasts) on the basis of the best available data and theories, and is capable of detecting discrepancies between such expectations and real behaviour, as well as of learning from such mistakes. Their third axiom is that of general equilibrium: all free markets would clear instantly.

All three postulates are at variance with the facts. The first – that everybody has the same utility function – is implausible because no two individuals are identical – particularly if they have very different backgrounds. The second (omniscience) is false as well: not even statistics bureaus possess all that knowledge. (Theologians might argue that not even God would care to amass that much information.) In particular, comparison of sales expectations with actual sales has shown that businessmen fall into two classes: the "perennial optimists" and the "perennial pessimists" (Lovell 1986, 115). Moreover, when making forecasts, managers typically do not use the information about their own sales history, let alone the publicly available information about the performance of the economy. The third postulate (general equilibrium) is refuted every time a recession occurs. In particular, the labour and financial markets are seldom in equilibrium. (Rational-expectation theorists attempt to save the postulate by adding the ad hoc hypothesis that most unemployment is voluntary – an assumption likely to bring more comfort to reactionary ideologues than to the jobless.) In short, the axioms of rational-expectation theory are false.

The three postulates jointly entail the thesis that fiscal policies are irrelevant. Indeed, omniscient people can anticipate the possible effects of such policies, acting so as to avoid their consequences, which they can do because prices and wages are flexible. This proposition too is at variance with reality. Suffice it to recall that the huge fiscal deficit and foreign debt accumulated by the US during the 1980s – not to mention the widening gap between rich and poor – were effects of the increased military expenditures and the tax cuts introduced by the conservative administrations (see Smithin 1990).

In conclusion, rational-expectations theory is spectacularly false. Moreover, it is pernicious in encouraging antisocial policies. (More in Blinder 1989; Dagum 1986; Frydman 1983; Malinvaud 1991; Hahn and Solow 1995; and Ericsson and Irons 1995.) This is not to deny the role of beliefs and expectations, whether reasonable or unreasonable. In fact, they are so important in social life that they ought to be studied scientifically – by social psychologists and in a variety of markets – rather than being the object of aprioristic amateur speculation. However, it would be unrealistic to expect that even a large army of competent social psychologists could find out the preferences, expectations, and decisions of every individual economic agent. Fortunately, we do not need such knowledge to make statistical predictions, just as the physicist does not need a complete knowledge of every atom or molecule in a body to specify its macrostate.

This is not to say that macroeconomics can stand on its own, let alone that it can be reduced to econometrics, as Sims (1980) and a few others have suggested in view of the failure of the rational-expectations speculations. Econometrics is a technique not a theory, let alone an explanatory one. Not even the most accurate time-series explains anything: only mechanismic theories, that is, theories describing mechanisms of some kind, have explanatory power (see Bunge 1996a, 1997b). Macroeconomics needs mechanismic theories, and these should make contact with microeconomics, if we are ever to understand and control macroeconomic processes. The reason is obvious: macroevents are effects of microevents – which in turn depend on macroconditions. For example, the shrinking of the workforce in the manufacturing sector, currently occurring in industrialized countries, results mostly from increases in productivity and decreases in fertility.

The failure of the four reduction attempts sketched above does not dash the macro-micro reduction project in question, for one might always hope to succeed where others have failed. What does dash the project is any of the following considerations. First, no realistic microsocial theory can be purely microsocial, because all microsocial activities are embedded in a macrosocial environment. Consequently, the very description of any business activity necessitates certain macroeconomic concepts, such as those of tax, interest, inflation, and unemployment rates. For example, the profit and wage rates in any sector are determined not only by such microeconomic factors as productivity and management style, but also by macroeconomic ones such as scarcity and plenty, discount and inflation rates, government regulations, political stability, and international relations. In general, every microeconomic variable depends not only upon other microeconomic variables but also upon some macroeconomic ones. Thus, if x and y are microeconomic variables (e.g., endogenous and exogenous respectively) and y depends functionally upon x, then y is bound to depend on some macroeconomic variable X as well: that is, $y = f(x, X)$. Second, the economy is ruled not only by economic activities but also by political factors, such as defence policies and public opinion, which influence policy makers – at least under a democracy. In other words, macroeconomists must reckon with political, ideological, and moral factors.

The moral of this story is that the micro-macro problems in economics are not to be solved either by denying the existence of the two levels or by attempting to reduce either to the other. Instead, they are to be approached by analysing the macro-macro relations in terms of macro-micro, micro-micro, and micro-macro relation – that is, by constructing Boudon-Coleman diagrams as explained in chapter 2. For example, the following diagram explains why a "healthy economy" (big profits) may involve high unemployment.

Macrolevel	Industrial unemployment	→	Increased aggregate output
	↑		↑
Mesolevel	Technological advance	→	Increased productivity

In sum, although macroeconomics and microeconomics must interact, the former is *in principle* irreducible to the latter. This is because (a) every microeconomic activity is subject to macroeconomic constraints; (b) far from being autonomous and self-regulating, the economy is intimately linked with both nature and the political system; and (c) the economies of countries at different stages of development can be remarkably differerent. (More in Malinvaud 1991.) A consequence of (a) is that macroeconomics must be studied on its own level, not only in relation to microeconomics. A consequence of (b) and (c) is that sound macroeconomics, positive or normative, is inseparable from political science. Normative macroeconomics will be discussed in chapter 10.

8 Ugly Facts versus Pretty Theory

In the "hard" factual sciences it is taken for granted that the problems to be investigated must have some relation to the real world. It is also tacitly admitted that, to be taken seriously, hypotheses, models, and theories must be empirically testable. Moreover, they must pass reality checks before being pronounced true or false to some degree – hence be accepted or rejected until further notice. Not so in mainstream economics. Here one may toy with ideas that have little if anything to do with the real world. Five examples follow. 1/ At a time of world-wide mass unemployment, T. Sargent (1987, 472), of rational-expectations fame, proposed a model of the labour market that assumes that it clears instantly at all times – that is, that there is no involuntary unemployment. 2/ There are no realistic theories of imperfect markets with price-setting (rather than price-taking) firms (Solow 1986). 3/ It is not yet known for sure whether wage rises destroy jobs (through cost increases) or create them (indirectly through consumption increases *à la* Keynes). In particular, it is doubtful that increase in the minimum wage kills jobs (Card and Krueger 1995). 4/ There are no realistic theories of the mechanisms of economic growth, business cycles, or inflation – let alone stagflation. 5/ Most economists overlook habit, custom, morals, and social norms (Koford and Miller 1991).

In economics, then, there are still plenty of hypotheses, models, and theories that have never been checked except for logical consistency, or that have been conclusively falsified, yet they continue to clutter reputable journals and popular textbooks. Neoclassical microeconomics is a case in point, as argued above. What holds for microeconomics also holds, though perhaps to a lesser extent, for macroeconomics and econometrics. Indeed, it is no secret that, unlike descriptive macroeconomics, macroeconomic theory and policy are in a state of disarray and far removed from reality (see, for example, Blinder 1989 and Hahn and Solow 1995). And most econometric models rest on data vitiated by large errors; they are seldom checked against large samples of data; and, when they are, they often founder (Hendry 1980; Leamer 1983).

Koopmans (1979) – who was far from heresy – once complained that nobody seems to keep track of the confirmations and refutations of economic theories. Most mathematical economists seem to be allergic to data, hence reluctant to put their models to the test. They thereby show indifference to truth, which is what scientists are supposed to look for. For example, Leontief (1982) found that over half of the papers published in the prestigious *American Economic Review* during the 1972–81 decade dealt with mathematical models without any data. What is the use of high-powered mathematics to build models that are not checked, and consequently cannot even be said to be false?

In a well-known paper, Gibbard and Varian (1978) thought they had taken economics off the hook by stipulating that the propositions constituting economic models are neither true nor false, the only task of the economic theorist being to analyse economic models. But if this were true, economics could not claim to be scientific. (Leontief [1966, 83] complained against this approach, calling it "second-hand theorizing" and contrasting it with Marx's "realistic, empirical knowledge of the capitalist system.") And in his Nobel lecture Stigler (1983, 542) stated with a straight face that "economists seldom choose between directly rival theories on the basis of critical empirical tests." Worse yet, some scholars, notably the members of the Austrian school, hold that economic theories are true a priori (Menger 1883; Robbins 1935; von Mises 1949) – hence in no need of tests. Hayek (1955) held that the only empirical part of economics concerns the acquisition of knowledge. Others, particularly those who regard economics as a decision science, claim that economic theories are not descriptive but normative, hence untestable. It would appear that it is ordinary people who must be tested to ascertain whether or not they live up to the allegedly high standards of rationality set by mathematical economists.

In 1908 Bagehot reproached his English colleagues for "not speaking of real men, but of imaginary ones." Nobody listened. Knight (1940) even boasted about the untestability of economic propositions, and dismissed all concern for truth. Martin (1957) protested to no avail. And Morgenstern (1972a, 703) accused mainstream economic theory of "studying largely hypothetical situations that have no similarity whatever with the real problem: 'free' competition, with free entry, arbitrarily large number of producers, sellers, and buyers, none of which has any influence on anything, each facing fixed conditions, hence able to maximize independently of others, etc. The real world is profoundly different." In short, main-line (or textbook) economic theory does not work because its assumptions, when testable at all, are wildly unrealistic.

Yet some economists, while paying lip-service to the requirement of empirical testability, regard the fundamental assumptions of an economic theory as useful fictions "because they need not conform to 'facts' but only to be useful in 'as if' reasoning" (Machlup 1955). Milton Friedman (1953) championed this fictionist (or instrumentalist, or pragmatist) variety of anti-realism. In an influential paper he stated that the antecedent A of a conditional hypothesis of the form "If A, then B" may be wildly unrealistic, while the entire statement may be true as shown by the predictions made with its help. Thus, it would not matter whether or not all businessmen do attempt to maximize their profits; all that would matter is that everything should happen *as if* they behaved in this manner (pp. 14ff.).

In short, Friedman's methodological watchword is "Never mind the assumptions: just watch for their consequences." This research strategy is logically flawed for the following reasons. First, rational people are supposed to care for both consistency and truth. Second, a false premise implies any number of consequences, some true, others false, and most of them irrelevant. (Medieval logicians called this the *Ex falso quodlibet* law.) Third, it is always possible to frame fantastic hypotheses that will account for anything. (Think, for instance, of the dogma according to which everything happens according to God's unfathomable designs: it accounts for everything without explaining anything. Remember that to explain a fact is to exhibit the mechanism that produces it.) Fourth, one may select the conclusions in such a way that the test outcome does not affect the assumptions. Consider this example. Assumption: "A and B." Logically valid conclusion: A. Perform a test bearing only on A. Test outcome: A confirmed. Since B has not been put to the test, nothing can be inferred about its truth value. Yet the unwary economist may believe that, since B is part of the hypothesis, it may be kept along with A, even though it has done no work and has not been tested. This is actually the case with the postulate of economic "rationality" (or utility maximization) in many theories: it does about as much work as incantation (Arrow 1987; Simon 1987).

In short, Friedman notwithstanding, assumptions do matter – provided they occur as premises in deductions. Hence, fictionism is methodologically untenable with reference to factual science. (It is tenable only in pure mathematics: Bunge 1997a.) Fictionism is also epistemologically untenable, for a goal of scientific research is to uncover reality beneath appearance. And it is technologically self-defeating for, if we use a hypothesis of the form "If A then B" to attain goal B through means A, we must check whether A is fact or fiction.

To be sure, not all mainstream economists share either Friedman's fictionism or the apriorism of the neo-Austrian school. However, very few of them bother to subject their theories to empirical tests. And even fewer pay any attention to relevant findings in neighbouring disciplines, such as social psychology and sociology. As for the predictive power of main-line economics, as we saw earlier it makes very few forecasts, and those few are seldom correct. (A classical example was the forecast that free trade would eventually reduce worldwide the differences in income per head. Actually, the ratio of incomes in rich to poor countries rose from 2:1 in 1800 to about 20:1 in 1970 [Bhagwati 1972]; and the gap keeps widening.) In short, economists would do well to adopt Hendry's (1980) three golden rules for econometrics: Test, test, and test.

That is not all. Economics exhibits five quaint features absent from the so-called hard sciences.

1. Even journals not specifically devoted to the history of economics contain frequent references to Turgot, Quesnay, Smith, Bentham, Ricardo, Mill, Cournot, Marx, Walras, Menger, Marshall, Pareto, Schumpeter, and other forerunners, as if they were our contemporaries. Thus, at least five generations of students seem to coexist happily in the economic pantheon, which doubles as the economic academy (see also Lekachman 1976, 264).

2. Disproportionate mathematical ingenuity is invested in formalizing, embellishing, and analysing untested or falsified assumptions.

3. Exceedingly small investments are made in theory "operationalization," that is, the linking of theoretical to observational variables via economic indicators. This holds in particular for the concepts of scarcity, utility, shadow price, and expectation. Instead, much energy is spent arguing about them – which takes economics suspiciously close to theology.

4. Extravagant claims are often made for certain behavioural and economic hypotheses (often called 'laws,' and occasionally 'a priori principles'); and even more so for sweeping theories – in particular consumer theory and general-equilibrium theory – that are seldom if ever put to the test – or that, when found false, are said to have great heuristic or else normative power.

5. Defunct entities, such as the free market, are often vividly evoked and sometimes even glorified, whereas important economic developments, such as capital concentration, cooperation, barter, deindustrialization, and stagflation, are neglected.

In confronting such anomalies, anyone trained in a rigorous science is bound to wonder whether economics is really the hardest of all social sciences, or even whether it is a science at all. In fairness, it must be admitted that an increasing number of economists have been voicing their misgivings about the current state of their discipline. They go from scathing criticisms (e.g., Robinson 1962) and the admission that the discipline is in a state of deep crisis (e.g., Phelps Brown 1972; Wiles 1973; Hutchison 1964; Blaug 1980; Thurow 1983; Allais 1995; and Rosegger 1995) or even dead (Ormerod 1994), to the statement that economics is not yet a science (e.g., Perroux 1972; Eichner 1983; and Hahn 1983), to the accusation that economics has become "the cloak over corporate power" (Galbraith 1973, 8). These criticisms of mainstream economics boil down to the thesis that it is at best a flat-earth theory, at worst a no-earth one.

To judge the degree of scientificity of economics we must first agree on a precise idea of a science. If the definition of a factual science proposed in chapter 1, section 2, is adopted, the following conclusions follow. Economics does meet the conditions that (1) it is cultivated by people who constitute a research community; and (2) this community is supported by society at large. But I submit that economics fails to satisfy fully the remaining conditions.

In fact, mainstream economics violates the condition 3 that science should deal exclusively with real (actual or possible) entities – notably when dealing with competitive markets in equilibrium. The apologists for the free market, as well as those for central planning, fail to abide by condition 4 concerning the ethos of science, which requires us to search for truth. (Indeed, the former ignore social costs and the latter inefficiency.) Condition 5 of logical and mathematical rigour is violated every time undefined utility functions are used. Condition 6 too is often violated: the psychological assumptions of neoclassical economics, in particular the ones of maximizing behaviour and of dislike for work, are at variance with the evidence (see, for example, Hebb 1953 and Juster 1991). In other words, economics lacks a firm specific background, for it makes little if any use of contemporary psychology, anthropology, sociology, or politology. The problematics of economics (condition 7) is a mixed bag: it contains authentic problems along with academic questions concerning non-existent objects or conditions, such as general equilibrium. Worse yet, most economic theorists ignore the fact that technology and management are factors of production, and overlook such pressing social issues as depletion of non-renewable resources, stagflation, mass unemployment, underdevelopment, the political connection, the military-industrial complex, alternatives to capitalism (e.g., cooperativism), and the ideological contamination of the discipline (see, for instance, Melman 1989).

In view of these numerous and serious errors of commission and omission, it should come as no surprise to find that the fund of knowledge of mainstream economics (condition 8) is not much to write home about. Indeed, the findings of theoretical economics are anything but sensational and robust. The same flaws explain why economists seldom satisfy the condition 9 of discovering or using regularities, in particular laws. And the condition 10 regarding method is fulfilled only partially: far too many economic hypotheses are untested or even untestable.

Nor are the two additional scientificity conditions met. Indeed, the condition of being a component of the system of the sciences is hardly met: mainstream economists pay no attention to non-economic variables, hence to neighbouring disciplines such as psychology, sociology, and political science. (For example, recent experiments show that, contrary to rational-choice-theory dogma, people who engage in repeated exchanges may form attachments and make commitments: see Lawler and Yoon 1996.) Hence, orthodoxy cannot help us understand, let alone control, such socio-economico-political facts as inflation, oil wars, narco-politics, and cleptocracy. Self-reliance is not a sign of maturity but a characteristic of pseudoscience, as exemplified by psychoanalysis, parapsychology, graphology, and homeopathy (Bunge 1991c, 1991d, 1996a.) Finally, economics meets only partially the condition of renewal: it evolves far too slowly to count nowadays as a lively science.

Let us tally the test results. To begin with, we may ignore the first two conditions (community of scholars in a receptive or at least tolerant society), for they apply nowadays to all academic disciplines, not only to the sciences proper. Next, we assign arbitrarily the same weight to all the remaining ten conditions, allotting one point to total fulfilment, half a point to partial fulfilment, and zero to failure. With some good will, on a scale from 0 to 10, the total is: $\frac{1}{2} + \frac{1}{2} + \frac{1}{2} + 0 + \frac{1}{2} + \frac{1}{2} + \frac{1}{2} + \frac{1}{2} + 0 + \frac{1}{2} = 4$.

If this result is accepted, it must be concluded that economics is a *semiscience* or *protoscience*, with some pockets of mature science and others of pseudoscience. (If this diagnosis is deemed to be too severe, recall that John Hicks's is even more so: to him economics is and will always be a discipline, never a science.) So, economics may well be the bag lady rather than the queen of the social sciences, particularly by comparison with anthropology, demography, sociology, and history. It remains to be seen whether it is a (very slowly) emerging science, or a discipline suffering from severe stagflation.

We have emphasized the flaws of mainstream economics, only to show that they have philosophical roots and can therefore be corrected through a philosophical reorientation. This is not to belittle the genuine advances of economics since the Great Depression – and largely thanks to it. Suffice it to mention the advances in bioeconomics, production models, information economics, human-capital theory, environmental economics, input-output analysis, economic indicators, national accounting, the Keynesian revolution, the post-Keynesian theories of growth, the emergence of socio-economics, and sundry mathematical refinements. However, only the latter have been associated with mainstream economics. All the other advances have been alien to orthodoxy. Moreover, economic theory is still plagued by such basic unanswered questions as, Why do firms emerge? What is money? What are the mechanisms underlying business cycles? and Why are financial markets unstable?

Our methodological analysis suggests that economics theory is still a semiscience. Worse, it is advancing far too slowly by comparison with the pace of the economy, whence it is of little help to businessmen and statesmen. What can be done to raise the standards of economics, facilitate its progress, and render it useful? I venture to suggest trying jointly the following moves.

1. Brush up your philosophy: do not adopt uncritically an obsolete philosophy, such as Thomism, positivism, conventionalism, dialectical materialism, or ontological and methodological individualism – let alone an openly antiscientific philosophy, such as Hegelianism, phenomenology, hermeneutics, or existentialism. Also, keep clear of relativism-constructivism, another antiscientistic philosophy. And do not embrace Popper's falsificationism either, for (a) it applies only to the null hypothesis, a trademark of infant science; (b) one may confirm a hypothesis while trying to falsify it, and conversely; and (c) scientific research aims not only at discarding error but also at attaining truth.

2. Study the economy more intensively than the economic literature. In particular, do not stay with the classics, let alone the neoclassics, for they did not face the unexpected and pressing economic issues of our time, such as quick increases in population, productivity, mass unemployment, capital concentration and mobility, and "North-South" inequalities.

3. Do your best to remain ideologically neutral in positive economics, but disclose your morals and politics in policy matters. (There is nothing subjective or dishonest about working with explicit value premises: see Hutchison 1964 and Myrdal 1969. What is dishonest is to try to conceal them or to pass them off as scientific findings.)

4. Don't take for granted any vulgar maxims on human nature and behaviour, for they may be false; and leave psychoeconomics to experimental psychologists, behavioural economists, and field anthropologists.

5. Keep on using mathematics to craft economic models and theories; but get rid of pseudoquantities, and refrain from using mathematics to clothe untestable or false hypotheses; and do not use economics as an excuse for doing mathematics.

6. Either abstain from using subjective concepts altogether or operationalize them.

7. Take time, dynamics, and disequilibria seriously: go beyond the short and the long terms, and regard equilibria as phases in a process – in short, study dynamical systems.

8. Focus on economic systems rather than on either individuals or unanalysed wholes; but do not ignore their environment, in particular the body politic and the natural resources – especially since many of these are becoming scarcer by the day.

9. Do not isolate the economy: treat it as a subsystem of society, hence as strongly coupled with the natural environment, the polity, and the culture.

10. Strengthen the links between economics and its neighbours, in particular

demography, sociology, political science, and history, for every social science studies only some aspects of a single whole, namely society, and all those aspects are interrelated, hence interdependent.

The last three pieces of advice lead us straight to the next chapter, on the science of politics. Indeed, political scientists know that wealth and power come together, whence economics and political science are sister disciplines.

4

Political Science

Just as the economy turns around work and its fruits, so politics is centred in power. Put bluntly, it is about "who gets what, when, how" (Lasswell 1958). And political science – or, more modestly, *politology* – is of course the study of politics. Since the marrow of politics is the struggle for and management of power, realists define political science as "the science of power" (Lasswell and Kaplan 1952, 82). In other words, political science asks who governs what for whom. More precisely, it is the scientific study of power relations in and among social systems. Hence, it attains the very heart of the agency-structure relation.

Power relations bind or oppose people in all social systems, even in families, schools, churches, business firms, and voluntary organizations. Therefore, political science should be conceived of in a broad manner, rather than be confined to the study of organizations such as states and parties. That is, political science should embrace the politics of family, business, culture, and more. In other words, politologists should study the struggle for, and maintenance of, political (in particular military), economic, and cultural power, all the more so since all three intertwine. Indeed, political power can dominate the economy and the culture; wealth can buy political and cultural influence; and cultural power can either enrich or impoverish the economy or the polity. Hence, the idea that domination can be avoided by keeping separate the spheres of power (Walzer 1983) is naive: for better or for worse, the three artificial subsystems of every society intersect. The tyranny of an unelected power elite can be avoided only if power is widely distributed in all three subsystems, and an enlightened citizenry is free and willing to work or even fight individually or in groups against every power concentration.

Unlike other social scientists, political analysts cannot confine their attention to facts: they must study the political discourse too, for it guides or misguides political action, and it manifests or masks the latter. Now, we all know that political discourse is a tissue of truths and lies, promises and threats, noble ideals and base interests; and that it now stimulates, now inhibits political action. Accordingly, the politologist cannot trust political documents any more than he can ignore them. Above all, he must avoid the hermeneutic mistake of identifying fact with text, in particular politics with political discourse. Instead, he should adopt a realist standpoint, regarding political documents as indispensable yet unreliable sources, as well as distorting mirrors and equivocal indicators of the political process. This is because the name of the political game is 'persuasion,' not 'education.' In politics what matters above all is *res, non verba*. In other words, beware of ideological labels, for most of them have become obsolete and perform a persuasive function rather than an analytical one. Just think of the words 'patriotism,' 'national security,' 'liberty,' 'democracy,' or 'socialism.'

The scientific politologist will also avoid the extremes of irrationalism and hyperrationalism. In particular, while recognizing that politics is often nonrational, he should not despair of the ability of rational analysis, based on reliable data, to uncover the nature and sources of political power, and even to examine rationally the merits and demerits of the various types of governance. But cultivation of his own rationality should not lead him to attribute rationality to all political agents, trying to account for political actions exclusively in terms of accurately informed, cold, and clever calculations of expected costs and benefits, for political action is influenced by ideological and emotional factors too. Shorter: Rational politological analysis, sí; rational-choice political theory, no.

Nor are these the only philosophical commitments that the politologist ought to make. Although he should strive for objectivity, he would be ill advised to underrate the power of beliefs, desires, values, ideals and norms in political life. And, when acting as a consultant to political parties or governments, he should declare his values and goals, as Myrdal (1969) urged, instead of claiming that his recommendations follow from a dispassionate and disinterested scientific study. Basic science is unbiased, technology is not.

Last, but not least, the politologist will also benefit from realizing that the individualistic approach, which focuses on politicians and solitary citizens, is just as shallow as the holistic one, which handles only political wholes, such as nation-states, without caring for leaders or for the hopes and fears that these can induce or reduce in their followers or subjects. Since citizens, politicians, civil servants, and political systems are distinguishable but inseparable from one another, political science benefits from adopting an explicit systemic approach. In sum, I submit that systemism, together with rationalism and epistemological realism, are philosophical preconditions for the maturation of political studies.

Not only political analysts but also ordinary citizens, politicians, and bureaucrats face the individualism-holism-systemism trilemma. Indeed, consistent individualists are either politically apathetic (e.g., Olson's "free riders") or favour piecemeal (rather than systemic) social reforms. By contrast, holists are either conservative or revolutionary, on the right or on the left: they wish either to keep the system or to change it overnight. Only systemists favour gradual yet integral change. They are integral reformers, realizing that in society everything hangs together, inertia is large, and "shock therapies" of all kinds are painful, hence likely to encounter passive resistance or elicit rebellion. (More in chap. 11.)

Politology was founded by Plato and Aristotle two millennia ago, and it has been cultivated by such luminaries as Aquinas, Machiavelli, Spinoza, Hobbes, Locke, Hume, Montesquieu, Rousseau, Condorcet, Bentham, de Tocqueville, Mill, Marx, Weber, and Lenin. (However, neither Marx nor Lenin had a theory of the state: see van den Berg 1988. And we still lack an adequate theory of democracy: see Sartori 1987.) Given this tradition, the pervasiveness of politics, and the public attention it draws in modern society, as well as the huge number of professors and journals of political science, one would think that political science is one of the fastest moving, more advanced, and useful of all sciences. Regrettably, political science is still at a primitive stage, particularly on the theoretical side (see, for instance, Greenstein and Polsby 1975 1: v; Waldo 1975, 114; and Lindblom 1982, 1990); so much so, that much of it consists in commentaries on the classics, and analogies are sometimes passed off as theories. For instance, the shallow analogy between political turmoil and atmospheric turbulence, together with allusions to chaos theory – without the writing down, let alone solving, of any relevant equations – has become fashionable (see, for example, Rosenau 1990 and Kiel and Elliott 1996).

Three reliable indicators of the progress of any social science are (a) its degree of emancipation from ideology; (b) the precision of its language and the logical organization of its assumptions and empirical findings; and (e) the number of true generalizations it has found. Let us see how the work of one of the foremost contemporary politologists fares in these respects. The *pièce de résistance* of Samuel Huntington's still influential *Political Order in Changing Societies* (1968) is the following system of "equations":

Social mobilization / Economic development = Social frustration,

Social frustration / Mobility opportunities = Political participation,

Political participation / Political institutionalization = Political instability.

Koblitz (1988) noted that Huntington had not bothered to inform his readers how any of the terms occurring in these "equations" can be assigned a numerical value, much less what the units of those pseudomagnitudes could be. Huntington "divided" phrases, not well-defined functions. Moreover, he claimed that the overall correlation between frustration and instability is 0.50 – a number that makes no sense unless the variables in question are well defined. On top of this, Huntington smuggled ideology under the cover of political science when stating, at the height of apartheid, that the Republic of South Africa was a "satisfied society." The upshot is clear: Huntington failed all three above tests.

However, political science has made some progress. Indeed, if the number of true generalizations is an indicator of the degree of advancement of a scientific discipline, it must be admitted that political science is on a par with economics. Indeed, it can boast of at least the following regularities. 1/ Rebellion is the stronger, the clearer the perception of inequity (Aristotle). 2/ Authority is likely to be challenged not at the height of power but when power begins to wane (Tocqueville 1856). 3/ By hindering adaptive social changes, tyranny ultimately weakens the very social order it is expected to shore up. 4/ All political parties are ruled by self-renewing and self-serving oligarchies (Michels). 5/ The likelihood that a government will tolerate an opposition increases as the expected costs of suppression increase (Dahl 1971). 6/ Agrarian revolutions are caused by great inequalities in land distribution together with a large peasant population (Midlarsky 1982). 7/ Military power requires a strong economic basis (Kennedy 1989). 8/ Political democracy can coexist with economic dictatorship (Galbraith 1992). 9/ Nationalism has been a powerful political force since the Napoleonic Wars (Alter 1994). 10/ "[T]here is nothing more difficult to carry out, nor more doubtful of success, nor more dangerous to handle, than to initiate a new order of things" (Machiavelli 1940[1513], 21).

True, these are only empirical generalizations: they are not included in theories proper, hence they do not qualify as scientific laws (see Bunge 1967a, 1996a). Still, they may be called *quasi-laws*, being highly plausible generalizations concerning important social processes. Hence, they are more valuable than all the rational-choice models put together, if only because none of these has suggested any politological generalization (see sect. 5).

What may have slowed down the progress of political science? I submit that there have been seven main obstacles to it: (a) a wrong approach (either holistic or individualistic rather than systemic); (b) focus on miniproblems and the concomitant neglect of larger issues, as is obvious from the exaggerated concern with the mechanics of the voting process at the expense of substance – real power; (c) conceptual fuzziness, as in the handling of the notions of people, nation, nation-state, and national security; (d) excessive attention to the thought of political theorists of bygone times, such as Hobbes and Locke, at the expense of the myths, ideals, and norms people actually live by and fight for; (e) ideological contamination; (f) isolation from the other social sciences; and (g) shallow metatheoretical analysis.

Whether morally or practically right or wrong, some political ideas help guide, misguide, or justify political action. Example of guidance: Montesquieu's principle of the division of the three powers helped shape the modern liberal state. Example of misguidance: Lenin's principle of the supreme role of the party helped shape communist dictatorships. Example of justification: Stalin's thesis that class struggles intensify after revolution – allegedly because the newly dispossessed fight back desperately – helped to legitimate the "red terror" and suggested inventing plots and setting up show trials to "confirm" that thesis. In sum, the ability of widely broadcast political ideas to mobilize or paralyse people underscores the value of serious political studies.

Let us start our study by examining the polity (or political system) and the peculiar relation that binds it together and may put it asunder, namely political power. We will then proceed to studying the nucleus of the modern political system, namely the state – which North Americans call 'government.' Subsequently we will glance at domestic and world politics. And later on we will examine three approaches to political theory and policy making currently popular in academic circles: game theory, public-choice theory, and social-choice theory. The rest of the chapter will be devoted to the explanation and prediction of political events, as well as to the moral justification for political action.

1 Units of Analysis and Power

Politology may be conceived of narrowly, as the study of the polity (or even only government), or broadly, as the study of power relations in all social systems, including business firms and non-profit organizations. Given that power relations are central to the structure of any social system, it is odd that much of contemporary political science is not about power and its "perceptions" but about such side issues as voting schemes and "rational" political choices – which are often treated as simple-minded and bloodless intellectual games. It is equally disappointing to find that few political analyses distinguish the mere holding of office from the wielding of power, which often operates behind the scenes. It is even more distressing to find that the very notion of power is seldom correctly analysed. This has led some politologists to treat power as a thing, and others to discuss the power-structure relation (see, for instance, Lukes 1977 and Debnam 1984). This is a pseudoproblem because power is a relation, and social structure is the collection of all social relations. (Recall chap. 2, sect. 1.) So, the power-structure relation is simply that of set membership.

Let us analyse the concept of power. Since there are three major units or levels of political agency – citizen, organization, and nation-state – there are six possible types of power relation: person to person, person to organization, organization to nation, and so on. However, regardless of level, to a first approximation power can be analysed as a binary relation: agent *a* wields power over patient *b*, or *Pab* for short. (The formal properties of *P* are obvious: it is irreflexive, asymmetrical, and transitive.) On second thought, power turns out to be at least a quaternary relation, for it is always exerted with some means *c* to some end *d* – or *Pabcd* for short. However, for any fixed <means, end> pair, the quaternary relation can be treated as a binary one.

The binary power relation may be defined as the ability to change the course of events, often against other people's wills. (Weber is often credited with having defined it as the *probability* of imposing one's will. But the original [Weber 1922, 28] reads *Chance*, which in German means possibility or opportunity – not probability. *Traduttore, traditore!*)

It is usual to distinguish two kinds of power: *to* and *over*. We define them as follows. An [individual or collective] agent *a* has *power to do b* = There is a thing *c* [inanimate, living, or social] such that *a* can cause change *b* in *c*. Next comes the concept of power over. We stipulate that an [individual or collective] agent *a* wields *power over* entity *c* if and only if *a* has the power to make *c* do or refrain from doing something. In other words, an agent wields power over another thing if and only if the former restricts the patient's freedom to act – that is, if it forces, hinders, or deviates his or its actions.

Note that the second concept (*over*) is just a subconcept or particular case of the first (*to*), whence the to/over distinction is not a dichotomy. In turn, the second concept subsumes two special concepts: those of Weber (coercion) and of exchange theory (dependence). Which is just as well, because they are two sides to the same coin. Indeed, coercion elicits dependency, which in turn invites coercion. Think of the parent-child, employer-employee, and political boss–client relationships.

Taking a cue from the potency-act distinction due to Aristotle, we distinguish potential from actual power. *Potential power* is the ability to change the course of events. (It may be quantitated as the difference in resources or means accessible to agent and patient. That is, $P(a, b) = k [R(a) - R(b)]$, where k is a constant.) *Actual power* is the effect that an agent actually has on events. An individual or organization may have a large potential power but may not make full use of it. By contrast, strong actual power is an indicator of large potential power. (Actuality implies potentiality, but not conversely.)

However, unlike physical forces, social forces pass through people's heads: that is, their effects depend upon the way they are "perceived." This holds, in particular, for power relations. In fact, experiments in social psychology (e.g., Zelditch and Butler Ford 1994) have shown that an agent "perceived" as powerful need not do anything beyond occupying an ostensible position of power, such as sitting quietly on his throne. That is, he may elicit or prevent changes without doing anything. Another important distinction is that between direct and indirect power. An (individual or organizational) agent exerts *indirect* power if he or it makes use of an intermediary. For example, in principle a deputy minister is expected to act only in the name of his minister, and the manager in that of his board of directors. But in practice such intermediaries may wield direct power, either by controlling the agenda, making important decisions on their own, or dragging their feet or even sabotaging when given instructions they do not like. Therefore, the scientific politologist will not confine his work to reading rules, decrees, minutes of meetings, and speeches, but will try to assess the actual impact of decisions and words on the social system concerned. He will keep in mind that most of the decisions taken by Gorbachev's government in the final days of the former USSR were never implemented.

We are now ready to examine the political system, or polity. We take the *polity* of a society to be the subsystem of the latter composed of all the persons making or influencing, implementing or frustrating, decisions affecting public goods: their creation, upkeep, utilization, or destruction. The polity of a modern society is composed of the state or government (including the military), intermediary organizations (such as bar associations), political parties, lobbies, and the citizenry. The modern state manages a hugely complex *res publica*, and it has the legal monopoly on coercion, both peaceful and violent – yet all governments are fractured rather than unitary.

The politologist who studies modern societies investigates the current state and evolution of the political system: he is expected to be an objective (though not necessarily disinterested) onlooker. If he knows anything about real people, and has any civic responsibility and moral sensibility, he is bound to have some political convictions, even if no party line suits him. But, if he wants to be taken for a scientist, he is bound to search for objective truth and tell it. He must resolve his inner conflict between objectivity and partisanship – something that church, party, or business intellectuals cannot do.

By contrast, the political practitioner and the insider expert – politician, activist, consultant, lobbyist, or public servant – attempt to shape the polity by designing, redesigning, or managing political systems or practices, in particular policies, plans, and procedures for administering the commonwealth. Unlike the politologist, who only searches for truth, the political commentator or analyst participates in the political process. And he is listened to for being a professional rather than an amateur.

Alas, we all know that few political analysts are learned politologists. Likewise, few learned politologists ever get to influence government, let alone public opinion. We all pay dearly for this mismatch between research and action, theory and practice. Hence, we should encourage a closer contact between the student of politics and the political practitioner. Provided the difference between science and ideology be kept in mind, such contact should encourage politologists to tackle important practical issues, and it should help political experts to design science-based policies and plans (of which more in chaps. 10 and 11).

The referents or units of analysis of political science come in three main categories or levels: individuals (e.g., leaders and followers), organizations (e.g., nation-states, governments, parties, and lobbies), and whole societies – from hamlet to nation to the world system. As far as political science is concerned, the central entities in this vast and variegated array are nation-states (countries): all else is either a component, a collection, or a supersystem of either. (Nation = <Territory, People>. Nation-state = <Territory, People, Central government>. There are about 5000 nations and 200 countries. Each people "comes" with its culture: the nation is thus partly an "imagined community" [Anderson 1983]. For the dubious opinion that the nation-state is dying, consult the vast recent literature. For the fantasy that the "global cyberspace" will replace the nation-state, see Negroponte 1996.)

Unless such level differences are drawn, confusion and oversight of the micro-macro links are bound to result. For example, one may attribute to political systems such features as beliefs and goals, which only persons can have. And one may forget that political preferences and actions are partly conditioned by education, status, and circumstance. In sum, political processes must be studied on all levels. For example, international crises should be placed in their wider context of great-power (or even global) politics, and analysed into their component actors, namely nation-states (see Brecher et al. 1988, 9).

Some political wholes, such as the electorate, are mere aggregates; others, such as the polity, are "organic wholes" or systems. (The present king of Morocco boasts that, although most of his subjects may oppose him, he faces no opposition – that is, no organized adversary.) But both political aggregates and systems can be characterized only in terms of certain political bonds that bind the parts together. For example, an individual is a citizen by virtue of his civil rights and duties. These would alter if the political system were to change.

What holds for individual political action also holds, with all the more reason, for any account of the vicissitudes of political systems. For example, the birth of the modern state in Western Europe has been explained as the outcome of two intertwining social processes. These are the concentration of both capital – in particular central control of fiscal resources – and means of coercion, in particular armed forces (Tilly 1990). Both were macrosocial processes involving individuals who were agents as well as patients of such changes. In a systemic perspective the individual is an active part of a whole, and the latter is ultimately the aggregate outcome of individual actions. Hence the bottom-up and top-down accounts are mutually complementary rather than exclusive.

The typical relationships among the members of a political entity on any level are those of cooperation, conflict, dependency, and influence, in particular power. Cooperation is sought to attain or restrain power, and power to induce or weaken cooperation, and in either way to resolve (or at least cover up) conflict or enhance it. Influence – in particular power – generates conflicts between those who wield it and their subjects. We will treat cooperation and conflict on a par because, unless checked by cooperation in some respect, conflict may result in the instability or even breakdown of the political system.

Cooperation, conflict, and power are rarely purely political: usually they also have biological (in particular psychological), economic, or cultural components, roots, or consequences. (Think of the platform of any modern political party.) Likewise biological, cultural, and economic power usually have political ingredients, sources, or effects. (Think of the political and economic power that some churches wield, and of the political and cultural clout of megacorporations.) Moreover, the four kinds of power may combine into one, as is the case with any modern tyranny. In this case one faces total power.

(Totalitarianism takes its name from the fact that a totalitarian government attempts to control all the activities, private and public, of its subjects. Total power is usually called 'absolute.' This is a misnomer because "absolute" is the opposite of "relative," whereas "total" is the opposite of "partial." Hence, Lord Acton's notorious dictum should be revised to read: "Power corrupts, and total power corrupts totally.")

In our systemic perspective the polity, the economy, and the culture take turns in initiating social change. (For example, governmental subsidies and regulations control the economy; business supports or fights political parties; education and technology serve the economy.) This could not be otherwise given that the political, economic, and cultural "spheres" (systems) interact and overlap partially with one another. (In other words, the politologist is supposed to identify and combine six different causal – feedforward or feedback – cycles: two generated by each of the three sources of power.) Clearly, this thesis is at variance with the popular view that each of the three artificial "spheres" is or ought to be autonomous. It is also at variance with all three reductionist theses: economicism (politics is an outgrowth of the economy), politicism (politics generates or cripples all economic activity), and culturalism (culture is the only fountain of politics).

Whatever the source of a given social change, it is initiated or used by a leader or an elite. Either may or may not resort to coercion. In modern societies there are leaders and elites of various kinds: political (in particular military), economic, and cultural. Normally the maintenance of a modern social system requires only a bureaucracy; but its reform and, a fortiori, its radical renewal, calls for leadership. Weak leadership is bad because it cannot stop the rot; but strong leadership may be even worse because it can easily degenerate into tyranny. The call for "strong leadership," so often heard in America, is an unwitting invitation to dictatorship. What we should aim for is competent leadership under democratic control. In other words, we should favour responsive, accountable, well-informed, and honest leadership.

Leadership is incompatible with power equality, not with democracy. Indeed, the democratic leader wields more power than the ordinary citizen, but he is expected to be freely elected, responsive, and accountable to his constituency, so that he may be removed. He is only *primus inter pares*. The greatest threat to democracy is posed by leaders who head elites that own or can mobilize sizeable economic resources, whether private or public. And the most dangerous among these leaders are those with more charisma, manipulative skill, and access to funds and the media than statesmanship and public-spiritedness. That combination is bound to result in lowering the democratic guard, a necessary condition for the transformation of leadership into dictatorship.

(A coarse measure of the power that an individual wields in any social system can be constructed by assuming that power boils down to generating, keeping up, or cutting social bonds among the individual members of the system. Calling m the number of such bonds and N the total of possible bonds of a given kind among the n individuals in question, I suggest that $P = m/N$, where $N = n \cdot (n - 1)/2$. Clearly, P ranges between 0 for utter powerlessness, that is, $m = 0$, and 1 for total power, that is, $m = N$.)

Recall our quadripartite or *BEPC* analysis of society into its biological, economic, political, and cultural subsystems (chap. 1, sect. 1). In line with it, we break down power – with regard to both means and ends – into biological, economic, political, and cultural. (For alternative analyses see Mills 1959; Galbraith 1983; Mann 1986, 1993; and Jouvenel 1993.) The biological means include the use of muscular force, charm, beauty, sex, intelligence, persuasion, or all-round personality. The economic means boil down to compensation in, or exaction of, goods, money, services, or votes. The political means include legal coercion, violence, patronage, and party discipline. And the cultural means include education, persuasion, and indoctrination. Correspondingly, the goals of the exercise of power are submission to biological, economic, political, or cultural aims. Hence, there are altogether sixteen possible means-ends combinations in the power relation. (The reader is invited to write the corresponding

4 × 4 matrix and supply an example of each entry.) However, because B, E, P, and C interact, neither of them comes "pure" either as means or as goal. In other words, every power relation is a combination – or entwining, as Mann (1986, 1993) would say – of all four basic kinds in varying proportions.

Most politologists confine their attention to the <P, P> pair. But obviously all seven combinations including a political means or end deserve their attention: that is, <B, P> (e.g., voter intimidation), <P, B> (e.g., sex and race discrimination), <E, P> (e.g., vote buying and business lobbying), <P, E> (e.g., industrial regulation and colonization), <C, P> (e.g., party membership out of ideological conviction), <P, C> (e.g., ideological persecution), and <P, P> (e.g., military threat).

Awareness of the relational nature of power encourages the politologist to look at the other side of the coin – the reaction of the subordinate unit. There are several kinds of reaction, from acceptance to passive resistance to rejection (see Simmel 1950 [1908], 181–6; Scott 1985). Thus, the slave (or POW or worker) may obey because his livelihood or even life depends on his submission; then again, he may drag his feet or even sabotage; and, given the will and the opportunity, he may escape or rebel. Likewise, the citizen of a modern nation may "opt out of the system" and adopt an unconventional lifestyle; and he may do so either individually or by joining with others in peaceful communes or in criminal gangs. Or he may attempt to change "the system" either peacefully or by violent means. (Recall Hirschman's [1970] exit-voice pair.)

What is philosophically interesting about all such reactions against the powers that be is that they may involve the rejection of some of the prevailing values and morals, particularly with regard to rights, duties, property, work, leisure, sex, religion, and family life. Characteristically, whereas the antisocial responses are accompanied by moral nihilism, the prosocial ones come with new moral codes that emphasize group solidarity and certain individual rights and duties not covered by the dominant moral and legal codes.

The reactions to the exercise of power must be taken into account if we want to evaluate the efficiency of power, define the concept of authority, and explain ungovernability, that is, the breakdown of authority. The *efficiency* with which an actor wields power may be defined as the benefit/cost ratio of the exercise of power. *Authority* is legitimate power: that is, the authority that an actor enjoys may be equated to the degree to which his power is accepted by his subordinate(s), willingly and according to the law or otherwise. (More precisely: If a and b are any social units, then a exerts *authority* over b in respect $c =_{df} a$ exerts power over b in respect c, and b admits a's power in respect c.)

Finally, we stipulate that authority is (a) *de facto* if it rests only on force; (b) *politically legitimate* if it abides by the laws and mores of the society concerned; and (c) *morally legitimate* if it does not infringe upon the rights of the people (Bunge 1992b). Ideally, authority is both politically and morally legitimate. (For an alternative see Bochenski 1988.)

Corresponding to the four basic kinds of power listed above, we distinguish four basic kinds of authority: biological, economic, political, and cultural. Total authority is authority in all four respects; when strong, it is of course the strongest and most evil of all. (Examples: The medieval bishops who doubled as barons, and the modern totalitarian governments.) Anything short of total authority is bound to make room for dissent or even rebellion. As Tocqueville (1856) noted, rebellion against abusive power is more likely to occur when the ruler's power starts to wane, and the oppressed's lot starts to improve. (Mechanism: only then will the ruled dare openly criticize the ruler and hope and begin to enjoy the freedom he needs to express and spread and organize dissent.)

Obviously, no social system can function without some authority. Equally obviously, no social system can function both efficiently and fairly without accountability and the possibility of arguing and of challenging authority. In other words, obedience can be either conditional (critical or rational) or unconditional (blind or non-rational). And, whereas the latter only serves the rulers (and even so only in the short run), the former serves everybody by allowing for criticism and encouraging constructive proposals for improvement. A repressive or aggressive army is a paragon of the first kind, whereas a good university is a paragon of the second. Under political democracy authority is checked with the help of rational debate, and the latter is moderated so as to save authority. Further, only dialogue makes common goods possible (Reed 1996) – whence the political relevance of rationalism and irrationalism: rationals engage in dialogue, irrationals either obey or rebel blindly (see Popper 1962 [1945] and Ackerman 1980).

Since political power can be exerted in a number of ways, as well as with a variety of results, there can be no single indicator of its strength. Rather, there should be at least one indicator for each of the kinds listed above. (The rider 'at least' is intended to indicate that, since most indicators are ambiguous, one should try to set up a whole battery of independent indicators for every feature.) Regrettably, current political analyses fail to draw the above distinctions and, correspondingly, they employ at best aggregate indicators of political influence. Thus, in a political democracy voter turnout is taken to be a reliable indicator of the interest people take in politics; and the relative number of elected representatives is assumed to measure the relative influence of a political party. Under political dictatorships, alternative indicators of political participation, such as voluntary participation in mass mobilizations or in the performance of collective tasks, might be suitable were it not for the difficulty in ascertaining that such participation is voluntary.

In recent years an increasing number of political indicators have been constructed and measured (see the *World Handbook of Political and Social Indicators*). For example, political strikes, protest demonstrations, and riots are recorded as indicators of political unrest. However, the number of participants reported in such events is not always reliable, for fear of reprisal. The numbers of political prisoners, tortures, and executions are indicators of the intensity of government repression – but, again, the figures may not be reliable or even available. Military manpower per thousand working-age persons is an indicator of military power – though a weak one unless accompanied by an armament inventory and an evaluation of the servicemen's professional qualifications. And the frequency of involvement in foreign wars, punitive expeditions, and "destabilizing" manoeuvres on foreign soil is an indicator of international aggressiveness. Yet all such indicators are fallible and, though fairly numerous by now, they are still incomplete. For example, we have no figures for the precise degree to which any given great power controls its client states, other than the size of its "aid" in arms and bribes.

2 Government and People: Autocracy to Democracy

Stateless societies have few and simple public affairs, which they manage with voluntary work coordinated by headmen or councils of elders. By contrast, the public affairs of a modern society are so multifarious, voluminous, complex, and expensive that they call for numerous experts – public servants and technologists. The state is not only the custodian and manager of the public goods of a modern society, starting with its territory; it is also the nucleus and powerhouse of the polity, the partner (or predator) of the economy, and the protector (or enemy) of the culture, as well as, ideally, nature's steward.

The contemporary state is a huge (often hypertrophied) system composed of many subsystems (branches, ministries, departments, etc.) that often compete with one another over functions and resources. Every one of these subsystems is expected to discharge a specific function: controlling social behaviour, managing public goods, or addressing social issues of some kind. However, occasionally some of those subsystems, particularly the security forces, attain autonomy and therefore turn into serious social problems instead of solving any. (This is why Mann [1986, 1993] regards the military as a separate "source of power" [powerful agent] on a par with the economy and the ideology. But in the contemporary democratic state the armed forces are led by statesmen and share power with the bureaucracy.) Unless made accountable, watched, and periodically reviewed, all bureaucracies – corporate as well as governmental – may end up by being inefficient, self-serving, and oppressive. Bureaucrats tend to forget that they are servants and that their privileges imply duties, just as the duties of the citizens they are supposed to serve imply rights. (This is a sufficient practical reason for encouraging, in an Aristotelian vein, the joint advancement of political science, political philosophy, and ethics.)

In his classic study of bureaucracy Weber (1922b) noted that democracy leads to bureaucratic power rather than popular power (see also Dahrendorf 1988). And he conjectured that citizens obey bureaucrats because they believe that these represent legitimate power. I submit that both assertions are debatable. The first is a correct historical generalization, but it only concerns political democracy, where everyone is mistrusted and almost anyone may become a bureaucrat; it does not affect integral participative democracy combined with technological expertise. However, there is no empirical evidence for or against this hypothesis. By contrast, Weber's conjecture about the source of obedience to the bureaucracy is empirically testable. Moreover, it has been put to the experimental test (Willer 1987, chap. 6). Not surprisingly, it turns out that bureaucrats are obeyed because they can effectively force people to do certain things against their will – for instance, they can impose fines or worse. That is, *pace* Weber, most people obey the government not out of belief in legitimacy but out of fear or from expediency. Justice is expensive: paying an unjust fine may be cheaper than contesting it.

Politology can be descriptive or normative. The former is expected to account for (describe, explain, or predict) the actual workings of political systems and processes. By contrast, normative political science, which ideally is a branch of sociotechnology, designs or redesigns political systems or processes: it is statecraft. (In his *Discorsi* Machiavelli draws practical morals from his histories.) But, whether descriptive or prescriptive, standard political theory eludes moral questions. For example, it tackles the problem of the political legitimacy of governments, not that of their moral legitimacy.

By contrast, political and moral philosophers, as well as ideologues, raise questions about the morally desirable or undesirable functions of government. As we all know, the answers to these questions cover a broad spectrum, from anarchism to statism (or totalitarianism). Moreover, there are at least two versions of each of these answers. Thus, in principle anarchism and statism can be left-wing or right-wing; conservatism can be mildly progressive or ferociously reactionary; liberalism can be purely political or integral, conservative or progressive; and socialism can be democratic or dictatorial, as well as either purely economic or integral. Can philosophers introduce some order in this apparent chaos, so as to facilitate rational discussion and objective evaluation? They can do so by analysing some key politological ideas, unveiling whatever moral correlates they may have, and debunking ("deconstructing") political rhetoric. And they must question the moral legitimacy of any political order. For example, one should find out and point out the virtues and defects of political democracy. Only an understanding of its values, goals, mechanisms, and limits will allow us to practise, perfect, and defend it.

Let us begin with the role of government. All except anarchists agree that, because of its complexity, every modern society needs a state, and that the latter's role is to manage and deliver public goods. These are things or services that are either indivisible (like public parks), or that cannot normally be administered or delivered by private individuals or business firms, either because they are economically unprofitable (like museums) or because they call for impartiality (like the judiciary) or central coordination (like defence).

The point in dispute is what the public goods should be. Thus, the ultra-conservatives (modern-day libertarians) argue for a minimal state run like a business, because they restrict the commonwealth to public order and, in particular, the protection of property rights. Thus, a champion of the "pure market economy" asserted that the latter "assumes that government, the social apparatus of compulsion and coercion, is intent upon preserving the operation of the market system, abstains from hindering its functioning, and protects it against encroachment on the part of other people" (von Mises 1949, 239). His student Hayek (1979, 65), an adviser to Thatcher and Pinochet, nodded. By contrast, democrats oppose the trend of letting the market rule politics (see Touraine 1994).

Progressive conservatives, such as Adam Smith (1776, bk. 5, chap. 1), add public works and schools to the sphere of public goods. Classical iberals and social democrats add much more, in particular relief programs (e.g., unemployment insurance) and public health care. And, of course, Marxist socialists go even further: they advocate the state control or even ownership of the means of production. In any event, all but the extreme individualists (anarchists both left and right) favour state intervention in the economy and culture to some degree or other.

Interventionist political philosophies have a long pedigree. Here is a tiny random sample. Aristotle (*Politics*, bk. 3, chap. 9, 1279) taught that "a state exists for the sake of a good life." Nearly one century later the Indian emperor Asoka promoted social welfare and spread the *dharma* (principles of right life). Bentham (1789, chap. 7) wanted the state "to promote the happiness of the society." Jefferson (1853–4, 8:165) put it thus: "The care of human life and happiness, and not their destruction, is the first and only legitimate object of good government." And Russell (1960, 54) wrote: "The *primary* aims of government, I suggest, should be three: security, justice [including economic justice], and conservation [of natural resources and cultural treasures]." In short, all enlightened political thinkers, except for the anarchists, have given the state the mandate of enhancing everyone's quality of life by managing and delivering public goods.

I submit that the question about the nature of public goods is part of the broader question, What is a good society? I also suggest that a good or humane society is one where everyone is able to meet his basic needs, is free to realize his legitimate aspirations, and feels compelled to discharge his duties and can get the means to do so (Bunge 1989a; Falk 1995; Galbraith 1996). Some of the roles of the state in such a society are to protect rights and enforce duties; to control social behaviour; to protect natural resources from private greed; to support science, the humanities, and the arts; to facilitate universal access to health care, education, and culture; to set standards of safety, public education, and health care; to stimulate political participation; to encourage cooperation and manage competition; and to control whatever is likely to have an impact on society, from mining and logging to technology. Such is the public-service state: one facilitating everyone's endeavour to enjoy life and help live. Though imperfect, it is perfectible.

Let us now look at the state as regards its "power sources" (most powerful agents) in the light of the foregoing. We distinguish six main types of state: theocratic (church → state), military (armed forces → state), fascist (big business → party → state), Stalinist (party elite→ state), democratic capitalist (people and business → state), and integrally democratic (people and co-operatives → state). (For a different classification and a detailed analysis see Crick 1971, chap. 4).

The first four have failed on all counts. The fifth, capitalist democracy, has so far been the most successful, but it coexists with the economic dictatorship of the very rich as well as with international inequities and conflicts. And admittedly integral democracy – that is, biological, economic, political, and cultural – is still only an ideal. However, this ideal may eventually spawn a political movement justifiable on moral grounds. This is because, unlike its rivals, (a) it does not involve the domination of any privileged group, and (b) it does not tell people how they should live, but just helps them pursue happiness as they see fit and as long as this pursuit does not harm others. We shall take a closer look at several social orders in chapter 10. Let us now discuss the place of democracy in the ladder of political development.

A politologist's conception of the degree of political development of a people depends on his own image of the ideal polity. If he favours only representative democracy, he is likely to equate political development with increasing electoral enfranchisement, the normal functioning of a multi-party system, and free elections at regular intervals. However, normal elections, though necessary, are insufficient for the following reasons: (a) the voter is offered options that he may not have proposed, and that may not be in his interest to favour – which may result in his abstention; (b) voting is episodic and it may result only in empowering a self-perpetuating political class: the voters are "citizens for a day and subjects for four years" (Jouvenel 1993, 288); (c) when in the hands of professional politicians, political parties may be mere electoral machines or tools of special-interest groups; and (d) in some countries, notably the United States, running for office is so expensive that candidates seek the backing of special groups in exchange for the promise of furthering their interests. Although representative democracy is morally and practically superior to dictatorship, it is only a beginning of total democracy, which involves the permanent participation of the entire citizenry in the entire political process: see chapter 10, section 8. (Caution: participative democracy ≠ direct democracy. The latter is possible only in small groups: large numbers require representation. See, for example, Bobbio 1991.)

Whoever equates democracy with self-government will ask, *Who votes where, for what, and how*? From this broad perspective, the student intent on assessing the level of democratic development of a society will look at steady (not just episodic) and voluntary participation and free contestation in both policy and decision-making matters leading to the formation, upkeep, or reform of governmental, paragovernmental, and nongovernmental organizations both political and nonpolitical. In principle, participation may be small, middling, or large, and it may or may not be come with freedom to compete for different political programs and offices. Hence we need some definitions.

Schumpeter (1950, 269) viewed democracy as a procedure "for arriving at political decisions in which individuals acquire the power to decide by means of a competitive struggle for the people's vote." (This has been dogma since the 1970s: Huntington 1991, 6.) By placing procedure before substance, the Schumpeterians forget that politicians are elected to manage public goods in the public interest. Hence, they will condone regimes where elections are periodic and clean, but the voters are prodded by the local bosses and the representatives serve the interests of the powerful. Thus, India's procedural democracy would be on the same level as Sweden's.

By contrast, Dahl (1971) has championed what he calls *polyarchy*: a combination of free contestation with popular participation – which alone gives the *demos* a chance. Note that these two components are separable. Thus, in capitalist democracies there is ample freedom to compete for public office but weak popular participation. Worse still, in the US, both in polls and in social surveys, "[t]he voices of the well educated and the well heeled sound more loudly" (Verba 1996, 4). In other words, the *res publica* is being privatized;

hence the need to preserve the equality–public good–contestation–freedom quadruple.

The separability and mutual complementarity of participation and freedom suggests that democratic political development be gauged by the pair <*degree of voluntary participation, degree of liberty of contestation*>. Whereas the first component of this couple is cooperative, the second is competitive. In other words, polyarchy (or participative democracy) combines cooperation for the common good with competition for individual or group advancement. And it is unique in combining top-down with bottom-up control, thus constituting a feedback loop – a necessary condition for the orderly development of the body politic. (See a compatible alternative in Tilly 1996.)

Both components of participative democracy, namely participation and freedom, come in degrees. To set up a quantitative concept of democracy we may proceed as follows (Bunge 1985b). We gauge the extent to which citizens participate freely and effectively in (α) determining both the long-term *goals* of their society (in particular of their government) and the *means* to attain such goals, and (β) making *decisions* (as voters, elected office-holders, or volunteers) affecting the various social groups. Various combinations of α and β are possible. Examples: All citizens participate about equally in both α and β (participative democracy); all adults participate in α but delegate β to special bodies (representative democracy); an elite monopolizes α but nearly everybody participates in β (populist dictatorship); or a ruling group monopolizes both α and β (authoritarianism).

Let us agree to assign the same weight to the two aspects α and β distinguished above, and call A and B respectively the number of citizens participating in them. Then the following *index of political democracy* can be introduced:

$$\Delta = (A + B - N)/N,$$

where N is the total number of adults in the given society. Δ varies between -1 (autocracy) and $+1$ (participative democracy). Here are some typical values:

Autocracy ("Obey me")	$A + B = 1 \Rightarrow \Delta = (1 - N)/N \to -1$
Totalitarianism ("Obey us")	$A, B \ll N \Rightarrow \Delta \cong -N/N = -1$
Populist dictatorship ("Follow me")	$A \ll N, B = N \Rightarrow \Delta \cong A/N > 0$ but $\ll 1$
Representative democracy ("Elect us")	$A = N, B < N \Rightarrow \Delta = B/N > 0$ but $\ll 1$
Participative democracy ("Let's govern")	$A = B = N \Rightarrow \Delta = N/N = 1$

Note that representative democracy (freedom without participation) gets a low mark, namely nearly 0, the same as populist dictatorship (participation without freedom). This should come as no surprise: civic rights without duties should not rank higher than civic duties without rights. In a just society rights imply duties and conversely (Bunge 1989a).

The upshot is that, if the above index of political democracy is accepted, participative democracy is the ticket. However, it does not suffice to build a good society, for democratic politics ought to be only a means to enhance everyone's quality of life in every respect – biopsychological, economic, and cultural. Participative democracy should be a component of *integral democracy*, the other components of which are biological, economic, and cultural democracy. In other words, integral democracy extends political democracy to all social spheres. It boils down to freedom to enjoy all the resources of society, as well as to the right and the duty to participate in social activities, subject only to the limitations imposed by the rights of others. (More in chap. 10.) This brings us to the matter of rights and duties, which lies at the intersection of political science and ethics.

Authoritarians are long on duties but short on rights, whereas libertarians adopt the opposite stance. In particular, the former want to suppress dissent whereas the latter wish to minimize duties. I submit that both views are morally objectionable. Indeed, the emphasis on duties at the expense of rights crushes the individual, whereas the focus on individual rights justifies selfishness. Moreover, as Tocqueville (1835 part 2, chap. 2) noted, radical individualism destroys civic virtue. (See also Bellah et al. 1985). Furthermore, both authoritarianism and individualism, in weakening the social bonds through undermining solidarity, are socially dissoving. To a just person rights and duties come in pairs: every right entails a duty and conversely. For example, my right to vote entails my duty to cast a well-informed ballot; and the taxes I pay entitle me to a share in the public goods.

Postulating that rights and burdens come in pairs amounts to stating that justice amounts to the balance of freedom and responsibility. My freedom to do X is limited by my responsibility to see to it that my doing X does not prevent others from meeting their basic needs. And my responsibility for Y involves my free access to the means required to discharge my duty with regard to Y without seriously jeopardizing my own well-being.

Now, I cannot exercise my rights and discharge my duties unless I have or can get the means to do so. If I am destitute, then others will take advantage of me, perhaps to the point of buying some of my rights (as in the cases of voluntary slavery, marriage of convenience, and the sale of blood, organs, or votes). My rights will be safeguarded only if I live among equals. And – according to the reference-group hypothesis – my burdens will not overwhelm me provided they are not heavier than other people's. In other words, only equality guarantees the free exercise of rights and the fair discharging of duties, and only freedom makes it possible to safeguard equality. Shorter: Freedom is possible only among equals, and equality is possible only among the free. But, since neither member of this pair can be total, trade-offs between them must be negotiated.

It follows that, far from having to opt between liberty and equality – as libertarians enjoin us to do – we should combine them, for equality ensures the free
exercise of rights and a fair distribution of duties; and in turn freedom makes it
possible to attain or defend equality. Equality and freedom are thus on a par, and
they are means as well as ends. By contrast, the concentration of political and
cultural power ends up by destroying whatever economic equality there may
have been at the beginning; and the concentration of wealth hinders the attainment of political and cultural freedom. Once postponed for the sake of freedom,
equality gets lost – until the next rebellion. And once postponed for the sake of
equality, freedom gets lost – until the next uprising. Not surprisingly, the noble
devise of the French Revolution – *Liberté, égalité, fraternité* – is the only political slogan to have survived, at least on paper, for two centuries. It also summarizes the ideal of integral democracy, which I take to be the highest stage in
political development.

Our next question is whether there is room for a political elite – that is, leadership – in an integral democracy. Whether primitive or advanced, democratic
or authoritarian, every social system breeds and needs leaders capable of proposing vision and direction, as well as exerting moral or legal coercion. It
breeds them because some individuals are better endowed, placed, or motivated
to lead (e.g., more competent, dedicated, ambitious, or crafty) than others; and
it needs them to gain direction and avoid confusion. A leader may trigger or
stem a social (political, economic, or cultural) process. He may do so by
embracing popular causes, proposing large-scale actions, or mobilizing people
and resources. But even if he manages to wield huge clout, a leader can do only
so much – which is just as well. Leaders propose: society disposes.

Some important political changes have been brought about by a combination
of grass-roots leadership with (domestic or foreign) state power. For example,
the democratization of the ex–German Democratic Republic (DDR) during the
last months of 1989 went roughly as follows: First in Leipzig and a few other
cities there were some small street demonstrations that were repressed by the
government (bottom-up and top-down actions). Second, the Soviet government,
too weak to shore up the DDR government, advised it to ease up on those
movements, and to introduce some democratic reforms (top-top action). Third,
the new-found liberties encouraged the leaders of small opposition groups to
organize mass rallies (top-middle-bottom), fuelled by mouth-watering promises
of the West German government. Fourth, the huge success of these demonstrations forced the DDR government to resign (bottom-up action). Needless to say,
such multilevel analysis is possible only in a systemic perspective.

What characterizes democracy is not the absence of elites but (a) free competition for leadership positions; (b) responsiveness to social issues and popular

demands; (c) accountability; (d) explicit and clear rules limiting the power of leaders; and (e) teamwork. In an advanced democracy the leaders sit at the centre of the power network rather than on top of it. And in a technodemocracy the leaders resort to social science rather than myth, as well as to rational debate and persuasion rather than deceit or sloganeering.

Finally, what is democracy to do with its enemies? Obviously, these should enjoy freedom of speech. But, since democracy is supposed to protect dissent, it can tolerate neither public hate speech nor actions aiming at suppressing dissent. Democracy should work and fight for its own preservation instead of going quietly to the gallows. In politics, as in science, boundless tolerance is just as intolerable as total intolerance.

3 Rational-Choice Politology

Politicians and journalists know that political allegiances and actions are prompted by a combination of affective and cognitive factors. In particular, the success of charismatic crooks and the survival of obsolete political ideologies and strategies should be reminders that all is not reason in politics. Moreover, some experiments suggest that, in battles for public support, appeals to emotions usually win (Kuklinski et al. 1991). One crafty TV spot is likely to win more votes than a hundred technical reports. This is the price we pay for unenlightened public opinion and non-participative democracy.

Notwithstanding the clear evidence for the power of emotion and prejudice in politics, politologists in growing numbers are toying with rational-choice models of political behaviour (see, for instance, Booth et al. 1993). These models are attractive for their apparent rigour, alleged generality, and manifest simplicity. But the rigour is not there, for, as will be shown below, those models involve arbitrary figures. The generality is deceptive, having been attained at the expense of depth. (For example, Olson [1993] claims that one and the same hypothesis – namely, that people are motivated exclusively by self-interest – accounts for both autocracy and democracy.) As for simplicity, it is not the seal of truth, for reality is complex (Bunge 1963). In particular, political decision-making processes are extremely complex. For instance, as Weber noted, the masses are likely to follow charismatic (populist) leaders instead of engaging in rational calculation. And many successful leaders are not very rational either, for they tend to be swayed by obsolete ideologies or to follow the advice of individuals, parties, or lobbies obsessed with a single issue, such as re-election, national security, abortion, or the containment of inflation at all costs – that is, at the cost of all. Besides, governments are mixtures of groups with somewhat different goals rather than unitary actors (recall sect. 2, and see Mann 1993).

As even a casual perusal of the *American Political Science Review* shows, the most fashionable rational-choice models of political life are couched in game-theoretic terms. At first sight game theory is an attractive alternative to neoclassical microeconomics, for unlike the latter it does not postulate the mutual independence of the agents. On the contrary, a correct assumption of the theory is that every individual action depends on what the agent believes the other "players" (partners or adversaries) are likely to do. Consequently, it makes room for both conflict and cooperation. This is why game theory is often hailed as *the* theory of both conflict and cooperation.

A consequence of the postulated interdependence of all the "players" in a "game" is that the utility of every one of them depends upon the utilities of the others. At first blush this seems reasonable enough. But game theory does not question the mathematical status of utility functions; it assumes both individualism and maximizing behaviour; it includes no robust findings of psychology or social science; and it makes no room for either causation or political debate. No wonder then that it fails to deliver what it promises, namely a mathematically well-defined, general, and realistic theory of social processes. (See also Rapoport 1968; Luke 1985; Bunge 1989b, 1991a; and Green and Shapiro 1994.)

Let us take a quick look at the case of international conflict. According to most game-theory experts, antagonism is best modelled as a constant-sum game, that is, one in which one side's losses are the other's gains. But this is the view of the pre-nuclear military, who could think only in terms of one-sided victory or defeat. A political scientist should know better: he should know that in an all-out war both sides stand to sustain heavy unforeseen losses of many kinds. Furthermore, in this case third parties – particularly if neutral or only lightly involved – may gain (or lose) much more than either of the main combatants. Worse yet, the victor may be left weaker than before – as was the case with Great Britain and France at the end of both world wars. Hence, building 2×2 payoff matrices to model modern warfare is just a simple-minded parlor game with only tenuous links to reality.

The game-theoretic models of international relations are not just simplistic: they are also quite arbitrary. So much so that, whereas one political scientist will model an international crisis as a prisoner's dilemma, another may model the same crisis as a game of chicken (brinkmanship). Moreover, "[i]t is quite possible for a crisis to be a prisoner's dilemma for one party and chicken for the other" (Snyder 1971, 91). The same author tells us (p. 93) that "[i]t is perhaps an open question whether the Cuban missile crisis [of 1962] was chicken or prisoner's dilemma for the United States." If the very choice of game is so arbitrary, what is the point of discussing any games at all?

One root of this arbitrariness lies in the utilities and disutilities involved in most applications of game theory. For example, suppose that a two-party nuclear confrontation were to be modelled as a prisoner's dilemma game, where each party adopts either of two strategies: cooperate (e.g., negotiate) or defect (e.g., strike), which shall be called C and D respectively. The pay-off matrix has the general structure

	C	D
C	<C,C>	<C,D>
D	<D,C>	<D,D>,

where the entry <C,D> is to be interpreted "Row cooperates, Column defects," and similarly the other entries. How does one assign numerical values, whether absolute or relative, to the entries of this matrix? In the original example, involving two prisoners held incommunicado, the judge determines (negative) pay-offs according to the law of the land: they are prison terms. But in political games there is neither law nor judge: there are only stipulations, guesses, wishes, and ideological blinkers. That is, the utilities are chosen a priori. Consider three such possible choices: hawkish ($\mathcal{H}$), doveish ($\mathcal{D}$), and realist ($\mathcal{R}$):

$\mathcal{H}$	C	D	$\mathcal{D}$	C	D	$\mathcal{R}$	C	D
C	<0,0>	<0,1>	C	<1,1>	<0,0>	C	<1,1>	<0,$\frac{1}{2}$>
D	<1,0>	<$\frac{1}{2}$,$\frac{1}{2}$>	D	<0,0>	<0,0>	D	<$\frac{1}{2}$,0>	<$\frac{1}{2}$,$\frac{1}{2}$>

Where do these numbers come from: experience or computation? Neither. They are assigned a priori. Indeed, they only *define* what is meant by a hawkish, doveish, or realistic strategy. In other words, the strategy is not a *result* of a game-theoretic model or analysis but its premise: one begins by assuming a solution to the problem – one *begs the question*. Thus, the game-theoretic approach to the study of politics is aprioristic, hence nonscientific. Consequently, while a game-theoretic model may well describe (in a simplistic fashion) a simple situation, it can neither explain nor foresee its outcome. Nor, a fortiori, does it have any use for planning a course of rational action. Yet game theorists claim that their approach to conflict situations teaches valuable lessons – only, there is no agreement on which these may be. Thus, whereas most theorists hold that defection is the best strategy, a few claim that cooperation is the best, and still others that a combination of the two is optimal. At best, game theory only provides a neutral if poor language or foil for such discussions.

Iterated games are somewhat more promising than single-shot games, for modelling (or rather simulating) processes rather than events. The best-known application of iterated prisoner's dilemma games is the attempt to explain the emergence of cooperation as a result of the consistent use of the tit-for-tat (TFT) strategy (Axelrod and Hamilton 1981; Axelrod 1984). Following this strategy, Row cooperates in the first move and watches Column's response. If Column too cooperates, then Row behaves loyally; otherwise he "defects," that is, counterattacks – and so on. But this strategy turns out to be unstable (Boyd and Loberbaum 1987). Worse: lions, supposedly the paragons of cooperation as well as of courage, sometimes lag behind their fighting partners, thus refuting this simplistic game-theoretic model (Heinsohn and Packer 1995).

(The original argument was this. Consider a sequence of n encounters, every one with gain g and probability p – which makes sense only for chance encounters. The expected gain of either TFT player over the course of n random encounters is

$$G_n = (1 + p + p^2 + \dots + p^n)\, g = g\,(1 - p^n)/(1 - p) \approx g/(1 - p) > g.$$

That is, the TFT strategy would seem to guarantee equal gains for both players, whence it is in their own interest to abide by it. But the assumptions that p and g are constant down the road are unrealistic. Indeed, the gain from each encounter is likely to depend upon the gain from the previous one, and it has got a probability only if random. If these factors are taken into account, TFT proves to be an unstable strategy.)

Nowak and Sigmund (1993) have further noted that TFT is not robust. In fact, it is vulnerable to unavoidable errors in the mutual "perceptions" or "interpretations" of the contender's behaviour. They propose an alternative strategy, which they call Pavlov and that, besides being robust, is based on the well-known psychological law that animals perform more rewarded than unrewarded behaviours. The Pavlov strategy is summed up in the rule "Win-stay, lose-shift." That is, cooperate if both players either cooperated or defected in the last round, and defect otherwise.

Kitcher (1993a) has proposed an even more realistic strategy that incorporates the possibility of opting out of the game – that is, of remaining neutral – and one whereby each player takes into account not only his own interest but also his contender's (or partner's). Moreover, computer simulation shows that individuals who adopt the optional strategy tend to cooperate more often than do animals playing the standard compulsory variant (Batali and Kitcher 1995). Whereas this finding is encouraging to those of us who believe in the possibility and desirability of combining freedom with cooperation, it must be kept in mind that it holds only for the prisoner's dilemma game, which is a highly idealized model of real-life situations. Moreover, here again, if one *assumes* both pay-off matrix and strategy, then such and such trend (e.g., cooperation) emerges in a population.

Game theory cannot *prove* that any given strategy, or some combination of them, is always superior to others in every respect – for example, the enemy's undoing, mutual benefit, stability, robustness, or what not. The reason is that the efficiency of every strategy depends critically upon the pay-offs (and probabilities) involved, and these are usually *unknown* – this being why they are *assumed*. By conveniently juggling with numbers one may "prove" almost anything. In particular, one may "prove" that "rational" (selfish) actors always attempt to maximize their own gains – or else maximize others' pain even at their own expense, as in Samson's Choice (Lichbach 1990). Likewise, Hirshleifer and Martínez-Coll (1988) claimed that sometimes either of the strategies "Always defect" and "Always cooperate" yields better results than TFT. Regrettably, their alleged proof rests on starting off with suitable pay-off matrices. And politologists who favour nuclear deterrence have used game theory to "prove" that mutual defection is the best strategy, well knowing that it may lead to mutual destruction (see, for instance, Campbell 1985). But of course by positing the utilities occurring in the payoff matrix they only "prove" what they have assumed.

What then is the possible function of decision-theoretic and particularly game-theoretic models of social processes? Let us listen to a master. First, "these models are at their best as exercises in mind stretching. They are seldom helpful in the construction of either descriptive or normative theories of human behavior in concrete social situations" (Rapoport 1990, 508). Second, these models, particularly the prisoner's dilemma, warn us against falling into the "social traps" into which we are dragged in the pursuit of self-interest – Adam Smith's "hidden hand" notwithstanding (Rapoport 1989a, chap. 14). Third, many such models "were most likely offered as *rationales* for proffered decisions, not as *bases* for rational decisions. Prognoses of war were couched in the language of probability to make it appear as if the principle of 'calculated risk' (a prestige phrase) guided the proffered decision" (Rapoport 1980, 51). Fourth, certain games have been used to design experiments to study animal and human behaviour. One finding of these experiments is that, when the participants are given the chance of playing repeatedly the same game, they usually adopt the less aggressive ("rational") strategy, that is, either unconditional or conditional cooperation. (See, for example, Milinski 1987 for stickleback and cichlid fish; and Rapoport 1989a for people.)

In conclusion, although game theory does not describe, explain, or predict political behaviour, it has some heuristic and analytic value. In particular, it may serve to (a) pose problems and display, analyse, and compare strategies, and (b) set up experimental situations to study the propensity of animals (in particular humans) to cooperate, defect, or cheat. (Ironically, game theory has proved far more useful in biology than in social studies, where it was born. This is because in biology "utility" is replaced with "Darwinian fitness," and "rationality" with "evolutionary stability" – both objective features [Maynard Smith 1982].)

Game theory involves too many oversimplifications and arbitrary posits to be able to fit any real-life social interactions, in particular international conflicts. Hence, it serves neither descriptive nor normative purposes. Worse still: unlike scientific theories, which can be revised by altering, dropping, or adding some hypotheses, game theory is so poor that it cannot afford to be plastic. Consequently, its ruin is not a monument worth being preserved in textbooks – except as a warning against apriorism and simplism.

What holds for the game-theoretic approach to politics also holds, *mutatis mutandis*, for the entire rational-choice approach. (For details see Bunge 1995a, 1995b, and 1996a.) Read or watch the news any day, and you will doubt that our most powerful political rulers and their supporters are "rational" in any of the many senses of the word. Here, governments continue to stockpile weapons while poverty, sickness, and illiteracy keep worsening. There, nations blessed with ethnic and cultural diversity burst at largely imaginary ethnic seams while their peoples do not have enough to eat or read. Almost everywhere politicians swear by moth-eaten economic and political doctrines that inspire disastrous environmental, economic, and cultural policies. And we, the voters, are taken in again and again by incompetent or dishonest professional politicians – or, worse, we do not bother to do anything about it. Are these instances of rationality? If not, what is the point of rational-choice models other than to maximize paper spoilage?

In sum, the rational-choice models in political science raise more problems than they solve. Although they have occasionally stimulated interesting new ways of looking at political systems and processes, they have failed to deliver realistic models that can be used to analyse effective policies, let alone design any. Last, but not least, the rational-choice approach to politics is elitist in seeking "the best" policy irrespective of public opinion – which must be kept in the dark if the policy is to be implemented.

4 Public-Choice and Social-Choice Theories

Let us now examine a different though related approach to politics, that of the public-choice school, gathered around J.M. Buchanan, G. Tullock, and the *Public Choice* journal. This school regards politics, particularly domestic politics, as an economic activity and, moreover, a rather dirty one. Hence, it exemplifies economic imperialism – much as Marx, Schumpeter, Beard, and F.C. Lane did in their own ways. (Recall chap. 2, sect. 5.)

The central thesis of this school stems from Anthony Downs's 1957 classic *An Economic Theory of Democracy*. The idea is that the political arena is nothing but the "market" of public goods, and that this market obeys the laws of all markets – whichever these may be. The sellers would be the politicians and the consumers the voters. The former promise to deliver certain goods, but their real goal is to reap the rewards of public office. By voting for a politician who promises to deliver good X, the citizen freely chooses to "buy" X, under the illusion that he thereby advances his own interests, while actually he is unwittingly supporting a parasitic class. (See Buchanan 1975; Buchanan and Tullock 1962; and Buchanan and Tollison 1972.)

The reduction of the polity to a market of sorts faces the following objections. First, it misses the marrow of politics, which is the struggle for, and exercise of, political power – which happens to involve passion and ideology, persuasion and coercion. Second, by treating voters as consumers, economicism makes a mockery of political debate and action, which are of the essence of democracy. Indeed, under democracy the citizen can protest and attempt to influence the political attitudes of his fellow citizens. By ignoring this option, economicism fails to explain why people who have no political aspirations support or even join political movements.

This is not to say that the polity is independent of the economy: we all know that money can hire advertising experts, buy TV spots, bribe politicians and civil servants; and that many people vote with their wallets. But it is one thing to admit that the polity is intimately connected with the economy, whence politologists should not overlook the economic factors, and quite another to include the political sphere in the economic one, and thus turn political science into a chapter of economics.

In addition to reducing politics to an economic activity, the public-choice school asserts that (a) individual voters are manipulated by politicians who favour special-interest groups represented by lobbies; and (b) all big governments are wasteful and primarily interested in the welfare of the state bureaucracy and the political class. The remedy for (a) would be to replace simple majority rule with something close to consensus or unanimity. The remedy for (b) would be to downsize government, and particularly to eliminate social services, which some conservatives call 'the human betterment industry.'

One problem with this view is that (a) and (b) are mutually inconsistent. Indeed, if all our elected representatives really defend special interests, then the government they form cannot be primarily self-serving – for, if it were, their bagmen would not solicit and obtain generous campaign contributions from those special-interest groups. A second conceptual problem is this. The rationale of the public-choice school may be compressed into the following reasoning:

Governments are composed of individuals.

All individuals act from self-interest.

Ergo, governments are self-serving.

The major premise is a truism. But, since it concerns only the composition of the state, while keeping silent about its structure and environment, it suggests that the state is just a collection of individuals – as if membership in a government department did not largely determine the bureaucrat's behaviour, and as if the state did not have (emergent) properties that its members lack – such as social policies and the monopolies on taxation, legal violence, and foreign relations.

The minor premise of the above argument is false. Indeed, individuals act not only from self-interest but also from habit or from a sense of duty, out of fear or hatred, solidarity or compassion, and occasionally are driven by curiosity or by ideals. Moreover, a public servant who were to serve only his private interests would soon be sacked, if only because he would be a burden to his colleagues. The traditional British, German, or French public servant serves not only the rulers of his country but also the public interest, reminding his political boss of his obligations under the law. In any event, he is no less public-spirited than his counterpart in the private sector.

Not surprisingly, the conclusion of the argument is equally false. First, the most powerful modern economies, particularly the American, French, German, and Japanese, were built with the active help of their respective governments. Second, in poor countries, where four out of five humans happen to live, the state is the only organization with sufficient funds, credit, and power to undertake large-scale projects of public interest. Third, the modern state is not a solid block, but is composed of a number of rather loosely linked departments that are often at loggerheads with one another. Because of such heterogeneity it is simplistic and unfair to pass value judgments about any given government as a whole.

Aside from these conceptual problems there are three practical problems with the public-choice school. One is that consensus can only be achieved in comparatively small communities with intense popular participation, such as the Amerindian communities. In modern society the consensus rule would often lead to paralysis or worse. Something near consensus could work only as a result of a profound social reform, involving a radical decrease in social inequalities, decentralization, and a combination of technical expertise with popular participation in addition to representation. But this is the last thing the public-choice school would like to see, for it is staunchly conservative.

A second practical problem with the political project of the public-choice school is that it is utopian. Indeed, political reform is not just a matter of political arithmetic and constitutional reform. The legislator cannot write the new constitution on a clean slate suspended in a social vacuum without a history (Albert 1985). Or are we talking about revolution rather than constitution?

A third and even more serious problem is that a drastic shrinking of the size and power of the state would entail eliminating most if not all of the public services now expected from any civilized government. Such change should be welcome only if it were compensated for by a thousand-fold strengthening of self-reliant cooperatives and non-profit organizations of all kinds. But the public-choice school advocates the replacement of the relief ("welfare") state with one restricted to providing only the legal framework for the operation of the free market – that is, strictly a law-and-order government. Why should the ordinary rational voter "buy" a political program so obviously geared to the interests of the few who stand to benefit (in the short run) from turning back the social clock?

The preceding criticism does not entail rejecting the public-choice school as a whole, for it does contain a few truths and some valuable advice. One of its merits has been to stress the intimate coupling between the modern state and the economy. It is true that Marx, Keynes, the Myrdals, Galbraith, Prebisch, Hirschman, Lindblom, Sen, and a few others have said much the same, but this does not detract from that merit. Still, one should not exaggerate the link between the political and the economic systems, for they are distinct and each has its own specific functions. Moreover, when politics weds business we get such monsters as corrupt governments, ruinous nationalized industries, and the military-industrial complex. (For an early analysis of the latter in Germany during the First World War see Weber's little-known 1918 [1988b] essay on socialism.) The aim of good government is not private profit but genuine social welfare – rather than relief, which only masks and perpetuates social injustice. Hence, running hospitals or jails, schools or museums as if they were grocery stores would be as preposterous as treating brain tumours like bunions.

A second contribution of the public-choice school is to have shown that, since simple majority is required to pass most bills, it suffices that five lobbies, each representing 10 per cent of the citizenry, join forces. In this way political democracy can work against the general welfare (see also Galbraith 1992). However, this shows only that political democracy, though necessary, is insufficient to protect the rights of the greatest number: we should work for integral democracy, or self-government with equity in all domains, as will be argued in chapters 10 and 11.

It is also important to have insisted that the state should be in the service of the public, not the other way round; and that one condition for doing so is to trim it, if only because large vessels are hard to steer. However, the democratic alternative is not to eliminate overnight the bureaucracy and the social programs – let alone to market votes, as Buchanan and Tullock have proposed. Rather, it is (a) to increase voter power (as recommended by the public-choice school itself); (b) to increase public participation in all domains; (c) to render relief programs gradually unnecessary, by redistributing equitably wealth and power; and (d) to foster the growth of non-governmental organizations of all kinds. Again, integral democracy is the ticket.

Finally, it is important to have stated (though not proved) that certain social programs in the United States have been instituted for purely electoral purposes, with disregard for their long-term consequences and in isolation from one another rather than in a systemic manner. However, I submit that the remedy for this is not across-the-board privatization but a combination of integral democracy with sociotechnology, a synthesis involving long-term participative and largely decentralized planning.

In conclusion, public-choice theory has the merit of having tackled some thorny issues in domestic politics, as well as the defects of adopting the economicist approach and of putting down social justice. It has delivered a realistic diagnosis of some of the flaws of the liberal state, but has exaggerated the adverse (in particular inflationary) effects of social programs (see M.R. Smith 1992). And the cure it prescribes is worse than the disease.

Let us now turn to an altogether different rational-choice theory, namely *social* (or *collective*) *choice theory* (see, for instance, Arrow 1951; Sen 1970a, 1987; and Bonner 1986). This is a theory of collective decision making, the kind of decision allegedly effected by the free market, as well as by such collective bodies as committees and constituencies. In effect, like public-choice theory, this one straddles economics and politology. And it too is normative rather than descriptive: it is offered as a policy tool to devise voting schemes, social programs, and the like.

Social-choice theory departs from other rational-choice models in that it is concerned exclusively with what may be called prohairetic rationality, that is, the completeness, reflexivity, and transitivity of preferences: it neither assumes nor prescribes utility maximization. But, insofar as it involves utility functions, social-choice theory is open to the technical objections raised elsewhere (e.g., Bunge 1996a). If anything, it makes things worse by assuming the existence of a welfare functional W supposed to aggregate the individual utilities u_i of the n

members of the society concerned: that is, $W = f(u_1, u_2, \ldots u_n)$. Since normally the independent variables u_i are undefined, so is W itself: it is the shadow cast by a ghost.

Fortunately, nearly all of social-choice theory can be stated and applied without utility functions. In fact, it can be couched exclusively in terms of preference relations. Its aim is to map individual preferences into social rankings. These mappings are called 'collective choice' or 'social welfare' functions (SWF). The input of a SWF is a set of propositions of the form "Individual i prefers social state A to social state B"; and the output is a set of propositions of the form "Social state X is collectively preferable to social state Y."

As hinted above, the rationale of the theory is to equip policy makers with an exact tool enabling them to make rational decisions in agreement with the wishes of the majority. Being rational, such decisions should be binding on all rational agents, thus rendering debate and bargaining superfluous. A technocracy would thus be able to implement democracy, or even to replace it. It would spare us the bother of arguing, attending political meetings and rallies, marching, and walking to the polling station: everyone could phone in or e-mail his choice. Politics would be lived in an aseptic political "cyberspace" complete with a "virtual political reality" nicely designed by a programmer-politologist.

For better or for worse this goal has proved elusive, for social-choice theory was sparked off by a paradox and has culminated in another, whence it is useless as a policy tool. Indeed, the triggering paradox is Condorcet's, and the centrepiece of the theory is Arrow's General Impossibility Theorem. According to the latter no rational and democratic procedure is possible. This negative result has been staple food for thought for thousands of scholars over nearly half a century. One cause of its popularity is that it is widely, albeit erroneously, believed to be the social counterpart of the Heisenberg and Gödel theorems.

A classical illustration of Arrow's theorem (1951) is one of the paradoxes of voting, first discovered by Condorcet in 1785. Consider three citizens who, when asked to express their preferences among three social states (or issues or candidates), A, B, and C, come up with the following rankings:

Voter 1 $A > B > C$
Voter 2 $B > C > A$
Voter 3 $C > A > B$

Clearly, A is twice preferred to B, which in turn dominates C twice – but C beats A twice too. That is, the collective ranking is cyclical: A > B > C > A. Hence, the transitivity that characterizes individual rational preferences is lost in social or collective choice. (This is a sad case of submergence – the opposite of emergence. A reactionary is likely to interpret it as confirming the thesis of the inferiority of the "crowd mentality.") Moreover, in this example every option obtains two votes: *A* those of persons 1 and 3; *B* those of 1 and 2; and *C* those of 2 and 3. This stalemate is said to paralyse the democratic process. And so it does unless the voters are open to argument, bargaining, or bribing, particularly if they are given a second chance to vote and form coalitions – as, for example, in France and Italy.

Arrow's impossibility theorem generalizes the above paradox and states that there is no social-welfare function (SWF), or collective-choice rule satisfying jointly certain mild and allegedly self-evident conditions. Stated somewhat loosely, these read as follows.

1. *Unrestricted domain*: For every (logically) possible set of individual orderings there exists a SWF.

2. *Weak Pareto principle*: For any two social states *A* and *B*, if everyone prefers *A* to *B*, then society (or government) too should prefer *A* to *B*.

3. *Independence of irrelevant alternatives*: Social choice depends only upon the orderings of the individuals over the given alternatives, and not on irrelevant alternatives.

4. *Non-dictatorship*: There is no individual whose choice the others must follow regardless of their preferences.

On closer inspection none of these conditions proves to be obvious, mild, or realistic. Condition 1 is unrealistic because in the real world preferences are limited: they are determined by a rather small number of factors, such as basic needs and aspirations, as well as occupation, position in a social network, and cultural background – so much so that a knowledge of these factors is often sufficient to predict the agent's choice. Therefore, there is no need to demand that every SWF accommodate all logically possible sets of individual orderings. Only realistic orderings, such as preferring full employment to handouts or the welfare state to raw capitalism, need be considered.

Condition 2 is threatened as soon as experts are given any say – as they always are in any modern state. (After all, the ancient demagogic saying *Vox populi, vox dei* can work well only with a fully informed and public-spirited citizenry.) Even if every individual were to prefer social state *A* to state *B*, the experts might offer solid grounds for the converse preference – or even for a new option *C*. In such case, an enlightened government informs the public, conducting hearings and organizing public debates, before asking it to vote. Or it might circumvent voting, as was the case with compulsory education and vaccination.

Condition 3 focuses on goals while overlooking the means (resources and strategies) for bringing about a desired social state. Indeed, since the domain of an SWF contains no information regarding such means, its output must ignore them as well – which leaves the decision maker without guidance or, worse, with a free rein. For example, the public may be asked whether it wants to improve its standard of living, but not whether this goal is to be attained through increased productivity, tax hikes, or plundering other nations.

The condition 4 of free choice is unrealistic as well. As a matter of fact, some of our basic preferences are distorted by a number of factors, from propaganda to arm twisting, from powerlessness to commitment.

In short, the hypotheses of Arrow's theorem are unrealistic. No wonder then that the theorem itself, and indeed the theory as a whole, has made no impact on political life (Tullock 1967). In particular, it has not discouraged anyone from engaging in democratic politics. At most, it is a reminder that that a one-shot election may result in a tie – a problem that is easily resolved by calling a second election. It is also a reminder that, in a mature science, when one derives a theorem that flies in the face of the available evidence, one normally re-examines the hypotheses of the theorem, relaxing some of them and altering or dropping others to avoid the unwanted result. This is in fact what uncounted students of social choice have been doing for several decades – to no avail.

One such revision is Riley's (1985), who undertook to alter Arrow's axiom system in order to remove the doubts it casts on democracy. Riley's version of liberalism is not libertarian but social-democratic, for it involves the principle of distributive justice that everyone must make only choices whose consequences promote his (and everyone else's) security or self-protection. Although I happen to agree with this principle, I believe that Riley has spoiled it by treating it in the spirit of social-choice theory and introducing a social-welfare functional defined on individual utility functions – themselves undefined. It is possible to give up this ghost while keeping the substance of Riley's axioms, which are in tune with the progressive ideology inherent in Mill's *Principles of Political Economy*.

So much for the technical troubles with social-choice theory. Others seem to have philosophical roots. To begin with, the theory is in tune with ontological and methodological individualism, which we have criticized before in several places. According to it individual behaviour in private – for instance, in the privacy of a polling booth – rather than social interaction (in particular group action) is the ultimate source of everything social, and therefore the only thing we need to know about. But this assumption is at variance with social psychology and sociology. (See chap. 3, sect. 6, and Bunge 1996a.)

Second, social-choice theory is subservient to positivism insofar as it demands that we stick to observable behaviour, in particular choice behaviour, without attempting to find out its roots – for example, need or aspiration, habit or social constraint, moral feeling or taste, propaganda or ideology. Social-choice theory is also relativist: it does not question individual preferences, which are precisely what admen, politicians, and clergymen are out to alter. Since such preferences are often non-rational, and even contrary to the agent's real interests, they are not sufficient to design a social policy. As Rescher (1975, 90) says, "The welfare or well-being of people is an objective condition that cannot be extracted from anything as tenuous and volatile as their preferences." The same holds for the choice of social order: it should not be a matter of uninformed opinion, but of political theory, sociotechnology, and massive participation in rational debate. But social-choice theory is silent here.

Third, the theory is too ambitious. Indeed, it attempts to tackle such different group-aggregation problems as those raised by committee decisions, social-welfare judgments, and normative (as opposed to descriptive) social indicators, such as those of inequality and poverty (Sen 1970a). But a Theory of Everything can account for nothing in particular.

If our diagnosis is correct, the main service rendered by social-choice theory is to have shown that no rational social-welfare function has so far been found. Whether the very project is realizable remains to be seen. (See also Elster and Hylland 1986; Iannone 1994; Luke 1985; Mortimore 1976; Rescher 1969; Sen 1995; and Tullock 1967.) We shall meet the theory again when discussing welfare economics in chapter 10, section 4.

5 Explaining and Predicting Political Events

Rational-choice models of political processes explain little and predict nothing. We must therefore look for alternative approaches. Two suggest themselves immediately: holism and systemism. Holism attributes political systems an existence independent of their members, and attempts to account for the behaviour of individuals in terms of the former: it adopts a top-down strategy. It accounts for conformity but not for leadership and rebellion, much less for the peculiar blend of conformity and protest inherent in populism. Let us examine the latter. Thereafter, we shall tackle the current decline of socialism.

Populism has baffled politologists at least since the time of Louis Napoléon, because it defies the traditional dichotomies left/right and democratic/authoritarian. These categorizations do not help to characterize populism because, like nationalism, it appeals more to emotion than to rationality, and because it is neither homogeneous nor consistent. Moreover, populism derives much of its strength from heterogeneity and inconsistency. Finally, its actions seldom match its rhetoric. This latter feature is likely to misguide the politologist who relies more on texts than on deeds. Indeed, focus on rhetoric may lead him to equating populism with either demagoguery or the popular cause. Both identifications are mistaken because (a) unlike the demagogue, when in power the populist does deliver part of what he has promised – this being why he can count on lasting popularity; and (b) unlike the powerless *ami du peuple*, such as Danton, the populist politician trades favours with law-and-order forces.

But what *is* populism? (Or, as a neopositivist would prefer: What does 'populism' mean?) Modern populist politicians are characterized (a) *psychologically* by their folksiness and charisma; (b) *economically* in that they "give something to popular groups without directly taking away from others" (Hirschman 1981, 196) – and without regard for long-term economic consequences; (c) *politically* in that they mobilize the masses around serious social issues, while keeping them under control and promising quick and painless solutions from above; and (d) *culturally* in that they shout simplistic recipes and flatter the uneducated – for instance, by flaunting contempt for the cultural elite.

This definition invites the following hypothesis to explain the emergence and waning of populist movements. I suggest that a vigorous populist movement emerges in a society if and only if (a) the society faces extremely serious social issues; (b) the ruling classes and the traditional political parties are unwilling or unable to address such issues, so that large popular groups feel alienated from them and perhaps even from the state; and (c) the movement is headed by a smart, charismatic, and unscrupulous manipulator of public opinion who broadcasts a handful of catchy slogans. Let me illustrate this conjecture.

The Argentinian president Juan D. Perón has been perhaps the most successful populist leader in modern times. An examination of Peronism, one of the least understood of all political movements, should teach us something about the poverty of both holism and individualism, and of the need to combine microsocial and macrosocial factors to explain social facts. Launched in Argentina in 1944, and still going strong more than half a century later, Peronism is one of the most powerful popular movements in modern Latin American history. It has resisted explanation in terms of left and right because, being a populist movement, it has components of both.

Methodological individualists have attempted to account for Peronism by saying that most of the Argentinian poor supported it in the belief that it defended their interests. This is undoubtedly true, but it does not explain why popular support for Peronism hardly diminished when the Peronist government started to impose economic sacrifices and repress strikes. Furthermore, it overlooks the institutional component, in particular the support of the armed forces, a docile judiciary, and free access to public funds.

Holists, in particular Marxists, have regarded Peronism as the child of the industrial bourgeoisie, the armed forces, and the Catholic church. This account does justice to the institutional setting; but it does not explain the genuine popularity of Peronism, any more than Dimitrov's characterization of fascism as "the terrorist dictatorship of financial capital" explains Hitler's huge popularity. (Besides, the Argentinian industrialists never understood that the Peronist protectionist policies favoured them; consequently, most of them have not supported Peronism until recently.) Let us try an alternative account, one of the mixed (bottom-up and top-down) type.

Peronism may be explained as the outcome of a number of convergent processes: (a) initially Perón and his friends sided with the industrial workers who demanded salary hikes but were being held back by their own labour unions – controlled by Socialist or Communist leaders; (b) the Peronists gained control – by hook or by crook – of the most militant labour unions; (c) they roused the shanty-town dwellers and the landless peasants, who had been ignored by the traditional politicians; (d) they opened their ranks to labour organizers and political leaders of all shades, who had no bright future in their original organizations; (e) they appeared to treat the poor as comrades, listened to their grievances, initially redressed some of these, and made uncounted promises; (f) once in power they enlarged considerably the scope of the incipient welfare state; (g) they gave women and the inhabitants of the territories the right to vote; (h) once firmly on the saddle, Eva Perón mounted a huge charitable organization of the Robin Hood type, whose slogan was "Where there is a need there is a right" (to assistance); (i) they controlled the judiciary and the media; (j) they proclaimed a somewhat original ideology, the *doctrina nacional*, which included the *tercera posición* (the third way) – allegedly intermediate between capitalism and communism; (k) they made the teaching of the "national doctrine" and the reading of Evita's autobiography compulsory in all schools; (l) they shouted anti-imperialist slogans and in effect adopted a non-aligned foreign policy; (m) they used charm and promises, together with lies and threats, far more often than violence; (n) they enjoyed the support of the armed forces and, for most of the time, that of the Catholic church as well; (o) Perón, popularly perceived as the Big Man, and Evita, seen as the Great Provider, made an unparalleled team with enormous charisma; (p) the US government obliged by fighting them – and the opposition (the present writer included) welcomed the interference of the American Ambassador Braden; (q) most political analysts diagnosed Peronism as a variety of fascism, and consequently they failed to furnish the opposition with the intellectual tools required to act intelligently and efficiently. (See also Di Tella 1988.)

This tentative explanation of the success of Peronism involves two general premises. One is the bottom-up generalization "Agents act on what they believe to be their own best interests." The second is the top-down generalization "Any populist party enjoying the sustained support of the armed forces, free access to the public treasury, and the privilege of exacting tribute, is more effective in winning the support of common people than any of its rivals." In other words, our explanation is systemic, referring to individuals as well as to the systems in which they are immersed.

Our second case is the current decline of socialism, whose classical slogan was "For a classless society through the socialization of the means of production." Democratic socialism looked unbeatable when the British Labour Party came to power in 1945, but it has been declining since about 1980. Why? My answer invokes processes on both micro- and macrolevels. In a nutshell it reads thus: Socialism is dying from five main causes, namely success, the relative contraction of the manufacturing sector, consumerism, TV – the contemporary opium of the masses – and lack of new ideas. Let me spell out this answer.

European socialism is a victim of its own success. Indeed, the welfare state has implemented the short-term program of the social-democratic movement, and has thus taken much wind off the sails of the socialist parties. Incomes above the subsistence level, a reduced work load, retirement benefits, unemployment compensation, universal health care and education, and liberty to unionize are now taken for granted in all socially advanced nations. (See, for instance, Moene and Wallerstein 1995.) It stands to reason that, once such minimal conditions have been achieved, there is no point in continuing to fight for them. If in Marx's time the workers had only their chains to lose, now they neither feel chained nor believe that they have much to win by making radical demands.

This is a clear case of action, or rather inaction, prompted by a change in the social structure and, in particular, a change in the distribution of benefits and burdens. A minority of people think that not enough has been achieved, and they continue to be active in labour unions, left-wing parties, or both. But most blue-collar workers are content with the status quo. Even if they grumble over local conditions, most of them do not question the social order. As Laski (1935, 128) wrote, "So long as the system of private ownership in the means of production produces a continuous improvement in working-class conditions which satisfies the workers' established expectations, the latter will accept, even if doubtfully, the state as it is."

A second cause of the decline of socialism is the contraction of the manufacturing sector and, consequently, the shrinking of the industrial proletariat relative to the total population to far less than half its share only half a century ago. (The contraction is in turn due to the enormous increase in productivity made possible by technological advancement, the quick expansion of the service sector, and the export of factories to Third World countries.) Since socialism is, at least historically, a working-class ideology, it stands to reason that it must decline with the shrinking of the industrial proletariat. True, a large fraction of the members of the European socialist parties have always been white-collar workers, professionals, and intellectuals. Still, most of the white-collar workers do not regard themselves as workers even when they earn less than skilled industrial workers. The absence of visible barriers between them and their bosses, with whom they have daily face-to-face encounters, gives them the illusion that they stand a better chance of advancing by personal effort than by unionizing. Consequently they usually identify with that ill-defined category the middle class, which also includes skilled workers, midlevel managers, small businessmen, and independent professionals. In Marxist jargon, they have developed a wrong class consciousness.

A third cause of the decline of socialism is consumerism. This is defined not only by mass consumption of goods but also by shopping as a sport or even an addiction. The rational consumer regards shopping as a necessary evil, and buys only what he needs at prices he can afford. By contrast, the addictive consumer regards shopping as a joyful occasion, and often buys what he does not need at prices he cannot afford, to the point that he may overbuy on credit. Once the privilege of the leisure classes, conspicuous consumption and chronic indebtedness are now rights and behaviour norms for the majority of the population in the industrialized countries.

Entertainment via television is one of the commodities, since about 1950, that we all consume in industrial quantities. Now, it is well known that an overdose of TV-watching numbs the brain and renders people passive: it hypnotizes, desensitizes, and paralyses. Even if we watched only educational programs, we would still be diverted from thinking hard and twice, daydreaming, going to the library, socializing, debating, and engaging in dicey and risky collective action. Those who can switch on at will the dreaming machine do not feel like taking to the streets.

I submit that a fifth cause of the decline of socialism is the lack of new (post-socialist?) ideas. The classical socialist ideology may have been suitable in facing classical capitalism, but it does not match welfare capitalism, and it contains no blueprint for a more just social order designed in the light of social science, social technology, and a realistic moral philosophy. The socialist parties have become so busy with electioneering that they have discouraged theoretical thinking. Moreover, they are reluctant to propose any new ideals and policies for fear of losing votes. They may assess correctly the conservatism of most employed workers, but they may also underrate the increasing insecurity felt by nearly everyone, the frustration felt by the workers forced to take lower-paying jobs, and the aspirations of the many young people without good and permanent job prospects.

So much for our attempt to explain the decline of socialism. If correct, it should make room for the eventual revival of socialism if the latter comes up with new ideas and succeeds in capitalizing on the growing gap between popular expectations and the actual performance of the capitalist economy and the welfare state – a gap that widens as the frequency and depth of economic recessions keep increasing, as they have since the late 1950s. Ironically, consumerism and TV may help such a revival, as people's declining purchasing power makes it increasingly difficult to buy advertised commodities and as their actual lifestyle becomes ever more remote from the carefree lives shown in soap operas. (Remember that the growing dissatisfaction of the East Europeans during the late 1980s was largely a product of comparing their own drab lives with the glittering daily lives shown by the West European TV networks.)

For what it is worth, our analysis has zigzagged between the micro and the macro, without regarding either of them as the ultimate source of either change or stasis. In some cases political events and movements originate from anomie – a mismatch between individual aspirations and macrosocial realities. In others they are triggered by mismatches between the political system on the one hand and the economic or cultural one on the other. Indeed, it is always discrepancies or imbalances of some kind or other, whether real or perceived as such, that trigger social action and, in particular, political action. Of all such imbalances, perceived inequity and perceived threat to security, rights, or privileges are among the most powerful motivations for political action.

A further major source of popular dissatisfaction and alienation from any ruling party is the latter's unresponsiveness to popular needs and demands – which, if real, may result from complacency over past victories. A case in point is the defeat of the Sandinistas in the 1990 Nicaraguan general election. This event took nearly everyone by surprise because the Sandinistas had overthrown a predatory, cruel, and corrupt dictatorship originally installed by an American occupation force; they had distributed much land among peasants; they had greatly improved public education and health care; and they did not execute any opponents. But the Sandinista leaders had become increasingly remote from the people. They did not listen to them, and consequently they became unresponsive to the economic harshness caused by the US embargo, the command economy, the guerrilla war, and the upkeep of an army that had become unnecessarily large once the "contras" practically ceased hostilities because the Bush administration had cut drastically their payroll. The anti-Sandinista vote was largely a vote against a government that had nothing further to offer except memories of its early achievements and groundless alarms against a US-backed invasion.

Our explanations of the fortunes of populism and of democratic socialism, as well as of the ultimate failure of the Sandinistas, are at variance with the views that all political action results from cold calculation and that it is a manifestation of blind passion. In our view, all human action partakes of both reason and passion: reason controls passion, which in turn fuels reason. In particular, even the smartest political action is under the influence of strong passions, such as anger, fear, hope, generosity, empathy, and moral indignation – which are in turn sustained by such cognitive processes as memory, learning, and the fixation of belief. Regrettably, the role of passion in politics is usually overlooked by politologists, particularly those of the rational-choice persuasion. It is, however, occasionally studied by social psychologists. For example, Sears and Funk (1990) found that, in the United States, self-interest seldom determines public opinion or voting behaviour.

Psychological factors play a far smaller role in international relations, where economic power and military might have always been the dominant forces and therefore the main explanatory variables. Take the case of the 1973 Oil Crisis and its economico-political causes and effects. A distal cause was the decision of the American government to decrease the country's dependence on foreign oil and, at the same time, to block the Soviet Union's access to the Persian Gulf and the Arabian sea. The American secretary of state, Dr Kissinger, found no difficulty in persuading the Shah of Iran to press OPEC for a substantial hike in the price of crude oil, and to use a large fraction of the oil revenues to buy American weapons, turning Iran into a forbidding fortress at the gate of the USSR.

The OPEC oil embargo and the rise in the price of crude oil had global economic consequences. First, it was a bonanza for the Texan oilmen, as much as it was a disaster for the German and Japanese economies – which were trade rivals of the US anyway. (Only the American consumers were hurt for a while.) Second, the American banks were flooded with petrodollars coming mainly from the Persian Gulf. Since they had to invest this money, they sent emissaries to Third World countries offering huge instant loans on attractive terms and without collateral. The borrowed money went partly into the pockets of generals and politicians and partly to buy weapons – in neither case a productive investment. A few years later the interest rates doubled or tripled – the origin of the monstrous debt that is still stunting the development of these nations. To fix the mess on behalf of the creditors, the International Monetary Fund and the World Bank imposed "readjustment" measures that, by cutting social expenditures, affected only the poor. This in turn caused serious domestic political crises.

In short, the last two decades of the history of the Third World, from Iran to Brazil to Afghanistan, was profoundly affected by a smart move undertaken by the US Secretary of State on behalf of certain short-run American economic and geopolitical interests. True, this calculated move did have some negative unforeseen side-effects, such as the Iranian Revolution, which in turn caused the Iraqui military build-up (supported by the US), which led to the eight-year-long Iran-Iraq war and subsequently to the invasion of Kuwait, which elicited Operation Desert Storm, which caused the ruin of the Iraqui people and the reinforcement of Saddam Hussein's dictatorship. But you cannot forecast and win them all. All you can do is paint them as victories in your memoirs.

So much for political explanations. Let us now say a few words about political forecasts. As regards their logical form, they are either conditional or unconditional. The former are of the form "If A happens, then B will (or is likely to) occur." For example, "If the agreement is signed, then the conflict will be averted." Unconditional forecasts are of the form "A will (or is likely to) happen." For instance, "It will take at least one generation to reconstruct the societies in the former Soviet Union."

Whether conditional or unconditional, political (and economic) forecasts are of either of two kinds: passive or active. Passive forecasts are made by political analysts: they foretell what is likely to happen. By contrast, active forecasts are made by politicians: they are direct or indirect calls to action, and are aimed at influencing public opinion and mobilizing some social groups. Example 1: "If you vote for my opponent, your standard of living will sink." Widespread belief in this forecast may decide an election. Example 2: "A showdown with nation X is unavoidable, whence we must arm against X." Belief in this prophecy will stimulate an arms build-up and prepare public opinion for hostilities.

We shall confine our attention to passive forecasts, for they befit political scientists. A simple example of this kind is the following: "As the world mineral deposits become depleted, the world powers will try to lay their hands on them, if necessary by military force – that is, further oil wars are to be expected." Correct passive political forecasts are hard to make for several reasons. One is that political attitudes are often shallow and therefore sensitive to comparatively minor disturbances or even politically irrelevant factors, such as a leader's smile, voice, dress, or private life. Such instability is in turn an effect of a low level of political sophistication and information on the part of the public.

A second reason that accurate political forecasts are hard to make is sometimes that the political system is unstable, either internally or because of external pressures. In a touch-and-go situation, a charismatic leader voicing a few simple appealing slogans can tip the balance one way or another. This was apparently the case of Russia in October of 1917. If Lenin had not returned from exile at that precise moment, and if he had been unable to persuade his comrades that this was their chance, the revolution might not have occurred.

A third reason for the difficulty in making accurate political predictions is that some of them are untestable, so that political events teach us next to nothing about the truth value of such forecasts. In fact, consider the following forecast schemata made by politicians and political analysts:

If party A wins, consequence(s) C will follow.   [1]

If party B wins, consequence(s) D will follow.   [2]

If party A happens to win, then [1] will eventually be confirmed or refuted, for consequence(s) C will either follow or not. But in this case [2] will remain untested – at least until a similar situation occurs.

A fourth and more serious reason for the difficulty in making accurate political forecasts is the current dearth of good political theories and the poverty of empirical political data. This is why the more cautious political analysts prefer to propose pairs of scenarios, for instance, an optimistic and a pessimistic one. For example, one may say that, if such and such governments sign a peace treaty, then there is likely to be peace in their region during the foreseeable future – whereas otherwise war is likely to occur (or to go on). Although such dual scenarios are pathetic from a scientific viewpoint, they may be practically effective, in showing politicians what they stand to gain or lose if they take or do not take certain actions. In other words, they are forecasts of the active kind. Whereas they hardly serve to test any theories, they may be useful warnings to political agents.

Of all political processes, wars are the least predictable, because they are not limited to military operations but engage entire communities over vast territories, affecting every aspect of their lives. In a complicated and tense situation, such as the one prevailing in the Middle East since the Second World War, even a limited military operation can have unforeseen consequences because of the instability of the total system. To be accurate, military forecasts would have to rely on detailed and adequate mathematical models of the communities likely to become involved in military conflicts. Since such models have not yet been constructed, the triggering of a war is politically irresponsible as well as morally reprehensible. After all, "Every one may begin a war at his pleasure, but cannot so finish it" (Machiavelli ([1513] 1940, 21). The causes were known to Ibn Khaldûn ([1377?] 1967, 2:85–6): "the causes of superiority [in war] are, as a rule, a combination of several factors," many of which are hidden and therefore unexpected. Consequently, organized violence should be approached in a systemic way (see Rapoport 1989b).

6 Politics, Ideology, Morality

In politics social values and norms, that is, ideas about what is good or bad for society, are at least as important as vested interests. Whether right or wrong, such ideas matter because they mobilize or paralyse people: they motivate them to initiate, join, oppose, or ignore social movements of various kinds. Some of these, such as abolitionism, the nineteenth-century *Narodnischestvo*, and the current "pro life" and Green movements, are incomprehensible in terms of self-interest. The participants in such movements, which cross class and party barriers, are public-spirited, not gain maximizers. Hence, their actions refute economicism (for which see chap. 2, sects. 5 and 6).

Politics is incomprehensible without ideology, both for what it reveals and for what it hides. Thus, some ideologues have presented colonialism as a civilizing mission, capitalism as coextensive with democracy, communism as a peace crusade, and so on. Not even the opportunistic politician is free from ideology: what he does is to change ideologies as he sees fit. Nor is political ideology the only cultural component of political action. Religion too has often played a role in both domestic and foreign politics.

Ideology is central to politics because every political ideology is centrally concerned with the struggle for power. This holds, in particular, for the most potent political ideologies of the last two centuries: liberalism, communism, fascism, and nationalism. Indeed, all four hold that conflict is not only inevitable but also beneficial, either because it promotes progress (liberalism and communism), or because it eliminates the "weak" or "inferior" (fascism), or because it promotes national interests (nationalism).

The difference between liberalism and its two extreme rivals with regard to conflict is that, whereas the latter push for "the final struggle," the former endeavours to contain and regulate conflict (see Lipset 1959 and Lyttelton 1973). And the main philosophical differences between fascism and communism are their mutually contradictory views on equality and reason and the fact that communism has an explicit metaphysics of universal conflict. This is dialectics, according to which conflict ("the struggle of opposites") is the source of all change on all levels of reality. (For a criticism see Bunge 1981a.) As for nationalism, it is so complex and so poorly understood that its treatment will be postponed to chapter 5, section 7.

Wherever conflicts of interests occur – as they do all the time in social life, particularly in politics and business – moral problems are bound to arise. With regard to the morality of politics, its practitioners and students have always been divided into pragmatists (or *Realpolitiker*) and the principled. In particular the latter, from Aristotle to Spinoza to Kant, have held that politics ought to be guided by morality, whereas the pragmatists, from Machiavelli to Smith, Hegel, Marx, Lord Acton, Weber, Lenin, Gramsci, and Kissinger – not to mention Mark Twain and Mencken – have held that all politics are amoral or even immoral. Machiavelli taught that politics is immoral, for in order to stay in power the ruler must "learn how not to be good"; Lord Acton coined his famous dictum; Lenin held that whatever advances the interests of the working class is good, and conversely; Weber stated that whoever engages in politics "signs a deal with diabolical forces"; and Mencken wrote that public functionaries constitute "a class of professional immoralists." Were any of them right?

The correct if non-committal answer is: it depends. Politics can be either clean or dirty, according as it abides by sound moral maxims or by none; and it can be realistic without being cynical – that is, political realism is not the same as *Realpolitik*. More precisely, the morality of a political action depends on the morality of the means and goals chosen by the politician, and on the type and extent of the detours – concessions and compromises – he is forced to make in his struggle for power. (We take it for granted that whoever sticks rigidly to his principles and is not prepared to make some detours is unlikely to have a political career.) If the goals are prosocial and the means are clean, then concessions and alliances are morally justified as long as they consist only in temporary postponements or in a temporary sharing of power with political rivals on the basis of a common platform that is made public and does not harm the public interest. It is well known that good intentions without power are impotent. It is harder and better to do a little good from a position of power than to criticize evil from a powerless opposition.

Though imperfect like everything human, democratic politics have several advantages from a moral viewpoint. First, under democracy intentions, deals, and deeds are open to public scrutiny, evaluation, and revision. Second, the quest for popularity motivates even the crooked to do some good or at least to appear to do so. (Remember Ben Franklin's dictum that, if scoundrels knew the advantages of virtue, they would be virtuous out of sheer roguery.) Third, moral lapses in democratic politics can be discovered, and often prevented, by the vigilance of concerned citizens, conscientious civil servants, journalists, and political rivals eager to exploit failures and scandals. In short, democracy involves some moral control – provided the citizens retain some moral principles and do not adopt the cynical view that all politics are unavoidably dirty.

Once in power, the morally sound politician will remember – and should he forget, his constituency may remind him – that good government is not only politically skilful and technically (e.g., fiscally) competent, but also morally right, management. Good government consists in serving the public interest, that is, the interest of everyone, rather than that of some interest group. In this sense, politics can be the long arm of morality. However, this arm can do more harm than good unless it is guided by sociotechnological expertise. In other words, democracy should work best when combined with morality and sociotechnology.

Since there are many moralities, the reader is likely to wonder which of them is being referred to. I am referring to the agathonist morality encapsulated in the maxim *Enjoy life and help live*, expanded on elsewhere (Bunge 1989a). The alternative moral philosophies are not much help to politics. In particular, the natural-law school does not have much to say to a highly artificial society like ours. Kantian deontologism does not tell us much beyond "Do what is right." Contractualism too is formalist, for it does not commit itself as to the content and moral worth of contracts. And utilitarianism does not instruct us on how to measure and add up utilities, and thus to maximize them. Not surprisingly, there are members of all four schools and more on both sides of all the great social issues of our time: environmental degradation, overpopulation, sex and race discrimination, capital punishment, the right to start wars, minority rights, duties to our posterity, and the plight of the Third World. All of these issues are involved in the conservative/liberal/socialist controversy.

Consider for example war, which from the agathonist viewpoint is the supreme crime for involving the most glaring violation of the maxim *Enjoy life and help live*. In war might is right: moral norms are suspended, and all is permitted where "the enemy" is concerned, so that people are encouraged to perpetrate the most infamous actions. As President Wilson noted cynically when he drafted the American people into the First World War, in wartime people "stop weighing right and wrong."

Yet neither of the standard moral philosophies involves an explicit condemnation of war. (True, Kant favoured perpetual peace, but at the same time he upheld the citizen's duty to obey his sovereign – right or wrong.) There are several reasons why these philosophies fail the politician. First, they are neither specific enough nor close enough to real-life moral conflicts: in particular, they do not speak to the immense moral problems peculiar to our age, such as those posed by overpopulation, mass poverty, neocolonialism, and nuclear weapons. Second, those moral philosophies are not intimately related to social science and technology. Third, moral sentiments, such as compassion and solidarity, as well as sheer ignorance and stupidity, and passions – such as greed and generosity – play a far greater role in practice than in most moral theories with the exception of emotivism – which is unacceptable for excluding reason and experience altogether from moral deliberation.

It is wrong to underrate the moral factor in war, because unjust wars end up by being unpopular at home and abroad. Thus, all imperial powers have taken the wrong moral side in attempting to foist their own interests and views on foreign peoples. This moral mistake has often had a negative practical outcome, for soldiers do not fight well unless they believe in the cause they fight for. Immorality is bad business – at least if the other side is strong and feels morally justified. At any rate, politicians cannot skirt moral issues, for whatever they do is bound to benefit some people while harming others.

What about political scientists? Can they praise or condemn political actions without surrendering scientific objectivity? They can and must whenever they can show that the action concerned harms innocent people. Take for instance modern imperialism, that is, colonialism, which can be political, economic, cultural, or a combination of these. Imperialism has been condemned not only by such foes of capitalism as Veblen, Bukharin, and Lenin, but also by such pro-capitalists as Adam Smith, Jeremy Bentham, James Mill, and Richard Cobden. Some of its critics, from Hobson (1902a) to O'Brien (1988), have documented the detrimental effects of imperialism upon the colonial powers themselves, involving trade imbalances, large military expenditures, the maintenance of a burdensome colonial bureaucracy, and the diversion of investment. Others have condemned imperialism for being morally wrong as well as economically and politically disastrous. They claimed that imperialism is morally wrong for involving the exploitation of the natives, the plundering of their natural resources, and the destruction of their cultures. Granted, these critics could have confined themselves to describing the negative effects of imperialism, stopping short of passing moral judgments, and letting the readers "draw their own conclusions." But had they done so we would accuse them of being timorous, hypocritical, or even insensitive. What is important about any moral judgment is whether it is justified. And moral justification presupposes truth. Example: "X harms someone. It is wrong to harm ∴ X is wrong." The conclusion is false unless the factual premise is true.

Contemporary political ideologies have been in trouble since the end of the Second World War II. Most political labels, particularly 'conservative,' 'liberal,' 'socialist,' and 'communist,' have become obsolete: they no longer denote the political ideologies and movements they used to half a century ago. Only 'fascism' and 'anarchism' stick, but the former is nearly universally repudiated for moral reasons even while being practised, and the latter only attracts a handful of naive intellectuals. We need new political labels to denote the current political trends. But above all we need a new political ideology inspired in both a new morality as well as in social science. This subject will be addressed in chapters 10 and 11.

7 Domestic Politics

Political scientists are expected to account for political conflict, change, and stasis. Here we meet again the holism-individualism-systemism trilemma. For instance, whereas conservative holists regard conflict as inimical to their ideal – the solid block society – individualists take it for the marrow of a free society. By contrast, for systemists conflict is inevitable, so we should make the most of it. In itself conflict is neither glue nor solvent: what matters is that it be adequately managed (Hirschman 1994). Thus, whereas protracted confrontation may lead to social breakdown, bargaining may enhance cohesion. This holds for family quarrels, class struggles, international conflicts, and more: we come together not by ignoring unavoidable (and often valuable) differences but by negotiating a *modus vivendi* in a rational fashion. Here again, systemism is an alternative to the communitarism/individualism dilemma.

Furthermore, whereas holists describe macropolitical facts and individualists focus on individual actions, systemists combine structure with agency. They emphasize that all political action takes place within a political system, and that the latter may change as a result of coordinated individual actions. In other words, the systemist combines micropolitical with macropolitical considerations. For example, he will state the important truism that, under democracy [macro], even a single vote [micro] may make a difference to the outcome [macro]. And he will stress that there is no political change unless some individuals, whether at the top or at the bottom, become sufficiently motivated by current conditions and get together in an effort to alter them. Seen in this perspective, individual action may make a social difference, whereas neither holism nor individualism offer hope.

From a systemic viewpoint the clue to both stasis and change is the stability or instability of the entire social system. If the system is stable, then only severe external shocks, such as natural cataclysms or foreign invasions, may alter it. Usually a shock causes adaptive reorganizations and alters individual behaviour. But if the system is structurally unstable, as is the case with deeply fractured societies, then – by definition of "instability" – even a comparatively small perturbation, internal or external, may trigger disaster, from riot to civil war.

The perturbation may occur either at the macro- or at the microlevel. Thus, a mere rumour about new austerity measures, if perceived as bound to increase poverty, may trigger street riots complete with looting and shooting. Such stimulus will trigger the process rather than causing it: it will be only the straw that breaks the camel's back. In other words, for an event, such as a political action, to have momentous consequences it must be exerted on an inherently unstable system – one ready to explode or implode. Let us examine one example of each of three kinds: riot, revolution, and national breakdown.

The famous Los Angeles riots in April of 1992 were triggered by the news of the acquittal, by an all-white jury, of the policemen who beat up a black man, Rodney King, most brutally and without provocation. An individualist explanation schema of this event might look like this: inexcusable beating → acquittal → increased frustration → individual violence → riot. This schema is correct but incomplete, because it does not include the background, namely chronic poverty and racial segregation, and the concomitant resentment and hopelessness of the people who took to the streets. The holist would include poverty and segregation, and propose instead the schema: chronic poverty and segregation → riot. But this schema too is incomplete, because it misses the psychological wellspring of social action, and because chronic poverty and segregation are compatible with resignation as well as with rebellion. Combining the two schemata one gets what in chapter 2 was called a Boudon-Coleman diagram:

Macrolevel	Chronic poverty & segregation			→		Riot
	↓					↑
Microlevel	Acquittal	→	Increased frustration	→	Individual violence	

In other cases, such as rebellions against despotism or austerity measures, the trigger lies on the macrolevel. Example:

Macrolevel	Political or economic oppression	→	Organized opposition
	↓		↑
Microlevel	Indignation	→	Communication

Let us now focus on organized mass actions ending up in social revolutions – to be distinguished from mere *coups d'état*, which do not change the social order except in weakening whatever democracy there may have been before. There are two kinds of social revolution: quiet and violent. Quiet revolutions are the effect of industry, legislation, or education, and they are the least well studied for not being dramatic. And yet the diffusion of electric energy, food canning, rapid transportation, telecommunications, mass-murder weapons, compulsory education, the refrigerator, the automobile, television, the computer, industrial pharmaceuticals, birth-control devices, advertising, and mass tourism have brought deeper and more lasting social changes than all the *coups d'état* put together. (Just think of the rise in individualism caused by the popularization of the automobile.) Something similar can be said of the legislative packages and social programs that gave birth to the modern welfare state. The combination of the latter with the industrial innovations mentioned above has given rise to a whole new civilization – alas, a fragile one because it is threatened by the irreversible loss of jobs caused by increasing productivity, as well as by the revolt of the "contented," and it draws on rapidly depleting natural resources as well as the massive conversion of citizens into shoppers and passive consumers of cultural junk.

Violent social revolutions are of course quite different from quiet ones. Sometimes they are advocated on the ground that they are the only way of changing an unjust social order protected by strong police or armed forces. This rationale may well be true, but it misses the following points. First, revolutionaries overrate the efficacy of violence because they underrate the unforeseen as well as social inertia, which stems from vested interests, habit, and neophobia. Second, the cost of a violent revolution can be staggering in lives taken or disrupted and in new divisions generated. Third, to stay in power the new political elite is likely to resort to terror, which it may continue to practise long after its enemies have disappeared. Fourth, for the same reason the revolutionary government is likely to postpone indefinitely some of its promised reforms. Fifth, unchecked power corrupts. The combination of these five factors is likely to result in failure – perhaps at the cost of many lives and the discredit of noble ideals. (See, for instance, Gurr 1980.)

The October 1917 Russian revolution is a prime example of a violent and profound social revolution that ended in failure. According to Marx it should have resulted from a mismatch of the political superstructure and the economic infrastructure, in particular a new mode of production. However, many similar mismatches have failed to trigger any revolutions. Lenin rejected this explanation and proposed his own: Russia was the weakest link in the imperialist chain. But this is just a metaphor. Moreover, it fails to take into account the specific political circumstances. The facts of the matter are as follows.

First, in 1917 the Russian people were enormously impoverished and demoralized by a long, bloody, and unpopular world war in which they had no real stakes. The czarist regime was so unjust, corrupt, and unstable that it fell at the first street demonstrations in a few cities. But Kerensky's incompetent, dithering, and insensitive self-styled socialist government went on fighting despite heavy losses and a rapidly declining morale. Second, and as a consequence, the new government grew quickly unpopular, particularly among soldiers, sailors, factory workers, and peasants. In short, public opinion became polarized and a power vacuum developed. Third, Lenin and his tiny party stepped into this vacuum, and promised to deliver what most people seemed to yearn for: an end to the war, democratic goevernment, and a redressing of blatant economic inequities.

Once in power the Bolsheviks made good on their first promise, reneged on the second, and took their time doing anything about social justice except as regards popular access to education and higher culture. This tardiness had several causes. First, the new government had a narrow political base. And, instead of attempting to broaden it, the Bolsheviks instituted the "red terror" and persecuted all their former allies as well as their adversaries. (They admired Robespierre, forgetting his ultimate failure.) Second, they had to repell the military aggression of fourteen different foreign armies. Third, in keeping with the anti-utopian stand of Marx and Engels, Lenin's team had no blueprint for building the new society. They had no idea of how to reconstruct the economy, devastated first by the world war and then by the civil war. In particular, they did not understand the key role of managers, engineers, and agronomists in rebuilding or even keeping factories and farms going – on top of which most of the experts had fled the revolution anyway. The Bolsheviks believed that revolutionary enthusiasm could replace technical expertise, and that socio-economic planning was "child's play." When they finally undertook to modernize the economy through a sequence of five-year plans starting in 1928, they succeeded in building a modern heavy industry as well as in equipping a modern armed force. They also succeeded in advancing public health and education at all levels and in all regions, as well as in promoting research in mathematics, physics, chemistry, and engineering. Their dismal failure in nearly everything else – particularly agriculture and light industry, self-management and political democracy, biology and psychology, social science and philosophy – helps to explain their ultimate failure. This may explain a world-shaking but, alas, failed revolution in terms of structural instability and the interplay of microlevel and macrolevel factors of three kinds: political, economic, and cultural.

Finally, let us take a look at political breakdowns or implosions, such as that of the Soviet state in the summer of 1991. It would be simplistic to attribute the failure of the Soviet "experiment" after seven decades to a single cause, such as defeat in the Cold War, inter-ethnic conflicts, collapse of the command economy, widespread disaffection and corruption, or the incompetence of a handful of leaders. After all, what went down was not just an administration but a whole social order, with its concomitant lifestyles, together with an empire spread over four continents. Moreover, the Soviets were not a giant with clay feet: they had withstood a civil war and foreign invasions (1917–22) and had won the Second World War nearly single-handed; the USSR was a superpower, which had climbed from near-medieval conditions to modernity, was free from business cycles, and pioneered the conquest of space; it guaranteed job security, built decent if not outstanding systems of universal social security, public education, and health care; and it enjoyed the lowest income inequality (Gini index) in the world. No wonder the foundering of the Soviet Union took everyone by surprise, from its own citizens to the CIA to the political-science community. How to explain such a precipitous fall?

I submit a platitude: The USSR had been suffering from severe systemic malfunction for decades, to the point of having become structurally unstable – a touch-and-go situation. It broke down for a number of interdependent causes of various kinds operating simultaneously on both macro- and microlevels. Here is a list of only fifteen such causes grouped into three clusters: political, economic, and cultural.

1. Political causes

(a) The "dictatorship of the proletariat," which was actually the dictatorship of the *nomenklatura* or political elite, destroyed what little civil society there had been earlier, and it stunted political development by drastically curtailing popular participation at all levels. It replaced voluntary allegiance with submission, fear, and the dilution of responsibility. Hence, it alienated most individuals from the government, which was rightly perceived as omnipotent and repressive. It divided the people into two new social classes with conflicting interests: "us" (the people) and "they" (the elite). It covered up social and ethnic conflict with rhetoric, and it betrayed the noble ideal of a classless society. In fighting to survive and advance in a climate of fear, denunciation, and mistrust, people became increasingly individualistic and corrupt – hardly the suitable material for an egalitarian and solidary society. The "New Man" sung in the early days became hardly distinguishable from the frightened, cynical, and self-seeking subject of a fascist regime.

(b) The fusion of state and party prevented the training of competent and politically independent civil servants capable of furnishing expert and objective information and advice except on secret-police matters. Censorship turned the mass media into agit-prop tools: people were uninformed or misinformed. Hardly anybody was honest or foolhardy enough to risk career or freedom, let alone life, in telling the truth, much less in publicly criticizing any major policy errors. Complicity, servility, and cowardice became habits.

(c) The enormous ethnic diversity inherited from the czarist empire gave rise to inter-ethnic conflicts that were temporarily muffled but never solved. As centralism worsened and Marxism-Leninism became increasingly discredited, nationalism got more virulent.

(d) The Soviet Union competed with the United States in pursuing the Cold War with unnecessary intensity. In particular, it was not really necessary to develop an overkill capacity or to keep the largest army in the world. This irrational military confrontation, expected and perhaps also sought by the leaders

of both superpowers, exacted enormous sacrifices on every citizen of a multination that was and had always been much poorer than the so-called West. Furthermore, it exacerbated a xenophobic attitude that prevented loyal (or merely
prudent) Soviet subjects from learning anything foreign, while inducing the dis-
affected citizens to imitate foreign ways, particularly if bad or in poor taste.

(e) The "Brezhnev doctrine" of solidarity of the "socialist" bloc diverted
huge resources to foreign aid and intervention (as in Afghanistan). This fuelled
the arms race, bled the economy, and was seldom reciprocated. In particular, the
unsuccessful military adventure in Afghanistan sapped the morale and tarnished
the public image of the USSR. The heroic underdog of the 1920s and 1930s had
become another world bully. To top it all, the sudden collapse of some satellite
regimes in 1989 worsened an already precarious situation.

2. Economic causes

(a) The means of production, transportation, trade, and communication were
owned by the state and managed by bureaucrats: nationalization was mistaken
for socialization, statism for socialism. Because it excluded self-management,
this economic order resulted, just like capitalism, in widespread alienation. In
particular, the agricultural workers did not have the responsibilities and incentives of the individual farmer, the manager of the capitalist agribusiness company, or the member of a self-governed cooperative concern.

(b) The market, though not entirely absent, was stunted by pervasive and
crippling state intervention. It lacked the advantages conferred by competition, such as relentless technological innovation, a "natural" (non-decreed)
pricing procedure, and personal initiative and responsibility (see chap. 10,
sect. 6). Worse, the economy was centrally planned in an authoritarian fashion. Planning was in the hands of a group of remote economists out of touch
with economic realities, to the point of disregarding cost/revenue ratios, thus
protecting enterprises that would have gone bankrupt anywhere else. Top-
down planning demanded unrealistically high production quotas, maintained
artificial prices, killed local initiative, and paid no attention to the wishes of
the consumers. (Giving priority to quotas discourages quality, depresses job
satisfaction, and encourages corruption, for example, through padding figures
and bribing.)

(c) The planners of the post-war period imitated those of the 1930s in paying
far more attention to heavy industry and weapons manufacture than to consumer goods and services. As a consequence, essential commodities were in
short supply, which in turn generated long line-ups, underground work, dissatisfaction, and corruption. At the same time, people started to get information,

mainly through foreign TV, about the far higher standard of living enjoyed by the workers in the advanced capitalist countries.

(d) Agriculture and industry were on the whole technologically backward and therefore of low productivity, which contributed to the scarcity of consumer goods. Because consumers were not consulted, there was no pressure to improve product design and quality control, and consequently most goods were shoddy. As well, skilled services of all kinds were in short supply and could be procured only in the black market. Consequently, the only flourishing sector of the civilian economy was the underground one.

(e) Because most consumer goods were scarce, only the powerful could obtain them. The economic inequalities, particularly those between the top bureaucrats and the rest, became ever more pronounced, notorious, and irritating. Owing to the lack of democracy there was no open class struggle, but the divergence of class interests was nearly as pronounced as in the capitalist countries.

3. Cultural causes

(a) The party dictatorship was guided and justified by Marxism-Leninism. This ideology, once innovative, had become stagnant and incapable of inspiring anyone, particularly in view of the inability of the regime to ensure a standard of living equivalent to that enjoyed by the West European workers. The gospel did not match reality: there was massive cognitive dissonance and anomie. The official ideology was taught as dogma on all three levels by teachers who were not even well versed in it, and consequently were neither enthusiastic nor willing to discuss it critically. Moreover, because it was the official credo of the ruling class, Marxism-Leninism was increasingly looked upon with boredom, suspicion, or hatred. The political consequence is obvious: people are unwilling to lift a finger for a regime inspired by a doctrine they no longer believe in.

(b) There was no cultural freedom: a clear-cut sectarian party line ruled in every single cultural domain ("front"), complete with censorship and persecution of unorthodoxy, real or imaginary. (For instance, historians had no access to archives, and no one had free access to copying machines.) All this curtailed inquiry and crippled the imagination of artists, philosophers, scientists, engineers, and managers. This repression lowered the quality of cultural production and slowed down its pace. Cultural terrorism severely stunted, distorted, or even wiped out entire research fields, notably biology, agronomy, psychology, social science, and the humanities, particularly philosophy.

(c) The Soviet intellectuals, technologists, and artists had limited access to foreign sources, and only the faithful – that is, unoriginal – were allowed to travel abroad. They were not full members of the international cultural community. Hence their knowledge was artificially restricted, they often reinvented the wheel, and they could not benefit from the criticisms of their Western counterparts.

(d) There was no new cultural project capable of mobilizing the *intelligentsia*. Worse, higher culture started to weaken because people became increasingly disillusioned with the party line or had not been trained in critical thinking. In particular, the earlier worship of science and technology began to be replaced with belief in esoterics, pseudoscience, and quackery. Indoctrination in Marxism-Leninism, and surfeit with it, proved to be an effective school of general gullibility. Enforce one dogma and breed every superstition.

(e) The founders of socialism had been inspired by the noble ideals of the French Revolution: Liberty, Equality, Fraternity. But Marxism-Leninism lacks a moral philosophy of its own. It boils down to a handful of pious slogans to be recited rather than implemented, and it includes a narrow version of utilitarianism. (Remember Lenin's dictum: Moral is whatever advances the cause of the proletariat.) As the distance between the *nomenklatura* and the common people increased, the slogans about equality, solidarity, and abnegation sounded increasingly hollow. Rampant cynicism and the attendant corruption ensued. (Remember the popular saying in the late USSR: "We pretend to work and they feign to pay us.") No moral problems were aired, and in the end no moral norms were left. Not surprisingly, morale sunk: after all, there is no morale without morals.

To be sure nearly every one of the above fifteen factors have been known for some time. But they were never before pulled together. They were kept separate because most political analysts adopt a sectoral approach. It is only when viewing those factors as forming a system that the structural instability and therefore vulnerability of the Soviet society and the Soviet Union can be properly understood.

The progressive reforms introduced by Gorbachev and his team in 1985 came too late, when the regime was already far gone. They came at a time of low morale, were neither clear nor radical enough, and were not carried out consistently and democratically. In particular, (a) they were not accompanied by open and detailed debates on the failing regime; (b) they did not involve an explicit criticism and denunciation of Marxism-Leninism as an obsolete and paralysing dogma; (c) they were decreed from above, without any grass-roots participation; (d) they did not include the creation of fully democratic town councils and regional parliaments, as well as freedom to organize new political parties; (e) they involved no clear ideas about the market, and consequently no incentives to produce for it; (f) they discouraged the organization of independent cooperatives; and (g) they were not part of a comprehensive and long-term national project including the radical redesign of all the subsystems of society.

As a consequence of (a), many of the flaws of the system were not even seen by the elite, which was too far removed from the people who suffered them. As a consequence of (b), there was no theoretical tool to help redesign society, nor did a process of self-criticism, re-education, and reform occur among the rank-and-file party members. As a consequence of (c), there was no organized mass movement capable of implementing the proposed reforms, or of evaluating and altering them as needed. As a consequence of (d), there was no democratic debate or decision making: the bosses continued to rule by decree, there were no authentic political alternatives, and the semi-democratic parliaments rubber-stamped nearly all the decisions the leaders had made. Perverse effects of the general liberalization were institutional vacuum, relaxation of discipline, and worsening of the shortage of consumer goods. As a consequence of (e), nobody had any clear idea as to what to do about the economy – except to ask for the advice of foreign experts, some of whom prescribed a "shock therapy" that they would not have dared propose in their own countries. As a consequence of (f), the unique opportunity was missed of organizing cooperative businesses on the largest scale ever – the obvious choice given the lack of domestic capital and the unlikelihood of foreign investments. And as a consequence of (g), the people remained apathetic when not distrustful. Suddenly there was liberty but hardly any democracy; nor was there a tradition of public rational debate, much less popular participation, that would help to clear the rubble of the old order and rebuild a new one. In short, Gorbachev's team of tinkerers lacked a grand and clear vision of the successor society.

Moreover, because Gorbachev's team had no coherent and systemic plan, *glasnost* and *perestroika* backfired. Indeed, the party and the central government lost authority as a result of the sudden emergence of freedom of speech and association in a country lacking democratic traditions. Party and government proved unable to keep discipline in the workplace or in the barracks, as well as to contain inter-ethnic strife or curb crime. Not even the crops were harvested. Disobedience, demoralization, and even panic and crime spread like fire. The central government was perceived as being incapable of securing the genuine achievements of the previous social order, particularly job security and fringe benefits, or even of guaranteeing safe streets. When Yeltsin, Gorbachev's successor, hastily issued *ukases* dissolving the Communist Party and severing the links among the Soviet republics, a power vacuum developed that was even worse than before the two revolutions in 1917. The Soviet order collapsed suddenly, unexpectedly, and without agony, just when oppression began to slacken – one more instance of Tocqueville's law.

In short, the Gorbachev team had no clear policy and consequently no clear blueprint for its orderly implementation. It could design neither because it had no theory to replace Marxism-Leninism, to which it continued to pay lip service. Worse, the central government changed course every few months: it was disoriented and did not inspire trust, hence it only worsened popular confusion and generated indiscipline. By tampering with an unstable system in a nearly trial-and-error fashion, the Gorbachev team unwittingly turned chronic disease into coma. His incompetent and autocratic successor made things even worse. In sum, *glasnost* and *perestroika* had unexpected perverse effects.

The following Boudon-Coleman diagram summarizes in an oversimplified fashion the myriad macro-micro processes involved in the last act of the Soviet tragedy:

Macrolevel   Gorbachev reforms   →   Collapse
                           ↓   ↑
Microlevel   Debate, confusion   →   Demoralization, indiscipline

The collapse of the pseudosocialist social order as well as of the Soviet mulination, was amazingly swift. It occurred neither for lack of natural resources nor because of military weakness; it did not result from a mismatch between new productive forces and the political superstructure; nor did it result from a class struggle. The regime crumbled for sheer want of a transition plan fired by bold new and adequate ideas capable of rallying the support of the Soviet people. The latter was made to pay dearly for the absence of a democratic tradition, the officialization and fossilization of Marxism-Leninism, the lack of a tradition of rational debate, and the backwardness of Soviet social science – for which the Soviet *intelligentsia*, particularly the philosophers, must take much of the blame. In the end the people were left with neither "real socialism" nor real capitalism. Worse, they were destitute, dispirited, divided, without compass or hope, without moral or legal norms, and at the mercy of political adventurers, improvised businessmen, gangsters, and Western preachers of palaeocapitalism.

All political scientists, East and West, were taken by surprise. In particular, neither rational-choice theorists nor Marxists made any correct important forecasts. (We discount the prophecies of doom that the anti-communist industry had been manufacturing since 1917.) True, Hélène Carrère d'Encausse (1978) – who is neither a Marxist nor a rational-choice theorist – did forecast the dismemberment of the Soviet Union; but she did not foresee the collapse of the pseudosocialist social order. And a few economic analysts did foresee an eventual economic crisis caused jointly by the rigidity of the command economy and the military over-expenditures. But nobody expected the collapse of both the social order and the multination to happen jointly, let alone so thoroughly, so soon, and so suddenly, particularly without a civil war and in peacetime. Not even the CIA expected or perhaps even wished the collapse, for the myth of the strength and stability of the USSR was handy to justify the West's huge arms build-up. So much for the fortunes lavished on spying, Sovietology, and "scientific communism."

Why this dismal failure of political science? My answer is in two parts. First, political science is not yet scientific enough. In particular, it fails to integrate political analysis with economic, cultural, historical, and psychological analysis; and it focuses too often on either personalities or political systems, with little regard for the "perceptions," needs, and aspirations of the common people. Second, when studying social orders politologists are sometimes blinded by ideology: witness the common confusions of free market with democracy, of market control with socialism, and of the various kinds of nationalism.

8 International Relations

The study of international relations has advanced since the Second World War to the point that a standard textbook (Russett and Starr 1981) assures us that it has undergone a revolution. For example, the International Crisis Behavior project (Brecher et al. 1988) has studied 278 international crises, comprising 627 crisis actors, between 1929 and 1979. It uses about one hundred variables, defines a crisis-severity index, and attributes a value of it to every crisis.

However, the field still suffers from ideological contamination and conceptual fuzziness. Whereas the first feature is understandable, though hardly justifiable, the second is inexcusable, for it generates unending barren controversy. Two examples should suffice. Consider first the much-debated Holsti-George hypothesis concerning international crises: "Moderate levels of stress improve decision-making performance while high stress may impair it." (Likely source: Dr Selye's popular recipe for managing stress in daily life.) How is one to test this hypothesis unless its key concepts of stress level and decision-making performance are elucidated and preferably quantitated? Our second example involves the debate between holists and individualists. Where the former see foreign policy as a contest between nation-states, the latter regard it as a tournament between leaders: the former see capabilities, the latter impute intentions. Fortunately, a systemic synthesis between the two extremes is emerging: neorealism (see, for instance, Waltz 1979 and Wendt 1987).

Let us try to clarify in systemic terms a few central concepts in the discipline, starting with that of the international community. This is of course the supersystem composed of about two hundred nation-states. The international *system* is even larger, for, in addition to nation-states, it comprises more than ten thousand international organizations, some governmental such as the UN and the IMF, and others nongovernmental such as the Red Cross and IBM. The relations among the components of the international system are not person-to-person ties but intersystem bonds – some of them cooperative, others conflictive. Of course all such relations are set up, maintained, or altered by individuals such as senior civil servants and top managers. But these individuals are not totally free, and they can be replaced with others enacting similar roles or functions. It is not that their personalities do not matter, but that they discharge certain functions in impersonal organizations.

Since every nation-state is constituted by an economy, a polity, and a culture, international relations can be economic, political, or cultural. An improvement (or deterioration) in a relation of any of the three kinds contributes to improving (or deteriorating) relations of other kinds. It is customary to describe such webs of links in terms of relations of two types, direct and indirect. The latter, also called 'cross relations,' are usually referred to as "relations among relations," the classical example being the relation between economic and political relations. Actually this is a logical muddle. Instead of positing ill-defined higher-order relations, we would do better to talk about relations among systems, such as the economy and the polity. For example, where politics influences the economy, two sets of relations among concrete systems are involved: the intranational and the international relations between the economic and the political subsystems of the national systems concerned. The same holds, *mutatis mutandis*, for the remaining dyadic relations.

The practical advantage of the systemic over the conventional approach is realized upon computing the number of dyadic international relations. In the former case, the total number of possible dyadic international relations among n members is $N = 9n(n - 1)/2$. This number is approximately 200,000 for nations-states and 450 million for the entire international system. Though very large, this number is far smaller than that arrived at on the conventional schema. In fact, in the latter case we would have $(\frac{1}{2}) 10^4 (10^4 - 1) \cong 50,000,000$ direct relations plus $(\frac{1}{2}) 5 \cdot 10^7 (5 \cdot 10^7 - 1) \cong 1.25 \cdot 10^{15}$ relations among relations (or "cross relations"), which is seven orders of magnitude greater than the figure calculated according to our schema (Bunge 1977b).

Even after eliminating the ghostly relations among relations, we are left with 450 million possible relations among the actors of the international system. This is a forbidding figure, but one that should challenge political scientists instead of paralysing them. Instead of complaining about the complexity of the task, or waiting for faster computers to be built, scientists try to craft theoretical models representing the main traits of the systems of interest. In the study of international relations, the two analyses of the actors (both in composition-environment-structure-mechanism and in economy-culture-polity terms), their groupings into partial supersystems (such as political blocs), and the selection of certain variables in preference to others facilitate the search for patterns, that is, precise functional relations among the variables. In short, the systemic view can play a potent heuristic role in the study of international relations and the design of foreign policies.

So far, foreign policies have been anything but systemic: most have been designed to foster the national interest as perceived by ill-informed, short-sighted, and greedy political leaders. Nor have foreign policies benefited much from political science. They have been largely inspired by ideological tenets as well as by partial and therefore misleading analogies of current situations with the recent past. For example, each side in the Cold War (1946–90) often saw – or at least described – the adversary as a version of fascism (May 1973). And both sides played the nuclear game of chicken (or brinkmanship) – the most dangerous, stupid, and immoral of all games. The concern for "national security" overrode prudence and morals. It even replaced political science with dogma. Thus, the American government waged the long and disastrous Vietnam War on the strength of a single political hypothesis, and moreover one that proved wrong, namely General Eisenhower's simplistic "domino theory."

Understandably, statesmen and foreign-policy analysts take national security to heart. Incomprehensibly, few of them tell us exactly what it means. And no wonder, for it is a slippery notion. Consider, for instance, the definition proposed by Galtung (1984, 84), the eminent peace researcher: The national security of party A relative to party B equals the invulnerability of party A minus the destructive potential of party B. This definition allows him to define another fuzzy notion, that of balance of power: There is balance of power between two parties if and only if their national securities are roughly the same. All this sounds clear until one attempts to "operationalize" (that is, set up measurable indicators for) the variables in question. Indeed, whereas destructive potential may be equated with firing power (or tons of TNT), invulnerability depends on such intangibles as organization and morale – as Galtung himself notes (ibid., 92). Unsurprisingly, the "experts" drop the second variable and focus on the first: that is, they plan for ever more-powerful weapons systems – which can only increase global insecurity. It does not occur to them that the best protection is non-offensive, promoting collective security (ibid., chap. 5). The hedgehog's defence can be just as effective as the leopard's – and it is far cheaper.

The idea that military preparedness is only one of the ingredients of national security is utterly alien to military experts. Yet, to anyone adopting a systemic approach, it should be obvious that national security is a vector with four components: bio-psychological (good public health), economic (strong economy), political (internal political stability, defensive capability, and enforceable international treaties), and cultural (high levels of popular education and technological development). Weakness in any of these components puts national security at high risk (see Renner 1997). The best defence is having and cherishing something worth defending.

The ethicist will notice the moral problems raised by international politics, in particular the principles and practices of national sovereignty, national security, the arms race, war, colonialism, the protection of human rights, and the fight for democracy. These moral problems are overlooked by all schools of political realism. (See, for example, Baldwin 1993.) Let us take a quick look at them in the light of the maxim *Enjoy life and help live* (Bunge 1989a).

The right to self-determination and, once this is attained, the protection of national sovereignty are usually regarded as self-evident and inalienable. But it can be argued that national independence is at best one of the means for national development, whence its possible costs must be taken into account as well as its doubtful benefits. For this reason national sovereignty should not be regarded as an absolute value, and many a violent fight for self-determination should be critically examined – particularly when fuelled by aggressive and undemocratic nationalism. If a people is actually being oppressed or threatened by another, as is the case with a colony, then the attainment or maintenance of sovereignty is a morally legitimate means for its development – particularly if sought by peaceful means. (For the distinction between defensive and aggressive nationalism, and their respective moral value and disvalue, see chap. 5, sect. 7.) But if two nations need one another – for example, because their economies are mutually complementary – then their political independence may be an obstacle to their development. (Possible examples: the members of the former Soviet Union, and of the Spanish colonial empire.) In this case political (and economic and cultural) interdependence is more valuable than independence – provided neither partner becomes dominant. In any event, national self-determination should be relaxed or even given up when it conflicts with peace, welfare, or democracy. Prudentially, as well as morally, sovereignty without peace, welfare, and democracy is not worth dying for.

National security can be interpreted either as defence of national sovereignty or as an excuse for aggression. In the latter case it is immoral, involving as it does the oppression of other people. But even in the former case the national-security system should be closely watched by the citizenry, for it provides an excuse for militarism, repression of dissent, secret (hence undemocratic) policy making, delays in addressing domestic social issues, education for war, and the awarding of juicy defence contracts. Lasting peace can only be attained through

(a) world disarmament, or at least the banning of aggressive weapons and strategies; (b) international trade and cultural cooperation; (c) educational reforms that aim at forming citizens of the world rather than jingoists; and (d) the formation of a world federation. If we had partners instead of enemies we would not fight them. And if there were no frontiers other than purely administrative ones there would be no point in defending or altering them. If you really want peace, work for it.

The principles of national sovereignty and national security are becoming increasingly obsolete owing to the strengthening of the economic and cultural ties among nations, as well as to the common interest in adopting policies to address such global life-and-death issues as overpopulation, energy overconsumption, and environmental degradation. The alternative is no longer sovereignty or dependence, but survival of all – through peace, international cooperation, and eventually world government – or extinction of all. Granted, global governance won't be easy to attain, but we are getting closer to it through a growing number of international organizations and agreements of various sorts, many of which limit national sovereignty. The alternative, namely universal annihilation, is still possible even after the end of the Cold War because of the growing hunger for natural resources, the proliferation of nuclear weapons, and the revival of aggressive nationalism.

Let us now address the problem of war. Ordinary mortals, particularly those likely to become cannon fodder, regard war as the ultimate disaster: they cannot admit the claim of Hegel, Nietzsche, Scheler, and Mussolini that war is morally uplifting. Still, according to an old tradition, there are just wars, such as those waged to liberate oppressed peoples (see, for instance, Walzer 1977). I submit that the expression 'just war' is an oxymoron, for war is mass murder, and modern wars harm civilians in even greater numbers than the combatants. Moreover, starting a war is irrational if only because its outcome is hardly foreseeable. Therefore, all wars are both unjust and irrational, hence to be averted or stopped through negotiation. But I also submit that there may be a just and rational *side* in a war, namely the victim of aggression if it risks annihilation unless it counterattacks.

More precisely, I propose the following norm: A party in an international conflict is morally justified in taking arms if and only if it acts (a) in reaction to armed aggression; or (b) to enforce an international security treaty; or (c) in order to save a people or a minority from annihilation, and in either case with a reasonable chance of not losing. Shorter: Only self-preservation or defence of an ally victim of aggression justifies acts of war. Accordingly, considerations of national sovereignty, political liberties, protection of foreign oil reserves, or international trade routes do not justify war.

We wind up this section by noting that international politics is often at odds with domestic politics, particularly with regard to political democracy. For one thing, matters of peace and war are never under the full control of the people: no citizenry has ever been asked to vote whether or not to go to war, or to offer or accept peace terms. In such matters the power elites have always had the first and last words. For another, even such mainstays of domestic political democracy as Great Britain and the United States have strived for world domination, and hence have often trampled democracy abroad. (See Gurr 1980 for the domestic-foreign connection.)

There are three main approaches to the study of politics: holism, individualism, and systemism. Holism focuses on political systems and movements: it overlooks the interests, feelings, and thoughts of their members. It may describe impersonal features, such as systemic properties and the substitutability of low-rank officers. But it fails to account for political leadership and following, loyalty and disaffection, enthusiasm and apathy, sacrifice and corruption because it overlooks personal interests and the ways, often distorted, in which agents and patients "perceive" social facts. Hence, holism cannot explain the emergence and decline of institutions or nations, all of which it must either take for granted or try to account for in terms of uncontrollable and inscrutable historical forces.

As for individualism, it may occasionally explain the action of an individual – for instance, in terms of ambition, vision, or charisma – but it does not account for the emergent properties of political movements and states. For example, individualists may guess why Mussolini turned from anarchism to socialism to fascism, but they cannot tell us what anarchism, socialism, or fascism are. In particular, by focusing on cold calculation, rational-choice theorists underrate solidarity, sacrifice, persuasion, coercion – in particular violence – ignorance, miscalculation, and of course sheer stupidity. Consequently, they cannot offer realistic accounts of such irrational actions as fighting for irrational beliefs or lost causes; warfare, political terrorism, or collective suicide (as in Massada and Numancia); or the stockpiling of nuclear arms far above what it takes to wipe out the human species.

Only a systemic approach to politics can account for the struggle for power, because such a struggle is carried out by some individuals to acquire, maintain, or increase their control over supra-individual systems, such as parties and nation-states – which systems in turn constrain or encourage those individual actions. (See Rosenau 1990 and Girard 1994 for micro-macro and macro-micro political "flows.") In other words, unlike holism and individualism, systemism combines microlevels with macrolevels, as well as agency with social structure. It also makes room for "perceptions" and feelings, such as fear and hatred, anger and love, along with interests and purposes. Hence, it can account for political loyalty and dissent, conformism, and rebellion. And it brings norms and ideologies down to earth, placing them in live individual brains.

Moreover, systemism rejects unicausal accounts of political events. In particular, it rejects as empirically inadequate the one-sided hypothesis that the intensity of domestic political conflicts depends nowadays exclusively upon the level of industrialization (modernization theory), or else on the position of the country in the core-periphery ranking (world-system theory). The available political and economic data favour instead a more complex structural model that refines and combines the preceding hypothesis (Moaddel 1994). According to it the intensity of political conflict depends linearly upon two political variables (regime repressiveness and separatism) and five economic ones (income inequality, economic growth, vulnerability to fluctuations of international prices, industrialization, and peripheralization). Moral: Join many-sidedness with quantitation.

However, most politologists are either individualists or holists rather than systemists. Moreover, most of them regard the political process as if it were independent of the economy and the culture. (For exceptions see Hobson 1938; Downs 1957; Lipset 1960; Dahl 1971; and Di Tella 1988.) No wonder then that only some of politology wrestles with important issues in a scientific manner. The rest falls into the following categories: data gathering without the benefit of theory; simplistic political model building; journalistic rather than scientific political analysis; policy making; political philosophy; political ideology; and political pseudoscience. Such fragmentation and contamination are unhealthy. Like any other discipline, politology should combine empirical and theoretical research with philosophical reflection (see Crick 1971). The ideal situation should be something like this:

Political philosophy ↔ Political science research in close cooperation with
economics and culturology ↔ Political analysis ↔ Policy making ↔ Politics

where the double arrow stands for reciprocal influence. Politics has been included in this circuit because its complexity is such that it calls for some politological knowledge.

In sum, politology should greatly benefit from adopting a proscience philosophy. This would encourage rigorous theorizing in tune with facts. It would also allow politology to avoid the silliest *ism*, namely simplism, or the belief that a single factor or force can explain all of politics. The science of power would also attain more clout by closing ranks with sister disciplines, particularly demography, sociology, economics, history, and the science of culture. For example, modern politics cannot be properly understood without analysing both the concepts and the powers of ideology, technology, and communication – neither of which is, alas, well understood. Hence the need to connect political science with culturology – our next subject.

5

Culturology

Recall our quadripartite or *BEPC* analysis of every society into its biological, economic, political, and cultural subsystems (chap. 1, sect. 1). Recall also that we have preferred the narrow sociological concept of culture to the broad anthropological one, which equates culture with society (chap. 1, sect. 7.) According to the former, the culture of any society, whether primitive or civilized, ancient or modern, is composed of such ingredients as language, stories, knowledge (in particular science, technology, and the humanities), art, morality, and ideology – including religion. In sociological (and materialist) terms, the culture of a society is the subsystem of it composed of the linguistic, epistemic, artistic, and ideological communities. Thus conceived, a culture is a concrete system, not a bunch of disembodied ideas (Bunge 1981a).

Being a social system, every culture has its distinctive structure and mechanism. The structure of a culture is constituted by the set of links among its members, in particular those of comunicating and training. And its peculiar mechanisms are those of producing and diffusing cultural products. This sociological concept of a culture differs from the psychological one of personal culture. A person's culture is what he has learned through living in some of the cultural communities that compose his society. Hence, no personal culture could develop in a cultural vacuum. This trite corollary of the definition of "personal culture" has interesting consequences. One is that the sociological concept of culture as an impersonal entity cannot be defined in a bottom-up fashion – that is, starting from the notion of personal culture. (In particular, the culture of a society cannot be defined as either the set or the union of the personal cultures of its individual components, if only because the resulting set is unstructured, whereas a culture is a system.) Shorter: Methodological individualism cannot cope with the sociological concept of culture.

A second consequence concerns the analogy between cultural and biological evolution based on the idea that cultural traits ("memes") replicate and mutate like genes (Dawkins 1976). This analogy is shallow, hence unhelpful. Indeed, to begin with, genes are material units, whereas cultural items – such as languages, legal codes, techniques, sciences, and myths – are not. (Only the respective communities and their individual components are concrete things.) Second, genes are subject to chance mutation, whereas cultural features are largely the result of deliberate (hence non-random) activities – they are artificial. Social systems, such as cultures, are to be studied sociologically.

The kinship system is studied by anthropologists, the economy by economists, and the polity by politologists. Who studies culture? Following Leslie White (1975), I call *culturology* the sociological, economic, political, and historical study of cultural systems, or cultures in the narrow or sociological sense of the word. Obviously, culturology can be synchronic or diachronic. In the former case it coincides with the anthropology, sociology, economics, and politology of culture. By contrast, diachronic culturology is a component of history.

Increasingly over the past few years, studies of culture have dealt with the only important cultural phenomena accessible to the layperson: the communications explosion, tricks of mass persuasion, and adulterated popularizations of science and technology. Most of these "cultural studies" are the work of literary critics or philosophers incompetent to study facts and theories at first hand. They are shallow dogmatic essays written in a pretentious and often esoteric prose. Instead of clear, interesting, and testable hypotheses, they propose barren metaphors, outrageous paradoxes, quotable but not always translatable phrases, and egregious howlers. (See, for example, Baudrillard 1988; Ross 1991; and the journal *Social Text*.) Common to all these essays is the inversion of sociolinguistics: instead of studying communication as a social relation, they view society as a text or "code" to be "deconstructed" (deciphered and debunked). Being shallow, the success of these essays is ephemeral. They leave behind only a few slogans, such as "the medium is the message," and "there is nothing outside the text." Moreover, deconstructionism can be parodied to the point of ridicule, as the physicist A. Sokal (1996) has shown in his hoax on "transformative hermeneutics of quantum gravity," published by the unsuspecting editors of *Social Text*. So much for unscientific culturology.

Serious culturology is a social science that can boast of a number of generalizations in addition to uncounted monographic studies. Let the following random sample suffice. 1/ In every society, however primitive, some people specialize in cultural activities. 2/ The great divides in the early stages of every culture are the invention of tool-making techniques, organizations, world-views, religions, and art forms. 3/ In stratified societies, the dominant values are those of the ruling class(es). 4/ Critical thinking has coevolved with civil liberties, the law, mathematics, the study of nature, trade, and travel. 5/ Critical thinking flourishes under political freedom and withers under tyranny. 6/ Superstition prospers with insecurity and fear. 7/ Ideological constraints damage art, science, and the humanities. 8/ Philistinism hinders the expansion of basic science and thereby that of science-based technology. 9/ The sustained growth of any branch of culture requires the simultaneous growth of all the others. 10/ Any void left by science or technology is filled by junk.

Two of the most basic and hotly debated issues in culturology are the idealism-materialism and the internalism-externalism controversies. The former is clearly a philosophical issue, and the latter has philosophical presuppositions as well as consequences. The traditional account of ideas is at once idealist and internalist (or asocial). In particular, mainstream history of ideas is still largely the story of ideas and their authors, precursors, commentators, and critics, with disregard for their social circumstances and, in particular, for the social stimuli and constraints all thinkers are subjected to. The accent is on ideas in themselves, the intellectual processes and influences that prompt their birth, development, or decline, and their influence on society at large. The latter is either ignored or regarded as clay in the hands of thinker-potters.

The traditional approach to culture is then strictly *internalist*: it regards external circumstances as purely anecdotal. For instance, it sees no connection between Galileo's work on the laws of motion and his employment by the Venetian arsenal; between Leibniz's obsession with harmony and his activities as a peace broker; between the music of Bach and his court and church; between the instant popularity of neoclassical microeconomics and the threat posed by socialism; between philosophy and political power – for instance, between rationalism and the liberal state, or irrationalism and fascism.

The very idea of a sociology (or politology or economics) of science, technology, the humanities, the arts, or ideology is repugnant to any consistent individualist, as well as to any consistent idealist. To these scholars ideas are either events in free individual minds impregnable to economic and political influences or inmates of Plato's Realm of Ideas, Dilthey's "objective spirit" or Popper's "world 3." They see the history of any ideas as a string of individual discoveries or creations influenced only by their precursors. They focus on individuals and schools, and are not interested in the communities of people engaged in such activities – for example, the religious, artistic, humanistic, scientific, and technological communities. Theirs is an asocial view. (True, Weber, a professed individualist and immaterialist, was one of the founders of the scientific sociology of religion – but this only goes to show that he did not practise the philosophy he preached: see Bunge 1996a.)

Not even mathematicians and astronomers live in a social vacuum. They are members of scholarly communities, and as such they are now stimulated, now constrained by their fellow workers, with whom they interact directly or through publications; and they are influenced by social factors, such as the ruling ideology and research budgets. Therefore, the internalist account of ideas is one-sided: it must be complemented with an account of the social matrix of research, belief, controversy, diffusion, and censorship. Art is parallel: it cannot be fully understood apart from patronage and marketing.

The sociology, economics, and politology of culture repels individualists and idealists but it attracts holists and vulgar materialists. These scholars view individual ideation and action as products of the social environment and, in particular, of social forces. Not for them inspiration, creativity, doubt, or heterodoxy: they only see adaptive or functional behaviour, with the occasional short-lived dysfunction. They underrate natural curiosity, devotion to truth, and the internal dynamics of ideation. In particular, they are hardly interested in the problems that spark off disinterested research, in the hypotheses invented to solve them, and in the methods employed to gather data or test guesses. Nor are they interested in questions of logical consistency, testability, or truth: they only look for social sources and for seals of social approval or disapproval. They are externalists, even behaviourists.

The externalists have the merit of criticizing the excesses of internalists. Their main defects are that they refuse to see the differences between ideas and other artefacts; underrate or even deny creativity; claim without evidence that abstract ideas have a social content or, indeed, a hidden (and often odious) political source or even content.

My objections to both externalism and internalism are the same as those against holism and individualism respectively: because, as stated above, each of them sheds light on a single side of the coin. Holism minimizes the role of individuals and disclaims analysis; individualism ignores material resources, social structures, and social movements. Hence, a synthesis of whatever is valuable in each of these extremes should be performed.

The alternative to both holism and individualism is systemism (see chap. 1, sect. 3, and Bunge 1979a, 1979b, and 1996a). Unlike holism, which regards all individuals as instruments of uncontrollable social or historical forces, systemism encourages the study of individual creators in their social environment. In particular, it suggests treating the history of ideas as neither more nor less than one of the many threads of the thick rope of general history. Systemism leads also to viewing professional communities and cultural organizations, such as orchestras, libraries, and universities, as systems composed of interacting individuals. Thus, an orchestra is not just a bunch of performers, but a cohesive system that behaves as a whole by virtue of the coordination of its components. If the system fails, cacophony results.

The adoption of this view facilitates the understanding of the transactions between cultural systems and other subsystems of society, in particular the economy and the polity. It helps in understanding, for example, the current vogue of biotechnology as a result of both the molecular-biology revolution – a piece of basic research – and the expectation of large medical benefits and commercial profits. Just think of the prospects, as frightening as marvellous, of cloning, which began as a tentative hypothesis.

As for the idealism/materialism divide, it fares similarly. Systemist materialists reject idealism but not ideas. They regard ideas as brain processes that are influenced by the social environment and which, moreover, are socially effective whenever they inspire social action. (Idealists not only rightly stress the potency of some ideas: they also share the magic belief in disembodied ideas acting upon passive matter.) And materialists regard social systems, in particular communities of speakers, thinkers, artists, or believers as concrete (hence material though supraphysical) systems, which differ from other material systems in that their components are often creative and act on the strength of their beliefs. (See Bunge 1979a.) Let us take a critical look at this controversy.

1 Idealism versus Materialism

Traditionally, culture has been viewed as a disembodied system of ideas, values, and norms: that is, as an autonomous ideal entity. This view has the merit that it invites one to examine ideas and cultural practices on their own merits or demerits, regardless of the individuals or groups that espouse or fight them. In particular, it favours the evaluation of consistency, content, and truth.

But cultural idealism is inadequate on three counts: methodologically, epistemologically, and scientifically. It is methodologically flawed because there is no empirical evidence for the existence of disembodied ideas. What is true is that, for analytical purposes – for example, to unveil meaning or to evaluate truth and consistency claims – it is advantageous to treat certain ideas *as if* they were self-existing. (Note that this kind of fictionism is only methodological: it does not question the reality of the external world or the objective truth of any scientific ideas.) Second, idealism is epistemologically inadequate for barring the investigation of the ways whereby real people come to create, improve, adopt, or discard beliefs, values, norms, or cultural practices. Indeed, when ideas are taken as given, there is no point in asking how they emerge, evolve, spread, or decline. Third, and consequently, the idealist concept of culture is inadequate for social-science research because it detaches culture from people and, hence, makes nonsense of the sociology, politology, and economics of science, technology, art, or the humanities.

Even Marxists, despite professing materialism, conceive of culture in a semi-idealistic way, by regarding it as "the ideal superstructure" of society – the material infrastructure being composed of the things and "forces" of production and reproduction. Theirs is then a dualistic view of culture, that is, one that joins materialism with idealism. The difference between Marxism and consistent idealism is that the former postulates that the material infrastructure somehow produces the ideal superstructure, which in turn may modulate (e.g., help organize and maintain) the former. But the mechanism whereby the "material basis" produces the "ideal superstructure" is not elucidated, except in vague functionalist terms. Indeed, it is assumed that every culture is adapted to the underlying material infrastructure; and that, when a mismatch between the two layers occurs, one of them is bound to alter, so that a revolution occurs that, if victorious, establishes a new balance – until the next "contradiction" appears. (See, for instance, Engels 1954 [1878].)

This dualist view of culture is inadequate on several counts. First, it shares the methodological and epistemological flaws of the idealistic view. Second, it overlooks the fact that, although science-based technology is a part of modern culture, it is also a potent input to both the modern economy and the state. (No wonder that Marxist scholars have been debating endlessly the question whether technology belongs in the infrastructure or in the superstructure. More on technology in sect. 5.)

From a systemic viewpoint the idealism/materialism debate is solved in a straightforward manner, namely thus: Every society, being composed of concrete entities, namely people, is conceived of as a concrete (material) system. The culture of a society is a subsystem of the latter, namely that composed of real-life individuals who – often with the help of artefacts such as signs and word processors – produce, consume, or diffuse cultural goods. (Examples of such goods: songs and theorems, chronicles and blueprints, legends and theories, myths and data, computer programs and economic policies, moral maxims and legal precepts, budgets and paintings.) Since cultures are composed of concrete (material) entities, they are concrete themselves. But, unlike purely physical, chemical, or biological systems, cultures happen to contain feeling, thinking, and willing individuals capable of creating or acting on the strength of their beliefs, hopes, fears, goals, and norms. If all rational animals were to become extinct, then books, paintings, musical scores, diskettes, and the like would cease to be cultural goods. This thought experiment refutes vulgar materialism (physicalism) and vindicates emergent materialism.

In sum, systemist (or emergentist) materialism is an alternative to both idealism (power of mind over body and society) and vulgar materialism (impotence of ideas). It places ideation in material brains that, by controlling some social actions, can contribute to shaping or destroying societies. And it situates those brains in such social networks as linguistic, scientific, technological, artistic, and religious communities. In this way systemist materialism can explain why some intellectuals play a direct social role whereas others do not.

2 Internalism versus Externalism

As mentioned in the introduction to this chapter, cultural life can be approached in either an internalist (or endogenous), an externalist (or exogenous), or an interno-externalist (or endo-exogenous) way. The first of these approaches, inherent in idealism, is the well-known traditional one, so it hardly calls for comment. Suffice it to recall that, while it rightly emphasizes individual creativity, it underrates social stimuli and constraints. Let us therefore turn to externalism. We shall confine our discussion of it to basic science. However, similar considerations apply to technology, the humanities, the arts, and ideology.

Externalism (or *sociologism*) is the thesis that context determines content, or even that there is no difference between them: that an individual's ideas and actions are fully determined by his social environment, or even that the latter "constitutes" the former. Since the expressions *social context*, *determines*, and *constitutes* are vague, the externalist thesis can be interpreted in several ways:

A. *Moderate or weak externalism*: All knowledge is socially conditioned.
- *ME1 (Local)* The scientific community influences the work of its members.
- *ME2 (Global)* Society at large shapes the work of individual scientists.
B. *Radical or strong externalism*: All knowledge is social.
- *RE1 (Local)* The scientific community constructs scientific ideas, all of which ultimately have a social content.
- *RE2 (Global)* Society at large constructs scientific ideas – whence the inside-outside, micro-macro (in particular person-group), content-context, and discourse-*praxis* distinctions must be erased.

Let us analyse, exemplify, and evaluate each of these approaches, starting with ME1 or *moderate local externalism*. This view presupposes that the scientific community is self-regulating: that it sets its own agenda and settles its affairs on its own. This thesis is so mild as to be hardly distinguishable from internalism. The only difference between the two is that – unlike the radical internalism inherent in the traditional science of science, which is individualistic – moderate local externalism postulates that individual scientists act not on their own but as members of their scientific communities, observing the norms and standards prevailing in such systems, seeking recognition from their peers, and in most cases following the scientific fashion of the day. By and large this is the view embraced by the Merton school in the sociology of science, to be examined in section 3.

Moderate local externalism is compatible with the internalist thesis that scientific research has its own rules and standards, and is driven mainly by curiosity. Moreover, it is the necessary complement of internalism (see Agassi 1981 and Bunge 1983a). In fact it deserves being called interno-externalist. Indeed, this view makes room for the social stimuli and inhibitions that act on the individual researcher, as well as for the reception that his work obtains. For instance, Schrödinger (1935), one of the founders of the quantum theory, noted that the *Zeitgeist* dominant after the First World War favoured radical novelty and thus heterodoxy in all fields: that even physics was affected by the *Umsturzbedürfnis*, or drive to subvert the discredited old order. But of course he did not claim that the demand for novel ideas can be met in the absence of original brains. In particular, he did not credit the *Zeitgeist* for the famous equation that bears his name.

The *moderate global externalist* thesis ME2 goes much farther: it asserts that science is subject to strict external social control rather than to the internal control exerted by the scientific community. It holds that science is a productive force, hence part of the economic infrastructure of society. More precisely, according to this school, (a) every scientific problem is one of production or trade; (b) science is only a tool for solving economic or political problems; and (c) the dominant ideology, which expresses the material interests of the ruling class, orients the scientist's research.

The best known product of this school is Boris Hessen's Marxist essay "The Social and Economic Roots of Newton's *Principia*," which caused a sensation at the International Congress of History of Science and Technology held in London in 1931. Though a global externalist, Hessen was moderate by comparison with today's externalists, for to him scientific research is an *intellectual* pursuit, hence one accomplished by individuals. He claimed that science has economic (and secondarily also ideological) inputs and outputs, but not that its content is social, or that it "emanates" from social groups. Hence, he might not have accepted any of the radical externalist theses (more on Hessen in sect. 3).

Radical externalism, in its two versions, is the thesis that all knowledge is social in content and function as well as in origin. In other words: Tell me the kind of society in which you live and I'll tell you what you think. This view is a generalization of the well-known Feuerbach-Durkheim thesis that all *religions* are symbolic translations and enshrinements of actual social structures – a thesis made plausible by a number of studies (e.g., Frankfort et al. 1946). If the same were true of *science*, we should be able to read society off scientific theories and experiments, much as Durkheim (1972 [1897], 250) claimed that "[i]t is through religion that we are able to trace the structure of a society." But actually nobody has ever discovered anything about social structure by studying, say, Newton's equations, or the way cell division is observed. It so happens that natural science is not built in the image of society and with the aim of reinforcing the social order: natural science is only expected to explore and represent nature as objectively as possible. (Reference: the entire literature in natural science.)

Radical externalism also comes in two ranges: local and global. The *radical local externalist* thesis RE1 is that every science and all of its referents are literally created by the corresponding scientific community. The classical statement of this view is Ludwik Fleck's *Genesis and Development of a Scientific Fact*, originally published in 1935, and which T.S. Kuhn rescued from oblivion. (See Kuhn's preface to the English translation of 1979.) The theme of Fleck's book is the history of popular and medical thinking about syphilis, which he called a *scientific fact*. Fleck denied that scientists study independently existing things: he was a radical social constructivist. In particular, he held that "syphilis, as such, does not exist," but is a "social construction" performed by the medical community. (If syphilis, why not smallpox, senile dementia, or even death?)

The claim that a disease is a *construction* or idea, rather than an objective condition, involves confusing a fact with its accounts, in particular disease with its descriptions, diagnoses, aetiologies, prognoses, and treatments. And the idea that disease is a *social* construction involves equating a medical condition with a social one. These elementary confusions could harm not only the study of science and medicine but also the health-care system. Indeed, if disease is not an objective biological process in an organism, but an idea in the physician's mind, in the medical community, or in society at large, then medicine is a myth, and the panacea is at hand: Outlaw the practice of medicine and close down all hospitals and all biomedical research laboratories. And, to be consistent, extend this policy to all other sources of trouble. Storms and earthquakes could be avoided by banning earth science, and social ills by hunting down all social scientists. In particular, poverty could be eradicated by persecuting socially concerned individuals, crime by dissolving the courts of law, and wars by banning military history. Obviously a bad philosophy, if adopted by policy makers, can have disastrous social consequences.

Fleck's general thesis is that every "scientific fact" is a social fact in being the product of a "thought collective" or community of individuals united by a "thought style." He rejects the idea that an individual can think, hence that persons matter. Moreover, according to Fleck there is no such thing as the external world: "objective reality can be resolved into historical sequences of ideas belonging to the collective" (1979, 41). This collectivist kind of subjectivism, called *social constructivism*, had been adumbrated by the later Husserl (1931). It was later adopted by a few sociologists (e.g., Berger and Luckmann 1966), as well as by the new crop of sociologists of science (e.g., Latour and Woolgar 1979; Knorr-Cetina 1981; and Barnes 1983). Characteristically, no *evidence* for this view has ever been proffered: it is an exercise in wild speculation. Moreover it is ludicrous, for by its logic biological evolution began with Darwin, class struggles with Marx, and the universe with astronomy.

Let us finally deal with *radical global externalism*, or RE2. This thesis is inherent in the "strong programme" of the Edinburgh school of sociology of science. The first principle of this project is that the sociology of knowledge should be "concerned with the conditions which bring about belief or states of knowledge," for knowledge "emanates from society"; it is "the product of collective influences and resources and peculiar to a given culture" (Bloor 1976). Clearly, this principle (a) focuses on external conditions, ignoring the inquirer's motivations and cognitive problems, or attributing them to external factors, thus making him appear as a mere pawn of social forces rather than as a creator; (b) ignores the fact – well-known to all but the classical behaviourists – that one and the same external stimulus may elicit different ideas, or none at all, in different persons or in the same person at different times; and (c) overlooks accident and luck – ever present inside the brain and out. We shall return to this school in section 4. For the moment we conclude that radical externalism is false for attributing to social groups functions that only individual brains can discharge.

Moreover, radical externalism is unsupported by empirical evidence. It does not even work for social science. To be sure, in this field social changes pose new theoretical problems, but (a) many students of society are unresponsive to such events, and (b) those who do tackle the issues posed by social change cannot expect society to deliver ideas: society can only challenge, reward, or punish social research. (See Stigler 1983 for economics.)

What holds for science also holds, *mutatis mutandis*, for the humanities. Here too some social conditions stimulate certain developments while inhibiting others – yet giving birth to neither. For example, Ingenieros (1923) noted that the academic fortunes of the nineteenth-century French philosophy professors followed the changing sociopolitical circumstances. (Possible mechanism: in France, as in Germany, university professors were civil servants, and every ideology has a philosophical nucleus.) Thus, whereas the victors of the 1848 revolution favoured idealism and intuitionism, the vanquished – particularly the best, Cournot and Renouvier – turned to Kantianism, which matched their liberal politics because it admitted free will (pp. 37–40). Closer to us, Gellner (1988, 28) wondered whether the Popper/Hayek vision of the open society was not inspired by the fact that the "individualistic, atomized, cultivated bourgeoisie of the Habsburg capital had to contend with the influx of swarms of kin-bound, collectivistic, rule-ignoring migrants from the eastern marches of the Empire."

However, the clearest cases of the influence of social forces upon philosophy are the totalitarian states. Because every such political system is intellectually legitimated by an official dogma, it cannot tolerate deviations from the latter. No wonder there is no original philosophical thought under such rules. Whatever original idea may occur to any philosopher living under any such a regime is promptly self-censored or censored. The same applies to social scientists. Only socially neutral fields, such as pure mathematics and natural science, can be cultivated in such circumstances; and even so with limitations because of the strictures of party philosophy and of the demand for practical results.

In sum, both internalism and radical externalism are false. Only individuals can have ideas; but, since every individual interacts with his society, and particularly with other members of his professional network, he is not immune to external influences, which may stimulate or inhibit his creativity. Hence, only a combination of internalism with externalism is appropriate. Such combination exemplifies the systemic approach.

3 Sociology of Knowledge: Marx to Merton

The sociology of knowledge may be characterized as the study of knowledge-producing and -diffusing communities, and their interactions with their host societies – in particular, the social constraints and stimuli on research and teaching – as well as the impact of scientific findings – via technology – on education, industry, and government.

The seeds of the modern sociology of knowledge were sown by Marx and Engels. They were the first to hold the following influential theses, which were both externalist and holist: (a) The social being of men determines their consciousness rather than the other way round (Marx 1859, in Marx and Engels 1986, 182). (b) "Upon the different forms of property, upon the social conditions of existence, rises an entire superstructure of distinct and peculiarly formed sentiments, illusions, modes of thought and views of life. The entire class creates and forms them out of its material foundations and out of the corresponding social relations. The single individual derives them through tradition and upbringing" (Marx 1852, in Marx and Engels 1986, 118–19). (c) All social studies are ideologically committed: they further the interests of some social class or other. In modern times there is bourgeois social science and socialist social science. However, whereas the former is "ideological" (in the sense of being full of error and illusion), the latter is objectively true as well as partisan, because the proletariat represents the interests of humankind.

These were certainly bold new ideas in the mid-nineteenth century, and each of them holds a grain of truth. In fact, (a) developmental and social psychology have shown that the social environment *conditions* a person's mental make-up – without however determining it fully, for both the nervous system and individual action (which sometimes goes against the current) do count for something, to put it mildly; (b) belonging to a social class does influence the *social* scientist's approach – but this does not entail either that he cannot overcome such limits or that his class does his thinking for him. (It is odd for a materialist to hold that a social class, which is brainless, can think. And it is simply false that all ideas emanate from the economic foundation of society.); (c) it is true that some branches of economics and political science, particularly those concerned with the management of the economy and with government, are tainted by the interests of the ruling classes. Suffice it to recall the "stabilization and adjustment" policies promoted by the International Monetary Fund, the doctrine of mutual nuclear deterrence, and the Leninist view of the state. However, even at the time of Marx and Engels there were objective social studies, such as some of their own. In short, whereas prescriptive or normative social studies are necessarily biased, basic or descriptive social studies can be objective. If they fail to be objective, they are unscientific.

The views of Marx and Engels on the social conditioning of knowledge and the partisanship of social science were fuzzy, sketchy, unsystematic, and above all unsupported by empirical research. For instance, what does 'determine' mean in the sentence "Social being determines consciousness"? That society as a whole *causes* mental processes, or that an individual's social position and behaviour strongly *influence* the way he thinks? And although at times Marx and Engels held that science and technology reside in the material *Unterbau* (infrastructure or economic basis), at other times they placed them in the ideal *Überbau* (superstructure). And whereas sometimes they held that *every* idea is the creation of a social class, and is thus distorted by class interests, at other times they admitted that mathematics and natural science are class-free, even while being conditioned by social circumstances. Such vacillations, sketchiness, and imprecision gave rise to a considerable variety of opinion and inconclusive scholastic controversy over these matters in the Marxist camp. However, most Marxists agree on radical externalism, or the thesis that only external (economic and political) circumstances matter to the genesis of ideas.

The programmatic ideas of Marx and Engels on the sociogenesis of ideas did not bear fruit until much later, when Hessen produced his much-acclaimed essay "The Social and Economic Roots of Newton's *Principia*," mentioned in section 2. Hessen held that Newton's work was a child of his class and time, and that his scientific work was an attempt to solve technological problems posed by the rise of capitalism. This thesis has a grain of truth: Newton did tackle scientific problems that had not even been posed before the modern era; he did so with the help of thoroughly modern methods; and the diffusion of his work was partly due to its usefulness to the technology required by the rapid transformation of industry and transportation, in particular navigation. However, this does not prove that Newton's equations of motion, let alone his contributions to optics and the infinitesimal calculus, had a social *motivation*, let alone a social *content*. Like any other first-rate scientist, Newton was primarily motivated by his curiosity over certain outstanding conceptual problems. Moreover, his theoretical mechanics concerns moving bodies in general, not machines, whereas his mathematical contributions were mainly about "fluxions" (time-dependent functions). Besides, how does one explain that Newton happened to be the only "child of his class and time" to build that monument? Why was there only one *Principia* rather than thousands of similar books written by as many contemporaries of Newton's? And why, if Newton was so keen on industry as Hessen claims, did he not design any machines or industrial processes? Why was he a theoretical physicist and mathematician, as well as a theologian and alchemist, rather than an engineer? And why did the same social class produce the atheist Hobbes, the sceptic Bayle, the deist Newton, the Protestant Boyle, and the nearly tolerant Locke, along with masses of religious fanatics and witch-hunters? Is it not just possible that the individual brain, as well as the social environment, has something to do with originality?

Hessen's paper won instant success. It helped shape the Western Marxist sociology of science, which flourished between the mid-1930s and the mid-1960s. The members of this movement published in the journals *Science & Society*, *The Modern Quarterly*, and *La pensée*. The most thorough and influential single study to come from this school was Bernal's *The Social Function of Science* of 1939. (See Goldsmith and Mackay 1964 for a representative sample of the work of this school.) However, neither Bernal nor his eminent friends and fellow members of the Royal Society – among them P.M.S. Blackett, J.B.S. Haldane, J. Needham, and E.H.S. Burhop – followed Hessen literally. They did stress both the social conditions of scientific research and the actual and desirable social uses of science, but they never claimed that mathematics and natural science have a social content. Being working scientists, they knew what they were writing about. Today they would perhaps be described (and denigrated) as naive internalists, not externalists.

What remains of those enthusiastic efforts? Very little except for the general ideas – now obvious to most students of science – that scientists do not work in a social vacuum, that they fulfil an important social function, and that they ought to discharge an even more important one. The main contribution of those students of science was to science policy. However, their proposal of planning all research elicited a backlash. In particular, the distinguished physical chemist Michael Polanyi (1958) rightly stressed the need for freedom of research and detachment from ideology.

The main effect of Marxism on the sociology of science, as on every other branch of social science, has been indirect. In fact, Marx is one of the three most important influences on the work of Robert K. Merton and his school – the other two being Weber and Durkheim. But, before it could be of any use, Marxism had to be watered down and activated: watered down, that is, stripped of its radical externalist thesis that context determines content; and activated, that is, transformed from dogma into research project.

Merton, a sociologist and historian of ideas by training, is the real founding father of the sociology of knowledge as a science and a profession; his predecessors had been isolated scholars or amateurs. (See, for example, Zuckerman 1988.) When Merton started his academic career in the mid-1930s, all the students of science, with the exception of the Marxists, were strict internalists. This applies in particular to H. Butterfield, A. Koyré, A. Mieli, C. Singer, and G. Sarton – Merton's teacher. Merton's doctoral dissertation, published in 1938, was titled *Science, Technology and Society in Seventeenth-Century England.* (The first four words denote nowadays an established academic field.) The central general hypothesis of that book is that "not only error or illusion or unauthenticated belief but also the discovery of truth is socially and historically conditioned." One of its key specific hypotheses was that the Puritan ethic promoted the rise of science in England – much as, according to Weber, Calvinism had favoured the emergence of capitalism. (See Cohen 1990 for an anthology of studies on Merton's thesis.)

A historian of the sociology of science might note that this idea had been "in the air," particularly in view of three fresh experiences. One was the popularity of Marxism among British and French intellectuals in the 1930s, and their enthusiastic reception of Hessen's externalist thesis about Newton's mechanics in 1931. A second fact was the vigorous support of scientific research given by the Soviet government before it imposed the detailed planning of research and embarked on the disastrous road of *partinosty* (partisanship) and scientific witch-hunting – a support all the more remarkable given the Soviet Union's economic underdevelopment and the miserly science budgets in Britain and France at that time. A third event was the rise of so-called Aryan science (*Rassenkunde*, German physics, etc.) and the persecution of so-called Jewish science in pro-Nazi Germany, as well as the role played by Nazi intellectuals in shaping the new anti-intellectualist atmosphere. (See, for instance, Kolnai 1938 and Farías 1990.)

Merton's reaction against the Nazi attempt to subdue and pervert German science was his seminal 1938 piece "Science and the Social Order" (see Merton 1973). In it he introduced the novel idea that science has its own *ethos*, which he summarized as follows: "intellectual honesty, integrity, organized skepticism, disinterestedness, impersonality." Four years later he reformulated the code of scientific ethics, stating that it comprises four "institutional imperatives": *universalism* or non-relativism, *communism* or unrestricted sharing of scientific knowledge, *disinterestedness* or freedom from economic or political motivations and strictures, and *organized scepticism* or emphasis on methodical doubt, arguability and testability (Merton 1942 in Merton 1957a and 1973). (This point was elaborated later on by Bronowski [1959] and myself [1960].) Little did Merton suspect that a few decades later the very existence of that ethos would be denied by the so-called post-Mertonian or constructivist-relativist sociologists of science, many of whom regard themselves as leftists and would consequently feel insulted if told that they have embraced, albeit unknowingly, a central part of the Nazi creed, namely contempt for pure science and rationality in general.

Much of the work of the Merton school would nowadays be described as a kind of *discourse analysis*. It consisted in analysing scientific documents, especially publications, and it involved only occasional empirical research, mainly by way of interviews and questionnaires. In the hands of these scholars, who knew what science is all about, discourse analysis has produced a number of classics, such as Merton's own "Singletons and Multiples in Science" (1961), "The Matthew Effect in Science" (1968), and "Age, Aging and Age Structure in Science," written with H. Zuckerman (1972, in Merton 1973). (For other jewels in the same style see Barber 1952; Barber and Hirsch eds 1962; and Merton 1973.) In addition to performing discourse analysis, some of the scholars in Merton's circle interviewed live scientists to discover what makes them tick (e.g., Hagstrom 1965; Zuckerman 1977.) They all confirmed Merton's hypothesis, that what drives scientists are chiefly disinterested curiosity and the desire for peer recognition.

All of these studies assumed the *uniqueness* of basic science deriving from its universalism, epistemic communism, disinterestedness, and organized scepticism. (Such uniqueness is denied by the pro-Kuhnian philosophers and sociologists of science.) This is not to say that all those studies were flawless. In my view some of them have been excessively externalistic: they have underrated the uniqueness of the contributions of men of genius. Thus, in his justly famous paper on singletons and multiples, Merton wrote that "scientists of genius are precisely those whose work in the end would be eventually rediscovered. These rediscoveries would be made not by a single scientist but by an entire corps of scientists. On this view, the individual of scientific genius is the functional equivalent of a considerable array of other scientists of varying degrees of talent" (1973, 366). How can we know that this is indeed the case? I submit that we cannot. We only know that (a) the work of many a genius has been recognized late; and (b) in the case of some breakthroughs, such as in the genesis of quantum physics, the synthetic theory of evolution, physiological psychology, molecular biology, and operations research, several geniuses teamed up to build a new discipline. To be sure, there are cases – precisely those studied by Merton – that fit his hypothesis, but they are seldom cases of scientific breakthroughs. An outstanding individual, no less than a science, is unique – by definition.

To sum up, the Merton school sinned, though only venially, in holding that quantity can compensate for quality; and, being structuralist, it occasionally exaggerated the power of the social matrix. But on the whole it practised a sound synthesis of externalism and internalism, it embraced neither subjectivism nor relativism, and it did not underrate the importance of ideas. This is why it produced the first scientific studies on the institutional aspect of science. And this is why, in my opinion, Merton's school attained the peak of the sociology of knowledge. When it began to be rejected in the 1960s, the discipline started to roll downhill, as will be argued in the following section.

4 The Antiscientific Reaction

The "post-Mertonian" or antiscientific movement in the sociology of knowledge emerged in the 1960s under the influence of T.S. Kuhn and P.K. Feyerabend, Wittgenstein's linguistic philosophy, and "Continental" (that is, German and French) irrationalism. (See Barnes 1977; Knorr-Cetina and Mulkay 1983; and *Social Studies of Science*.) It quickly won popular appeal by denying that basic scientific research is peculiar, rational, objective, disinterested, and benign. This movement is characterized by radical externalism, constructivism, relativism, pragmatism – and amateurism. We shall show below that externalism implies constructivism, which in turn implies relativism and pragmatism.

As we saw in section 3, radical global externalism – as exemplified by the "strong programme" of the Edinburgh school (see Bloor 1976) – holds that every single bit of knowledge is a social construction. Moreover, it would be somehow *about* society, that is, it would have a *social content* – so that, ultimately, there would be no distinctions between content and context, natural science and social science, or even discourse and praxis. This would hold even for mathematics, traditionally regarded as the purest of all sciences: "[I]f mathematics is about number and its relations and if these are social creations and conventions then, indeed, mathematics is about something social. In an indirect sense it therefore is 'about' society. It is about society in the same sense as Durkheim said that religion is about society. The reality that it appears to be about represents a transfigured understanding of the social labor that has been invested in it" (Bloor 1976, 93).

Let us pass over the howler that mathematics is just "about number and its relations" – an even poorer characterization than the ancient description "the science of number and form." Let us ask instead for the *evidence* in support of the thesis that "mathematics is social through and through" (Restivo 1992). The answer is that there *is* no such evidence. Of course mathematics is a social creation, in the sense that it is constructed by a number of people who inherit a tradition, interact, and learn from one another. But this does not entail that the mathematical postulates, definitions, or theorems refer even indirectly to society, let alone describe it. The application of any reasonable theory of reference (e.g., Bunge 1974a) yields the unsurprising result that set theory is about sets, abstract algebra about algebraic systems, topology about topological spaces, number theory about whole numbers, analysis about functions, geometry about manifolds, and so forth. In short, pure mathematics is about mathematical objects and nothing else. In turn, mathematical objects, though not arbitrary fantasies, are fictions, not facts (Bunge 1985a, 1997a).

If mathematics were actually about society it would be a *social* science. Consequently, (a) it could not be used in physics, chemistry, biology, psychology, or engineering; (b) it would be tested empirically the way social-science hypotheses are supposed to be checked; and (c) social science proper would be redundant. In any event, any serious claim of the form "A refers to [or is about] B" is substantiated with the help of some theory of reference. But the new crop of sociologists of science have no such theory: they proceed in this crucial matter in a non-technical and dogmatic manner.

The best known fruit of the "strong programme" is Latour's and Woolgar's 1979 account of laboratory work. Consider the following gems. Just because scientific laboratories are public institutions partially open to laypersons (even to journalists trying to pass for sociologists), they have no walls, but mesh in intimately with society at large, so that what goes on in them is quite ordinary (Latour 1983). And, just because in a laboratory thought and action intertwine, "context and content merge" (Latour 1987), and there is no distinction between discourse and *praxis* (Woolgar 1986). Moreover, just because scientific research – like any other institutionalized activity – involves some politicking and, when mistaken for technology, it may be seen as the most potent source of power in modern society, "science is politics pursued by other means" (Latour 1983, 168). Thus, ultimately, the micro/macro distinction too is lost in the big magma that the new sociologists of science call 'science.'

Radical global externalism is shared by a number of currents in the counterculture and "postmodernist" movements. For instance, Wright (1992, 7) asserts confidently – but of course does not prove – the theses that physics is actually a social theory in disguise and that the whole of science must be understood as referring to the structure of language rather than to things out there. And the feminist philosopher Harding (1986, 127) assures us that "the social order creates the biological conceptions that are thought to serve the needs of those holding, aspiring to, or defending power." (But she omits to explain how a social order, which is mindless, can create biology.)

Such shift from interior to exterior comes in handy for anyone who insists on talking about science without bothering to learn any. It even nourishes the illusion that the outsider is able "to explain [to] the insider how it all works" (Latour 1987, 15). For example, a "semiotic analysis" enables Latour (1988) to discover that Einstein's special relativity is not about bodies moving in an electromagnetic field, as its creator naively believed, but about "communication among long distance travelers." An original finding indeed – but an utterly false one, as anyone who has analysed even a single formula of relativistic physics knows. For example, is "$E = mc^2$" being used to communicate with Antipodians?

To sum up, the radical externalist is right in holding that scientists do not live in a social vacuum. It is also true that the search for truth is personal and often passionate – but truth is neither. The detachment of scientific ideas and practices from individual researchers and their social circumstances is just an analytic device – albeit an indispensable one if one is to understand and evaluate them *as* ideas or practices. And stating that social circumstances *constitute* scientific ideas and practices is like saying that, since we must breathe to stay alive, we are made of air – presumably hot. (More on externalism and relativism in Shils 1982; Gellner 1985; Boudon 1990b; and Boudon and Clavelin 1994.)

Radical externalism implies the collectivist version of subjectivism called *social constructivism*. According to it all things, from atoms to stars, are consequences of cognitive processes: they are cultural objects – just because they are studied in certain branches of culture. Thus, Knorr-Cetina (1983, 135) stated that scientific research is "the process of secreting an unending stream of entities and relations that make up 'the world.'" Feyerabend (1990, 147) concurred: *"Scientific entities* (and, for that matter, all entities) *are projections and are thus tied to the theory, the ideology, the culture that postulates and projects them"* (emphasis in the original). Since manifest facts "are the response of an (unknown) material to human action, we may say that ... Nature is a work of art" (Feyerabend 1995, 264). (See also Latour and Woolgar 1979, 237; H.M. Collins 1981, 3; Barnes 1983, 21; and Lynch et al. 1983.) Do not ask for empirical evidence: constructivists need none because, far from exploring the world, they claim to build it. But of course there is overwhelming evidence against constructivism, from palaeontology and archaeology to evolutionary biology and the study of perception and action.

If ontological constructivism – whether individualist or collectivist – were true, there would be no point in checking any representations of real things. There would be no difference between map and territory, portrait and person portrayed, Picasso's *Guernica* and the ruins of Guernica: what there is is what you feel or think. Nor would there be any difference between appearance and reality, primary and secondary properties, atoms and gods, history and myth. Illusion, dream, hallucination, and story would be indistinguishable from reality, and science and technology would be mythical. Thus, the *Entzauberung* (de-enchantment) peculiar to modernity would have to be reversed. As a matter of fact, Berman (1981) has demanded the "re-enchantment" of the world. And Feyerabend (1990, 152) held that the "drab material world" can be repopulated with gods "if its inhabitants have the heart, the determination, and the intelligence to take the necessary steps." In sum, ontological constructivism is a regression to magical thinking.

In turn, constructivism implies epistemological *relativism*, that is, the view that there are no objective truths. Indeed, if all facts are created by some social group or other, there can be no objective truths about them. And if this is the case, there can be no truth tests or "reality checks." That is, what counts as valid method or as relevant evidence for one social group need not count as such for another. In sum, evidence and truth are relative to the social group. Because of such plurality of truths there must be as many belief systems as there are social groups, and neither of them can be said to be objectively superior to any other, precisely because there are no objective – hence universal – truth tests. This view – perhaps first expounded by Nietzsche – has been adopted by the Frankfurt school, Foucault, Rorty, Ross, Aronowitz, and most other "postmodernists." All of them deny the existence of objective truths and assert that scientific knowledge does not map the world but is only a tool of power. But none of them has explained why mathematics, science, and technology often succeed, regardless of social order, when all else fails.

For example, according to epistemological relativism, a modern critical mind is not superior to a primitive one; a magic world-view is just as valid as a scientific one; and science is no better than pseudoscience: "anything goes" (Feyerabend 1975). In particular, evolutionary biology would not be superior to creationism, and medicine would not be better than faith healing. In fact, most constructivist-relativists have defended some pseudoscience or other (see, for example, Pinch and Collins 1979, 1984; H. and S. Rose 1974; Ezrahi 1972; and M. Mulkay 1972).

Epistemological relativism has also been embraced by leading "feminist philosophers." Thus, Nye (1990) claims that logic is "gendered" because the textbook examples of inference rules have only male names in them – as in "All men are mortal, Socrates is a man, hence Socrates is mortal" – a claim that betrays a crass ignorance of formal logic. Others hold that a "feminine science" (organicist, qualitative, intuitive, and caring) should have its rightful place along with or even above male science (mechanistic, analytic, "linear," quantitative, and power-hungry). Regrettably, no achievements of "feminine" science are ever cited. Nor is it explained how genuine philosophy, mathematics, and science, which are universal, can be sexed. As Lynn McDonald (1993) states, this is "both poor scholarship and counter productive." Which is not to deny that many scientists (female as well as male) have overlooked experiences and issues peculiar to women. But, precisely because these experiences and issues are just as important as neglected, they should be tackled scientifically not irrationally.

As we have just seen, relativism and pragmatism are logical consequences of social constructivism, which in turn was shown to be implied by radical externalism. This chain is logically impeccable, but every link of it happens to be false: it is a chain of errors. Moreover, these are both gross theoretical and practical mistakes. They are theoretical errors because they do not match the practice of scientific research, which is the search for objective, hence cross-cultural (though not necessarily eternal) truths. And they are practical mistakes because they encourage superstition and quackery, and consequently undermine any efforts to raise the cultural level and increase social welfare.

What may explain the current vogue of this error? I conjecture that it is due to the confluence of three contemporary currents: exacerbated individualism ("Everyone is entitled to their beliefs and habits"), utilitarianism ("Good or true is only that which helps live"), and uncritical non-conformism ("Everything related to the establishment is bad"). Each of these currents imperils the explorers: their confluence is sure to drown them.

In conclusion, the post-Mertonian sociology of science is false, shallow, and antiscientific. It is critical of genuine science but gullible about pseudoscience, as well as being guilty of ideology. It draws on irrationalist philosophies, in particular philosophical hermeneutics, phenomenology, and existentialism – that height of uncommon nonsense. It has made no single solid contribution to the field. And it ignores all of the most interesting problems in the sociology and political science of science, such as the participation of outstanding scientists in the Cold War, the recent cuts in research budgets (particularly in the social sciences), the universal reluctance to fund large-scale social experiments, the distorting effects of fast publication and grant-hunting, the economic interests behind the Human Genome project, the decline in the enrolment in science schools, the growing hostility of humanities students to science, and the vogue of New Age thinking and other superstitions. In particular, the constructivist-relativists have not asked themselves what the social roots of their own popular success are. (Further criticisms in Boudon 1990b and 1995; Bunge 1991c, 1992a, and 1996c; Holton 1992; Kitcher 1993b; Gross and Levitt 1994; and Gross et al. 1996. And for some recent defections from that camp see Forman 1995.)

In short, the sociology of science has derailed. There is only one way to put it back on track: Back to Merton!

5 Technology in Society

Any social study of technology presupposes some idea of technology. Regrettably, most conceptions of technology are flawed. Indeed, some confuse it with science, others with applied science, still others with craftsmanship or even industry; most restrict technology to engineering, and many mistake diffusion for invention. The first of these confusions is typical of philosophical pragmatism, of much post-Mertonian sociology of science, and of "critical theorists" such as Marcuse and Habermas. It amounts to mistaking truth for efficiency, or even to proposing the replacement of the former with the latter. This is an elementary error. In fact, scientific hypotheses are checked mainly for truth, whereas artefacts – from machines to organizations – are tested for efficiency, reliability, durability, safety, affordability, profitability, user-friendliness, or some other non-cognitive feature.

The second confusion – that is, "Technology = Applied science" – ignores the fact that applied science (such as pharmacology, medical sociology, and pedagogy) is the bridge between basic science and technology. And it underrates the role of imagination and research in design and planning, which happen to be the hub of technology. Hence, the confusion in question breeds the false expectation that scientific findings will lead automatically to "applications." This fallacy is exploited by many scientists when asking for research grants, in the hope of fooling the science bureaucrats. This deceitful practice should be discouraged: civil servants and politicians should be taught that basic research meets primarily the important social need of raising the general cultural level.

The third confusion – of technology with either craftsmanship or industry – leads to underrating the input of science to technology. Indeed, modern technology is science-based and, unlike craftsmanship and industry, it produces ideas, such as blueprints and plans, rather than concrete things such as machines or services such as health care.

Fourth, equating technology with engineering overlooks the sociotechnologies, from management science and normative economics to education and law. These are technologies because they aim at the control of human behaviour through the design, redesign, or management of social systems, such as business firms, government departments, schools, hospitals, armies, and jails. (See part C.)

Finally, invention – a brain process – must not be confused with diffusion – a social process – since the latter consists in the implementation and adoption of an invention. Nor must the improvement of an existing artefact be confused with the conception of its prototype. The former responds to some shortcoming: it corrects failure Petroski (1993). By contrast, radical invention – as in the cases of artificial selection, vaccination, the electric motor, telecommunications, and the electronic computer – involves leaps of the imagination on a par with the inventions of mathematics and religion. (I invent, you perfect, they copy.)

In view of the popularity of the above-mentioned confusions, let us perform the philosophical task of defining the concept of modern technology. We define it as the branch of knowledge concerned with the design and test of systems or processes with the help of scientific knowledge and with the aim of serving industry or government. (See also Susskind 1973; Agassi 1985; Bunge 1985b; Quintanilla 1988; Wiener 1994; and Mitcham 1994).

Let us note some of the differences between basic science and technology. Scientific knowledge, the goal of basic research, is a means for technology. The former aims at understanding reality, the latter at supplying tools for altering nature or society. Science produces priceless cultural goods; technology produces cultural goods that double as merchandises. Hence, whereas scientific findings are public goods, technological items can be privately owned. To be sure, every so often both science and technology will produce "lemons" (shoddy items). But eventually the scientific community weeds them out, whereas there is always a market for technological "lemons" because businessmen and consumers are seldom as rational and honest as scientists. A further difference is that, whereas science only enhances our intellectual powers, technology also supplies means to strengthen our power over nature or over men. Hence technology, rather than science, can help to either solve or originate social problems.

The preceding elucidation should help us tackle three philosophically interesting problems: the alleged neutrality of technology, the claim that it is a "social construction," and the view that it is just as lawless as basic science. Let us start with the first problem. Because of its potential for both good and evil, technology – unlike science – is morally, ideologically, and politically committed. (Frisk the technologist, not the basic scientist, for concealed wealth or power.) Therefore, it may be argued that technology should also be socially responsive. In a fully democratic society, technology – unlike basic science – should be subject to public scrutiny and control (Agassi 1985; Bunge 1989a). In particular, the public is entitled to assess the potential of new technologies for good or evil, and even to nip in the bud any technological developments that threaten public welfare.

There have been a few scattered and half-hearted efforts to pass off technology as a social construction (e.g., Bijker et al. 1987). They are unconvincing because intellectual creativity is a feature of brains, not of social groups. The latter can only stimulate or inhibit intellectual creativity. Technological designs, plans, proposals, and recommendations must certainly match the economic and political realities and possibilities. But "demand-pull" results only in improvements of existing artefacts. Radical inventions are ultimately motivated by the passion for solving problems, trying out new ideas, or just tinkering.

Our third and final problem is whether there are any laws of technological development. No laws of scientific evolution are known, other than that every scientific finding makes it possible to pose new problems – whence the exponential growth of science as long as scientific research is carried on. By contrast, a number of plausible candidates for the status of generalization about technological development can been exhibited. Here is a sample. 1/ Every artificial thing or process can be improved upon, but only up to a point: there are natural and social (in particular economic) limits. 2/ Every technological innovation has unpredictable and undesirable side effects. 3/ Every such defect can in principle be fixed with the help of either more knowledge or social reform. 4/ Every breakthrough in high tech exploits some scientific findings. 5/ Only a small fraction of basic science gets to be applied, and only a small fraction of applied science finds use in technology. 6/ There is usually a delay of several years between scientific findings and their technological use. 7/ Most inventions are never put into practice. 8/ Military technology has minimal civilian spin-offs, and it slows down the development of civilian technology because it diverts brains, natural resources, and funds. 9/ In developing nations technology starts by being imitative. 10/ Technological innovation as a function of firm size is an inverted U: it grows at first and then declines.

These are mere empirical generalizations or quasi-laws. But some of them can be explained in terms of social mechanisms. For example, the growth part in the tenth quasi-law is explained by the need for an organization to attain a critical mass before it can afford to engage in R&D; and the downturn part is explained by the large layouts required by retooling, reorganizing, and (not least) rethinking. Caution: Some of the key variables occurring in the preceding, particularly the epistemic ones, are somewhat fuzzy. (This caution is necessary in view of the existence of certain models of the economics of R&D containing variables, such as the fund of knowledge and the likelihood of a technical breakthrough, that have not been properly quantitated and therefore measured.)

In conclusion, the budding social sciences of technology are bound to cast light on one of the three engines of modern culture – the other two being science and ideology. Moreover, those disciplines are required to design suitable technology policies, which are in turn necessary to design efficient industrial policies. But those social sciences are unlikely to make the requisite advances without the assistance of a philosophy of technology capable of tackling the peculiar problems posed by technology, starting with the very definitions of "artefact" and "technology."

6 Social Science in Society

Every social science can be studied from a social-science viewpoint. As a matter of fact a number of new sciences of social science have emerged in recent years – for instance, the political sciences of anthropology, politology, and history, and the sociology of the economics profession. Some of these studies have confirmed Marx's claim that, unlike the study of nature, the social studies can be ideologically contaminated or even politically committed. For example, even when scientific, politology can hardly avoid social pressures. Thus, mainstream political science and legal theory are far more interested in problems concerning law and order than in questions of social conflict and social justice.

Anthropology has long been suspected of ideological contamination, having initially been sponsored by colonial administrators eager to learn the ways of the natives to better control them, or to prove the myth of the White Man's Burden (see, for example, Harris 1968). In particular, it has been held that anthropological functionalism and relativism were largely the children of the colonial policy of not meddling with the native social organizations in order to avoid rebellions. For example, Malinowski (1926) opposed the persecution of native sorcerers, believing that "sorcery remains a support of vested interest [...] It is always a conservative force." But functionalism could also have been used to justify native revolt: since the imperial powers have imposed severe dysfunctionalities, let us throw them out. Still, this ambivalence has not prevented contemporary anthropologists from finding a number of objective truths about their subjects.

History has often been suspected of "patriotic" bias. For example, up until the end of the First World War, French historians could hardly trust their German colleagues, and conversely, and neither of them trusted their English counterparts. Every national community of historians seemed pre-eminently concerned with singing the glories of its respective nation and hushing up its iniquities. (Such bias is still conspicuous among textbook writers and nationalist ideologues.) And, as Lewis H. Morgan showed in 1877, the early European descriptions of the Amerindian peoples suffered from (mostly unwitting) ideological contamination: those chroniclers could not help seeing the New World through the lens of their own political and religious beliefs. (See, for instance, León-Portilla 1980 for ancient México, and Rostworowski de Díez Canseco 1983 for ancient Perú.) And the Huron historian Georges E. Sioui (1989) has charged European students of the Amerindians with distorting their history in having overlooked the moral values of the aboriginals, which he finds superior to those of their European conquerors. However, one should beware against distortions in the opposite sense, such as the claim that all pre-Columbian agriculture was environmentally benign, while in fact it sometimes caused roughly as much soil erosion as plough agriculture (O'Hara et al. 1993).

Our next example of ideological contamination is the instant popularity earned by the marginalist "revolution" in economic thinking shortly after 1871. (Recall chap. 3, sects. 5 and 6.) Surely such success could not be due to the scientific exploits of neoclassical microeconomics, for this theory did not solve any of the problems left over by the classical economists. Worse, it constituted a return to eighteenth-century mercantilism, overlooking as it did production and consequently labour and technology as well. It was epistemologically reactionary in overrating the subjective aspect of economic activity at the expense of its objective sources, impacts, and constraints. And it was politically conservative in playing down business cycles, market disequilibria, and imperfections; in ignoring the social costs of private enterprise and the problem of income distribution; and in consistently advising against government intervention to treat what Gini (1952) called "economic pathologies." In particular, it is no accident that nearly all the studies of income distribution have been conducted outside the neoclassical school (see, for example, Asimakopulos 1988).

According to Robinson and Eatwell (1974, 35) and Pasinetti (1981,12–14) – all three prominent non-Marxist economists – it was precisely its conservatism that made marginalism so attractive to an establishment scared by the first Socialist International (1864), Marx's *Das Kapital* (1867), and, above all, the Paris Commune (1871). This conservatism may be one of the reasons that, despite its inadequacies, neoclassical microeconomics is still the central vein of mainstream economics. It may also be one of the reasons that "it is the essential glue by which the economics profession as a social system is held together," and that its critics are usually marginalized (Eichner 1983, 233).

Occasionally a good scientific idea is pressed into ideological service. For example, Darwinism has been misused for over a century to justify social inequality: the rich and powerful are seen to be naturally superior to others, and thus the legitimate winners in the struggle for existence. A more recent case is that of human-capital theory. This is the correct and important thesis (hardly a theory) that people are wealth, so that education is an investment (Schultz 1961; Becker 1964). Regrettably, no sooner was this idea launched than it was used to justify economic inequality in terms of differences in education: "Laborers have become capitalists ... from the acquisition of knowledge and skill that have economic value" (Schultz 1961, 3). Accordingly, initial endowments and social connections play no role in social differentiation. (More in Blaug 1976.)

Marxism – a rich and interesting if largely obsolete mixture of social science, philosophy, and ideology – poses another problem. Scholars have occasionally puzzled over the bewildering diversity of twentieth-century Marxisms and their growing divergence from one another. Anderson (1976) has grouped them into two main clusters, classical and Western, and has claimed that this division has political roots. The former used to be cultivated mainly by Communist Party intellectuals – which explains why it stressed the unity of theory and practice, and it employed a non-technical vocabulary. By contrast, Western Marxism is the creature of sophisticated academics – which explains why it emphasizes grand theory and employs an esoteric jargon.

All this rings true, but it fails to explain why neither of the two strands of Marxism got rid of the Hegelian nonsense; why both have failed to come up with bold and true new theories; and why Marxism is seldom interested in quantitation. (There have been a few honourable exceptions, notably P.A. Baran, M. Kalecki, O. Lange, and P.M. Sweezy – but they were all unorthodox and thus hardly listened to.) Yet the explanation is obvious: no novelties can be expected if the bulk of the original doctrine is accepted, new problems are skirted, and most of the energy of its adherents is devoted to attacking rivals instead of listening to what they have to say. Only an internalist analysis, focusing on dogmatism, fuzziness, and disregard of logic and evidence, may account for the decadence of Marxism, all the more so since it has occurred under "real socialism" as well as under capitalism.

All students of society, not only Marxists, run the risk of confusing science with ideology, particularly if they have no clear idea of either. This is obvious in the case of the externalist sociologists of science, who see the fangs of power even in the most innocent mathematical formula. There is only one way of checking whether a statement has an ideological connotation, namely to perform a semantic analysis of it and, in particular, to reveal what it is about. If the statement is about actions likely to affect a particular sector of society, then of course it belongs to either ideology or social policy. (Example: any social program.) Otherwise it is ideologically neutral, as is the case with truthful social statistics.

Still, this test is insufficient to spot the ideology that may be lurking behind a given statement. Indeed, it may well be that the statement is simply false, and that such falsity is employed to shore up an ideology or a social policy (see, for instance, Hutchison 1964). Thus, the contemporary apostle of monetarism and his closest co-worker have been accused of doing precisely this. In fact, the econometric analyses of the American and British economies performed by Milton Friedman and Anna Schwartz (1982) were explicitly designed to prove the benefits of tight monetary policies – but on examination they proved not to accomplish anything of the sort (Brown 1983; Hendry and Ericsson 1983).

Our last example of ideological contamination of social studies will be the fashionable "feminist theory." This is not to be mistaken for feminism, a progressive social movement with no particular philosophical attachment. Nor is academic feminism to be confused with the scientific (in particular sociological) study of the feminine question, in particular the issues of sex roles and discrimination. "Feminist theory" is an ideology with philosophical pretensions that attacks "official" science alleging (but of course not proving) that it is inherently "androcentric" (or "phallocentric"). Worse, it has unknowingly rehashed the irrationalism inherent in the counter-Enlightenment. It does not care for truth tests because it rejects the very idea of objective truth; and it claims that reason, quantitation, and objectivity are damnable male features. Moreover, it exaggerates sex differences and sees male domination nearly everywhere. Thus, Harding (1986, 113) holds that it would be "illuminating and honest" to call Newton's laws of motion "Newton's rape manual." The rape victim would be Nature, which of course is feminine. Moreover, basic science would be indistinguishable from technology, and the search for knowledge would be just a disguised struggle for power.

The "feminist theorists" ask us to believe that philosophy, mathematics, science, and technology have so far have been "gender-laden" and, moreover, tools of male rule. Of course they offer no evidence for their thesis – presumably because the concern for objective truth is androcentric. Nor do they offer a glimpse of the ideas and methods that would characterize, say, feminine inference rules or feminine celestial mechanics by contrast to the generally accepted ones. Obviously, it is far easier to discuss imaginary "male paradigms," and to dismiss what one does not understand, than to construct the so-called successor science, an allegedly superior replacement for the only science we have got – and one that is increasingly being cultivated by women. In short, there is no more feminine science than there is Aryan science; what passes for such is just an academic racket. So is feminist philosophy: genuine philosophy is just as sexless as authentic mathematics and science. (More in Weinberg 1993 and Gross and Levitt 1994.)

In conclusion, social studies have always run the risk of ideological contamination. (See Zeitlin 1968 for a history of the sociology-ideology connection.) But, if authentically scientific, a study in basic social science will be ideologically neutral even though it may be used to justify or indict social policies. Therefore, we must beware of blanket condemnations of all social studies as being distorted by the ruling ideology (as Ross [1991] has claimed); much less as being just a political phenomenon and a product of the state (as charged by some Marxists). There are enough serious social studies to hope that some social protoscience and semiscience will eventually mature into social science.

7 Ideology

A sociopolitical ideology is an explicit system of values and ideals concerning both the prevailing and the desirable social orders. In their youth Comte and Marx believed that ideology and philosophy were obsolete and would soon be replaced with science. But in due time they invented their own ideologies and philosophies. Before and since then uncounted civil wars and international conflicts have been fought in the name of some ideology or other. When the Cold War was in full swing Daniel Bell (1960) announced the end of ideology. But in fact ideology has never ceased to influence lifestyles, fan political conflict, distort social studies, and feed uncounted intellectuals ready to lie for king and country, church or party. (See Benda's [1927] classical denunciation of the betrayal of the good scholar's universal values: reason, truth, and justice.)

Bell is right in holding that no *new* broad ideologies are in sight. In fact, all of the grand extant ideologies are intellectually senile or dead. Moreover, no party, once in power, can afford to abide strictly by its own ideology, for it soon finds out that the real world is far too complex and changeable to be depicted accurately by any orthodoxy – and because the exercise of power calls for bargaining and compromising. However, this is another story.

What intrigues the culturologist more is why even "dead" beliefs – that is, beliefs that have proved to be irrelevant, inefficient, false, or even harmful – can draw the living. (In social matters we seem to invest more effort in fooling ourselves and others than in searching for new ideas and testing them.) Apparently all social ideologies outlive the societies they are born in: that is, every social ideology ends up by lagging behind social reality. (This, incidentally, falsifies functionalism.) Witness the resilience of religious fundamentalisms, laissez-fairism, Marxism-Leninism, fascism, and nationalism, even at the height of what is supposed to be the Age of Science and Technology.

These belief systems have proved to be not only impervious to rational debate but also largely insensitive to hard fact. (Incidentally, since they defy cultural selection, they falsify the much-talked-about yet still unborn "evolutionary epistemology.") Hence, Huntington's (1993) prophecy, that the conflict of political ideologies is being replaced with a clash of civilizations, is unlikely to come to pass. (However, given the laxity of Huntington's concept of civilization – which makes room for an "African civilization," as if Africa were a solid block – any large-scale international conflict may be taken to confirm his prophecy.) If the past is any guide, every serious international conflict is likely to be multifaceted: territorial, ethnic, political, economic, and cultural – in particular ideological.

In any event, although ideologies should be analysed as conceptual systems, they should not be evaluated independently of historical circumstances, for they are flags of social movements and, therefore, tools of either stasis or change: so much so that one and the same ideology can discharge one function at one time and another in a different epoch. Thus, economic liberalism, which had been progressive between about 1750 and 1850, became increasingly conservative after the birth of the labour movement and the welfare state. Marxism, born as an emancipation ideology, ended up by being a tool of oppression. And nationalism can serve as a flag of national independence, an appeal to a return to the past, or an excuse for oppressing minorities or other peoples. (More on this in a while.) What holds for political ideologies also holds, *mutatis mutandis*, for religions.

Whoever is minimally interested in politics cannot do without some ideology. Every citizen and every culture is guided or misguided by at least one ideology – religious or secular. Not even the most enlightened culture can dispense with some ideology, for an ideology is a way of perceiving and evaluating facts, and consequently it plays a role in our social choices and actions. Thus, rather than being alien to social reality, ideology is part of it. Moreover, ideology contaminates some social studies or even masquerades as such. But it can also motivate social research. For example, a number of people are attracted to history because of their radical politics. Never mind the motivation: the point is whether the end product is neither false nor trivial (see Hobsbawm 1972, 1).

Given the political importance of ideology, its serious study falls to politologists. Let us proceed to examining a particular ideology, or rather a family of ideologies, that looked quite dead a few years ago, namely, nationalism. This should prove a useful exercise in the analysis of an idea that derives much of its appeal from its fuzziness. Indeed, *nationalism* is a catch-all word, whence it should never be used without qualification (see, for example, Alter 1994). In fact, nationalism can be *defensive* or *aggressive* – the former being often a reaction against the latter. And in either case nationalism can be territorial, biological, economic, political, cultural, or a combination of two or more of these basic kinds.

Territorial nationalism (T) favours either the defence of the national territory or the conquest of foreign territory. *Biological (ethnic) nationalism* (B) urges either the protection of an ethnic group or the oppression of one or more alien ethnic groups. *Economic nationalism* (E) presses for either economic protectionism or economic expansionism (whether peaceful or violent). *Political nationalism* (P) advocates either the political emancipation or the political oppression of a nation or part of it. And *cultural nationalism* (C) advocates either the preservation of a nation's cultural heritage or cultural domination, in particular cultural imperialism.

There are then five basic types of defensive nationalism, and another five of aggressive nationalism. These can combine, forming ten couplets, ten triplets, five quartets, and one quintet (integral nationalism), each of which is in turn either defensive or aggressive:

T, B, E, P, C
TB, TE, TP, TC, BE, BP, BC, EP, EC, PC
TBE, TBP, TBC, TEP, TEC, TPC, BEP, BEC, BPC, EPC
TBEP, TBEC, TBPC, TEPC, BEPC
TBEPC

Thus, there are altogether $2 \times 31 = 62$ nationalisms. (Addition of the left/centre/right trichotomy yields 186 logically possible kinds of nationalism. But the point of nationalism is that it seeks to rally everyone around the flag, regardless of social class and political orientation.) No wonder that nationalist movements are heterogeneous and likely to change course rather erratically under the influence of successive cliques or leaders who are bound to assign different weights to the five basic components. No wonder, too, that all studies of nationalism have been inadequate. Indeed most of them, even Gellner's (1983) and Mann's (1993), have treated nationalism as a single entity rather than a numerous family. Hence, the unavoidable functionalist question 'What is the function of nationalism?' is imprecise. And any imprecise question invites many one-sided answers.

Philosophers, as such, are not competent to pass political judgment on nationalism. But they can analyse the underlying concepts and the empirical validation proffered – particularly where the latter is bookish. Philosophers should also pass moral judgment. In particular, they should condemn all thirty-one varieties of aggressive nationalism, for unprovoked aggression deprives the victims of some or all of their basic rights. Besides, aggressive cultural nationalism impoverishes the aggressor as well as its victim by erasing the latter's culture, in particular its language, from the aggressor's picture. Another victim of aggressive nationalism, as of every other nonscientific ideology, is critical thinking – notoriously treasonable – in particular, rational debate and objective evaluation. In sum, the flag is no substitute for the brain. Hence, rational-choice analyses of nationalism (as in Breton et al. 1995) are shallow, both because they lump all sixty-two varieties of nationalism into one, and because they overlook non-rational factors such as the feeling of "identity."

Let us examine next a by-product of the neoliberal or free-market ideology.

8 The Market Approach to Culture

The school that calls itself "economic imperialism" treats all social processes as economic and moreover as trade activities (chap. 2, sects. 5 and 6). In particular, it holds that every cultural activity, from religious worship to philosophizing, is market-driven. Thus, the "religious market" is supposed to be composed of religious "firms" (churches) competing for "rational" consumers of non-rational commodities, such as indulgences and the promise of an afterlife, and endowed with a religious capital, or investment in religious learning. For example, Iannaccone (1991, 156) claims that "the benefits of competition, the burdens of monopoly, and the hazards of government regulation are as real in religion as in any other sectors of the economy." However, his data can be "interpreted" in alternative ways – that is, they can be explained by alternative hypotheses. For instance, poor and declining church attendance in some countries might be due to rising standards of living and levels of education rather than to religious monopoly. And large church attendance in the southern US and in the Republic of South Africa may be largely due to the fact that for most whites it has become a social occasion, whereas for blacks it is a show of solidarity and combativeness against racial segregation.

It is unreasonable and offensive to treat religion as a sector of the economy, and it is incorrect to treat it in isolation from social features such as wealth distribution. And it is unrealistic to ignore tradition and overlook social factors such as status, as well as political circumstances such as political oppression. In fact, it is well known that there is high church and low church, and that in North America there are white, black and aboriginal Christian congregations with different social gospels. It is also well known that church attendance soars when the church defends the underdog. In short, the data do not support the thesis of Locke and Smith that religious competition promotes religiosity.

Another example of economicism is the idea of the education market, where schools compete for parents, and – on the advice of Milton Friedman (1962, chap. 6) – government gives out vouchers enabling parents to choose schools for their children, to the delight of private schools and the dismay of public-spirited civil servants. At the microlevel the school has been regarded as a market place where students trade homework for grades (Coleman 1990, 706–9). This may well be true of bad pupils in bad schools: they do attempt to maximize grades while minimizing effort. But the very *raison d'être* of schools, which happens to be learning, is lost in this perspective. Nor does that analysis account for the organization of any school with more than one teacher into subsystems, such as academic staff, non-academic staff, student body, and administration. The cooperation and competition that take place both within and between these subsystems are left in the dark. In real life students "trade" among themselves scraps of information and trivia, and they do so largely in a disinterested manner. But good students "trade" with their teachers only questions for answers, and challenge for praise – priceless "commodities." Imagine a school principal at the end of the day engaged in toting up the "volume of trading" in his school, and trying to figure out whether the "school market" is bullish or bearish.

Student-teacher interactions are not reducible to trading, because schools are not trading posts. They are places where teachers are expected to share knowledge and stimulate learning; and students are expected to learn, rediscover, reinvent, question, and socialize, all the while having some fun in the process. This is not to discourage the study of the economics of education. Since scholastic achievement and choice of school are largely determined by economic status, and since the educational system does have economic inputs and outputs, educational economics is a legitimate field of study, particularly when joined with educational sociology. But the economic aspect of education should not be exaggerated to the point of reducing education to a commodity, and of overlooking its specific function as well as its relations to social stratification and mobility.

Focusing on the economic aspect of education leads one to forget that the "business" of education is learning. It also leads one to overlook the fact that, although education is strongly correlated with occupation and is therefore a "positional good," scholastic achievement is largely determined by social status, and that in the industrialized countries schools tend to transmit and strengthen social inequality rather than promoting equality. (See, for example, the reviews of Bidwell and Friedkin 1988 and Halsey 1990.) In short, education has several intertwined strands: psychological, social, economic, and political. Therefore, it should be approached in a systemic rather than a sectoral manner.

What about technology? Could it profitably be studied from an economic point of view? Yes, but only partly so. Yes because, unlike basic science, technology is a potent input to the modern economy (as well as to the modern state). Hence, (a) some technological inventions have a market value; (b) the transformation of an idea into a viable product may call for expensive R&D; and (c) a viable product will disseminate only through suitable marketing and under favourable business circumstances. (For the economics of technology see Rosenberg 1982 and Rosegger 1996.) But economics cannot give a full account of innovation because what makes the creative technologist tick is not radically different from what motivates the scientific investigator. Indeed, in both cases the main drive is curiosity, not profit: curiosity about artefacts in the former case and about nature, society, or ideas in the latter. After all, an invention, whether technological or of any other kind, is a system of ideas – and this only well-trained, curious, imaginative, and strongly motivated individual brains can produce. The market is not creative: it only selects by stimulating or inhibiting – and it does not always select the best or kill the worst. Moreover, it encourages improvements (a.k.a. induced innovations) rather than radical novelties (recall sect. 5).

Undoubtedly, the market stimulates improvements in the design of goods and services: it pulls technology, which in turn is pushed by science. (But many such improvements are merely cosmetic and designed only to boost sales.) The market does not drive the invention of radically new products: these have to be imagined, designed, tested, produced, advertised, and taken to market before they can be evaluated by their potential customers. For example, Gutenberg created the book market, Watt the steam-engine market, Bell the telephone market, Marconi the radio market, Edison the electric-bulb market, Ford the popular-car market, and IBM and Apple computer engineers the personal-computer market. In short, technology creates new markets rather than the other way round. Thus, the modern market is largely technology-driven, rather than conversely. (For balanced views on the push-pull and the invention-diffusion questions, see Dosi 1982; Basalla 1988; Rosegger 1990, 1996; and Wiener 1994.)

The reason for this fact is obvious: whereas nature precedes basic science, modern artefacts are preceded by technology. (Which is one more reason for not confusing technology with science, and consequently their respective philosophies.) Moreover, new technologies, when adopted by industry or government, may alter relations of production, lifestyles, and even social orders. For example, the steam engine helped spark off the Industrial Revolution, which led to the rise of industrial capitalism, which, together with democracy and the expansion of education, transformed the social order.

Moreover, although industry often follows technology, at other times it stunts it. The economic cause of such resistance to innovation is well known. Once a corporation – or for that matter any other large social system – has succeeded, it becomes conservative, for any radical change requires hard rethinking and expensive retooling and reorganizing. For example, the patents of the tape recorder and television were not used for a long time for fear that they would compete with the record and the radio industries respectively.

Most technologists are not inventors but work in maintenance or at most engage in improvements rather than in original design or planning. Even though he may have the brains, the technologist seldom has the opportunity to work on a radically new project. Typically, he is not a self-employed adventurer or entrepreneur but a nine-to-five employee in a business firm or a government department. Hence, unlike his employer, who feels the market (or the political) incentives as well as its constraints, the technologist only feels his employer's or client's demands and constraints. He is not free to dream or tinker on his employer's time; he may do this on weekends. He is expected to make recommendations likely to increase the economic or political power of his employer. Furthermore, while the latter's demand for profitability – hence for productivity and competitiveness – is likely to stimulate the design of improvements (mainly in efficiency), it may rather inhibit the quest for better quality and radical innovation – particularly in the case of big corporations. Getting first to market is very risky: so much so that the mean market share of technological pioneers is only 10 per cent (Tellis and Golder 1996).

To be sure, some of the technologist's products – particularly designs, plans, recommendations, and operating manuals – are marketable commodities. But know-how, or tacit knowledge, being locked in the brains of technologists, technicians, foremen, and middle managers, is not marketable with equal ease. Besides, the technology market is far from free: it is severely distorted by secrecy and patents. (In the case of military technology, fat R&D government contracts add to market imperfection.) Moreover, most technological commodities are the property of the technologist's employer. And yet the technologist won't deliver anything out of the ordinary unless he is allowed some freedom to dream and explore and tinker, and is innerly motivated to tackle challenging problems and see new things or processes fashioned.

In sum, the economic approach to technology must be supplemented with the psychology of technologists. And, because the latter interact among themselves as well as with scientists, technicians, managers, foremen, and workers, the sociology of technology too has an important contribution to make. The economic approach to technology will at most cast some light on one of the sides of this multilateral process. But neoclassical economic theory, by focusing on subjective preference, choice, and decision, ignores technology as a factor of production and a major engine of economic change (see, for instance, Pasinetti 1981; Freeman 1988; Rosegger 1996). Hence, it would be mistaken to approach technology from the point of view of neoclassical economics.

Science is likely to be the next target of economic imperialism. We may soon be told that there is a science market: that scientists produce commodities – namely problems, concepts, hypotheses, data, and methods – that can be imputed shadow prices; that they trade these commodities among themselves; that they sell them to universities, business firms, or governments; that every scientist attempts to maximize his utilities by producing the largest possible quantity of papers with minimal creative effort – or even by stealing them; that scientific creativity is market-driven ... and so on and so forth.

Such a picture of science would be grotesque. Indeed, as Merton showed long ago, scientific research is driven mainly by curiosity and the desire for peer recognition, and it is controlled by truth tests. Moreover, the outcome of a reasonably ambitious research project is unforeseeable: only small findings can be premeditated and commissioned. Furthermore, the products of research, such as theories and empirical findings, are shared, not privately owned; scientific competition is not for clients but over ideas, priorities, or research funds; and the profit motive, when it exists, is subordinated to the knowledge motive and it is constrained by scientific desiderata and norms, such as accuracy and coherence, predictive and explanatory power, and corrigibility. (See, for instance, Hagstrom 1965; Bunge 1967a; Merton 1973; and Medawar 1988.)

Still, it must be admitted that in recent years two anomalous trends have emerged in the scientific community: academic industries and foul behaviour. Let us address them briefly. An activity may be called an *academic industry* if and only if (a) it benefits only its practitioners or their employers, without making any real contribution to the fund of genuine knowledge; but (b) has some of the accoutrements of authentic scholarship (e.g., plenty of footnotes, symbols, or use of computers); and (c) is tolerated by academia for nonscientific reasons – for example, because it is generously funded or has been endorsed by some well-known academics. Two obvious examples have been, for over half a century, Sovietology in the West and official Marxism in the East. Another academic industry is what passes for measurement theory in psychology, social science, and philosophy (see, for example, Suppes and Zinnes 1963). This theory does not tackle measurements proper, which are empirical operations, and therefore require specific factual theories rather than a single and moreover a priori mathematical theory (Bunge 1973c). And the mathematical embellishment of the false assumptions of neoclassical microeconomics (recall chap. 3) is still a flourishing academic industry.

The second deviation alluded to above is the mounting number of cases of breach of the scientific moral code first described by Merton (1938b). A small but increasing number of scientists devote all their time to management while claiming to do research; others engage in open piracy or, worse, data forgery. As a consequence, the output of poor papers, and even fraud and plagiarism, has been mounting, particularly in the biomedical sciences. In short, science is being mercantilized to some (small) extent. But this behaviour is anomalous and, when reported, is usually regarded as immoral, and occasionally denounced and punished as such. A lonely wart does not spoil beauty.

The market approach to basic science is doomed to fail because, unlike technology and quackery, science and mathematics are not for sale. This is why their funding must be public, not private. Let us keep basic research this way if we wish it to continue growing and enriching culture and feeding technology. Let us expel the merchants from the temple of disinterested inquiry, thus saving it from resembling the economicist cartoon that someone is likely to have in mind.

How about art? Can the market be trusted to promote genuine and original art, and thus render patronage dispensable, as the neoconservatives claim? Hardly. Whoever wishes to make money out of art must aim at the least-educated social strata. He must produce either pop art or corporation art, not art. He must cater to mediocrity or advertising instead of trying to raise the artistic level of the public. He must conform, not rebel – except perhaps in physical appearance or dress. He must put himself in the hands of an agent, a gallery, a show-business or pop-music entrepreneur, or a marketing agency, whose goal is to make big money, not great art. The contribution of the market to art lies not in inpiring artists but in diffusing their work: in making it possible that, once genuine art is freely created, it may reach the public through mass media, large exhibitions or concerts, or myriads of books or records. Art, like science and technology, feeds the market. Without paintings there would be no art dealers. Great art can occasionally be commissioned, never mandated.

As for the humanities, they cannot hope to attract investors. Therefore, universities and governments should fund them instead of attempting to turn them into business or political enterprises. This should be done because culture is a system: if any of its components weakens, other parts are bound to suffer. For instance, where kitsch reigns, the demand for high-quality industrial design declines; and where antiscience philosophies spread, enrolments in science schools drop.

Finally, could religion be explained in economic terms? Surely some churches have occasionally embarked on profitable adventures. But sincere religious belief and worship, particularly offering, is economically wasteful. Like art, religion is not just a commodity. And its survival in the age of science and technology is an open problem in culturology.

Ironically, the market approach is rarely adopted to study junk culture, although some of it is a growth industry that rivals and contaminates authentic culture. Ordinary garbage is a public good and recyclable; cultural rubbish is neither. It is not mere honest, corrigible error but wrong-headed nonsense, falsity, or worse – and often costly to boot. (Think of the thousands of students who waste the best years of their life taking courses in such academic frauds as existentialism, deconstructionism, or feminist philosophy.) To err is human; to exploit error is criminal. Whereas the belief that 13 is an unlucky number is an unprofitable superstition, the alternative medicines are profitable and often hazardous varieties of quackery.

We have just mentioned specimens of three kinds of cultural garbage: naive, commercial, and academic. The former is a heap of popular superstitions. These emerge more or less spontaneously out of unchecked speculation, hasty induction, or faulty reasoning. Many of them are vestiges of primitive cultures, and they have currently no market value. As for commercial junk culture, such as New Age, it is a jumble of wrong beliefs, values, and practices deliberately manufactured and marketed for mass consumption: it is big business. Finally, academic rubbish is the product of academics or para-academics intent on gaining celebrity, or at least promotion, by performing verbal tricks and without doing their homework – for instance, science-bashing without knowing science. There is no big money in this business. Nor does it confer political clout: real subversion takes place in the street or in governments, not in classrooms. Only ephemeral prestige and influence upon the unwary are to be gained by it – often at the taxpayer's expense.

All three kinds of cultural junk are advertised as alternatives to "establishment culture." This attracts rebels as well as those unwilling to undergo rigorous apprenticeships. And all three constitute shortcuts as well as obstacles to the advancement of knowledge. But whereas garbage of either of the first two kinds is easily identified, academic rubbish may fool those who tend to admit uncritically the entire output of academe.

To sum up, the economics of culture is a legitimate field of scholarship. By contrast, the market approach to culture is blinkered and distorting – except of course when it deals with authentic merchandise, such as industrial or political secrets, pseudoscience, alternative medicine, pseudophilosophy, and junk culture.

The importance of serious social studies of culture hardly needs to be extolled, particularly at a time when cultural novelty – mainly in the domains of science and technology – has an increasingly strong impact on the rest of social life. This makes it mandatory for the philosopher to dig up the philosophical presuppositions of culturology, as well as to evaluate the intrinsic worth of the various fields of culture, pseudoculture, and counterculture – particularly when cultivated in the hallowed groves of academe.

So far we have focused on the major synchronic social and biosocial sciences. All of them converge to history, or rather historiography, which in turn sheds light on the former. Let us then take a philosophical look at historiography.

6

History

The study of human evolution is only one of the historical sciences: others are cosmology, geology, and evolutionary chemistry and biology. All the historical sciences have the same aim, namely, to discover what happened and why it happened: they seek truth and explanation, not just yarn. Moreover, the historical sciences investigate the past not only out of curiosity but also to better understand and influence the present, and thus help to shape the future, on the obvious assumption that today is the child of yesterday and tomorrow that of today. All of them abide by Charles Darwin's famous dictum, "If we know not how a thing became we know it not." This thesis is sometimes called 'historism.'

(Regrettably the term 'historism' – or 'historicism' – is not used consistently in the literature. Sometimes it is taken to denote the hermeneutic school founded by Dilthey, which held not only that all human affairs must be viewed in the light of history, but also that man is outside and above nature. This usage is incorrect because Hegelians and Marxists, as well as evolutionary biologists and historians, are historists in holding that nothing can be understood except as a stage in a process: they are all historists in the broad sense of the term. Nor shall I adopt Popper's [1957, 3] characterization of historicism as the view that society has laws of its own that, once discovered, render social prediction possible. Through this idiosyncratic usage of the word, the idealist Hegel, the positivist Comte, and the materialist Marx end up in the same bag. All three were holists as well as historists; but, whereas Hegel and Comte believed in the primacy of ideas, Marx held that the economy is the engine of history. In any event, the three were so different from one another that it is not helpful to characterize them only or even predominantly as historists.)

Historism is explicitly or tacitly rejected by rationalists, in particular rational-choice theorists, who hold – alas, against empirical evidence – that all human beings, in all societies, circumstances, and periods, act in the same way, namely so as to maximize their expected utilities. Thus Menger (1883), one of the founders of neoclassical economics and a critic of historism, introduced the concepts of ideal type and of typical relation, and regarded them as universal and cross-cultural, that is, ahistorical. The consequence, stressed by his disciple L. von Mises (1949), is obvious: good economic theory holds for all societies at all times. But this is false. In fact, historians have shown conclusively that different economies follow different patterns. Indeed everything human, from lifestyle to longevity, and from mode of production to mode of thinking, is subject to change.

Historism is true but it should not be exaggerated to the point of holding that historiography encompasses everything, or at least is prior to every other discipline. This radical historist thesis is false because, to find out how or why something has evolved, we must have some preliminary knowledge of *what* has evolved. Knowledge of the present helps us to understand the past, which in turn sheds light on the present. For example, historical sociology both presupposes and enriches sociology. Synchronics precedes diachronics, which in turn enriches synchronics: this process is not linear but spiral.

Historians study social change. That is, they study social events and processes of all kinds in social systems of all sizes, from family to nation, as well as social activities of all types, from farming to communication. Their field is thus just as broad as the anthropologist's: they can be said to engage in diachronic anthropology. However, most historians specialize in some type of social system (e.g., the nation), activity (e.g., trade), or period. Indeed there are specialists in social history, economic history, historical linguistics, history of philosophy – and so on. And there are also a few historical generalists, who attempt to encompass nearly everything. These are the philosophers of history.

In this chapter we shall touch on some of the philosophical problems raised by the scientific study of the past. Although these problems rarely draw the attention of contemporary philosophers, they are occasionally discussed, sometimes acrimoniously, in the historical and archaeological literature, particularly in the journals *History and Theory* and *Past and Present*. (See also Klibansky and Paton 1936; Aron 1961; Gardiner 1959; Meyerhoff 1959; Gilbert and Graubard 1972; Barraclough 1979; Bunge 1985b; Binford 1989; Trigger 1978, 1989, 1991; Tilly 1984; Kozicki 1993; Lloyd 1991; Wandsnider 1992; Renfrew and Zubrow 1994; and Murphey 1994.) One reason for the interest in this subject among historians is that they all use certain general principles about the past and its study. Another is that their subject is being renewed from time to time by some new approach, method, or result: think of the *Annales* school, quantitative history, recent findings and controversies in palaeoanthropology and archaeology, and the fashionable flirt with literary criticism.

History raises a number of ontological and methodological problems. Accordingly, one may distinguish two aspects of the philosophy of history: the substantive, or ontological, and the analytic, or methodological (Danto 1965). The problems of the role of individuals in history and of the existence of historical patterns belong in the former, whereas the problems of historical interpretation and explanation belong in the latter. Every historian entertains some views about these subjects. He does so, for example, when wondering about the driving forces of history, the place of accident, the role of knowledge of the present in guiding the exploration of the past, the place of narrative, or the importance of quantitative (e.g., geographic, demographic, epidemiological, and economic) data.

The *substantive* philosophy of history can be largely speculative, like that of Vico, Hegel, Comte, Marx, Spencer, Spengler, or Toynbee. Or it can be "based on" (that is, suggested and checked by) historical data. The former was the precursor of modern sociology (Mauss 1968, 18). It has now been superseded by the theories of social change, usually grouped under sociology, social history, and historical sociology. These theories are just as general, hence philosophical, as the old philosophies of history. This apparent shift from philosophy to social science has had two effects. One is that social change is nowadays studied by professionals rather than amateurs – which can only be to the good. The other is that, for this reason, people tend to overlook the fact that the contemporary theories of social change are so extremely general that they qualify as philosophico-scientific: they are frameworks for crafting specific theories and searching for evidence.

These theories are similar to the (general) theory of evolution, in that they cannot, without further ado, explain anything in particular (Boudon 1984). However, just as the general theory of evolution, when enriched with special assumptions and data, can yield explanations and forecasts (or hindcasts) concerning particular biopopulations, so a general theory of social change might be used in like manner with regard to specific social groups. To pooh-pooh general historical ideas as metaphysical nonsense is sheer flippancy (see Gellner 1988). They guide or misguide historical research, and they can be evaluated by the fruits of such research. For example, the thesis that all social changes are powered by ideas is falsified by any instance of environmental, biological, or economic causes. Another example: if we assume that there are patterns, we will try to guess and test them. In other words, some metaphysics of history are empirically testable.

As for *analytic* philosophy of history, it is nothing but the epistemology and methodology of historical research. It tackles such problems as the nature of historical evidence and historical hypotheses (often called 'interpretations'); the differences between historical explanation and hindcast; and whether archaeology is a separate discipline, an auxiliary one – or the merger of anthropology with history. We shall examine some such problems in each of the two branches of the philosophy of history.

1 Historical Objectivity, Lies, and Forgeries

No sooner do we utter the word 'history' than we face the old philosophical problem of distinguishing facts from their representations. Indeed, the word 'history' is notoriously ambiguous: it denotes both a process and its study. When necessary to forestall confusion, historians use the word *historiography* to designate the study of history.

The concept of history – as different from that of historiography – is important and cross-disciplinary: it belongs in ontology as well as in all the factual sciences. It may be elucidated as follows. The *history* of a complex thing – such as a star, an ecosystem, a machine, or a social system such as a family, a firm, or a nation – is the temporal sequence of its states (or of its changes of state) over the period under consideration (see Bunge 1977a). The records of such states are largely sunken and often irretrievably lost, hence impossible to reconstruct except conjecturally. And historical conjectures are dicey because one and the same observed fact may have alternative hidden causes. (When $C_1 \vee C_2 \vee ... \vee C_n \rightarrow E$, there are n suspects.) Besides, historians work with traces or indicators of human behaviour, all of which are ambiguous. In particular, they may conceal as well as reveal: think, for example, of such social-status indicators as dress, jewellery, or graves.

A historiographical account of any historical process is a hypothetical, hence fallible, reconstruction of it on the strength of bits and pieces of historical traces, such as debris, hearths, and tools, in the light of general hypotheses concerning human behaviour. We may distinguish two main types of historical reconstruction: in terms of outstanding ("historical") events and in terms of key properties, such as population, total production, volume of trade, and degrees of literacy and numeracy. The former is the traditional historical account of kings and battles. A historiography of the second type will contain a sheaf of time-series, such as those reconstructed by demographers and economic historians. If there are objective patterns, they are more likely to show up in time-series than in sequences of heterogeneous events. In sum, historical records are pieces of (true or false) knowledge that have occurred outside the historian's head, usually before his time.

Subjectivists – in particular those who claim that all facts are "social constructions" – are bound to conflate both concepts, holding that history (as a process) results from the historian's work (historiography). Thus, Simmel (1923), Carr (1961), Steele Commager (1966), Furet (1972), and Goldstein (1977) rejected the belief in historical "hard facts" occurring independently of the historian. They did so presumably just because the modern historian, far from being a mere chronicler, has got to search for, select, and "interpret" his data in the light of contemporary knowledge – a process in the course of which "new facts come to light" (that is, are discovered) whereas some "old facts disappear" (that is, are shown never to have occurred). Oakeshott (1983) and the "post-processual" archaeologists (e.g., Tilley and Shanks 1987) have even claimed that people create their own past – in fact multiple pasts. Mercifully, they refrained from coining the slogan "For a better past!"

The vast majority of historians know the difference between fact and fiction, as well as between historiography and literature: they toil in dusty archives to discover truths about the past. Yet Novick (1988), a philosopher and historian of social studies, claims that the idea of historical objectivity is "confused," and the ideal of historical objectivity nothing but "a noble dream." He formed this opinion after examining hundreds of statements of contemporary American historians about their own discipline, rather than from checking their substantive work. Yet, presumably Professor Novick "has got his facts right," that is, he has not made them all up.

A recent fad is the hermeneutic (or semiotic) school, which is said to have brought about the "linguistic [or rather literary] turn" in historiography. According to it, all there is or ever was is a collection of texts and texts about texts: there would be no real world to be explored, no facts to be discovered, no past to be dug up. This idealist conflation of fact with sign implies equating past with archive, document with story, history with historiography, and the latter with literature. Since there would be no facts to be discovered, there would be no truth either – or, if preferred, there would be as many truths as historians. Even those who, like Hayden White (1978), admit that what historians write about may actually have happened, claim that "historiography is a form of fiction-making," hence a form of literature or rhetoric not science. This school calls itself the New Historicism, but in fact it is old hat, namely subjectivist philosophy contemptuous of empirical evidence. (See, for instance, Kozicki 1993.) What *is* new about it is the cheek of literary critics posing as historians, the unprecedented jettisoning of causality (Zagorin 1990), and the "dehistorization of history" (Spiegel 1990). So much is clear. What is far from clear is why such pseudohistorical sallies of literary critics misguided by pseudophilosophers are tolerated in universities that would not appoint alchemists, soothsayers, or faith healers.

The expression *subjective history* is as much of an oxymoron as *true fiction*.

Nobody can claim to be a historian – as different from a storyteller – unless he seeks to find out the (most likely) truth about the past. Surely Carr, whose subjectivist opinion we recalled a moment ago, reported on hard facts (though sometimes through soft evidence) when writing his monumental *History of Soviet Russia* (1950–69), a standard work of reference. Moreover, if subjectivism were true, then the very concept of *the* past would be empty: there would be as many pasts as historians. And there would be no way of distinguishing historical reality from historical narrative, or even authentic document from forgery or myth.

Mercifully, historical subjectivism is a minority view. When on the job, historians distinguish between fact and fiction, document and hypothesis, the past and its hypothetical reconstructions. They modestly admit that, far from making history, they only uncover, reconstruct, narrate, and explain it. (To be sure, historical research is itself part of history, but only a very minor part – except when it produces lies designed to prop up a shady cultural or political movement.) Indeed, most historians take it for granted that (a) the past has really existed; (b) the past has ceased to exist and cannot be relived or "re-enacted" (contrary to what Collingwood thought); (c) the past is unlike the present in at least some respects; (d) human history can end only with the extinction of the human species; (e) parts of the past can be known (reconstructed) at least partially; and (f) every historical reconstruction is conjectural and consequently imperfect; but (g) every historical account is perfectible in the light of new data, techniques, or approaches; and (h) some reconstructions have permanent components, whence everyone can build on some past historiographic findings while correcting or discarding others – whence historians can and, in fact, do make progress.

That is, historians adopt, more or less explicitly, a dynamicist or processual ontology and a realist and fallibilist (though not radically sceptical) epistemology. Moreover, most of them are scientistic, in that they adopt the scientific method and, in particular, try to exhibit evidence for or against their hypotheses. In short, they regard historiography as a social *science*, namely the scientific study of social change. Thus, they tacitly reject the opposition between historiography and science introduced by the Romantics, stressed by Dilthey and Collingwood, adopted by Popper and by Wittgenstein's followers, and recently revived by the self-styled "new historians" and "interpretive archaeologists."

Historiography was the first branch of the social studies to attain maturity: in fact it was fathered by Thucydides four centuries BCE. Moreover, history is arguably the most rigorous of all the social sciences. Indeed, in no other social science is factual truth – the adequacy of discourse to fact – sought so painstakingly and held in such high esteem: so much so, that any deliberate departure from historical truth – as is customary among "patriotic" and nationalist historians – is unanimously censored as dishonest. In particular, no historian would dream of following Lakatos's (1971) injunction that the history of science ought to be subjected to "rational reconstruction." Revision whenever necessary, yes; deliberate distortion, no. (More in sect. 7.)

Historical revisionism – the rewriting of "official" history – has got a bad press. Such negative evaluation is justified whenever well-documented facts, such as the Jewish Holocaust, are denied. But blanket antirevisionism is unjustified, because all original historians are revisionists, that is, innovators, even while revisiting old ground. This is unavoidable and desirable, for historical knowledge advances through new findings (data), new hypotheses, new techniques, and even new approaches, any of which may require the correction or even rejection of some of the previous results. It is not that, as a constructivist-relativist might say, the past isn't what it used to be. Rather, its successive reconstructions are bound to differ from one another simply because they are the work of inventive but fallible beings working on incomplete records with imperfect methods and limited resources – though sometimes misled by a wrong philosophy.

Consider first the case of the revision of "sources," that is, data. The ancient and medieval chroniclers relied exclusively on their own observations and on reports of (authentic or putative) witnesses. This procedure is flawed for, as Marc Bloch (1949, 47) put it, there are no good witnesses, but only good (or bad) testimonies. And even good testimonies may be of little help for describing all the minute facts that make up a historical process. In any event, contrary to received opinion, indirect (circumstantial) evidence may be more important and reliable than the direct evidence supplied by (putative) witnesses (Fogel 1982b). For example, parish, manorial, and notarial records, paymaster's lists, and tax rolls may be more useful and reliable than many an eyewitness report or official document. In any event, the kind and value of evidence the historian is after depends largely on his previous knowledge of the case, on the hypotheses he entertains, and on his general approach: documents never "speak for themselves" (Bloch 1949, 26).

As for the revision of hypotheses, two recent examples come to mind. One concerns the popular hypothesis that hominids and primitive human beings made their living mainly by hunting. This hypothesis had several sources: the hunting scenes painted in caves about 20,000 years ago, the incomplete observation of some modern gatherer-hunters, the tradition of military history – and male bias. Binford (1981) has argued that our ancestors were too small, weak, and dull-toothed to compete for prey with the great cats. His view is that our ancestors were plant foragers and "the most marginal of scavengers." Evidence for this hypothesis is both fossil and experimental. The former consists in the absence of weapons among the tools used by the protohuman hominids. The second is the finding that scavenging in the riparian woodlands of East Africa is rather difficult, thus challenging and promoting of social skills (Blumenschine and Cavallo 1992). However, the hypothesis in question is still in limbo, in view of the finding that wild chimpanzees supplement their plant diet with meat obtained seasonally through group hunting (see, for instance, Stanford 1996). Maybe this is one of the historical questions that can have no conclusive answer.

Our second example is the new light shed on the causes of the English Revolution by Jack Goldstone (1991). He has argued, in a Braudelian vein, that his predecessors failed to realize the impact of the sustained population growth during the years 1500 to 1640. This growth caused inflation, which increased elite mobility and caused a rise in fiscal distress; in turn, population growth and inflation enhanced the potential for mass mobilization. The product of the latter by mobility and fiscal distress equals the political stress indicator, which peaked shortly before the breakdown of the state (1991, 141–5). This is an instance of the power of cliometrics – no pet of the innumerate.

Every generation of historians is thus bound to rewrite history. Consequently, as long as there are historians left there will be no definitive historiography. Contemporary historians know this: they "expect their work to be superseded again and again" (Clark 1957, xxiv). Such progress comes not only from new data but also from new ways of "interpreting" old data and from searching for data of new kinds. Thus, important new developments in historiography may be expected from looking at the past "from the other side" – for instance, that of the female, the loser, or the oppressed rather than that of the male, the victor, or the ruler respectively. We may also expect novelties from the reassessment of popular and persistent scholarly errors, such as Weber's Protestant ethics thesis and Foucault's claim that the liberal penal reforms were actually illiberal (see Hamilton 1996). In sum, the historian's task is unending.

This view does not entail the conclusion that objective historical truth is unattainable and that, as the literary critic Barthes claimed, historical discourse is in its essence a form of ideological elaboration. First, every historical account can in principle be checked for accuracy and consistency, and it may thus be improved upon. Second, one expects different historical accounts of a given event or process to overlap to some extent, for one admits that there are some robust historical findings. Third, one expects alternative historical accounts to converge to a single story. In short, historical fallibilism and meliorism, sí: historical relativism, no. In this regard history and natural science are one: both care for truth.

Where the historian differs from the natural scientist is that – contrary to the positivist credo but as stressed by the *Verstehen* school – the former may try to guess the beliefs, value judgments, intentions, and decisions of his subjects. For example, in explaining a popular rebellion against X, a historian may note that X was generally seen as unjust, oppressive, corrupt, or just weak. However, unlike the *verstehende* historian, the scientific historian attempts to check whether his conjecture is correct. If he exhibits evidence that it is, the historian takes sides without thereby abandoning scientific objectivity. On the contrary, he broadens the scope of objective inquiry, because all deliberate behaviour – including his own – is guided by value judgments, which are not necessarily subjective or biased. In particular, it would be vain to try to explain social reforms, revolutions, or counter-revolutions without resorting to the (generally perceived) ideas of justice and injustice, equality and inequality. (Incidentally, holists disagree. Thus, according to Skocpol 1985, ideology plays no role in revolutions, which would be purely "structural" affairs. This view makes no room for leadership, and it fails to explain why rebels are willing to risk their lives.) In sum, the historian's quest for truth is compatible with, nay it requires, explicit value judgments. Hence, Objectivity $\neq$ Impartiality.

Another difference between historiography and natural science is that, unlike rocks and trees, people can cheat. They can do this in three ways: by fabricating evidence – that is, by committing forgeries; by deliberately suppressing or mis-interpreting authentic evidence; or by inventing myths. (See Caro Baroja 1992.) Examples of the first kind of lie: forged relics, the Donation of Constantine, and the alleged evidence used in religious and political witch-hunts. Examples of the second kind are the standard depictions of Descartes as an idealist despite his materialist cosmology; of J.S. Mill as a champion of classical liberalism despite his warm defence of socialism; and of Popper as one of "Thatcher's men" despite his praise of the welfare state.

As for the suppression and falsification of historical documents, they have been common under dictatorships and during wars, and are characteristic of official histories under all regimes. For example, some decades before the Spanish conquest, the wily Mexica statesman Tlacaélel ordered the burning of documents and the rewriting of history to consolidate the power of the new ruling class (León-Portilla 1980). Napoléon ordered his minister of police to oversee the work of the French historians. The lies of the "patriotic" historians have been exposed several times (see, for example, Benda 1975 and Taylor 1963). Alperowitz (1965) has discussed the real motive of the Truman administration in dropping nuclear bombs on a country whose government had asked for terms of surrender a couple of weeks earlier. And half a century later the Smithsonian Institution was ordered to remove all the photographs in a public exhibition showing the effects of those bombs on the civilians of Hiroshima and Nagasaki.

Finally, the deliberate manufacture of myths is exemplified by hagiographies and by the Romantic inventions about the Celts and the early Germans. Similar fabrications are the old myth that the 1815 to 1914 period was one of uninterrupted world peace and Stalin's version of the history of the October Revolution and the Soviet Communist Party.

Unlike the subjectivist (particularly the constructivist-relativist), who rejects the very idea of objective truth, the scientific historian regards all such deliberate distortions as intellectual crimes – no less heinous when animated by patriotism.

2 Materialism versus Idealism

Philosophy, in particular ontology, is the source of the splitting of historiographic schools into two main currents: materialist and idealist. Each of them proposes its own answer to the old question, Which are the driving forces of history? Materialists (whether Marxists or not) hold that the ultimate determinants of social change are material (that is, environmental, biological, or economic), whereas historical idealists postulate the primacy of ideas (ideological, political, or technological), or even of supernatural agencies.

Consider for instance the following problems. First: How did proto-Indo-European spread westward from Anatolia begining around 9000 BP? Idealists have offered no plausible answer. A plausible materialist answer is that proto-Indo-European spread westward and ramified along with farming, which forced people to occupy new territory (Renfrew 1988). The vast geographic-demographic-genetic investigation of Cavalli-Sforza and co-workers (1994) has confirmed this hypothesis. Second problem: Why was Attica, at the time of the Peloponnesian War, homogeneous and free from political disunity? Thucydides's answer was materialist: The would-be invaders were repelled by the poverty of Attica's soil, whereas refugees of invasions found sanctuary in it.

There are several versions of the materialist philosophy of history. Most of them are monistic or unifactorial, that is, they assert that there is a single first mover of social change – for instance, hunger, sex, conflict, greed, lust for power, trade, technological innovation, economic expansion, or institutional dysfunction. The best-known materialist philosophy of history is the Marxist kind of economic determinism, according to which production and trade constitute "the basis of all social structure," and "the final causes of all social changes and political revolutions are to be sought ... in changes in the modes of production and exchange" (Engels 1954, 369). In short, according to Marxism, "in the last analysis" the economy determines the course of history.

Undoubtedly, the Marxist version of historical materialism has been confirmed in some cases. Let the following examples suffice. (Some counterexamples will follow shortly.) It is generally admitted that the Persian Gulf war (1990–1) was an oil war. The Germans fought two world wars to grab territory rather than to spread German philosophy. The Spanish, Portuguese, British, French, Dutch, Russian, and American empires were built by violent means to loot natural resources and exploit natives. Venice, Genoa, and Barcelona built and kept each a string of fortresses along the Mediterranean coast to defend their international trade. The Crusaders looted every town they took, whether Moslem or Christian. Ancient Rome destroyed Carthage to secure the trade lanes in the Mediterranean and beyond. (See Lane 1958 for an economic analy-- sis of military campaigns.) Likewise, most civil wars have been class wars. Witness the German Peasant Wars; the French, Russian, and Chinese Revolutions; the 1848 revolutions in Europe; and the Spanish Civil War: all of them pitted poor against rich.

However, there may be just as many counterexamples to economic determinism as there are examples. Indeed, all the social events and movements triggered by environmental disasters, plagues, fertility changes, literacy, numeracy, technical innovations, religious fanaticism, racial prejudice, nationalism, political opportunism, and the thirst for freedom constitute counterexamples to economic determinism – even though, admittedly, some of those changes affect people mainly through their impact on production or trade. A handful of examples follow. 1/ The Neolithic revolution, that is, the introduction of agriculture, gave rise to a population explosion, which in some places gave birth to civilization, which changed drastically people's lifestyle and gave rise to the state and to a far richer culture. 2/ Crowding in cities led to the spread of contagious diseases, some of which decimated or even wiped out entire populations. Such epidemics may have caused the major genetic differences between ourselves and our ancestors of 10,000 years ago, namely inheritable changes in the immune system (Keyfitz 1984). Our present immune systems are thus a product of both natural and social evolution. (Incidentally, the first to point out the relevance of health considerations to history, in particular the importance of plagues, was not a historian, but the novelist H.G. Wells.) 3/ The doubling of the population of the Mediterranean basin between 1500 and 1600 may have been the major factor in all the other revolutions during that period. Had it not been for that "biological revolution," the Turkish conquest, the discovery and colonization of America, and Spain's imperial "vocation" would not have happened (Braudel 1972, 1: 403). 4/ The diffusion of the automobile and television has transformed worldwide everyday life, political attitudes, and the struggle for power almost as radically as the replacement of subsistence economies by market economies. 5/ The downfall of most dictatorships since the end of the Second World War was not an effect of changes in the mode of production or of class struggles, but the work of people who longed for some freedom. 6/ Strategic considerations – in particular the maintenance of continental hegemony – and domestic politics have played a more important role than the protection of private interests in determining the US Latin American policies (Blasier 1985). 7/ The civil wars in the former Yugoslavia and the USSR are political, ideological (in particular religious), and above all stupid pseudo-ethnic conflicts with no economic justification.

In short, economic determinism is falsified by a number of counterexamples. Besides, the Marxist version of historical materialism has the following flaws. First, it overrates the importance of conflict – in particular class struggle – at the expense of cooperation, which is just as important. Indeed, no social system could emerge or subsist without a modicum of cooperation. Since social conflict occurs within or between social systems, cooperation precedes conflict. Moreover, many an attempt to repair social systems is an attempt to restore cooperation on a new basis. Second, Marxism makes far too much of the "laws of motion of society," which have yet to be discovered. Not that there are no such laws, but Marxists have failed to find any and have overlooked norms, which are social inventions and therefore mutable. (See sect. 2.) Third, the claim that "in the last analysis" the economy is the first mover condemns beforehand any alternative "interpretation" of history. Fourth, like every doctrine purporting to explain everything in unicausal terms, Marxism wins the loyalty of people who like to spend more time defending it and attacking its rivals than doing original research. This, and the fact of having been endorsed by a once-powerful political movement, transformed an incipient science into a dogma.

However, Marxism has been very productive outside the Marxist camp. It has inspired or at least reinforced the radical rewriting of history "from the bottom up": from peasant to lord, from manual worker to cleric, and from oppressed to oppressor. Moreover, according to a well-known non-Marxist scholar, "Marxism is the only coherent theory of evolution of man in society, and in that sense the only philosophy of history, which exercises a demonstrable influence over the minds of historians today" (Barraclough 1979, 164). However, only a few of Marx's very numerous faithful followers have made serious contributions to historical scholarship – and no wonder, for dogma stifles creativity. The main beneficial effect of Marxism on historiography has been indirect: it has reinforced at least three important contemporary scientific developments.

One of these movements is materialist archaeology, which is flourishing nearly everywhere and focuses on work rather than on either kinship or belief systems (see Trigger 1989). Another is the so-called New Economic History, particularly active in the United States, which makes intensive use of econometrics (see, for instance, Andreano 1970; Aydelotte et al. 1972; and Temin 1973). The third is the French school of the *Annales*, officially launched in 1929, and whose best-known members were March Bloch and Fernand Braudel, famous for their classics *La société féodale* (1939) and *La Méditerranée* (1949) respectively. This school focuses on the social structure of societies: it owes much to Marx, a little to Durkheim, and nothing to Weber. Its members have done important original research into the material (environmental, demographic, and economic) aspects of a number of medieval and modern societies, though without overlooking their mores, mindsets, politics, and culture. They have tacitly adopted the systemic approach characteristic of the best anthropology. That is, they have studied entire social systems – small like the village of Montaillou or large like the Mediterranean basin – at all levels and in all their aspects, from domestic life and trade to politics and culture. In short, the *Annales* historiography is total, serial, and analytic rather than sectoral, event-oriented, and narrative.

Although the achievements of all three schools prove the centrality of economic history, neither of them is monistic, in particuar economicist. Historical monism holds that there is a single engine of historical change. Whether materialist or idealist, monism is at best partially true because society is not a solid block but a system of systems embedded in nature. Environmental, biological (in particular demographic), economic, political, and cultural "factors" (conditions, events, or processes) take turns in initiating social change, and they influence one another. Example 1: Overpopulation → conflict over land tenure → civil war → loss of life and property → increased poverty → cultural disaster. This happened in Rwanda in 1994. Example 2: Technological progress → productivity rise → unemployment → rise in social expenditures → reaction of the contented → trimming of the welfare state. This is happening at the time of writing in all industrialized countries.

Since society has many components and undergoes processes of many kinds, any monistic philosophy of history (such as environmental, biological, economic, political, or cultural determinism) is at best partially true, at worst a gross distortion. We need a pluralist perspective. The pluralist alternative to be proposed is systemic materialism, which will concern us in the next section. (For an alternative pluralism see Mann 1993.)

Let us now peek at historical idealism. This view – held by Hegel, Ranke, Droysen, and Dilthey among others – is that ideas are the prime movers of history. One of the most articulate and influential historical idealists was the versatile essayist Georg Simmel (1923). His main theses are these: (a) every historical fact is the expression of a mental process; (b) consequently the historian's task is to ferret out the ideas and feelings of the historical agents; (c) however, individuals are born into environments that they do not create, and that contribute to shaping their ideas and sentiments, whence the historian has to take them into account. (Since Simmel does not attempt to analyse these "situations" or "forms" in terms of individual actions, his individualism is only programmatic.)

For all his anti-idealist rhetoric, the philosopher R.G. Collingwood (1975 [1946], 115) adopted Simmel's main tenets, in particular the thesis that the thought in the agent's mind is "the inside of the [historical] event itself," whence the historian's task is "not knowing what people did but understanding what they thought." The eminent archaeologist I. Hodder (1992) concurs: he claims that, in order to understand our ancestors, we must start by finding out what was in their minds. But how can such initial knowledge be garnered, if all the student of the remote past can ever come across are material remains? These come first: the rest is more or less plausible conjecture that one may hope to test. For instance, a burial site containing food remains suggests belief in the afterlife.

No doubt, historical idealism holds a grain of truth, as many social actions are guided or misguided by ideas of various kinds. (Oriana Fallaci wrote that there is a book behind every large-scale infamy.) But ideas do not emerge in a social vacuum: many people contribute to fashioning, elaborating, and spreading them. Moreover, ideas about social action are not easily adopted unless they either match the existing social structure or promise to alter it in a way beneficial to some social group or other. In short, ideas do not move the elites, much less the masses. As Marx stated, only people with ideas of the "right" kind, and acting at the right time in the appropriate environment, are likely to exert an influence on other people. But this innocent-looking shift from ideas in themselves to thinkers-in-society amounts to a shift from idealism to sophisticated materialism.

Let us look at a celebrated instance of historical idealism, namely Weber's thesis that "the spirit of capitalism," in particular Calvinism, promoted modern capitalism. According to Weber (1920a, 53) "[w]herever this spirit comes to life and cares to actualize itself, it produces the sums of money as a means for its action, not the other way round." (However, he suggested no mechanism for the transmutation of ideas into money.) This thesis has been hailed as a refutation of the Marxist thesis that the economy always precedes and shapes the ideology. (Ironically, the first to propose "Weber's thesis" was Engels, who held that Protestant asceticism favoured the primitive accumulation of capital.) However, Weber's thesis faces the following objections.

First, early capitalism flourished not only in Protestant countries but also in Catholic ones such as France, northern Italy, and southern Germany – whereas it did not take in Calvin's Geneva or in Lutheran Sweden. Second, although it is true that asceticism favours postponed gratification, and therefore the accumulation of capital, it is also true that the Old Masters have documented the luxurious lifestyle of their Dutch Calvinist patrons. Third, the positive attitude towards learning, manual work, money-making, and the active life – as opposed to the contemplative one – emerged in the Renaissance, particularly in Catholic Florence, one century before the Reformation. Fourth, "Protestant" capitalism, which was predominantly commercial, was modelled largely on that of Catholic Venice and Genoa, and it grew thanks to the migration of southern capitalists to the north under the pressure of Catholic intolerance (Trevor Roper 1967; Braudel 1982). Fifth, surely the conquest, plunder, and colonization of America did more than either the Reformation or the Counter-Reformation towards shifting the centre of business from the Mediterranean to the Atlantic around 1600. Sixth, the diffusion of capitalist behaviour and activities owed much to the "desperate search for a way of avoiding society's ruin [by frequent wars and civil wars], permanently threatening at the time because of precarious arrangements for internal and external order" (Hirschman 1977, 130).

In short, the Protestant (in particular Calvinist) ideology was only one of the components of the emergence of the modern world. (Curiously, Weber 1920a, 83) himself admitted that the view that capitalism is a product of the Reformation is a *töricht-doktrinäre These*, a foolishly doctrinaire thesis.) Further factors in the rise of the modern world were the expansion of industry and commerce, the calculating attitude they involve, and the increase in skilled manpower they promote; the exploitation of the Third World; the insecurity caused by war and civil war; the spread of literacy and the rise of science, technology, and the humanities. Nevertheless, there is no question but that, *once* capitalism was under way, it was helped by the ascetic, activist, and utilitarian Puritan ethic. In particular, as Merton (1938a) has documented, Puritanism promoted the cultivation of science as a means for glorifying God and enlarging the control of nature. In short, capitalism, the growth of the cities, the voyages of discovery, the Reformation, rationalism, the Scientific Revolution, modern technology, secular philosophy, and new morals were so many intertwining strands of a single process: the birth of the modern world. This is our sytemic view of the matter.

Another case of historical idealism is rational-choice theory. This view attempts to explain all historical events by attributing them exclusively to the deliberate calculations of leaders. (Recall chap. 4, sect. 5.) This approach is individualist as well as idealist. It is individualist because it underrates matters of social structure, and idealist because it focuses on the mental processes pre-ceding action, thus overlooking the so-called material resources and constraints. (More in Bunge 1996a.)

The conspiracy "theory" of history is perhaps the earliest and coarsest ver-sion of rational-choice historiography. Indeed, it holds that all social changes results from plots, whether successful or failed. Material constraints and acci-dents would play no role, except in foiling conspiracies. This view has been rejected and even ridiculed by most political theorists and philosophers of his-tory. Yet, conspiracies do happen from time to time even under political democ-racy; and they are rife in any authoritarian regime because the opposition is forced to go underground to plot against the powers that be. In sum, some polit-ical changes can be explained in terms of conspiracy. (See Pigden 1995.) But conspiracy itself, particularly if successful, cries for explanation.

Contemporary rational-choice historiography is at first sight far more sophis-ticated, making use as it does of decision theory or game theory. It may even appear to be scientific by involving numbers. Consider, for instance, any rational-choice approach to the Persian Gulf conflict of 1990–1. (For two ear-lier essays see Malitza 1971 and Bunge 1973b.) To dispel any illusions about the rationality of the Persian Gulf war, suffice it to recall the three major miscal-culations involved in it: (a) the political and moral mistake of the American administration in supporting, till the very last moment, the brutal dictatorship headed by Saddam Hussein; (b) Iraq's invasion of Kuweit without pausing to think that, sooner or later, the Americans would intervene to protect their access to the richest oil deposits in the world; and (c) the decision of the Coalition to launch a massive air and land attack despite the CIA's report that the economic blockade imposed by the United Nations was effectively strangling the Iraqi economy, whence a military action would be unnecessary.

No doubt, the American decision to attack Iraq was calculated. But in what sense was this calculation rational? Was the massive offensive proportionate to the declared aim of forcing the Iraqi dictatorship to regurgitate Kuweit? If not, which was the real goal? To restore the rule of international law as proclaimed, or else to secure the continuous supply of cheap oil as well as a permanent mil-itary basis in the Persian Gulf, impose a lasting peace on the region, exclude the USSR from any post-war negotiations, cause a further division of the Arab world, bring the Palestinians to their knees, test new "smart" weapons, give the arms manufacturers a chance, distract public attention from burning domestic issues, restore the self-confidence lost in Vietnam, remind the world who was Top Dog – or perhaps a combination of some or all of these aims? And how rational was it to cripple an entire people, antagonize the whole Islamic world, and destabilize the region without prompting the UN Security Council to design a comprehensive and rational plan to solve the endemic problems of the whole Near East? Can anyone seriously believe that the American administration, let alone the ad hoc Coalition, proceeded throughout on the basis of a precise over-all rational-choice model, rather than in accordance with an American diplomatic and military plan superbly designed to win a battle without solving any of old political issues of the region? (See Rubinstein 1991 for some data.)

Let us now move on to a general and much-lauded game-theoretic approach to military history, namely Bueno de Mesquita's (1981). Mesquita's goal was to find laws of war, assuming that all the agents are expected utility maximizers and – for a welcome change – attempting to use objective utilities and probabilities rather than subjective ones. Regrettably, the author assigns these on dubious empirical information. For example, he assumes that the calculations of the war starters have usually been correct. But the contemporary historical record falsifies this assumption. Indeed, those who started both world wars and the Vietnam War lost; and the Korean and Iran-Iraq Wars ended up in draws with heavy losses to both sides.

Consider the following finding concerning contemporary wars: "In the 20th century, starters on the average have won 39 percent of the wars. In the current decade [the 1980s], however, only 11 percent of the starters of wars appear to be winners" (Sivard 1987, 28). Bueno de Mesquita ignores these data. As if this were not enough, he estimates utilities to three decimal points, when even one may be excessive. But he is not the only or even the worst sinner: pseudo-exactness, joined with neglect of adverse factual information, is pandemic among rational-choice modellers (see Bunge 1996a).

Historians and politologists know something applied game theorists and military strategists don't, namely this: Whereas one may find out – albeit only in outline – how a war starts, one may seldom predict how it will finish – as Machiavelli (1940 [1513], 21) warned. Hence, one may seldom forecast the utilities and disutilities of the contenders. One reason is that one can never know exactly the enemy's strengths and weaknesses, particularly its determination to go on fighting after a certain point. Another is that wars are not one-shot events – as assumed by most game-theoretic models – but processes; and one must expect accidents, hence surprises, in every protracted social process. One should prepare for them if only because of the quick turnover of people, new internal alignments, the changing mood of the combatants and the civilian population, and the shifting goals and alliances as the conflict proceeds. In short, waging war is, in Weber's terms, neither *Wertrational* nor *Zweckrational*. War is the ultimate irrationality as well as the supreme immorality. Hence, it is irrational to try to account for such folly in terms of rational action.

Greed, lust for power, and sheer stupidity are far more important in war than cold calculation (Kolko 1994). This explains why all the rational-choice models of international-conflict initiation have fared poorly (Huth and Russett 1993). Moreover, no modern war, civil or international, has resulted from the decision of a single individual intent on maximizing his own gains. Even when the final decision is made by a head of state, he acts with the consent and support of his co-workers as well as on behalf of special economic, political, or cultural interests, such as those of arms manufacturers, businessmen with colonial or neo-colonial interests, the military establishment, or the ruling political party or church. Hence, attributing a vast social event to a single leader, or even a tiny elite, is a mark of shallowness. So is overlooking accidents and, in particular, the unanticipated – often perverse – consequences of deliberate actions. (See Ibn Khaldûn 1967, Machiavelli 1940, and Boudon 1984 for the places of "fortune" and "disorder" in history.)

Two examples should suffice to emphasize the importance of unforeseen perverse effects. It has been argued that, except for Gustavus Adolphus of Sweden, all of the leaders of the Thirty Years' War fought to achieve a durable peace (Wedgwood 1967). Three centuries later the Versailles Treaty, designed to dismantle the German military-industrial complex, only succeeded in breeding *revanchisme*, which fuelled Nazism, which started the Second World War. Like the rational choice theorists, those politicians and generals ignored the fact that social action may have unintended consequences. They did not know that nearly all large-scale military calculations turn out to be erroneous in overlooking such important non-military factors as weather, supply of raw materials, and morale, and in ignoring the interests and feelings of the "enemy."

So much for the idealism-materialism controversy in historiography. We shall see next that systemism joins the valid contributions of both rivals.

3 Systemism versus Individualism and Holism

I submit that the systemic approach to history joins the valid contributions of historical materialism and historical idealism. Indeed, systemism asserts that overall social change is the effect of a myriad of individual actions occurring within systems ("structures"), and that social (structural) change can be triggered by environmental, biological, economic, political, or cultural factors – or a combination of either. Example 1: Climate deterioration, overcultivation, or their combination may lead to desiccation, soil erosion, or salinization. In turn, either of these environmental disasters results ultimately in poor crops, which, if recurrent, are bound to cause demographic, political, economic, and cultural decline – as seems to have been the case with the Sumerians and the ancient Mayas, not to speak of modern Africa. Example 2: The diffusion of literacy and public education facilitate the development of industry, which may in turn lead to either a population explosion or to birth control, depending on the standard of living and level of education. Example 3: Civil liberties favour culture, which in turn promotes industry and trade.

Systemists view every society as embedded in a natural environment, as well as being composed of four main subsystems: the biological, economic, political, and cultural ones – the *BEPC* model introduced in chapter 1. Hence, they see human history as a process composed of five intertwined strands, every one of which has in turn several constituents. A few of them are listed in the following table.

Environmental	Biological	Economic	Political	Cultural
Climate	Nutrition	Gathering & hunting	Government	Language
Soil	Shelter & clothing	Agriculture & husbandry	Public goods	Ideology
Water & minerals	Population	Crafts	Political strife	Technology
Flora	Fertility & mortality	Industry	Law & order	Science
Fauna	Morbidity	Trade	Foreign affairs	Humanities & arts

This view is at odds with the traditional idea of historiography as a linear narrative of successive-point events. The modern historian is not just a chronicler or storyteller. When narrating an episode or the life of a person, he does so "not for its own sake, but in order to throw light upon the internal workings of a past culture and society" (Stone 1979, 19). By placing the particular in a sequence, and adopting a broad perspective, the systemist overcomes the idiographic/ nomothetic duality we examined in chapter 1, section 3, as well as the concomitant narrative/structural opposition. The historian looks at the social world now through a microscope, now through a telescope (Hobsbawm 1980, 4).

The systemic historian weaves large tapestries like that of Bayeux. Or, to change the metaphor, he paints pentaptychs, that is, pictures on five panels placed side by side. Thus, sytemism is not monist but pluralist: it favours integral historiography. However, it is consistent with a materialist ontology provided it conceives of every culture not as a set of disembodied values and norms (Parsons's definition) but as a concrete system. Like all social systems, a culture is composed of live people whose emotions, perceptions, and ideas are brain processes, some of which elicit items of social behaviour. Hence, systemism can account for the interactions between the so-called material and ideal features of social change – as we saw in the previous section with regard to the relation between the rise of capitalism and the birth of modern culture.

One-sided historians are bound to make gross mistakes. For instance, the eminent historian A.J.P. Taylor (1961) denied that Nazi Germany had a "system" (plan) for conquering the world: he held that it stumbled into the Second World War by accident. He reached this conclusion from reading exclusively the political and diplomatic documents of the time – that is, a pile of lies. A look at the statistics, which show the vigorous arms build-up and the economic recovery, along with the intense Nazi hate propaganda, would have saved him from that error. A line segment is not a true model of a pentagon.

Like other social scientists, historians begin by choosing their referents or units of analysis. These lie between two extremes: the individual, studied by biographers, and the bloc of nations or even the world-system, studied by the *Annales* school and the world-system theorists, such as Wallerstein (1974). Actually biography is not a branch of history, just as developmental biology is not a branch of evolutionary biology. However, each of these disciplines needs the other. The good biographer places his characters in their social and historical contexts, and the good historian resorts to biographical data in order to reconstruct the past of social systems. Biography is a literary genre that uses historiography as an auxiliary discipline, whereas historiography is a branch of social science that utilizes biographies as sources along with traces of other kinds.

The units of analysis of historiography are social systems, sometimes also (wrongly) called social *structures* or *institutions* (see, for example, Mandelbaum 1955; Gellner 1973; Bunge 1985b; and Lloyd 1991). Because social systems come in all sizes, there are different levels of historiography. There is microhistory (e.g., that of a village or an industrial firm), mesohistory (e.g., that of a nation), and megahistory (e.g., that of Europe). However, micro- and mesohistories are shallow unless embedded in larger historical currents.

To be sure, one may also reconstruct the past of unstructured aggregates, such as children or women; of practices, such as birth control or voting; or of norms, such as those accompanying property rights. But, if realistic, these histories will be embedded in the general histories of the corresponding social systems or even entire societies. In sum, historiography is centrally about the evolution of social systems: it is about social change. But in turn social change, far from hovering above individual lives, is made of changes in the lifestyles of the components of the social system in question. And "social change" is to be taken in the broadest sense: as comprising demographic, economic, political, and cultural change. In this sense all historiography, even the history of ideas, is social.

As historians move upwards in the size scale, they unavoidably recede from individuals and their beliefs, feelings, and intentions and move towards impersonal concrete things or features such as the environment, the means of production, and the state. However, even when dealing with individuals, the historian cannot ignore their social setting and the trends of their time, which idealists call *Zeitgeist* (spirit of the time). Likewise, when dealing with entire nations historians cannot ignore elites, ideologies, or customs. In either case the historian cannot help adopting the systemist strategy of zig-zagging between the micro-, meso-, and macrolevels.

In particular, the historian has plenty of opportunities to construct Boudon-Coleman diagrams (chap. 2, sect. 3). For example, all the large migratory movements, from the Aryan (or Vedic) and Hun hordes down to our days, have presumably been flights from enviromental calamity, resource scarcity, war, demographic pressure, oppression, or poverty. And whereas a few such mass movements have been led by religious or military leaders, such as Moses and Attila, others are likely to have been the aggregate outcome of thousands of nearly independent individual decisions. (Much the same holds for cultural diffusion.) Both cases are covered by the following Boudon-Coleman diagram:

Macrolevel	Oppressive conditions $\rightarrow$ Large immigrant population	
	$\downarrow$	$\uparrow$
Microlevel	Desire for change $\rightarrow$ Migration	

The question of the role or weight of the individual in history is a classical problem in the philosophy of history. Once again, the best-known solutions are individualism (or voluntarism) and holism (or structuralism). The former is of course the view that the individual is everything, and the latter that he is nothing but "the involuntary tool of History" (Tolstoy). Individualists view individuals as distinct persons freely pursuing their interests; holists view them as indistinguishable units marching in step to an inaudible tune. Individualists hold that history is a sheaf of biographies – especially those of heroes and villains – whereas holists claim that history unfolds above individuals and drags them along. Whereas the former stress action and ideas but overlook the natural and social constraints upon them, holists emphasize the latter to the point of rendering individuals mere tools of obscure forces. Unsurprisingly, individualists may account for some successes (e.g., in terms of character features), but they certainly do not explain failures (e.g., in terms of adverse circumstances), whereas the converse holds for holists. Neither makes room for accidents, which will occur whenever the paths of a myriad of nearly independent individuals or systems cross. Nor do they allow for human errors.

Most contemporary historians subscribe to neither view: they adopt, albeit tacitly, the systemist thesis. This is the view that there are three types of "historical" (large scale) events and processes as regards their causes. *Type I* facts, or disasters, are triggered by natural "forces" such as earthquakes (e.g., the destruction of Pompeii) and plagues (e.g., the Irish potato blight and the subsequent mass migration). *Type II* facts, or mass movements, are caused by groups of people acting in unison – as in the cases of invasions and political upheavals. Finally, *Type III* historical facts are initiated by particular individuals, that is, leaders in some field – or some dwarf surfing a huge wave.

Moreover, the systemist historian does not attempt to reduce either of the three types to the others. Instead, he will explore their interrelations. In particular, he views Type III events in the light of Type II events. For example, he realizes that a leader can succeed only to the extent that he (a) puts himself at the head of a social group or process; (b) voices the needs or desires, or else fires the imagination, of a good many members of the system undergoing the process concerned; and (c) wins the trust of these individuals – whether by hook or by crook. The moment the leader stops meeting either of the last two conditions, he falls or else turns into a tyrant.

In any event, not all historical facts (that is, social changes) are initiated by identifiable leaders: much of history is anonymous – as emphasized by the *Annales* school – even if it results from a myriad of individual decisions. For example, Stone (1972) and Goldstone (1991), though disagreeing on the causes of the seventeenth-century English "Great Rebellion," agree that it was a mass movement that did not result from any individual will and had a number of unforeseen effects. However, this view is at odds with the holistic idea that history is a supra-individual movement or even a force that drags individuals and societies – usually a progressive force at that. Thus, Marx had asserted that, in carrying out the "revolutionary transformation" of India through its conquest, England had been the "unconscious tool of history." Systemists, as well as individualists, reject any such personification of history, not only because there is no evidence for it, but mainly because it is a category mistake and it leads to fatalism.

Another feature of systemic historiography is the shift from the isolated event to the process (string of events) and, moreover, the *longue durée* or protracted process (Braudel 1969). The adoption of a systemic and processual approach alters the very manner in which historical problems are posed. Consider, for instance, the question of the origins of modern science and, in particular, the question, "What caused the Scientific Revolution in the seventeenth century?" From a systemic and processual viewpoint this question is ill conceived, for it regards the birth of modern science as a point event caused by one or more events, rather than one of the strands of a whole braid of social processes. To be sure, the Scientific Revolution was the work of a few hundred exceptional brains. But these worked, and could only have worked, in a society that tolerated and occasionally rewarded the exploration and control of nature, as well as the invention and rational discussion of secular ideas about the world.

In a systemic and processual perspective, the proper question to ask is the more comprehensive one: What begat the modern world? Here is a sketchy answer. The modern world is the society that emerged in sixteenth-century Europe from a large number of interacting processes: the decline of rents and the rise of prices, and the consequent weakening of the aristocracy; the growth of manufacture and trade, and the consequent rise in the political and cultural power of the bourgeoisie; the voyages of discovery and conquest expeditions, and the subsequent looting of the Third World; the Thirty Years' War and the Revolt of the Netherlands, and the consequent decline of Spain and Austria and the rise of England; the creation of nation-states; the Renaissance and the Reformation, and the concomitant stretching of the mind; the strengthening of secularism and the diffusion of literacy and learning; and last, but not least, the emergence of modern science and technology, and a secular philosophy. (See Braudel 1972 and 1982; Wallerstein 1974; Hall 1985; and Kennedy 1989.)

To conclude this section. Historians, like any other students of society, are split into three ontological camps: the individualists, who claim that history is the doing of a few individuals (in particular heroes and villains); the holists, who assert either that history makes itself or that it is made by social groups – and in either case is something that happens to individuals; and the systemists, who maintain that history is made by individuals acting in and upon social systems that pre-exist and shape them. Moreover, both individualists and holists are monists: they propose unifactorial explanations. By contrast, systemists are pluralists: their explanations are multifactorial. (However, not all pluralists call themselves systemists; for instance, Mann [1993] does not.)

4 Law, Accident, Luck

Are there historical laws? Holists, such as Hegel, Comte, and Marx, tend to answer in the affirmative; and individualists, such as Dilthey, Weber, and Popper, tend to answer in the negative. The former assume that men are swept by lawful supra-individual forces: for them, history is a nomothetic science concerned exclusively with large processes. By contrast, individualists assume that individual decisions and new ideas, which are hardly predictable, are the ultimate movers: for them, history is an idiographic discipline concerned exclusively with particular events.

Now, the only proper way of establishing a universal is to exhibit instances of it. The US Committee on Historical Analysis, of the Social Science Research Council, came up with but a meagre crop of historical generalizations (Gottschalk 1963). And the examples that holists offer evaporate on inspection. Thus, Zhukow (1983) cites only two "laws" of history: that class warfare is the source of all progress and that human history has been one of continual progress. But technological innovations are counterexamples to the first "law"; and the setbacks brought about by overpopulation, plagues, wars, and the persecution of new ideas refute the second "law." To be sure, there are some definite worldwide trends, such as the expansion of capitalism, democracy, bureaucratism, literacy, secularism, and science over the past five centuries. But trends are not laws.

Still, the failure of holists to substantiate their claim does not entail the triumph of the antinomianist party. In fact, we know of a number of correct if somewhat crude historical generalizations. Here are a few. 1/ *Primum vivere, deinde philosophari.* 2/ Agriculture $\rightarrow$ surpluses $\rightarrow$ class division. 3/ All social systems deteriorate unless overhauled from time to time. 4/ No institution discharges exactly the tasks it was originally set up to do. 5/ No revolution alters all institutions. 6/ "The rich and privileged, when also corrupt and incompetent, do not accept rescuing reform" (Galbraith 1987, 56). 7/ All ideologies are eventually superseded by social changes. 8/ Every artefact is eventually displaced by an improved version of it or by one of a different kind. 9/ The diffusion curve of any cultural novelty is roughly sigmoid (S-shaped). 10/ "[E]minent scientists get disproportionately great credit for their contribution to science while relatively unknown ones tend to get disproportionately little for the occasionally comparable contributions" (Merton 1968).

There are, then, historical regularities: historical trajectories are not of the random-walk type. If they were, the future would not depend on the past, and the present could not be a clue to the past. Historical regularities have two sources. One is that all people are similar, have the same basic needs, and are willing to do something to meet them. Thus, during a famine most people do not lie down, but scavenge for food, beg, steal, loot, or move elsewhere. Another source of pattern is that humans are innately sociable, whence they get together into social systems of various kinds. And the social systems of any given kind discharge peculiar functions and therefore "come" with their own patterns – this being why we care to set up, maintain, or reform social systems and behaviour patterns. Thus, because schools are not the same as banks, the history of education differs from that of banking.

But there are irregularities along with regularities. They originate in idiosyncrasies, inventions, and individual or collective actions at cross purposes, as well as in internal instabilities and random external shocks. History is thus a tangle of causal lines and their intersections (see, for instance, Childe 1947 and Di Tella 1988). Consider any chain of this form: A caused B, which gave C the opportunity for D to happen. The presence of agent C was neither necessary nor providential: it was an accident. If C (or someone like C) had not been at the right place and time, the final outcome D would not have happened. Thus, individuals are not dispensable and therefore expendable any more than they are omnipotent. (Incidentally, the holistic counterfactual that if some "great man" had not been available to do something, someone else would have done it, is untestable.)

What holds for persons also holds, *mutatis mutandis*, for environmental (e.g., climatic), biological, economic, political, or cultural accidents. For example, bad weather in France in 1787–8 caused a crop failure, which brought famine and contributed to the mysterious "great fear," which in turn contributed to the 1789 revolution. From a social (though not a meteorological) viewpoint bad weather was an accident. But it caused a poor harvest, which in turn bred fear and increased discontent, which in turn eased the work of the revolutionaries – who had appeared earlier, as the *ancien régime* had begun to slacken. An example of a lucky accident is Margaret Thatcher's accession to power at about the time when North Sea oil started to produce the wealth that compensated for the fall in revenues caused by the tax cuts. This was a political accident, but of course neither a geological nor a technological one.

Accidents, or unexpected events, are particularly effective when the system concerned is in a state of unstable equilibrium, because in this case small causes can have large effects. (Examples: the balance of military power among the great powers in 1914, and the USSR in 1990.) Such situations are of the "touch-and-go" kind. Still, one should not exaggerate the role of accident in history, as the famous revisionist historian A.J.P. Taylor (1961) did when claiming that the Second World War started by accident (recall sect. 4). No large-scale war can be improvised: it must be planned and prepared. Still, the final outcome will be dicey. Ibn Khaldûn (1967, 2: 85) warned that only "[v]ictory and superiority in war come from luck and chance."

There are, then, plenty of historical accidents. However, few if any of them are frequent enough to allow us to use the concept of probability and its calculus. Indeed, large-scale events are unique. Hence, instead of saying that a certain historical event was *probable*, we should say that it was *likely* to happen; and instead of saying that some historical evidence is *probable*, we should say that it is *plausible*. Thus, it may well be that, as Clausewitz said, war is the realm of chance, but it is certainly not that of randomness.

Now, we call some accidents lucky and others unlucky. Is luck for real and, if so, does it play any role in history? (For the place of luck in biological evolution see Raup 1991.) The answer depends critically upon the meaning we attribute to the word 'luck.' Before proposing a definition let us offer a couple of examples. Good luck: A farming community enjoys unusually good weather, which allows it to reap a bumper crop and thus set aside a large surplus. Bad luck: News of this good luck reaches a neighbouring warrior tribe, which attacks, loots, and decimates the prosperous community.

Luck (good or bad) may be regarded as nothing but a (favourable or unfavourable) circumstance that is not a consequence of the agent's own actions: this is what Machiavelli meant by *fortuna*. We talk of good luck when circumstances offer an opportunity for beneficial action, and of bad luck when circumstances get in our way. A person may be lucky, yet fail to seize the opportunity; or he may be unlucky and still skilfully skirt or overcome the hurdle. What holds for individuals holds, *mutatis mutandis*, for entire social systems. For example, in the twentieth century many a country was lucky to discover that it had rich oil deposits – and unlucky in being ruled by an elite that appropriated and squandered the newly found wealth, leaving the country poorer or more divided and vulnerable than before.

Needless to say, being accidental, luck does not last. Good luck lasts only as long as the corresponding opportunity does, and as long as one takes advantage of it. Moreover, sometimes an agent can create a favourable circumstance or obviate an unfavourable one. Occasionally this happens unintentionally. For example, it was largely by a combination of good luck with hard work and ingenuity that comparatively backward Western Europe – rather than China, India, or Islam – became the cradle of modern civilization. In fact, modern Europe rose by a unique *concours de circonstances*, among which historians have listed the following: a temperate climate favouring a diversity of agricultural produce, and geographical accidents favouring political decentralization and discouraging foreign invasions; numerous waterways, and the roads and bridges left by the Romans; small families and a low population density; social inventions such as the free city and the guild, banking, and the university; the Renaissance and the Reformation; the substitution of secular goals (e.g., wealth and pleasure) for religious ones; innovations in agriculture and mining; the invention of the firearm and the printing press; advances in nautical instruments and navigation; the birth of modern science and a philosophy attuned to it rather than to theology; the lure of the Orient and the desire to keep up with it; the voyages of discovery and the subsequent ransacking of the Third World; the import of cheap eastern European grain; the rise of nation-states and the emergence of trade rivalries among them; the birth of science-based technology and technology-based manufacture and transportation; the birth of a few hundred exceptionally talented individuals unhindered by quietism and pietism; and last, but not least, the rapid decline of the last bulwark of feudalism, namely the Habsburg bloc, as a consequence of the overextension of its territory, the squandering of its wealth in wars and in the consumption of luxuries, as well as its adhesion to the Counter-Reformation (see Wallerstein 1974; Jones 1981; Hall 1985; Kennedy 1989; and Tilly 1990). England, France, and the Netherlands made the most of these intertwining opportunities; the other European countries missed nearly all of them. And nobody intended or foresaw the rise of Europe: far from being the outcome of rational choices, it came as a surprise and it does not cease to amaze us. And it is a reminder that great progress results from parallel advances in the economy, the polity, and the culture.

In short, there are a few true historical generalizations. However, most of them are spatio-temporallly bounded, none of them involves the absolute primacy of a single "factor," and all of them mingle with accidents, some lucky and others unlucky (see also Mann 1993). The occurrence of accidents of both types explains why human history – unlike historical narrative – is just as irreproducible as biological evolution. It also explains why the future cannot be predicted from the past. Which is just as well: not being predetermined, the future is uncertain, so we can help make it ourselves.

5 Trends: Progress, Stagnation, Decline

History has no purpose ("meaning"), but it is not haphazard either. Indeed, every period is characterized by some definite trends – typically, of growth, stagnation, or decline of certain features, such as population, prices, and cultural output. The "general drift of events" may escape the chronicler but not the scholar who, following the *Annales* school, looks at large expanses and long periods. Paradoxically, as Tocqueville (1985 [1857], 351) pointed out, only trends and their "general causes" are clearly discernible and certain, whereas "all that is particular is always more or less doubtful." In particular, progress, stagnation, and decline (in certain respects) are rather easily diagnosed – alas, usually only in retrospect. However, we are nowadays not as sure about the very concepts of progress and decline as the Enlightenment *philosophes* were. Therefore, it may be worthwhile to try to elucidate these concepts.

Recall what was said about luck in the previous section. Sometimes lucky (or unlucky) events come in isolation, at other times stringed. A streak of good (or bad) luck may continue for a while or stop altogether. If good luck prevails on the whole for a while, one speaks of progress, otherwise of stagnation or decline. However, the concept of progress is problematic. For one thing, the three artificial subsystems of a society may not "move" – advance or recede – in step. Thus, for a while cultural splendour may occur during economic recession or political turmoil – as were the cases of the Italian Renaissance, the Spanish Golden Century, and the Scientific Revolution. Besides, progress can be quantitative, qualitative, or both. That is, it may consist in the growth of the quantity of goods, an improvement of their quality, or both.

Scholars under the spell of mainstream economics focus on quantitative marketable goods regardless of their quality and their possible harmful side-effects. Until recently they gauged advancement by value or level attained – for instance, territory size, GDP, volume of foreign trade, and market share. Later on they added growth (or decline) rates – for example, percentage change in consumer spending, unemployment, illiteracy, or infectious diseases. Nowadays accelerations too are occasionally reckoned: demographers, economists, and politicians worry about the upward or downwards trends of rates of change. Thus, we are told that we may expect the current rise in population, unemployment, or voter apathy to slow down in the near future.

Such increasing quantitative precision is all to the good, yet insufficient because of two important facts. One is that growth is not always desirable. For instance, it is definitely malignant if it involves overpopulation, overconsumption, the depletion of natural resources, or the exploitation of persons or nations. Second, we should aim for improvement in the quality of goods and services – for instance, increase in the durability of artefacts and a better quality of printed matter and TV programs. Third, we should improve our lifestyles: better diets, improved education, better-informed voting, and a more just distribution of wealth. The upshot of the foregoing is that progress cannot simply be equated with quantitative growth.

I submit the following definition: A historical trend is *progressive on the whole* if and only if it involves the increasing satisfaction of the basic needs and legitimate aspirations of an increasing number of people, together with decreasing exploitation, oppression, and neglect, without jeopardizing the chances of future generations. Shorter: there is progress only insofar as integral democracy expands on the whole. (The rider "on the whole" is intended to take into account temporary setbacks due to natural disasters, wrong decisions, or unpredictable perverse effects, as well as the unavoidable costs of every advancement.)

A trend is not a law but a stretch of history, and thus the outcome of the working of a multitude of patterns (laws and norms), circumstances, and accidents. For example, the world market share of British manufacture has been declining steadily since about 1850; and the decline of the American world market share started one century later. There is no law stating that either country had to suffer such decline. However, there are several quasi-laws underneath both trends: (a) success breeds complacency; (b) all social systems become obsolete and deteriorate unless overhauled once in a while; (c) civilian industry goes down as military industry goes up; (d) the conquest and maintenance of new large markets requires the cooperation of business with government; (e) as new competitors enter a race, the chances of any one of them winning drop; and (f) the winners in the world market are those who either offer the most reasonably priced high-quality products in more demand, or gain a monopoly.

Social decline is no more inevitable than progress: both can be arrested or prodded. Moreover, neither excludes the other. On the contrary, progress in any respect requires some sacrifice, hence decline or stagnation in other respects. For example, advances in public health care and education may require higher taxes, which, if collected, may in turn lower in the short run the level of consumption or the volume of investment. Thus, all progress is partial. For this reason it will always be painful to the members of some social groups. This is why it is usually resisted by its prospective victims.

As with progress, so with decline and with cycles or "waves." One of the most intriguing historiographic problems has been tackled by Kondratieff, Schumpeter, Kuznets, Braudel, and a few others. This is the question whether there are "long waves" of economic growth followed by decline and, if so, what the underlying mechanisms could be. The problem of their existence may be solved by more accurate data and finer econometric analysis, whereas that of mechanism calls for social and technological history as well. So far neither study has brought conclusive results. Yet a study of the British and American economies between 1790 and 1990, conducted by Berry and the Kims (1993), proposes the following interesting hypotheses. Kinematics: The long (or Kondratieff) waves are price cycles lasting for about half a century each; the short (or Kuznets) waves are national income cyles of about a quarter-century each. Moreover, the short cycles nestle in the long ones; and every such cycle has the logistic shape both upwards and downwards. Dynamics: Obsolescence of the dominant techno-economic system (e.g., coal-steam-rail) → new techno-economic system (e.g., electricity-chemicals-automobiles) & social changes → market saturation → drop in prices. Whether these findings will hold remains to be seen. If they do, they are likely to encourage both serious techno-economic history and long-term speculative prophecy. (Still, such cycles may be Ptolemaic fictions. After all, any irregular curve can be analysed as a sum of regular waves with different frequencies.)

We close with three old but still open questions: whether history repeats itself, it keeps a constant pace, and there are unchangeable or ahistorical societies. My answer to all three is in the negative. Social processes, like the biological processes underlying them, are irreversible if only because of environmental changes, people turnover, and the wear and tear of all artefacts – not to mention the emergence of new ideas, customs, and institutions. Not even counter-revolutions can succeed in fully re-establishing the *status quo ante*, because people and circumstances will have changed in the meantime, new interests may have emerged, and new traditions will have become ingrained.

As for the pace or *tempo* of history, no such thing has been found or is likely to be found. Human history, just like biological evolution, is gradual (or continuous) in some regards and discontinuous in others. However, the similarity between history and evolution should not be exaggerated. First, because there is no design in biological evolution, whereas many human actions are planned. Second, because, whereas most biospecies eventually become extinct, few institutions ever disappear totally. Some of them adapt to new circumstances, and others – called 'vestiges' – continue out of sheer inertia even long after they have ceased to be functional. Functionalism notwithstanding, social matter is less functional than living matter. This is because vested interests, ignorance, and false beliefs, in particular ideologies, can delay the recognition of dysfunctionalities, unresolved conflicts, and new opportunities.

Anthropologists and sociologists contrast societies in transition with stagnant societies. Some of them – in particular Lévi-Strauss – hold that all primitive societies are structurally immutable. This is a replay of the nineteenth-century Romantic opposition between *Naturvölker* and *Kulturvölker*. As a matter of fact all societies, like everything else in the real world, are in a state of flux. The so-called stagnant (or traditional) societies are actually in a near-steady (or stationary) state: one where institutions change too slowly for the outsider to notice. In any event, all of the contemporary primitive societies are in quick transition, if only because of their (usually disastrous) interactions with advanced societies.

6 Interpretation or Hypothesis?

Archaeologists, prehistorians, and historians never face brute facts: they face only traces of past facts, from fossil bones and footprints to garbage and legal documents. These are their only sources or data: all else is conjecture. Worse, some data, particularly those supplied by court or party chroniclers or journalists, are suspect of bias or even wilful distortion. Hypotheses do not fare better. In particular, some historical conjectures proposed long ago are still in limbo. For example, the famous Nazca lines in the Peruvian Andes are clearly visible and they have been carefully photographed and measured, but they remain unexplained at the time of writing: all of the numerous hypotheses proposed to account for them seem to have been falsified (see Aveni 1990).

Data do not speak for themselves: they can only suggest and constrain. They must be "read" in the light of hypotheses, some of which suggest looking for further data of certain kinds. Yet the role of conjecture in historical reconstruction is often underrated under the influence of both empiricism and hermeneutics. Indeed, the standard view is that the student of the past "pieces the data together," "draws conclusions" from them, or "interprets" them. A methodological analysis shows that he does neither. What the historian does is to frame guesses or hypotheses, concerning, say, the use of artefacts found in a site. (Think, for instance, of Stonehenge.) Moreover, whenever possible he goes on to test such hypotheses – for example, by making and trying out replicas of ancient tools, or by proposing hindcasts and checking them. Thus, historians employ the scientific method. They have no use for arbitrary hermeneutic "interpretations" of actions of inaccessible protagonists, such as the untestable fantasies of psychohistorians.

All historiography is hypothetical reconstruction. And every such reconstruction calls for more than data and disciplined imagination. As Hempel (1942) argued, it also requires a number of apparently trite but actually potent generalizations. Some of these are "All humans, at all times, have similar basic needs," "Complex tasks call for knowledge, communication, and social organization," "Similars are likely to have similar origins or uses," "Every artefact is a component of some system – that is, there are no stray artefacts," "Every type of human society has its peculiar norms," and "All new challenges call for social changes." These generalities help to invent specific hypotheses, which in turn are tested in the field or the laboratory. Such tests may be direct, as in the case of a microscopic examination of pollen found in a site. Or they may be indirect, as in the case of hindcasts that guide the search for further traces in the same site or nearby. In this regard the historian and the natural scientist proceed similarly: both attempt to explain data by hypotheses, and both check the latter by looking for further data (see Carr 1961; Goldstein 1977; Albert 1988; and Trigger 1989).

True, unlike the physicist, the historian attempts to reconstruct unrepeatable facts, and he has access to a hopelessly incomplete and often severely distorted record. But the geologist, the cosmologist, and the evolutionary biologist are in the same predicament: they too deal with ex-facts on the strength of small samples of traces – and moreover non-random ones. (Furthermore these traces, though seldom deliberately distorted, suffer the ravages of time. In particular, fossils evolve; this evolution is the object of an auxiliary discipline: taphonomy.) The real difficulty lies elsewhere, namely that – as C.F. Hawkes pointed out in 1954 – there is a scale of difficulty in "interpreting" the archaeological or historical record in terms of human activities: technique–economy–social organization–political organization–culture. The reason for this escalating difficulty in "inferring" (guessing) human behaviour and thought from archaeological data is that the lower levels impose constraints on the higher ones without fully determining them (Trigger 1989, 392–5). For example, one and the same environment can support two different economies, each of which is compatible with two different cultures and political organizations. This partial autonomy of the higher levels relative to the lower ones refutes geographic, biological, and economic determinism.

The framing and testing of historical hypotheses is becoming increasingly rigorous as a result of two trends: systemism and concern for accuracy. A systemic approach, unlike a sectoral one, has the advantage that it demands that every hypothesis be examined in the light of several disciplines – for instance, geography, demography, and economics. This requirement decreases uncertainty. As for the concern for accuracy, it has led to cliometry. This involves not only the gathering of quantitative data but also their statistical analysis. For example, two rival hypotheses concerning the French Revolution of 1789 – the Taine-Dollot and the Tocqueville ones – were subjected to quantitative tests. Both presuppose that the revolution was basically a revolt of the bourgeoisie against the nobility. But Taine and Dollot hypothesized that the bourgeoisie hated the *ancien régime* for barring its upward mobility. By contrast, Tocqueville conjectured that the ennoblement procedure increased the hatred of the commoner against the *gentilhomme* to the point that the bourgeoisie demanded that the procedure be narrowed rather than widened. Neither of these hypotheses had been tested before, and the former had been preferred for seeming the more reasonable. Shapiro and Dawson (1972) studied the *cahiers de doléances* (grievances lists) in order "to discover whether, in places where ennoblement opportunities were plentiful, the bourgeoisie was more or less radical than where ennoblement opportunities were scarce" (ibid., 169). Their statistical analysis of the data revealed a strong positive correlation between radicalism and objective opportunities for ennoblement. This finding vindicated Tocqueville's counterintuitive hypothesis – until new notice. (Incidentally, it is most unlikely that a social revolution could have a single cause: see chap. 4, sect. 3, and Mann 1993.)

Whether or not a hypothesis looks at first sight plausible ("probable") has little to do with its truth value. In fact, all the hypotheses in the advanced sciences are counterintuitive on inception, particularly if they refer to hidden mechanisms. What is characteristic of scientific hypotheses is that they are (a) compatible with the bulk of antecedent knowledge (including the philosophical presuppositions of science) and (b) empirically testable. The first condition excludes resorting to the supernatural and the paranormal, and it encourages the search for compatible evidence and hypotheses belonging to neighbouring fields. The second condition demands the search for new data that cannot be "covered" by rival hypotheses.

Note that, unlike Popper (1959), I do not equate "testability" with "refutability" (see Bunge 1998). Of course counterexamples, if repeatedly corroborated, weaken or even falsify general hypotheses. But we want more than just to weed out falsities. We also want to know the truth, and this requires *positive* evidence. For example, since "not yet found" is not the same as "non-existing," no amount of digging and dating can refute the currently unsupported conjecture that America was peopled 100,000 years ago. This hypothesis is at present disregarded for lack of positive findings, not for having been refuted; but new findings may confirm it. In short, confirmation is just as valuable as refutation. (By contrast, refutability is weightier than confirmability.) This holds for history as much as for physics (see Bunge 1967a, 1973a, 1985b, and 1996a).

In conclusion, although historians and natural scientists employ different special methods, and even though the latter have powerful and exact theories that the former cannot even dream of, both groups employ the scientific method to find truths. By the same token, both are realists rather than either apriorists or empiricists, intuitionists or hermeneuticians: they all attempt to model reality, past or present, by framing testable hypotheses capable of explaining their data. More on explanation anon.

7 Historical Explanation

Historiography is to chronicle as biology is to natural history. Whereas the chronicler only describes some of what happened, the historian seeks to explain why it happened, for he wants to understand rather than just to know (see, for instance, Bloch 1949). In particular, he seeks to find out how and why a given social system or social process emerged or disappeared there and then – and even why certain conceivable events failed to happen.

Historians explain in terms of generalizations (laws, norms, or both) and data. But, to count as explanations proper, the generalizations in question must describe or hint at some mechanism or other (Bunge 1967b, 1983b, 1996a, 1997b). And some of them, in particular those regarding human nature, are general, whereas others are special, or space- and time-bound. A handful of examples follow. 1/ The cold spell in 1879 ruined English agriculture for decades because, under the free-trade terms, it opened the door to cheap Russian and American wheat – for not even patriots prefer dear domestic goods to cheap imported ones of the same quality. 2/ Great empires do not last, either because the upkeep of military power drains the economic and cultural resources, or because long distances from the centre of power hinder coordination and facilitate corruption and sedition in the outlying regions. 3/ Radically new ideas are so often introduced by newcomers or outsiders because these are not shackled to the field's tradition. 4/ A disproportionate number of natives of Extremadura – a backward land-locked Spanish province – distinguished themselves for their valour, entrepreneurship, endurance, and brutality in the conquest of America because they were very poor and used to the hardships of outdoors living. 5/ The dairy industry did not develop in China or in black Africa because most of the adult natives of these regions lack the enzyme required to digest dairy products. 6/ Agriculture developed as a consequence of the increase in population, which was due, in turn, to the increase of habitable areas brought about by the end of the last Ice Age. In all of the preceding cases events are explained in terms of specific mechanisms, and non-events by their absence.

The general schema in the preceding explanations is this:

$$\text{General hypotheses}$$
$$\downarrow$$
$$\text{Agent(s)} \rightarrow \text{Action(s)} \rightarrow \text{Trace(s)} \rightarrow \text{Historiography} \rightarrow \text{Fact to be explained}$$
$$\uparrow$$
$$\text{Special hypotheses}$$

In this regard the historian's job does not differ from that of the natural scientist. True, the historian seldom makes explicit use of historical generalizations. More often than not he borrows generalizations from other disciplines – mainly biology, psychology, sociology, economics, and political science. But so does the chemist when explaining certain chemical processes in physical terms; the biologist when resorting to physics and chemistry to explain certain biological processes; and the psychologist when explaining mental processes in biological or social terms.

Finally note that the rejection of historical monism (sect. 2) involves distrust of unifactorial explanations. Consider, for instance, the problem of why a few hundred Spaniards, mostly uneducated to say the least, were able to conquer America, a continent inhabited by between 20 and 100 million people, many of whom lived in civilized societies. The correct explanation seems to be multifactorial rather than unicausal. The conquerors had no chance of advancement at home, they were pulled by the (largely imaginary) riches to be had, and they were technically superior to the natives, particularly in weaponry, organization, and transportation. The Ameridians were shocked by and in awe of the Spanish weapons, horses, and strategy; they had been divided and often at war with one another; and the Amerindian (particularly Mesoamerican) religions and myths were particularly pessimistic and fatalistic.

In sum, historians, just like physicists, are not content with maximally accurate (true) descriptions. They also want to explain what they describe. To do so they hazard and check hypotheses, in particular conjectures of the causal kind; in turn, such hypotheses guide their search for evidence. Regrettably, hypotheses are often called *interpretations*. This suggests to the methodologically naive that history is a hermeneutic discipline – or rather indiscipline. But this is a mistake, because historical events are just as meaningless as physical events. Only ideas and the symbols representing them can be meaningful.

8 Uses of History

Like every other field of knowledge, historiography can have good, bad, or indifferent uses. It can help in understanding the present and thus assist in designing the future; it can perpetuate superstitions, grudges, and rivalries; or it can be intellectually rewarding or just fun to read.

Most North American politicians do not care for the past – at their peril and ours. And some of those who read history do so in the mistaken belief that the future will be roughly like the past because human nature is invariant. This is actually how many a foreign policy has been designed (May 1973). But of course human history, like biological evolution, is irreversible: it is both creative and destructive rather than either repetitive or cyclical. That, then, is not a good reason for studying history.

There are several excellent reasons for studying history. One is that the present is a consequence of the past and in turn unfolds into the future. Consequently we must know the past, if only in outline, to understand the present and have an intelligent say in shaping the future. Of course, we never fully master our "destiny," much less that of our society; still, in a democratic society every one of us does have some say, and this had better be an enlightened one.

A second reason for cultivating historical studies is that, although history never repeats itself, some historical events and processes have analogues, and such analogies allow one to form certain general concepts and propositions (recall sect. 3). Although no generalizations will instruct us on how to tackle current issues, some may warn us against repeating past follies. For example, if we know that arms races enhance the possibility of war, and impoverish everyone except for the arms manufacturers and dealers, we will try to solve international conflicts by peaceful means. (Wallace [1979] found that, of the twenty-eight arms races between great powers during the 1816 to 1965 period, twenty-three ended up in war. So much for the slogan *Si vis pacem, para bellum*.)

A third reason is that only the study of history helps to discover the mechanisms underlying macrosocial dynamics. (This is why historical sociology and economic history are so important.) Such knowledge has a practical as well as an epistemic interest. Indeed, knowledge about social mechanisms can be used to either steer change or prevent it. (This is why historiography is a hobby of both reformers and conservatives.) For example, macroeconomists still study the German hyperinflation in 1922 and the 1929–39 depression: they wish to uncover the (still poorly known) inflation mechanisms, as well as ascertain the role of fiscal (in particular monetary) policies.

A particularly instructive use of history is to learn the mechanisms of the emergence of successful societies, in order to ward off bad advice concerning the so-called developing nations. Thus, when economists and politicians advise those nations to adopt "economic shock therapies," so as to introduce overnight a capitalist market without state intervention, they should be reminded that all the capitalist economies were built over many generations with vigorous state support, which often included military force. For example, British trade and industry expanded, and then declined, in synergy with British colonialism; and the American railroads, highways, dams, water-distribution networks, and arms industry were built with substantial state investment. Free enterprise indeed!

Another important practical use of history could be to uncover the mechanisms of the decline and fall of earlier civilizations, to help us preserve our own. No previous civilization has had a social science to speak of, and consequently the possibility of identifying the causes of decline so as to prevent or reverse it. We are fortunate in having some social science, and, as a matter of fact, some of the threats to our civilization are well known: overpopulation, depletion of natural resources, poverty, neglect of education and health care, militarism, irrationalism, and aggressive nationalism. Such knowledge could be used to save modern civilization from those bent on destroying it.

A fourth good reason to study history is to evaluate claims concerning the viability or otherwise of certain social orders. For example, the famous tale of the "tragedy of the commons" (Hardin 1968) has been used not only to illustrate the bad consequences of the pursuit of self-interest. It has also been used to "prove" the unavoidable vulnerability of public ownership. But historians tell us that the actual tragedy was the reverse of the imaginary one, and it happened all over Europe since medieval times. It consisted in the forced enclosure (privatization) of the communal fields, which deprived poor peasants of their livelihood. Schematically, the actual (as opposed to the imaginary) tragedy of the commons was this: enclosure → eviction → destitution → starvation or emigration.

Not only the study of the past, but also counterfactual speculation is occasionally enlightening, for pointing to missed opportunities or to policy mistakes. Think, for instance, of such contrary-to-fact hypotheses as "If Napoleon had liberated the serfs as his troops advanced towards Moscow, he might have won the war, and the Holy Alliance would never have been put together" and "If Gorbachev's team had designed a plan for the gradual but integral democratization of the Soviet society – including the transformation of state enterprises into self-governed cooperatives – the USSR might not have split and sunk."

We may learn more from such rational fantasies than from many a reliable but uninteresting document: though logically intractable and empirically barren, counterfactuals can be heuristically fertile. However, this is not to say that counterfactual historiography is on a par with historiography proper. For example, Robert W. Fogel's thesis that the economic development of the US would not have been much different without railways is just interesting speculation, although it is buttressed by the very same statistics that measure the actual economic impact of the railroad. Even though intelligent fiction can occasionally steer the search for fact, historiography is about fact not fiction.

To conclude. We can learn something about society by studying social change, that is, history. However, the "lessons of history" are ambiguous. What we learn from the past depends largely on our world-view, interests, and attitude to the future. The conservative "learns" that social reform is pointless or worse because so many previous attempts have failed or backfired. The revolutionary "learns" that certain social reforms failed because they were not radical enough. The nationalist and the hawk "learn" to nurse their hatred for "the other" and thus to march backwards. The pacifist and the internationalist "learn" the virtues of peace and international solidarity. In short, much of what we "learn" from the study of history we already knew or believed in to begin with: by and large we see what we look for. Still, a critical brain can learn from history to uncover recurrent social mechanisms, dispel illusions, support hopes – or at least "raise the level of the debate" (Hirschman 1977, 135). In particular, one can learn to mistrust the claims that the current social order is eternal and that there is a quick fix for every social issue.

History may also be put to evil uses. Thus, obsession with the past may make us lose sight of the present and neglect preparing for the future. As well, historiography – whether truthful or not – can be used to prop up regressive political movements. In particular, the biased history textbook is the mainstay of xenophobia and all manner of aggressive nationalism – hence a tool of aggressive policies. But this is not the prerogative of history: every piece of knowledge, even an innocent mathematical formula, may be put to evil uses. Basic knowledge is intrinsically neutral and, for this reason, it may be put to either good or evil uses (Bunge 1989a). It is also good in itself, for assuaging "mere" curiosity. Thus, only the history of the geographic distribution of human genes brought about by the great migrations explains their present distribution and some of the peculiarities of the various modern ethnic groups and languages (Cavalli-Sforza 1994). In short, historiography has its uses – some good, others evil.

Contemporary historians are divided roughly into two schools: the traditionalist or humanistic and the modern or proscientific. The former's approach and method are close to classical philology, literary criticism, law, and art history, whereas the approach and method of the proscientific historians are close to those of evolutionary biology. Some of the differences between the two camps are shown in the following table (see, for example, Braudel 1969; Andreano 1970; Bogue and Fogel 1972; Gilbert and Graubard 1972; McClelland 1975; Barraclough 1979; Fogel 1982a, 1982b)

Feature	Humanistic	Proscientific
Philosophy	Mostly idealist	Mostly materialist
Referents	Individuals, ideas, institutions	Social systems
Facts	Exceptional events	All processes
Favourite strands	Politics and culture	All
Favourite region	Europe	The world
Generalizations	Truisms	Truisms, laws, and norms
Quantities	Innumerate	Numerate
Models	Implicit, informal	Explicit, occasionally formal
Type of source	Archive and library	Multiple
Relatives	Literature	All social sciences
Goals	Description or apology	Description and explanation
Controversy	Destructive	Constructive
Ideology	Frequent	Rare
Research mode	Individualist	Often teamwork
Style	Narrative	Narrative combined with tables, etc.

A scientific look at the past has the following six philosophical or methodological characteristics: it is realist, materialist, systemic, interdisciplinary, quantitative, and nomothetic as well as idiographic. This look is thoroughly *realist*, like the best traditional historiography and unlike the nationalist, jingoistic, partisan, religious, or "postmodern" stories. In other words, it seeks to reconstruct the past in the truest possible manner. This does not mean that it is necessarily "dry as dust": far from being a positivist hoarder of "facts," the realist historiographer hazards hypotheses to explain some facts – but, being a scientist, he attempts to check his conjectures. The proscientific approach is *materialist* in the broad sense, not in the economicist one: it studies concrete things – social systems – not disembodied ideas, though it does not underrate the power of the latter when they guide or misguide social behaviour. The combination of materialism with realism suggests systemism, whose device is: *Everything is either a system or a component of one.*

The new look is *systemic*, for it focuses on social systems rather than individuals, and on long-drawn-out processes rather than isolated and exceptional events. And when it does study exceptional events or characters, it places them in their social context. This is of course necessary for historiography to count among the *social* sciences.

Systemicity entails increasing *interdisciplinarity*: proscientific historiography draws on geography, demography, epidemiology, social psychology, sociology, economics, political science, and culturology. However, we still have a long way to go. Thus, most of the papers in the *Journal of Interdisciplinary History* fall into one of the traditional fields.

Interdisciplinarity, and particularly intimate contact with demography, economics, and sociology, has facilitated *quantitation* – and conversely. Numeracy is necessary for several reasons. First, because several key historical variables (such as population, fertility, GDP, and volume of foreign trade) are quantitative. Second, because quantitation makes for conceptual precision: it elucidates such vague concepts as "some," "most," "frequent," "growing," "declining," "fast," "slow," and so on. Third, some statistical correlations suggest causal connections. (For example, if population and prices rise concurrently, it may be conjectured that population growth causes demand inflation.) Fourth, tables of figures may exhibit trends or even quasi-laws. Fifth, cliometrics (quantitative history) may yet grow into cliomathematics (the building of mathematical models of historical processes).

Quantitation and interdisciplinarity have jointly stimulated the search for historical patterns (trends, laws, and norms), thus reinforcing the *nomothetic* aspect of history. We have come to suspect that history, like the evolution of climate and biopopulations, is a result of underlying generalities and circumstances, even if the histories themselves do not exhibit obvious regularities because of the importance of circumstance and accident.

The preceding considerations suggest that the new historiography (not to be confused with the New History advertised by some literary critics) is a science, albeit an emerging one. Admittedly, it is not nearly as rigorous as atomic physics or molecular genetics. However, it is no less rigorous than cosmology or psychology. And it is far more rigorous, deep, and interesting than mainstream economics or political science. In conclusion, the old opposition between history and science, proclaimed by Dilthey and stressed by Weber, Popper, and

Berlin among others, applies to much of traditional history though not to proscientific historiography – including Thucydides, Ibn Khaldûn, and Machiavelli.

This is not to say that traditional or humanistic history lacks a future. Because they focus on social changes, that is, anonymous processes, social historians cannot account fully for the evolution of art, technology, medicine, science, and the humanities, all of which are cultivated by craftsmen. The student of culture must try to discover the problems that the individual creator tackled; the flashes of insight that punctuated his endeavour; the wrong starts and blind alleys that slowed down his work; the missed opportunities; and the social constraints and stimuli under which he worked. Hence, the history of culture will continue to be largely a branch of the humanities. Yet, although the culturologist may have little use for the peculiar methods employed by the scientific historian, he will ignore the latter's findings only at his risk, for no creator, however original, starts from scratch or works in a social vacuum. In short, proscientific history provides culturology with some scientific knowledge of the large social currents in which the individual creator swims.

Our examination of the proscientific school of historical research suggests that we are witnessing an important new shift: from fragmentation to unity. In the past most students of society and most philosophers stressed the autonomy of the various social sciences. In particular, Aristotle, Machiavelli, Hobbes, Spinoza, and Condorcet saw politology as detached from economics and history – not to speak of sociology, which hardly existed in their own times. Comte and Durkheim ignored sociology's sisters. And the neoclassical economists, in particular Menger and Pareto, stressed the autonomy of economics.

By contrast, scholars as different as Mill and Parsons, as well as the contemporary socio-economics movement, have stressed the ties between economics and sociology. Ibn Khaldûn, Marx, Weber, Schumpeter, Myrdal, Merton, Braudel, Tilly, and a few others went even farther, conceiving of all the social sciences as different strands of a single braid. There are no autonomous social sciences because all of them study the same thing: society. Hence, all of the social sciences are interdependent: the borders between them are largely artificial. Worse yet, a stress on borders hinders progress, for it blocks the flow of different perspectives about a single subject matter. Awareness of this artificiality favours a unified approach to both the study of social facts and the tackling of complex and serious social issues. And all of these are, by definition, multidimensional and hard to solve. Which leads us to sociotechnology.

PART B

Sociotechnology

In this part of the book we shall examine some of the philosophical problems raised by social technology, or sociotechnology for short. This discipline studies ways of maintaining, repairing, improving, or replacing existing social systems (e.g., factories, hospitals, and schools) and processes (e.g., manufacture, health care, and education); and it designs or redesigns social systems and processes to tackle social issues (e.g., mass unemployment, epidemics, and crime). Accordingly, social medicine, social work, management science, normative macroeconomics, and the law are sociotechnologies; so are the disciplines that study environmental protection, welfare, education, work, social control, city planning, finance, and public policy in general. These sociotechnologies are on a par with electrical engineering, biotechnology, and knowledge engineering.

What can philosophers say about social issues and ways of tackling them? A lot. Let two examples suffice. We just met one of them when suggesting that the study of the management of social systems is, or ought to be, a branch of technology on a par with engineering. The irrationalists of all hues will disagree: they favour tradition, common sense, intuition, or gobbledygook – neither of which can cope with the unfamiliar. So will the hyperrationalists, for they believe that one can make do with a priori theories that, like those of decisions and games, make no room for parameters to be determined empirically. By contrast, a scientific realist would advocate carrying out the following sequence of operations:

Perform a scientific study of the issue of interest → design policies and plans in consultation with all the interested parties → try out the preferred plan on a small- to medium-scale pilot plant → evaluate the results, again in close consultation with the stakeholders → make the necessary corrections → implement the corrected plan on a large scale → monitor continuously the implementation of the plan, review it periodically, and alter or even drop it in case of failure.

Our second example involves the individualism-holism-systemism trilemma. It is that of mass homelessness, an increasingly serious issue, and one about which hundreds of studies have been published in recent years. These studies can be split into individualist, holist, and systemist. The individualist's diagnosis is that homelessness is caused exclusively by personal characteristics such as mental illness, drug addiction, and a criminal record. Hence, if liberal he will advocate rehabilitation programs; and if conservative, jailing. By contrast, the holist attributes homelessness exclusively to macrosocial circumstances: changes in the economy and the social-security system during the1980s, lack of affordable housing, and the massive closing of psychiatric wards in earlier years. Consequently, he will favour large-scale social reforms. Finally, the systemist will acknowledge the operations of causes on both the micro- and the macrolevels; moreover, he will combine them. For example, drug addiction, criminality, and drift are favoured by structural conditions, which in turn are reinforced by the former – the "infernal cycle of poverty." Hence, the systemist is likely to advocate a mixed strategy combining rehabilitation programs with social programs such as building low-rent houses and organizing community centres and work cooperatives where the homeless can start to get hold of their own lives. In short, different conceptions of society are bound to inspire different diagnoses and treatments of social ills. The choice among them is philosophical, and it can make the difference between social stagnation, degradation, and progress.

But back to the epistemic status of the sociotechnologies. Let us start by noting the salient similarities and differences between basic science and technology. To begin with, whereas science – whether natural, social, or socionatural – studies the world, technology devises ways to change it: it is the art and science of getting things done in the most efficient way. If preferred, technology devises rational ways of leaping from *is* to *ought*. In science deliberate change, as in experiment, is a means to knowledge. In technology it is the other way round: here knowledge is a means to alter reality. For example, social medicine uses medicine, toxicology, and epidemiology to recommend measures likely to improve public health.

In particular, whereas in science theories are expected to model reality, in technology they are also tools for altering reality – for better or for worse. (Still, in both cases theories are supposed to be at least approximately true. A bridge or a corporation built on an utterly false model is bound to collapse. Truth precedes efficiency.) Whereas scientists work on epistemic problems, technologists face practical issues. In particular, sociotechnologists wrestle with such social issues as pollution, overpopulation, poverty, unemployment, waste, bad health, illiteracy, violence, and corruption. (More on technology in Agassi 1985; Bunge 1985b and 1996a; Quintanilla 1989; and Mitcham 1994.)

However, just as engineers design machines but are not expected to assemble them, sociotechnologists do not engage in practical actions: they only study social issues and recommend solutions to them. Those who do tackle social problems in a practical fashion are politicians, civil servants, managers, business consultants, lawyers, social workers, teachers, and others. All these individuals perform services, ideally in the light of studies and recommendations of sociotechnologists. The parallel with medicine is clear. Here too three types of work must be distinguished: research (human biology, in particular pathology), technology (therapeutics and social medicine), and health care – a service.

We must distinguish and interrelate, then, three different fields: science (S), technology (T), and praxis (P). The relations among them can be summed up as follows: $S \leftrightarrow T \leftrightarrow P$, where '$\leftrightarrow$' denotes interaction. To spell it out, (a) every practical activity can be the object of a technology, and in turn every effective technology can be grounded on, and justified by, one or more sciences, (b) every science can be used to construct or strengthen the corresponding technology, which (c) can be used to steer the corresponding practical activity. For example, resource management makes use of biology and geography.

Unlike scientific problems, which exist only in the brain of the curious student, social issues – such as shortages, dysfunctions, and conflicts – are objective features of the social world. Such issues are out there to be discovered and studied, though they won't be without a modicum of social sensibility. Think, for example, of poverty, unemployment, illiteracy, marginality, colonialism, political oppression, and the manipulation of public opinion: usually they are not "perceived" by the powerful and their intellectual courtiers (see Lindblom 1990, 217). Moreover, there is no one-to-one correspondence between issues and problems: some issues fail to be addressed, hence they have no scientific correlates.

Unlike the traditional crafts (or technics), modern technology utilizes some scientific knowledge, to which it adds some new knowledge: it is never an automatic product of basic research. Think, for instance, of management science, which at its best uses some social psychology, sociology, and economics to diagnose the state of business firms and make recommendations for their maintenance, improvement, rescue, or dismantling, on the basis of rules as well as laws, or at least quasi-laws. (Example of a quasi-law: As division of labour increases, the costs of communication increase. Example of a rule: Improve coordination as the division of labour increases.)

Basic research is both objective and impartial: it collects data, makes conjectures, and crafts (approximately) true models of real things, taking no side other than that of intellectual honesty. Its task is to describe, explain, and if possible forecast as well: it prescribes nothing. Technology too is objective, but not impartial. It is objective because it starts by finding out how things really are: it has no use for myth. But technology is likely to be biased when prescribing change, for nearly all change – whether in nature or in society – is likely to benefit or harm some people more than others. In other words, whereas basic science is value-free, technology is value-bound. For this reason technologists face moral problems that do not arise in basic science, all of whose moral problems are internal (see Merton 1973, chap. 4). Besides, technology may raise political problems, which basic research does not pose at all. (Political decisions can benefit or harm basic science, but the latter is politically powerless; whereas technology, when controlled by business or government, is a potent tool for either stasis or change.)

Technologists design artificial systems or processes but do not produce them: they just make recommendations. The adoption and actual production or reform of artificial systems and processes is a function of business or politics, in particular government. Think, for example, of factories, transportation networks, schools, courts of law, jails, safety standards, legal norms, or international treaties: none of them emerges spontaneously, and all of them can benefit from sociotechnology. And yet the very existence of social artefacts, and consequently the need to handle them in the light of sociotechnology, is in dispute.

Whereas some social systems and behaviour patterns – such as the family, communication, instruction, and small markets and towns – emerge spontaneously, others are the execution of human design. Both occur in primitive as well as in civilized societies, but pervasive social design and large-scale organization are peculiar to civilization. It suffices to think of such social inventions as city and state, factory and road, school and hospital, court of law and temple, army and political party, labour union and club, old-age pension and medicare, unemployment insurance and family allowance. Or think of farms, workshops, business firms, banking, insurance, and cooperatives, as well as of writing, printing, publishing, and broadcasting – and of course policy-making, planning, accounting, and chronicling. All such systems and processes are artificial rather than spontaneous: they have been invented and set up or controlled according to plan.

The advantage of design over spontaneity is that it makes explicit and intensive use of knowledge, and consequently may spare us the waste and sluggishness of natural selection. The disadvantage of the artificial is that it may not be strictly necessary, or it may cease to be such, and consequently it may fail to command loyalty and dedication. (For the differences between the natural or "organic" social formations, and the artificial or "mechanical" ones, see Tönnies 1979.)

The sociotechnologies handle all social systems, in particular what may be called sociotechnical systems, such as modern factories, banks, armies, and hospitals. A *sociotechnical system* may be characterized as a social system where work is done with the help of devices designed by technologists (see, for instance, De Greene 1973; Pasmore and Sherwood 1978; and Quintanilla 1989). A bank run by financial experts and operated by clerks with the aid of computers is a sociotechnical system – not so a bank where everything is done by hand and with empirical rules. By contrast, only some components of a university – such as its workshops and accounting offices – are sociotechnical systems. Which is just as well, for original research is not work done to rule, let alone on an assembly line: it is eminently artisanal and driven by curiosity rather than profit.

All sociotechnical systems are products of design: of invention and deliberate and particularly rational action, that is, action carried out in accordance with deliberate policies and plans designed in the light of expert – if sometimes flawed – knowledge. (The fact that they sometimes fail is beside the point.) The main difference between spontaneous and designed social systems lies in the modes of social control: whereas in the former social control consists in social and moral norms, in designed systems control consists in legal norms, incentives, and sanctions imposed by designated agents (see Coleman 1993).

Artificial social facts and systems have been valued differently by different philosophies and ideologies. Thus, the classical economists, from Quesnay to Smith to Marx, and even more so their Austrian foes, from Menger to Mises to Hayek, stressed social spontaneity, and the latter even self-regulation. By contrast, rational-choice theorists, policy makers, designers of norms and standards, planners, management scientists – in particular operations research experts – as well as praxiologists (action theorists) and pragmatist and voluntarist philosophers stress the need for deliberation, decision, design, and governance.

The choice between spontaneity and design is nowadays partly motivated by ideological considerations. Thus, conservatives (or "neoliberals") hold that the *laissez-faire* policy is "natural" because it allows for the free pursuit of self-interest, which would be more natural and efficient than solidarity, cooperation, and state intervention. (They conveniently forget that the *laissez-faire* policy was the object of nearly two centuries of political struggle, and that capitalism in the UK, US, France, Germany, Japan, and elsewhere developed under vigorous state protection.) Conservatives, like Hayek, love to quote Adam Ferguson's 1767 dictum that social facts are "the results of human action, but not the execution of any human design." Moreover, they claim that all planning inter- feres with the "natural" development of society, involves inefficiency, and leads unavoidably to serfdom – presumably even if it involves the abolition of serf- dom. They also hold – rightly so this time – that detailed planning calls for knowledge we do not possess, and that even the most carefully planned course of action is bound to have unintended or even perverse consequences. By con- trast, the partisans of government intervention – regardless of their political views – insist on the need to control the economy and plan all large-scale endeavours, at least with regard to public goods. (See, for instance, Wootton's 1945 anti-Hayek.)

I suggest taking the middle-ground view that every one of the above posi- tions holds a grain of truth: that in civilized societies all social facts are partly spontaneous and partly the products of design. For example, "[w]hile *laissez- faire* economy was the product of deliberate state action, subsequent restrictions on *laissez-faire* started in a spontaneous way. *Laissez-faire* was planned; plan- ning was not" (Polanyi 1944, 141). A more recent example is this. The reforms initiated by Gorbachev in 1985 triggered confusion, spontaneous popular reac- tions, and a paralysis that five years later culminated in the crumbling of both state socialism and the Soviet Union (recall chap. 4, sect. 3). In general, as Pop- per (1962, 2: 143) wrote in a classic often mistaken for a neoliberal manifesto, "*institutions* can be planned; and they are being planned. Only by planning, step by step, for institutions to safeguard freedom, especially freedom from exploita- tion, can we hope to achieve a better world." (For Popper's social philosophy see Bunge 1996b.)

Moreover, I claim that, because serious social issues are (by definition) sys- temic (or structural) and endemic rather than isolated (or sectoral) and episodic, they call for systemic and sustained action. And such action, particularly when funded by the taxpayer, had better be based on social-science findings rather than armchair ("humanistic") social essays. However, this does not commit us to the view that social processes can be predicted and planned in detail – much less to the view that all policies and plans necessarily involve the loss of free- dom. Furthermore, we shall claim that, while rational-choice theories may have little if any descriptive power, some of them are necessary for prescriptive pur- poses. At a minimum, we need cost-benefit analyses and the periodic evaluation and review of programs.

I also take the view that description, analysis, and theorizing should precede prescription and proscription: that law-making and social policy-making are bound to be at best inefficient, and at worst disastrous, unless based on social science. In other words, I suggest turning Marx's famous apothegm upside down, to read as follows: "So far, politicians (and economists) have attempted to change society; their failures suggest that one should study society, empirically as well as theoretically, before attempting to change it." Shorter: Observe, think, analyse, model, design, and test before and during, not only after, taking action. Even shorter: First learn, then act. After all, this is how modern medicine proceeds: to find a cure for any disease it starts by attempting to uncover its mechanism.

The observation of large social systems is notoriously difficult. But this difficulty is not due to the alleged impossibility of distinguishing the observer from the observed. Such systems are hard to observe mainly because they are not in view. (Who has ever seen a corporation, let alone a nation?) Not even their individual (human) components are fully observable, because the outsider has no direct access to what is going on inside their skulls. (The insider has some, but he is seldom a disinterested scientific observer.) Second, many social systems, particularly business corporations and governments, as well as some political parties and churches, are deliberately opaque. Their operations are seldom open to public scrutiny, and they do not regard their actions as accountable to the public at large even when their actions affect the latter. (This is an obvious flaw of the restriction of democracy to politics.)

As a consequence of this opaqueness, the student of economic and social policies and plans seldom has access to the data required to build realistic models of organizations. For example, he does not know for sure how corporate managements deliberate, make forecasts, reach decisions, and have them implemented – or fail to do so. The negative consequences of such secrecy for management science and political science are obvious. It is equally obvious that this boomerangs into the very administration of business and government organizations. Thus secrecy, originally aimed at protecting the interests of the organization, ends up by harming it, by blocking the advancement and diffusion of the very knowledge and criticism needed to arrest decline. Moreover, secrets do not last: see appendix 5.

Normative social science wrestles with social issues such as social dysfunctions. Social issues come in many kinds and sizes, from faulty bus services and poor schools to economic crises and international conflicts. Such issues may be classed into structural and circumstantial. The former derive from serious defects in the social structure, such as blatant social inequalities, that call for radical reforms. By contrast, circumstantial issues are temporary dysfunctions that, if addressed in time, may be repaired with comparatively mild reforms – though, if not corrected, may turn into structural defects. In turn, circumstantial issues may be partitioned into deficiencies, such as local shortages of food or skilled labour, and surpluses such as overpopulation and bureaucratic fat.

As with everything social, we must distinguish between facts and the way they are "perceived" (conceptualized and evaluated). For example, social psychologists have found that the poor usually overrate their own social status and underrate their own needs and rights, whereas the rich tend to exaggerate their own needs and burdens. One of the professional and moral duties of the far-sighted manager and the honest politician is to correct such misperceptions, for people will not act efficiently or fairly on the strength of distorted perceptions. Once again, truth precedes efficiency and fairness. (But, in turn, concern for fairness may motivate the search for truth about social issues.)

Rational and realistic people are expected to plan and perform their actions in an intelligent and well-informed fashion rather than routinely or on impulse. The aim of rational-choice theories is precisely to provide rational guidance to action. Regrettably, such theories go only halfway in confining their attention to the choices and decisions that precede action, as well as to the risks and prospective rewards of action. Neither the sweat and stench of real action nor the attending pains and joys reach the lofty abode of rational-choice theory. Nor, for that matter, does painstaking data collecting.

Moreover, rational-choice theorists hold that individual action is the only source of everything social, and that all actors are identical in all relevant respects – in particular, they have the same utility function (see, for example, Stigler and Becker 1977). These theorists do not realize that these two hypotheses lead to the conclusion that only environmental factors (the "situation") can account for differences in individual action – a typically externalist and holistic thesis. Thus, rational-choice theory is inconsistent besides being unrealistic. (More in Bunge 1996a.) Moreover, because choice is only a prolegomenon to action, rational-*choice* theory should be only a chapter of rational-*action* theory. A realistic theory of rational action should encompass all the stages of rational action, from problem and conception to action and the outcome evaluation; and it should be based on scientific studies of social behaviour instead of being an a priori speculation.

Regrettably, in the field of social studies the time lag between scientific findings and their utilization in social practice does not parallel the ever-shrinking time lag between natural science and engineering or biotechnology. There may be three main causes for such persistent and injurious lag. One is that most policy makers and planners have no scientific background. However, this gap is being closed as government policy makers commission and use scientific reports on social issues. A second cause is that most academic economists and politologists are more interested in printed matter than in real action – but this mismatch too is avoidable. The third cause is that there is a large wedge between social science and sociotechnology, namely, ideology. Though unavoidable, this is not deplorable in itself because, unlike science, technology is not value-free and morally neutral (see Iannone 1987 and Bunge 1989a). There would be no problem with a proscience and morally right ideology. The trouble is that most ideologies are unscientific, morally wrong, or both, despite which some of them have political clout.

So much for the *apéritif*. Let us now tackle praxiology as a prolegomenon to the study of a sample of sociotechnologies.

7

Action Theory

Human action is a legitimate subject of philosophical reflection because, when deliberate and rational, it has philosophical presuppositions. Indeed, we would not act at all unless we thought that our actions might have consequences – that is, unless we embraced some version of determinism. Nor would we ever take extra precautions unless we also believed that unexpected side-effects and accidents might happen. Moreover, we would not care to study action unless we believed that the knowledge garnered through such study might help improve our actions – that is, unless we adopted epistemological realism. And we would have no qualms about the possible effects of our actions upon others unless we thought that every actor is morally or legally responsible for what he does – or fails to do when action is called for. (Inaction may have consequences – namely, the outcome of the process that one refrains from interfering with.) In sum, purposive action and inaction have tacit ontological, epistemological, and moral presuppositions.

Praxiology, or action theory, is the study of the general features of human individual and collective action. It may be regarded either as the foundation of sociotechnology or as the most basic and general of all social theories – though, alas, not the most advanced of them. And in either case action "theory" is actually a whole family of half-theories. These are so different from one another that they do not even share the principle that humans are active beings rather than either pure consumers, decision makers, or contemplatives. Moreover, praxiology has so far been more analytical than systematic. And it has yet to produce laws of its own beyond Murphy's: "If anything can go wrong, it will."

The oldest and most general doctrines of action are Marxism and pragmatism, each of which has been called a *philosophy of praxis*. Actually, neither of them is an action *theory* (hypothetico-deductive system). They are only doctrines that emphasize the importance of practice in social life as well as in the genesis and testing of ideas. They do this to the point of exaggeration, for they minimize the role of theory. And both of them regard praxis as the criterion of the worth of any theory. That is, they hold that a theory – even one in basic science – is only as good as its practical fruits. (Engels identified truth with success, and William James replaced truth with "cash value.") Hence, neither Marxism nor pragmatism is adequate as a philosophy of science or even of science-based technology. First, because truth (or falsity) is a property of propositions (or sets of such), whereas efficiency can only be predicated of human actions, artificial things, or man-controlled processes. Second, because nowadays the design of the latter calls for some basic (or pure) science.

The Marxist philosophy of praxis is original and important, in rightly stressing the centrality of work and collective action, and in promoting the combination of manual and intellectual labour – all taboos to the postmoderns (e.g., Baudrillard 1973). Unlike everyone else, Marx held that work can be not only a means but also an end in itself: that it can be a source of pleasure and a way of self-realization rather than a disutility. Moreover, his analysis of labour (1867: 1, part 3, chap. 7, sect. 1) is more realistic and profound than any of the philosophical action theories. However, Marxism does not amount to a theory proper: it is a jumble of propositions containing incurably fuzzy concepts borrowed from Hegel, notably those of ontic contradiction and dialectical process (Bunge 1981a). Furthermore, its holistic (and muddled) view of the individual as a set of social relations, as well as the unwitting tool of suprapersonal social forces and historical laws, belittles the roles of creativity, thought, debate, initiative, leadership, and, ironically, rebellion. All this makes it impossible to build an orthodox Marxist theory of *rational* action.

Philosophical pragmatism (or instrumentalism) fares even worse than Marxism. For one thing, except for John Dewey, pragmatists have overlooked the social context as well as social conflict. For another, their overemphasis on praxis at the expense of theory involves ignoring the indirect practical impact of disinterested inquiry. Thus, ironically, though originally a reaction to empty verbiage, groundless speculation, and inoperative idealism, pragmatism has not delivered an adequate theory of rational action. Moreover, it cannot inspire any because of its irrationalist contempt for analysis and theorizing, and its insistence on the primacy of action. Shorter: It is impossible to build a pragmatist *theory* of action, rational or not. Worse yet, pragmatism condemns us to blind praxis.

Given the failure of both pragmatism and Marxism, it should come as no surprise to learn that most contemporary work in action theory is neither pragmatist nor Marxist. Nowadays action theory is being cultivated by philosophers – in particular philosophical (armchair) psychologists – and social scientists and technologists. Regrettably, the two parties seldom listen to each other. This is not because philosophers tend to be apriorists whereas social scientists tend to keep close to data. As a matter of fact, most action theorists in either camp care little about data or, indeed, about action proper. For example, the concept of work is conspicuously absent from most of the contemporary literature on action theory. Another conspicuous absentee is the mass of experimental findings concerning work of certain kinds as a source of satisfaction – and forced idleness as a source of unhappiness and anomie. (See, for example, Veblen 1961; Hebb 1953; Scitovsky 1976; and Goldsmith et al. 1996.)

A reason for the lack of interest in empirical data on the part of most action theorists is that they espouse (usually in a tacit manner) philosophical idealism. In this perspective, it is only natural to focus on the discursive antecedents of action and, in particular, on what Dilthey and Weber misleadingly called the 'meaning' (meaning 'purpose') of action, as well as on communication, text, and text interpretation, at the expense of material conditions, social constraints, and practical outcomes. The point of action, which is to get things done, and thus control or alter reality, gets lost. Thus, the end result is apraxia rather than praxis.

Most contemporary students of action in both camps also share the unrealistic assumption that all action is voluntary and calculated. This hypothesis holds approximately for most economic transactions, but not for actions constrained by tradition, social norms, family bonds, loyalty to friends, allegiance to boss, coercion by the state, and so on. They also share the simplistic view of agents as nondescript individuals, without a past, utterly selfish, and free from social bonds.

Typically, the agents referred to by rational-action theory ponder and worry about action, but they seldom get caught *doing* anything. Indeed, most contemporary students of action are more interested in the subjective determinants of action – that is, tastes, beliefs, intentions, evaluations, reasons, and decisions – than in the entire process triggered by such subjective determinants and ending up in the outcome of practical action. By so doing they miss the feedback loop that allows the rational agent to adjust his course of action in the face of error or unexpected environmental challenge. For this reason, those studies are of little help to flesh-and-bone decision makers, in particular managers and statesmen. Action theory will have to deliver some useful goods before it deserves being included in the curricula of business or government schools.

In particular, most action theorists overlook protest, whether individual or collective, peaceful or violent, as well as its effect on society. In a classic book, Hirschman (1970) emphasized the role of protest in preventing, halting, or reversing the otherwise inevitable decline of all human creations when left to their own devices. He distinguishes two kinds of protest: *exit* (or silent) and *voice* (or vocal). In fact, when dissatisfied with a product, service, or organization, we may protest either by giving up the item concerned or by complaining – or in both ways at the same time. Getting divorced, emigrating, and switching brands, jobs, churches, or political allegiances are examples of exit. By contrast, complaining to the people in charge, criticizing them publicly, or fighting them are instances of voice.

When justified protest is ignored or suppressed, rot sets in. When listened to, protest of either kind – exit or voice – may trigger a reorganization process that may succeed in correcting malfunctions, such as declining efficiency, quality, competitiveness, or satisfaction. In short, protest is an important correction mechanism that should be explicitly incorporated into all social systems. Regrettably, most economists know only of exit, whereas most political scientists know only of voice, and both overlook the vocal threat of exit, which is or should be a human right. Only the well-rounded social scientist will take both exit and voice into account when studying social systems of all kinds. So much for the failure of conventional action theories to tackle important kinds of social action.

Philosophers and social scientists tend to approach action somewhat differently with regard to both subject matter and form (see, for instance, Fløistad 1982; and Seebass and Tuomela 1985). Ordinary-language philosophers do action theory as a branch of folk psychology and avoid do-or-die situations, dealing almost exclusively with trivial actions, such as getting dressed, spilling coffee, and picking up the newspaper (see Kenny 1964 and Davidson 1980). Baudrillard (1973) goes even further: he deals only in symbols, "codes," and simulations. Accordingly, he proposes to replace the economy of work and commodity with the "economy of the sign" – whatever this may be. Likewise, Habermas (1981) focuses on "communicative action," that is, speaking and writing. Both writers view the world as a communication network, where nobody produces anything but signs.

By contrast, the anthropologists, sociologists, economists, and politologists interested in action theory claim to deal with all kinds of social behaviour, though they seldom look beyond the preparation for actual action. Indeed, they usually restrict their task to the preambles to action proper, that is, preferences, intentions, and decisions. And when they do study praxis, as in the cases of the ethnomethodologists (e.g., Garfinkel 1967) and the post-structuralists (e.g., Bourdieu 1977), they eschew work and collective action. They focus on the gentle arts of conversation, gift exchange, and rite. Moreover, they propose no theories proper and write in an opaque idiosyncratic style informed by irrationalist and subjectivist (in particular phenomenological) philosophy. In either case, the net result is that no reasonable and full-fledged general theory of rational praxis is available.

I shall start by sketching a systemic praxiology. Subsequently, I shall examine some of the most popular rational-choice theories of action, namely decision theory, Olson's theory of collective action, and Austrian economics – which is often presented as a general theory of action. The examination of these theories will be critical. We shall criticize them not for being rational but for being neither rational enough nor in agreement with facts. However, some constructive suggestions will be advanced too. Let us start with the latter.

1 Systemic Praxiology

Let us sketch a systemic action theory. This theory receives inputs from both social science and philosophy (in particular ontology and ethics). And its main function is to help analyse and even reconstruct the sociotechnologies. Our praxiology may then be seen as both sink and source: see figure 7.1.

The key concepts of our theory are those of social system, action in and upon a system, its consequence(s) or effect(s), instrumental (though not necessarily economic) rationality, and social morality. We start by postulating that every human action is produced by some individual agent (or his proxy) in a social system or network, and either upon the same or another system. The "patient," or object of the action, can be natural, social, or mixed, and it can be part of the agent or external to him. The consequence or outcome of an action is a set of events in both patient and agent. (For a formalization of the general concepts of action and consequence, see appendix 7. For a congenial alternative see Burt 1982.)

We start with the general concept of a system, which we shall then specialize to that of a social system. Two or more different concrete things may be said to be bound, linked, or coupled together into a *system* if and only if at least one of them acts upon the other. Note the difference between a relationship, tie, or coupling, which affects the relata, and a mere relation, such as being to the left of something else, which does not. However, a non-bonding relation may be a necessary condition for a bond to emerge. (For instance, spatial proximity and temporal contiguity favour interaction.) Bonds may be ephemeral or lasting, weak or strong. In either case bonds give rise to concrete systems such as molecules, organisms, and social networks. (For details see Bunge 1977a and 1979a.)

Not all complex things are systems: some, such as a crowd attracted by a large fire, are unstructured aggregates. A complex thing is a *system* if and only if every one of its parts is bonded to at least one other part of the same thing. (Examples: molecule, organism, business firm, machine.) If all the ties in ques-

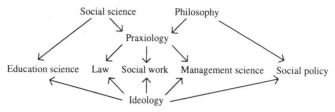

Figure 7.1 The system of sociotechnological knowledge

tion are ephemeral, so is the corresponding system. The cohesiveness of a system depends on the strength of the bonds among its parts. If a system is representable by a graph, as in chapter 1, section 1, the simplest measure of its cohesiveness is the ratio of the number of edges (joining lines) to the number of nodes (intersections). A more refined measure is obtained by assigning every edge a weight representing the strength of the corresponding bond. A common measure of such strength is the frequency of interactions. An alternative is the size of the intersection of the social groups concerned (Bunge and García-Sucre 1976).

A system composed of people and the artefacts they use to communicate is called a *social system*. Social systems emerge, change, and break down as the components and the bonds (social relations) among them alter. Thus, the features of a social system depend upon the nature, strength, and variability of social relations, which in turn are reducible to social actions. Some of the properties of a system are *emergent*, that is, they are not possessed by the system components, even though they emerge (or submerge) as a result of their interactions. Whereas individualists deny emergence and holists admit it but regard it as unexplainable, in our systemic perspective emergence is intelligible in terms of actions among individuals. Moreover, we explain the whole in terms of its parts, and the latter in terms of their actions in the whole. (For example, a social system is stable if the cooperative ties among its components are stronger than the conflictive ones, unstable otherwise. And the inertia of a social system is proportional to the number of its components and inversely proportional to its cohesiveness.) This strategy is particularly useful in accounting for micro-macro relations in social affairs. (Recall chap. 2, sect. 3.)

So much for generalities. Let us now consider the special case of purposive human action. A *deliberate action* may be characterized schematically as an ordered couple <goal, means>, or $\mathcal{A} = \langle G, M \rangle$ for short. However, once attained, goals may become means for further aims. (Here, as elsewhere, Distinction ≠ Detachment.) Besides, the outcome of an action may differ from the envisaged goal: the action may have unintended side-effects, some counterproductive (perverse) and others welcome – as is so often the case when complexity is overlooked. Therefore, we represent an actual action by an ordered quadruple: <goal, means, outcome, side-effect>, or $A_+ = $<G, M, O, S> for short, where S is included in O.

An action is successful only if its outcome is close to its goal, unsuccessful otherwise. If the action is unsuccessful but repeatable, G, M, or both will have to be altered. Moreover, far from being rigid, means and goals change with the individual and his circumstances. What is a means in one context or situation may be a goal in another and conversely. For example, earning money may be a goal on the job, and a means at home; political clout is a goal in politics and a means in business. One may surmise that this holds generally: every means-end distinction is situational or context-dependent.

Rational action is of course a special case of deliberate action, and instrumentally rational action is a special case of rational action. We stipulate that a means M to a goal G is *a priori instrumentally rational* if and only if M is both necessary and sufficient for G, that is, $M \Leftrightarrow G$. But since, as noted above, the outcome O may not coincide with G, we correct the preceding formula to read: $M \Leftrightarrow O \& S$. This forces us to supplement the previous definition of (prior) instrumental rationality with the following convention: M proves a posteriori to be an *instrumentally rational* means for G if and only if (a) M is necessary and sufficient for G, and (b) O is far more valuable than S (which may be disvaluable). For example, having an inflamed appendix removed meets both conditions. By contrast, since smoking satisfies the first condition but not the second, it is not instrumentally rational. The preceding will be refined in a while.

So far we have overlooked morality. But we must include it because evil can be just as rational as goodness. In fact, the road to hell is paved with rational no less than with evil or stupid actions. We stipulate that a goal G is *morally rational* if and only if G contributes to meeting either a basic need or a legitimate want (that is, one whose satisfaction does not jeopardize someone else's chance of meeting his basic needs). Ditto for means. The twin concepts of instrumental and moral rationality of means and ends allow one to define the concept of action rationality *tout court*. As before, let $A_- = $<G, M> and $A_+ = $<G, M, O, S> represent the envisaged and the corresponding actual actions. We stipulate that (i) A_- is *rational* if and only if M is instrumentally rational and G is morally rational; and (ii) A_+ is *rational* if and only if (a) M is instrumentally rational, (b) both M and G are morally rational, and (c) O is far more valuable than S.

In some cases it is possible to quantitate the values of means, goals, side-effects, and needs or wants. For these particular cases we postulate that

(i) the degrees of *prior and posterior instrumental rationality* of an action are

$$\rho_-(A_-) = V(G) / V(M) \text{ and } \rho_+(A_+) = V(O) / V(M), \text{ respectively;}$$

(ii) the degree of *prior moral rationality* of an action is the value of the basic need or legitimate want N that G is expected to meet; and the corresponding degree of *posterior moral rationality* is the value of the N that O actually meets plus the value (positive or negative) of S; in symbols:

$$\mu_-(\mathcal{A}_-) = V(N), \text{ and } \mu_+(\mathcal{A}_+) = V(N) + V(S) \text{ respectively};$$

(iii) the degrees of *prior and posterior rationality of an action* equal the products of the corresponding instrumental rationality and moral rationalities:

$$\alpha_-(\mathcal{A}_-) = \rho_-(\mathcal{A}_-) \cdot \mu_-(\mathcal{A}_-), \alpha_+(\mathcal{A}_+) = \rho_+(\mathcal{A}_+) \cdot \mu_+(\mathcal{A}_+).$$

We also stipulate that an action is (fully) *rational* if and only if $\alpha > 0$, *non-rational* if $\alpha = 0$, and *irrational* if $\alpha < 0$. Note that (a) an extremely disvaluable side-effect or a very costly means may offset a valuable goal, and (b) an action is either non-rational ($\alpha = 0$) or irrational ($\alpha < 0$) if it is instrumentally or morally non-rational or irrational respectively. Note also that an action judged to be rational when first envisaged (that is, one for which $\alpha_- > 0$) may in retrospect prove to be irrational (that is, $\alpha_+ < 0$). Finally, we define the *error* of an action as the absolute value of the discrepancy between the prior and posterior degrees of its rationality: $\epsilon = |\alpha_- - \alpha_+|$. The *relative error* is $\epsilon / |\alpha_-|$. An unwanted error should prompt a revision of M, G, or both. However, unlike errors in knowledge, not all action errors are bad: the outcome of an action may accidentally be better than its goal. But then, unlike an error in knowledge, a practical one may not be corrigible.

Any instrumentally and morally rational course of action is based on a sufficiently true model of the system concerned, such as a business firm or a government agency. If such model is quantitative, it allows the decision maker to infer precise rules of action that, once implemented, can be evaluated (both practically and morally) in the light of the outcomes of the action. In other words, a sufficiently precise and true description allows one to derive rules of efficient action. The following simplistic example suggests how this can be done at least in principle.

Suppose that a variable y representing a property of the system of interest is known to depend linearly upon another variable x that the agent can manipulate at will. That is, assume that $y = ax + b$, where a and b are real numbers to be found by empirical (e.g., epidemiological, econometric, or politological) research. The agent's goal is to force y to attain a preassigned desirable value y^* by varying the strategic variable x. (For example, x may be the discount rate and y the national income.) The value x^* of x that delivers the goods (that is, the means to y^*) is such that the discrepancy between the desired y^* and the actual y is minimal. (More precisely, the expectation value of the discrepancy is to be a minimum.) Since only the absolute value (equivalently, the square) of such discrepancy matters, the mathematical problem amounts to finding the value of x that minimizes the quantity $(y - y^*)^2$. A necessary condition for this to happen is $y^* - y = 0$, which amounts to $y^* - ax^* - b = 0$. This in turn implies $x^* = (y^* - b)/a$. This, then, is the rational (supposedly efficient) rule derived from the supposedly true model of the system (or rather one aspect of it). Incidentally, this is how sociotechnologists – in particular, operations research experts and normative macroeconomists – actually proceed. Contrary to most philosophers, they do not erect a wall between what *ought* to be and what *is*. On the contrary, they bridge the value-fact gap.

We assume that, in general, the rules of (instrumentally) rational action in or on a system are derivable from a sufficiently true representation of the latter: truth precedes efficiency. Likewise, the morality of such rules can be estimated a priori by computing the relevant forecasts; and they can be checked a posteriori by observing the consequences of the actions on the persons or groups affected by them. In short, a scientific study of action can bridge the overblown is-ought (or fact-value) gap. Equivalently: *Rational-action rules are based on laws*. The moral for science and technology policy is obvious: Scientific truth shall make you efficient, and perhaps free and even good to boot.

The above sketches a systemic and objective study of deliberate human action. This is not to say that we can afford to overlook the subjective sources of action: views, tastes, intentions, evaluations, and decisions. It only means that subjectivity combines with material resources and circumstances to yield real changes in the agent's environment. In particular, our approach encompasses the so-called self-referential or reflexive nature of human action, that is, the fact that we can refer to ourselves and make self-fulfilling and self-defeating prophecies, and that we depend partly on our self-image – which, though inevitably more or less distorted, is a real feature of every conscious being.

Let us finally approach two intriguing and important praxiological problems: those of inaction and of the unintended (in particular perverse) consequences of deliberate action. Taken in itself, that is, regarded in isolation, inaction is inconsequential: no cause, no effect. How then can anyone be justly blamed or even punished for not having done something? Is it not like attributing to nothingness positive properties and even powers, as with darkness in the Middle Ages? The answer is of course that people are not isolated, whence if anyone takes no action on some issue that concerns him, physically or morally, he allows others to carry on – and these actions do have consequences. This, then, is why negligence can be criminal: because everyone is a component of some social system or other. Though obvious, this result does not fit in with individualism, for this view denies the very existence of social systems and, consequently, the social embeddedness of actions.

Every social action is performed in a system that the actor can never control fully. Consequently, no social action can have exactly all its intended consequences. In other words, every social action is bound to have some unpredictable and often undesired consequences (see appendix 7). In particular, an action may have unintended consequences – some bad and others good. The occurrence of unintended consequences may be due to one or all of the following: (a) other people's interference, especially if the action in question harms their interests; (b) miscalculation owing to imperfect information, as in the case of ignorance of the social embeddedness of the action; (c) unforeseen changes in the system to be acted upon.

The size and frequency of unintended consequences, whether good or bad, is bound to increase with the importance of the action, which in turn depends on the size of the system in question. Building a nationwide health-care system or waging war is not quite the same as throwing a birthday party. The more numerous the people affected by an action, the less well-informed one is bound to be about motives and behaviour, hence the less predictable the outcome of the action is likely to be. This is one of the reasons that large business mergers and downsizings, as well as wars and revolutions, seldom have the desired consequences. It is also one of the reasons that highly centralized global plans are usually inefficient – whence the desirability of decentralization together with self-management and overall coordination – of which more in chapter 10.

So much for our praxiology embryo. The next four sections will be critical of mainstream rational-action theory. It will be found conceptually fuzzy, empirically unsupported, and ignorant of the facts of life that all agents are subject to structural constraints and the world is not a casino.

2 Decision Theory

Human affairs are ruled by tradition, necessity, and choice, all of which are subject to either law or rule (in particular social convention). Besides, as Keynes (1936, 162–3) noted, risky decisions are also guided by more or less irrational hopes and fears. Moreover, neuropsychologists know that, because the cerebral cortex interacts with the limbic system, reason is now compelled, now impaired by emotion. In particular, they have found that decisions are often preceded by nonconscious feelings and hunches (or intuitions) – processess that do not occur in patients with prefrontal damage (Bechara et al. 1997).

We shall presently tackle the matter of choice, which is both a preference indicator and an action trigger. Even in the absence of both external compulsion and complete information, choice need not be arbitrary. (When it is we may as well flip a coin.) Indeed, choice is constrained by opportunity and goal, and it ought to be guided by the best available knowledge. (The knowledge in question may be general – in particular theoretical – or specific – that is, about the situation in hand. In either case it is often imperfect.) When we must choose among alternatives, and wish to do so in the light of relevant knowledge, we tackle a decision problem that merits study. (However, since some of the requisite knowledge may be expensive, we may be driven to either imitate others or proceed by trial and error.)

Decision problems are the object of *decision analysis*. Any such analysis starts by recognizing and breaking down the problem in question; it then proceeds to identifying options and drawing a decision tree and evaluating every one of its branches; and it ends up by recommending a desirable course of action. Such analysis is performed in the light of data and desiderata, as well as generalizations and rules. Ordinarily we imitate, apply some well-tried rules of thumb, or ask for in-house advice. In more difficult cases we resort to outside expertise. In extremely difficult cases, particularly when the system exhibits persistent defects suspected of being structural rather than circumstantial, we hire an operations research expert. This specialist studies the system in question, perhaps crafts a mathematical model of it, runs it on a computer, and makes recommendations on the basis of the outcome of the simulation. (See chap. 9, sect. 4.) If rational, the expert will discuss the matter, from beginning to end, with all the interested parties or their representatives. Management may accept the recommendations, reject some or all of them, or propose modifications that will render them better suitable to its means and ends.The final decision will be an outcome of such deliberations and negotiations. Still, the decision should be regarded as corrigible in the light of experience.

Consider the following typical case. The R & D laboratory of a computer firm comes up with a new personal-computer model that has passed all the technical tests: it is powerful yet affordable, versatile yet user-friendly, has definite advantages over its competitors, and so on. However, the engineer proposes, and the market disposes. Hence, the firm's manager is faced with the dilemma: to have the new product market-tested or not. Being a rational agent, he begins by drawing (or just imagining) a decision tree, that is, a graph containing nodes of two types: the possible decisions and the events that may result from having them implemented or not (see, for instance, Hammond 1967). A responsible decision-maker will disregard the branches attached to no market testing: he will commission product testing on a modest scale. If the test results are unfavourable, he will shelve the project at least for the time being. But if they are favorable he faces another decision fork: to mass-produce or not to. If he decides to produce, he will encounter the further problem of financing the production and publicity costs. But if he decides not to produce he may be blamed for incurring opportunity costs – and so on. Every tree node represents new opportunities and the concomitant risks. The branching is likely to go on until the given production line is discontinued.

In all this decision-making process rational agents behave as *risk-averse persons intent on minimizing uncertainty with the help of expert knowledge*, rather than as gamblers willing to take foolish risks in an attempt to maximize their expected utilities. If unable to reduce the uncertainties below some acceptable risk level, the rational agent refrains from acting. This is not the view taken by the enthusiasts of decision theory. They believe this to be a universal theory dispensing with both general causal relations and a detailed empirical study of the system in question. (In particular, they usually assume that all agents have the same utility function. Moreover, the function is usually one of the following: $u = \log x$, $u = \log(x - a)$, $u = ax^{\frac{1}{2}} + b$, and $u = ax - bx^2$, with a, b > 0. Neither of these is empirically validated.) Let us take a quick look at decision theory, or DT for short. (See von Neumann and Morgenstern 1953; Savage 1954; and Luce and Raiffa 1957.)

DT is generally assumed to be the most general and best possible theory underlying "rational" (utility maximizing) decision making under uncertainty. Uncertainty may derive from limited knowledge or from the objectively random nature of the process occurring in or around the system in question. And anything may be at risk, from material possessions and peace of mind to the future of humankind. DT is rather unique in that it claims to be at once universal, descriptive, and normative. We shall find that it is neither.

Because it is concerned with rational social-action, DT would seem to belong in sociotechnology. But in fact it does not, because it makes no use of social-science findings. Indeed, DT is an a priori and thus unrealistic, theory because it assumes, against all available empirical evidence, that (a) all decision problems are reducible to lotteries; (b) the agent can list and assess all his possible options and the corresponding outcomes, assigning them precise probabilities and payoffs; and (c) everyone is a gambler intent on maximizing his expected utilities. Psychologists and management scientists have refuted these assumptions (see, for instance, Kahneman et al. 1982; March and Shapira 1987; and Rapoport 1989a). In particular, they have shown that real people shrink their menus of choice, imitate more often than they calculate, learn from mistakes, and seldom if ever calculate expected utilities or count on the self-interested maximization of others (see, for example, Olshavsky and Granbois 1979; Berk et al. 1996; and Beard and Beil 1997). But such empirical evidence is systematically ignored or dismissed by most DT students.

The basic concepts of DT are those of decision maker, preference, possible course of action and outcome of the latter, and probability and value of such outcome to the decision maker. These six concepts are sketched implicitly by some set of postulates. There are several axiom systems for DT, but all of them share the assumptions that every rational agent (a) has a complete and constant preference order of all options, and moreover has his own (subjective) utility function and knows it; (b) can assign a (subjective) probability to every possible outcome; and (c) always opts for the course of action that maximizes his expected utility, defined as the sum of the products of the probabilities of the possible outcomes in question by their respective utilities.

According to DT, if two alternative courses of action have the same expected utility, the choice between them is a matter of indifference: a small chance is compensated for by a large pay-off and conversely. But if the expected utilities are different, then, according to axiom (c) above, DT predicts and prescribes that the rational agent chooses the alternative with the greater value regardless of the risk involved. Maurice Allais disproved this axiom in 1953 with a simple counterexample that the decision theorists across the Atlantic ignored for three decades (Allais and Hagen 1979: 89). Let us review it.

Suppose a person is offered two alternatives, A and B. If he chooses A he gets $1 million for sure. If he chooses B he has a 10 per cent chance of winning $5m, an 89 per cent chance of winning $1m, and a 1 per cent chance of winning nothing. The expected utility of choice A is $1m, whereas that of B is $(0.1 \cdot 5 + 0.89 \cdot 1 + 0.01 \cdot 0)m = \$1.39m$. According to classical DT, B is the better choice by 39 per cent. And so it is if the alternative is offered *repeatedly* – say 100 times. But if the occasion is unfrequent, particularly if it is unique, any sane person will choose the "sure thing" A, that is, $1m, contrary to what classical DT predicts and recommends. That is, authentic rationality is risk-averse and therefore at odds with decision-theoretic "rationality," which is that of the compulsive gambler. This is called the *Allais paradox* or, rather, counterexample. It was ignored by mainstream decision theorists (and economists) until Allais got the Nobel prize in economics in 1988. However, even four decades later most classical DT users continue to ignore Allais's criticisms.

The falsity of classical (or expected utility) DT has prompted the construction of alternative (non-expected utility) decision theories, as well as the design of further experiments (see, for instance, Machina 1987; Munier 1988; Tversky and Simonson 1993; and Machina and Munier 1994). These alternatives are in some respects more realistic than the standard theory. For example, they may not require knowledge of all the options, the transitivity of preferences, or assume maximizing behaviour, and they are not preached as gospel. Being descriptively more adequate than traditional DT, the unorthodox decision theories are of interest to the psychology of decision making. However, it is debatable whether they are relevant to the art and science of decision making in, say, business or politics. Let me explain why, in my opinion, the new theories lack prescriptive power.

All of the extant theories of decision under uncertainty share the notions of subjective utility and personal probability. These notions can be shown to be mathematically either fuzzy (undefined) or arbitrary, as well as empirically slippery (see Du Pasquier 1926; and Bunge 1988a and 1996a). Now, it is practically irrational to act on the strength of subjective figures: they are groundless and cannot be improved upon. Let us see how these two basic flaws of DT, whether old or new, can surface in practice.

A tacit assumption of all decision theories under uncertainty is that chance is king in social life, and moreover that all the possible courses of action, as well as their outcomes and their corresponding probabilities and utilities, are knowable. In short, DT assumes that man is basically an omniscient gambler. This assumption is unrealistic on three counts. First, in real life we are not repeatedly faced with the same betting choices that a casino offers the well-heeled (and reckless) gambler. Second, it is not true that uncertainty implies randomness, hence legitimate use of probability. (Only the converse is true.) We may be uncertain about the outcome of an action because of incomplete knowledge. In fact, we can forecast only some of the possible outcomes of our own actions, and fewer of other people's. And even after the event we get to discover only some of the effects of our actions or inactions – alas, sometimes too late. Third, it is incorrect to attribute probabilities to the possible outcomes of any action other than operating a randomizing device: no probability proper without randomness (Bunge 1988a.) Gambling is irrational when the outcome is uncertain and risky, and immoral when it is predictable and risk-free for the gambler but hazardous for his opponent.

A simple example will clarify this point. A young woman is uncertain as to whether to study either of two subjects – say, management or the law. She is equally attracted to both subjects, but is not sure for which of the two she is more gifted, or which of them will offer the best prospect of employment upon graduation. This is not a game of chance. In fact, scholastic inclination and proficiency are matters of family background, brainpower, will-power, health, and environmental factors. All of these are more causal than random. As for employability, it depends on competence, having the right connections, and market demand at the time of graduation. The young woman must make a decision based on incomplete knowledge, hence under risk. But decision theory won't help her, because her predicament is not a lottery: neither the odds nor the ticket price are known in advance. Hence, betting would be irrational.

A manager's predicament is often less dramatic, but it is not reducible to a game of chance either. In fact it would be just as disastrous for a company to hire a gambler as to hire someone ignorant of the plain fact that every course of action is subject to unpredictable disturbances. Of course everyone runs and takes risks when engaging in action – as well as when failing to act when action is called for. (See Rescher 1983 for the distinction between running a risk, as when crossing the street, and taking a risk, as when launching a new business.) It is equally obvious that the rational agent only takes "calculated" risks. However, in this case the word *calculated* must not be taken literally. It only means that the agent is aware of the possibility of failure, yet he estimates (or rather guesstimates) that both the "chances" of success and the "utility" of the latter are so great that the risk is worth taking. However, these estimates are qualitative or comparative. It would be (epistemically) irrational to pin down numbers on such possibilities and utilities, because there are no firm grounds for doing so: business is risky but not a form of gambling. Moreover, the manager was presumably hired to steer the company and attempt to reduce as far as possible the role of chance, or at least keep it under control.

Even the notion of preference, though much weaker than that of cardinal (numerical) utility, is problematic. Indeed, the transitivity condition, which any preference relation satisfies by definition, may not be met in practice. (Recall that a relation $\geq$ is transitive in a set S if, for any members a, b and c of S: $a \geq b$ and $b \geq c$, then $a \geq c$.) The observance of transitivity is indeed rational in the case of objects exhibiting a single feature of interest. But it is not when we are asked to choose among heterogeneous and many-sided items, such as food, music, love, entertainment, and pain avoidance, without specifying the respect. In these cases cycles, such as $a > b > c > a$, may occur. Such cycles have been known for two centuries (see, for example, May 1954 and Tversky 1969).

A common reason for the intransitivity of some preferences is that many-sided objects can be ordered in as many different respects as they have sides. For example, one item may be economically preferable to another, but the converse may be the case from a political or a moral viewpoint. That is, when asked to rank a collection of items we may do so in different though mutually compatible respects: we may inadvertently employ different preference relations. (In obvious symbols, we may have at the same time $a \geq_R b$ and $b \geq_{R'} a$, where $\geq_R$ and $\geq_{R'}$ are two different preference relations.) Mere data about Samuelson's "revealed preferences" (actual choice behaviour) is unlikely to reveal the cause of such apparent inconsistency. Moreover, these are bound to occur whenever the subject is risk-averse or has a stake in the events in question (Karni and Safra 1995).

DT does not allow explicitly for such multiple concurrent valuations. Consequently it is hardly relevant to the choices we face in real life. In particular, it does not cover the case of the undecided. It may well happen that, faced with two personal, business, or political choices, an agent may be unable to make up his mind, seeing virtues and flaws in both options. (Remember the American president who wished economists were single-handed.) Hence, instead of asking a subject whether he prefers *a* to *b* or conversely, one should ask him whether he prefers *a* to *b* in a given respect, and moreover which respect he values most – that is, how he ranks his preference rankings (Sen 1982). This is precisely what well-designed commercial and political opinion polls do.

In sum, classical DT has failed critical empirical tests, such as those of Allais (1979); Hammond (1967); Kahneman and Tversky (1979); and Tversky (1975). And its rivals may be of value to psychology but not to action. For these and other reasons DT is hardly used in management science, as will be seen in chapter 9, section 3. The same applies, for similar reasons, to its close relative, game theory.

3 Collective-Action Theory

Let us begin with the obvious. First, human action may be physical, as in lifting a weight; cognitive, as in problem solving; or both, as in machining a part of an artefact. Second, human action may be individual, as in walking, or collective, as in marching. In turn, collective action may be organized, as in choir singing, or spontaneous, as in rushing for cover from a bomb attack. Third, whether spontaneous or organized, human actions do not usually add or compose like vectors: they tend to interact, as a consequence of which they often result in effects that neither of the agents intended. Boudon (1979, 130) rightly regards such effects as emergent. Clearly, whereas some of them are positive, others are negative or counterproductive.

In his famous book on collective action, Olson (1971) did not distinguish between organized or concerted action, on the one hand, and the effects that individual actions (e.g., food hoarding on hearing the news of a crop failure) may have on all the members of a social group. Moreover, Olson (1971, 1982) is mainly interested in the "perverse" outcomes of "rational" (that is, maximizing) behaviour when undertaken by the members of a group. (So are Schelling [1978] and Frank [1988] in their equally famous books.) For example, if upon the onset of a fire in a theatre everyone stampedes to the exit, attempting to leave before all the others, instead of lining up in orderly fashion, most may not make it. Likewise, if many businessmen decide to manufacture the same popular product, most of them are bound to make only modest profits, and some are likely to go bankrupt: "[I]f the firms in an industry are maximizing profits, the profits for the industry as a whole will be less than they might otherwise be" (Olson 1971, 10).

These are examples of the so-called paradox of "rational" (that is, selfish) behaviour: namely, that it may lead to outcomes that go against the group interest by eroding the very rationale of its existence. Shorter: Individual "rationality" may turn out to be collectively "irrational" or self-defeating. This illustrates the idea of emergence, or occurrence in a whole, of a feature absent from its components. More to the point, Olson's finding refutes Adam Smith's postulate of the "hidden hand," according to which individual "rationality" (selfishness) guarantees collective or market "rationality." It highlights what Hardin (1982) has called "the back of the invisible hand." So far, so good: no phony mathematics, no untestability, and no ideology.

Trouble starts when Olson applies cost-benefit analysis to actions and outcomes that can hardly be quantitated, let alone added up. This is the case with the benefits of various kinds that may accrue from participating in a voluntary organization, a strike, a political campaign, a revolution, or any other social movement. Such benefits cannot merely be toted if, as is usually the case, they are heterogeneous. Indeed, in this case only some of these benefits may be reckoned in dollars. Others must be reckoned in additional leisure hours, greater safety or job security, cleaner air, less stress, greater peace of mind, ideological satisfaction, or what have you (Barry 1970).

This is not to dismiss cost-benefit analysis in all its guises. We often do perform such analyses even with regard to items that cannot be conventionally priced – that is, that are literally priceless, as in the case of aesthetic or moral satisfaction. But in such cases we employ tacitly a qualitative notion of utility that lies between the concepts of ordinal and cardinal (numerical) utility. The gist of it is this: the utility of an action equals the set of its positive (or pleasurable) consequences, and its disutility equals the set of its negative (or harmful) outcomes. (For a formalization of this concept see Bunge 1996a, appendix 7.)

Another problem with Olson's analysis of collective action is that, in tune with most other rational-choice theorists, he assumes that each agent makes his decisions independently of all other actors. This assumption is false. In real life we are constrained by the social networks in which we are embedded – hence, by other people's actions as well as by the opinions and expectations they hold about our own actions. In particular, all individual contributions to common goods (or bads) are interdependent, and they depend critically upon the actor's position (leader or follower) in his social network. (See Gould 1993 for a mathematical model of collective action constrained by network structure.)

Moreover, when becoming members of an organization, individuals enter into contracts and adopt solidary attitudes that may lead them into deep personal trouble, as when engaging in subversive action. If people behaved in accordance with rational-choice theory, revolutions would never occur. Or, if they did occur, they would never mobilize the masses: revolutions would be watched by the "free riders" who would reap their benefits without risking anything (Tullock 1971). But mass revolutionary movements do occur once in a while, which refutes the theory. One may attempt to save the latter by postulating that "The group will act if the expected benefits of acting (gains − losses) exceed the value of the conditions at the status quo" (Goldstone 1994, 150). But why do desperate upheavals occur again and again? And who is in a position to make such cost-benefit calculations anyway?

The trouble gets even worse when the rational-choice theorist shifts from description to prescription with regard to public goods and collective actions. In particular, being a committed individualist, he is likely to claim that the rational agent is a "free rider" or parasite who will attempt to benefit from public goods and collective action without paying his dues. Rational people would be loners, not joiners: only "zealots anxious for a particular collective good are more likely to act collectively" (Olson 1982, 34). This is how Olson explains voter apathy in the United States and the decline in the membership in American labour unions since the end of the Second World War – as if US = World.

There are several flaws in this reasoning. First, a "free rider" can prosper only if there are conscientious citizens who participate in organizations that produce collective goods. So, the parasite *is* interested in the continual existence of such public-good organizations, just as the thief is the most enthusiastic supporter of private property. Hence, there can be no *society* of free riders. (This is a crypto-tautology, as there is no rider without a mount.)

Second, as every social psychologist knows, sociality is an essential feature of human nature: so much so that normal people are willing to make some sacrifices in exchange for being able to feel that they "belong" in a group and are protected by it, even if they derive no material benefits from their membership. This is why so many people bother to vote even when not forced to. That is also why voluntary organizations of all kinds multiply and prosper in all democratic societies, particularly in the US. After all, there is subjective as well as objective strength in numbers, particularly in the pursuit of goals perceived as beneficial. (See Kim and Bearman 1997.) And such moral feelings as solidarity, altruism, and the sense of duty can powerfully motivate involvement in public causes (Knoke 1988).

Third, the "rationality" of abstaining from joining a labour union does not explain the strength of the Canadian and West European labour unions, or why the American labour movement grew vigorously before the Second World War. By contrast, the following facts, overlooked by Olson, do jointly help explain the subsequent decline in membership that he noted : (a) the decline of the manufacturing sector in relation to the service sector and, more recently, the wholesale export of American industries to the Third World; (b) the institutionalization, via social programs, of many of the goals that had been pursued by the labour movement during the earlier period, thus taking much of the wind off its sails; (c) the bonus offered by management in many industries to their personnel in exchange for refraining from unionizing; and (d) the disillusion with some union leaders who proved to be parasites or crooks. (For additional causes see Farber 1987.)

In short, because of their attachment to individualism and utilitarianism, as well as their obsession with free-riding, Olson, Tullock, and other rational-choice theorists miss the most powerful motivations people have to organize or join associations of various kinds, namely to attain goals that no individual could reach by himself, as well as to feel integrated, protected, and wanted. (For further criticisms of Olson's speculations see Hardin 1982; Hirschman 1982; Marwell and Ames 1981; Oliver et al. 1985; and Oliver and Marwell 1988. For the marginal impact of Olson's work on the sociology of social movements see, for example, McAdam et al. 1988.)

Olson (1982) blames "distributional coalitions," that is, associations aiming at controlling the distribution of wealth, for all that is wrong in the world, in particular for the decline of nations. In principle he indicts them all equally for representing vested interests. But he is more worried about labour unions than about the military-industrial complex; about protectionist tariffs and immigration restrictions than about unemployment; and about the redistribution of wealth through taxation and social programs than about poverty and overall social decline. And he suggests making it more difficult for small groups to organize – which would only reinforce the existing cartels and would render social invention and innovation all but impossible, since all things new have small beginnings.

Unlike most rational-choice theorists, Olson professes to be interested in the empirical test of his views. In particular, he claims that they are confirmed by the rapid post-war growth of West Germany and Japan. But most economic historians favour an alternative explanation, namely one in terms of the Marshall Plan and the MacArthur reform, nearly no military expenditures, the substitution of modern industrial equipment for the obsolete machinery largely destroyed by the war anyway, and the availability of skilled and disciplined workforces anxious to overcome misery. (In post-war West Germany an additional contributory factor has been the welfare state or "social market." In the case of Japan, two important factors have been the underground survival of the powerful pre-war cartels and their long-term planning in collusion with the government – a case of "distributional coalition," though one with positive as well as negative effects.) A moral of this story is that, because of the complexity of society and the diversity of histories, all uniform (cross-societal) and unifactorial (or unicausal) explanations of social facts are bound to fail.

In conclusion, we owe to Olson's "logic" of collective action just one important insight. This is that "rational" (that is, selfish) individual behaviour may lead to collective harm or "irrationality" to the detriment of all concerned. Shorter: The pursuit of self-interest may lead to "social traps" (Cross and Guyer 1980). But this finding is marred by Olson's wholesale disapproval of nearly all collective actions – which, followed to its logical conclusion, leads to either anarchism or totalitarianism. If either unsavoury conclusion is to be avoided, an alternative approach to collective action is needed, in particular one that does not assume the rationality postulate. (See Macy and Flache 1995 for alternatives.)

4 Austrian Praxiology

Let us now turn to the Austrian school of praxiology (or action theory) and economics. Though founded by Menger in the 1870s, it is still being widely discussed. (See, for instance, Dolan 1976 and Auspitz et al. 1992.) This is not because it is a buzzing research hive but because it is one of the theories underlying the *laissez-faire* policies.

Ludwig von Mises, Menger's successor and von Hayek's teacher, regarded the "pure theory of economics" as a special case of praxiology, or the science of rational action, revolving around the rationality postulate (recall chap. 3, sect. 6, Axiom 1): so much so that his most popular book is titled *Human Action: A Treatise on Economics* (1949). Following his teacher, von Mises (1949, 3) conceived of this discipline as the a priori and subjective general theory of human choice – nay as "the science of every kind of human action." However, since he believed that all choice is guided by (economic) rationality, his *homo agens* is nothing but the old *homo œconomicus* – a clear case of the "economic imperialism" we met in chapter 2, section 5. He makes no room for non-rational factors: "Action is, by definition, always rational" (1962, 35). What sometimes happens is that your reasons differ from mine, because our respective goals or means do not coincide (ibid.).

In short, according to the Austrian school all rationality is subjective, every action is individual and "rational," and its outcome logically necessary. Hence action theory, like logic or geometry, is a priori. The advantages of this view are obvious. First, one need not bother with empirical data. Second, people can be made to follow one's social-policy recommendations with the same awe in which they bow to pure mathematics.

The heart of the theory is "rational economic calculation," which bears on money (market) prices, that is, on values in exchange. Of course, where there is no free market, no rational economic calculation is possible. This is von Mises's and von Hayek's favourite argument against socialism, planning, and even mere governmental regulation. Characteristically, both authors and their followers blame socialism for all evils. And yet authentic socialism did not start most of the major social calamities of the last hundred years: the two world wars, Nazism, militarism, and the further looting of the Third World – not to speak of the Great Depression, the subsequent recessions, involuntary mass unemployment, and the disappearance of permanent jobs. Were these results of "rational economic calculation"? Or is this an impertinent question to ask of an allegedly a priori science? Or are we dealing with ideology rather than science?

The main methodological idea of the Austrian school is that praxiology, in particular economic theory, should be regarded as a "pure theory," that is, one uncontaminated by empirical data and immune to them though referring to concrete action. Economic theory would be in the same boat with Euclidean geometry as (mis)interpreted by Kant: its principles would be synthetic a priori. (That is, although they concern experience they hold in spite of it.) Moreover, such an a priori economic theory would be the permanent foundation of both descriptive and prescriptive economics.

In case the reader suspects this to be a caricature of the Austrian philosophy of economics, let us check the sources. In his remarkable, though all-but-forgotten monograph on the epistemology of economics, Menger (1883) mistakenly conflates "theoretical" with "a priori," "formal," and even "general." Moreover, he opposes "theoretical" to "realistic," and asserts that theoretical economics is only concerned with "rigorous types and typical relations (laws) among phenomena," not with the phenomena themselves. (Following Ricardo, Marx too claimed that only abstraction can reach the reality underneath the economic phenomena – and so did Weber. But neither of them regarded economic theory as a priori and therefore immune to data.)

So as not to leave any doubts about his aprioristic approach, Menger writes: "Testing the exact theory of the economy through full experience is just a methodological absurdity, a [token of] disregard for the foundations and presuppositions of exact research, as well as for the special goals of the exact sciences. Wishing to test the pure theory of the economy by experience in its full reality is a procedure analogous to that of a mathematician who were to correct the postulates of geometry by measuring real objects, without taking into account that the latter are not identical with the magnitudes assumed by pure geometry, and forgetting that every measurement necessarily involves errors" (1883, 54).

Ludwig von Mises (1949, 39), Menger's disciple, concurs: "The theorems attained by correct praxiological reasoning are not only perfectly certain and incontestable, like the correct mathematical theorems. They refer, moreover with the full rigidity of their apodictic certainty and incontestability, to the reality of action as it appears in life and history. Praxiology conveys exact and precise knowledge of real things." How do we know this, since statistical data are reputed to be irrelevant to the pure theory? Presumably we must assent because this is a matter of pure reason.

It is not surprising that Menger should have been a Kantian at a time when neo-Kantianism was the dominant academic philosophy – and intellectually more progressive than either of its rivals, Thomism and Hegelianism. What is rather astonishing is that the Austrian school went on undaunted by the (few) critics who – in agreement with Einstein (1923) – pointed out the differences between a mathematical geometry, such as Euclid's, and a physical geometry, such as that obtained by interpreting lines as light rays and surfaces as boundaries of extended bodies.

These differences are both semantic and methodological, and the former entail the latter. Indeed, whereas a mathematical geometry is about concepts ("point," "line," "angle," "incidence," etc.), a physical geometry is about spatial relations among physical things. Hence, whereas the former can be checked only by conceptual procedures, such as deduction and the finding of counterexamples, the test of a physical geometry calls for measurements as well. Remember Einstein's famous dictum: "As far as the laws of mathematics refer to reality, they are not certain; and as far as they are certain, they do not refer to reality" (Einstein 1923).

In general, if a hypothesis or a theory refers to factual items, then it must pass empirical tests before being pronounced true or false. This is the central rule of the scientific method. Compliance with this rule is what distinguishes factual science from pure mathematics, theology, pseudoscience, and art. The rationale for the rule is the following: (a) Factual truth amounts to matching with fact; so that (b) in order to be justified in claiming that proposition p about fact f is true, p must have been contrasted with f (or some evidence for f); and (c) this comparison must have yielded a positive result, that is, (nearly) every observation of f must have confirmed p. The necessary refinement involving indicators, errors of observation, the rejection of outlying empirical values, and the eventual introduction of bona fide ad hoc hypotheses, is left to the reader. The only point in recalling the rule in question was to emphasize the semantic and methodological chasm that separates an authentically a priori science, such as logic, from a factual discipline such as economics. (More in Bunge 1985a and 1997a. For the "Factual content (or reference) – Testability – Actual test – Truth valuation" sequence see Bunge 1974b.)

The neo-Austrian school not only went ahead unmindful of criticism, but it is nowadays prospering in its adoptive homeland, the United States. This anomaly may be explained in socio-political terms, namely as follows. First, apriorism is rampant in mainstream economic theory, where few care for rigorous testing. (Still, the arrogant proclamation of apriorism is anomalous. Even the mathematical economists who could not care less for data do pay lip-service to an empiricist methodology.)

Second, while claiming to provide a universal theory of action, the Austrian school, from Menger to Mises to Hayek, has emphasized the dangers of actions of a certain kind, namely progressive collective or governmental action. In this regard the school engages in what Hirschman (1991) calls "the rhetoric of reaction." In particular, L. von Mises, F. von Hayek, G.L.S. Shackle, M.N. Rothbard, and other members of the school have endeared themselves to the Right by criticizing economic planning, socialism, and even the welfare state and democracy, in the name of rationality and liberty. By contrast, they keep silent about the New Deal and the Marshall Plan, as well as about the planning of the post-war German and Japanese economic recoveries.

Third, by lashing out at "scientism," and particularly by ridiculing those who claim that economics is or ought to be an objective science, the Austrian school is music to the ears of the softies in philosophy as well as in social studies. To be free to choose, and to choose "rationally," is said to be the ticket in the market of material goods and services. But when it comes to ideas we must beware "the abuse of reason" and, moreover, we must denounce "scientism" as a "counter-revolution of science" – presumably much more vigorously than irrationalism and pseudoscience (see Hayek 1955).

In conclusion, the Austrian school has been intellectually barren from birth. It proposes no research project and, paradoxically for an alleged theory of action, it proposes no course of social action – except of course good old *laissez-faire [les riches]*. It is nothing but a rusty piece of the conservative armour. This intellectual failure should serve as a warning: it is futile to write about action without studying real actions and without tackling some genuine open problems of individual and collective action – and inaction.

5 Reasons for the Failure of Rational-Choice Action Theory

I have argued that the three best-known rational-choice action theories –

namely decision theory, Olson's collective-action theory, and Austrian praxiology – fail to account for real action. I shall presently argue that *all* rational-choice models of action are bound to fail in their attempt to describe real action, and are consequently useless as policy tools. They are bound to fail for three reasons: in being idealist (in the ontological sense), in underrating the importance of non-rational factors, and in minimizing or even ignoring the importance of social constraints and norms. Let me spell out these charges.

That rational-choice action theory is idealist is obvious, since (a) it regards ideas, in particular reasons, as the main source of action (or deliberate inaction, as the case may be); and (b) it pays far more attention to the agent's preferences, beliefs, and goals than to the material means at his disposal and to his environmental (natural and social) constraints. (Paradoxically, at the same time rational-action theory ignores technology, in particular engineering and management science. So does mainstream economics.)

This is not to say that a realistic action theory should adopt a behaviourist viewpoint, focusing on overt behaviour and ignoring subjectivity altogether. This would be mistaken because people are not just reactive: they have an inner life, can take the lead and be creative, often devise new ways of meeting their needs and wants, and occasionally come up with new wants. In short, it is true that beliefs (correct and incorrect) steer action, though always jointly with habits and norms, as well as under social constraints.

However, it is not true that all beliefs are free creations. Some, particularly in economic, political, and ideological matters, respond to either objective situations or ideological bias. For instance, as Feuerbach suspected, and Durkheim, Weber, and others confirmed, certain religious ideas conveniently match the structure of the society where they are born. Another example: as Weber showed, instrumental rationality coevolved with the economy and the polity. In particular, modern engineering and management science would be unthinkable except in an industrialized country.

As for the non-rational sources of action, underrated by rational-choice action theory, we only need to recall that prosocial action may be motivated not only by enlightened self-interest. It may also be driven by tradition, fear of (social or divine) retribution, wish for peer recognition, a sense of duty, the pride of a job well done, the pleasure of "belonging" (to some social group), empathy, or even love – whose force rationalists and utilitarians seem ashamed of admitting. (See Elster 1989 and Koford and Miller 1991 for the power of norms.) These and other non-rational sources of action must be reckoned with because cognition and emotion are interdependent. Passion activates or obfuscates reason, and cognition arouses or dims emotion. See figure 7.2 (over).

```
                  Cognition      ←    ←    ←    ←    ←    ↑
Stimulus → Problem → ↓      ↑   →  Decision → Behaviour → Outcome → Evaluation
                  Emotion         ←    ←    ←    ←    ←    ↓
```

Figure 7.2 Exogenous and endogenous determinants of action. The stimulus (external or internal, physical or social) generates the practical problem that activates the agent's cognitional and emotional organs. Values and goals, as well as the agent's model ("perception") of the situation he finds himself in, are included in his cognitive equipment.

The large variety of motivations of human action helps to dissolve some of the paradoxes that paralyse rational-choice theory. Among these are Olson's "paradox" of collective action (sect. 3), the "paradox" of voting (why people bother to vote even knowing that a single vote is unlikely to make any difference), the "paradox" of public goods (why people are willing to support public services), and the fact that most people prefer to cooperate rather than to defect. Only hardened criminals, conquerors, dictators, and rational-choice theorists share Hobbes's pessimistic view of man as the wolf of man.

Because it is individualistic, rational-choice action theory underrates the social matrix – or worse, it takes the social structure for granted and thus does not analyse it. This is mistaken because, by definition, a social action is one that affects others and is affected by others: it occurs in a social network not in a social vacuum. As Parsons (1940b) put it, economic activity is "a phase of institutional behavior," whence it cannot be understood independently of the institutional framework (see also Polanyi 1944). Real agents act within several social systems, most of which pre-exist them. True, some individuals can change such systems to some extent. To have recognized this fact against holistic fatalism is a virtue of individualism. But the rational-choice version of individualism does not make the most of this virtue because it shifts attention from action to deliberation.

The deliberations, interests, and intentions of an agent explain what moves him to act or to refrain from acting, but they do not account for the success or failure of his actions or inactions. Only an analysis of his social ties – that is, of his status and roles in certain social networks – as well as of the state of the system in or upon which he acts or refrains from acting, can explain his success or failure in attaining his goals. (Think of a businessman who intends to launch a new product, or of a politician who intends to run for office on a new electoral platform.) But rational-choice theories, being individualistic, underrate the social context of action, and therefore discourage its investigation. As a consequence they are of no help in steering effective action or preventing action.

The same holds for the unanticipated consequences of purposive social action. Even if fortunate in attaining his goal, an agent is bound to bring about some unanticipated side-effects as well – some of which may be so negative as to render the attained goal worthless. Shorter: Every social action has unanticipated consequences, some of which may be counterproductive (recall sect. 1). This becomes particularly apparent in the case of social traps such as the arms race and environmental degradation (see Iannone 1994).

As Merton (1936) noted long ago, "[P]recisely because a particular action is not carried out in a psychological or social vacuum, its effects will ramify into other spheres of value and interest." Consequently, every "rational" calculation of the utility to be derived from a course of social action is bound to be in error. Only a systemic approach can yield a realistic action theory. However, it must be admitted that systemist action theory, sketched in section 1, is still at an embryonic stage.

In conclusion, rational-choice action theory is on the whole false and amoral when not immoral. This is so because it is under the spell of a narrow economicist notion of human action, namely, that which maximizes either the expected subjective utility or the benefit/cost ratio for an agent placed in a social vacuum. We need alternative theories making room for social values, passion, and tradition as well as for calculation; for social structure as well as for agency; for social forces as well as for leadership. Furthermore, we need action theories allowing us to optimize morality as well as efficiency. And we need not only realistic general action theories but also substantive theories addressing specific social issues – such as overpopulation, unemployment, poverty, militarism, environmental degradation, illiteracy, and drug abuse. However, the construction of such theories involves certain general philosophical concepts, such as those of policy, plan, value, and norm. We proceed therefore to examine some of these general praxiological ideas.

6 Values and Norms

Human action, whether individual or social, is controlled by valuation, explicit or tacit. Indeed, our actions are triggered by the need or desire to attain valuable goals or avoid disvaluable outcomes. And, when rational, our actions are planned and monitored in the light of value judgments; moreover, their outcomes are evaluated for efficiency, morality, or both. The generic concept of efficiency may be compressed into either output/input or benefit/cost formulas. And the specific concept of moral efficiency may be defined as the ratio of the number of needs (not just wishes) met to that of total needs (Bunge 1989a).

Experience and deliberation about values and the ways to realize them are eventually compressed into rules or norms. A norm or rule is of course a prescription for doing something. The general form of a rule is: *To attain goal G, perform action A.* A somewhat more explicit formula is this: *To attain goal G with resources R, select or construct means M from among R, and perform action A with the help of M.* A rule is *social* if any of its three constituents – goal, means, or action being envisaged – is social or, when implemented, has a social impact. And a social rule is a *moral rule* if the actions it steers enhance the welfare of others without preventing anyone from meeting their basic needs.

A pristine society of gatherer-hunters observes few social norms; most of them are tacit rather than explicit and change slowly over time. Hence, such a society neither needs nor has any special formal organizations charged with the observance of norms. By contrast, a civilized society is ruled by a large (often excessive) and changing (often too slowly) body of explicit norms. Since not all of these are efficient ("rational"), as well as equitable and mutually consistent, some members of any society feel confused and boxed in. A few of those who do, rightly or wrongly, feel feel so attempt to break away through either evasion or crime, while others attempt to alter the box itself through political action. For better or for worse, the vast majority of criminals and politicians are at best competent craftsmen rather than creative sociotechnologists: they lack the knowledge and imagination required to stage original and grandiose coups.

There are laws of nature but not natural norms – *pace* natural-law theorists and utilitarians. In other words, nature is lawful but unruly and unconventional, whereas social matter is subject to rules. All rules, whether social or not, are inventions, hence subject to change or disuse. However, whereas some norms are purely conventional, others look like laws in being mandatory if one hopes for success. These are the most efficient known rules, such as those used for repairing cars or hernias, teaching how to swim or read, handling legal conflicts, or tackling logistic problems.

There are two kinds of rule: rules of thumb or traditional norms, and well-grounded or justified rules. A *rule of thumb* is an empirical rule adopted or kept because it is (rightly or wrongly) believed to work, or because its violation would cause unproductive social strains. Anyone would be hard put to explain why we should observe such a rule other than out of deference to tradition or authority. By contrast, a *grounded rule* is one consistent with science, morals, or both, even though it may not have yet been tried for either efficiency or social impact. The technological norms are expected to be of this kind. But some techniques, such as the ones for mass persuasion, pose moral dilemmas that most technologists ignore, but social scientists ought not to overlook (see Merton 1971).

Whereas etiquette rules are mere social conventions, observed only in some social circles at certain times, the technological norms are supposed to be universal in being based on scientific laws. For example, in setting up small work teams or committees we shall do well to avoid triads, on the strength of the well-known sociological finding that triads of equals tend to be unstable (because two of the members may gang up against the third). Likewise, in prescribing a medical treatment we shall do well to follow the advice of biomedical research rather than that of medical quackery. The reason is that research can come up with (total or partial) truths about the sickness mechanism and, once a mechanism is known, it may be possible to repair the corresponding system.

To generalize: Because efficient action implies truth, though not conversely, technology should be based on science. (Recall the introduction to part B.) This is what I mean by the *scientific justification* of a technological norm or rule: that every such prescription should be consistent with the relevant (natural or social) laws, and subject to efficiency tests. In particular, a scientifically justified social rule may be called a *sociotechnological* rule. Such a rule has the same epistemic status as a correct medical prescription or a good engineering design.

The expression "Rule R is based on law L" signifies this. Let L be an empirically well-confirmed general hypothesis belonging to a scientific theory. Suppose, for the sake of definiteness, that L = "If A, then B," and that L can be interpreted as "If A is the case, then B will (necessarily or probably) happen." Assume further that we can make A happen at will, and that the outcome B of A is either desirable or undesirable rather than indifferent. Then one and the same law L is the scientific basis for two rules:

R^+ = "To make B happen (always or with a given frequency), do A."

R^- = "To avoid B (always or with a given frequency), abstain from doing A."

We say that R^+ and R^- are *duals* of one another. Thus, if a given law has a practical application at all, it supports both a rule and its dual.

Laws have thus an ambivalent practical import. Basic science, which is centrally concerned with laws, is morally neutral. By contrast, technology, which is essentially a guide to action – and therefore a rule-directed activity – calls for values and morals whenever the action in question is likely to have a social impact (see Bunge 1988c).

A social action is, by definition, an action likely to affect not only the agent but other people as well. In order to either prevent unnecessary harm to others or optimize (not necessarily maximize) social benefits, we ought to subject our intentions and actions to ethical scrutiny. Consequently, whereas some technological rules, policies, plans, and technology-based actions are morally justified, others are not. (For example, compulsory vaccination and quarantine are morally justified because they are the only ways to prevent the outbreak and propagation of epidemics. By contrast, massive automation without a concomitant reduction of working hours is morally questionable in times of massive chronic unemployment.) We stipulate that a technological rule is *fully justified* if and only if it is both scientifically and morally justified. This suggests that sociotechnology is inseparable from ethics. We shall return to this point in the following section.

Like laws, norms may profitably be analysed in terms of the possible states of the (natural or artificial) system concerned. In fact, every law and every norm restricts the set of possible states, hence the possible histories, of a concrete system. (It confines them to a box within the state space – or space of possible states – representing the system. Unlike ordinary space, a state space – and any box within it – may have a very large number of dimensions.) We stipulate that a *good* norm or rule is one that minimizes the set of practically and morally undesirable states of the system concerned – hence, the collection of the events and processes occurring in the system.

However, a good norm or rule may leave too much latitude and may thus complicate the decision process instead of expediting it. Besides, there may be more than one good norm. Ideally, we want not just good norms but the best among them in terms of both efficiency and morality. That is, we want to shrink the set of states both practically and morally undesirable. This has the added advantage of simplifying the decision process, perhaps to the point of programming it into an expert system.

Norms or rules are central to deliberate human action. We must then expect to find them in policies or strategies, to which we now turn.

7 Policy

A *policy*, strategy, or action "philosophy," is a system of principles or guidelines underlying either the planning of some personal course of action or the operation or transformation of a social system such as a hospital, a factory, or a government agency. Thus, the policy of a given unit – person or organization – may be to ensure self-reliance through hard work; that of another, maximum profit by all means; and that of a third, public service through volunteer work. In general, to a first approximation a policy or strategy may be construed as a <goals, means> pair, where each component is only sketched. The details are left to planning, which will concern us in the following section.

However, a <goals, means> pair is insufficient to characterize a policy, because goals and means do not come in a vacuum. Indeed, all practical means and goals are prompted by some issue and devised, analysed, debated, assessed, and reviewed in the light of some empirical information, value judgments, general principles, and specific hypotheses concerning the system concerned. Suppose, for example, that a liberal politician knows that about 20 per cent of the population of his country lives below the poverty line (datum); he finds this state of affairs unfair and therefore immoral (value judgment); he wants to redress this injustice (goal); he adopts the (debatable) hypothesis that education is the source of all social goods in society; he assumes further that people are not poor by choice but because they do not find jobs for want of skills (hypothesis); he also posits (adopts the hypothesis) that education, in particular job-training programs (the means), can reduce substantially the poverty rate; finally, he argues that basic education is a public good that should be provided by the state (policy norm or metapolicy). This example suggests the following characterization. A policy (or strategy) is an ordered sextuple: *Policy = <Data, Value judgment(s), Goal(s), General principles, Specific hypotheses, Means>*. The general principles include policy norms (or metapolicies).

A policy for an artificial system, be it machine, organization, or an entire economy, concerns directly the control mechanism(s) of the system. In turn, the (efficient) controller of a system is the subsystem of it whose specific function is to regulate the functioning of the overall system in such a way that it may correct internal dysfunctions and adapt (within bounds) to external disturbances. Shorter: Efficient control optimizes stability (not immobility) and thus viability.

(In the classical cybernetics literature, systems control is equated with the reduction of variety: see, for instance, Ashby 1963. For example, a thermostat confines temperature variations within a narrow interval. Likewise, laws and government regulations reduce the variety of decisions that business managers may make. So much for the received view. This view overlooks the fact that in some cases control aims at conserving or even increasing diversity rather than reducing it. This is the case with the conservation of biodiversity through environmental controls, and of the increase in cultural diversity through investment in education and research. I therefore propose to generalize the standard definition of control to read: "The goal of artificial control is to reduce undesirable variety and conserve or increase desirable variety." Note, incidentally, the occurrence of the value term 'desirable' and its dual 'undesirable,' both absent from cybernetics.)

Like organisms and machines, social systems are subject to decay owing to both internal and external factors. If we wish to prevent an artificial system from decaying we must attach to it monitors and controls. Moreover, we must be prepared to repair the system and, should it become hopelessly obsolete, be prepared to redesign or scrap it.

The internal monitors and controls of an industrial firm are its managers, engineers, foremen, and accountants. In principle, the state is the supreme control of a modern society. (In both cases the correct biological analogue is the brain. The other control systems of the body operate automatically, whence they are hardly affected by small decisions.)

When the controls of a system are defective or fail, the system operates in a less efficient manner or even risks breakdown. In the case of artificial controls, such as those of machines and social systems, control failure may call for a review of the control's design or implementation, or even for changes in the policy guiding the design and operation of the control. For example, when the law-and-order forces in a community fail to keep the peace, they may have to be reformed. However, when crime becomes endemic, social controls of that type may prove to be counterproductive. In this case the entire society may have to be redesigned to cut the roots of crime rather than putting a lid on it.

The following flow diagram exhibits the pride of place held by metapolicy and policy-making in the design, organization, maintenance, or reform of any artificial system:

$$\begin{array}{ccccccccc}
\text{Policy norm} & \rightarrow & \text{Policy} & \rightarrow & \text{Plan} & \rightarrow & \text{Decision} & \rightarrow & \text{Action} & \rightarrow & \text{Control} & \rightarrow & \text{System} & \rightarrow & \text{Output} \\
\uparrow & & \uparrow & & \uparrow & & \uparrow & & \uparrow & & \uparrow & & \uparrow & & \downarrow \\
\leftarrow & & \leftarrow & & \leftarrow & & \leftarrow & & \leftarrow & & \leftarrow & & \leftarrow & & \text{Evaluation}
\end{array}$$

Figure 7.3 The feedback circuit whereby the outcome of an action upon a system is determined by policy ideas, and its evaluation leads to altering the latter

A policy can be of either the short- or the long-term kind, depending on the urgency and severity of the issue it addresses. However, "short term" should not be regarded as the opposite of "long term": rather, every short-term policy should nestle inside some long-term policy. Otherwise the very existence of the system concerned may be jeopardized. For example, recurrent famines can be avoided only by restructuring agriculture and land tenure. But in the meantime the hungry have got to be fed: the long-term plan must be supplemented with emergency action. Likewise a business firm cannot "survive" unless its stake-holders derive some benefit from it. But maximizing short-term returns on investment or labor is disastrous in the long term because it can be achieved the easy way – that is, by refraining from using new technologies, updating facilities, or reforming management style – which is to say, by allowing the rot to set in. In sum, a combination of short- and long-term policies is required both technically and morally.

Like any other proposal, a policy may be designed with or without the benefit of expert (scientific or technological) knowledge. (Still, no policy, however scientific, can cover all items: it must focus on essentials and decide on priorities.) And, once adopted, a policy may or may not be tested on a small scale (for instance, in a pilot plant or school) before being implemented on a large scale. Any responsible and effective policy is designed with the help of science and technology, and it is tested on a small scale before being implemented on a large scale. If the policy is grounded on a precise model, and the required data are available, it can be simulated on a computer.

(Computer simulation can afford only a preliminary test. No simulation, however sophisticated, can replace the actual testing on a sample of the total population or on a subsystem of the social system concerned. The reasons are obvious. First, simulation is a computer-aided conceptual operation, not an empirical one: it does not contrast ideas to facts, hence it does not test for either factual truth or efficiency. Second, given the backwardness of social science, the model involved in a simulation is likely to omit a number of relevant variables and, a fortiori, a number of relevant formulas as well. Moreover, the formulas occurring in the model are likely to be simplistic. Moral: Never attempt to terminate debates over social matters saying, 'Computer *dixit.*')

What is the methodological status of policies? Since a policy is a system of proposals, not of propositions, it can be neither true nor false. But it may be timely or untimely, as well as effective, ineffective, or counterproductive; and it may be moral, immoral, or morally neutral. Hence, a policy can be tested, first through experiment, then in pratice. Regrettably, most social policies are neither designed nor monitored and evaluated in the light of social science. Not surprisingly they often fail and, just as often, we do not even know whether they have accomplished their goal.

All policies should be checked for efficiency, but any such checks are necessarily indirect. Indeed, as shown in figure 7.3, there is a long stretch between policy and outcome. Moreover, any given policy may be spelled out in a number of plans or programs, and every one of these can be implemented in alternative ways according to circumstance. (Shorter: the policy-plan and plan-implementation relations are one-to-many, not one-to-one.) Hence, what can actually be subjected to the test of practice is an implementation of one of the conceivable plans whose intersection is the given policy. The failure of a plan might be attributed to its defective implementation; and its success might be due to unforeseen favourable circumstances. What holds for plans also holds, a fortiori, for the underlying policies: failure hardly indicts them, and success hardly vindicates them. However, this somewhat discouraging conclusion does not prove that policies are useless: it only suggests that they should be justified and monitored rigorously.

So much for policy in general. Let us now approach the problem of social policy. Social-policy research started in the 1880s with the birth of the welfare state in Germany, Austria, and Great Britain, and it received a great impetus in the United Kingdom in the 1950s under the first Labour government, and in the USA in the 1960s in conjunction with the so-called Great Society programs. (The US General Accounting Office includes a Program Evaluation and Methodology Division.) The practical rationale for this branch of sociotechnology is the following. A serious social issue – such as sex and race discrimination, chronic poverty, teenage pregnancy, illiteracy, violence, and drug addiction – is, by definition, a multidimensional problem affecting large numbers of people and having often deep historical roots, such as slavery and chronic unemployment. Because of their complexity, there are no quick fixes for such problems. They can be addressed only in the light of solid social studies and long-term social policies. Moreover, their solution demands large public expenditures, which in turn call for political will and public support.

A *social policy* is obviously a policy whose goal is to control certain social variables. Social policies can be scientific or nonscientific: that is, they may or may not be designed in the light of empirical information and social theory. Regrettably, most social policies and programs designed so far have been nonscientific: they were either improvised in the heat of political circumstances, or designed on the strength of dogma. They have seldom been justified by serious intellectual debate based on solid data and theory. (For a brief survey of both kinds of policy see Chelimsky 1991.) In particular, most conservative public policies presuppose uncritically that humans are utility maximizers, hence only sensitive to carrots and sticks, and always ready to free-ride, and therefore reluctant to comply with those very policies (Steward 1993). And, of course, no antiscientific school in social studies has a potential usefulness for informing effective social policy-making. Moreover, ignorance is the more dangerous the more complex a society.

A *scientific social policy* draws half of its components – namely data, general principles, and specific hypotheses – from basic social science. The last component of the sextuple – the means – is the specific concern of sociotechnology. As for the last two components – value judgments and goals – they are distinctly moral and ideological. In an epoch-making study, Myrdal (1942, appendix) emphasized that "practical conclusions" from social studies – that is, policies and plans – can be drawn only from data jointly with value judgments. For example, "In country X blacks are discriminated against. Racial discrimination is wrong. Hence, measures should be taken to curb racial discrimination in X." Thus, the social scientist who looks for practical solutions to social issues should state explicitly his value premises (Myrdal 1969, 63; Titmuss 1976, 14). Does this contradict Weber's injunction to keep social studies free from value judgments? Let us see.

Social policies have nonscientific components, but the latter can be supported or undermined by empirical research. For example, although social science cannot tell us that poverty and discrimination are unfair, it does teach us that they (a) are objectively degrading; (b) weaken social cohesion by causing alienation and anomie; (c) waste human capital; (d) are generally perceived as demeaning and unfair; and (e) may trigger social unrest. Hence, social science supports the goals of eradicating poverty and discrimination. By the same token, social science undermines conservative ideologies – which is why conservative governments are reluctant to fund social research. However, basic social science is not concerned with devising means to eradicate poverty or discrimination: this is a task for sociotechnology and, particularly, for social policy-making. Shorter: whereas basic social science is value-neutral (though not ignorant of values), social policy-making, and in general sociotechnology, is value-laden. This should resolve the apparent conflict between Weber and Myrdal.

A public policy may be either structural or short term. It may address clusters of long-standing and serious social issues, such as those of underdevelopment, overpopulation, chronic poverty, endemic sickness, and environmental degradation. Or else the policy may attempt to correct a partial or temporary malfunction, or even only mask some symptoms. In metaphoric terms, a public policy may prescribe surgery, specific medication, or aspirin. Land reform combined with the organization of farmer cooperatives, technical assistance, and credits is an instance of the first; massive inoculation against a threatening epidemic exemplifies the second; and the jailing of opponents, beggars, vagrants, or prostitutes typifies the third.

Paradoxically, a symptomatic (or stop-gap) public policy may have profound and lasting effects – some beneficial and others harmful. This is the case with two rival policies: those that favour a welfare state including a safety net and those that prescribe dismantling it. Indeed, the former decreases social inequality, and it may even eliminate abject poverty, by using progressive taxation to redistribute wealth and fund social programs. But, since the roots of social inequality remain, what we get is relief rather than welfare. Worse, in the case of the chronically unemployed, relief addiction is demoralizing besides increasing the tax burden on the active segment of the population.

The rival symptomatic policy with profound and lasting effects is the standard prescription of the International Monetary Fund for healing the sick economy (particularly the financial system) of a Third World nation – never that of an industrialized country. This recipe boils down to freezing wages (not prices or profit rates), reducing social services (perhaps to the point of ripping the safety net), trimming the state bureaucracy (not the armed forces, though), privatizing state enterprises (even if profitable), stopping all public works, regulating the money supply – and, of course, serving the debt punctually and at all costs. (After all, the Fund speaks on behalf of the creditors.)

The Fund's policy is sectoral, short-sighted, and conservative. It does not go to the roots of economic dysfunctions, and is not interested in the biological, political, and cultural consequences of the measures it recommends. In particular, the Fund seldom if ever recommends land reform, helping farmers and small businesses, reducing military expenditures, protecting natural resources, increasing the production of staple foodstuffs, or investing in human resources. No wonder that, when implemented, the Fund's recommendations lead at best to short-lived economic boom at enormous social costs (including bread riots), at worst to long-term stagnation or decline together with political instability. They betray a combination of sectoral vision and shallow thinking with moral turpitude and conservative ideology rather than sound socio-economico-political theory.

All social policies and plans are designed on the basis of more or less explicit and justifiable socio-economic, political, ideological, moral, and philosophical considerations (see, for instance, Reich 1988). The first of these inputs is obvious: Social policies are designed to either solve or mask social issues, and these appear clearly only upon examining the current social situation as revealed directly (but uncertainly) by public dissatisfaction, and indirectly (but more securely) by such socio-economic, political, and cultural indicators as rates of population growth, joblessness, illiteracy, morbidity, school drop-out, crime, and political unrest (or its dual, apathy). Regrettably, most empirical research on the possible advantages and disadvantages of social policies has had little or no impact upon social policy-making (Stromsdorfer 1985).

The political input to social policy-making consists in politicians assessing the weight that advocacy for certain social policies may have on the chances of staying in power, winning the next election, or retaining power or grabbing it by undemocratic means. For example, it has been noted that during electoral campaigns certain politicians focus on unemployment and advocate job creation and easy credit terms; but once in power they shift attention to inflation and fiscal debt, forgetting the rest. That is, their electoral social policies are geared to their struggle for power.

Public policy-making depends upon political factors because it is favoured or resisted by political parties or special-interest groups, and it is carried out by the state. Yet many economists pretend that they can design apolitical economic policies. This pretense is not just mistaken: "[i]t is also a cover for the reality of economic power and motivation. And it is a prime source of misjudgment and error in economic policy" (Galbraith 1987, 299).

The ideological input to public policy-making is complex, for one and the same social issue may look differently from different ideological standpoints, so that alternative solutions are bound to be advocated to solve it. For example, liberals and social democrats are likely to admit the existence of most social ills while disagreeing on the degree of radicalism with which they should be tackled. Likewise, conservatives and fascists agree that socioeconomic inequality is unavoidable or even desirable; but, unlike fascists, conservatives are reluctant to suppress civil liberties to defend privilege.

Moral input is the most subtle of all inputs to social policy-making, and therefore the more neglected, but it is no less important than the others. In fact, socio-economic issues raise moral problems because they involve the inability of large numbers of people to meet their basic needs or satisfy their legitimate wants. In short, all social issues are problems of inequity, which is the enemy of fairness and a source of social conflict. Hence, anyone committed to social justice and peace is expected to admit the need for social policies designed to decrease inequality. But the social reformer knows that social policy-making has powerful enemies – not only the outspoken defenders of privilege but also the schools of thought to be discussed anon. (For a different analysis of the "rhetoric of reaction" see Hirschman 1991.)

The fiercest enemy of any social policies aimed at decreasing social inequalities is the neoconservative, neoliberal, or modern-day libertarian. He claims that such policies, in levying new taxes to finance social programs, involve risks and restrict individual liberties. Now, it is certainly true that social policies involve risks, particularly when ill grounded, inflexible, or untested. But the risks of social inaction to everyone are not less than those of intervention: after all, rioting and social revolution originate in the perception of inequity, or of the indifference, incompetence, or corruption of the powers that be. (Incidentally, we do not know yet how to quantitate social risk. The whole field of risk assessment is ruled by the narrow problematics of actuaries and finance experts. Both use hard data but, whereas the former employ suitable mathematical tools, most finance experts make do with the standard "market model," which involves only linear functions. And the "rational"-choice approach to risk assessment, though general, is nonscientific in involving subjective utilities and probabilities.)

As for the burdens accompanying social policies, they are intolerable to anyone who, like the libertarian, holds that liberty is the supreme good – particularly if he shares Hegel's view that property embodies the idea of liberty (see also Radnitzky 1993, 54). But the libertarian principle is vulnerable to the following criticisms. First, no society is viable unless people comply with some social duties. Second, liberty is possible only among equals. In fact, as soon as one individual or group dominates others in any way, the dominant unit (by definition) limits the freedom of others. As Pound (1954, 168) put it, we need to balance the desire to be free and the desire to be equal. In short, libertarianism is not a viable political (or moral) philosophy, because it undermines the roots of social cohesion, namely participation and value sharing. (More in Bunge 1989a.)

A second party hostile to social policy holds that the latter is futile because "rational" – that is, well informed, prescient, and maximizing – individuals will offset the effects of any policy to their own advantage. In particular, those who wield economic power always manage to avoid paying for new social programs. For example, the businessman passes tax increases on to the consumer, so that in the end nobody benefits. This line of argument is pursued vigorously by the rational-expectations school of macroeconomics (see Lucas and Sargent 1981), which we first met in chapter 3, section 8. This school rose briefly to prominence around 1980 for two quite different reasons. The first is that it rightly emphasizes that human action is (partly) determined by expectations. The second is that it falsely claims to provide a scientific basis for *laissez-faire* economic policies.

The rational-expectations line of reasoning is unsound for the following reasons. First, it conceives of rational expectation as using not only all the relevant data but also the theorist's model to forecast prices, rates of inflation, and other variables. This assumption is unrealistic: indeed, most successful businessmen do not use mathematical economics, in particular Lucas's mathematically sophisticated theory; and no economic agent can be infinitely well informed and prescient, as the school demands. A second unrealistic hypothesis is that every agent supposes that the other agents share his own expectations. (The only function of this hypothesis is to save the theorist the trouble of facing the problem of higher-order expectations – for examples, mine about yours, which in turn depends upon mine, and so on in unending loops.) This hypothesis is false because information is no substitute for experience, smartness, and especially clout, so that different businessmen are bound to form different expectations. (This is suggested by common sense and it has been confirmed in market laboratories: see Vernon Smith 1991.) Consequently, few if any individuals succeed fully in offsetting the effects of social policies. Third, businessmen are never completely at liberty to price what they sell: they can charge only what the market will bear. Further, they are tied by contracts or promises, and they form loyalty bonds. Fourth, consumption rises with income, whence – as Keynes (1936) argued – business stands to gain from a rise in the standard of living brought about by non-confiscatory wealth redistribution and public-works programs. Fifth, macroeconomic policies do have consequences: think, for instance, of the success of any zero-inflation policy and the recession it often causes. (More in chap. 3, sect. 7; see also Frydman 1983; Thurow 1983; Fisher 1983; Dagum 1986; Blinder 1989; Rowley 1995; and Ericsson and Irons 1995.)

A third school holds that all social policies are counterproductive: that they have perverse effects. Thus, compulsory immunization saves lives, which increases population, which increases poverty, which in turn increases morbidity. Second example: An unemployment compensation equivalent to the going minimal salary discourages people from seeking employment, which has negative effects on everything else. All this is true: some social policies do have perverse effects. Think of welfare addiction, rent freezing, and unconditional state support for unwed mothers and unemployed youngsters. Does it follow that all social policy is necessarily inefficient or even counterproductive? Not at all. Rather, the failure of partial social programs suggests that *sectoral* (rather than systemic) and *symptomatic* (rather than radical) social policies are ineffective or even counterproductive. Let us look briefly into this matter.

The sectoral approach to social issues tackles them one at a time. It presupposes that such issues are mutually independent, so that they can be resolved independently from one another. But as a matter of fact social issues come in clusters or systems. The various members of the cluster may certainly be distinguished, but we would be ill advised to separate them. Indeed, every social issue affecting a large segment of the population involves at least two of the following features: environmental, biological, economic, cultural, and political. Think, for instance, of soil erosion, sex discrimination, hunger, poverty, ignorance, or political oppression.

In short, all social issues are *systemic*: they involve all the main features of a social system. Consequently, to be effective and sustainable, social policies and programs must be package deals, whereas sectoral measures are at best short-lived. For example, charity may save some people from starvation for a while, but it does not affect the roots of poverty: worse, it may perpetuate them. Only a multilateral social policy, one involving job creation, the teaching of skills, and organization for self-help (such as savings, work, and housing cooperatives of various kinds), may eradicate poverty. Social policy may be likened to a four-wheel chariot pulled by politics. The wheels are environmental, biological, economic, and cultural, neither of which turns independently of the others.

For example, health policy may be approached in three different ways: individualist, holist, and systemist – or cure, prevent, and prevent-and-cure respectively. The first stresses intervention in disease processes, pinning its hopes exclusively on biomedical research. By contrast, the holist reminds us that historical epidemiology shows that "[t]he improvement of health during the past three centuries was due essentially to provision of food, protection from hazards, and limitation of numbers" (McKeown 1979, 197). And the systemist claims that health depends on environmental and social factors (e.g., clean air, sanitation, and massive vaccination), socio-economic status (e.g., income, rank, and type of work), genetic endowment, individual prevention (lifestyle and personal hygiene), and intervention in disease processes (e.g., dental care and surgery). The ticket is "Healthy body in a sound society" (see Evans et al. 1994). And the moral for social policy-making is equally obvious: Ignore the relevant sciences (e.g., epidemiology and demography) and put social welfare at risk.

What holds for social policies holds also for one of the technical tools used in the design and monitoring of any social policy, namely cost-benefit analysis. Most such analyses are sectoral. For example, when studying the performance of a rural post office, the "lean and mean" zealot looks only at economic efficiency: he overlooks the fact that the post office doubles as source of information, civic centre, and informal social club. A systemic (or inclusive) cost-benefit analysis involves social costs and benefits, and concludes that the social benefits of rural post offices may outweigh their cost.

To return to the moral basis of social policy. I submit that the key moral variables in social-policy design and planning are *concern* and *respect* for others. The reason is that "[c]oncern without respect is at best paternalism and can lead to tyranny. Respect without concern is the cold world of extreme individualism, a denial of the intrinsically social nature of humanity" (Arrow 1992, 45). We may accordingly distinguish four types of social policy with regard to moral underpinnings:

Concern and respect → Social welfare and democratic participation
Concern and no respect → Charity and elitist (authoritarian) policies
No concern but respect → No social policies at all
Neither concern nor respect → Antisocial public policies

The last three types of policy are the easiest to design and implement. But, like anything cheap, they have neither deep nor lasting beneficial effects. This is because they fail to involve all the stakeholders, and thus to redress a major universal social ill, namely marginality. In particular, the implementation of policies of the second or top-down type may have unexpected undesirable effects. A classical example of a perverse effect is that of prohibition, which begat gangsterism, corruption, and toxic liquor.

Policies of the concern-together-with-respect kind are the most difficult to design and put into practice: so difficult, in fact, that they may fail in buying welfare at the price of economic viability, or democracy at the price of expertise. Which shows that, in order to live up to our moral philosophy in public matters, we must become knowledgeable about social science and sociotechnology.

Moreover, we ought to favour intensive public participation in the discussion of policies and the evaluation of the resulting programs, and this for moral as well as prudential reasons. Indeed, if program X is bound to affect individual Y, then Y is entitled to have a say in the design and implementation of X. Moreover, Y knows best where the shoe pinches and where X might fail, so Y is well placed to propose criticisms or constructive suggestions. However, individual action is likely to be ineffective. This is why so many public-spirited non-governmental organizations (NGOs) have sprung up since the nineteenth century, many of which have become militant organizations with long-term agendas – unlike democratic governments, whose horizon is the next election.

Let us finally touch on the philosophical input to public policy-making. An example will suffice to bring home the relevance of philosophy to public policy. The monumental Los Angeles riots in April 1992 are generally regarded as an indicator of a deep crisis in American society. However, the diagnosis of this crisis is still under debate. Whereas conservatives blame the "breakdown of family values," others point to chronic poverty and racial discrimination, which weaken social bonds, erode good traditional values, and cause anomie, hopelessness, and delinquency. Clearly, the former interpretation is idealist, whereas the latter is materialist (recall chap. 6, sect. 1).

The implication of the idealist/materialist contrast for public policy is obvious. Idealism leads to recrimination and preaching, or even to proposing the dismantling of the welfare state, regarding it as the culprit. In any event this view does not encourage the scientific study of the socio-economic causes of the crisis because it denies that there are any. By contrast, the materialist view favours the objective study of the socio-economic roots of the crisis, as well as the design of social policies that aim at job creation, improvement of education and health care, and the strengthening of community organizations.

The materialism/idealism cleavage, which is of an ontological nature, has an epistemological concomitant, namely the realism/anti-realism one. Indeed, any scientific study of social facts starts by admitting the reality of social facts as well as the possibility of knowing them, if only partially. By contrast, an anti-realist – whether positivist, constructivist, conventionalist, phenomenologist, or hermeneuticist – is interested only in appearances and subjective phenomena such as individual perceptions and intentions, as well as in symbolic interaction or "communicative action," such as conversation. Consequently, far from proposing public policies to solve any social issues, he will tend to favour the *laissez-faire* non-policy – which in practice amounts to letting do those who can, and forgetting about those who lack the power to redirect their own lives except for the worse. (True, many anti-realists call themselves progressives, but this only proves their incoherence.)

In short, the public policy maker or consultant faces at least four philosophical dilemmas: rationalism/irrationalism, systemism/sectoralism, materialism/ idealism, and realism/anti-realism. For this reason sociotechnologists, statesmen, and civil servants will ignore philosophy at their own risk and at the cost of us all. This will happen not only if they adopt an irrationalist, intuitionist, or pragmatist stand, but also if they make use of rational-choice theory. Indeed, the latter grasps the wrong horn in each of the last three above-mentioned philosophical dilemmas. (See Bunge 1996a for these dilemmas as well as for a detailed analysis of rational-choice theory.)

However, one might admit that rational-choice theory fails to describe, explain, and predict, while still claiming that it is the correct normative theory, being about ideally rational people, which is what we all should try to become. This is in fact what some practitioners of decision theory have claimed, at least when cornered. But then a new question arises: Can the said theory prescribe successful courses of action? My answer is that it cannot because it has the ambition of being a Theory of Everything Social, hence a theory of nothing in particular. Indeed, the injunction "Maximize your expected utilities!" is no more helpful a guide for solving technical problems than Kant's injunction "Do what is right!" in facing moral problems.

Particular decisions call for much more than general theories. In fact, they call for empirical information, specific models, and rules. A manager intent on upgrading a corporation is better advised to hire an operations research consultant capable of constructing a mathematical model of the company than a rational-choice theorist likely to play around with utilities and probabilities drawn from a hat. Successful rational action requires specific models consistent with sufficiently true scientific theories, as well as with plenty of reliable data of both the "hard" and "soft" kinds. (Examples of the former: production volume and cost; of the latter: management style and worker morale.)

Finally, do social policy makers actually use rational-choice theories to design social programs? Not to my knowledge, and for good reasons. Indeed, an authentically rational (and moral) social policy depends more on a right combination of reliable data with worthy goals than on any detailed theoretical models. For example, assume that the Secretary of Health and Welfare is intent on improving the health of the people in his country. What should he do: invest in medical care or in preventive health care, that is, social medicine? If he is a genuinely rational individual he will begin by reading the relevant literature, not by building an a priori rational-choice model. And if he does so he will find that medical care only contributes about 10 per cent to health improvement. The remaining 90 per cent is due to improvements in public sanitation, pollution control, nutrition, housing, work conditions, the reduction of tobacco, alcohol, and fat consumption, and access to public parks and sports facilities. In short, any reduction in morbidity and mortality is mainly due to preventive care. Consequently, the policy maker is confronted with a rather simple choice that requires far more data, ideology, and morality than theory. This is not to suggest that the design of an efficient program can be atheoretical: once the basic choices have been made there is plenty of room for crafting specific models.

Second example: the Secretary of Education is faced with an even tougher problem, and he too will find no use for rational-choice theories. If he skims the literature in the sociology of education, he will find that improvements in the level of public education depend not only upon the quantity and quality of schools but also upon the socio-economic status of the students and their employment prospects. The best school, if placed in a poor ghetto, cannot change the fact that malnourished and unmotivated children of poor, uneducated, disillusioned, and anomic parents are poor learners. (For example, Head Start – an American pre-school program aimed at poor children – has improved the education of whites, but not of African Americans: see Currie and Thomas 1995). If knowledgeable and honest, the Secretary will recommend that his school-reform program be a component of a comprehensive and radical social reform aimed at raising the standard of living of the population – for instance, by stimulating job creation and local initiative helped by government funding. But rational-choice theorists won't be able to help design such a social reform, for they are not concerned with macrosocial issues – and because on the whole they are rather conservative, trusting as they do in unconstrained individual choice and free enterprise, the "hidden hand," the power of charity, and similar mirages.

It is doubtful that any major social policy has been designed exclusively in the light of some rational-choice model (Iannone 1994). What is certain is that, if any policy were so designed, it would be bound to fail because of its oversimplifications as well as the very principle that has got us all into a number of "social traps," namely that of economic "rationality" or utility maximization: recall section 2. The design, adoption, and implementation of any effective public policy involves not only realistic modelling and calculation, but also regard for others, restraint in the search for personal gain, public education, popular participation, and bargaining – with its concomitant threats, emotionally charged arguments, and rhetorical tricks. (For the latter see Majone 1989.)

In sum, rational-choice theories are unrealistic and, partly for this reason, they are unpractical. These serious flaws in what passes for hard social science encourage the backlash of the soft, in particular non-quantitative, approaches inspired in irrationalist or simply muddled philosophies. Faced with these two suboptimal options, the authentically rational decision maker will not opt for one of them but will attempt to create a third one, both formally rigorous and empirically adequate. In general, genuinely rational agents avoid being impaled on the horns of dilemmas.

8 Planning

Conservatives would have us believe that planning on a large scale is part of the red conspiracy to destroy liberty, which they tend to equate with selling and shopping rights. Actually, large-scale planning was practised in Sumer, ancient Egypt, and pre-Columbian Perú, where the state took care of the collection, storage, and redistribution of grain, as well as of public works. Hippodamus, an early city planner, designed a number of ancient Greek cities, among them Miletus, Priene, and Piraeus. And in every modern nation the state regulates, coordinates, and to some extent even organizes the national economy. Hence, the debate over "free" versus "planned" economies is largely artificial and barren (Myrdal 1960). In particular, the foreign policy of any great power is largely designed (planned) to favour its own interests in foreign resources and markets, thus strongly influencing the domestic economy. Economic planning has become so widespread that planning theory is academically respectable. (See, for instance, Malinvaud and Bacharach 1967; Heal 1973; and Seni 1993.)

Whenever there are alternatives, reasonably well-informed and rational choices can be made, and planned action becomes possible. Whenever certain alternatives look definitely better than others, planning is mandatory. And whenever planning is requisite, it is necessary (a) to resort to the appropriate sociotechnology; (b) to monitor the implementation of the plan so as to adapt it to new circumstances or new findings; and (c) to involve, for both prudential and moral reasons, all those likely to be affected.

Now, popular involvement is impossible under centralized, rigid, and authoritarian planning, for it ignores consumer needs and tastes as well as local interests; furthermore, it suppresses local initiative and makes no room for unforeseen changes of any kind. To be successful, any planning on a national, regional, or global scale must be sketchy, adaptive, and participative. That is, the central-planning agency (not authority) ought to inform, suggest, and help to coordinate rather than command. More precisely, (a) its function should be to collect, process, and distribute information about the quantities and prices of the goods in question; and (b) its goal ought to be an approximate (never perfect) balance of supply and demand for each commodity. This kind of planning is a component of the social order to be called *technoholodemocracy*, combining integral democracy with technical expertise (chap. 11).

Planning is philosophically interesting if only because, as G. Myrdal (1960, 7) noted, it has three philosophical presuppositions. These are trust in reason, freedom of choice, and the possibility of altering the course of events. Besides, planning raises certain logical, epistemological, and ontological problems, as will be seen in the sequel to this chapter.

From a logical point of view a planning problem is the inverse of a forecasting problem, in the sense that the givens in one case are the unknowns in the other. Indeed, a simple forecasting problem looks like this: Given the law or trend of the process of interest, together with the current values of the relevant variables, compute their future values. The corresponding inverse or planning problem is this: Given the law or trend of the process of interest, and the desired values of the relevant variables at a future time, compute their requisite present values. (In more complex cases these values will depend on both the past history of the system and on the trajectory joining the initial and final points.)

What the direct and the inverse problems share is the law or trend of the process of interest. The trouble is that this item of knowledge is usually missing in today's sociotechnology. This does not prove that planning is impossible, but only that it is not an exact science. In fact, we plan all the time: man is the planning animal par excellence. Planned activities, however, are not like bullets: one must readjust frequently both direction and speed. Acting intelligently according to plan is like driving in an overcrowded Indian city: it involves making frequent snap decisions.

Nor is our almost total ignorance of the laws of social change the only reason that planning is not an exact craft. Another is that purposive social action has unanticipated consequences, being socially embedded rather than carried out in a social vacuum (Merton 1936). Indeed, we are constituents of social networks, some of which are so closely knit that, if one of the threads is pulled, others are likely to be affected as well. This embeddedness is, by the way, one of the reasons for preferring participative to authoritarian planning.

All planning calls for forecasting (see Bunge 1973d). Now, a rigid plan requires exact forecasts – which, alas, are not to be had in human affairs. Consequently, a reasonable plan is flexible rather than rigid, as well as sketchy rather than detailed. In other words, when laying out a plan we must count on unpredictable events that may force us to alter the plan or even abandon it altogether. Such events may be unpredictable for either or all of the following reasons. One is plain ignorance – an ever-present though partially remediable handicap. A second is that, as we go ahead, the world around us keeps changing, sometimes to the point of rendering our initial goal irrelevant, or our means insufficient or obsolete. A third reason is that we experience accidental encounters with new people, fresh information, or even new problems, any of which may force us to reconsider our initial plan. A fourth is that the outcomes of our action may prove unsatisfactory. The occurrence of unpredictables of any of these kinds suggests the need to design flexible plans, that is, plans that can be quickly altered as needed.

Given that all our actions have unforeseeable side-effects, some of them perverse, it is only fair to ask what is the point of planning. The answer is that, by contrast to social forecasting, which is passive and dicey, planned action is self-fulfilling, provided it is based on realistic models and data, as well as readjustable. Shorter: realistic and flexible plans and budgets are self-fulfilling prophecies. This is why it may pay more to redesign and build the future than to forecast and wait for it (see Lowe 1965 and Ackoff 1974). After all, although we cannot know the future, we make it happen, if seldom to exact specification.

By monitoring and examining critically the implementation of a plan, we are often able to readjust it at the first sign of error, altering course accordingly. And, as suggested a moment ago, both monitoring and correction are more effective if the stakeholders become involved in the deliberations as well as in the actions than if the plan is imposed from above, which is one of the advantages of the democratic spider-web social organization over the pyramidal or hierarchical one.

What holds for planning in general holds in particular for social programs, from the earliest German national health-insurance plan (1883) to the multitude of social programs currently in place all over the civilized world. The implementation of any social policy calls for some action that, if authentically rational, will be guided by some plan or program. A social plan has an input and an output. The input consists of the resources, and the output of the regulations and measures taken to implement the policy. Let us attend briefly to each side in turn, emphasizing the moral aspect.

The resources are human and financial. The former are government workers, such as bureaucrats and professionals. As for the financial resources, they derive from taxation, borrowing, or both. Conservatives object to any taxes other than those required to pay for national security, law, and order. They do so in the name of liberty, but actually they are only motivated by near-sighted greed. ('Libertarianism,' which used to be a synonym of 'anarchism,' has become a euphemism for selfishness.) Social expenditures are called for by prudence as well as by solidarity. A society that prefers destitution to taxation is not worth defending. Nor is it fully civilized: no civilization without taxation.

However, let us not exaggerate: overtaxation will not necessarily lead to the pinnacle of civilization – particularly if much of the tax revenue is spent on armed forces, bureaucracy, and symptomatic social remedies. Taxation is necessary but it is not the cure-all that some economists prescribe for social ills. In particular, the famous welfare neoclassical economist Pigou and his followers proposed that antisocial behaviour (e.g., polluting) be taxed rather than prohibited and punished. Others, such as Becker (1976), propose that crime be punished mainly by fines. A tacit assumption of both proposals is that everything, including vice and virtue, can be priced and licensed. This assumption is objectionable in overlooking morality. Moreover, experience shows that in many cases offenders prefer to pay taxes or fines than incur the expenditures required to avoid harming others. Everyone is likely to benefit more from the prevention of antisocial actions than from their punishment, particularly where the tax or fine moneys do not go to teachers, health and social workers, and community organizations, or to compensate the victims.

As for government borrowing (e.g., in the form of issuing treasury bonds), the only genuine moral problem is this: will it pay for productive expenditures, and will these benefit not only ourselves but also our descendants rather than throwing a burden upon them? For example, borrowing in order to pay for health care, education, the eradication of poverty, the creation of useful jobs, the building or rebuilding of the infrastructure, or authentic defence is morally justified. By contrast, borrowing to finance military aggression or to support a parasitic bureaucracy is not.

So much for the input side of social planning. Its output side raises general practical and politico-moral problems. Among the former stands out the problem of evaluating the efficiency of a social program. In principle it is a simple problem of cost-benefit analysis. But in practice this problem is tougher because the data are often missing, and some of the outcomes are intangible, or they take several years in appearing. As for the politico-moral problems posed by any new social programs, they boil down to the following: do the concomitant regulations restrict our rights or increase our burdens? If either, are we morally bound to accept the consequences, and willing to pay the price? The answer depends on the moral code one adopts and on the kind of society one favours.

The future belongs to those who design and make it rather than to those who wait for it. Whence the centrality of planning in the governance of any social system, from family to firm to state. However, plans have got to be justified if they are to be both efficient and acceptable to others. I submit that the justification of a plan is sixfold: (a) *epistemic*: the plan must be supported by some plausible theory, however sketchy, as well as by some data; (b) *experimental*: the plan should be tried and evaluated on small groups before being adopted on a large scale; (c) *economic*: the plan must be shown to be economically viable and beneficial; (d) *political*: the plan must be politically feasible, that is, able to earn the support of public opinion and political organizations; (e) *environmental*: the actions envisaged by the plan must be shown to be minimally detrimental to the environment; (f) *moral*: the actions envisaged by the plan must observe the basic principle *Enjoy life and help live*.

Now, a large fraction of the social programs instituted in the United States have proved to be ineffective or even counterproductive. (See, for instance, Bennett and Lumsdaine 1975; Mosteller 1981; and the journal *Evaluation Research*.) This suggests that they failed to comply with the above-mentioned conditions and, in particular, that they were sectoral and politically expedient. However, even a well-grounded social program should be evaluated periodically, for it might work even better if properly modified over time.

A realist, moral, and useful theory of rational social action should centre around the twin concepts of policy and plan. However, not even the best action theory could contain an algorithm allowing us to design foolproof plans protecting us from uncertainty and sparing us the trouble of making snap decisions in the face of unforeseen catastrophes and opportunities. Blind faith in planning is just as stultifying as trust in improvisation.

We must find a middle course between spontaneity and the central, detailed, rigid, and elitist social planning typical of utopian thinkers from Thomas More to Charles Fourier to the bureaucrats of the defunct USSR's *Gosplan*.

Although action theory ought to be either the basis or the culmination of sociotechnology – or perhaps both – it still is in diapers. This immaturity is largely due to philosophical obstacles. One of these is philosophical idealism, which leads most students to focus on the mental processes that precede deliberate action and to neglect the social matrix of individual action. A related cause is individualism, which suggests focusing on isolated actions that attempt to accomplish one result at a time. Given the dismal failure of the idealist, individualist, and sectoral approaches to human action, it is time to work out and try the rationalist, realist, and systemic alternative sketched in section 1.

A rationalist, realist, and systemic praxiologist acts on the strength of sight, insight, and foresight. He also attempts to track down action from sources (internal and external) to design, to performance, to evaluation and review. Moreover, he tries to place all of these stages in their wider social and historical context. One of the offshoots of this approach to action is the realization that "[w]e can never do merely one thing" (Hardin 1982, 58). The reason for this is that one always acts in or upon a system, so that, by altering any of its components, one affects several others, often in unforeseeable ways. However, such a realist and systemic theory of action is yet to be born. (Yet see section 1 for a theory in embryo.)

We conclude with two cautions. First, we are not always required to make decisions. Occasionally we are free not to make decisions. (And yet abstention may have dire consequences: for example, many a hotly contested election is decided by the so-called undecided vote.) Second, sometimes wisdom lies in refraining from taking action. A case in point is the Mackenzie Valley Pipeline Inquiry, conducted in northern Canada between 1974 and 1977 (Berger 1988). A huge consortium had proposed the largest construction project ever to be undertaken by a private concern: a 2600-mile-long pipeline from Alaska to the US Midwest. The Canadian government, though initially eager to approve the project, instituted a commission of inquiry. The commissioners started from the systemic premise that "the proposed natural gas pipeline is not to be considered in isolation" – as the engineers had done. Inspection of the vast fragile ecosystem, as well as interviews with a thousand natives, led the commissioners to recommend (a) against the megaproject and (b) for keeping the aboriginal subsistence economy, the only self-sufficient and sustainable one in that region.

Since in civilized societies every social action matches or breaks some legal norm, it will pay to examine the law before any other sociotechnologies. Let us do it.

8

Law

The law is a means for guaranteeing rights, enforcing duties, resolving conflicts, attaining justice, exercising social control, and conserving or reforming the social order. However, far from being a neutral tool, law has many philosophical and ideological presuppositions (see, for instance, Feinberg and Gross 1991). For example, the old philosophical clash between idealism and materialism appears in legal theory and jurisprudence under the guise of the conflict between conventionalism – in particular legal positivism – and legal realism, or sociological and historical jurisprudence. (For formalism see Kelsen 1945 and Hart 1961; for realism see Pound 1954; Llewellyn 1930; Lundstedt 1956; Stone 1966; and Black 1989.)

Legal formalism views law as a dry book; realism sees it as a throbbing engine. Whereas formalists focus on norms and systems of norms in themselves, legal realists focus on the social function of lawmakers, judges, and lawyers. Whereas formalists regard law as a "pure" and self-contained discipline (yet in the service of the powers that be), legal realists treat it as a branch of science-based social engineering. Their respective slogans are "The law is the law" and "The law is a tool for social control and reform." Unsurprisingly, the formalist is legalistic and conservative, while the realist is flexible and progressive.

Regarded exclusively as a body of ideas, and understood in a broad way, the law *is* a system of norms (in particular laws), metanorms, expert opinions, legal precedents, and debates about permissible, forbidden, and obligatory social behaviour. (For the narrow construal of law as a system of disembodied norms or laws see, for example, Kelsen 1945 or Raz 1970.) However, far from being an isolated field, lawmaking and jurisprudence may be regarded as an emerging branch of technology on a par with management science, and law practice as a service on a par with medical practice and engineering consulting. According to this view, contemporary jurisprudence is a budding sociotechnology, for it seeks justice and social control with the help of some of the knowledge garnered by social studies, particularly social psychology, sociology, economics, political science, and history. (This view should not be mistaken for Kelsen's [1941–2] conception of law as "the specific social technique of the coercive order," or Hart's [1961] as "a set of rules that constrain our actions in everyday life." This view overlooks rights and social ills, and it makes no room for social science. Pound called it "mechanical jurisprudence.")

We shall construe the law as *both* a body of legal precepts and data – though not a self-contained one – and as an institution. In the latter construal the law may be analysed as the family of concrete (by contrast to abstract) legal systems, such as courts of law, every one of which is a sociotechnical system. (Parallel: the institution of the family may be regarded as the collection of all families.) In turn, a concrete legal system may be characterized as a social system composed of people linked by the relations of contract, litigation, observing or breaking the law of the land, arraigning, passing sentence, fining, jailing, and the like (Bunge 1979b). In this sense law is – along with education and organized religion – a device to maintain, repair, or alter the social order from above.

Being a tool for both social control and social engineering, "law in action," in contrast to the corpus of "paper rules," is part of the body politic – even though the courts of law are expected to steer clear of partisan politics. This holds not only for the bulk of law, which in modern society is in the hands of the state, but also for the by-laws that regulate non-governmental organizations. Hence, the law cannot be correctly understood apart from its extralegal context. This is why the sociology, economics, politology, and history of law are just as important as the internalist (analytical) study of legal texts. This explains also why these disciplines have been cultivated since the days of Savigny and Jhering – though never intensely enough. (However, see Black 1984 and the *Law and Society Review.*)

But jurisprudence draws also on philosophy, particularly logic, epistemology, moral philosophy, political philosophy, and, of course, legal philosophy as well. In fact, history shows that, for better or for worse, philosophy has always been a strong pillar of the law. For example, logical consistency is universally regarded as being a necessary condition for any legal code and any legal argument. As well, at the stages of fact-finding, litigation, and sentencing jurists make more or less tacit use of epistemological principles – alas, not always correct ones. For instance, the jury system relies on the view that belief, if strongly held and "beyond the shadow of a doubt," is a more reliable truth indicator than objective evidence. As well, some judges resort to the "intuitive appeal" of certain testimonies, as if intuition had more weight than mere guess. And some criminal codes require the death penalty when "there is a probability that the defendant would commit criminal acts of violence" – as if such "probability" (actually mere intuitive plausibility) could be either measured or calculated. Thus, sometimes freedom or even life hang on epistemologies that would not stand a chance in science, engineering, or management science.

Legal philosophy makes use of logic, and it lies at the intersection of political philosophy and ethics. However, legal philosophers have tended to focus on legal texts detached from legal practice, the social behaviour that such texts are supposed to rule, and social-science research. Such internalist study is interesting and necessary, for it allows the student to examine such conceptual issues as the possible contradictions and gaps in a legal corpus, as well as the moral underpinnings (or lack thereof) of legal principles. Still, because law originates in social issues and discharges social functions, its internalist study should be supplemented with the social study of the rights and duties that the law enforces or violates, as well as with the lawmaking and law-enforcing institutions and, above all, the interactions between law, morality, and politics. The following diagram exhibits the salient relations (causal or informational) among legal and extralegal items.

Figure 8.1 The system of legal knowledge, decision, and action: from lawmaking to sanction

1 Norm and Truth

When concerned with matters of fact, scientific reasoning blends factual truth with logical validity. That is, it combines (possibly) true data with (reasonably) valid inference. (The qualifiers in parentheses take care of the conjectural nature of most factual knowledge, as well as of the shortcuts involved in most arguments, even in mathematics.) Whether valid or fallacious, legal reasoning is apparently more complicated than scientific reasoning, by referring to social facts rather than natural ones, and consequently involving values and norms in addition to factual statements and inferences. And norms, even when couched in the declarative mode, are not so much truths as precepts. Hence, they are not checked against facts in the same way as either empirical data or natural laws. Rather, they are empirically testable in the same way as technological rules, namely by either their efficiency or their compatibility with the ruling morality.

This is not to say that in legal matters the concepts of right and wrong displace those of truth and falsity. Far from it, the very first task of lawyers and judges is "to establish the facts," that is, to find out the relevant truth(s) – as the great Beccaria (1973) emphasized long ago. In particular, witnesses are admonished to tell "the truth, the whole truth, and nothing but the truth," and are warned that perjury is punishable. Veracity, or at least lip-service to it, prevails even in attempts to "cover up" the facts (that is, conceal the truth). This is so because facts and our knowledge of them determine whether or not there is legitimate cause for litigation and, if there is, what legal norms are relevant to the problem.

Because the application of any statute book presupposes that the relevant truths must be established, the judge has the moral duty to admit only scientifically certifiable evidence, such as that provided by ballistic and forensic experts or psychiatrists and social workers. Yet some judges, obviously ignorant of the abyss that separates pseudoscience from science, have admitted or even sought "evidence" supplied by psychics, psychoanalysts, and the like. Thus, in recent years the American courts have heard many "repressed memory" therapists in lawsuits initiated by women against their fathers. The basic idea of such pseudotherapy is Freud's dogma that there is no such thing as forgetting: there would only be repression of painful memories. Thus, if a woman does not remember having been sexually abused by her father in her childhood, this only proves that the abuse did take place. Hence, the analyst's duty is to help the patient retrieve repressed memories, with the help of drugs if necessary – and it is his right to partake of the spoils. (The similarity with witchcraft tests is obvious.) Fortunately, in the early 1990s some of the victims fought back, arguing that most "repressed memories" are just false memories. They got the support of a number of scientific psychologists (notably Loftus 1994), who reminded the courts that memory can be not only incomplete but also creative, when not planted. As a result, the number of lawsuits of that kind has begun to decrease. The legal moral is clear: it is the judge's duty to laugh pseudoscience out of court.

Yet truth can be elusive, not only because appearances can lie but also because we often lie deliberately. In fact, research has established that most of us lie with some frequency, and yet few of us are able to detect when others are lying (Miller and Stiff 1993). In particular, the jurist knows from experience that some of his information about nearly every case is unreliable as well as incomplete. In fact, such information is likely to consist of more or less distorted and mutually inconsistent versions of the facts. Such versions are offered by, or extorted from, individuals – litigants, defendants, witnesses, experts, and law enforcers – who are often incapable of telling, or unwilling to tell, the truth. What is the jurist to do in the face of this uncertainty about the facts of the matter: examine and cross-examine witnesses, trust his flair, rely on plausibility ("probability"), or commission further fact-finding? Let us see.

The unreliability of witnesses is proverbial, and it has been confirmed experimentally by social psychologists. The reason is that perception and memory are limited and creative, as well strongly coloured by interests and emotion. As for cross-examination, sometimes it confuses the honest witness, who may come across as a bad witness. And at other times it gives a crook the chance of putting up a well-rehearsed show.

Should the judge trust his gut feeling, intuition, or insight? This would amount to tossing a coin, for we all know how coarse and undependable intuition is. It can only give the jurist (or anyone else) preliminary clues or conjectures that an intellectually and morally responsible person will refine and put to the test before acting on them (see Bunge 1962). As Schumpeter (1954) said, intuition or insight (which he called 'vision') is a "preanalytic cognitive act that supplies the raw material for the analytic effort."

As for probability, the so-called New Evidence Scholarship, which emerged in the mid-1960s, has revived the eighteenth-century idea of using probability to measure credence, in particular the credibility of evidence. In this connection there is even talk of "trial by mathematics" (see Tillers 1991 and the subsequent papers). I submit that probability hardly belongs in legal arguments, because probability only measures the likelihood of *chance* events, not the plausibility of a piece of evidence, the veracity of a witness, or the likelihood that a court of law will produce the right sentence. Propositions can be more or less plausible or true, but they cannot be attributed probabilities in an objective manner, if only because there are no rules for doing so. In view of this impossibility, talk of probability in law is pseudoscientific.

More precisely, probability theory applies legitimately only to objectively random events that are not within the purview of the law, such as the outcome of rolling dice, shuffling cards (or genes), or drawing random samples from large populations (see du Pasquier 1926; Fréchet 1946; and Bunge 1951, 1985a, and 1988a). And these probabilities are independent of the degree of truth of our statements about them. For example, the truth value of the proposition "The probability that a fair coin tossed randomly will land head up is 0.5" is 1.0. But the proposition itself cannot be assigned a probability, any more that it can be assigned an area or a temperature. In short, propositions are more or less plausible (judged in the light of extant knowledge) and more or less true (in relation to the evidence), not more or less probable. In science and technology it is usual to estimate or measure the error – that is, the departure from the truth – made in quantitative statements. And knowledge of this error allows one to estimate the degree of truth of the proposition in question – never its probability. For example, if someone's age is estimated as 45 years, when he is actually 50, the relative error is 5 in 50, that is, 0.1. Ergo, the truth value of the proposition "She is 45 years old" is $1 - 0.1 = 0.9$.

The law does not deal with chance events. In particular, any crime of either commission or omission is ultimately a result of deliberate choice – which, in the case of negligence, is that of refraining from taking action when action is due. There is nothing objectively random about facts in legal matters. Only our knowledge of such facts is more or less short of completeness and truth, hence somewhat uncertain. Chance (or randomness) implies uncertainty about the individual case, but the converse is false. Judges and attorneys wishing to proceed scientifically when dealing with uncertainty should therefore abstain from playing with the unscientific concept of the probability of a testimony or of a juror's being correct. In particular, they need not bother with Condorcet's famous Jury Theorem, according to which the probability of the competence of a jury increases with its size. A jury of incompetent or biased people, or one of competent and fair people supplied with incomplete, ambiguous, or false evidence, is likely to reach an incorrect verdict regardless of its size. How likely? There is no way of knowing beforehand: probability theory can only help handle chance events, and crime is not one of them.

Talk of the probability of conviction of crimes of a certain kind by a given court of law is unwarranted: we can only talk about the rate (or relative frequency) of conviction. One reason for this is that the conviction process is – let us hope – anything but random. Instead, it is supposed to be the outcome of a rational debate involving legal principles, empirical evidence, and sometimes bargaining as well. A second reason is that probabilities can sometimes be approximated or estimated by long-run relative frequencies, but the latter do not imply the former. (Think of the frequency of departure of Japanese trains, famous for their punctuality: it warrants no probability. In short, probability implies frequency, but the converse is false.)

Since neither intuition nor probability can help, what then is a court of law to do when the body of evidence is scant, ambiguous, or contradictory. Obviously, it should perform or commission further inquiries. But, since most officers of the law have no scientific training, the court may have to resort to outside experts. But the Anglo-American legal system – unlike others – does not allow such independent inquiry: the judges are forced to rely only on the evidence that the litigants see fit to present. They are thus driven to getting their job done even if the knowledge at their disposal is insufficient to do a good job.

At any rate, in every society observing the rule of law, the legal system presupposes the possibility of finding out the truth of the matter, even if it is only partial and fallible. That is, the law assumes *epistemological realism*. (Legal pragmatists disagree: see Posner 1990.) By contrast, what matters to a kangaroo court is not truth but whether or not the accused might pose a (real or imaginary) threat to the powers that be. Such courts "construct" (invent) crime instead of reconstructing it: they unwittingly abide by a constructivist-relativist epistemology (see chap. 5, sect. 4).

Where constructivism-relativism does hold to some extent is in the lawmaking process, because the latter concerns social facts not natural ones, and the former belong in the made world. Thus, whereas death is a natural event, murder is a social fact: it exists only by virtue of certain moral or criminal codes. In other words, these facts are relative to the legal system, which depends on place and time, whereas natural facts are absolute (context-free). Still, this does not fully vindicate constructivism-relativism, because the natural fact underlying a social fact – for instance, the wound that caused death – must be established objectively in the first place rather than made up. For example, the mass murders occurring in a war are objective even though war is yet to be outlawed.

A *norm* or rule, whether legal, moral, or technological, is a prescription for action. Typically, the form of a norm is "To attain goal of type G in circumstances of type C, perform action(s) of type A." Even a legal norm that is never actually observed can prompt people to act. For example, Latin Americans have sometimes invoked some of the noble principles enshrined in their constitutions as a legal excuse for revolting against oppression. This virtue of good norms that fail to match facts contrasts with false propositions, which at best are harmless. However, both are cases of idea-fact mismatch.

A norm can be spontaneous or designed, and in either case it can be either arbitrary or well grounded. We stipulate that a *well-grounded norm* is one based upon both (natural or social) laws and value judgments. For example, the norm "Never put your opponent in a corner" can be justified as follows: (a) cornered individuals are prone to reacting violently (psychological law); and (b) violence is bad (value judgment). Likewise, the injunction to oppose capital punishment is based on (a) "Capital punishment has no deterrence effect" (social law); and

(b) "Murder of any kind is evil" (value judgment). Ideally, all legal norms ought to be just as well grounded on scientific knowledge as the best environmental, safety, and health standards. (Kelsen [1945, 113] explicitly rejects this idea, and states that "Legal norms may have any kind of content.")

In addition to norms there are metanorms, in jurisprudence as well as in ethics. A *metanorm* (or metarule) is a norm that regulates the construction or application of norms of some kind. For example, Kant's universalizability metanorm (the Categorical Imperative, often mistaken for the Golden Rule) enjoins us to adopt only rules of conduct applicable to all human beings. And the legal principle that whatever is not explicitly forbidden is permitted is a metalaw in all law-ruled societies. Of particular sociological interest are the rules for changing rules. They occur in all democratic constitutions.

The way well-grounded rules are derived fits no deductive inference rule: the inference is praxiological rather than logical, for it bears on actions, not propositions. We postulate the following two basic *praxiological inference patterns* (Bunge 1989a, 301):

	Modus volens
Law	If A (is the case, or is done), then B (results).
Value judgment	B is good (or right) and, on balance, better (or more right) than A.
Norm	: : A is good (or right) [that is, A ought to be (the case, or done)].

	Modus nolens
Law	If A (is the case, or is done), then B (results).
Value judgment	B is bad (or wrong).
Norm	: : A is bad (or wrong) [that is, A ought to be avoided or refrained from],

where A and B name facts and ': :' stands for the relation of normative entailment – a relation partially defined implicitly by the above praxiological inference patterns.

This approach to the construction of well-grounded norms is at variance with the standard view that *all* practical inference differs from theoretical argument only by the content of premises and conclusions (see, for instance, Raz 1978). The reasons for our departure from orthodoxy are that, in moral and legal matters, values are pivotal and the bearers of value are actions, not propositions. Our unorthodox approach has the following features. First, it exhibits explicitly the grounds for adopting or rejecting norms – something rationalists as well as empiricists should welcome. Second, it validates uncounted inferences that we make in everyday life, and which are not covered by ordinary logic. Third, it bridges the fact-value and is-ought gaps, for it combines laws with value judgments to produce norms. Fourth, it strengthens the bonds between the normative disciplines – in particular ethics and the law – and value theory. Fifth, it makes no use of deontic logic, which has become a *cul de sac* (Weinberger 1985) and is anyway irrelevant to the law. (The two main principles of deontic logic are "If A is obligatory, then A is permissible" and "If A is not obligatory, then not-A is permissible." By contrast, the basic norms in the existing legal corpora are of either of these forms: "A is punishable by B," "If C [is the case], then D is permissible," and "If E, then F is obligatory." Moreover, whereas the latter concern actions, in standard deontic logic the operators "may" and "ought" are oddly assumed to act on propositions or sentences – an interpretation that might interest only censors. Only a normative-action theory, in which "permissible" and "obligatory" act on actions, could be a genuine theory of permissions and obligations.)

The status of norms and normative systems has been endlessly debated in legal philosophy as well as in meta-ethics (see, for instance, Kelsen 1945; Ross 1968; Raz 1970; and Alchourrón and Bulygin 1971). According to the received view a norm is logically, epistemologically, and ontologically different from a factual statement such as "The cat is on the mat." Indeed, norms are said to be imperatives of the form "Thou shalt do A!" or just "Do A!" rather than declaratives such as "You are (or you will be) doing A." Hence, norms are supposed to have a logic of their own, which would differ from ordinary logic. However, a look at any legal code suffices to raise serious doubts about this view. Thus, a common pattern of the legal precepts occurring in US codes is this: "Whoever does X shall be fined not more than $Y or imprisoned not more than Z years, or both." Surely this statement form is equivalent to the conditional "If a person does X, he will be subjected to penalties Y or Z [inclusive 'or']." And of course this pattern fits ordinary logic. This allows lawyers and judges to argue coherently without waiting for philosophers to come up with a cogent system of deontic logic – which has eluded their efforts for half a century anyway.

2 Law and Morality

The law is about justice, which can be retributive (corrective) or distributive (social). Now, these are primarily moral concepts, as they concern rights and wrongs, hence goods and bads. In particular, legal obligations should be binding only if they enshrine moral duties. Consequently, law overlaps partially with ethics. (This assertion is sometimes called "legal moralism.") In other words, whereas some legal norms specify (are applications of) certain moral principles, others violate them. Moreover, different moral philosophies underpin different legal systems. Thus, deontologism – a duties-only doctrine – is bound to inspire harsh laws. By contrast, utilitarianism, centred as it is on the "pursuit of happiness," is bound to inspire a legal system that minimizes duties. The alternative to both is agathonism, according to which every right implies a duty and conversely (Bunge 1989a).

Lawyers and judges face and solve moral problems all the time, because every legal code is about rights and wrongs, benefits and burdens, equities and inequities, fairness and unfairness, all of which can be evaluated in moral terms as well as in legal and prudential ones. Moreover, every body of law contains or presupposes certain general principles that are at once moral and legal, such as "Only moral agents can stand trial," "No crime without law, no punishment without crime," and "The burden of proving the defendant's guilt rests upon the prosecution." In short, morality and the law overlap in part. (The legal positivists, such as Kelsen and Hart, disagree: they conceive of the law as a morally neutral political instrument laying down legal obligations rather than defending rights or entrenching moral duties.) Consequently the corresponding philosophies – legal philosophy and moral philosophy – have a non-empty intersection too. I call this overlap *nomo-ethics*, and proceed to sketching it. (More in Bunge 1989a.)

A first problem in nomo-ethics is to ascertain whether the law includes morality or conversely, or else whether they overlap partially. The former view would be that of a consistent contractualist: if such a person existed, he would hold that ethics is a branch of contract law. This view is factually and morally wrong: the former, because some laws are inconsistent with certain moral principles; the latter, for subordinating morality to whatever special interests may be entrenched into the law. Furthermore, contractualism is at variance with two important and notorious facts. One is that fair deals are possible only among equals: under inequality the stronger can dictate their own conditions. The other fact is that not even equality before the law (isonomy) is practically possible where economic and political power are unevenly distributed. Moreover, boasting about legal equality may mask social inequalities. (As Anatole France said, the law, in its infinite wisdom, gave both poor and rich the right to sleep under the bridges.)

The converse view, that law is or ought to be included in morals, is indefensible too. Indeed, whereas a legal code may boil down to a set of prohibitions and sanctions, a moral code may lend support to the pursuit of welfare and justice, and it may encourage people to perform supererogatory actions, as well as to refrain from committing moral faults. In conclusion, law neither includes morality nor is included in. But the two do overlap partially. Moreover, every bill (or charter) of rights belongs in the intersection of the two.

I submit that, in addition to sharing some common ground, law and morals ought to interact vigorously, whence their respective philosophies too should interact. As a matter of fact the two fields have always interacted. Indeed, many a piece of legislation has been proposed or repealed on moral grounds, and some moral codes have been refined in the light of jurisprudence. (Suffice it to think of the abolition of slavery, child labour, and capital punishment.) Moreover, such interaction is beneficial, for it gives lawmakers the chance to act as moral reformers, and the latter a say in law reform. This results in the moralization of the political process and the institutionalization of morals, while keeping both evolving together with society.

An early example of such interaction was the reform of criminal law and incarceration conditions in the light of Bentham's social utilitarianism. Recent examples are the current public debates over welfare programs, abortion, homosexuality, the financing of political parties, environmental protection, and state terrorism. Every one of these debates originates in a mismatch between a legal norm and its moral counterpart. And some of them have shown that legal and political philosophy often lag behind jurisprudence. For example, few theorists dare challenge the principle of equality before the law; yet many a piece of legislation is rooted in the diversity of needs among individuals (e.g., children and adults) or groups (e.g., aboriginals). Moreover, the entire affirmative-action legislation aims at giving a chance to groups that have been discriminated against. Whether it has significantly decreased social inequalities is another matter.

Still, since there is no universally accepted moral code, not all moral considerations are compelling. Consider religious blasphemy and pornography. Both are condemned by authoritarians but tolerated by liberals. No doubt, both offend certain groups, but neither harms anyone – unlike hate literature, which incites the persecution or even extermination of ethnic, political, or cultural groups. By contrast, whereas there is empirical evidence that religious criticism promotes religious tolerance, there is none that pornography is a source of violence against women. Since the law is supposed to protect from harm, not from offence, hate literature should be banned whereas religious blasphemy and pornography should be tolerated. Moreover, all attempts to censor either should be resisted, because what bigots regard as heinous attacks upon religion may only be rational criticisms; and what they take to be pornography may be only art, or material discussing sexuality or birth control. In short, the rule should be: Outlaw what threatens or harms, not what offends; leave offence to rational debate.

Lastly, a word on the codes of moral conduct of the legal profession. Apparently they are all similar except with regard to the lawyer's duties to client and society. In the Anglo-American tradition the lawyer's main obligation is to his client, whereas in the European tradition his main duty is to society. This is but one instance of the individualism-holism conflict. A systemist would advocate a synthesis: Lawyers have the duty to defend their clients within the limits of just laws, and the duty to challenge unjust verdicts and laws.

3 Legal Code and Legal Theory

A body of law, such as a civil code, is a system of factual statements couched in the declarative mode and concerning social facts that, at first sight, are covered by the law. Most of these statements are conditionals of the form "If X does Y, then X is liable to sanction Z." Value judgments and norms are conspicuous by their absence in the codes ruling social behaviour under the rule of law. However, as we saw in the preceding section, legal codes are supported or undermined by custom and morality.

No legal code suffices to handle any legal case. To study any particular case, a jurist needs also (a) a body of empirical data concerning the facts to be legally evaluated; (b) the corresponding jurisprudence (a body of legal precedents and opinions relevant to the case); and (c) a legal theory facilitating the "interpretation" (gap-filling) of the legal corpus – in particular, helping to evaluate the "sizes" of the offence and of the corresponding sanction. The role of legal theory is also paramount in the process of introducing, reforming, or repealing legislation.

A *legal theory* is a hypothetico-deductive system of statements of two kinds: factual and valuational. For example, a statement of the form "All criminal actions are punishable by law" is factual. By contrast, a statement of the form "All acts of kind C are criminal" is a covert value judgment and more particularly a moral one. Not surprisingly, alternative legal codes are inspired in, or justified a posteriori by, different legal theories that presuppose different value systems and moralities differing from one another in some respect or other. For example, individualist legal theorists emphasize rights, whereas their collectivist counterparts emphasize collective duties. Again, whereas some theories favour selfish behaviour others extol altruism; and, whereas some legal theories only admit duly checked direct evidence, others admit circumstantial evidence, confession, or even mere accusation. Correspondingly, there are alternative legal philosophies.

One such legal philosophy is legal positivism – a kind of formalism – according to which all values are relative, whence right is might and, accordingly, justice equals the law of the land (see, for instance, Kelsen 1945 and Hart 1961). Seen in this light, the very idea of an unjust law is self-contradictory, and any effort to introduce or abrogate any piece of legislation in the name of justice would be preposterous and subversive. Not surprisingly, totalitarians – both left and right – have favoured legal positivism. However, since legal positivists stress blind obedience to the state at the expense of civil rights, actually their discourse is neither value-free nor morally neutral: it is committed to the powers that be.

It should be obvious that the law does not hover above political power, if only because it is a tool of the latter. What is far from clear is which came first in history. According to the vulgar materialist legal philosophy, custom is prior to law, which only enshrines the former. For example, all property rights were preceded by property; hence, wherever there is no private property there are no property rights, and consequently no violations of the same. But an idealist legal philosopher could exhibit exceptions, such as the laws restricting property rights: they had to be passed before being enforceable. So who is right? Obviously each of the two views has a grain of truth. Maybe the full truth is that sometimes custom is legalized and at other times laws induce new customs – and, when they don't, they are impotent. (More on law's impotence in sect. 7.)

So far we have discussed legal codes as if they were self-existing. This fiction is useful for the logical examination of codes. But if we wish to find out the social function of a legal code we must relate it to the concrete legal system of the society where it is supposed to be observed, infringed, or discussed. From a sociological viewpoint the legal system of a society is the subsystem of it composed of people whose specific function is to enforce, bypass, or violate the legal codes. That is, a concrete legal system (unlike a body of legal norms) is composed of judges, clerks and jurors, litigants and witnesses, defendants and suspects, attorneys and experts, policemen and prison wardens, and so on. Obviously, the legal system lies at the intersection of the culture and the polity of any civilized society. Seen in this systemic light, a body of law – including the constitution and the attendant jurisprudence – constitute a manual for operating and repairing the legal system and thus, to some extent, society at large.

Up to now all legal systems have grown with little or no assistance from social-science studies. For instance, the jury system has been in existence in the Anglo-American legal tradition without much empirical information about (a) the way juries reach their verdicts (since their deliberations are expected to be secret) or (b) the fairness and efficiency of juries, which are increasingly expected to be representative samples of the community rather than impartial deliberative teams. Recent empirical work with covert recordings and mock jury experiments (MacCoun 1989) have supplied a first answer to question (a). By contrast, question (b) is still open – in fact it is hardly ever raised. Which goes to show that the law is still far from being scientifically mature.

4 Legal Reasoning

Legal reasoning seems to have been the earliest example of conceptual rationality. (Moreover, I guess that formal logic was an offspring of legal reasoning and political democracy in the first society to recognize freedom of speech and litigation, namely the ancient Greek city-states.) Although there has been much talk about legal logic, actually legal reasoning does not differ formally from scientific or technological argument. In fact, it boils down to the deduction of consequences (e.g., verdicts) from generalities (laws, moral maxims, and procedural norms) and data (concerning, for example, precedents and criminal actions). Consequently, any application of a positive law obeys the same logic as an application of a scientific law to explain or predict a fact. That is, in both cases the inference pattern is: Generalization(s) & Evidence about fact(s) ∴ Conclusion.

True, much has been made of the need to "interpret" the law. But, being somewhat subjective, legal "interpretation" can generate injustice and corruption (Beccaria 1973 sect. IV). What is true is that supreme courts and judges are often obliged to fill gaps in the existing codes of law. But, since such actions usurp a function of the legislator, they should ultimately be subject to revision by a legislature. An ideal law is so clearly formulated and detailed that it requires no "interpretation": *clara non sunt interpretanda*.

In a court of law only the facts of the matter, as represented by the total available evidence, should be the subject of scrutiny and debate. However, all laws are necessarily sketchy, and some of the relevant facts are extralegal: they constitute the aggravating or extenuating circumstances that jurists and jurors must establish and weigh. Hence the need for legal "interpretation" – a matter of gap-filling, not of hermeneutics.

What is peculiar to legal reasoning is not the form but the *content* of its premises and conclusions. In fact, these contain concepts that occur nowhere else, such as those of (positive) law, contract, justice, equity, proxy, crime, criminal negligence, attenuating circumstance, legal case, litigation, prosecution, defence, defendant, legal code, court of law, fine, penalty, sentencing, and appeal. Moreover, unlike the technological statements, those occurring in any legal code are subordinated to higher-level principles of at least six different kinds: (a) high-level legal principles such as "No crime without a law"; (b) meta-law principles such as "No law with retroactive effect is valid"; (c) constitutional precepts specifying basic rights and duties; (d) value judgments such as "Premeditated murder is the worse crime"; (e) moral maxims such as *"Lex iniusta non est lex"*; and (f) ideological principles such as "Property rights can be infringed upon only in the public interest." These principles combine with data as shown in figure 8.2, following.

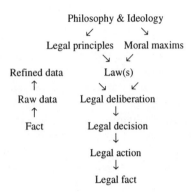

Figure 8.2 The process of legal deliberation, decision, and action

The reasoning leading to a legal decision (right-hand side of the above tree) is then strictly *deductive*. This holds in both Roman law and common law, even though the latter is usually said to be inductive. This appearance is deceptive. Indeed, when an Anglo-American court of law makes a decision on the basis of a precedent of the form "X vs. Y, year Z," it presupposes that the paragon case was one where certain more or less tacit general principles had been well applied. Thus, common law may may be said to be *cryptodeductivist*. This is not to deny the differences between the two schools. Roman law is logically superior to common law in being the simpler of the two, and in that its principles are clearly in evidence. By contrast, common law is empirically superior to Roman law in paying far more attention to experience, and in allowing the courts to break new ground – which may originate interesting conflicts with parliament. A sound explicit synthesis of the two legal styles is yet to be formulated.

Just as in science, technology, and the humanities, the source of any legal process and the concomitant legal reasoning is some problem. In turn, a legal problem consists either in a contrast between fact and law or in a conflict between two or more laws – just as in science. (Actually, not facts but only descriptions of facts, that is, data, can conflict with legal principles, because statements can only be confronted with one another.) The initial or raw data supplied by litigants or officers of the law are subjected to scrutiny in the light of the law. Such scrutiny is likely to alter the raw data, sometimes to the point of denying them – just as in the case of science. The legal decision-making process is a (logically valid or invalid) argument that, in turn, is an object of critical examination. For example, a judicial verdict may be challenged either in the name of some higher-level legal or moral principle, or in that of a mere procedural rule. Notice the similarity with the evaluation of a scientific or technological argument.

So much for the similarities between legal and scientific reasonings. The dissimilarities concern not only the occurrence of moral and ideological principles, but also the strength of evidence and the practical consequences of the conclusion of a legal argument. The burden of proof is usually much lighter in the legal case than in the scientific one, even though it is easier to correct scientific errors than judicial ones. As for the consequences of a legal verdict, they are likely to affect the lives of the people whose behaviour is being judged. For example, a legal decision may consist in a prison sentence; and the resulting legal action (incarceration) turns a free person into a prison inmate (social fact). This outcome is unlike the final result of a scientific reasoning, but similar to a technological reasoning that results in the manufacture of an artefact whose use alters people's lives.

5 Private and Public

Private equals personal, and public equals shared. The private sphere is of course the domain of action that does not affect others. It is tacitly characterized by Mill's (1859) "simple principle" that the only legitimate exercise of power over any individual, against his will, is to prevent harm to others. And the public sphere is the domain of social (prosocial or antisocial) actions.

Nowhere is the dependence of the law upon politics more evident than in the private-public distinction. Under dictatorship whatever is not prescribed is proscribed, whereas under democracy whatever is not forbidden is permitted. Under dictatorship there is no private sphere. In a democratic society it is "protected": free from legislation, surveillance, and interference by law-enforcing agencies.

However, far from being mutually disjoint, the two "spheres" overlap partially. This is so because even privately a person may engage in actions that affect others. For example, smoking and taking narcotics, and even overeating or overdrinking, are not strictly private actions wherever health-care costs are borne at least partly by others, for instance, relatives or taxpayers. Refusing to follow a treatment prescribed for an infectious disease is to engage in antisocial behaviour and thus to invite coercion. And a business firm, whether it be a corporation or a cooperative, is private with respect to ownership and management, but public with regard to its impact upon society. It is public in so far as it affects the lives of individuals through buying or selling, as well as through using up natural resources and public goods, polluting, and so forth. Even the most secret society is public to the extent that it intends to benefit society or take advantage of it.

An even more controversial subject is the partial overlap between the private and the public sectors of the economy. The former supplies goods and services to the public sector, and in turn the state constrains some private activities while supporting others. Actually, the modern state does much more than this: in most cases it also supplies and keeps up, or at least controls, the material infrastructure (water and sewage works, roads, bridges, etc.), the quality of food and drugs, transportation safety, and the public education and health-care systems, without which no modern civilization could function.

There is consensus that the specific function of government is to render public service, that is, to organize and manage public goods. It follows that the government has no business meddling in private matters. But it does not follow clearly that the government has no business running businesses of the public kind, such as the mail, communications, road maintenance, health care, or education. Yet, although such enterprises serve the public, they need not be owned and operated by the state. It was suggested earlier (chap. 9, sect. 4) that this problem should be approached pragmatically rather than in a doctrinaire fashion. I submit this rule: "If either the state or a private company renders a given service in an efficient and affordable way, do not innovate. Intervention is called for only if the public service in question is inefficient, unaffordable, or both." Yet even in the latter case nationalization is not the only or even the best possible solution. Alternative solutions are possible, such as regulation of the private sector and cooperative ownership and management – as will be argued in chapter 9, section 5.

Even the market is a public institution, not only in that (in principle) it is open to everyone with the means to participate in it, but also legally. Indeed, market operations are protected and at the same time constrained by laws and regulations designed to guarantee fair play and to prevent private interests from prevailing over the public interest. For example, a customer who has been sold an adulterated product can resort to litigation. Whether he will get satisfaction depends on his clout as well as on the legal system. (More in sect. 7.)

Free-marketers claim that the market should be subjected to no regulations at all, for these restrict liberty. However, if their views were to prevail, many a market would eventually crash for lack of either restraint or support. The realistic options are not freedom and serfdom, but efficient and fair regulations on the one hand and their opposites on the other. "On questions of economic regulation, the contest almost invariably will be, not between freedom and restriction, but between freedom and freedom. The issue will be whose freedom and which freedom should be protected or curtailed in which situation" (Borovoy 1988, 159). Such conflicts among rights are, along with conflicts between rights and duties, a major and unending source of conflict, litigation, legal argument, and moral debate – the more explicit and clear the better.

6 Rights and Duties

Legal and moral problems concern conflicts between rights, between duties, or between rights and the correlative obligations. Now, rights and duties may be legal or moral. Given that humans are largely artefactual, and that societies are changeable, the expressions 'natural law' and 'natural right' are oxymorons. By contrast, the concepts of moral and legal rights are clear-cut, for the former are specified by moral codes, and the latter by legal codes. Now, every such pair of codes holds in some society or other, seldom in all societies. This is why radical relativists hold that all codes are equivalent: that no legal or moral code is superior to any other, whence there can be no legal or moral progress. Radical relativists are thus legal and moral positivists: they wittingly or unwittingly subscribe to the maxims "Might is right" (Hegel) and "The law is the law" (Radbruch).

To be sure, for better or worse might does make (legal) right. But it is up to us to fashion political might so that only what is morally right gets enshrined in the law. This is not the view of legal positivism, which is relativist because it questions no powers, however unjust or despotic. I submit instead that there are some basic cross-cultural human rights and duties – such as the right to life and the duty to be useful – and that the best legal codes are those that entrench such basic rights and duties. I shall argue for this view by placing the discussion in the wider context of the relation between individual and society.

In the matter or rights and duties, as in every other aspect of social life, we face the individualism-holism-systemism trilemma. (See Bunge 1996a.) Individualists claim that individual rights are sacred and stand above the public interest, whereas holists maintain that individual rights must be subordinated to (what they call) the general (or higher) interest. Ironically, both views have been used to condone exploitation and oppression. The systemist offers the following alternative. Any conflict between the right of an individual and the public interest indicates that at least one of them is being ill conceived or wrongly practised. A legal right will be at fault if it involves harming others, as with the alleged rights to reproduce without restraint, own handguns, or hoard food during famines. And the public interest is not such if it infringes upon basic rights, as are the cases with the alleged rights of the state to draft soldiers and repress dissent. When any such conflict occurs, it should be debated democratically with a view to reforming the pertinent law(s).

Ultimately rights and duties are about interests. Hence, moral and legal issues arise ultimately from conflicts of interests. Now, interests can be morally or legally legitimate or illegitimate. I shall propose a few principles that presuppose the distinction between needs and wants (or desires). But first we must define these concepts. A *basic need* is a need that must be met to survive in good health and in good social standing. A *want* is a desire that may or may not match a basic need. Hence, wants may be legitimate or illegitimate. In particular, a *legitimate want* is one whose satisfaction does not jeopardize anyone else's ability to meet their own basic needs – though it may frustrate wants. So much for definitions. (Methodological remark: Basic needs – e.g., in nutrition, health, and security – are objective, whence they can be found out without resorting to questionnaires. By contrast, wants or desires are subjective, whence they can be discovered only by questioning or observation. True, wants can be manipulated to the point of being "perceived" as needs. But the point is that scientists are expected to tell needs from wishes, just as they are expected to distinguish survival from happiness.)

As for principles, here is our heptalogue. 1/ A moral right is the ability to meet a basic need or a legitimate want. 2/ A requirable moral duty is an obligation to help someone else exercise his legitimate moral rights. 3/ Every moral right implies a moral duty. 4/ A moral norm is justified if and only if it supports either basic needs or legitimate wants, or requirable moral duties. 5/ The supreme moral principle is *Enjoy life and help live*. 6/ A legal norm is morally justified if and only if is consistent with the corresponding moral precept(s). 7/ In case of conflict between moral and legal norms, the former ought to take precedence over the latter. (More in Bunge 1989a.)

Let us see how these principles apply to property rights, which have given rise to one of the most hotly debated topics in legal philosophy. Property rights originated in surplus or in scarcity, and were secured by force. But the concepts of private ownership and property right are legal categories, and they raise a number of problems of various kinds. Only the following problems in legal philosophy will be touched on here. Is private property a natural (or, as we say nowadays, a human) right? If so, are property rights boundless, as prescribed by Roman law (the *ius utendi et abutendi*), or should they be limited? If there ought to be limits, which human rights or duties set them? In particular, is private monopoly on means of production and communication compatible with political democracy? This system of problems lies at the intersection of ethics, ideology, law, and politics. In fact, it is at the very core of the disputes over public goods, state intervention, liberalism, and socialism.

The answer to the above problem system depends on both the kind of property and the moral code in question. Property for personal use, such as homes, clothes, and domestic artefacts, is not in question. Nor are public goods such as streets and courts of law. What are in question are the means of production and communication, such as land, energy sources, mineral deposits, heavy machinery, TV networks, and information. But even here opinion is divided. Thus, many thinkers above the suspicion of socialism, such as John Locke, Henry George, and Herbert Spencer, held that, because there is only so much land, it should be public property. Others have given a similar reason for advocating the public ownership of all energy sources and non-renewable resources. Likewise, in the nineteenth century the Brazilian planters favoured the abolition of slavery when the upkeep of slaves became too expensive compared with the seasonal hiring of free hands. However, these are practical reasons rather than moral ones. Philosophers must ask what if any are the morals behind or against property rights.

The pro-property theorists point out that any limitation on property rights is a limitation on liberty. This was in fact the main argument of the anti-abolitionists: they denounced the emancipation of slaves as a violation of property rights. Obviously they were right. But, because rights form a system, the exercise of any one right may limit or even block that of some other right, perhaps a more basic one, such as that of owning oneself. The moral and legal problem is this: Which of the rights and duties in a given conflict are overriding?

The unfairness of the right to own people has been clear for over a century: one can enjoy the freedom to own slaves only at the price of depriving them of most of their own human rights. The case of land ownership is similar for a different reason: ever since land became scarce, when it is owned privately the great majority of people are deprived of it. Besides, the value of a piece of land increases automatically through the work of all those who live and toil in and around it. In short, the case of land ownership is one of conflict between an individual's property rights and the ownership rights of several others.

There seems to be only one fair and practical alternative to the private ownership of land, namely state ownership – though without state management. The state (at the appropriate level) could lease land to whoever – individual, business firm, or cooperative – can work it best to the benefit of everyone, posterity included. The case of other natural resources, such as mines, oil deposits, waterfalls, forests, and fisheries, is similar. Contrary to what mainstream economists claim, there is only so much of these resources, and what there is does not suffice to be distributed equitably among six billion people. Hence, those resources should be owned collectively and managed rationally in the interests of all. If natural resources were to be declared public property, the state should see to it that their managers – individuals, business firms, or cooperatives – act as competent and accountable stewards or trustees.

The above suggests formulating the following general principle: "Anybody can own or use anything as long as, in doing so, he does not deprive others of its use (or that of something similar), harm anyone, or restrict anyone else's basic (human) rights." This maxim combines private interests with the public good. It may be called the *principle of restricted property rights*. It is just a special case of the moral principle of bounded rights, according to which my rights end where yours start.

In short, "there is no natural property" (Bentham). That is, private ownership is a social invention, not a basic (or human) right. This is why it is not included in either the American Constitution or the Canadian Charter of Rights. A consequence of this view for the law is that there is a chasm between economic crimes and all others, in particular (individual or mass) murder. Like inequality, private ownership is a privilege to be granted only when it benefits the overwhelming majority of people. An additional argument for limiting economic freedom is this: private property is an endless source of division and strife, as well as a powerful motivation for dishonesty and violence on all scales. Last, but not least, great wealth threatens political democracy, for it can buy power (see Dahl 1985).

However, the substitution of public (or state) property for private property fails to solve all the above-mentioned problems, for it only shifts economic power from owners and shareholders to politicians and civil servants. A better solution consists in extending the property rights from a small minority to the entire working population. That is, the ticket is cooperative ownership of the means of production. This solution involves democracy in the workplace and it does not jeopardize political democracy (see chap. 9, sect. 8).

7 Crime and Punishment

A criminal action may be defined as an action that, either deliberately or out of negligence, causes harm, violates basic rights, or hinders the discharging of basic duties. This definition excludes suicide but it includes child abuse and neglect, economic exploitation, financial speculation to the detriment of the public, political oppression, war-mongering, hate propaganda, and terrorism (by either political groups or governments).

The traditional criminal codes knew only of such crimes as theft, the causing of physical harm (in particular small-scale murder), sedition, or slander. Nowadays an increasing number of people are prepared to impose sanctions against social crimes such as deliberate environmental degradation, the incitement to racial hatred and sex discrimination, the fanning of religious intolerance, and above all war-mongering and military aggression.

In line with our world-view, we propose the following typology of crimes:

environmental (e.g., large-scale pollution and deforestation); *biological or psychological* (e.g., murder, torture, child abuse, and slander); *economic* (e.g., theft, exploitation, and destruction of public property); *political* (e.g., political persecution and abuse of power); and *cultural* (e.g., the deliberate propagation of lies and the destruction of cultural associations). These basic kinds can combine with one another, as in murder with theft. Modern or total warfare combines all five kinds of crime and is thus the total crime.

The traditional view is that all crime must be punished, and that all punishment should be "commensurate" with, or "proportional" to, the enormity of the crime. Thus, there are many degrees of punishment, ranging from admonition to fine, and from incarceration to death. This doctrine is conceptually fuzzy, revolving around such vague concepts as those of "degree" of a crime and of punishment "commensurate" with it. It is also aprioristic in making no use of observation, experiment, or statistics concerning the deterrent effect and cost of punishment. The question whether punishment works is an empirical one. What if punishment turned out to be ineffective or even counterproductive, as some behaviourists (e.g., Skinner 1938), exchange theorists (e.g., Homans 1974), and rational-choice theorists (e.g., Tsebelis 1990) have held? Let us peek at the evidence.

Ethologists have shown that social animals use punishment not only to establish or maintain dominance, but also to discourage parasites and cheats, and to enforce cooperation (Clutton-Brock and Parker 1995). Some experiments on humans suggest that, when properly administered, punishment is just as effective as reward (see, for instance, Molm 1994). And an increasing body of empirical evidence suggests that the expectation of informal sanction (e.g., by family or community) has a more potent deterrence effect than perceived formal sanction. In any case, some social control is necessary to counter antisocial behaviour. The problem is to devise techniques of social control that are effective yet humane and morally acceptable, and do not endanger civil liberties.

Now, the traditional stick-and-rope doctrine is morally as well as epistemically flawed in overlooking the social roots of criminality, such as anomie, unemployment, ignorance, growing up in a poor neighbourhood infested with criminals, and a tradition of violence (see Clark 1971). Since criminality is to a large extent a result of such social conditions, our main efforts should be directed to crime prevention rather than crime repression. (The parallel with health care is obvious.) In turn, crime prevention amounts to designing and implementing social reforms rendering crime unnecessary and unrewarding. Such reforms, successfully pioneered by Sweden, are currently unthinkable in the US owing to the popular misperception of the "crime wave" and to the fact that jails have become big business.

The most blatant case of impracticality joined to immorality is the death penalty – all the more so since it does not apply to large-scale murder, that is, war or state terrorism. Statistics show that the deterrence effect of the death penalty is nil or even negative. (Mechanism: where murder is punishable by death, witnesses run the risk of being eliminated.) And its immorality should be obvious to anyone who agrees that two wrongs do not make a right. It is for such prudential and moral reasons that the death penalty has been eliminated in nearly all civilized nations. In the US, belief in the morality and efficacy of capital punishment is a popular article of faith defended by the Supreme Court, according to which the death penalty "is not a cruel and unusual punishment" [*sic*]. Its promotion by some politicians is a reminder that law is not politically neutral, and that morality is the first casualty in the struggle for power.

The "economic imperialists," whom we first met in chapter 2, take what at first sight looks like a more humane and practical stand: they favour fines and taxes. But in practice an economicist criminal law could be enforced only on those who can afford paying fines or taxes. And for such people it might be economically profitable to buy the right to harm. Besides, the proposal rests on the false and wrong assumption that all harms can be priced. This is obviously wrong of crimes with irreversible effects, such as murder and the destruction of non-renewable natural or cultural resources. The so-called green taxes and fines, or monetary penalties exacted for environmental harm, constitute a case in point. First, some environmental crimes, such as dumping toxic waste and clearing tropical forests, are irreversible. Second, some managers are willing to pay fines or taxes as long as they are allowed to go on looting nature or polluting.

The liberal view on crime, pioneered by Beccaria in 1764, opposes both the traditional legal school and "economic imperialism." It holds that emphasis should be shifted from punishment to prevention and rehabilitation. If a crime is committed despite preventive measures, the offender should be re-educated and forced to do socially useful labour. This view is morally and practically enlightened in reducing criminality as well as the staggering costs of keeping up a huge and obsolete law-enforcement system. By contrast, the sporadic "wars" on crime and drugs, favoured by demagogues who choose to ignore sociology and criminology, have been ineffective or worse. In particular the United States, which spends more on jails than on crime prevention, has about one million prison inmates at the time of this writing – the price for replacing sociotechnology with ideology and demagoguery.

In short, in the matter of crime, as of everything social, we face the individualism-holism-systemism trilemma. In fact, we can blame either the criminal, society, or the individual-in-society. The respective solutions are: punishment, waiting for a better world, and prevention cum rehabilitation. The first two solutions are impractical and morally reprehensible; only the third has been shown to be efficient and consistent with our maxim *Enjoy life and help live*.

8 Law's Impotence

Lawmakers, jurists, and legal philosophers tend to believe that legislation is omnipotent: that the law not only regulates but rules. For example, Dworkin (1986, vii) starts his *Law's Empire* as follows: "We live in and by the law. It makes us what we are: citizens and employees and doctors and spouses and people who own things." This is a special version of the theses that ideas rule the world (idealism) and that there is no private sphere where people can behave to mutual advantage without the supervision of the state (statism). This view is false and it invites totalitarianism. Let us see why.

In the first place, the law does not give us life, skills, jobs, mates, property, or even incentives: it only regulates social behaviour – sometimes for the better, at other times for the worse. (Recall Pound 1954; Lundstedt 1956; and Stone 1966.) Second, the law is irrelevant to behaviour that is neither prosocial nor antisocial. Third, the law does not always regulate the settling of disputes, which in most communities is direct and smooth (see Ellickson 1991). In other words, social control is largely extralegal self-control. Fourth, the law is impotent to prevent such perfectly legal acts of business piracy as dumping and hostile take-overs. Fifth, laws do not deter unless they are widely known – which is seldom the case. In sum, on top of being false, legal idealism *cum* statism distorts the political process, leading lawmakers to try to solve all social issues through legislation, and it tempts them to invade all corners of life.

Not even the most advanced social legislation can change society by itself. Such legislation is impotent, and occasionally counterproductive, unless accompanied by economic and cultural changes capable of changing certain attitudes and habits. Take for instance the minimum-working-age law. By criminalizing child labour it condemns poor children to working in illegal sweat shops or worse – delinquency, prostitution, or starvation. Likewise easy divorce: it solves hopeless marital problems but throws unskilled divorcées into destitution. All partial remedies are similar.

In view of the perverse effects of some social legislation, should it be scrapped altogether as the conservatives demand? Of course not: this would amount to destroying civilization. The remedy is not to abolish social legislation but to supplement it with integral social reforms aimed at cutting the very roots of the social symptoms that such legislation intends to remedy. The law can trigger, steer, crown, or stunt social progress, but it cannot make it happen. Remember our dictum: *Leges sine potestas vanae* (sect. 5).

In sum, there is no such thing as law's empire. The law cannot *do* much: it can only either permit (and thus tolerate or encourage) or prohibit (and thus deter) social actions of certain kinds. It is sometimes necessary but never sufficient. Besides, under democracy legal norms, far from being above society, are subject to scrutiny, debate, and review: they must be justified or challenged in the light of both experience and morals. This applies particularly to unjust laws. When these threaten life, welfare, or liberty, citizens have the moral right and duty to fight them. This precept contradicts the Roman dictum *Dura lex, sed lex*, as well as legal positivism, both of which bow to the status quo even if unjust.

In short, laws can be important but never potent, let alone omnipotent. Only social groups, with or without laws, can have clout.

Lawmaking and the study of the law may be regarded as a sociotechnology on a par with management science, social work, and education science. An advantage of this approach is that it encourages cooperation between law and the social sciences. A disadvantage of it is that, if technology is regarded as being value-free – hence morally and politically neutral – then the law-ideology connection is obscured. But of course such a view of technology is mistaken, for technology empowers to modify human behaviour, and technologists are servants rather than masters. It is equally mistaken to believe that sound social knowledge "will inevitably find its way into legal doctrine" (Selznick 1959, 117). This will never happen because of inertia, ideological blinkers, and special interests, as well as because any practical application of basic knowledge requires additional research.

Whether or not the law is regarded as a sociotechnology, it has philosophical – in particular logical, epistemological, and ethical – inputs. Some of these are obvious: There is no litigation without causation and ratiocination, and no justice without truth and equity. Other inputs, particularly those about the moral underpinnings and nature of legal reasoning, are still under vigorous if not always enlightening debate. The law-ideology connection is even darker, if only because there is no sanction without power. A virtue of the systemic approach to the law is that it is bound to shed light on all the extralegal ties of the law, as exemplified by such hotly debated topics as the right-duty relation, the nature (or artifice) of property rights, the out-of-court settling of disputes, and the practical and moral worth of capital punishment.

Any study of a legal corpus in itself, however sophisticated, is bound to be shallow. To bring understanding and efficiency, the internalist approach must be joined with the view that law, far from being a disembodied corpus of ideas, is included in the social structure. This systemic and materialist view of the matter – which is that of the legal realists – makes it obvious that any substantial change in law is either cause or effect of some social change. And, since modern society changes rather quickly, we must expect legal reform to be part of any social reform. The latter will be the subject of the last chapter.

9

Management Technology

All social systems, even the voluntary ones, need to be managed, though of course not necessarily in an authoritarian fashion. Management expertise can be of either of three types: (a) *oracular*, or following the advice of self-styled experts in how to run other people's businesses, a.k.a. gurus; (b) *empirical*, or following tradition; or (c) *scientific*, that is, using experience, analysis, statistics, and occasionally mathematical modelling as well, to craft and discuss policies and plans, as well as to monitor their implementation. Each of these management styles presupposes its own theory of knowledge: intuitionism (or even magic thinking), empiricism, and ratio-empiricism respectively. I will disregard the first two management practices as being neither philosophically interesting nor efficient. (Witness the flops of Detroit gas-guzzlers, subliminal advertising, and mindless downsizing.)

The more complex an organization, the more numerous and difficult the problems it poses. And the more difficult a problem, the more expert knowledge it takes to be solved correctly. Small wonder then that the emergence of Big Business at the beginning of the twentieth century gave rise to management science (see, for instance, Chandler 1977). This is actually a craft struggling to become a sociotechnology. Management technology includes not only accounting and statistical analysis but also planning, forecasting, and simulation on the strength of sophisticated if often unrealistic mathematical modelling. But it is still in diapers and, like every emerging social discipline, it is a methodological, philosophical, and ideological battlefield. In this chapter we shall look into some of these controversies.

Management technology is so young that there are still spirited controversies on such questions as the role of the economic theory of the firm (which overlooks management technology); the relation between productivity and competitiveness; the proper task of managers, accountants, and financial analysts; the nature and role of strategies, plans, and forecasts; the functions of intuition, experience, and mathematical modelling; and the status of the discipline and its relations to other social studies, in particular economics and sociology. And, whereas some of the discussants adopt a scientific attitude, others are pundits long on anecdote but short on theory; and still others are long on mathematical modeling but short on real-life cases. And then there are the scribblers who dazzle the innocent with such high-sounding but irrelevant words as 'chaos,' 'fractal,' 'autopoiesis,' and 'neuronal network,' or even esoteric doctrines such as Taoism (e.g., Gerken 1994). Some firms hire graphologists, psychics, or astrologers to screen job applicants. And many experts peddle gospels, such as those of unfettered competition, which favours only the strongest, and "re-engineering," which destroys the firm's social fabric and undermines society. How are students to find their way in such a thicket?

Some management experts underrate strategy and planning, whereas others overrate them. Again, some swear by experience, others by intuition, and still others by reason. Many take the view that the study of management is reducible to psychology – in particular the study of consumer behaviour. Some experts regard management as an art, others as a science, and still others as a technology. Only a few adopt the latter view and realize that, though aiming at eminently practical targets, management should be firmly based on statistical analysis, social psychology, sociology, economics, and political analysis. Again, only recently has it begun to dawn on managers that they should adopt a comprehensive or systemic approach rather than a sectoral or point-like one, because they head complex and vulnerable sociotechnical systems that require much more than flair, experience, connections, and scrupulous accounting and auditing.

Like any other field of study, management technology raises a number of philosophical problems. Regrettably, few management experts realize this fact, and consequently they often adopt uncritically a wrong philosophy, or attempt to spin their own without the benefit of a look at the latter venerable (if still immature) discipline. A couple of examples should make this point. One is the question of the nature of the business firm. Where a philosophical idealist sees in the firm only a bundle of papers, a materialist will regard it as a social system, hence a concrete thing – though of course one constituted by thinking and feeling people acting upon one another under the constraint of contracts, legal codes, and social events. The methodological consequence is obvious: the former will only draft or read documents, whereas the latter will monitor the behaviour of real people and the performance of systems and their subsystems and supersystems.

Our second example of the relevance of philosophy to management is the set of views on the manager's proper role. The intuitionist will trust flair for business, and the empiricist experience: the former will be impulsive, the latter reactive. Since both are shackled to the past, neither of them will be able to tackle successfully any new challenges – for instance, those posed by new technologies or new social issues. A fortiori, neither the intuitionist nor the empiricist will be able to design the changes required for survival, let alone growth. As for the hyperrationalist, he will place excessive trust in theories and policies regardless of their past performance. Only the ratio-empiricist will check such performance and will try to design or commission theoretically and empirically well-grounded policies and plans.

In sum, it is no exaggeration to state that the performance of any organization, in particular a business firm, depends upon the philosophy inspiring its leadership and underlying its policy. In other words, philosophy makes a difference to the balance sheet.

1 Strategy: Policy

A policy or strategy for an organization is a design of the operation and governance of the organization in its environment. Most managers are hired to implement given policies, hence they seldom feel the need to inquire into the nature of a policy. Such neglect is unwise, because important changes in technology, social structure, legislation, public attitudes, or the international situation may require drastic and quick policy (strategy) changes. In a swiftly changing social world like ours, the good manager is a quick learner capable of taking the lead in proposing alterations in policies and plans, as well as in motivating others to learn and become involved in the process of overhauling the organization accordingly. In this regard, the good manager resembles the successful political leader: so much so, that the good statesman is a competent manager as well as a devoted public servant and a skilful politician.

To a first approximation, a *policy* or *strategy* is a goal together with a means (chap. 7, sect. 7). The goal of the policy of an organization is to help the latter discharge its specific role(s) by applying suitable organizational principles and techniques. In particular, whereas the central goal of a business firm is to make profit, that of a state organization is to render public service. However, the profit motive need not be incompatible with the service motive or with employment-equity practices. Indeed, some business firms and public-sector organizations are socially beneficial. A business firm is socially beneficial if it makes profit by delivering useful commodities at affordable prices. A socially beneficial state organization renders genuine public service by performing useful tasks that no private organization is willing to discharge, doing so at low cost to the taxpayer – as well as being in principle accountable to the public. In short, the optimal organization, whether in the private or in the public sector, is one that combines profit with service and performance with accountability. (At first sight, the existence of the so-called non-profit organizations refutes the previous statement. Actually it does not, because some voluntary organizations make profits – only they do not distribute them.)

An organization that makes no profit of any kind for self or others is at best useless, at worst a social burden, and in any case an instance of bad management. Examples of the latter are corporations that have to be bailed out by the government and state enterprises that sustain repeated losses, render poor public services at non-competitive rates, or are useless burdens on the taxpayers – like large standing armies in peacetime. For example, the International Monetary Fund and the World Bank have often been berated for poor management on a global scale: for having sponsored projects and programs that all too often have increased poverty and its biological and cultural concomitants, deteriorated the environment, or propped up dictatorships. These failures are attributable to poor strategy (sectoral as well as politically conservative), social insensitivity, and deficient monitoring.

The keys to pecuniary profit are cost, price, discount rate – and luck. This observation, though obvious, is not very helpful, because costs are seldom known accurately, the price-setting mechanism is often veiled, and different people evaluate future gains and losses in different ways. According to mainstream economics, prices are determined by the market alone, and all future costs and benefits should be discounted at the same rate. But in fact large corporations are price setters, not takers (see chap. 3, sect. 6). And experiment suggests that, contrary to orthodoxy, the discount rate differs among individuals and categories of goods (see, for example, Knetsch 1995b).

Of course the market has some say in price determination, for there is a limit to what the market (actually the consumers) will bear. In other words, the market sends "signals," however weak and distorted, to all concerned – this being one of its virtues. But the point is that the conventional theory of the market is of limited use to the policy maker because it ignores the distortions resulting from imperfect competition and externalities. Likewise, that theory does not help to determine discount rates, for these depend on the macroeconomic situation as well as on individual preferences and expectations. In short, the policy maker cannot rely on economic orthodoxy. Business schools will have to reconstruct economic theory *da capo* on the basis of business experience. Meanwhile, policy design will remain at the artisanal stage – except when coupled with operations research (sect. 4).

Whereas most economists keep preaching the competition gospel, good management consultants and smart managers know better. They know that ceaseless improvement yields diminishing returns and can be ruinous, because the rivals attempt to outperform one another to the sole benefit of the consumers. This is why Porter (1996) recommends staking out a unique position by delivering products that no one else offers. Shorter: Don't join the race, for you may lose it; instead, go it solo or in partnership with peers.

One of the most important problems of strategy is that of the right size. Military strategists and politologists have known this since antiquity, but management experts are still debating this point. Up until recently many of them swore by the Pharaonic slogan "The bigger the better," which used to be justified in terms of economies of scale. But technological advances, particularly in information systems, as well as recent negative experience with some megacorporations, such as GM, IBM, and Philips, have shown that diseconomies of scale may offset economies of scale, mainly because of inertia, bureaucratization, poor coordination, or excessive diversification. Decentralization improves governance, facilitates innovation, decreases reaction times, and spreads risks. This explains the healthy current trend towards splitting giants into semi-autonomous yet centrally coordinated units, every one of which is a nearly self-managed team – so as to enhance personal initiative, responsibility, and morale. A parallel trend is that of partnerships to command advanced technology or conquer a new market. In short, the formula for success involves combining decentralization with coordination.

There is no reason to believe that there is a single optimal size for economic systems of all kinds. For each type of system there is likely to be a size that optimizes performance through a wise mix of technology, local autonomy, and overall coordination. Thus, whereas day-care centres are necessarily small and labour-intensive, steel mills cannot help being large and capital-intensive. The right formula is neither "Small is beautiful" nor "The bigger the better," but rather "Efficiency and fairness result from combining local autonomy with overall coordination." Thus, finding the right size of an organization of a given kind is a task for operations research (sect. 4), not ideology.

It may be assumed that every business of a given kind in a given society has an optimal size. This size is "natural" in the sense that it depends on the task and organization of the unit, as well as on the competence and motivation of the personnel, whence it cannot be determined a priori. This point is overlooked by the fanatics of downsizing ("restructuring") for the sake of profits – an operation that has perverse effects in involving the sacking of supervisors and middle managers, the dismantling of R&D laboratories, and a decline in consumption. Indeed, the following suicidal loop is often seen in the 1990s: push for profit maximization → downsizing → fear and demoralization among employees →

quality decline → drop in market share → decline in profits (see New York Times 1996).

Well-known consultants, such as Nonaka (1991) and Hamel and Prahalad (1994), recommend thinking harder and tapping the ingenuity of employees instead of sacking them. The top consultancy firm Arthur D. Little (1995) also rejects mindless downsizing and recommends an alternative strategy: internal service quality → employee satisfaction → productivity → external service value → customer satisfaction → customer loyalty → profitability.

Our last problem, still open after having been debated for over three decades, is this. What comes first: strategy or structure? (See, for instance, Hammond 1994.) There are two rival theses: "Structure follows strategy" and its opposite, "Strategy follows structure." This impasse is solved upon noting that the concept of a problem has been conspicuously absent from the debate – as befits the empiricist approach dominant in management science. When the missing concept is included, each of the rival views is seen to hold half of the time:

Given structure 1 → strategy 1 → problem 1 → new structure 2 → ...

Given strategy 1 → structure 2 → problem 2 → new strategy 2 → ...

2 Tactics: Planning

As Smith (1776, 278) noted, businessmen "during their whole lives ... are engaged in plans and projects." Nearly all management experts admit the need for planning: they only differ with regard to the best kind of plan, as well as to who should do it – a special department or all those in the know? (See Porter 1980, 1990; Deming 1982; Makridakis 1990; Drucker 1991; Seni 1993; and Rumelt et al. 1994. And see Stacey 1992, Mintzberg 1994, and Aaker 1995 for dissenting voices useful as warnings against rigid planning.)

Perhaps only small shopkeepers – an endangered species anyway – can afford not to plan their business operations: their management is of the reactive rather than proactive style. They hardly need planning, having no capital to expand and being largely at the mercy of their suppliers. (They are often regarded as price setters just because they post their prices. Actually they are price takers, since the prices they post are mainly determined by their suppliers.) Being in a subordinate position, they can only react from moment to moment to external stimuli. By contrast, the same persons are likely to plan carefully, and way ahead, their own lives and those of their dependents: they know that, unless they plan their lives, others may do it for them. If they did not plan at all they would neither schedule, budget, save, nor buy insurance; they would neither immunize their children nor send them to school, and they would scorn the planting of trees.

Responsible managers do not improvise, but plan, forecast, and budget. They carry out these tasks on the strength of the best available knowledge. However, far from relying on their forecasts and sticking to their plans, they update the latter, trying to adapt the organization to internal and environmental changes as revealed by social studies: they favour flexible over rigid planning. They are learners as well as doers. For example, the American tricycle manufacturer who did well in the 1960s, when there were two children for every elderly person, would be well advised to go into wheelchairs nowadays, when the ratio of children to the elderly has been inverted.

The epistemology underlying such concern for keeping up to date with social change and technical knowledge is realism. By contrast, a consistent apriorist would go on as if nothing new happened. And an empiricist (in particular a pragmatist) would go by the past, sticking to observable features only, and improvising responses to external stimuli as they come. Actually this is how most *small* businessmen behave, if only because of poor resources. In particular, their sales forecasts are anything but scientific: they are of the form "Same as last year plus or minus a certain (rather arbitrary) quantity." Optimists increase, whereas pessimists decrease: guts prevail over brains (see Lovell 1986).

(At first sight a more scientific business forecast is made on the basis of both past sales and past forecasting performance: it is said to be *adaptive*. More precisely, the routine forecast is of the form: $F_t = A_{t-1} + b$, where F_t is the value of F forecast at time t, A_{t-1} the actual sales during the previous period, and b a positive or negative number. By contrast, the so-called *adaptive forecast* is of the form: $F_t = A_{t-1} + c(A_{t-1} - F_{t-1})$, with $c > 0$. However, since the weight c of the discrepancy between past actual and forecast sales remains just as unspecified as b, adaptive forecasts are no more scientific than the intuitive ones after all. Mathematical ignorance is still ignorance.)

In real life, large corporations do not just forecast but set their goals, design scenarios, and plan and monitor their operations so that their forecasts become self-fulfilling. They attempt to fulfil them with the help of business connections, market research, and advertising campaigns. In other words, their forecasts are active, not passive: contrary to what Stacey (1992) claims, they do not rely on "the spontaneous self-organizing interaction between people." Surely, some large corporations fail in that endeavour. But most of the time this is so because their structure (organization) is hierarchical, as a consequence of which their plans exclude participation and criticism, are based on insufficient knowledge, or are rigid rather than adaptive (see Aoki 1986). Such rigidity is an unavoidable concomitant of excessive size and centralization, as both make for inertia, bureaucratization, alienation, and waste. These features weaken private firms and kill cooperatives (see Craig 1993).

In closing, a word of caution. Planning is bound to fail when in the hands of a planning staff removed from managerial and operational tasks (see, for example, Wilson 1993). Likewise nation-wide central planning, typical of the late "socialist" economies, failed mainly because of the remoteness and unaccountability of the central planning bureaucracy. This implied ignorance of local conditions, insensitivity to rapid changes in the latter, and lack of involvement of the stakeholders in making decisions – hence, limited personal responsibility and low creativity. Planning should be of the hands-on, not the hands-off type. That is, it should not be detached from management but part of it. More on this next.

3 Management

Management is the governance of social systems of any kind. The study of management is not a science, but it can become just as scientific as engineering or medicine. When scientific, it deserves to be regarded as a branch of sociotechnology tapping social psychology, sociology, economics, and political science. However, it is not reducible to either of these sciences, if only because its ultimate goal is utilitarian rather than cognitive.

Like any other branch of learning, the study of management raises a number of broad conceptual problems, some of which are properly philosophical. (See, for instance, Simon 1970; Mattessich 1978; Kliksberg 1978; Wand and Weber 1990; Moessinger 1991; Seni 1993; and Mintzberg 1994.) Here are a few examples. 1/ Are all self-managed organizations bound to end up as hierarchical and therefore incompatible with moral autonomy? 2/ How can one find out whether success (or failure) is due to proper (or improper) management rather than to favourable (or unfavourable) circumstances? 3/ Can managers afford to treat production, quality control, financing, accounting, marketing, planning, and human relations as separate departments, or should they look upon them as constituting a single system? 4/ Does marketing make use of the concepts of real world and objective truth, or does it condone some anti-realist philosophy? (See Hunt 1990.) 5/ Is the search for profit the only goal of management, or just the foremost of several goals? (See Drucker 1993.)

Business and administration students are seldom if ever asked the above questions, or even trained to face the complexities and uncertainties of real-life firms. For one thing they are usually required to learn mainstream economic theory, which they are unlikely to use on the job because it describes an ideal world of free and "rational" (maximizing) agents who participate in markets in equilibrium and free from social (in particular political) constraints. The real-life manager faces "imperfections" of various kinds, such as technological and organizational obsolescence, resistance to change, and supply bottlenecks. Above all, he must monitor and coordinate the activities of his employees; delegate responsibilities and stimulate learning and cooperation; "see," evaluate, and seize opportunities; repair malfunctions; listen to grievances; negotiate (fight and bargain) with employees, suppliers, banks, and customers; satisfy or elude government regulations; plan for product diversification or the opposite, as well as for expansion or shrinking; and must always be on the alert and improvise solutions to unexpected problems. None of these realities is covered by general equilibrium theory. Worse, the latter is individualistic, whereas mainstream management theory is not. Fortunately, a systemic (or "structural") view that makes room for individuals as well as networks and "holes" in them (i.e., opportunities) is gaining ground (Granovetter 1985; Doz and Pralahad 1991; Burt 1992; and Uzzi 1996).

Another theory supposed to be of capital importance to managers is decision theory (DT), the classical and new versions of which we met in chapter 7, section 2. But, although real-life managers may draw decision trees, they seldom if ever use DT in any of its versions. In particular, insurance companies handle risk on the basis of actuarial tables, not DT (see, for example, Borch 1988). There are two good reasons for this. One is that DT handles only unitary decisions, such as whether or not to buy a chocolate bar, whereas managers and other sociotechnologists usually confront bundles of interrelated decision problems, that is, systems of such (see Ackoff 1970). A second reason is that DT assumes, mistakenly, that all practical situations involving uncertainty can be modelled as lotteries to be understood in terms of subjective probabilities – whence all business decisions would be choices among lotteries with "known" (actually only conjectured) probabilities and pay-offs. (Its classical version is also wrong for assuming, contrary to fact, that it is always "rational" – that is, practical – to attempt to maximize one's expected utilities: see Bunge 1996a.) To be sure, one must always reckon with accidents, both lucky and unlucky, random and non-random. Hence, a realistic management model is likely to involve random variables, such as environmental "noise." (However, these variables are beyond management control.) If the main processes in a social system were like games of chance, the system might as well be put in the hands of a croupier rather than a manager. Which, on second thought, might not be a bad idea, for the croupier would use objective probabilities and pay-offs rather than subjective hence arbitrary ones.

The manager's task is to steer the system in his charge, and this involves repairing its defects, minimizing the amplitude of the random fluctuations within the system, and protecting it from environmental shocks instead of regarding it as an uncontrollable roulette wheel and watching it passively. As March and Shapira (1987, 1415) noted in a well-known study, "Perhaps the most troubling feature of decision theory ... is the invitation it provides to managerial passivity. By emphasizing the calculation of expectations as a response to risk, the theory poses the problem of choice in terms appropriate to decision making in an uncontrollable world, rather than in a world that is subject to control."

Much the same applies to game theory – or GT for short – which we met earlier (chap. 4, sect. 5). GT, a close relative of DT, is becoming fashionable in management science and elsewhere. The theory makes the unrealistic assumptions that each "player" (agent) is a utility maximizer and has perfect knowledge of the rules of the "game," the utility functions of the players, the options, possible outcomes, and the corresponding pay-offs. (See von Neumann and Morgenstern 1953; and Luce and Raiffa 1957.) Hence, GT can encompass only oversimplified games, such as the prisoner's dilemma, a two-person game in which each player has only two options: to cooperate or to "defect" – with no possibility of face-to-face bargaining. Worse yet, GT makes success or failure depend exclusively on the players' moves: it ignores structure, environment, causality, and history (see Porter 1994).

For these reasons, GT discourages the empirical investigation of the complexities of the real system of interest, such as a business firm in a changing environment: GT models are largely when not wholly a priori, hence outside time. This is one of the (bad) reasons for their current popularity. Given such popularity, some cautious dissenters present their own alternatives as mere reforms of GT. Thus, Sebenius (1992,19) describes his own contribution, negotiation analysis, as "nonequilibrium game theory with bounded rationality and without common [that is, shared] knowledge [among the actors]." But the GT faithful will not fail to see through this triple heresy, similar to a religion without gods.

Still, GT can be of some use in extremely simple situations, particularly if stated in qualitative terms, that is, dropping the unrealistic assumption that prospective gains and losses can always be assigned precise numerical values. For example, the qualitative version of prisoner's dilemma captures correctly certain important features of social behaviour – ironically, those denied by the free-market zealots. In fact, it encapsulates the rule that cooperation (or at least refraining from aggression) is beneficial, unbridled competition (mutual "defection") maximally disastrous, and unilateral restraint on competition beneficial to the scoundrel and harmful to his victim (the "sucker"). Thus, GT may have been helpful in recent years by giving cooperation a veneer of intellectual respectability in a business community used to reciting the gospel of unrestrained competition. In fact, this is how strategic alliances and joint ventures are sometimes being justified nowadays. But GT was not really necessary to realize that sharing information, or forming joint ventures, with one's competitors is more prudent and advantageous than engaging in cut-throat competition.

Trouble with GT starts when attempting to quantitate the pay-offs, for the assignment of precise numerical values to the pay-off function is seldom possible in real-life situations. For example, what is "squealing" (backstabbing) worth to each player when, as in real markets, there is no umpire competent to allot rewards and punishments? And what exactly is the benefit that rival business firms may expect if they refrain from engaging in trade warfare with one another? This is anyone's guess, not a matter of either calculation or measurement. The manager or business consultant will at most hazard that "if firms are cooperative they all can make a reasonable profit. However, if one firm makes a self-interested strategic move to which others do not retaliate effectively, it can earn even higher profit. If its competitors retaliate vigorously against the move, though, everybody can be worse off than if they were all cooperative" (Porter 1980, 89).

In sum, even though they face decision problems all the time, neither real-life managers nor business consultants have any use for either DT or GT – except perhaps as vague frameworks and languages. Their decisions are supposed to steer the social system under control along a satisfactory (if possible optimal) path. Their recommendation depends not only on the firm's policy but also on the circumstances, in particular the available resources and the state of the market, or perhaps even the state of the world. Therefore, keeping up to date with the state of the firm and the state of the world will help managers and consultants far more than guessing probabilities and utilities.

In any case, the rational manager looks for realistic or at least reasonable figures, and checks and updates them periodically instead of playing games with subjective expectations. In other words, he makes no use of DT, GT, or any other alleged general problem solver. This does not entail, however, that he lets his "gut feelings" (or intuition) guide him: after all, he is supposed to be a rational animal, hence one who, though often primed by intuition, is careful to process and test it. Above all, he is expected to observe at all times certain general principles. But what kind of principles: rules of thumb or rules based on scientific observation, analysis, modelling, and perhaps even experiment or at least computer simulation? The answer depends on the type of firm. Any firm, of any size, employing advanced technology requires more than empirical rules, particularly at a time of rapid social and technological change: it calls for management science, complete with statistical analysis, quality control, marketing, and eventually operations research as well.

Management scientists have come up with a number of general principles, among them those proposed by Greiner (1972), Simon (e.g., 1977), Deming (e.g., 1982), Politz (1990), and Drucker (e.g., 1991). For instance, W. Edwards Deming is credited with having revolutionized management science in the 1950s with his principle that – contrary to received wisdom – productivity increases with quality. (Mechanism: Less rework and waste, more pride in workmanship, and higher consumer satisfaction.) His recipe for good management is the following chain reaction: Better quality → increased productivity → lower costs → larger market share → stay in business → job creation.

Here we are interested only in the methodological status of management principles, good or bad: are they laws, hypotheses, or rules? They cannot be laws because, unlike laws, principles can be altered – though not arbitrarily, for they must be compatible with the relevant laws if they are not to be disastrous. (Fancy a management principle that would violate the law of conservation of energy.) The principles in question cannot be hypotheses either, because they prescribe what ought to be done rather than describing what there is or can be. A fortiori, they cannot be theories, that is, hypothetico-deductive systems, although they are often called such. (Of course there are hypotheses and theories about the firm, but they are not management maxims.)

I submit that management principles are *sociotechnical rules* subject to empirical tests, compatible with the relevant psychological, sociological, economic, and politological theories, and conforming to the principle of common decency. The rules should be kept if they pass these three tests, and dropped otherwise. Moreover they should be revised once in a while instead of being worshipped – as they often are when coming from the lips of the Management Guru of the year. In other words, in principle one should accept only scientific management principles. As will be argued in section 5, such principles are based on scientific models of the firm together with practical and moral desiderata.

Like any other human activity, management can be routine-bound or creative. The routinish manager follows custom, goes by hearsay, and follows his nose; he limits himself to reacting to the stimuli he happens to perceive, and plans only for the short term. In short, he is a bureaucrat rather than an entrepreneur. He is well adapted to a slowly changing environment, but is incapable of facing, let alone initiating, radical changes: these require vision, foresight, research, and long-term planning. Some of the expertise can be supplied by outside consultants. What cannot be bought is the ability to realize in time that outside help is required: an intimate knowledge of the firm is required for this.

The creative manager studies the organization he is in charge of, identifies in time its trouble spots, charts its course for the long term, and endows it with efficient feedback mechanisms – in particular through employee and customer involvement – that keep him well informed about successes, failures, and threats. He takes the lead and tries to foresee opportunities and risks, and prepares for them, if necessary with outside help.

Since all decisions involve risks, risk assessment and control are part of the manager's job. He faces, among others, the methodological problem of risk measurement. There are two standard solutions to this problem: the inductivist and the decision-theoretical ones. The inductivist or empiricist rule – popular until a few decades ago – is simple: "Look at the past performance of similar systems or actions, and assume that the future will resemble the past." This rule is reasonable in the absence of information about mechanisms. But in this case, adopting the rule is itself risky, for the system concerned may be about to start declining. Besides, if followed slavishly, the inductivist prescription will deter us from undertaking any innovating action. In short, induction is, paradoxically, too risky precisely for focusing on the past. After all, opportunity lies ahead.

The decision theorist is likely to propose that the risk of an action (or inaction) be estimated in terms of failure probability. But, since except in the case of random processes, such as games of chance, we ignore the objective probabilities in question, his subjective estimate is a recipe for disaster. Responsible risk management involves objective risk assessment, such as the one practised by insurance companies, which rely on the relative frequencies handled by actuaries.

But outside natural science, casinos, and insurance companies, objective probabilities are hard to come by. For example, suppose a DT enthusiast asks a nuclear engineer to estimate the probability of meltdown of a particular reactor, so as to calculate the expected disutility of such an accident. He may expect three answers. One: The consultant concocts a subjective probability or degree of certainty – an irresponsible answer for being intuitive. Two: The consultant attempts to find out the frequency with which reactors of the same type and age, and similar performance, have melted down in the past. This datum may be hard to find because of the cover-ups of past accidents; or because the precise cause of past accidents (flawed design? faulty operation?) is unknown; or because the reactor in question is of a new type. If the real meltdown frequency is unknown, the expert cannot pass a serious judgment; if known, he cannot conclude to an objective probability, because meltdowns are not random processes – and, no randomness, no probability. Three: The consultant produces a report like this: "Given that the specifications in force are the best to date, and that the inspectors have ascertained that your reactor complies with them, I predict that it is very unlikely to melt down provided it is operated in accordance with the operating manual. However, don't ask me to pin numbers on this unlikelihood, because I could only make them up, and specious accuracy is both a swindle and an invitation to complacency." If a report of this kind is accepted, it was unnecesary to commission it to begin with, for it relies entirely on the reports of the inspectors who authorized the operation of the reactor. In sum, DT is of no use whatever in making decisions under uncertainty: it only serves to incur consultancy fees.

Another management activity of interest to philosophers capable of touching ground is bargaining (see, for instance, Gauthier 1986). Bargaining is theoretically interesting because it transforms conflict (actual or potential) into cooperation, and involves a modicum of tolerance and trust. Most bargaining theories are linked to DT and consequently ignore the moral aspect of the bargaining process, and are committed to subjective and therefore untestable utilities and probabilities. However, if couched in terms of objective values, the bargaining problem can be put in simple terms, namely as follows: The desirable outcome of a bargaining process is a deal between two parties, each of which concedes the other something (e.g., labour) in exchange for something else (e.g., wages). The deal will be fair or equitable if and only if the values of the items being traded are roughly the same – that is, if neither of the parties stands to gain at the expense of the other.

Now, the outcome of a bargaining process is not just a matter of goodwill – as Kant might have argued – but also of bargaining power. Indeed, a fair deal is possible only when there is a balance of bargaining power. But this is not the rule in negotiations between unequals, such as men and women, employers and employees, or developed countries and Third World ones. In short, the morality of a deal depends on the balance of power, not the other way round. Still, occasionally an unfair deal may be preferable to either no deal at all or to protracted confrontation. When the latter threatens, arbitration is called for. The philosophical interest of arbitration lies in that the arbiter is supposed to be impartial by introducing the moral viewpoint in a situation where each participant is likely to disregard the other party's interests (Rescher 1975: 59ff.).

Policies, plans, and good management are necessary but insufficient, for nothing can replace good luck. Luck has nothing to do with fate and it is not mythical. Good (bad) luck is just the accidental matching (mismatching) of ability and circumstance beyond our control, such as natural catastrophes and the opening up of new niches (see chap. 5, sect. 3, and Raup 1991). A lucky (unlucky) individual is one who happens to be at the right (wrong) place at the right (wrong) time. This holds not only for people and other organisms but also for organizations. In the case of business firms, even the best of brains, policies, and plans cannot make up for unlucky circumstances (Kaufman 1985).

But of course there is a crucial difference between a manager and a sub-human creature, namely that the former can "see" opportunities, exploit them rationally, assess risks, buy insurance, prepare for threats (both looming and unforeseen), and alter course when necessary. However, these advantages can be offset by negative character traits, such as neophobia, unwillingness to learn, short-sightedness, greed, lust for power, ruthlessness, groundless optimism, and improvidence. It is not for nothing that Dun and Bradstreet has made good business in publishing its yearbook *Business Failure Record* – according to which 67 per cent of all new American firms last less than five years.

Finally, what about the moral aspect of management? Does the manager have any moral and social responsibilities? The traditional answer is of course that his only duty is to make a profit. This view has been challenged in recent years by consumer and environmentalist groups, as well as by responsive civil servants and even some management experts (e.g., Scott and Rothman 1992; Messick and Bazerman 1996). Indeed, it is increasingly being admitted that the manager of a business firm is answerable to all of the firm's stakeholders: stockholders and employees, consumers and suppliers, creditors and neighbours, living or to be born. For this reason, 'business ethics' has ceased to be an oxymoron (see, for instance, Snoyenbos et al. 1983; and Iannone 1989). Still, to expect business to give up the search for profit as its main goal – as the Catholic Church has been advising of late – is like preaching vegetarianism to the tiger. Social justice does not consist in eliminating gains but in distributing them fairly.

Prudent and socially responsible management and technology are not wholly market-driven but abide by the norms of common decency. Any cunning crook can make a fast buck by cheating – for example, supplying junk. Only a combination of suitable technology and scientific management with social responsibility can supply what the public really needs and can afford, and thus earn its loyalty. Still, since high quality is not always affordable, a compromise must be worked out between quality and price. The business firm intent on supplying good-quality products or services at affordable prices will proceed roughly as follows: find out what people need or want, and what they can afford $\rightarrow$ decide what the firm can supply $\rightarrow$ design the product $\rightarrow$ make a prototype $\rightarrow$ test $\rightarrow$ redesign if necessary $\rightarrow$ make a new prototype $\rightarrow$ test $\rightarrow$ make $\rightarrow$ control quality $\rightarrow$ advertise $\rightarrow$ sell $\rightarrow$ find out market reception $\rightarrow$ alter design or marketing as needed. (See Deming 1982.) And all the while remember this platitude: Honesty, if affordable, is the best long-term policy.

4 Operations Research

Management problems come in all sizes. The biggest of all are strategic problems – that is, policy and planning ones – , in particular, problems of survival posed by unexpected radical novelties in technology or in the business or political environment. Such problems may defeat experience and flair: they may require consulting with teams of operations research experts. These are likely to propose studying the system and, among other things, identifying dysfunctions, performing a statistical analysis of the quality and sales of its products, using linear programming techniques, running a computer simulation of the model, and redesigning the firm. Some or all of these studies are expected to result in a set of feasible recommendations for addressing the issues in question.

Operations (or operational) research, or OR for short, was created in the 1940s by an Anglo-American interdisciplinary team faced with submarine warfare (see Morse and Kimball 1951). It was initially conceived of as the application of the scientific approach to large-scale logistical operations and weapons-systems evaluation beyond the reach of the military mentality. Subsequently it became the most sophisticated approach to management problems in all fields. And it uses mathematical tools as well as some substantive scientific knowledge, computer simulation, and the occasional small-scale experiment. Its philosophical attraction derives from having adopted the scientific and systemic approaches (see, for instance, West Churchman, Ackoff, and Arnoff 1957).

Hundreds of useful OR models have been built over half a century: for production, resource allocation, inventory, queuing, location, forecasting, and so on. Far more is in store given the increasing complexity of sociotechnical systems and the opaqueness of their operations to all but insiders and experts. In fact, OR is currently facing the challenges of the globalization, quality, employee involvement, and technological unemployment "revolutions." At the same time, no sooner did OR become an academic discipline than a stream of papers devoid of practical interest started to appear (Geoffrin 1992). This inward-looking trend has brought undeserved discredit upon the whole of OR. (Similar trends can be observed in theoretical physics and economics: here too mathematics, the best of servants, is becoming master.) The popularity of management gurus long on big words but short on specifics has not helped. However, the right reaction to high-sounding verbiage is not to discourage rigour but to encourage the crafting of mathematical models both relevant and empirically supported.

The best way of getting a feel for the OR approach is to consult a standard textbook (e.g., Nahmias 1989; Taha 1992) and sample the journals in the field. For our philosophical concerns it will suffice to analyse three examples requiring only elementary formal tools. Our first example is this: Given that a company needs a certain product and could produce it, should it make or buy ("outsource")? Obviously, the answer depends on the quantity and cost of the product. But this evasive answer is not enough for making a rational decision. Such a decision calls for a modicum of algebra. Suppose that the cost to the firm to make x units of the product in question is $ax + b$, whereas that of purchasing the same quantity is cx, where a, b and c are positive real numbers. (These formulas must be altered in the cases of both very small and very large quantities.) The break-even condition is given by the number x^* of units for which both costs are the same. This condition is $ax^* + b = cx^*$. Solving for the critical value we find $x^* = b/(c - a)$. Hence the rule: "Buy if you need less that $b/(c - a)$ units, and make if you need more." Methodological moral: When quantity is of the essence, precise and efficient rules of action can be derived only from exact and true models of the system in question.

Our second example is this: An academic committee is asked to recruit new professors in a given discipline for a total of \$Q per year. Predictably, the committee splits evenly into the partisans of quality and those of quantity. To break the tie, the dean hires an OR consultant. This expert recommends a mix: a few strong scholars to set standards and train students, and three times as many young unknowns, some of whom may mature into good scholars and may eventually replace retiring senior staff. The model is as follows.

Budget constraint $Q = mp + nq,$ [1]

where

m = # of senior scholars, n = # of young unknowns
p = average going senior salary, q = average going junior salary.

Further,

Desirable junior/senior ratio $n = 3m$ [2]
Going average salaries $p = 3q$ [3]

Substituting [2] and [3] into [1] yields

$Q = 2mp,$

which in turn implies

$m = Q/2p,$ $n = 3Q/2p.$ [4]

Since both Q and p are given, the last two formulas solve the given problem. The methodological status of [4] is that of a rule of action based on two data, [1] and [3], and one hypothesis, namely [2]. This model, though extremely simple, is quite general. Moreover, it is likely to satisfy at least partially the two factions in the hiring committee. If not, all that has to be done is to examine the hypothesis [2] in the light of the available statistics about the frequency with which new graduates become independent productive scholars – a tough task given the tendency to protect incompetent academic buddies.

Our third and last example concerns culture management. About the simplest model for it is the following. Postulate 1: The rate of investment in a given cultural product is proportional to the difference between the desired and the current values. Postulate 2: The rate of production is proportional to the product of the production volume by the investment. The formalization of these assumptions yields the volume of investment required to close the initial gap (see Bunge 1983b, 250–1).

Reflecting on the foregoing suggests that OR involves the following tacit philosophical assumptions. 1/ Every management problem concerns some social system(s), whence it involves considerations about resources and interests. 2/ The more complex a system, the more fields of knowledge must be tapped to understand and control it. 3/ All management problems can be spotted, and they can be formulated precisely, often mathematically. 4/ All clearly formulated management problems can be handled and solved scientifically, that is, through data collecting, analysis, modelling, and occasionally computer simulation and small-scale experiment as well. 5/ Since management problems involve people, they are bound to have moral aspects – which, alas, are all too often overlooked by OR experts. (In the early days of OR it was also assumed that every feature of any organization can be quantitated. This assumption, which sometimes led to pseudoquantitation, has now been relaxed.)

In short, management can be rendered scientific without adopting Taylor's "scientific" principle that everyone's work should be so simplified that even an idiot could do it.

5 Private and Public

By definition, private goods are personal and often divisible, whereas public ones are shared and usually indivisible. The line between the private and the public depends not only on the nature of the good in question but also on the social order. Thus, whereas toothbrushes are naturally private, seas are not. And, whereas in some primitive societies everything sharable is shared, in modern societies many items that ought to be public – such as non-renewable resources – are in private hands. Everywhere the line is drawn by social forces and conventions rather than by technical considerations (e.g., efficient allocation) or moral principles (e.g., equity). Yet both have a say in a good society.

A popular argument for the means of production being private property is that private business firms are maximally efficient because the owner takes a personal interest in his business. This is indeed the case with microbusinesses, such as small farms, cottage industries, retail stores, and professional practices. In these cases the owner-worker plans and executes or supervises all tasks, does not toil to enrich others, and is accountable to nobody but himself or his family, and his income depends mainly on his performance. In short he is, or at least believes himself to be, his own boss – even though in fact he may be largely at the mercy of his suppliers, the banks, or "protection" rackets.

However, the advantages of small-scale private business are not peculiar to it. In fact, the case of the cooperative enterprise is similar. Here, although nobody owns the whole firm, every cooperant owns an equal part. Moreover, every cooperant is accountable to every fellow cooperant and is more or less involved in management as well as interested in the success of the enterprise. However, when a cooperative firm becomes so successful that it grows beyond a certain size, it resembles a private corporation, in that its managers end up losing contact with the workers and the public. However, the remedy is at hand: if a cooperative becomes unmanageable in a collegial manner because of large size, it should be split into two or more semi-independent units.

The cases of the large corporation and the large government agency are totally different. The managers and executives of these organizations are far removed from the action: they only see papers, fellow executives, and their secretaries. They are essentially bureaucrats, and in most cases their income does not depend on the firm's or agency's performance. As for the sleeping partners and stockholders, they are even farther removed from the work process, in many cases their livelihood does not depend on the success of the company, and they are seldom if ever invited to participate in decision making. Owning a piece of the cake does not entail getting involved.

Whether an organization is private or public, excessive size makes for rigidity and waste, as well as for insufficient involvement and unaccountability (abuse of power). However, the moral is not "Small is beautiful" but rather "Giantism is ugly" (recall sect. 2). Hence, the remedy lies neither in extreme fragmentation nor in merger. Instead, it lies in choosing the right size of the component units, and in coordinating them so that they function flexibly, smoothly, efficiently, and fairly to all the stakeholders. In other words, the right size results from combining available (or obtainable) resources with coordination, adaptation, and participation to produce both optimal efficiency and fairness.

6 Resource Management

The management of natural resources, such as land, water, mineral deposits, forests, and fish banks, has two aspects: private and public. Those who specialize in the former aspect tend to overlook the latter and conversely. No wonder then that resource economics is just as fractious as the rest of economics: in fact, it is divided along philosophical and ideological lines.

Resource management raises ontological, epistemological, and moral problems in addition to technical and political issues. Here is a small sample of this problematics. Can every natural resource be priced? Can economic efficiency be reconciled with environmental protection? Should environmental protection be combined with social reforms, and if so how? What kind of discipline is resource management: natural, social, or biosociological? And is it scientific, technological, or both?

The first of the above questions is tacitly answered in the affirmative by the experts who use cost-benefit analysis as the sole tool for evaluating the impact of human action, in particular agriculture and manufacture, on nature. Clearly, whereas some natural items can be priced, others cannot. For example, the losses caused by overcultivation and deforestation are hard to quantitate. In particular, there is no way of putting a price tag on irreversible insults such as the loss of topsoil and the elimination of biospecies. Hence, there is no way of imposing fair taxes or fines on the perpetrators of such disasters.

Yet, welfare and rational-choice economists propose fines and tax disincentives as the only means to curb environmental degradation (recall chap. 7, sect. 8.) But, in societies ruled by economically and politically powerful elites, seeking pecuniary compensations for such crimes only perpetuates them: it is just as wrong as punishing murder exclusively with fines. The only practical and moral solution to such issues is prevention through a combination of education, vigilance, regulation, and coercion if necessary. An exemplar of this kind is the 1987 Montreal Protocol on Substances That Deplete the Ozone Layer (Prather et al. 1996).

As for the conflict between exploitation and conservation, it is no secret that, in its search for economic efficiency at the price of the depletion of exhaustible resources and environmental degradation, industry has been aided by mainstream economists (see, for instance, Heal and Dasgupta 1979; and Soderbaum 1987, 1990). Since we are finally learning that, if humankind is to survive, nature must be protected from irreversible depredation, it stands to reason that the search for economic efficiency must be constrained by environmental (and demographic) concerns. This suggests introducing radical changes in economic theory as well as in policies and plans at both the micro- and the macroeconomic levels. For one thing, the very concepts of self-interest and economic efficiency ought to be honed. We should consistently distinguish between short-term and long-term – in particular between generational and intergenerational – self-interest and economic efficiency. As concerns resource management, we may defend the pursuit of economic efficiency only as long as it is taken in the long run and placed in a social context.

The answer to the question whether resource problems can be separated from social issues is a loud 'No!' The reason is that the former are consequences of our actions – in particular overcultivation, overlogging, overfishing, over-mining, and overindustrialization fuelled by greed, population growth, and con-sumerism. Neither conservation biology (the science of biodiversity), nor technology, nor the "green" movement can solve by itself the problems of resource management, for these are social problems. Indeed, managing any resource amounts to governing our own actions upon the resource. And manag-ing it intelligently requires a lot of science, both natural and social, that is scarcely available. Therefore, an efficient change in resource management involves not only more research but also political mobilization and legislation aimed at effecting certain deep changes in the social order, such as alleviating poverty, restricting reproduction and property rights, and altering consumption habits. (See, for instance, Dasgupta and Mäler 1994.) This is particularly evi-dent in the Third World, where environmental degradation is only one compo-nent of a system of social issues centred on poverty:

$$
\begin{array}{ccccc}
 & & \text{Low level of education} & & \\
 & & \updownarrow & & \\
\text{High fertility rate} & \leftrightarrow & \text{Poverty} & \leftrightarrow & \text{Environmental degradation} \\
 & & \updownarrow & & \\
 & & \text{Militarism} & &
\end{array}
$$

If resource management is viewed in a systemic manner, it becomes environ-mental (or ecological) socio-economics – an emergent discipline. But this is not a technical subject that can be approached in a politically neutral way, for it poses the problem of the limits to economic growth imposed by the conflicting desiderata of human survival and social development. However, the political connection deserves a separate section.

7 Management and Politics

Everyone knows that business is conducted not in a political vacuum but in close interaction with the body politic. Moreover, it is no secret that politicians, statesmen, and civil servants are beleaguered and tempted by business lobbies, and that some political campaigns are funded by corporations who expect eventual reciprocity. Moreover, in critical situations business leaders get together to design and promote pro-business or even antisocial policies. And occasionally they can grab power overnight through massive smart publicity: recall the victory of the Italian tycoon Silvio Berlusconi in 1994.

What is the middle manager freshly graduated from a business school to do in the face of political threats and promises to business? Can he pretend that politics does not exist, or must he play the game of political corruption? If he adopts the first attitude he behaves like an ostrich, if the second like a member of a less reputable species. He will consult his textbooks to no avail. Indeed, most management schools steer clear from political science, and teach the neoclassical myth that the economy is an "autonomous sphere." Hence, they do not prepare their students for wrestling with the external politics, or even the internal one, of the business firm. But the experienced entrepreneur and the high-ranking civil servant know about struggles for power within any large firm or government department, as well as about the ties and conflicts of his organization with other organizations, private and public. They learn political skills the hard way.

Any realistic management school should take the bull by the horns: it should teach that business is bound to interact with politics. It should also teach that such interaction is bound to be synergic at times and confrontational at other times. Furthermore, it should teach that management has the right and the duty to try to influence macroeconomic and social policy makers, though not secretly and as the privileged party but openly and in concert with labour and consumer groups. And that, in the long run, there is more to be gained from a mediocre but fair deal than from huge profits obtained through craft.

However, let us face it: in a society dominated by corporate capitalism, driven as it is by greed rather than service, that is only wishful thinking. It will be argued later on (chap. 10, secs. 7, 8) that only economic democracy, which involves the substitution of cooperatives for corporations (private or state-owned), can protect everyone's interests.

8 Rationality in Action

The rational-choice school enjoins the manager to engage in unfettered competition and maximize the economic gains of his enterprise. This policy is short-sighted: first, because only strong firms can afford to compete – and even so only within limits; second, because in any social system there are non-economic factors to be considered. To realize the importance of these factors it will suffice to consider a simple practical problem: that of the efficiency of government departments, starting at the municipal level.

Suppose two towns have grown so close together that the border between them exists only on paper. Anyone imbued with the maximization dogma is bound to propose that the two towns fuse into one. The resulting economies of scale seem obvious: one city council instead of two, one town hall instead of two, and so on. However, the merger might induce an equally obvious diseconomy of scale: the increase in size might decrease the involvement of people in municipal government, thus strengthening the power of the bureaucracy. The end result would be weakening of self-government and increase in waste and corruption. Save one penny and lose one freedom.

In conclusion, authentically rational managers attempt to optimize overall and long-term efficiency and market share rather than to maximize short-term gain. Still, management decisions are often distorted by non-rational factors, such as overly timid choices derived from excessive loss aversion, and overly optimistic forecasts due to short memory and neglect of external factors (see, for instance, Kahneman and Lovallo 1993). Good policies and plans, together with careful monitoring of their implementation, will not prevent all mishaps, but at least they will facilitate the timely correction of many mistakes.

Management science is not only an important sociotechnology: it is also a source of methodological and philosophical problems, and therefore a testing ground for philosophical doctrines. Among other things, it has shown the fertility of the systemic approach and the barrenness of its alternatives. In particular, management science has shown the inadequacy of the holistic-intuitionistic approach, with its hostility to rationality, quantitation, and planning. Likewise, it has exhibited the futility of rational-choice theories – not because of their rationality but because of their contempt for social norms, real-life problems, and empirical tests. Lastly, management science has found no use for irrationalism and idealism: it is tacitly ratio-empiricist, materialist, and systemist. Still, management science is no substitute for initial endowment, entrepreneurship, and luck.

Let us now turn to the management of entire economies.

10

Normative Economics

The task of normative economics is to design, analyse, evaluate, and update policies that aim at controlling the production and distribution of goods, whether martketable or public, at all levels. Such policies are of interest to philosophy on several counts. First, they involve broad assumptions about human nature and society, in particular ideas about the right social conduct and the good society. Second, because they affect individual welfare and freedom, economic policies give rise to conflicts between individual and public interests, as well as among social groups, so that they raise moral problems. Third, the very idea of a public policy, in particular an economic one, poses the problem of its foundations: is it based on sound economics and on acceptable moral norms? Fourth, how should economic policies be evaluated: by their benefits to business, to the public, or both? Or is it possible that, as the libertarians (neoliberals) claim, the very idea of a public policy is incompatible with freedom? Or else, is it true that – as the once-influential rational-expectations school holds – economic (in particular fiscal) policies are impotent, and governments should let the "market forces" operate freely? Or, finally, could it be that, as the organicists and the neo-Austrians claim, the economy is a self-controlled system that can only be wrecked by political interference?

Let us deal briefly with the latter school because, if right, normative economics should be buried rather than studied. The neo-Austrian arguments against state intervention are that a free society is one where people can compete and choose freely, and that in the process the more efficient win to the benefit of all. Hayek adds, rightly, that the modern economy hinges on knowledge. He then goes on to claim that competition is "the only method which we know for utilizing the knowledge and skills that other people may possess" (Hayek 1979, 75). However, this is notoriously false: the best means for sharing knowledge are publication, discussion, and cooperation – for example, in workshops, research teams, seminars, professional meetings, and strategic alliances. Besides, co-operation does not exclude competition: the two are sides of the same coin (see appendix 3).

Now, Hayek knows that perfect competition is an ideal type: in the real world there are oligopolies, monopolies, and monopsonies in addition to govern-ments. However, instead of condemning such concentrations of economic power in the name of free enterprise, he justifies them and attacks all anti-trust legislation. Hayek reasons as follows. He holds that it is "desirable not only to tolerate monopolies but even to allow them to exploit their monopolistic posi-tions – so long as they maintain them solely by serving their customers better than anyone else" (Hayek 1979, 73). But since under monopoly there *is* no one else, the phrase 'serving their customers better than anyone else' makes no sense. It would have been more forthright for Hayek to admit that what really interests him is not so much freedom in the broad sense as free enterprise. As a matter of fact he comes near to saying this much four pages later: "[I]t seems at least likely that unlimited democracy will destroy it [a functioning market] where it has grown up" (ibid., 77). He put this idea into practise when he advised the fascist dictator General Pinochet (see Prebisch 1981b). However, "When the enterprises are really free, the people are not" (Mintzberg 1996a, 75).

Given the inconsistency of the most radical of all enemies of economic poli-cies, let us take a look at these, particularly since they are not the exclusive concern of economists. Indeed, such policies are also of interest to political sci-entists and the public at large, for their discussion and implementation are polit-ical processes. Indeed, the entire field of public policy-making is part of the political process, whence it is intimately related with morals and is conse-quently of interest to moral and political philosophy. For example, fighting inflation at all costs may succeed, but at the price of unemployment and its sequels (sect. 2).

Since the immediate target of an economic policy is the control of the macro-economy, it will pay to start by taking a look at the study of the latter.

1 Normative Macroeconomics

As we saw in chapter 3, section 7, macroeconomics – the study of entire econo-mies – can be either descriptive (positive) or prescriptive (normative). If descriptive, it will attempt to model the economy. If normative, it will design and monitor policies regulating taxes, tariffs, interest rates, public expenditures, and employment rates. Unlike descriptive macroeconomics, but like any other sociotechnology, normative macroeconomics has ideological and political inputs, and it can be relevant or irrelevant to socio-economic issues. For example, it can either tackle or overlook the two major issues of the day: under-development nearly everywhere, and chronic mass unemployment everywhere – particularly the fast disappearance of permanent jobs (see Gorz 1982 and Rifkin 1996). And, like any other technology, normative macroeconomics can be scientific or unscientific. It will be scientific if it relies on the corresponding basic science(s), and if it monitors and evaluates the results of its recommendations; and it will be unscientific if it fails both tests.

The hub of normative macroeconomics is the design and evaluation of policies and plans that aim at acting on the economy as a whole so as to favour certain sectors of the population. Although the macroeconomist is supposed to be an unbiased technologist, the advice he offers can be a political tool. If retained by a conservative government, he will tend to favour big business, for instance, by cutting corporate taxes and social expenditures. And if in the service of a progressive government, he will recommend redistributing wealth through social services financed by income taxes. These examples suggest that normative macroeconomics is sandwiched between positive macroeconomics and politics *cum* morality and ideology. This explains why, by contrast to mainstream microeconomics, normative macroeconomics is cacophonic and strident. It explains why the only robust finding in the field seems to be this: Given any policy P, firmly endorsed by a Nobel laureate in economics, there is at least another Nobeal laureate who, with equal authority and conviction, will dismiss P as quackery.

Regardless of its political and moral motivation, for an economic policy to be efficient it must be based on sound positive macroeconomics. Now, most mainstream economists, particularly those of the neoclassical persuasion, feel no need for macroeconomics because they share Adam Smith's individualist dogma that the economy is merely the aggregate of households and firms, every one of which must look only after itself – the Hidden Hand looking after everyone. The Great Depression caught them (as well as the institutionalists) napping, and it raised the political and moral issue of doing something on the macrolevel to improve the condition of the many millions who had failed to maximize their expected utilities.

This challenge was taken up by Keynes (1936), who put real people – particularly the poor – back into economics. This he did by constructing a macroeconomic theory that relates aggregate demand to the rate of employment, and national income to government spending (recall chap. 3, sect. 7). Keynes used this theory to urge on governments the adoption of vigorous macroeconomic policies aimed at reducing unemployment through public works and the stimulation of aggregate demand. Whether Keynesian policies are still advisable at the time of writing is debatable, because they are strictly economic rather than systemic, and because not every rise in consumption is healthy. But this is beside the point. The point is that Keynes fathered modern macroeconomics, both positive and normative, and that he emphasized its political and moral components.

Obviously, only sound positive macroeconomics can be a reliable guide to responsible normative macroeconomics (or economic policy). Regrettably, positive macroeconomic theory is still dismally underdeveloped despite the spectacular increase in the database since the last world war. Moreover, the unexpected stagflation that started about 1970 threw macroeconomic theory and policy into disarray. The following laundry list should suffice to confirm this pessimistic assessment. 1/ There is no generally accepted theory of money, hence no solid theoretical foundation for any monetary policy (see Hahn 1981a, 106). 2/ There is no good theory of inflation, let alone stagflation. 3/ There is no generally accepted theory of economic growth, in particular one making room for the statistical data showing that, whereas during certain periods economic growth is accompanied by inflation, during others the two are inversely correlated. 4/ GDP estimates fail to include the undeclared housework performed mostly by women – which Statistics Canada estimates at 46 per cent of the GDP. 5/ Most macroeconomists care more for the total GDP than for its composition, to the point that certain economic dysfunctions, such as large military expenditures during peacetime, the clearing of tropical forests, the cost of mopping up oil spills, and the building of jails are recorded as increases in GDP. 6/ The standard national accounting system, influenced as it is by neoclassical economics, does not take into account the depreciation of natural resources caused by their depletion or degradation, let alone the waste in human resources caused by poverty and persistent mass unemployment. 7/ Monetarist theorists and most monetary authorities are more interested in the total quantity of money circulating in an economy than in the way it is distributed and used – whether it goes to investing in sound businesses or in buying bonds, to healthcare or to defence, to education or to law enforcement, to pollution control or to polluting industries, and so on. 8/ Hardly any macroeconomists doubt that economic growth is the *summum bonum* – even if it benefits only a minority and is achieved at the cost of the irreversible degradation of the environment. 9/ Economic policy makers continue to debate whether the American economy suffers a competitiveness crisis. This deadlock is due not so much to a dearth of data as to confusion between competitiveness, as indicated by market share, and productivity, as measured by output/input ratio (see Papadakis 1994).

Evidently, the effectiveness of normative macroeconomics depends on whether or not these and other flaws of mainstream positive macroeconomics are acknowledged and corrected. For example, if the depreciation of natural resources is included in a system of national accounting, the policy maker may propose changes in the rate of exploitation of those resources (see the *Ecological Economics* and *Environment and Development Economics* journals). However, positive macroeconomics is only one of the inputs to normative macroeconomics. Ideology, morals, and politics are further inputs: see the following.

2 Economic Policy

Economic policies constitute the best-known kind of public policies. And monetarism is the oldest, simplest, and best-known example of an economic policy. But at the time of this writing it is generally discredited for three reasons. First, for lack of a sound theoretical basis (see, for instance, Hahn 1981a; Hirschman 1981; Hendry and Ericsson 1983; and Bunge 1985c). Second, for having failed to check inflation while increasing poverty and unemployment (see, for example, Dow and Saville 1988). Third, for having increased or generated staggering fiscal deficits according to the mechanism: war on inflation → higher interest rates → economic slowdown → falling tax revenues → increased fiscal borrowing.

(For one thing, it is false to contend that there is a single type of inflation and therefore a single cure for it, namely tight-fisted monetary and fiscal policy. In fact, there are several kinds of inflation: demand, cost, and government-induced. Moreover, demand inflation is largely fuelled by advertising [Triffin 1980]; cost inflation is partly the creature of low productivity, which in turn derives from technological backwardness and low wages; and most governments fan inflation by maintaining needlessly large armed forces and bureaucracies. Neither of these sources of inflation is much affected by monetary measures. Even the International Monetary Fund (IMF) has occasionally admitted that the latter, though necessary, are insufficient to check inflation. In general, single-target policies are bound to fail.)

Notwithstanding both statist and *laissez-faire* rhetorics, economic policies are intrinsically neither good nor bad. Some policies are stabilizing and promote development, whereas others are ineffective or counterproductive. For example, the New Deal policy may have helped the US economy get out of the Great Depression (see sect. 2); by contrast, Churchill's decree that one pound was worth five dollars triggered a severe recession. The neoconservative claim that government policies "are the only source of shocks to an intrinsically stable mechanism is a proposition that could be seriously advanced only by persons with extravagant faith in their own abstract models and with historical amnesia" (Tobin 1980, 46).

Any social policy has five possible inputs: socio-economic, ideological, moral, political, and philosophical (chap. 7, sect. 7). Take, for example, the "shock therapy" that the International Monetary Fund and the World Bank have been advocating for the Third World as well as for the ex-"socialist" nations. This therapy consists in the sudden dismantling of both the social-security system and the institutional (in particular legal and bureaucratic) obstacles to the free market. The various inputs of this policy are as follow: (a) Socioeconomic = neoclassical economics; (b) ideological = conservatism; (c) moral = selfishness; (d) political = opposition to the welfare state; (e) philosophical = ontological and methodological individualism (inherent in neoclassical economics). The outputs of this policy are well known: checking inflation and (sometimes) reducing the fiscal debt, at the price of increased misery, cultural degradation, and political instability often followed by repression – or by the return of the old guard in the case of the former Soviet empire (see Danaher 1994). However, let us analyse the various inputs to economic policy-making listed above.

Ideally, the socio-economic input to macroeconomics is sound social science, in particular descriptive macroeconomics. The trouble is that this discipline is still rather backward, as we saw in chap. 3, section 7. No wonder that many economic advisers to governments base their recommendations on rules of thumb, dogmas, or even hunches (Malinvaud 1984, 78, 102). Take, for instance, the tax cuts favoured by conservative politicians. The historical record shows that, while tax cuts always force cutbacks in social expenditures, they do not always have the same economic effects. In fact, depending on current circumstances and expectations, a tax cut may stimulate investment in either business, spending, or saving. This suggests that tax cuts (or hikes) cannot be detached from other factors. (The motion of a feather in air is analogous: it will fall down, float, or move upwards according to the prevailing local air currents.) The moral is obvious: only (sufficiently) true macroeconomic models, together with reliable data, can provide a sound basis for economic policies: not the only one, though, because the economy is just one of the three artificial subsystems of society – the others being the polity and the culture.

Next in our list comes the ideological input to economic policy-making. It is so obvious as to hardly require comment. If in doubt, look at any of the principles (actually rules of thumb) that guide economic policy-making (see, for instance, Hutchison 1964). Thus, an empirical rule sometimes adopted by the World Bank is this: "If producer poverty exceeds consumer poverty, increase the producer price above the world level." (Incidentally, this rule is at odds with the free-market principle favoured by the same agency.) But since a rise in price is likely to reduce demand, which may be disastrous in the case of food staples, a further rule has to be introduced: "Subsidize the commodities necessary for survival." The two rules combined are designed to alleviate poverty – which is an ideological and moral issue, not just an economic one. Another example is the economic "shock therapy" designed for ex-communist countries. This strategy is undemocratic in being of the top-down type; and it is immoral in disregarding the suffering and cultural deprivation it causes. Not surprisingly, it is seldom successful (Pickel 1993, 1997).

The moral component of macroeconomics is often overlooked or even denied, particularly by those who focus on the market and sidestep the issue of wealth distribution. This stand is scientifically, technically, and morally indefensible. It is scientifically indefensible because production and distribution come together – except of course in either a subsistence economy or a super-abundance one. (In the former case there is no surplus to be distributed, and in the latter there is no burden to be shouldered.) The view is technically objectionable because, unless the distribution of wealth is minimally fair, there won't be the wherewithal to consume, hence the incentive to produce. And the opinion in question is morally indefensible because every macroeconomic policy raises the problems of distributive justice and recognition of merit.

Unlike its descriptive basis, normative macroeconomics is morally committed. This commitment becomes obvious upon reflecting on such issues as social expenditures, environmental degradation, and fiscal debt. Only the most myopic reactionary will deny that the state should provide social services above and beyond the maintenance of territorial integrity and internal security. And no altruistic moral code will forgive us for bequeathing our offspring a depleted and degraded environment or a huge fiscal debt. Hence, if we abide by any such code we shall work, or at least vote, for a conservationist resource management and a fiscal policy involving debts contracted exclusively to invest in the future, in particular to pay for overhauling the national infrastructure and the public health-care and education systems.

The political input to economic policy-making, though usually masked by rhetoric, should be obvious to any political analyst. Indeed, every economic policy is both child and parent of political circumstances and movements. It is partially dictated by political interests and, if implemented or merely adopted for political expediency, it will strengthen some political parties while weakening their opponents. (Think of the differences among reactionary, conservative, liberal, and socialist economic policies and their effects on public opinion.) When motivated by purely electoral interests, economic policies can be disastrous (e.g., inflationary) in the long run. After all, the unborn do not vote.

Certain economic policies have profound and lasting political consequences. For example, if an underdeveloped nation lifts its customs barriers, its industry is bound to decay at least in the short run, as a consequence of which both its industrial bourgeoisie and industrial proletariat will drop sharply in numbers, which in turn will weaken the unions and political parties representing their respective interests – to the joy of the parasitic sectors.

The fifth and last input to economic policy-making is of a philosophical nature. It consists of the philosophical presuppositions of the socio-economic, ideological, and moral inputs. For example, whereas a central command-economic policy is based on a holistic social philosophy, *laissez-fairism* is based on an individualistic social philosophy.

The five above-mentioned inputs have different weights: heretofore the socio-economic one has been the lightest. In fact, once a philosophical, moral, political, and ideological stand has been adopted, all the macroeconomic policies inconsistent with it are automatically discarded. For example, since mainstream economists assume that natural resources are infinite, they can be trusted to oppose any budget including environmental protection measures. And, since they are obsessed with equilibrium, they can be relied upon to defend balanced fiscal budgets come what may, and thus oppose any reconstruction plans involving large public expenditures, even if these are required to rebuild a nation or region ravaged by natural disaster, war, chronic unemployment, long neglect – or disastrous economic policies.

A clear case of a controversial economic policy is the bitter pill that the IMF and the World Bank (WB) prescribe for all the "developing" and ex-"socialist" countries regardless of their particular situations and traditions and the welfare of their peoples. (Such bitterness and uniformity remind one of the two universal remedies of Molière's physicians: laxative and bleeding.) This policy of "stabilization and structural adjustment" is designed in the light of mainstream economics, which (a) does not even work for reasonably stable and prosperous capitalist countries (chap. 3); and (b) makes no room for transition processes, in particular from statism or semi-statism to the "free" market (Przeworski 1991). Furthermore, the policy in question is sectoral rather than systemic: in particular, it does not care about unemployment, welfare, health, education, civil rights, democracy, or even domestic industries. No wonder that it fails except in opening the doors to financial speculators and transnational corporations.

It is instructive to contrast this policy with the paths followed successfully by the developed nations in earlier times. These paths are characterized by two major features: protectionism and steadfast parallel progress in the economic, political, and cultural domains. Since only the former is controversial, let us take a look at it. Economic history shows that all the developed nations have practised protectionist policies even while preaching free trade. In this way they ensured the take-off and growth of their own industries as well as a monopoly on their internal markets; at the same time they protected the plundering of

Third World countries, and sometimes deliberately crippled the latter's industries. (Great Britain blazed the trail by enacting the monopolistic Navigation Acts in the seventeenth century, and by wrecking the Indian textile industry in the eighteenth.) To this day free-trade rhetoric has often only masked expansionist policies. This is not to deny the benefits of free trade among peers, such as the members of the European Union and some Third World blocs, such as Mercosur. Regional free trade, sí, global, no – as long as glaring disparities persist.

The IMF and the WB recommend that Third World and ex-"socialist" nations embrace the free-trade policy supposedly practised by the industrialized countries, thus abandoning fledgling industries to their own devices and engaging in impossible competition with powerful industrialized nations: they tell toddlers and the disabled to race athletes. To top it all, the IMF and the WB do not keep track of the performance of their own programs, and are never punished by their mistakes, so they do not learn from them. Nor do they bother to answer the charges that their policy not only cripples local industries and favours mostly transnational companies, but also increases social inequalities and causes political unrest that invites repression. This is why the IMF and the WB have been accused of attempting to treat disease without regard for life.

In conclusion, the "structural adjustment and stabilization" policy championed by the IMF and the WB is open to three charges. First, it is sectoral rather than systemic – hence doomed to fail in addressing severe systemic ("structural") issues. Second, in many cases that policy has blocked development by increasing misery, dependence, political instability, and cultural decline. Third, the policy is immoral in increasing social injustice and safeguarding only the interests of the creditors (see, for instance, Dagum 1990).

What are the so-called developing nations to do if they can neither follow profitably the recommendations of the IMF and the WB nor replicate the original conditions that made the rise of the West possible? Clearly, they must design their own development policies in their own interests, by their own lights, and within their own means. Now, as we saw in chapter 7, section 7, one of the conditions for any public policy to succeed is that it be systemic rather than sectoral. This is how the West (or rather some of it) rose: by developing simultaneously its own economy, polity (in particular democratic institutions), and culture (in particular education, science, technology, and the humanities) – and exploiting the rest of the world in the process. In short, the West followed a systemic not a sectoral development path – albeit, not always deliberately, and long before systemic thinking emerged. (Recall chap. 6.) It should be instructive and amusing to speculate on where the West would be today if it had been under the thumb of the IMF and the WB.

Finally, when should economic policies be evaluated? Answer: before, during, and after being implemented. Before, to ascertain whether the policies address the major issues and whether they are consistent with the extant socioeconomic knowledge; during, to allow for unforeseen events and to correct mistakes; and after, to check whether they have been effective. The latter task is perhaps the more difficult, and this for two reasons. First, it is always possible to argue that the policy only seems to have succeeded (or failed) because of the occurrence of unforeseen events. For example, Keynesianism is usually credited with having stimulated the recovery from the Great Depression. However, the Second World War started while the recession was still on; hence, the huge military build-up may have done more to end the recession than any investments in public works and social programs. A second reason is that it is always possible to argue either that (a) the policy was not correctly implemented (the usual excuse of monetarists), or (b) the policy succeeded (or failed) because of the presence of mechanisms other than those it envisaged. For example, maybe the German post-war economic "miracle" would have occurred even without Ludwig Erhard's monetary reform. Indeed, one can argue that the recovery was a result of six major concurrent factors: (a) massive American assistance (the Marshall Plan) and investment; (b) self-imposed austerity; (c) strict fiscal controls; (d) absence of military expenditures; (e) sound social programs; and (f) the eagerness of ordinary people to resume normal life after a period of carnage, devastation, deprivation, and insecurity – not to mention the taming brought about by Nazism. In short: hope, hard work, and labour restraint may have been at least as important as monetary policy in effecting the recovery. The Japanese case seems to have been similar.

In sum, it is hard to evaluate objectively the results of economic policies. Only the triplet constituted by a social (not just economic) policy, the accompanying plan, and the mode of its implementation can be evaluated. Parallels: the recovery of surgery patients and the rehabilitation of criminals.

Having taken a quick look at the general features of economic policies and plans, we are now ready to examine the main theoretical contenders.

3 Economic Planning

Planning is a means for shaping the future through the control of natural or social systems. (Recall chap. 7, sect. 8.) All rational individuals, in particular business managers and statesmen, act according to some plan or other: this is well known. What is far from obvious is whether the economy as a whole should be planned and, if so, what kind of plan should be adopted: sectoral or global, centralized or decentralized, direct or indirect, detailed or sketchy, rigid or flexible, authoritarian or participative, and so on. Let us start by considering the classical "liberal" (or *laissez-faire*) case against economic planning.

The neoliberal (conservative) objection to planning rests on the assumption that the market is a closed system always in or near equilibrium thanks to the play of supply and demand. Being a self-controlled system, and more precisely one in which any deviation from equilibrium self-corrects (clears) almost instantly, intervention can only worsen things. In particular, regulations and subsidies that distort real prices or wages cause inefficiency or graft. Hence, they should be lifted wherever they are in force.

The Great Depression and the subsequent recessions falsified the assumption that the economy is a self-regulated system, and prompted a number of strict regulations in addition to welfare programs: recall the New Deal. Moreover, the successful reconstructions of the West European and Japanese economies after the Second World War were planned. All these plans aimed at full employment, a fairer income distribution, equilibrium of the balance of payments, and price stability (see, for instance, Malinvaud and Bacharach 1967). The sensational growth of the Japanese economy between 1945 and 1990 is usually credited, at least in part, to the clever plans and strict regulations designed jointly by business and government. By contrast, some of the spectacular bankruptcies and swindles that characterized the American economy during the greedy 1980s are attributable to the massive deregulations introduced by the conservative government administrations.

Every modern government, whether dictatorial or liberal, conservative or socialist, takes charge of the macroeconomy. In particular, by determining government expenditures – especially those of the social and military kinds – and by dictating the discount rate, every government has a big say in demand, investment, and employment. (For instance, the restrictive monetary policies adopted by the US government in the early 1980s were explicitly designed to "cool down" the economy in order to avert inflation. Actually, they caused a deep recession and the irreversible loss of millions of industrial jobs. The moral is not that all intervention is bad, but that monetarism is catastrophic. Second example: When the first signs of another recession appeared in 1990, *The Economist* [6 October 1990, 24] declared: "The coming recession may not be deep enough to do good." Actually it turned out to be disastrous, particularly in Europe.) Finally, nearly every time an American megacorporation gets in the red, it begs the government to bail it out. In short, it is simply false that the modern capitalist economy does or can do without some planning and some state intervention. Nowadays *laissez-faire* is more ideological slogan than political fact (see Hobsbawm 1995 and Gellner 1996).

Conservative scholars, in particular von Mises and Hayek, have coupled economic planning to totalitarianism, and have claimed that democracy requires a totally free market. Actually, in itself planning is consistent with any social order. The cases of the state-controlled economies of the UK and the USA in war time, as well as the post-war planning of the most advanced West European economies, refute the neoliberal assertion. Second example: The Soviets began planning their economy only one decade after the 1917 revolution. Marx, Engels, and Lenin had refused to sketch a blueprint of the socialist society. They believed that socialism would unfold unavoidably from capitalism, and that what little planning was needed would be, as Lenin put it, "child's play." The result was catastrophic. This did not deter the Communists from indulging in prophecy: abundance, overnight birth of the non-acquisitive and well-rounded New Man, withering away of the state, and all that. So much for "scientific communism."

At the time of this writing, few dispute the need for central economic planning to rebuild one of the many casualties of the Cold War: the infrastructure of the industrialized countries, both East and West. Such need becomes even more obvious as the economy gets globalized and, above all, as we move towards an economy of scarcity owing to the depletion of non-renewable resources and increasing overpopulation. In an economy of scarcity social inequality will be even less justifiable – politically and morally – than in an economy of abundance.

The question then is not whether we need any economic plans but what kind of plan is best, and who should design it. The answer depends of course upon the socio-economic order to be favoured or achieved. For example, the building of an industrial economy demands, in the early stages, a protectionist policy combined with tax breaks and the encouragement of savings and investment. By contrast, welfare capitalism in an advanced industrialized nation only requires "indicative" planning and the occasional price and wage control measure. But vigorous expansion into overseas markets requires much more: it calls for definite industrial and trade policies – for instance, covert protectionism combined with the demand that others abide by free trade. (It also used to require colonial war and gunboat diplomacy.) And "socialist" statism involves detailed, rigid, and top-down central planning, and the concomitant stunting of initiative and freedom.

What kind of nation-wide planning would be most effective and socially just? I submit that planning should be global, sketchy, flexible, technically sound, and participative. And its implementation should be continuously monitored, evaluated, and revised with the participation (mostly indirect) of all concerned. Let us see why.

A plan should be *global* in the sense that it should concern not just the economy but the whole of society and its environment. The reason for this is that "there are perhaps no practical questions ... which admit of being decided on economical premises alone" (Mill 1871, xcii). More precisely, "Economic reasoning, alone, cannot offer a solution for any economic problems, for all involve political, social, and human [moral] considerations that cannot be reduced to 'the lore of nicely calculated less and more'" (Robinson and Eatwell 1974, 293). The reason is that, far from being a closed self-controlled system, the economy is open: it interacts strongly with the environment, the polity, and the culture.

In other words, there are no purely economic issues: there are only social issues with salient economic features. Consequently (a) the so-called economic problems do not have purely economic solutions; and (b) sound economic planning is only a component of comprehensive social planning. (A strictly economic plan, of the type promoted by the IMF and the WB, is bound to sacrifice the environment, health, the culture, the polity, or all four.) For example, the overhauling of an economy may involve, among other things, rebuilding the infrastructure, retraining workers and managers, and upgrading the healthcare and education systems – all of which call for public enlightenment and mobilization. Hence, such a plan should be designed by a multidisciplinary team of sociotechnologists concerned about people, their offspring, and the environment.

However, such a plan should be *sketchy* rather than detailed, in order to make ample room for local talent and initiative, as well as unforeseen obstacles and opportunities. Any detailed social plan is foolish if it ignores unpredictable changes and restricts the involvement of people and therefore their imagination and initiative, as well as in imposing either sluggishness or excessive growth.

The plan should be *flexible* or corrigible rather than rigid, to accommodate learning as well as unforeseen circumstances. (A rigid plan leads one headlong regardless of unforseen obstacles and opportunities.) That is, the plan should be altered as needed in the light of experience – just like a scientific research plan and unlike an algorithm.

The plan should also be *technically competent*. That is, far from being either improvised or dictated by ideologues, the plan should be designed by competent managers and sociotechnologists in close consultation with the representatives of all the stakeholders. (Democracy without technology is inefficient, and technology without democracy can be diabolical.) For example, following Allais, to avoid inflation the rate of interest should equal the growth rate of the economy. Hence in a zero-growth economy the interest rate should be 0 per cent, and in a declining economy it should be negative – that is, new and socially beneficial investments should enjoy fiscal incentives.

The plan should be *participative* rather than authoritarian, and this for three reasons. First because, as the Japanese and European experiences show, employees can make positive technical contributions to production, particularly to work design in high-technology industries (Alic 1990). Second, because the modern economy depends increasingly on "knowledge workers," who cannot be supervised effectively, let alone ordered about the way routine (manual or service) workers can (Drucker 1993; Handy 1994). Third, because self-governance is of the essence of democracy. (Plans designed from above are bound to ignore at least some of the real needs, aspirations, and spontaneous contributions of the people, and they are unlikely to get them involved voluntarily, intelligently, and enthusiastically over a long period.) In other words, the single plan designed by a central state agency should be shunned. The state should only coordinate and perfect the various local planning proposals. A combination of top-down and bottom-up procedures is thus in order (see Nove 1983).

Finally, the implementation of any plan should be continuously *monitored and evaluated* to check for efficiency and detect and correct flaws in the application or even the conception of the plan. Such continuous evaluation is particularly necessary in the case of large-scale social services and programs administered by large bureaucratic bodies, since these tend to be inert and to develop a vested interest in the status quo. (For the problem of program evaluation see Mosteller 1981; Caro 1983; Herman 1987; Aguilar and Ander-Egg 1992; and *Evaluation Studies Review Annual*.)

Obviously global, sketchy, flexible, technically sound, participative, and monitored planning is necessary but not enough to build or sustain a just and efficient social order, because plans are only means to attain a goal. In this case the goal is to build or manage a just and sustainable society where everyone can enjoy life while helping others live.

To get a feel for the kind of economic planning required by a just, efficient, and durable society, let us sketch an oversimplified model of the relation between income and expenditure. We first postulate the equity condition: In a just social order the total contribution of an able-bodied person to society (in the form of work and taxes) should equal the sum total of his needs and those of his dependents, both taken over his lifetime. (That is, every family gets as much as it gives.) Our second postulate is that, for every person, the need-versus-age curve is J-shaped, whereas the contribution-versus-age curve is an inverted U. (That is, one's needs are greatest when very young or very old, and one's contributions increase at first and then declines with age.) In a just (and simple) world the two postulates together should suffice to plan for wages and social expenditures. The point of philosophical interest is that, whereas the first postulate has a moral content, the second is a sociodemographic hypothesis. This illustrates the thesis that, though different, fact and norm can be combined: the *is/ought* gap can be bridged (Bunge 1989a).

(The above model is easily formalized. The assumptions are that the functions for the need N and social contribution C versus age A for the "average person" are a J and an inverted U respectively, that is,

$$N = a - bA + cA^2 \quad , \quad C = d + eA - fA^2$$

where all six parameters, from a to f, are positive real numbers. The equity condition laid down above amounts to the equality of the areas under the N and C curves over the life expectancy of the average person in the population concerned. The economic planner's task is to determine the values of the six parameters.)

Being descriptive, social statistics will not do all the job for the planner. For example, he must estimate not just what the actual costs of child care and care for the elderly are. He must also determine whether they are adequate and are the best that society can afford. In short, his main task is prescriptive. But he won't do a good job unless he teams up with education, health-care, and social-work experts, and consults public opinion about such delicate matters as birth control and extraordinary medical services for premature babies, the handicapped, and the elderly.

Having taken a quick look at the general features of economic policies and plans, we are now ready to examine the main theoretical contenders.

4 Welfare Economics

Welfare economics is normative macroeconomics that aims at enhancing social welfare within the market economy and uses some neoclassical economics. (*Locus classicus*: Pigou 1927.) It aims at mitigating economic inequality through increasing aggregate income, reducing income fluctuations, and redistributing wealth through social programs financed by taxation. Hence its propositions, unlike those in positive economics (chap. 3), are morally coloured (Fellner 1960, 10). We shall discuss only a few of the philosophical problems raised by welfare economics. These are the concept of Pareto optimality, the fundamental theorem of welfare economics, the status of social-welfare functions, Arrow's impossibility theorem, and the proper way of testing theories.

Pareto optimality (or efficiency) is the state of a society (in particular the economy) in which anyone's gain can only occur at the expense of someone else's loss: it is an equilibrium state. Equivalently: The state of a society is Pareto optimal if no one can be made better off without someone else being made worse off. In game-theoretic terms, Pareto optimality amounts to a zero-sum game. Mechanical analogue: the see-saw. This is no coincidence, for Pareto used statics as a source of inspiration for his economic theory.

An example of Pareto optimality is perfect competition. No wonder then that the *fundamental theorem* of welfare economics states that every perfectly competitive market in equilibrium is Pareto optimal. Equivalently: If some agents gain and others lose from participating in a market, then the latter is either imperfectly competitive or in disequilibrium (or both). Hence, the free-market economy would be the best of all possible worlds. Only a grouch could complain about such an ideal state of affairs. Dr Pangloss nods.

The idea of Pareto "optimality" has been widely discussed not only by economists (e.g., Dobb 1969) but also by politologists and moral philosophers. In particular, Sen (1970b) claimed to have shown, by means of a famous counterexample, that Pareto "optimality" is inconsistent with libertarianism, or the view of the primacy of individual rights. Others (e.g., Barry 1986) have denied such a contradiction. Still others (in particular Gibbard 1974) have proposed that, if an individual right conflicts with Pareto optimality, the right in question should be given up. In my opinion these are academic games of no relevance to economics or political science, because Pareto "optimality" is seldom actually optimal. By dropping it we are spared many a paradox. (See also Allén 1988.)

An even more persuasive reason for giving up Pareto "optimality" is the following (Moessinger 1988). Strictly speaking *any* distribution, whether fair or not, is Pareto optimal – that is, any way of slicing the pie automatically satisfies Pareto optimality. Indeed, any alteration in the sizes of the individual slices will favour someone at the expense of someone else. Consequently, Pareto optimality enshrines the status quo and discourages all policies of wealth redistribution. In any case, Pareto optimality is not a *moral* desideratum, hence not one that should guide any economic policy except a conservative one.

I submit that the fundamental theorem of welfare economics is irrelevant to both economic efficiency and social welfare, for neither is attainable through unrestrained competition. Indeed, both efficiency and social welfare call for a modicum of sharing, cooperating, and regulating, so that everyone's gains (or losses) are (nearly) everyone else's gains (or losses). Think of mutual societies, cooperative enterprises, joint ventures, strategic alliances, and social movements, in contrast to trade and military wars, colonial plunder, or exploitation. Or think of common goods such as public services. In sum, in a just society *non*-zero "games" are the ticket. Equivalently: In a just (or merely viable) society no one can be made better off without eventually someone else being made *better* off too; the welfare of any is accompanied by the welfare of all.

Our next topic is the status of *social-welfare functions* (SWF). A social-welfare (or utility) function is assumed to represent the utility of something, such as a piece of legislation or a social program, for a whole social group. According to utilitarianism, from Bentham to Pigou, A. Bergson, Samuelson, Arrow, and beyond, a social-utility function is a function of the individual utilities (or else the individual preferences) of all the members of the social group concerned. In particular, it is usually postulated that the social welfare of a group of people equals the sum of their individual utilities.

There are two problems with this idea. One is that, in the vast majority of cases, the individual utility functions are mathematically undefined, empirically unknown, or both, if only because they are subjective by hypothesis (see Bunge 1996a). Another difficulty is that, even if the individual utilities were known, their sum would be just as meaningless as the addition of the temperatures of the group members. (Utilities, like densities, are presumably intensive magnitudes, not extensive ones like areas.) Hence, any social-welfare function constructed out of individual utilities is the shadow of a ghost. (For further criticisms of the additivity hypothesis see Myrdal 1954 and Sen 1979.)

These objections do not touch Arrow's (1951) version of welfare economics, which uses the concept of ordinal utility (or preference) rather than the cardinal (or quantitative) one. The centrepiece of Arrow's theory of social choice is his famous Impossibility Theorem, according to which the aggregation of individual transitive preferences need not be transitive (hence rational) itself. We claimed earlier (in chap. 4, sect. 6) that the premises of the theorem are doubtful, to put it mildly, and that it is politicaly unimportant anyway. For better or for worse, four decades of research on this theorem have not improved the situation: individual "rationality" does not guarantee collective "rationality." The major consequence for normative macroeconomics and sociotechnology in general is that individualist (in particular rational-choice) welfare economics is kaput.

This failure of individualist welfare economics suggests adopting a systemic approach to the problem of collective choice. One systemic idea is to combine sociotechnology with democracy, that is, to design and try out a technodemocratic procedure whereby the expert proposes and the public debates and disposes, or the citizens propose and the expert advises. In the simplest case, this procedure would consist in having the economic authority design two or more alternative economic policies to be submitted to a popular referendum preceded by a campaign devoted exclusively to explaining and debating the merits and demerits of the proposals, and succeeded by periodic evaluations and eventual readjustments (see, for example, Reich 1988). It should be noted that technodemocracy is not utopian. In fact, some Swiss cantons have been practising it for decades, though seldom with the benefits of previous organized grass-roots debate as well as subsequent periodic reviews. We shall return to technodemocracy in chapter 11.

Finally, how should theories in welfare economics be tested? According to de Graaff (1967, 3), "whereas the normal way of testing a theory in positive economics is to test its conclusions, the normal way of testing a welfare proposition is to test its assumptions." I submit that, if we are talking science, both the premises – particularly the tacit ones – and the conclusions of such a theory should be checked. Moreover, they should not only be checked against the relevant data: they should also be tested for precision, internal consistency, and external consistency, that is, compatibility with findings in neighbouring fields. And even all of this, though necessary, is insufficient, for the ultimate output of normative macroeconomics is not a model of reality but a set of policy recommendations. And the ultimate test for a policy, as for a strategy, is practise: Does it work? And does it work morally and politically as well as economically?

Since standard welfare economics is centred in its fundamental theorem, which in turn involves Pareto optimality, the question whether it works can be recast as follows: Does capitalism work both economically and morally – that is, is it both efficient and fair? However, this question deserves a separate section.

5 Capitalism: Old and New, Pro and Con

Let us start with a few definitions. *Capitalism* is the socioeconomic order characterized by the private ownership of the means of production, free (individual or collective) contracting of labour, and markets that operate competitively at set prices. *Industrial capitalism* is the kind of capitalism characterized by large-scale manufacture informed by science-based technology, and with a market that delivers basic necessities at low prices. *Corporate capitalism* is the kind of industrial capitalism in which comparatively few large firms, some of them transnational, control the bulk of production, trade, and finance. And the oxymoron *post-industrial capitalism* denotes the variety of corporate capitalism wherein at least half of the workforce is engaged in services – nowadays most of it increasingly lowly paid or temporary – some of which require the application of fairly advanced knowledge. But, wherever it exists, capitalism coexists with non-capitalist economic activities, such as those of cooperatives, state-owned-and-operated firms, and rural communities with a subsistence economy. Hence, the various concepts of capitalism are so many ideal types.

Where a capitalist economy of some kind is dominant, it is the nucleus of a whole social order. In this case we may speak of a *capitalist society* characterized by the following features: (a) most of the means of production, exchange, and finance are privately owned by individuals or firms; (b) by and large private interests override the public interest; (c) the wages and prices of most commodities are mainly determined either by the market (when free) or by a handful of oligopolies; (d) the state, in particular the legal system, secures the exercise of property rights – if necessary by violent means – and on the whole favours the capitalist class; (e) the culture, in particular the public school system, upholds the values and norms favourable to so-called free enterprise; (f) industry, trade, and government utilize science-based technologies.

(Note that this characterization does not include political democracy, even though the latter was originally a sibling of capitalism – but so were modern science, science-based technology, and modern philosophy. The numerous cases of dictatorship coupled to capitalism – nay, deliberately engineered to shore up capitalism in times of social unrest – prove that democracy is not the natural mate of capitalism. Democracy in its various guises was invented by politicians and intellectuals not by businessmen. Moreover, it may be argued that "capitalism creates pressures [for democratization] in spite of capitalists, not because of them" [Rueschemeyer et al. 1992, 271]. Finally, an increasing number of apologists for classical capitalism [e.g., Crozier et al. 1975; Hayek 1979; Seldon 1990; and Radnitzky 1993] claim that politics, in particular democratic politics, may become or are already an obstacle to capitalism. In sum, industrial capitalism and modern political democracy, though siblings, are mutually independent. This is why there is more than one pro-capitalist ideology and more than one pro-democratic ideology.)

The market is a subsystem of any economy, namely the one whose specific function is the exchange of commodities (recall chap. 3). In other words, the market is the system composed of buyers and sellers and held together mainly by the bonds of trade and credit, most of which are ephemeral. (The capitalist market has an additional function: that of pricing wages and commodities.) But no market is autonomous and apolitical. First, because all trade activities, whether or not in capitalist economies, are embedded in society at large and are channelled through social networks of various kinds (Granovetter 1985). Second, because the state is present in the modern market as builder and manager of a huge infrastructure and a complex culture, as well as lawmaker, regulator, umpire, guarantor, competitor, policeman, educator, partner in business or in R&D, and so forth. Consequently, the "market versus state" rhetoric masks reality (see Hollingsworth et al. 1994).

In principle, the market can be either free or regulated to some extent or other. If self-propelled by the profit motive and unfettered by government rules, the market is said to be free (or "savage") even when actually controlled by a handful of oligopolies. Under communist rule the market is almost totally controlled by the state, so that the so-called laws of the market do not apply at all. But it is still a market of sorts because it is composed by sellers and buyers. However, the prices are artificial instead of being determined by costs, revenues, competition, and the concentration of wealth.

The question whether the free-market economy works is a loaded one, for it presupposes the existence of such a market. Now, it is common knowledge that the free market is an ideal type, in fact an increasingly ideal one. Indeed, in every contemporary economy there are restrictions to private property, free enterprise, or both, such as those imposed by governments and labour unions – not to speak of barriers to entry and exit, cartels, and oligopolies. (Recall chap. 3, sects. 6 to 8.) There are then *degrees* of market freedom and, correspondingly, different types of capitalism, from raw ("savage") to welfare ("humane") – or palaeocapitalism and neocapitalism respectively.

However, our present task is not to describe capitalism but to assess the claim that it works better the less government interferes with it. If the market works, does it work for everyone and always, or at least for most people most of the time? And if there are market failures and externalities, are all of these due exclusively to either government interference or imperfect competition, that is, departures from the ideal type? Or are they inherent in the very principles of private property and decentralized profit-seeking?

The conservative (or neoliberal or libertarian) thesis, that a healthy market calls for a non-interventionist state, is false. In fact, the state is needed to guarantee minimally fair economic play, and even to protect the market from itself, particularly when in severe disequilibrium. The Committee for Economic Development (1996), a loud corporate voice, favours social expenditures in addition to private investment in economic security, health insurance, and on-the-job training. Two Mancunian politologists go even farther: "[T]he more brutally competitive are market processes, the more vital is the role of state power. Markets have to be defended: against intellectuals, against the losers in competitive struggles, against capitalists and against workers" (Moran and Wright 1991, 284).

The market has undeniable virtues. One of them is that its pricing procedure, even when heavily distorted by oligopoly, is economically preferable to the arbitrary pricing instituted by a central bureaucracy that pays insufficient attention to costs and revenues, and is therefore likely to shore up technically bankrupt enterprises. Second, the market encourages personal initiative and responsibility – though only at the top. Third, the market rewards technological and managerial ingenuity – though not consistently and, again, only among the top decision makers. (Most new enterprises fail within five years: the market selection pressure is more ruthless than rational. Moreover, Tellis and Golder

[1996, 73], experts in the economics of technological innovation, have found that "[m]arket pioneering is neither necessary nor sufficient for long-term success and leadership.") Fourth, by stressing competition, the market keeps people on their toes – though it often brings them to their knees. Fifth, over most of the past century the capitalist market has raised remarkably the absolute standard of living of the majority of the population in the industrialized countries – not elsewhere, though. Sixth, the market has increased the fraction of the population with access to private property – though most people have no assets to speak of. Seventh, the market offers an astonishing variety of commodities – some of them superfluous or harmful, though. (More on market virtues in Arndt 1984, 124–5.) Since the market has so many virtues and defects, we should try to perfect it: see sections 7 and 8, and Miller 1989b.

Sometimes the capitalist market works, though not equally well for rich and poor. The market has worked well for the majority of the population in the advanced industrialized countries equipped with welfare systems, offering plenty of commodities in great (often excessive) variety at accessible prices, as well as opportunities for gainful employment and advancement. But this happens only in periods of prosperity, such as the 1946 to 1973 period in the West – an era of post-war reconstruction and growth guided by Keynesian macroeconomic policies. Even so, from Columbus onwards the prosperity of the First World has been achieved largely at the expense of the Third World, which has been supplying cheap raw materials and foodstuffs, as well as cheap labour and a market for industrial goods – and bads.

Paradoxically, the market works best in barter economies and in the underground sector, as well as for goods and services that are not essential to survival, such as guns, narcotics, alcoholic beverages, cigarettes, fancy food, mouthwashes, TV sets, and cars. Even in normal times the market is not always the best mechanism for price determination and resource allocation for essential commodities. For example, were it not for state subsidies, the farmers in the US, Canada, Western Europe, and Japan would produce either too much or not enough, at low prices. Likewise, without state support, health care and education would be prohibitively expensive, while science, the humanities, and the arts would languish or even perish. In these cases *laissez-faire* amounts to *laissez-mourir*.

Obviously, the market fails dramatically during recessions. Even large firms have been known to go under at such times. And even in good times market failures – such as glut and scarcity, mass unemployment and underemployment, high barriers to entry and exit, pollution, and the depletion of non-renewable natural resources – are so serious and constant that they are the object of a vast literature. In most nations they are also the object of a large body of legislation. In short, the market does not effect an *efficient and sustainable* allocation of resources, particularly of human resources. Ironically, the capitalist market does not even effect an efficient allocation of capital: witness the large percentage of either underpriced or overpriced stocks, as well as the stockmarket "bubbles" and crashes – particularly before the regulations introduced in the 1930s. In short, the so-called less-developed market is both technically and morally flawed.

In the so-called developing nations the free market has seldom worked well. First, the introduction of capitalist or semi-capitalist market economies to these peoples has often changed their ways of life in a catastrophic manner. In fact it has (a) encouraged people to work mainly for the market (notably cultivating cash crops) instead of working to support their families; (b) ripped the traditional social networks that had been formed for their own protection; and (c) substituted an imitative culture for the traditional one. (For example, the dumping of English textiles on India ruined its domestic looms; the encouragement of cash crops for exports in Africa distorted its agriculture to the point of causing famines [Moore Lappé and Collins 1988]; and low-grade international commercial culture is replacing genuine culture everywhere.) Second, in these countries the state is often the main or even sole source of funds (through taxes, bond issues, or foreign loans) to build an infrastructure, exploit on a large scale natural resources (in particular energy sources), and help small enterprises. Third, only the state may have the power to (a) protect the natural resources, (b) correct extreme economic inequalities, and (c) offer modern education and health care to everyone. At any rate, the statistics are eloquent: capitalist development increases income inequality within and between communities (see, for instance, Smith 1991). To put it mildly, capitalism has not been kind to the Third World. Hence, preaching the free-market gospel in that region amounts to condemning it to backwardness and dependency.

In addition to its technical deficiencies, namely market failures and externalities, as well as the widening of the North-South gap, the so-called free market – or raw capitalism – has serious social and moral shortcomings. These derive ultimately from the selfishness that it encourages. Indeed, since the motor of capitalism is private profit-seeking, it encourages antisocial behaviour – though within bounds in peacetime. Under raw capitalism what money says goes. Hence, it is neither willing nor able to secure certain basic social desiderata, or even the survival of humankind.

For example, capitalism thrives only with economic growth – which is accompanied by consumerism and environmental degradation. The capitalist market does not filter out junk commodities: on the contrary, it encourages their consumption. It won't minimize waste: on the contrary, it thrives on the discarding of short-lived products and on energy waste. It has not brought about full social justice: on the contrary, it has entrenched or even exacerbated economic inequality. It won't secure full employment: on the contrary, some unemployment is inevitable as a result of increased productivity; moreover, unemployment is useful to check inflation (sometimes), depress wages, and keep the labour unions down.

The market won't prevent a handful of nations from exploiting most of the rest: on the contrary, capitalism and colonialism (or neocolonialism) go hand in hand. It won't curb the looting of natural resources: on the contrary, it started such pillage on a global scale five centuries ago. It won't prevent wars: on the contrary, being inherently expansive, capitalism is to be blamed for two world wars and an untold number of colonial wars. It does not secure democracy: on the contrary, it has prompted a large number of authoritarian and even fascist regimes – as well as uncounted communist and populist backlashes. It won't interfere with the population explosion, for it welcomes droves of new consumers. It won't secure universal health care, because it abhors tax hikes. It won't foster any disinterested pursuits, such as the basic sciences, the humanities, the arts, or even education, beyond what is strictly necessary to train skilled workers, physicians, technologists, and managers.

Last, but not least, the market is not a morality school: although it requires a modicum of decency, the market breeds more scoundrels than saints. After all, a place where "too smart" is the same as "crooked" is a permanent source of strong temptation for evildoing. Remember Keynes's celebrated complaint that, in the present society, we must pretend that "fair is foul and foul is fair; for foul is useful and fair is not." (For further shortcomings of capitalism see, for instance, Schumpeter 1950; Macpherson 1973; Balogh 1982; Schotter 1985; and Wiener 1994.) In short, capitalism is morally flawed as well as the most destructive (and at the same time the most creative) social order in world history. So much for the evils of palaeocapitalism.

An honest rejoinder could be this: "The above may be true but it is irrelevant, for the only function of the market is to make exchanges possible and, through them, to control the supply of commodities, their quality, and their prices. The social functions alluded to above could be discharged by cooperatives or governments." True enough, but this is not the line taken by the free-market advocates. In particular, G. Becker, J. Buchanan, D. Gauthier, M. Friedman, F. Hayek, L. von Mises, R. Nozick, and many others – in particular Ronald Reagan, Margaret Thatcher, and uncounted economic journalists – have claimed that the "free" capitalist market is a neutral and self-regulating system that satisfies the desires of all human beings, and thus external interferences, in particular government regulations, can only damage it to everyone's loss. But they have not proved their thesis.

Free-marketeers conveniently overlook the fact that the so-called free market is part of a social order that has bred uncounted wars, small and big, and has failed to give the vast majority of people the chance of doing what they want – such as working for the pride and joy of a job well done as well as for a decent livelihood; of living without fear of bankruptcy, destitution, violence, or humiliation; of owning their own home; of being able to give their children a good education; of having a say in managing their workplace and their community; or even of breathing clean air and inhabiting pleasant surroundings. The apology for raw capitalism is insensitive to the basic needs and legitimate aspirations of the losers in the economic rat race – who happen to be the vast majority of human beings, because only a few become and remain prosperous businessmen. It results from deliberate moral and political choices: those of defending private interests, and of pretending that normative macroeconomics is morally and politically neutral.

The said apology results also from wilful ignorance of the possibility, noted by Schumpeter (1950), that raw capitalism may be killed by its own economic success. Indeed, raw capitalism succeeded to the extent that it stimulated waste, exploited or underused human resources, polluted the environment, looted the Third World, and expanded through trade wars or military adventures. If only because it fouls the wellspring of its own success, raw capitalism is economically unsustainable on top of being politically vulnerable because of the domestic and international inequalities it involves. This is why in the most advanced nations it has been superseded by welfare capitalism.

Indeed, the economic and moral deficiencies of the so-called free market, or palaeocapitalism, are so severe that they prompted a number of social reforms carried out in the so-called West roughly between 1880 and 1960 (see, for instance, Hicks et al. 1995). Some of these reforms were favoured not only by the European social democrats and Christian democrats, but also by the British "red Tories," such as Disraeli, and by such notorious subversives as Otto von Bismarck, Henry Ford, Franklin D. Roosevelt, and Lyndon B. Johnson. The last two men had the benefit of the advice of Keynes's disciples, who were intent on saving capitalism from itself. Keynes (1926, 53) himself had earlier advocated and prophesied the end of *laissez-faire* or raw capitalism. He found it "in many ways extremely objectionable. Our problem is to work out a social organisation which shall be as efficient as possible without offending our notions of a satisfactory way of life."

The result has been what is called welfare capitalism, the social market, or neocapitalism, of which there are several varieties (see Esping-Andersen 1994). Statistics show that capitalism works best, economically as well as politically and morally, where it combines economic efficiency with a good measure of social justice watched by vigorous labour unions – for example, in Australia, post-war Austria, Belgium, Canada, France, Germany, the Netherlands, and Scandinavia. And it has fared worse in the UK, the US, and Latin America since the neo-"liberal" (conservative) counter-revolution of the 1980s. In fact, social statistics show that this social regression has worsened everyone's lot except that of the upper crust; it has deteriorated the public health-care and educational systems; it has increased unemployment and underemployment, which have caused a sharp increase in criminality; it has increased income inequality; and it has intensified selfishness and created a cynical and despondent mood among the young.

Neocapitalism combines capitalism with socialism. It keeps private property but limits some of the damage it causes; and it institutes a moderate version of socialism in the form of transfer payments (a redistribution of profits) that ensure a satisfactory standard of living for most. In some places, notably in Sweden, it also institutes a good measure of democratic governance in the workplace, which enhances work satisfaction to the benefit of all concerned (see Buber-Agassi 1985). Besides, welfare capitalism involves a strong public sector, particularly in banking, insurance, transportation, and communications – not to mention health care, education, science, technology, the humanities, and the arts. The state-owned enterprises are socialist to the extent that their goal is to serve the public rather than to make profit for a few. But of course they are not and could not be self-managed: they are run by technocracies or bureaucracies that are sometimes excessively expensive and authoritarian, and are seldom if ever accountable to the users.

The welfare state exercises legal paternalism: it protects the individual against others and even against himself. But, if liberal, the state refrains from exercising moral and religious paternalism, that is, from imposing official moral or religious canons ruling individual behaviour in every domain. (Ironically, neoconservatives and religious conservatives tend to favour moral and religious control while rejecting legal paternalism when the latter attempts to check social injustice through social programs.) The rationale of legal paternalism is concern for fairness to all; that of moral and religious paternalism is concern for obedience. However, legal paternalism can become almost as pernicious as moral and religious paternalism by taking over the responsibility of welfare recipients to chart the course of their own lives. This is one reason for regarding the welfare state as a makeshift to be eventually superseded by integral democracy – of which more in section 8.

Let us now tackle the nationalization/privatization dilemma. Economic "liberals" – who are not necessarily politically liberal – preach the privatization of all state-owned enterprises on the following grounds. They claim that such enterprises cannot help being inefficient and that all profitable businesses should be conducted by private firms. The first argument, of a practical nature, is shaky, for in Western Europe and elsewhere there are plenty of extremely efficient state-owned enterprises in transportation, communications, banking, insurance, health care, and education. The second conservative argument is of a principled nature and it is reasonable. In fact, the specific function of the state should not be business but government, in particular legislating social behaviour, managing essential public services – such as defence, security, justice, education, health care, and environmental protection – and providing relief to the needy. By assuming business functions, the state limits private initiative and it may grow to the point of becoming an economic burden and a threat to liberty. This is true, but it should only apply to proposed new inessential public services. It is not in the public interest to privatize public services that are run efficiently. Indeed, the defining feature of a public service is that it serves the public. If it does so efficiently, it should be improved rather than destroyed.

Anyhow there is an alternative to the nationalization/privatization dilemma, namely this: The state should manage all, and only the essential, public goods, leaving all others in the hands of private firms – preferably cooperatives – which it should oversee in the public interest. The state has no business running factories, farms, supermarkets, transportation firms, banks, or even utilities, all of which could be owned and run by cooperative enterprises. But the state of any civilized nation does have the obligations to (a) defend the population from foreign attacks; (b) optimize internal security; (c) protect the weak and minorities; (d) guarantee the exercise of all the basic liberties; (e) protect natural resources; (f) supply essential services that would otherwise be accessible only to the wealthy; (g) coordinate production, finance, and trade, protecting the public from the predatory tendencies inherent in private business; (h) modulate competition and promote cooperation; (i) protect future generations against the greed of the living; and (j) support education, basic science, the humanities, and the arts – none of which can be run by business firms. The preservation of civilization and even the survival of humankind require states that are capable of discharging these tasks in an efficient manner. By contrast, the total privatization envisaged by radical conservatives puts both goals at risk. (Ironically, the same ideologues do not worry over the growing invasion of private life that businesses as well as governments engage in. How about privatizating private life?)

Fortunately we are not always at the mercy of either the state or business for, in addition to these, in all democratic nations there are plenty of voluntary or nongovernmental organizations (NGOs). For example, in Britain, Canada, and other countries blood banks are run by charities and depend on voluntary donations, whereas elsewhere blood has become a commodity. To the surprise of many, the voluntary system is not only the fairest but also the cleanest as well as the most efficient in economic terms (Titmuss 1971). The case of the organs market is similar. In both cases, private enterprise may involve unsanitary conditions, exploitation, sometimes even murder; and it always leaves out the needy and erodes solidarity.

To conclude. Neocapitalism (a.k.a welfare liberalism) is the most advanced social order tried so far, but it is still imperfect. In particular, it has not avoided business cycles and military conflicts originating in economic interests; and it has yet to be shown that it could thrive without exploiting the so-called developing nations, which supply cheap raw material and labour, and constitute a large market for the industrialized nations – especially for guns, cigarettes, and beer. Moreover, welfare capitalism cannot improve beyond certain limits. Indeed, (a) the welfare state only lessens socio-economic inequality; in particular, it relieves poverty but does not eradicate it; (b) though it saves lives, it does not eliminate drudgery or drabness, underemployment, or unemployment; (c) it often involves a fat, inefficient, and self-serving bureaucracy; (d) it creates welfare-dependency, which is fiscally burdensome and morally degrading; and (e) it undermines solidarity by relieving citizens of their obligations towards each other (Kropotkin 1902, 227).

Worse has been happening since about 1980: everywhere the welfare state is in crisis. This is due to a combination of three factors, one biological, the second technological, and the third political. The first is increasing longevity and the consequent increase in welfare expenditures. The second is increasing productivity, which is causing irreversible mass unemployment and underemployment that might be offset only by a drastic reduction of the work week accompanied by a drop in wages – unless the extra wealth created by the rise in productivity were equitably distributed, which of course would endanger capitalism. The third is the pressure of neoconservative political parties and fundamentalist churches. These three factors together have persuaded many that the welfare state has become too expensive. These same people seem to forget other staggering costs, such as the unending arms build-up and business aid – which at the time of this writing amounts to about $150 billion in the USA. In any event, the welfare state is being dismantled in many nations. Thus, the much-touted final triumph of (palaeo)capitalism is threatening the precarious balance between private interests and public interests that had been achieved by welfare capitalism (see Mintzberg 1996a).

Are there technically and morally preferable alternatives to welfare capitalism? Let us examine two candidates: totalitarianism and cooperativism.

6 Statism: Fascist and Communist

Statism, or *totalitarianism*, is the social order in which the state monopolizes all political power, proscribes all dissent, rules the cultural life, and invades the private sphere. The earliest totalitarian states were military (as in Sparta) or theocratic (as in Tibet). In modern times there have been two kinds of statist social orders: communist and fascist. The former began as a revolt against exploitation (and in the Soviet case against war as well), whereas fascism was the child of the very rich and the military caste. Though initially these two social orders were poles apart, under Stalin's clique state socialism became increasingly closer to fascism. In fact, the Soviet order ended up by being a class society where a minority exploited and oppressed a silent majority. In both cases the state was in the hands of a tiny non-elected and therefore unaccountable and unresponsive elite.

However, there were important differences between the two forms of statism. Under communism the means of production were nationalized (not socialized), while under fascism they remained mostly in private hands. Communist statism not only set up a modern industrial economy, a powerful military machine, a prepotent bureaucracy, and a police state. It also built a welfare system that eliminated misery and provided job security, low rents, and free education and health care for all, in exchange for political and cultural submission. Under fascism the welfare system was either far weaker or non-existent, and prosperity for all was promised after the final victory. Under communist statism most people benefited both economically and culturally, although its main beneficiaries were the high-ranking party officials: they owned little but controlled everything. Fascism only benefited the high-ranking party officials and the big industrialists and landowners. In both cases, the vast majority of the population had no say whatsoever in public matters: they were handcuffed and gagged. This alone suffices to indict both forms of totalitarianism as morally reprehensible.

I call 'socialist statism' what communists call 'real [as opposed to ideal] socialism.' I submit that socialist statism is bogus socialism (or communism), because (a) the means of production were not socialized, that is, put in the hands of the workers: they were owned and managed by the state; and (b) except for a short initial period, no business enterprise and no cultural institution was self-managed. Ironically, Engels (1878, 385) had warned against mistaking nationalization for socialization, calling the state ownership of industrial establishments *spurious socialism*. He was right, because under state socialism the state is the boss, and as such it can impose unfair inequalities of all kinds, whereas the gist of genuine socialism is egalitarianism. But neither Engels nor Marx proposed any clear alternatives: both derided the drawing of blueprints as utopian. They offered their followers no guidance for the reconstruction of society (see Popper 1962, chap. 13). They offered only the mirage of a society without conflicts – mirage because conflict is just as inevitable (and sometimes productive) as cooperation.

When they seized power in 1917, the Bolsheviks had neither a theory of the state nor a clear vision of the new society they wished to construct. Moreover, the struggle to consolidate their power made them forget Marx's and Engels's moral motivations for changing the social order, namely their abhorrence of exploitation. Eventually they came up with a project that was technically as well as morally flawed. It was technically deficient because Lenin and his comrades had a simplistic vision. In fact, their formula was "Socialism = Soviet power + Electrification." Moreover, they equated Soviet power with the nationalization of the means of production together with the "dictatorship of the proletariat." But, as we saw above, nationalization does not equal socialization, for it excludes self-government. And the "dictatorship of the proletariat" proved to be nothing but the tyranny of a minuscule elite. The noble ideal of the classless and solidary society, where every individual would have the means to meet his needs and actualize his potentialities, as well as the willingness to help his neighbour, was never put into practise. Worse, this ideal has become discredited for having served the rhetoric of an oppressive, largely inefficient, and corrupt regime. The moral of this story is clear: Ideology is impotent without technology, and it is evil when it overlooks morality.

In sum, the Bolsheviks resorted to improvisation, and they spent more energy fighting enemies, both real and imaginary, than in redesigning society. They failed largely for lack of a scientific political theory and a comprehensive social policy. If this be admitted, it follows that the failure of the Soviet Union does not prove the failure of genuine socialism.

7 Socialism as Cooperativism

The word *socialism* denotes both a political ideology and the social order it advocates. The latter may also be called *socialist society*. In view of the bewildering variety of kinds of socialism and the current worldwide crisis of various kinds of socialism, we had better start by defining what we mean by 'authentic socialism.'

Authentic socialism is a classless social order, that is, one wherin all the goods and burdens are equitably distributed. It is characterized by (a) the cooperative ownership of the means of production, trade, and credit and (b) the self-management of all business firms – that is, democracy in the workplace. Shorter: Authentic socialism = Cooperative property together with self-management. This kind of socialism has never been tried on a national scale, and it has nothing to do with "real" (actually surreal) socialism.

Authentic socialism is more in line with the ideals of Mill and Kropotkin than with those of Marx or Lenin. In fact, we read in the former's *Principles of Political Economy* (1965, 775): "The form of association ... which if mankind continue to improve, must be expected in the end to predominate, is not that which can exist between a capitalist as chief, and workpeople without a voice in the management, but the association of the labourers themselves on terms of equality, collectively owning the capital with which they carry on their operations, and working under managers elected and removable by themselves." (See also Vanek 1975; Miller 1977, 1989b; Clayre 1980; Zwerdling 1980; Carens 1981; Louis 1981; Dahl 1985; Elster 1989; Elster and Moehne 1989; Le Grand and Estrin 1989; Przeworski 1991; Flakierski 1995; Pierson 1995; *Annals of Public and Cooperative Economics*; and ILO's Cooperative Development series.)

Cooperativism may be regarded as a socialized and updated version of Locke's (1681–9, 2: chap. 5, sect. 27) principles that (a) the natural resources belong by rights to "mankind in common"; (b) the worker owns by rights the fruits of his labour; and (c) my property rights stop where your right to self-preservation begins. These principles are egalitarian in restricting the control of wealth to those who produce it. But principle (b) is one of qualified or meritocratic rather than literal or radical equality, for it rewards competence, leadership, and dedication. Taken together, the three principles are akin to the ideas of social justice as fairness, and of democracy in the workplace.

Locke's first principle need not be revised for our time. Actually it is more topical than ever, given the increasing scarcity of arable land, forests, water, mineral deposits, fish banks, and other natural resources. His second principle must be revised in light of the social character of modern manufacture and farming, which makes it seldom possible to ascertain what exactly are the fruits of each individual's work. Given the complexity and extreme division of labour of the modern business firm, Locke's second principle might be revised to read thus: "The firm as a whole owns the fruits of the labour (manual, clerical, or managerial, productive or commercial) of its members." Finally, Locke's third principle needs only a slight extension, to read as follows: "The property rights of every individual or cooperative are limited only by the rights of others."

How are we to choose between authentic socialism and capitalism? Pareto (1906, 257) admitted that such a choice depends upon non-economic reasons. The following political, psychological, and moral reasons favour cooperativist socialism over capitalism. Cooperativism (a) eliminates the root of class conflicts (some of which have led to civil wars); (b) relies on reciprocity, a far stronger and lasting social bond than either subordination or impersonal market relations (see Polanyi 1944); (c) substitutes personal initiative, responsibility, and open debate for both blind obedience and confrontation; (d) offers all members the incentives deriving from participating in management as well as profits; (e) increases job satisfaction by facilitating the flexibility of job specifications and shifts; (f) supports entrepreneurship while decreasing its risks; (g) could solve the problem of technological unemployment and underemployment by decreasing the work week; (h) involves the decentralization required to make grass-roots participation possible as well as to endow the firm with the agility required by a rapidly changing environment; (i) makes machinery and technology accessible to all cooperants; and (j) cuts down on bureaucratic waste and unjustified salaries and perks paid to top-level megacorporation officers.

The spectacular and sustained success of the Mondragón network of about one hundred highly diversified cooperatives in the Basque country shows that cooperatives can perform well even in a capitalist environment (Thomas and Logan 1982; Whyte and Whyte 1988; Le Grand and Estrin 1989; Flakierski 1995). Moreover, cooperativism is spreading around the corporate world, where strategic alliances are formed to decrease transaction costs and share costly and risky R&D (see Granovetter 1994). On a far more modest scale, think of the thousands of successful carpools in the United States (More in Craig 1993.)

The reason for the economic success of some cooperative firms is that they involve the following virtuous circle: worker participation → worker effectiveness → customer value → customer satisfaction → customer loyalty → shared profit → worker satisfaction → worker effectiveness. Empirical studies (e.g., Hodson 1996) have shown that worker participation is effective, even when unaccompanied by collective ownership, because greater responsibility enhances job satisfaction, learning, pride in work, and productivity.

Cooperativism is also morally superior to its alternatives in being fair to all cooperants and giving them a say in the way their own lives are run, particularly at the workplace. In fact, whereas under all other social orders only a few are propertied and empowered, under cooperative socialism everyone is both owner and manager. This is not only morally desirable but also psychologically effective, for no one looks after property better than its owner-manager-user.

The next question is whether this kind of socialism is desirable and viable. I submit that it is neither – not because it is excessive but in being insufficient. In fact, in its original form cooperative socialism (a) ignores the inevitability, indeed desirability, of (regulated) competition alongside (coordinated) cooperation; (b) is sectoral rather than systemic, for it concerns only the ownership and management of the means of production: it is silent about politics and culture; (c) ignores the problem of coordinating the cooperatives on a national, let alone regional or global, scale; in particular, it does not address the problem of the unequal receipts of unequally wealthy cooperatives – for example, those that mine uranium and those that publish philosophy books; and (d) it keeps silent about the management of public goods, such as security, defence, public health and education, environmental protection, science, the humanities, and the arts – that is, about the state.

In sum, cooperative property and self-management are desirable but insufficient, for being narrowly economicist. We need a social order inspired in a more comprehensive view of society: a systemic one. This alternative to the known social orders, namely integral democracy coupled with technical expertise, will be sketched in the following.

8 Alternative: Integral Technodemocracy

In the preceding sections I have argued that none of the known social orders is both economically efficient and socially just, hence morally justifiable. In particular I have submitted that statism (or totalitarianism), in both its left-wing and right-wing versions, is (a) morally inadmissible because it involves oppression, hence alienation; and (b) practically inefficient in the long run because it suppresses individual and local initiative as well as rational debate. I regard capitalism in its various forms, even at its best, as being (a) socially unfair, and therefore morally flawed, because it involves exploitation within and between nations; (b) practically inefficient, as it involves destructive business cycles and disequilibria, in particular unemployment; and (c) practically and morally objectionable because it gives rise to organized violence. And I regard market socialism as superior but inefficient because (a) it is one-sided (economicist) and (b) overlooks the global issues. In view of the shortcomings of both socialism and capitalism, alternatives to both should be explored.

Since the time of Richard Owen's New Lanark (1813) there have been a few theoretical or practical attempts to combine the positive features of capitalism with those of socialism. (The "Third Way" proclaimed by some fascist and populist movements is not one of them.) One of the oldest is profit sharing without worker participation in the firm's governance (see, for instance, Weitzman 1984). Its dual, labour-management co-determination, is enshrined in contemporary German law. A third is Halal's (1986) "new capitalism," which "fosters both cooperation and competition" through participative business leadership, worker safety, environmental and health protection, and the decentralization of the state. This blend of free enterprise with democracy is a step beyond welfare capitalism. It can also be highly profitable (Semler 1993). But, in keeping most means of production in a few hands, it still falls short of social justice and full democracy.

I have praised the political democracy inherent in welfare liberalism – that is, popular representation together with accountability. I have also praised cooperative socialism for involving economic democracy (economic power together with self-management). Political and economic democracy are both necessary to build a just social order, as stressed by Macpherson (1973), Lamont (1982), and Dahl (1985). In turn, these three were preceded by Mill (1924, 162), who wrote that the problem is "how to unite the greatest individual liberty of action, with a common ownership in the raw material of the globe, and an equal participation of all in the benefits of combined labour." Half a dozen varieties of market socialism, first sketched by Oskar Lange in the 1930s, have been advocated to attain those aims, in particular the labour-managed or bottom-up one (see Miller 1989a; Bardhan and Roemer 1993; Roemer 1994; Flakierski 1995; and Pierson 1995).

However, though necessary, political and economic democracy are insufficient because (a) the former only concerns the polity whereas the latter is only about the economy, so that neither tackles the environmental, biological, and cultural issues; and (b) modern society is extremely complex, our planet is overpopulated, and the environment is at risk. Since society is composed of four interlocked subsystems (the biological, economic, political, and cultural ones), every one of which is highly complex, and since population growth and the natural resources must be managed in a scientific manner, we should strive for integral democracy combined with technical expertise. In other words, the idea is to expand democracy and join it with sociotechnology (management science, normative macroeconomics, law, and so on). Let us examine this idea.

Technoholodemocracy (or *integral technodemocracy*) is the social order that ensures equality of sexes and races, as well as access to wealth, culture, and political power, with concern for the environment and the future. This is the goal. The means is, to paraphrase and qualify Lincoln, the enlightened rule of the people, by the people, and for the people in all social matters – and only in them. Shorter: Technoholodemocracy is equal opportunity through biological (sex and race) equality, participative democracy, cooperative property, self-management, technical expertise, and free access to culture.

The above schema calls for a few clarifications. First, technodemocracy is not to be confused with technocracy. Under technocracy – hardly viable because technicians serve power rather than wielding it – the experts would propose, the legislators would rubber-stamp, and the people would be remote and therefore even more alienated than under democracy. By contrast, under technodemocracy the lawmakers and state bureaucrats would consult the experts: such government would thus be more efficient than most. But one of the main threats to democracy nowadays, namely the growing political cynicism, apathy, and disaffection of the governed, would remain. Though respected, good housekeeping is never loved. Only a drastic expansion of the set of rights and duties of all kinds could stimulate mass participation, command loyalty, and moralize habits.

Second, integral technodemocracy does not involve literal egalitarianism, let alone forced equalization à la Khmer Rouge: it only involves what may be called *qualified* or (*undominated*) *equality*, a combination of egalitarianism with meritocracy (Ackerman 1980; Bunge 1989a). This results from combining four principles: (a) article 25 of the UN Universal Declaration of Human Rights (1948), according to which everyone has the right to an adequate standard of living; (b) Marx's maxim "To each according to his needs, from each according to his abilities"; (c) Locke's principle of the rightful ownership of the fruits of one's labours (sect. 6); and (d) Rawls's (1971, 62) principle according to which the sole inequalities justified in the distribution of goods and burdens are those that benefit all, namely the reward of merit and the punishment of misdeed. For example, if an individual is twice as competent and dedicated as his homologue, then it is in the interest of everybody that the former should earn (or be otherwise rewarded) more than the latter, for his extra ability and dedication result in everyone's benefit. (In a non-market economy, just as in a community of scholars, the extra rewards consist of prestige and honours.)

Third, technoholodemocracy involves combining cooperation with competition. In particular, it joins cooperative ownership with the market. The former is needed to strengthen solidarity and avert exploitation and privilege. And we need competition to encourage emulation, initiative, creativity, excellence, selectivity, and advancement. However, competition ought to serve the public as well as private interests. This kind of competition may be called *coordinated* or *managed competition*, in contrast to the cut-throat competition typical of raw ("savage") capitalism. And controlled competition calls for coordination, regulation, bargaining, and strategic alliances. In short, we need the social or controlled market rather than the free market. (For a history of managed competition in the US since about 1850 see Chandler 1977; for a mathematical model see appendix 2.)

Fourth, every large-scale system calls for the central coordination of its component units: it requires setting up federations and governments at all three levels, and eventually a federal world government. All of these macrosystems should deliberate democratically with the help of expert advice, and they should act in the interests of their components. In particular, the state should be the neutral umpire and provider of information, technical advice, safety standards, and financial assistance in the service of all. It should facilitate grass-roots coordination rather than impose it bureaucratically or by force, and it should act sometimes as a buffer and at other times as a catalyser.

Fifth, integral technodemocracy would require a far smaller and weaker state than any other social order since the dawn of the industrial civilization, and this for the following reasons. First, in a good society the overwhelming majority of organizations are voluntary and self-governing. Second, democratic economic planning does not command but only coordinates: it informs and makes suggestions about quantities and prices, so as to maintain equilibrium or restore it (recall chap. 9, sect. 8). Third, (nearly) full employment economy has no need for relief programs. Fourth, equity, reciprocity, solidarity, cooperative property, and grass-roots political participation render big law-enforcement agencies all but redundant. Fifth, well-educated, public-spirited, and morally upright citizens can supervise competently and honestly the administration of the common good. Sixth, a just and peaceful society needs at most a modest professional armed force.

In sum, a technoholodemocratic society would require only a comparatively small, highly competent, responsive, and accountable state. It would put in practise Lincoln's dream: "The legitimate object of government, is to do for a community of people, whatever they need to have done, but can not, *at all*, or can not, *so well do*, for themselves – in their separate, and individual capacities. In all that the people can do individually for themselves, government ought not to interfere" (Lincoln 1953, 2: 220).

Fifth, liberty, which is very restricted in a class society, and contracts, which often constitute only a fiction in it, should flourish in an integral democracy. Indeed, freedom – in particular the liberty to enter into fair contracts – can flourish only among equals. It is illusory wherever power of any kind is highly concentrated.

So much for integral democracy. (More in Bunge 1985b, 1989a; Dahl 1985, 1989; and Mathews 1989.)

Unlike basic economics, which has legitimate if frustrated scientific ambitions, normative economics is a socio-technology, for it is expected to tackle socio-economic issues as well as to recommend definite policies and programs to fix them. Some of these issues, such as the full employment–inflation dilemma, are of the short-term kind; others concern no less than the socio-economic order that it would be both rationally and morally desirable to strive for. Hence, normative economics makes room for both the fixer and the dreamer.

But, of course, the responsible fixer will worry about long-run consequences, in particular perverse effects. (For example, stimulation of consumer demand may help get out of a recession, only to invite demand inflation and further environmental degradation.) And socio-economic dreams are bound to turn into nightmares unless based on solid knowledge of the present situation, a clear grasp of the material and moral features of accessible means and attainable goals, and awareness that there can be no such thing as the final solution, that is, the perfect society dreamed up by some genius.

The central debates about long-term issues in normative economics over the past few decades have revolved around the socialism (or collectivism) – capitalism (or market) axis. Moreover, it has usually been assumed that no alternatives are possible. Hence, every criticism of (unregulated) capitalism has wrongly been taken to constitute an endorsement of (authoritarian) socialism and conversely. Yet, *tertium datur*. Indeed, in all advanced countries welfare capitalism is in place, though it is somewhat in trouble these days.

However, this particular combination of capitalism with socialism has failed to address, let alone solve, the issue of "survival" or sustainability, which all societies, rich or poor, advanced or backward, are facing. Indeed, neither of the social orders tried so far has tackled simultaneously the issues of overpopulation, depletion of natural resources, pollution, war, technological unemployment, social injustice, political marginality, and cultural poverty. This is a system, not just a set, of social issues: they are interrelated and therefore cannot be tackled one at a time.

Economists cannot tackle this system of issues because it overflows economics. In fact, it is a pentagonal problem: it has environmental, biological, economic, political, and cultural – in particular, moral and ideological – sides. Consequently, addressing responsibly the system of social issues requires the collaboration of all the social and socionatural sciences and technologies. Only thus can we hope to design a better future.

11

Designing the Future

The future of a natural thing beyond our reach "comes" without our assistance: it unfolds lawfully from present circumstances. Not so the future of a made object, such as an institution. The future of such a thing does not "come" at all: we make it, if not always deliberately, let alone rationally. We shape the future of society by acting now and by preparing for later action. But we are not all equally effective in modifying the present conditions in such a way that they will evolve into what we want. Some of us are forced to wait for the future, others dream it, and very few design it, even though all of us labour at the construction site.

Nearly everyone has come to realize that all our societies – rich or poor, advanced or backward, democratic or authoritarian – are imperfect. Witness environmental degradation, overpopulation, poverty, poor health, unemployment, political unrest, corruption, anomie, and cultural pollution. Scholars in increasing numbers have warned that humankind is in the throes of a severe global crisis that threatens industrial civilization and even human survival (see, for instance, Kurtz 1989).

However, social criticism, though necessary, is insufficient. Some of us believe that society can and must be reformed to forestall global catastrophe. And we add that any proposals for social reforms should be based on social studies, not just on electoral considerations. For example, social policy makers should know that social equality is a more reliable indicator of public health than are health-care expenditures (recall chap. 7, sect. 7). Hence, if genuinenly interested in public health, they will promote increases in social expenditures aimed at reducing social inequality, rather than increasing only health-care expenditures. (In general, input alone is a poor predictor of output or system performance simply because, by definition, Efficiency = Output / Input.)

I submit that to improve any contemporary society with maximal efficiency and minimal pain seven conditions must be met: (a) adequate knowledge of the main mechanisms of social stasis and change; (b) adequate knowledge of the current state of society, including its resources and ills; (c) adequate knowledge of the needs and aspirations of the people; (d) an imaginative but feasible vision of a better society; (e) the sociotechnical expertise and moral sensitivity required to design a worthy project; (f) an enlightened and popular leadership capable of "selling" the project; and (g) enough people eager to rally around their elected leaders to work for the project and monitor its implementation.

It is well known that the time lag between scientific findings and their application to engineering and biotechnology is getting ever shorter. Obviously, this is not the case with the sociotechnologies: these seldom benefit from recent findings of social studies. Why? One cause is that most social policy makers and planners mistrust social science and lack a scientific background: more often than not they are professional politicians or bureaucrats with, at best, a background in law or commerce. Another is that there is a wedge between social science and sociotechnology, namely, ideology. This is unavoidable and not deplorable in itself, because technology is neither value-free nor morally neutral. There would be no problem with a proscience and morally right ideology. The trouble is that most ideologies do not meet these conditions.

At any rate all the traditional ideologies are bankrupt. But, since we need some ideology to design social policies and plans, we should attempt to build a suitable new ideology. The latter should be based on both sound sociotechnology and sound morals, and it should be capable of helping us address social ills and work for a better social order: a fair, progressive, and sustainable one.

1 Macrosocial Issues and Their Inherent Values and Morals

Think of any of the threats to civilization or even human survival, such as overpopulation, rapid depletion of non-renewable resources; overindustrialization and consumerism in the rich countries, and underindustrialization and underconsumption in the poor ones; hunger and thirst; mass unemployment and underemployment; inadequate public education and health care; militarism and aggressive nationalism; race and sex discrimination; universal commodification and junk culture. Every one of these is a macrosocial issue and it poses a moral problem, for it affects us all, directly or indirectly, and it jeopardizes the future.

How have we come to the brink while at the same time making sensational advances in mathematics, natural science, engineering, medicine, and other fields? I submit that we have been misled by the prevailing value systems and the concomitant moral codes. It is not that these or any other ideas rule the world, but that – to indulge in a Platonic idiom – they are embodied in some of our key institutions.

The dominant value systems and moral codes can be grouped into two large families: individualism (or egocentrism) and holism (or sociocentrism). Whereas individualism promotes individual interests at the expense of the public good, holism sacrifices the individual to a whole that is not necessarily noble, and that is often invoked to disguise private interests. Ironically, both individualism and holism can promote either indifference or destructive conflict. Moreover, neither individualism nor holism meets the Socratic ideal of the good individual in a good society.

Only the systemic approach suggests a value system whose supreme good is species survival and reasonable personal happiness in a just social order. The corresponding supreme moral norm at the individual level fits this goal by combining selfishness with altruism, and welfare with justice. This norm is *Enjoy life and help live* (Bunge 1989a).

2 Utopianism and Ideals without Illusions

A social utopia is a vision of a perfect society unaccompanied by a specification of the means to build it. Utopianism is usually motivated by flaws (real or imaginary) in current societies, which it criticizes in a more or less veiled fashion. However, utopian fantasy need not be barren: a utopia is a sort of thought experiment or simulation prompting the examination of questions of the type, What would happen if such and such institutions were altered or even eliminated? This is why some social utopias, from Thomas More's (1518) on, have involved proposals that have fired social movements and reforms.

There is nothing wrong about imagining a better society even if one does not know how to build it. Others may suggest the appropriate means. A noble utopia is better than "realistic" (opportunistic and unscrupulous) politics. Still, dreamers do not accomplish much. Worse, they may seriously mislead those who adopt uncritically their diagnoses and prognoses, and even more so those who strive for the final society. These utopians ignore the fact that social conflict and value conflict are unavoidable features of any society – just as unavoidable as cooperation and partial value harmony. As Hutchison (1964, 127) wrote, "It is the main characteristic of Utopian thinking that, if only a particular Utopia is adopted, no hard choices between values and objectives are necessary, since the particular Utopia will provide *all* real *desiderata*, liberty, equality and fraternity, or freedom, social cohesion, stability economic and political ... and if there *are* any other *desiderata* they are not really worth desiring. In the communist Utopia all conflicts are, allegedly, abolished, and in the liberal Utopia they are all optimally mediated through the price mechanism." (See also van den Berg 1988.)

Between the traditional utopian and the *Realpolitiker* stands the realist and progressive social reformer. He may be called a *neo-utopian*: a realist without illusions, who begins by identifying the issues, and uses social science and sociotechnology to uncover their roots and treat them: first study, then act. He proceeds by analogy with the scientific physician: identify the problem cluster – study it scientifically – diagnose – plan – treat – check – revise if necessary.

Regrettably, in many cases the very first step, namely correct social diagnosis, is yet to be taken. Consider, for instance, income inequality as measured by the Gini index. It has been conjectured that this variable depends on GDP (national wealth), school enrolment, political regime, percentage of the population under fifteen, position in the world-system, and so forth (see, for example, Simpson 1990). But the precise form of such dependences is still under debate. In particular, the famous Kuznets hypothesis, that an inverted U-relation obtains between income inequality and GDP, has recently been refuted. In fact, Deininger and Squire (1996) have found no systematic (functional) relationship between the two variables in about 90 per cent of the 108 countries investigated. However, in the United States there is such relation; but, since 1969, it is one of increasing inequality (Harrison and Bluestone 1988). Some of the mechanisms of this U-turn seem to be racism, educational heterogeneity, and urbanization (Nielsen and Alderson 1997). Morals: (a) before designing a social reform, collect and interrelate relevant and good-quality data; and (b) economic growth alone is no recipe for overall social progress – more on which in sections 6 and 7.

To conclude: no society is perfect, some imperfections are defects, and some of these can be repaired. Some imperfections, that is, deviations from either the ideal type or the norm, are welcome because the type or the norm themselves may be undesirable – for example, because they are mediocre. Without imperfections there would be neither biological nor social evolution. Hence, we should not wish for a perfect society fitting a preconceived blueprint, but rather an imperfect but progressive society fitting successive visions, each better informed and fairer than the preceding, and every one of them viable. Such a neo-utopian program calls for as much social engineering as enthusiastic dedication and participation.

3 Social Engineering: Piecemeal and Systemic

One may attempt to change society through either revolution or reform. The former procedure promises a "quick fix," but it has well-known disadvantages:

It is hard to bring about, painful, dicey, costly, and has unforeseeable consequences – among them counter-revolution and degeneration into long-lasting dictatorship. Far from solving social problems, collective violence is one of them. For these reasons progressives and rationalists should prefer social reform to both revolution and counterrevolution.

Now, there are two kinds of social reform: piecemeal and systemic. The former is sectoral: it tackles social issues one at a time, introducing successively one social program per issue (see, for instance, Popper 1957). This procedure is ultimately ineffective or even counterproductive. First, because it attacks symptoms rather than causes. Second, because society happens to be a system of interdependent subsystems, not an aggregate of mutually independent individuals (see Bunge 1980, 1996a, 1996c and Hirschman 1990). As the historian E.H. Carr (1961, 207) noted, "Progress in human affairs ... has come mainly through the bold readiness of human beings not to confine themselves to seeking piecemeal improvements in the way things are done, but to present fundamental challenges in the name of reason to the current way of doing things and to the avowed or hidden assumptions on which it rests."

Any feasible, effective and lasting social reform with (roughly) foreseeable effects must then be radical and global (or systemic) as well as gradual. That is, it must be a slow but thorough and total change affecting the structure of all the four main subsystems of society and eventually, through these, the way people feel, think, and evaluate. Now, only political democracy offers the possibility of carrying out a reform of this kind. Dictatorships inhibit original social thinking, ban public rational debate of any reforms, and do not motivate personal effort.

The best-known nationwide social policies and plans are those designed for the "development" (economic growth) of Third World countries. Most of them have failed. (True, some of the emerging stock markets are doing well at the time of writing. But in the long run dependency on volatile foreign investment slows down economic growth and increases income inequality: see Dixon and Boswell 1996.) The failure of those plans is attributable to five major causes. One is the piecemeal (non-systemic or "one thing at a time") strategy. Another is that most development plans are national: they assume that national self-reliance is both possible and desirable. This nationalist assumption is false, for all peoples live on the same planet and are either dependent or interdependent. Only regional development plans, involving trade and cooperation among peers, can succeed. A third cause of failure is that none of the reforms envisaged so far has been radical enough. In particular, they have seldom included land reform and demilitarization. A fourth cause is the so-called Washington Consensus urged by the World Bank and the International Monetary Fund: Pay promptly the foreign debt, embrace the free market, invite foreign investment, cut social expenditures, and clip the wings of the labour unions. But, where the infrastructure is poor, and most people are unemployed or underemployed, ill nourished, in poor health, and unskilled, total reliance on the market only increases poverty and therefore "must be judged an unmitigated disaster" (Dasgupta and Ray 1986). A fifth cause of failure is weak or non-existent popular involvement in the design of most policies and plans, and the resultant lack of political support (Pettis 1996).

If this diagnosis is correct, it suggests that development policies and plans ought to be systemic rather than sectoral, as well as regional, radical, participative, and autogenous rather than imported. Although we can only take *one step* at a time, we must try to do *all things* at a time, because no component and no feature of society is independent of all its other components and features. (Parallels: child rearing and business management.)

4 Top-Down Planning

A social project is a plan to change the social structure, the lifestyle, and the associated value system of a whole society. It can be moderate or radical; it can be local, national, regional, or global; it can be rigid or flexible; and it can be authoritarian or democratic. Examples: The Meiji dynasty plan to have Japan catch up with the West; the Soviet Five Year plans aimed at modernizing the country; the Nazi plan to rearm and conquer; and the Marshall Plan to reconstruct Europe after the Second World War.

Social projects are of interest to philosophy because they pivot around value systems – existing or newly proposed, noble or despicable. The success or failure of a social project depends on the ability of the political and cultural elite to persuade most of the people to adopt the project. The project is likely to win popular support if it is perceived as answering the needs and desires of the people – even if in fact it does not. And the project may succeed if it enjoys such support, is realistic, and does not threaten other nations (Stern 1967, 270). If a social project succeeds, it reinforces the associated value system. If it fails, the underlying values sink along with it, at least for a while.

The transformation of a social order may be attempted from below, from above, or from the middle. The first way cannot work because, to succeed, every social movement needs competent leaders. The second or elitist way does not work either in the long run because it marginalizes the people by replacing one ruling class with another. In our time we have witnessed the ultimate failure of elitist attempts of three kinds: communist, fascist, and the authoritarian economic-development policies, such as the "shock therapy" currently advocated by mainstream economists to rebuild the ex-Soviet republics. It will be worth our while to take a quick look at the latter because it raises some philosophical issues.

An economic "shock therapy" to transform the former pseudosocialist economies is a social counter-revolution consisting in privatizing all public firms, creating an uncontrolled market, containing inflation as well as balancing the budget at all costs, and destroying whatever safety net may have existed to guarantee the survival of the neediest – all of this overnight. This treatment is recommended on the following assumptions: (a) any social order can be transformed radically from above and at one go; (b) nineteenth-century or raw capitalism is best; (c) mainstream economic theory is true; and (d) once "the economy" gets going the rest follows. But these assumptions are technically controversial, and the therapy is both sectoral and undemocratic, for it overlooks politics, culture, and morality.

The assumption (a) of nil social inertia is plainly false: the more drastic a social change, and the more people it involves, the longer it takes to implement, for old habits must be unlearned, unwanted social organizations must be dismantled, and new ones must be designed and set up. Assumption (b) too is false, for raw capitalism involves exploitation and often oppression as well – this being why it has been tempered in all advanced countries. Assumption (c) is false as well, as we saw in chapter 3. Ditto assumption (d): the economy is not autonomous and consequently it won't move in the desired direction unless the polity and the culture go along. In particular, successful economic reform calls for popular support, hence political democracy, rather than authoritarianism (Pickel 1993).

At the time of this writing the nations in the late USSR have no clearly defined social projects and no definite legal frameworks; there are plenty of demagogues and political gangs but no democratic political parties; there is some freedom but no democracy, that is, self-government; the state at all levels is weak and in disarray; and the culture – once strong if ideologically distorted – is a shambles. Under these conditions the *ukases* of an economic czar are at best bound to fail and add to the misery – except for the handful of adventurers with the cash required to buy shares of the newly privatized state firms. This is no transition from real socialism to real capitalism, but from unreal socialism to unreal capitalism – financeering, speculating, racketeering, and murdering. Unless the present trend is checked, the defunct Soviet Empire will end up by becoming just a source of cheap labour, raw materials, and energy for the West (see Sardar and Wyn Davies 1992).

In short, the so-called economic shock therapy is not working, and it is unlikely to work because it is sectoral and elitist – in countries that need productive work, democratic debate, participation, and hope. Besides, it is antisocial because it rips the safety net, and immoral in disregarding the welfare of the vast majority. The solution does not lie in substituting one authoritarian scheme for another, but in involving the people in the implementation of a social project of incremental but integral (not just economic) reconstruction over an entire generation. Such involvement requires trust in a new ideology that makes realistic promises of well-being and fairness, and that encourages using the newly won liberties to design and set up democratic (self-governed) organizations – in particular cooperatives – in all sectors of society. No such ideology is in sight in the former USSR.

5 Systemic Democratic Planning

As we saw in chapters 9 and 10, all large firms and all modern states plan even while their leaders engage in *laissez-faire* rhetoric. In particular, every state designs and implements plans when it hikes or cuts taxes or tariffs; when it regulates or deregulates, penalizes or subsidizes, certain sectors of the economy; when it adopts or scraps social programs; when it favours or prohibits family planning; when it spends either more or less money on education, health care, public works, defence, and so on. The modern statesman, like the manager and the housewife, has no choice but to plan (see, for instance, Lewis 1949 and Seni 1993).

The question is not whether to plan but how and for what. I submit that the only realistic and moral choice before us is between sectoral, authoritarian, and rigid planning, on the one hand, and systemic, participative (hence multilevel), and flexible planning, on the other. The costly failure of plans of the first kind suggests trying flexible social policies and plans that make ample room for free democratic debate and voluntary popular participation. Shorter: Any progressive, thorough, effective, and lasting transformation of a social order calls for *systemic, participative, multilevel, and flexible planning.*

Social planning should be systemic rather than sectoral because both society and social science are systems composed of a number of interdependent subsystems. And it must be participative, multilevel, and flexible, for technical as well as political reasons. The former is that only "the man on the spot" has the requisite knowledge of the local circumstances and people (Hayek 1949). The political (and moral) reason is that the imposition of a plan from above is inefficient as well as undemocratic. Instead of central command planning we need local plans coordinated at the centre – not the top.

Still, systemic, participative, multilevel, and flexible planning is not enough. Goals matter at least as much as strategy, since means and goals determine one another: recall chapter 7. The very first questions we must ask about any global, nationwide, or regional plan are these: (a) what kind of society we want to plan for: the jail (holism), the auction house (individualism), or the orchestra (systemism); (b) whether the plan is feasible; (c) which social changes are its implementation expected to bring about; and (d) whether these changes are likely to improve the quality of life of the greatest number without jeopardizing the welfare of future generations. That is, we must start by examining the project of a new society and the policy underlying the plan. In particular, if the target is growth, we must begin by asking, Growth in what respect(s) and for whose benefit?

6 Growth and Development

Growth is usually understood in a narrow sense, namely as economic growth, that is, output increase. Engineers, management scientists, and economists are supposed to know how to bring about such increase. And most of them take it for granted that economic growth is always a priority. But this assumption is questionable on both moral and political grounds. First, economic growth can be achieved through either increased exploitation of the workforce or techno-logical innovation. ("The economy," as reflected by purely economic indica-tors, may be flourishing along with a high poverty level.) Second, in many nations a large fraction of the output is due to the "informal" or underground economy, which involves self-exploitation or even exploitation in sweatshops and undermines the state (see Portes 1989). Third, the growth of most industri-alized nations has always derived largely from the exploitation of Third World countries. Fourth, these countries have the right to grow economically until the basic needs and legitimate wants of their people are met. Fifth, given that mili-tary expenditures, the production of luxury items, overcultivation, and overin-dustrialization are gobbling up the world's resources, economic growth should be checked in the developed nations. Sixth, economic growth without birth con-trol and cultural and political development is unsound, as will be argued below. In sum, economic growth alone is undesiderable.

Most development theorists are economists, and most economists equate development with economic growth, disregarding demographic factors, wealth and income distribution, public health, culture, politics, and the environment. (Notable exceptions: Lewis 1955; Hirschman 1958; Myrdal 1968; Prebisch 1981a; and Ekins 1986.) The idea is that, as long as the cake is small, there is little to distribute, whence the advice: Bake a larger pie, and everyone will eventually get a larger slice. But statistics suggest that inequality harms economic growth (Persson and Tabellini 1994). The mechanism is clear: (a) poor people are under-nourished and in poor health, thus incapable of performing efficiently; (b) lowly paid workers are not motivated to increase their productivity; (c) when land is in few hands there are few agricultural jobs – particularly where cattle displace people; (d) the internal market does not grow as long as the purchasing power of the majority is low. Hence one of the keys to development is to set up the chain reaction: equitable income distribution → work incentive → productivity increase → economic growth → higher profits and wages.

The sectoral vision has led to well-known disasters, such as hunger in countries with agricultural surpluses. Purely economic growth is likely to create new imbalances – for example, between manufacture and agriculture, urban and rural populations, the skilled and the unskilled. As long as development is lopsided it is bound to generate more imbalances than it corrects. In short, Development ≠ Economic growth.

To generalize, we characterize a *one-dimensional* development policy as one dealing exclusively with either the environment, the economy, the culture, public health, or the polity. For example, the World Bank was set up on the tenet that development equals economic growth, whereas UNESCO was set up on the assumption that the engine of progress is cultural (in particular educational) development. According to our systemic view of society, one-dimensional development policies can succeed at best in the short term, and even so they may cause severe disequilibria – for instance, between population growth on the one hand and the training of teachers and doctors on the other.

An integral or *multidimensional* development policy or plan is one favouring biological, economic, political, and cultural development jointly with scientific management of resources. Because every human society is composed of living beings organized in economic, political, and cultural subsystems embedded in a natural environment, only integral development policies and plans are likely to succeed in the long run (Bunge 1980; Perroux 1981; Max-Neef et al. 1990).

Regrettably, there is no generally accepted indicator of integral development. The human development index (HDI) adopted by the UN in 1990 comes closest, combining life expectancy, education level, and income: it is a systemic indicator. But – perhaps in deference to the undemocratic governments represented in the UN – it does not include political participation – the only effective means to steer and defend development. In any event, since authentic development is multidimensional and unequal across countries, it should be indicated by a vector or list of numbers rather than by a single number (Bunge 1981c).

7 Integral and Sustainable Development

Our five-wheel-drive model of development suggests that an integral development plan for the twenty-first century should include the following major goals:

Environmental: Energy saving; search for and exploitation of clean renewable energy sources; environmental clean-up; drastic reduction of domestic and industrial waste and pollution; repair and protection of the ozone layer; reforestation; desert reclamation; reversal of the acidification of lakes and streams; protection of biodiversity; globally coordinated environmental protection; and global management of mineral and marine resources.

Biological: Adequate nutrition, shelter, and health care for all; family planning that aims at adapting the world population to the planet's (unknown but already strained) carrying capacity; and incentives to resettle it rationally and humanely.

Economic: Full employment through shorter work weeks; mutual adjustment of work force and technology; multiplication of cooperatives, mutual societies, and joint business ventures; regulated markets; prevention of food hoarding; control of business cycles; free trade among peers; support of sustainable farming; progressive taxation on consumption; and drastic decrease of the consumption of beef, alcohol, and tobacco.

Political: Enforcement of human rights and duties, as well as of sexual and racial equality; protection of children and minorities; greater popular participation; effective liberty to compete for public office; universal disarmament; effective international peace-keeping; and increased international cooperation (e.g., in disease and pollution control).

Cultural: Primary and secondary education for all; lifelong learning; rewarding of workmanship; creative (as opposed to consuming) leisure; rehabilitation of criminals; cultural freedom; stronger public support for science, the humanities, and the arts; restriction of technology to the design of socially useful artefacts (e.g., well-insulated houses and controlled thermonuclear fusion plants) and processes (e.g., soil-preserving cultivation methods and minimally polluting transportation means); and exposure of cultural junk.

None of these objectives may be attained by authoritarian methods, by the market alone, or without the help of technology. Some of them require private (in particular cooperative) initiative, others state intervention, and still others global coordination, as no single nation can do all that. And unless all that and more is done, civilization and even human survival may be at serious risk by the mid-twenty-first century: see, for instance, the annual reports of the Worldwatch Institute.

Still, though necessary, integral development is no guarantee of lasting advancement. Indeed, it is possible for a society to advance for a while on all fronts while jeopardizing the livelihood of its posterity. To be morally justifiable, development must be sustainable. By definition, "[s]ustainable development is development that meets the needs of the present without compromising the ability of future generations to meet their own needs" (World Commission on Environment and Development 1987, 43). (Caution: 'Sustainable' should be taken to mean conserving the carrying capacity of the planet rather than its resources, some of which will be unavoidably depleted, so that substitutes will have to be found for them well ahead of time.) And, to be sustainable, development must be systemic (well balanced) rather than lopsided. In short, sustainability entails integrality though not conversely. Any policies and plans for sustainable development are integral: they have environmental, biological, economic, cultural, and political components (see Falk 1995). Moreover, they are based on scientific studies of natural and human resources and their interactions, such as sustainable land use (see, for instance, Thomassin et al. 1991).

For example, the design of any efficient and feasible policy to slow down global warming must join environmental and macroeconomic studies. For example, the rate of emission of greenhouse gases is roughly proportional to the volume of economic activity. The value of the proportionality constant depends on the environmental policy: it may be left as it is or it may be reduced. Thus, at any given time, $E = a(1 - b)P$, where E is the volume of greenhouse-gas emissions, a is a constant, b the emission control rate, and P the GDP. The task of the policy maker is to find a value of the control rate b that is environmentally safe and economically viable. In particular, he must find the tax rates on the consumption of coal, petrol, and other pollutants that will result in the desired value of the emission-control rate (see Nordhaus 1992). The point of mentioning this mini-model is to stress that development issues should not be left to amateurs, be they politicians, environmental activists, or even ecologists blind to social issues and social science. Since they are many-sided, the issues in question should be tackled by interdisciplinary teams, such as those working at once on ecological and development issues.

The environment is at risk as a result of uncontrolled human activity, in particular free industrial enterprise. Indeed, "[r]esource problems are not really environmental problems: They are human problems" (Ludwig et al. 1993, 36). Therefore, the focus of the discussion over sustainable development should be shifted from environmental protection to resource management, and from saving this or that particular endangered species to saving entire ecosystems. This tall order can only be met through a radical and global reform of consumption habits and social order. This, in turn, requires further social studies.

8 The Future of Social Studies

If we wish to correct social ills and rebuild society in an effective, sustainable and humane manner, we need the truest and deepest possible social knowledge, theoretical as well as empirical. This requires not only cleansing and enriching the fund of social knowledge, but also taking stock of it once in a while, to see whether social studies are on the right track. In particular, every generation of social scientists and philosophers should ask, how far have social studies come, what are their main flaws, and where are they going?

My answers to these questions are as follows. First, social studies have made great strides but by and large are still at a protoscientific stage; moreover, they contain pockets of pseudoscience that are seldom diagnosed and exposed as such. Second, social science has flaws of two kinds: philosophical and substantive; and the former are a source of many a fault of the second type – as argued throughout this book. Third, nobody can predict the future of social studies. However, students of society can do better than imagining the future of their own field: they can make it happen. In particular, they can steer such studies from semiscience to either science or nonscience. Only the future will tell which of the two attempts will prevail. Let me spell out these answers.

Everyone agrees that the study of society is not nearly as advanced as that of nature. The most popular explanations of this disparity are as follows. (a) "There can be no social science because people act according to their own free will, which is lawless." This is false: willing is a neural process and as such a lawful if mostly unexplored one. Besides, human action results from circumstance as much as from deliberation. (b) "There are no social laws to be discovered: every social fact is unique." False too: all facts can be grouped into kinds (equivalence classes), and we do know a few social laws or at least quasi-laws. Granted, most of these are empirical and spatio-temporally bounded, that is, inherent in societies of certain types during certain periods rather than being universal. But then the chemical and biological laws too are local rather than being universal. In any event, there is no science without laws. (c) "Social science cannot be mathematized." This is not true: There are plenty of mathematical models in social science. The trouble lies not with formalization as such but with the irrelevance of many mathematical models, and the hostility to precision inherent in the obscurantist philosophies currently fashionable in social studies. (d) "Society is far more complex than nature – so complex, in fact, that it is intractable." Partially true, but then any complex object can be studied on several levels of organization and to different approximations. And the study of nature teaches that complexity on one level is compatible with simplicity on a neighbouring level. (e) "All social studies suffer unavoidably from ideological contamination." This is only partially true. When scientific, basic social studies are ideologically neutral – by definition of 'scientific.' Only their sociotechnological application has an ideological component, and this one can easily be spotted. (f) "The scientific approach was adopted much later for studying society than in the study of nature." True. This is precisely what is wrong with too many social studies: they are not yet scientific enough. (More in Allais 1995.)

I submit that the main obstacles to the advancement of social science are insufficient funding and philosophical deficiencies – logical, ontological, epistemological, and ethical. The major logical flaws are conceptual fuzziness and invalid inference. The main ontological culprits are individualism and holism. Atomism is to blame because it shifts the student's attention from social systems to their individual components; and collectivism is wrong for underrating individual actions and rejecting the very attempt to explain emergence as their result. I have argued at some length that the cure for the ills of both extremes is systemism. So much for the logical and ontological culprits.

The main epistemological culprits of the underdevelopment of the social studies are sectoralism, subjectivism, apriorism, pragmatism, and irrationalism. Sectoralism, or tunnel vision, leads to viewing every aspect of society separately from the remaining aspects. A result is the fragmentation of the social studies into dozens of weakly related or even mutually independent disciplines. This fragmentation is artificial because (a) every one of the major subsystems of society – the biological, economic, political, and cultural ones – is intimately coupled with the other three; and (b) every social science looks from its own standpoint at one and the same thing, namely society (see Schumpeter 1934; Braudel 1969; and Fox 1989). Because of such interactions no major feature of either of the four subsystems, and none of the special sciences of society, can be correctly understood in isolation from the others. Ibn Khaldûn (1377?) realized this. Yet most social policy makers are narrow specialists who ignore the fact that experts in different fields will offer alternative (and sometimes conflicting) recommendations (see Keyfitz 1995). A necessary condition for unified social policy-making is a unified social science.

As for subjectivism and apriorism, they suggest neglect of fact-finding and empirical tests. Hence they tolerate wild speculation. Pragmatism demands subordinating social research to the practical solution of social issues. The result is ignorance of social mechanisms and, consequently, inability to repair or replace them. Finally, irrationalism is not just one more philosophical school: it is antiphilosophical, in rejecting clear and cogent discourse and, consequently, in being dogmatic. This holds even for the mildest form of irrationalism and the most prevalent one in social studies, namely intuitionism. Indeed, faith in the possibility of instant and unerring "understanding" or "interpretation" (*Verstehen*) of human action is dogmatic. Moreover, it leads to overlooking social systems or even denying their existence – hence, perversely, to misunderstanding social action, since the latter is always performed within and upon some social system or other. Intuitionism also discourages rigorous theorizing and the gathering of non-trivial data.

Finally, there are two major moral culprits of the backwardness of social studies. One is the frequent violation of the ethos of science, first ferreted out by Merton (1938b). Such violation occurs, in particular, when the universality of scientific knowledge is denied, dogmatism is substituted for "organized scepticism" – that is, rational discussion, in particular criticism – and rigorous testing, or at least testability, is jettisoned. The second moral culprit is the attempt to pass off ideology (left, centre or right) for science in basic research, and the pretense of moral or political neutrality when tackling practical issues.

If this diagnosis of the philosophical sources of the shortcomings of social studies is correct at least in part, then the answer to our third initial question – namely, "What is the future of social studies?" – becomes obvious. These studies will become whatever the students of society decide and do right now, which in turn hangs largely on the philosophy they adopt. Depending on the latter, the study of society will eventually either mature into full-fledged science or decay into irrelevant and arbitrary "postmodern" (in particular "constructivist-relativist") speculation, or even degenerate into uninhibited gobbledygook.

What can be done to improve the scientific standing of social studies? Our diagnosis suggests the following treatment.

1. *Replace both ontological individualism and holism with ontological systemism*: view every person as a member of several social systems (in particular networks) and each social system as coupled with other social systems and with their natural environment.

2. *Replace methodological sectoralism with methodological systemism*: favour the transdisciplinary study of problems and even the merger of social disciplines – reward trespassing instead of punishing it.

3. *Adopt scientific realism* and criticize irrationalism, subjectivism, apriorism, conventionalism, positivism, and pragmatism.

4. *Observe the moral norms of basic scientific research* and, when recommending social policies, *declare and justify your preferences* (morally as well as practically).

The success of this treatment will depend in turn on the observance of one last precept:

5. *Dig up, analyse, systematize, and review periodically your philosophical presuppositions*: check whether they match the best substantive research, and whether they help or hinder it. That is, attune your philosophy to the best scientific research.

Observance of these rules in working on important unsolved problems in social studies is more likely to help bring about a bright future for them than attempting to foresee that future. In general, people are far better at making their own future than at predicting it.

The social world is everywhere in a mess, global issues are piling up, and the traditional ideologies are not helping – on the contrary. But at least we know some of what is wrong with our societies. We also possess something our ancestors lacked, namely emerging social sciences and sociotechnologies, as well as the means to promote their further advancement – namely, more rigorous research. So, there is ground for hope. In particular, one may hope that the expansion of democracy – to encompass the biological, economic and cultural features of social life in addition to the political one – will succeed where other social orders failed, particularly if the expansion of democracy is guided by social science and sociotechnology. That is, one may hope that the technoholo-democratic project will be worked out and attempted because, far from being one more utopian fantasy, it is based on a systemic, realist, and ethical study of society.

Regrettably, the sustained advancement of social studies, which seemed secure only a couple of decades ago, is being jeopardized by a counter-revolution in philosophy that has spilled over the former. This consists in a revival of irrationalism, wild speculation, apriorism, subjectivism, conventionalism, relativism, and pragmatism, combined with intellectual laziness and an obsession with words and metaphors, symbols and myths (see Gross et al. 1996). These antiscientific philosophies are pernicious because they repudiate the search for objective if partial truths supported by empirical tests and rational discussion before and after tests. And, of course, those who do not believe in truth won't find it; or, if they do stumble accidentally upon a truth, they may not recognize it as such. It is equally evident that those who do not care for a better life will not care for the redesign and reconstruction of our more or less unjust, fractured, ailing, and ill-managed societies.

In sum, the advancement of social studies and the design of responsible social policies depend critically upon the adoption of a sound philosophy congenial with science and technology. One such philosophy has been sketched in the companion volume *Finding Philosophy in Social Science* (Bunge 1996a).

PART C

Appendices

APPENDIX 1 Modelling Competition: A Systemic Approach

The action that an agent exerts upon another modifies both, though seldom in the same manner. These changes can be represented as follows. Consider a social system composed of two agents, 1 and 2. Call F_1 and F_2 their respective state functions. (A state function for things of a certain kind is a function, or list of functions, whose value at a given time represents the state of a thing of the given kind. Example: the simplest state function representing a market for a commodity X is the ordered couple <Quantity of X, Price of X>.) Owing to the mutual actions of agents 1 and 2, the rate of change of each state function will depend upon both state functions. That is,

$$dF_1/dt = f(F_1, F_2) \quad , \quad dF_2/dt = g(F_1, F_2)$$

Dividing the second equation by the first yields

$$dF_2/dF_1 = g(F_1, F_2)/h(F_1, F_2).$$

This is the analytic representation of a family of curves (open or closed) in the state space spanned by F_1 and F_2. If the interaction ceases, so does the mutual entanglement of the two state functions, and each equation can be solved separately. In this case, the family of curves collapses into a family of straight lines on the $F_1 - F_2$ plane.

Competition is one side of the social coin, the other being cooperation. The well-known Lotka-Volterra model of biological competition can be interpreted in economic terms. Let the agents 1 and 2 be either individuals or firms competing for some resource, natural or human. Call $F_1(t)$ and $F_2(t)$ respectively the amounts of the resource that they control at time t. Assume that the rates of growth of these amounts satisfy the following non-linear conditions:

$$dF_1/dt = k\,F_1(a_1 - b_1 F_2), \quad dF_2/dt = kF_2(a_2 - b_2 F_1), \quad \text{with } k, a_i, b_i > 0 \text{ for } i = 1,2,$$

where k is a dimensional constant, a_1 and a_2 are the relative growth rates in the absence of competition, b_1 the strength of the inhibiting influence of 2 upon 1, and similarly for b_2. Dividing one of the equations by the other and integrating entails

$$a_2 \ln F_1 - a_1 \ln F_2 + b_1 F_2 - b_2 F_1 = \text{constant}.$$

This equation represents a family of closed curves on the $F_1 = F_2$ plane around the equilibrium (zero growth) point. It shows clearly that the size of each competitor depends on that of the other. Near the zero-growth point the curves approximate ellipses, and the solutions, as functions of time, are sinusoidal curves one-quarter cycle out of phase. (Warning: This model does not represent business cycles, for these are roughly synchronic for all firms.) In the absence of competition, that is, for $b_1 = b_2 = 0$, every agent grows exponentially. In this case, the graph of the "system" (actually an aggregate) becomes a straight line.

Although the above model is only a crude first approximation, it has some heuristic power. It suggests that interaction involves entanglement and nonlinearity. In other words, the state function of a system does not equal the sum or even the product of the state functions of the system components. Hence, methodological individualism is not a suitable strategy for investigating closely knit social systems.

APPENDIX 2 Modelling Cooperation: A Systemic Approach

Individualists extol competition, whereas collectivists praise cooperation. Neither of them imagines that sometimes cooperation could override competition; that struggle might combine with solidarity; or that cooperation in some respects might emerge in a conflict-resolution process. In the real world competition in some regards usually goes hand in hand with cooperation in others. For example, rival members of a social system agree tacitly to cooperate in holding the system together, by observing a minimal set of norms. Moreover, conflict may have to be moderated in order to prevent its becoming destructive. This is one of the functions of heads of family, managers, bargainers, arbitrators, governments, industrial alliances, and federations of all kinds.

Two simple types of cooperation will be sketched in the following.

1 Cooperation to Stave off Decline

Assume that two units (e.g., business firms) decline exponentially in the course of time as long as each minds only its own business. They can survive either by asking for state subsidies or by helping one another, thus constituting a system. We model this system by inverting the signs of the parameters in the Lotka-Volterra equations occurring in the previous section. Now a_1 and a_2 are the decline rates, whereas b_1 represents the strength of the help that partner 1 gets from partner 2, and similarly for b_2. (This mutual help may consist in an exchange of expertise.) Near the zero-growth point F_1 and F_2 are sinusoidal curves one-quarter cycle out of phase.

2 Competitive Cooperation

Consider again the case of two units engaged in producing or consuming goods or services of the same kind. When on its own, each unit operates at a constant rate, and it may or may not break even. But when cooperation sets in, each unit is sure to attain its optimal level. This cooperation is the stronger the more it is needed, it ceases when no longer needed, and from then on it turns into competition, so that growth remains under control. Such process can be formalized as follows (Bunge 1976b). The equations are

$$dF_1/dt = a_{11} + a_{12}(\alpha - F_1) \, F_2, \, dF_2/dt = a_{22} + a_{21} \, (\beta - F_2) \, F_1,$$

where $a_{ij} \geq 0$ for $i, j = 1,2$, and the initial values $F_1(0) = c_1$, $F_2(0) = c_2$ are positive. The parameters are interpreted as follows: α and β are the optimal or satiety levels (of production or consumption); a_{11} and a_{22} are the rates in the absence of interaction; a_{12} measures the strength of the help that unit 1 gets from unit 2, while a_{21} measures the help 1 lends 2. At the optimal point $<\alpha,\beta>$ there is neither help nor hindrance, so the system breaks down. But no sooner does unit 1 attain its optimal level than its partner 2 turns against 1, forcing it to slow down. When the two partners behave in exactly the same way, that is, for $c_1 = c_2 = c$ (neither has an initial advantage), $a_{11} = a_{22} = a$ (equal individual rates), $a_{12} = a_{21} = b$ (symmetric help), and $\alpha = \beta$ (same requirements), we are left with a single equation of evolution for both units, namely

$$dF/dt = a + b(\alpha - F)F, \text{ with } F(0) = c > 0.$$

The general solution to this equation is

$$F(t) = at + \alpha c/[c + (\alpha - c) \, exp(-b\alpha t)].$$

If each partner is self-sufficient ($a > 0$), cooperation only speeds up the growth process up to the optimal point, and curbs it after that point. Otherwise, that is, if $a = 0$, mutual help makes the process possible. In fact, the second term of the last equation represents the growth of F from its initial value c towards the asymptote $F(\infty) = \alpha > c$. From this point on rivalry prevents unchecked growth. In fact, it ends up by imposing zero growth. The model combines the virtues of cooperation with those of competition.

APPENDIX 3 A Production Model

Economic theorizing *can* be both precise and fairly realistic. This is the case with the standard linear production model (see, for instance, Gale 1960). Unlike the neoclassical models, this one involves only measurable variables and it is actually used by industrial economists. It can be characterized as a quadruple $L = <W, P, G, A>$, where W denotes the staff employed by a given firm, $P = \{P_1, P_2, ..., P_m\}$ is a set of specific activities of members of W, $G = \{G_1, G_2, ..., G_n\}$ a set of commodities, and $A = \|a_{ij}\|$ is the production (or input-output) matrix. The element a_{ij} of A is the amount of commodities of kind G_j consumed or produced by activity Pi, according as a_{ij} is positive or negative.

So far we have only listed and interpreted the variables. Let us now introduce a few assumptions, that is, some relations among the variables P, G, and A. (W, the staff, will remain unspecified or anonymous except for its activities P.) The model assumes (simplistically) that there is a one-to-one correspondence between the set P of activities and the set G of goods: that is, one industry–one good and conversely (whence $m = n$). Call p_i the intensity of activity P_i, and g_i the number of units of commodity G_i produced by that activity. Further, collect the two sets of numbers into the row matrices (vectors)

$$p = <p_1, p_2, ..., p_n>, \quad g = <g_1, g_2, ..., g_n>.$$

The net production of the firm, that is, its production minus its consumption, is represented by the difference $p - pA$, which in turn equals the "bill of goods" g :

$$p - pA = g, \text{ or } p(I - A) = g,$$

where I is the $n \times n$ unit matrix. This is the basic premise of the model. It is a typical black-box assumption, because it says nothing about the production mechanism except that the volume of every product is a linear combination of all the activities. (E.g., for $n = 2$, $g_1 = p_1A_{11} + p_2A_{22}$, and $g_2 = p_1A_{12} + p_2A_{22}$.) Moreover the model presupposes no law except for "Nothing for nothing," that is, the principle of conservation of energy.

Usually the givens are the production matrix A and the demand (or goal) g. The theoretical problem is to find the activity vector p, that is, to determine the suitable level of each activity or industry. Mathematically, this problem consists in inverting the matrix $I - A$ to obtain $p = g (I - A)^{-1}$ The tasks of collecting the information summarized by A, and of inverting the matrix $I - A$, are so time-consuming that the modeller has little energy left for any more accurate, let alone deeper, theorizing. Still, the above model can easily be rendered more realistic by including the rates or production and depletion of all stocks.

Note the following methodological points about the above model of production. First, it is a free model, rather than a bound one, not being based on any general theory. Second, it is a purely descriptive or black-box model: it describes production but does not explain how it works; that is, it exhibits no mechanisms. Yet, it is not just a data summary, for it involves the deduction of the level of activity p. Third, despite its purely descriptive character it can be used to program economic activities. Indeed, by setting g and solving for p, the economic planner, consultant, or manager finds the suitable level of activity necessary and sufficient to satisfy the demand g – a case of norm deduction. Fourth, the model does not contain any moral, ideological, or political elements. Only setting the demand g and recommending the economically desirable level of activity p may give rise to social and moral issues – for example, hiring, firing, or transferring personnel. (For models of various kinds see Bunge 1996a.)

APPENDIX 4 Humbug Mathematical Economics

In the mature sciences mathematics discharges honestly a number of jobs, from honing concepts and systematizing to deriving consequences from given premises. Elsewhere mathematics can be used for self-deception, or to fool and intimidate the layperson. In fact untestable, untested, or false propositions, when clad in mathematical form, look respectable and even unassailable. Yet nothing is easier, and few things are more amusing, than to construct mathematically correct but factually empty theories. The following is offered as an example. It is an application of classical Hamiltonian dynamics to microeconomics – a fashionable occupation among mathematical economists.

Let q_i and p_i be $2n$ functions of time, interpreted as the quantities of n commodities and their corresponding unit prices respectively. These variables may be regarded as the axes of a $2n$-dimensional abstract space: the state (or phase) space of the market for the given commodities, or "market space" for short. Further, let H be a function of the q_i and p_i as well as of time (t). H is assumed to be once differentiable with respect to every one of its variables, and subjected to the following $2n$ equations of motion of the market:

$$dp_i/dt = - \partial H/\partial q_i, \; dq_i/dt = \partial H/\partial p_i, \text{ where } i = 1,2, ..., n.$$

Aside from these conditions H is both formally and semantically indeterminate: that is, we stipulate nothing about its form or its meaning. However, we can choose whatever form of H will lead to the desired results, so that H will be mathematically well defined even though it may continue to be semantically indeterminate. This won't prevent the humbug economist from pronouncing H the Hamiltonian of the market, or even of an entire economy.

Example 1 Demand curve for a single commodity:
Setting $H = apq$, with a a positive real number, results in

$$dp/dt = - \partial H/\partial q = - ap, \; dq/dt = \partial H/\partial p = aq,$$

whence

$$dq/dp = -(\partial H/\partial p)/(\partial H/\partial q) = -q/p, \text{ or } pdq + qdp = 0.$$

Integrating we obtain $pq = c$, with c a positive real number. This is a standard assumption for the demand function – though one that is notoriously unrealistic (Morgenstern 1963).

Example 2 Supply curve for a single commodity:
Setting $H = (a^2/2)p^2 - aq$, where a is a positive real number, we obtain

$$dp/dt = -\partial H/\partial q = a, \ dq/dt = \partial H/\partial p = a^2 p,$$

whence

$$dq/dp = ap, \text{ or } dq = apdp.$$

Integrating we obtain

$$q = \tfrac{1}{2}ap^2 + constant,$$

which is one of the standard supply curves for perfectly competitive markets.

We could go on subsuming any number of curves, true or fantastic, under the Hamiltonian formalism. And all the while we would not care what the humbug function H stands for, except that it is accommodating enough and yet looks respectable because of its enviable track record in physics.

That is not all. On the basis of the preceding one may introduce the Lagrangian function

$$L = \Sigma_i p_i(dq_i/dt) - H,$$

which in turn allows one to introduce a Jacobi function S satisfying the Hamilton-Jacobi equations

$$p_i = \partial S/\partial q_i, \ \ \partial S/\partial t + H = 0.$$

The second equation may be regarded as the single equation of motion of the market. In the particular case $H = E =$ constant, we get $S(q, t) = -Et + W(q,d)$, with $d =$ constant. In this case the state of the market is represented by a surface $W =$ const. propagating in the n-dimensional "commodity space." W may be pictured as the front of a shock wave in this space propagating at speed dq/dt – a pretty but useless analogy.

All this, though mathematically rigorous and high-sounding, is economically mean-ingless because we ignore what properties, if any, H, L, and S represent. (We only know what the q_i's and p_i's represent, namely quantities and prices respectively.) Moreover, the formalism is just an ad hoc rationalization devoid of explanatory or predictive power. The whole thing is an academic game. So is much advanced mathematical economics.

APPENDIX 5 Modelling Secrecy Leaks

There are a number of quantitative models of political processes (see, for instance, Alker et al. 1973). But most of them – in particular those of the game-theoretic type – involve no blanks (parameters) to be filled by empirical data. I shall presently sketch a quantita-tive model that does admit data and can be tested.

All governments, particularly the authoritarian and corrupt ones, are obsessed with secrecy. But in large bureaucracies secrets are hard to keep. This assertion can be proved mathematically (Bunge 1979c) – admittedly with tongue in cheek. The proof is repro-duced here for fun, as well as to suggest that some features of government activity can be modelled mathematically.

Call D the collection of government documents and C the subset of D constituted by "classified" documents. The numerosity of either collection may change in the course of time. Call f the fraction of secret documents at a given time – that is, the ratio of the numerosities of C and D at t. Suppose that the government is prepared to do whatever it takes to protect the classified documents. Let us examine how this is attempted – to no avail in the long run.

We start by defining the concept of degree of secrecy. Let T be an arbitrarily long period of time, and call $N(t)$ the number of persons who, at time t in T, have access, whether direct or indirect, lawful or unlawful, to the classified documents C. Then the effective degree of secrecy achieved is assumed to be the value of the fraction of secret documents divided by the number of persons having access to them. That is, for any t in T, $S(t) = f(t)/N(t)$. In words: Effective secrecy is proportional to the secrecy index and inversely proportional to the number of people in the know. The bounds of S are (a) $S = 0$ for either $f(t) = 0$ or $N(t) \to \infty$; (b) $S = 1$ for $f(t) = N(t)$.

In order to protect the documents in C the government hires a number E of security guards commensurate with the relative bulk of C, that is, proportional to $f(t)$ or some other function of $f(t)$. We choose the linear approximation, setting $E(t) = af(t)$, where a is a large real number. Substituting into the above axiom yields

$$S(t) = E(t)/ aN(t).$$ [1]

Now, N increases with E, and the more security guards are sworn in, the more leaks are bound to occur. Calling $n_i(t)$ the number of persons that have been tipped off by the *i-th* security employee by time t, the total number of persons who have had access to C at time t is the sum of the $n_i(t)$ from $i = 1$ to $i = E$. Assume now that every one of these persons passes on secrets to at least two other people in the course of a time unit on the order of one week – whether as part of his job, as irresponsible gossip, or treasonably. After m such time units (weeks) we have $n_i(m) \geq 2^m$ for every i. Therefore, the lower bound of $N(m)$, or the total number of persons in the know at the end of m weeks, is $N(m) \geq E2^m$. Substitution of this result into [1] yields the degree of secrecy attained at the end of m weeks:

$$S(m) \geq 1/a2^m \qquad\qquad [2]$$

Consequently, the degree of effective secrecy approaches 0 as m increases. That is, in the long run no secrets are left. This result is reinforced upon recalling that all secrets become naturally obsolescent. The only well-kept secrets are those that are so well kept that they are useless.

APPENDIX 6 Newcomb's Problem

A number of social scientists and philosophers have been intrigued by Newcomb's Problem, the classical statement of which is due to the political philosopher Robert Nozick. Suppose there is a rich, supremely intelligent and well-informed, though not omniscient, being called Wise, who proposes the following game to You. He places before You two boxes, labelled A and B. A is transparent and seen to contain $1000, whereas B is opaque and known to contain either one million dollars ($1m) or nothing, depending on your choice disposition, as described anon. You have two options: taking what is in both boxes, or taking only the contents of the black box B. Wait, there is a catch.

If Wise suspects that You will greedily take what is in both boxes, he won't place $1m in box B. But if Wise suspects that You will take the risk of choosing only box B, he will put $1m in B: he likes to reward the foolhardy and punish the greedy. What will you do? Take into account that, for all his wisdom, Wise cannot be certain about your choice disposition, whence You cannot in turn be totally sure about his decision: both You and Wise will operate under uncertainty.

Moreover, the uncertainty is such that neither Wise nor You can assign (objective) probabilities to your choices. Consequently, no (objective) expected utilities can be calculated, and therefore it is impossible to pick the course of action that will maximize the expected utility. That is, *the problem is not well posed.* Therefore, no unambiguous solution for it can be expected without further information. In particular, I cannot give You a rational piece of advice unless I am reliably informed as to whether You are needy or wealthy.

Precisely because it is not a well-posed problem, Newcomb's has given rise to a spate of learned if undecisive papers (see, for instance, Campbell and Sowden 1985). For instance, David Lewis has argued persuasively that the Prisoner's Dilemma amounts to two Newcomb Problems side by side, one per prisoner. And Jordan Sobel has shown, just as forcefully, that only some Prisoner's Dilemmas are reducible to a couple of Newcomb's Problems. In any event, opinion seems to be equally divided as to which of the two possible decisions is the more rational. Can anyone think of a more exciting problem?

In my opinion the question of rationality concerns not so much the solution as the very formulation of Newcomb's Problem, which, on top of being fuzzy, is utterly artificial. It is so unrealistic that it does not even take your present needs into account. Indeed, none of the students of the Problem has asked himself whether You can afford *not* to win $1000. All of them assume that You are a well-heeled gambler who can afford to take the risk of attempting to maximize your utility.

In real life the needy individual, and even the merely risk-averse person, will forfeit the chance of becoming a millionaire and will grab the contents of both boxes, which at least will buy him a few meals. And he is likely to think that Newcomb's Problem is a only a show of academic acrobatics as a substitute for wrestling with real-life issues.

APPENDIX 7 A General Concept of Action

One way of formalizing the general notion of action is this (Bunge 1977a, 256ff.). Call a an arbitrary concrete thing, and $F_a(t)$ the value of its state function at time t. (A state function for things of some kind may be defined as the list of the known properties of the things. It may be visualized as an arrow in state space.) I define the *history* $h_T(a)$ of thing a over period T as the trajectory of the tip of $F_a(t)$ on the $t - F_a(t)$ plane, that is, the collection of ordered pairs $<t, F_a(t)>$ for all t in T. That is, $h_T(a) = \{<t, F_a(t)> \mid t \in T\}$. Similarly, the history of another thing b over the same period will be called $h_T(b) = \{<t, F_b(t)> \mid t \in T\}$, where F_b is a state function for thing b. Further, let $H_{ab} = g(Fa, Fb)$ be a third state function, depending on both F_a and F_b, and call

$$h_T(b|a) = \{<t, H_{ab}(t)> \mid t \in T\}$$

the corresponding history of b in the presence of a. Then thing a will be said to *act* on thing b, or $a \triangleright b$ for short, if and only if, for any state function F determining the trajectory, $h_T(a|b) \neq h_T(a)$. Here $h_T(a|b)$ is the history of a when acted upon by b, and $h_T(b|a)$ is that of b when under the action of a. In other words, $h_T(a)$ is the free or spontaneous trajectory of a, whereas $h_T(a|b)$ is the forced trajectory of a under the action of b. Two different things a and b will be said to *interact* if and only if each acts upon the other. In symbols, $a \lhd\rhd b =_{df} a \rhd b \mathbin{\&} b \rhd a$. The concept of *human* action is only a special case, namely when at least the agent a is a person. If both agent and patient are humans, or if one of them is a person and the other a social system or a public good, the action in question is said to be *social* (in particular, prosocial or antisocial).

The concept of consequence of an action is easily defined as follows. The *consequence* or *effect* of the action of a on b equals the (set-theoretic) difference \ between the forced and the free trajectories of the patient b. The total *reaction* of b upon a is the difference between the free and the forced trajectories of the agent a. And the *total interaction* between a and b is the (set-theoretic) union of action and reaction. The corresponding symbolizations are

$$A_T(a,\ b) = h_T(b|a)\backslash h_T(b) =_{df} h_T(b|a) \cap \overline{h_T(b)},$$

$$A_T(b,a) = h_T(a|b)\backslash h_T(a) =_{df} h_T(a|b) \cap \overline{h_T(a)},$$

$$I_T(a,\ b) = A_T(a,\ b) \cup A_T(b,\ a),$$

where \ stands for the set-theoretic difference, and the horizontal bar designates the set-theoretic complement operation.

We now formalize the concept of unintended or unanticipated consequence of an action. Call $A(a,\ b)$ the effect of agent a's action on patient b over a given period, and $A_f(a,\ b)$ the forecast or intended outcome of the same action over the same period. The *unintended consequences* $U(a,b)$ of the action of agent a on b over the given period are those in $A(a,b)$ but not in $A_f(a,b)$, that is,

$U(a,\ b) = A(a,\ b)\backslash A_f(a,\ b)$.

So much for individual action. Let us now formalize the concept of collective action. To this end we start by introducing the concept of "sum" of concrete things, such as persons. The "sum" of a and b, that is, the entity (either aggregate or system) composed of things a and b, will be denoted $a \nabla b$. (This concept is exactified in Bunge 1977a, 28ff.) Naturally, the action of agents a and b on patient c is denoted $A(a\nabla b,\ c)$. The simplest cases are of course

Additivity $\qquad\qquad A(a\nabla b,\ c) = A(a,c) \cup A(b,c)$,

Constructive interference $A(a\nabla b,\ c) \supset [A(a,c) \cup A(b,c)]$,

Destructive interference $A(a\nabla b,\ c) \subset [A(a,c) \cup A(b,c)]$.

In particular, two agents may act so as to counteract one another's actions, that is, in such manner that $A(a \nabla b,\ c) = \varnothing$. In other cases the outcome will not be comparable to the sum of the effects of the separate agents. In particular, as a result of constructive interference (cooperation) the resulting trajectory may lie in a state space involving new axes (properties). That is, something qualitatively new relative to the separate outcomes may emerge as a result of the joint action of the two agents. The generalization to an arbitrary number of agents is trivial.

References

Aaker, D.A. 1995. *Strategic Market Management*. New York: John Wiley & Sons.

Ackerman, B. 1980. *Social Justice in the Liberal State*. New Haven, CT: Yale University Press.

Ackley, G. 1961. *Macroeconomic Theory*. New York: Macmillan.

Ackoff, R. 1970. *A Concept of Corporate Planning*. New York: Wiley-Interscience.

– 1974. *Redesigning the Future: A Systems Approach to Societal Problems*. New York: Wiley.

Adams, R.N. 1975. *Energy and Structure: A Theory of Social Power*. Austin: University of Texas Press.

Adler, P.A. and P., eds. 1984. *The Market as Colletive Behavior*. Greenwich, CT: Jai Press.

Adorno, T.W., K.R. Popper, et al. 1976. *The Positivist Dispute in German Sociology*. London: Heinemann.

Agassi, J. 1971. "Tautology and Testability in Economics." *Philosophy of the Social Sciences* 1: 49–63.

– 1981. *Science and Society. Studies in the Sociology of Science*. Dordrecht: Reidel.

– 1985. *Technology: Philosophical and Social Aspects*. Dordrecht and Boston: Reidel.

Aguilar, M.J., and E. Ander-Egg. 1992. *Evaluación de servicios y programas sociales*. Madrid: Siglo Veintiuno.

Aiello, L.C. 1993. "The Fossil Evidence for Modern Human Origins in Africa: A Revised View." *American Anthropology* 95: 73–96.

Akerlof, G.A. 1984. *An Economic Theorist's Book of Tales*. Cambridge: Cambridge University Press.

Albert, H. 1985. *Treatise on Critical Reason*. Princeton, NJ: Princeton University Press.

– 1988. "Hermeneutics and Economics. A Criticism of Hermeneutical Thinking in the Social Sciences." *Kyklos* 41: 573–602.

Alchourrón, C., and E. Bulygin. 1971. *Normative Systems*. Wien: Springer-Verlag.

Alexander, J.C., B. Giesen, R. Münch, and N.J. Smelser, eds. 1987 *The Micro-Macro Link*. Berkeley: University of California Press.

Alic, J.A. 1990. "Who Designs Work?" *Technology in Society* 12: 301–16.

Alker, H.R., K.W. Deutsch, and A.H. Stoetzel, eds. 1973. *Mathematical Approaches to Politics*. San Francisco: Jossey-Bass.

Allais, M. 1979 [1953]. "The Foundations of a Positive Theory of Choice Involving Risk and a Criticism of the Postulates and Axioms of the American School." In Allais and Hagen, ed., 27–145.

– 1995. "The Economic Science of Today and Facts: A Critical Analysis of Some Characteristic Features." In Götschl, ed., 25–38.

Allais, M., and O. Hagen, eds. 1979. *Expected Utility Hypotheses and the Allais Paradox*. Dordrecht and Boston: Reidel.

Allén, T. 1988. "The Impossibility of the Paretian Liberal." *Theory and Decision* 24: 57–76.

Alperowitz, G. 1965. *Atomic Diplomacy: Hiroshima and Potsdam: The Use of the Atomic Bomb and the American Confrontation with the Soviet Power*. London: Secker & Warburg.

Alter, P. 1994. *Nationalism*. 2nd ed. London: Edward Arnold.

Althusser, L. 1965. *Pour Marx*. Paris: F. Maspéro.

Alvarez, J.R. 1991. *La racionalidad hexagonal*. León: Universidad de León.

Amir, Y., and I. Sharon. 1988. "Are Social Psychological Laws Cross-Culturally Valid?" *Journal of Cross-Cultural Psychology* 18: 383–470.

Anderson, B. 1983. *Imagined Communities*. London: Verso.

Anderson, P. 1976. *Considerations on Western Marxism*. London: New Left Books.

Andreano, R.L., ed. 1970. *The New Economic History: Recent Papers on Methodology*. New York: John Wiley & Sons.

Andreski, S. 1984. *Max Weber's Insights and Errors*. London: Routledge & Kegan Paul.

Aoki, M. 1986. "Horizontal vs. Vertical Information Structure of the Firm." *American Economic Review* 76: 971–83.

Arato, A., and E. Gebhard, eds. 1978. *The Essential Frankfurt School Reader*. Oxford: Basil Blackwell.

Aristotle. *Politics*. In R. McKeon, ed., *The Basic Works of Aristotle*. New York: Random House, 1941.

Arndt, H. 1984. *Economic Theory vs. Economic Reality*. Trans. W.A. Kirby. East Lansing: Michigan State University Press.

Aron, R. 1961 [1938]. *Introduction to the Philosophy of History*. Boston: Beacon Press.

Arrow, K.J. 1951. *Social Choice and Individual Values*. New York: Wiley.

– 1987. "Economic Theory and the Hypothesis of Rationality." In J. Eatwell, M. Milgate, and P. Newman, eds, *The New Palgrave*, 2: 69–74.

- 1992. "I Know a Hawk from a Handsaw." In Szenberg, ed., 42–50.
- 1994. "Methodological Individualism and Social Knowledge." *American Economic Review* 84 (2): 1–9.

Arrow, K.J., and M.D. Intriligator, eds. 1982–91. Handbook of Mathematical Economics. 4 vols. New York: North Holland/American Elsevier.

Arthur D. Little. 1995. "The Best of the Best." *Prism*, 4th quarter.

Ashby, W.R. 1963. *An Introduction to Cybernetics*. New York: Science Editions.

Asimakopulos, A., ed. 1988. *Theories of Income Distribution*. Boston: Kluwer.

Atkinson, P. 1988. "Ethnomethodology: A Critical Review." *Annual Review of Sociology* 14: 441–65.

Aumann, R.J. 1964. "Markets with a Continuum of Traders." *Econometrica* 32: 39–50.

Auspitz, J.L., W.W. Gasparski, M.K. Mlicki, and K. Szasniawski, eds. 1992. *Praxiologies and the Philosophy of Economics*. New Brunswick, NJ, and London: Transaction Publishers.

Aveni, A.F., ed. 1990. *The Lines of Nazca*. Philadelphia: American Philosophical Society.

Axelrod, R. 1984. *The Evolution of Cooperation*. New York: Basic Books.

Axelrod, R., and W.D. Hamilton. 1981. "The Evolution of Cooperation." *Science* 211: 1390–6.

Aydelotte, W.O., A.G. Bogue, and R.W. Fogel, eds. 1972. *The Dimensions of Quantitative Research in History*. Princeton, NJ: Princeton University Press.

Bain, B., ed. 1983. *The Sociogenesis of Language and Human Conduct*. New York: Plenum Press.

Bain, J.S. 1956. *Barriers to New Competition*. Cambridge, MA: Harvard University Press.

Baldwin, D.A., ed. 1993. *Neorealism and Neoliberalism*. New York: Columbia University Press.

Balogh, T. 1982. *The Irrelevance of Conventional Economics*. New York: Liveright.

Baran, P.A, and P.M Sweezy. 1966. *Monopoly Capital: An Essay on the American Economic and Social Order*. New York: Monthly Review Press.

Barber, B. 1952. *Science and the Social Order*. Glencoe, IL: Free Press.

Barber, B., and W. Hirsch, eds. 1972. *The Sociology of Science*. New York: Free Press.

Barceló, A. 1990. "Are There Economic Laws?" In Weingartner and W. Dorn, eds, 379–396.

- 1992. *Filosofía de la economía*. Barcelona: Economía Crítica.

Bardhan, P.K., and J.E. Roemer, eds. 1993. *Market Socialism: The Current Debate*. Oxford: Oxford University Press.

Barkley, P.W. 1984. "Rethinking the Mainstream." *American Journal of Agricultural Economics* 66: 798–801.

Barnes, B. 1977. *Interests and the Growth of Knowledge*. London: Routledge & Kegan Paul.

– 1983. "On the Conventional Character of Knowledge and Cognition." In Knorr-Cetina and Mulkay, eds, 19–51.

Barnes, B., ed. 1972. *Sociology of Science: Selected Readings*. Harmondsworth: Penguin.

Barraclough, G. 1979. *Main Trends in History*. New York and London: Holmes & Meier.

Barry, B. 1970. *Sociologists, Economists, and Democracy*. Chicago: University of Chicago Press.

– 1986. "Lady Chatterley's Lover and Doctor Fischer's Bomb Party." In Elster and Hylland, eds, 11–43.

Basalla, G. 1988. *The Evolution of Technology*. Cambridge: Cambridge University Press.

Batali, J., and P. Kitcher. 1995. "Evolution of Altruism in Optimal and Compulsory Games." *Journal of Theoretical Biology* 175: 161–71.

Baudrillard, J. 1973. *Le miroir de la production*. Paris: Casterman.

– 1988. *Selected Writings*. Ed. M. Poster. Cambridge, UK: Polity Press.

Baumol, W.J., 1977. *Economic Theory and Operations Analysis*. 4th ed. Englewood Cliffs, NJ: Prentice-Hall.

Baumol, W.J., and M. Stewart. 1971. "On the Behavioral Theory of the Firm." In R. Marris and A. Woods, eds, *The Corporate Economy*, 118–143. London: Macmillan.

Beard, T.R., and R.O. Beil, Jr. 1994. "Do People Rely on the Self-Interested Maximization of Others? An Experimental Test." *Management Science* 40: 252–62

Beaumont, J.G., M. Rogers, and P. Kenealy, eds. 1966. *The Blackwell Dictionary of Neuropsychology*. Oxford: Blackwell.

Beccaria, C. [1764]. *Dei delitti e delle pene*. Firenze: Mursia, 1973.

Bechara, A., H. Damasio, D. Tranel, and A.R. Damasio. 1997 "Deciding Advantageously Before Knowing the Advantageous Strategy." *Science* 275: 1293–5

Becker, G.S. 1964. *Human Capital: A Theoretical and Empirical Analysis*. New York: Columbia University Press.

– 1976. *The Economic Approach to Human Behavior*. Chicago: University of Chicago Press.

Becker, G.S., and W.M. Landes, eds. 1974. *Essays in the Economics of Crime and Punishment*. New York: Columbia University Press.

Bekoff, M. 1978. *Coyotes: Biology, Behavior, and Management*. New York: Academic Press.

Bell, D. 1960. *The End of Ideology: On the Exhaustion of Political Ideas in the Fifties*. Glencoe, IL.: Free Press.

Bell, D., and I. Kristol, eds. 1981. *The Crisis in Economic Theory*. New York: Basic Books.

Bellha, R.N., R. Madsen, W.M. Sullivan, A. Swidler, and S.M. Tipton. 1985. *Habits of the Heart: Individualism and Commitment in American Life.* Berkeley: University of California Press.

Benda, J. 1975 [1927]. *La trahison des clercs.* Rev. ed. Paris: Bernard Grasset.

Bendix, R., and S.M. Lipset, eds. 1966. *Class, Status, and Power.* 2nd ed. New York: Free Press.

Benn, S.I., and G. W. Mortimore, eds. 1975. *Rationality and the Social Sciences.* London: Routledge & Kegan Paul.

Bennett, C.A., and A.A. Lumsdaine, eds. 1975. *Evaluation and Experiment: Some Critical Issues in Assesssing Social Programs.* New York: Academic Press.

Bennett, R.J., and R.J. Chorley. 1978. *Environmental Systems: Philosophy, Analysis and Control.* London: Methuen.

Ben-Porath, Y. 1980. "The F-Connection: Families, Friends, and Firms and the Organization of Exchange." *Population and Development Review* 6: 1–30.

Bentham, J. 1982 [1789]. *An Introduction to the Principles of Morals and Legislation.* Ed. J.H. Burns and H.L.A. Hart. London and New York: Methuen.

Berger, P., and T. Luckmann. 1967. *The Social Construction of Reality.* London: Allen Lane.

Berger, T.R. 1988. *Northern Frontier, Northern Homeland.* Vancouver and Toronto: Douglas & McIntyre.

Bergson, H. 1932. *Les deux sources de la morale et de la religion.* Paris: Presses Universitaires de France.

Berk, J.B., E. Hughson, and K. Vandezande. 1996. "The Price Is Right, But Are the Bids? An Investigation of Rational Decision Theory." *American Economic Review* 86: 954–70.

Berlin, I. 1957. "Two Concepts of Liberty." In *Four Essays on Liberty.* Oxford: Oxford University Press, 1969.

Berlyne, D.E., ed. 1974. *Studies in the New Experimental Aesthetics.* Washington: Hemisphere.

Berman, M. 1981. *The Re-enchantment of the World.* Ithaca, NY: Cornell University Press.

Bernal, J.D. 1939. *The Social Function of Science.* New York: Macmillan.

Bernard, C. 1952 [1865]. *Introduction à l'étude de la médécine expérimentale,* 2nd ed. Paris: Charles Delagrave.

Berry, B.J.L., H. Kim, and H.-M. Kim. 1993. "Are Long Waves Driven by Techno-Economic Transformations?" *Technological Forecasting and Social Change* 44: 111–35.

Bettinger, R.L. 1991. *Hunter-Gatherers: Archaeological and Evolutionary Theory.* New York and London: Plenum Press.

Bhagwati, J.N., ed. 1972. *Economics and World Order.* New York: Macmillan.

Bhaskar, R. 1979. *The Possibility of Naturalism. A Philosophical Critique of the Contemporary Human Sciences.* Brighton, UK: Harvester Press.

Bickerton, D. 1984. "The Language Bioprogram Hypothesis." *Behavioral and Brain Sciences* 7: 173–88.

Bidwell, C.E., and N.E. Friedkin. 1988. "The Sociology of Education." In N.J. Smelser, ed., *Handbook of Sociology*, 449–71. Newbury Park, CA: Sage.

Bijker, W.E., T.P. Hughes, and T. Pinch, eds. 1987. *The Social Construction of Technological Systems*. Cambridge, MA: MIT Press.

Bindra, D. 1978. *A Theory of Intelligent Behavior*. New York: Wiley.

Binford, L.R. 1981. *Bones: Ancient Men and Modern Myths*. New York: Academic Press.

– 1989. *Debating Archaeology*. San Diego and London: Academic Press.

Black, D. 1989. *Sociological Law*. New York: Oxford University Press.

Black, D., ed. 1984. Toward a General Theory of Social Control. 2 vols. Orlando, FL: Academic Press.

Blair, J.M. 1972. *Economic Concentration*. New York: Harcourt, Brace, Jovanovich.

Blalock, H.M., Jr. 1989. "The Real and Unrealized Contributions of Quantitative Sociology." *American Sociological Review* 54: 447–60.

Blasier, C. 1985. *The Hovering Giant: U. S. Responses to Revolutionary Change in Latin-America 1910–1985*. Pittsburgh: University of Pittsburgh Press.

Blau, P. 1968. "Sociological Analysis: Current Trends and Personal Practice." *Sociological Inquiry* 39: 119–30.

Blaug, M. 1976. Human Capital Theory: A Slightly Jaundiced Survey." *Journal of Economic Literature* 14: 827–55.

– 1980. *The Methodology of Economics*. Cambridge: Cambridge University Press.

Blinder, A.S. 1989. *Macroeconomics under Debate*. New York: Harvester Wheatsheaf.

Bloch, M. 1939. *La société féodale*. Paris: Albin Michel. Trans.: *Feudal Society*. Chicago: University of Chicago Press.

– 1949. *Apologie pour l'histoire, ou Métier d'historien*. Paris: Armand Colin.

Bloor, D. 1976. *Knowledge and Social Imagery*. London: Routledge & Kegan Paul.

Blumenschine, R.J., and J.A. Cavallo. 1992. "Scavenging and Human Evolution." *Scientific American* 267(10): 90–6.

Bobbio, N. 1991. *Il futuro della democrazia*. 2nd ed. Torino: Einaudi.

Bochenski, J.M. 1988. *Autorität, Freiheit, Glaube*. München: Philosophia Verlag.

Bogue, A.G., and R. Fogel, eds. 1972. *The Dimensions of Quantitative Research in History*. Princeton, NJ: Princeton University Press.

Bonacich, P., and J. Light. 1978. "Laboratory Experimentation in Sociology." *Annual Review of Sociology* 4: 145–70.

Bonner, J. 1986. *Politics, Economics and Welfare: An Elementary Introduction to Social Choice*. Brighton, UK: Wheatsheaf Books.

Bonner, J.T. 1980. *The Evolution of Culture in Animals*. Princeton, NJ: Princeton University Press.

Booth, W.J., P. James, and H. Meadwell, eds. 1993. *Politics and Rationality.* Cambridge: Cambridge University Press.

Borch, K. 1988. "Insurance Without Utility Theory." In G.L. Eberlein and H. Berghel, eds., *Theory and Decision: Essays in Honor of Werner Leinfellner*, 191–202. Dordrecht and Boston: Reidel.

Borovoy, A.A. 1988. *When Freedoms Collide.* Toronto: University of Toronto Press.

Boudon, R. 1979. *La logique du social. Introduction à l'analyse sociologique.* Paris: Hachette. Trans.: *The Logic of Social Action: An Introduction to Sociological Analysis.* London: Routledge & Kegan Paul.

– 1980. *The Crisis in Sociology: Problems of Sociological Epistemology.* New York: Columbia University Press.

– 1981. *The Logic of Social Action.* London: Routledge & Kegan Paul.

– 1984. *La place du désordre: Critique des théories du changement social.* Paris: Presses Universitaires de France.

– 1990a. *L'art de se persuader des idées fausses, fragiles ou douteuses.* Paris: Fayard.

– 1990b. "On Relativism." In P. Weingartner and G. Dorn, eds, *Studies on Mario Bunge's Treatise*, 229–43. Amsterdam: Rodopi.

– 1995. *Le juste et le vrai.* Paris: Fayard.

Boudon, R., and F. Bourricaud. 1986. *Dictionnaire critique de la sociologie.* 2nd ed. Paris: Presses Universitaires de France.

Boudon, R., and M. Clavelin, eds. 1994. *Le relativisme est-il résistible?* Paris: Presses Universitaires de France.

Boulding, K.E. 1985. *The World as a Total System.* Beverly Hills, CA: Sage.

Bourdieu, P. 1977 [1972]. *Outline of a Theory of Practice.* Trans. R. Nice. Cambridge: Cambridge University Press.

Boyd, R., and J.P. Loberbaum. 1987. "No Pure Strategy Is Evolutionarily Stable in the Repeated Prisoner's Dilemma Game." *Nature* 327: 58–61.

Braudel, F. 1969. *Écrits sur l'histoire.* Paris: Flammarion.

– 1972 [1949]. *The Mediterranean and the Mediterranean World in the Age of Philip II.* 2 vols. New York: Harper & Row, 1973.

– 1977. *Afterthoughts on Material Civilization and Capitalism.* Baltimore, MD: Johns Hopkins University Press.

– 1982 [1979]. *Civilization and Capitalism 15th–18th Century.* Vol. 2: *The Wheels of Commerce.* New York: Harper & Row.

Brecher, M., J. Winkenfeld, and S. Moser. 1988. *Handbook of International Crises.* Vol. 1: *Crises in the Twentieth Century.* Oxford: Pergamon Press.

Breton, A., G. Galeotti, P. Salmon, and R. Wintrobe, eds. 1995. *Nationalism and Rationality.* Cambridge: Cambridge University Press.

Brock, W.A. 1990. "Chaos and Complexity in Economic and Financial Science." In G.M. von Furstenberg, ed., *Acting under Uncertainty*, 423–50. Boston, Dordrecht, and London: Kluwer.

Bronowski, J. 1959. *Science and Human Values*. New York: Harper & Brothers.

Brown, A.J. 1983. "Friedman and Schwartz on the United Kingdom." In *Bank of England Panel of Academic Consultants*, Paper no. 22, 9–43. London: Bank of England.

Brown, R. 1973. *Rules and Laws in Sociology*. London: Routledge & Kegan Paul.

Buber-Agassi, J. 1985. *The Evaluation of Approaches in Recent Swedish Work Reforms*. Stockholm: Department of Psychology, University of Stockholm.

Buchanan, J.M. 1975. *The Limits of Liberty: Between Anarchy and Leviathan*. Chicago: University of Chicago Press.

Buchanan, J.M., and R.D. Tollison, eds. 1972. *Theory of Public Choice*. Ann Arbor: University of Michigan Press.

Buchanan, J.M. and G. Tullock. 1962. *The Calculus of Consent. Logical Foundations of Constitutional Democracy*. Ann Arbor: University of Michigan Press.

Buckley, W. 1968. *Modern Systems Research for the Behavioral Scientist*. Chicago: Aldine.

Bueno de Mesquita, B. 1981. *The War Trap*. New Haven: Yale University Press.

Bunge, M. 1951. "What Is Chance?" *Science and Society* 15: 209–31.

– 1960. *Etica y ciencia*. Buenos Aires: Siglo Veinte.

– 1962. *Intuition and Science*. Englewood Cliffs, NJ: Prentice-Hall. Repr.: Westport CT: Greenwood Press, 1975.

– 1963. *The Myth of Simplicity*. Englewood Cliffs, NJ: Prentice-Hall.

– 1967a. *Scientific Research*. 2 vols. Berlin, Heidelberg, and New York: Springer-Verlag.

– 1967b. *Foundations of Physics*. Berlin, Heidelberg, and New York: Springer-Verlag.

– 1968. "The Maturation of Science." In I. Lakatos and A. Musgrave, eds, *Problems in the Philosophy of Science,* 120–37. Amsterdam: North Holland.

– 1973a. *Method, Model and Matter*. Dordrecht: Reidel.

– 1973b. "A Decision Theoretic Model of the American War in Vietnam." *Theory and Decision* 3: 328–38.

– 1973c. "On Confusing 'Measurement' with 'Measure' in the Behavioral Sciences." In M. Bunge, ed., *The Methodological Unity of Science*, 105–22. Dordrecht: Reidel.

– 1973d. "The Role of Forecast in Planning." *Theory and Decision* 3: 307–21.

– 1974a. *Treatise on Basic Philosophy*. Vol. 1: *Sense and Reference*. Dordrecht and Boston: Reidel.

– 1974b. *Treatise on Basic Philosophy*. Vol. 2: *Interpretation and Truth*. Dordrecht and Boston: Reidel.

– 1974c. "The Concept of Social Structure." In W. Leinfellner and E. Köhler, eds, *Developments in the Methodology of Social Science*, 175–215. Dordrecht and Boston: Reidel.

– 1976a. "The Relevance of Philosophy to Social Science," In W.R. Shea, ed., *Basic Issues in the Philosohy of Science*, 136–55. New York: Science History Publications.

– 1976b. "A Model for Processes Combining Competition with Cooperation." *Applied Mathematical Modeling* 1: 21–3.

– 1977a. *Treatise on Basic Philosophy.* Vol. 3: *The Furniture of the World.* Dordrecht and Boston: Reidel.

– 1977b. "A Systems Concept of the International System." In M. Bunge, J. Galtung, and M. Malitza, eds, *Mathematical Approaches to International Relations,* 291–305. Bucharest: Romanian Academy of Social and Political Sciences.

– 1978. Review of W. Stegmüller's *The Structure and Dynamics of Theories.* In *Mathematical Reviews* 55: 333, no. 2480.

– 1979a. *Treatise on Basic Philosophy.* Vol. 4: *A World of Systems.* Dordrecht and Boston: Reidel.

– 1979b. "A Systems Concept of Society: Beyond Individualism and Holism." *Theory and Decision* 10: 13–30.

– 1979c. "A Model of Secrecy." *Journal of Irreproducible Results* 25 (2): 25–6.

– 1980. *Ciencia y desarrollo.* Buenos Aires: Siglo Veinte.

– 1981a. *Scientific Materialism.* Dordrecht and Boston: Reidel.

– 1981b. Review of L. Fleck's *Genesis and Development of a Scientific Fact.* In *Behavioral Science* 26: 178–80.

– 1981c. "Development Indicators." *Social Indicators Research* 9: 369–85.

– 1983a. *Treatise on Basic Philosophy.* Vol. 5: *Exploring the World.* Dordrecht and Boston: Reidel.

– 1983b. *Treatise on Basic Philosophy.* Vol. 6: *Understanding the World.* Dordrecht and Boston: Reidel.

– 1984. "Philosophical Problems in Linguistics." *Erkenntnis* 21: 107–73.

– 1985a. *Treatise on Basic Philosophy.* Vol. 7, *Philosophy of Science and Technology,* part I: *Formal and Physical Sciences.* Dordrecht and Boston: Reidel.

– 1985b. *Treatise on Basic Philosophy.* Vol. 7, *Philosophy of Science and Technology,* part II: *Life Science, Social Science, and Technology.* Dordrecht and Boston: Reidel.

– 1985c. *Economía y filosofía.* 2nd ed. Madrid: Tecnos.

– 1988a. "Two Faces and Three Masks of Probability." In E. Agazzi, ed., *Probability in the Sciences,* 27–50. Dordrecht and Boston: Reidel.

– 1988b. "The Scientific Status of History." In U. Hinke-Dörnemann, ed., *Die Philosophie in der modernen Welt,* 1: 593–602. Frankfurt: Peter Lang.

– 1988c. "Basic Science Is Innocent, Applied Science and Technology Can Be Guilty." In G.E. Lemarchand and A.R. Pedace, eds, *Scientists, Peace and Disarmament,* 245–61. Singapore: World Scientific.

– 1989a. *Treatise on Basic Philosophy.* Vol. 8: *Ethics.* Dordrecht and Boston: Reidel.

– 1989b. "Game Theory Is Not a Useful Tool for the Political Scientist." *Epistemologia* 12: 195–212

– 1990a. "What Kind of Discipline Is Psychology: Autonomous or Dependent,

Humanistic or Scientific, Biological or Sociological?" *New Ideas in Psychology* 8: 121–37.

– 1990b. "The Nature and Place of Psychology: A Reply to Panksepp, Mayer, Royce, and Cellerier and Ducret." *New Ideas in Psychology* 8: 177–88.

– 1991a. "Charges against Applied Game Theory Sustained: Reply to C. Schmidt." *Epistemologia* 13: 151–4.

– 1991b. "The Power and Limits of Reduction." In E. Agazzi, ed., *The Problem of Reductionism in Science*, 27–49. Dordrecht: Kluwer.

– 1991c. "A Skeptic's Beliefs and Disbeliefs." *New Ideas in Psychology* 9: 131–49.

– 1991d. "What Is Science? Does It Matter to Distinguish It from Pseudoscience? A Reply to My Commentators." *New Ideas in Psychology* 9: 245–83. Criticisms: 151–44. Replies: 245–83.

– 1991e. "A Critical Examination of the New Sociology of Science, Part 1." *Philosophy of the Social Sciences* 21: 524–60.

– 1992a. "A Critical Examination of the New Sociology of Science, Part 2." *Philosophy of the Social Sciences* 22: 46–76.

– 1992b. "Morality Is the Basis of Legal and Political Legitimacy." In W. Krawietz and G.H. von Wright, eds, *Öffentliche oder private Moral?* 379–86. Berlin: Duncker & Humblot.

– 1993. "Realism and Antirealism in Social Science." *Theory and Decision* 35: 207–35.

– 1995a. "The Poverty of Rational Choice Theory." In I.C. Jarvie and N. Laor, eds, *Critical Rationalism, Metaphysics and Science,* 1: 149–68. Dordrecht and Boston: Kluwer.

– 1995b. "A Critical Examination of the Foundations of Rational Choice Theory." In Götschl, ed., 211–28.

– 1996a. *Finding Philosophy in Social Science*. New Haven, CT: Yale University Press.

– 1996b. "The Seven Pillars of Popper's Social Philosophy." *Philosophy of the Social Sciences* 26: 528–56.

– 1996c. "In Praise of Intolerance to Charlatanism in Academia." In P.R. Gross, N. Levitt, and M.W. Lewis, eds, *The Flight from Science and Reason*, 96–115. New York: New York Academy of Sciences.

– 1997a. "Moderate Mathematical Fictionism." In E. Agazzi and G. Darwas, eds, *Philosophy of Mathematics Today*, 51–71. Dordrecht and Boston: Kluwer.

– 1997b. "Mechanism and Explanation." *Philosophy of the Social Sciences* 27: 410–65.

– 1997c. "A New Look at Moral Realism." In E. Garzón-Valdés, W. Krawietz, G.H. von Wright, and R. Zimmerling, eds, *Normative Systems in Legal and Moral Theory*, 17–26. Berlin: Duncker & Humblot.

– 1998. *Philosophy of Science*. 2 vols. New Brunswick, NJ: Transaction Publishers.

Bunge, M., and R. Ardila. 1987. *Philosophy of Psychology*. New York: Springer.

Bunge, M., and M. García-Sucre. 1976. "Differentiation, Participation and Cohesion." *Quality and Quantity* 10: 171–8.

Bunge, W. 1962. *Theoretical Geography*. Lund: Royal University of Lund.

Burt, R.S. 1980. "Models of Network Structure." *Annual Review of Sociology* 6: 79–141.

– 1982. *Toward a Structural Theory of Action*. New York: Academic Press.

– 1992. *Structural Holes: The Social Structure of Competition*. Cambridge, MA: Harvard University Press.

Cacioppo, J.T., and R.E. Petty, eds. 1983. *Social Psychophysiology*. New York and London: Guilford Press.

Campbell, R. 1985. "Background for the Uninitiated." In R. Campbell and L. Sowden, eds, 3–41.

Campbell, R., and L. Sowden, eds. 1985. *Paradoxes of Rationality and Cooperation: Prisoner's Dilemma and Newcomb's Problem*. Vancouver: University of British Columbia Press.

Caplow, T. 1986. "Sociology and the Nuclear Debate." In Short, ed., 321–33.

Card, D., and A. Krueger. 1995. *Myth and Measurement: The New Economics of the Minimum Wage*. Princeton, NJ: Princeton University Press.

Carens, J.H. 1981. *Equality, Moral Incentives, and the Market: An Essay in Utopian-Politico-Economic Theory*. Chicago: University of Chicago Press.

Caro, F.G. 1983. "Program Evaluation." In H.E. Freeman, R.R. Dynes, P.H. Rossi, and W.F. Whyte, eds, *Applied Sociology*, 77–93. San Francisco: Jossey-Bass.

Caro Baroja, J. 1992. *Las falsificaciones de la historia*. Barcelona: Ariel.

Carr, E.H. 1961. *What Is History?* Repr. New York: Vintage Books, 1967.

Carrère d'Encausse, H. 1978. *L'empire éclaté: La révolte des nations en U.R.S.S.* 2nd ed. Paris: Flammarion.

Carroll, G.R. 1984. "Organizational Ecology." *Annual Review of Sociology* 10: 71–93.

Catton, W.R., G. Lenski, and F.H. Buttel. 1986. "To What Degree Is a Social System Dependent on Its Resource Base?" In Short, ed., 165–86.

Cavalli-Sforza, L.L., P. Menozzi, and A. Piazza. 1994. *The History and Geography of Human Genes*. Princeton, NJ: Princeton University Press.

Chagnon, N. 1977. *Yanomano: The Fierce People*. 2nd ed. New York: Holt, Rinehart & Winston.

– 1988. "Life Histories, Blood Revenge, and Warfare in Tribal Population." *Science* 239: 985–92.

Chamberlin, E.H. 1933. *Theory of Monopolistic Competition*. Cambridge, MA: Harvard University Press.

Chandler, A.D., Jr. 1977. *The Visible Hand: The Managerial Revolution in American Business*. Cambridge, MA: Harvard University Press.

Chelimsky, E. 1991. "On the Social Science Contribution to Governmental Decision-Making." *Science* 254: 226–31.

Childe, G. 1947. *History*. London: Cobbett Press.

Chomsky, N. 1972. *Language and Mind*. New York: Harcourt, Brace, Jovanovich.

- 1981. "Principles and Parameters in Syntactic Theory." In N. Hornstein and D. Lightfoot, eds, *Explanation in Linguistics*, 32–75. London: Longman.

- 1995. "Language and Nature." *Mind* 104: 1–61.

Clark, C.M.A. 1992. *Economic Theory and Natural Philosophy: The Search for the Natural Laws of the Economy*. Aldershot, UK, and Brookfield, VT: Edward Elgar.

Clark, G. 1957. General introduction to *The New Cambridge Modern History*, vol. 1. Cambridge: Cambridge University Press.

Clark, R. 1971. *Crime in America*. New York: Pocket Books.

Clayre, A., ed. 1980. *The Political Economy of the Third Sector: Cooperation and Participation*. Oxford: Oxford University Press.

Clutton-Brock, T.H., and G.A. Parker. 1995. "Punishment in Animal Societies." *Nature* 373: 209–16.

Cohen, I.B., ed. 1990. *Puritanism and the Rise of Modern Science: The Merton Thesis*. New Brunswick, NJ: Rutgers University Press.

Coleman, J.S. 1990. *Foundations of Social Theory*. Cambridge, MA: Belknap Press of Harvard University Press.

- 1993. "The Rational Reconstruction of Society." *American Sociological Review* 58: 1–15.

Coles, J. 1973. *Archaeology by Experiment*. New York: Charles Scribner's Sons.

Collingwood, R.G. 1975 [1946]. *The Idea of History*. Oxford: Clarendon Press.

Collins, R. 1981. "On the Microfoundations of Macrosociology." *American Journal of Sociology* 87: 984–1014.

- 1987. "Interaction, Ritual Chains, Power and Property." In Alexander et al., 193–206.

- 1989. "Sociology: Protoscience or Antiscience?" *American Sociological Review* 54: 124–39.

Collins, R., ed. 1983. *Sociological Theory 1983*. San Francisco: Jossey-Bass.

Committee for Economic Development. 1996. *American Workers and Economic Change*. Washington: CED.

Condorcet, M.-J.-A.-N. Caritat, marquis de. 1976. *Selected Writings*. Ed. K.M. Baker. Indianapolis, IN: Bobbs-Merrill.

Coser, L.A., ed. 1975. *The Idea of Social Structure*. New York: Harcourt Brace Jovanovich.

Craig, J.G. 1993. *The Nature of Cooperation*. Montréal: Black Rose Books.

Crick, B. 1971. *Political Theory and Practice*. London: Allen Lane.

Cross, J.G. and M.J. Guyer. 1980. *Social Traps*. Ann Arbor: University of Michigan Press.

Crozier, M.J., S. Huntington, and J. Watanuki. 1975. *The Crisis of Democracy*. Trilateral Commission Report. New York: New York University Press.

Currie, J., and D. Thomas. 1995. "Does Head Start Make a Difference?" *American Economic Review* 85: 341–63.

Cyert, R., and J.G. March. 1963. *A Behavioral Theory of the Firm*. Englewood Cliffs, NJ: Prentice-Hall.

Dagum, C. 1986. "Analyzing Rational and Adaptive Expectations Hypotheses and Model Specifications." *Economies et Sociétés*, sér. EM, no. 10: 15–34.

– 1990. "On Structural Adjustment and Stabilization: A Comment." In G. Bourgoignie and M. Genné, eds, *Ajustement structurel et réalités sociales en Afrique / Structural Adjustment and Social Realities in Africa*, 87–92. Ottawa: University of Ottawa Press.

Dahl, R.A. 1971. *Polyarchy: Participation and Opposition*. New Haven, CT: Yale University Press.

– 1985. *A Preface to Economic Democracy*. Berkeley and Los Angeles: University of California Press.

– 1989. *Democracy and Its Critics*. New Haven, CT: Yale University Press.

Dahrendorf, R. 1959. *Class and Class Conflict in Industrial Society*. Stanford, CA: Stanford University Press.

– 1988. *The Modern Social Conflict: An Essay on the Politics of Liberty*. London: Weidenfeld & Nicolson.

Dallmayr, F.R., and T.A. McCarthy. 1977a. "The Crisis of Understanding. In Dallmayr and McCarthy, eds, 1–15.

Dallmayr, F.R., and T.A. McCarthy, eds. 1977b. *Understanding and Social Inquiry*. Notre Dame, IN: University of Notre Dame Press.

Damasio, A.R., H. Damasio, and Y. Christen, eds. 1996. *Neurobiology of Decision-Making*. Berlin, Heidelberg, and New York: Springer.

Danaher, K., ed. 1994. *Fifty Years Is Enough: The Case against the World Bank and the International Monetary Fund*. Boston: South Bend Press.

Danto, A.C., 1965. *Analytical Philosophy of History*. Cambridge: Cambridge University Press.

Dasgupta, P.S., 1979. *Economic Theory and Exhaustible Resources*. Cambridge: Cambridge University Press.

Dasgupta, P.S., and K.-G. Mäler. 1994. *Poverty, Institutions, and the Environmental-Resource Base*. Washington: World Bank.

Dasgupta, P.S., and D. Ray. 1987. "Inequality as a Determinant of Malnutrition and Unemployment: Policy." *Economic Journal* 97: 177–88.

Davidson, D. 1980. *Essays on Actions and Events*. Oxford: Clarendon Press.

Davis, D.D., and C.A. Holt. 1993. *Experimental Economics*. Princeton, NJ: Princeton University Press.

Dawkins, R. 1976. *The Selfish Gene*. Oxford: Oxford University Press.

Debnam, G. 1984. *The Analysis of Power: A Realist Approach*. London: Macmillan.

Debreu, G. 1991. "The Mathematization of Economic Theory." *American Economic Review* 81: 1–7.

de Graaff, J. 1967. *Theoretical Welfare Economics*. Cambridge: University Press.

de Greene, K.B. 1973. *Sociotechical Systems: Factors in Analysis, Design, and Management*. Englewood Cliffs, NJ: Prentice-Hall.

Deininger, K., and L. Squire. 1996. "A New Data Set Measuring Income Inequality." *World Bank Economic Review* 10: 565–91.

Deming, W. Edwards. 1982. *Out of the Crisis*. Cambridge, MA: MIT Center for Advanced Engineering Study.

Deutsch, K.W. 1986. "Substantial Advances: Real but Elusive." In Deutsch, Markovits, and Platt, eds, 361–72.

Deutsch, K.W., A.S. Markovits, and J. Platt, eds. 1986. *Advances in the Social Sciences, 1900–1980: What, Who, Where, How?* Lanham, MD: University Press of America; Cambridge MA: Abt Books.

Deutsch, K.W., J. Platt, and D. Senghaas. 1971. "Conditions Favoring Major Advances in Social Science." *Science* 171: 450–9.

DeVillé, P. 1990. "Equilibrium versus Reproduction: Some Queries About Dynamics in Social Systems Theory." In F. Geyer and J. van der Zeuwen, eds, *Self-Referencing in Social Systems*, 155–74. Salinas, CA: Intersystems Publications.

de Waal, F. 1989. *Chimpanzee Politics: Power and Sex Among Apes*. Baltimore: Johns Hopkins University Press.

Dilthey, W. 1959 [1883]. *Einleitung in die Geisteswissenschaften*. In *Gesammelte Schriften*, 4: 318–31. Stuttgart: Teubner.

Dimond, J. 1997. *Guns, Germs, and Steel: The Fates of Human Societies*. New York: Norton.

Di Tella, T.S. 1988. *Sociología de los procesos políticos*. 3rd ed. Buenos Aires: Eudeba. Engl. trans.: *Latin American Politics: A Theoretical Approach*. Austin: Texas University Press, 1990.

Dixon, W.J., and T. Boswell. 1996. "Dependency, Disarticulation, and Denominator Effects: Another Look at Foreign Capital Penetration." *American Journal of Sociology* 102: 543–62.

Dobb, M. 1969. *Welfare Economics and the Economics of Socialism*. Cambridge: Cambridge University Press.

Dohrenwend, B.P., I. Levak, P.E. Shrout, S. Schwartz, G. Naveh, B.G. Link, A.E. Skodol, and A. Stueve. 1992. "Socioeconomic Status and Psychiatric Disorders: The Causation-Selection Issue." *Science* 255: 946–52.

Dolan, E.G., ed. 1976. *The Foundations of Modern Austrian Economics*. Kansas City, MO: Sheed & Ward.

Dosi, G. 1982. "Technological Paradigms and Technological Trajectories." *Research Policy* 11: 147–62.

Dosi, G., C. Freeman, R. Nelson, G. Silverberg, and L. Soete, eds. 1988. *Technical Change and Economic Theory*. London and New York: Pinter Publishers.

Dow, J.C.R., and I.D. Saville. 1988. *A Critique of Monetary Policy: Theory and British Experience*. Oxford: Oxford University Press.

Downs, A. 1957. *An Economic Theory of Democracy*. New York: Harper & Row.

Doz, Y.L, and C.K. Prahalad. 1991. "Managing DMNSCs: A Search for a New Paradigm." *Strategic Management Journal* 12: 145–64

Drucker, P.F. 1991. "The Emerging Theory of Manufacturing." In *The New Manufacturing*, 2–10. Cambridge, MA: Harvard Busines Review.

– 1993. *Post Capitalist Society*. New York: Harper Business.

Dumont, L. 1966. *Homo hierarchicus. Essai sur le système des castes*. Paris: Gallimard.

Dunbar, R.I.M. 1993. "Coevolution of Neocortical Size, Group Size and Language in Humans." *Behavioral and Brain Sciences* 16: 681–735.

Dunn, J. 1994. "Introduction: Crisis of the Nation State?" *Political Studies* 42: 3–15.

Du Pasquier, G. 1926. *Le calcul des probabilités, son évolution mathématique et philosophique*. Paris: Hermann.

Durkheim, E. 1972. *Selected Writings*. Trans. and ed. A. Giddens. Cambridge: Cambridge University Press.

Dworkin, R. 1986. *Law's Empire*. Cambridge, MA: Belknap Press of Harvard University Press.

Dyke, C. 1981. *Philosophy of Economics*. Englewood Cliffs, NJ: Prentice-Hall.

Eatwell, M. Milgate, and P. Newman, eds. 1987. *The New Palgrave*. 3 vols. New York: Macmillan.

Eichner, A.S. 1991. *The Macrodynamics of Advanced Market Economies*. Armonk, NY: M.E. Sharpe.

Eichner, A.S., ed. 1983. *Why Economics Is Not Yet a Science*. Armonk, NY: M.E. Sharpe.

Einstein, A. 1923. *Geometrie und Erfahrung*. Translated selection in H. Feigl and M. Brodbeck, eds, *Readings in the Philosophy of Science*, 189–94. New York: Appleton-Century-Crofts, 1953.

Ekins, P., ed. 1986. *The Living Economy*. London: Routledge & Kegan Paul.

Ellickson, R.C. 1991. *Order without Law: How Neighbors Settle Disputes*. Cambridge, MA: Harvard University Press.

Elster, J., 1989. *The Cement of Society: A Study of Social Order*. Cambridge: Cambridge University Press.

Elster, J. and A. Hylland, eds. 1986. *Foundations of Social Choice Theory*. Cambridge: Cambridge University Press; Oslo: Universitetsvorlaget.

Elster, J., and K.O. Moene. 1989. Introduction to J. Elster, and K.O. Moene, eds, *Alternatives to Capitalism*, 1–35 Cambridge: Cambridge University Press; Paris: Editions de la Maison des Sciences de l'Homme.

Engels, F. 1940 [1876]. "The Part Played by Labour in the Transition from Ape to Man." In *Dialectics of Nature*, 279–96. New York: International Publishers.

– 1954 [1878]. *Anti-Dühring*. Moscow: Foreign Languages Publishing House, 1954.

– 1973 [1845]. *The Condition of the Working-Class in England*. Moscow: Progress Publishers.

Ericsson, N.R., and J.S. Irons. 1995. *The Lucas Critique in Practice: Theory without Measurements*. Washington: Board of Governors of the Federal Reserve System. International Finance Discussion Paper no. 506.

Esping-Andersen, G. 1994. "Welfare States and the Economy." In Smelser and Swedberg, eds, 711–32.

Etzioni, A. 1987. "On Thoughtless Rationality." *Kyklos* 40: 496–514.

– 1988. *The Moral Dimension: Toward a New Economics*. New York: Free Press.

Etzioni, A., and P.R. Lawrence, eds. 1991. *Socio-Economics: Towards a New Synthesis*. Armonk, NY: M.E. Sharpe.

Evans, R.G., M.L. Barer, and T.R. Marmor, eds. 1994. *Why Are Some People Healthy and Others Not? The Determinants of Health of Populations*. New York: Aldine de Gruyter.

Ezrahi, Y. 1971. "The Political Resources of American Science." Repr. in Barnes, ed. (1972), 211–30.

Falk, R. 1995. *On Humane Governance*. University Park: Pennsylvania State University Press.

Farber, H.S. 1987. "The Recent Decline of Unionization in the United States." *Science* 238: 915–20.

Farías, V. 1990. *Heidegger and Nazism*. Philadelphia: Temple University Press.

Faulhaber, G.R., and W.J. Baumol. 1988. "Economists as Innovators: Practical Products of Theoretical Research." *Journal of Economic Literature* 26: 577–60.

Feinberg, J., and H. Gross, eds. 1991. *Philosophy of Law*. 4th ed. Belmont, CA: Wadsworth.

Fellner, W. 1960. *Emergence and Content of Modern Economic Analysis*. New York: McGraw-Hill.

Festinger, L. 1957. *Cognitive Dissonance*. Stanford: Stanford University Press.

Feyerabend, P.K. 1975. *Against Method*. London: Verso.

– 1990. "Realism and the Historicity of Knowledge." In W.R. Shea and A. Spadafora, eds, *Creativity in the Arts and Science*, 142–53. Canton, MA: Science History Publications, U.S.A.

– 1995. "Nature as a Work of Art." In Götschl, ed., 255–67.

Fisher, F.M. 1983. *Disequilibrium Foundations of Equilibrium Economics*. Cambridge: Cambridge University Press.

Flakierski, H. 1995. "Market Socialism Revisited. An Alternative for Eastern Europe?" *International Journal of Sociology* 25(3).

Fleck, L. 1979 [1935]. *Genesis and Development of a Scientific Fact.* Foreword by T.S. Kuhn. Chicago and London: University of Chicago Press.

Fløistad, G., ed. 1982. *Contemporary Philosophy.* Vol. 3: *Philosophy of Action.* The Hague: Marinus Nijhoff.

Fogel, R.W. 1982a. "'Scientific' History and Traditional History." In L.J. Cohen et al., eds, *Logic, Methodology and Philosophy of Science* VI, 15–61. Amsterdam: North-Holland.

– 1982b. "Circumstantial Evidence in 'Scientific' and Traditional History." In D. Carr, W. Dray, T.F. Geraets, F. Ouellet, and H. Watelet, eds, *La philosophie de l'histoire et la pratique historique d'aujourd'hui / Philosophy of History and Contemporary Historiography*, 61–112. Ottawa: University of Ottawa Press.

– 1994. "Economic Growth, Population Theory, and Physiology: The Bearing of Long-Term Processes on the Making of Economic Policy." *American Economic Review* 84: 369–95.

Foot, D.K. 1982. *Canada's Population Outlook.* Toronto: James Lorimer.

Forman, P. 1995. "Truth and Objectivity." *Science* 269: 565–7, 707–10.

Foucault, M. 1969. *L'archéologie du savoir.* Paris: Gallimard.

Fox, R. 1989. *The Search for Society: Quest for a Biosocial Science and Morality.* New Brunswick, NJ: Rutgers University Press.

Frank, R.H. 1985. *Choosing the Right Pond: Human Behavior and the Quest for Status.* New York and Oxford: Oxford University Press.

– 1988. *Passions within Reason: The Strategic Role of the Emotions.* New York and London: W.W. Norton.

Frank, R.H., T. Gilovich, and D.T. Regan. 1993. "Does Studying Economics Inhibit Cooperation?" *Journal of Economic Perspectives* 7: 159–71.

Franke, R.H., and J.D. Kaul. 1978. "The Hawthorn Experiment: First Statistical Interpretation." *American Sociological Review* 43: 623–42.

Frankfort, H. and H.A., J.A. Wilson, and T. Jacobsen. 1946. *Before Philosophy: The Intellectual Adventure of Ancient Man.* London: Penguin, 1949.

Fréchet, M. 1946. "Les définitions courantes de la probabilité." In *Les mathématiques et le concret*, 157–204. Paris: Presses Universitaires de France.

Freeman, C. 1988. Introduction to G. Dosi, C. Freeman, R. Nelson, G. Silverberg, and L. Soete, eds, 1–8.

Freeman, D. 1983. *The Making and Unmaking of an Anthropological Myth.* Cambridge, MA: Harvard University Press.

Friedman, M. 1953. "The Methodology of Positive Economics." In *Essays in Positive Economics,* 3–43. Chicago: University of Chicago Press.

– 1962. *Capitalism and Freedom.* Chicago: University of Chicago Press.

– 1970. "A Theoretical Framework for Monetary Analysis." In R.J. Gordon, ed.,

Milton Friedman's Monetary Framework, 1–62. Chicago: University of Chicago Press.

– 1991. "Old Wine in New Bottles." *Economic Journal* 101: 33–40.

Friedman, M., and A. Schwartz. 1982. *Monetary Trends in the United States and the United Kingdom 1867–1975*. Chicago: University of Chicago Press.

Frydman, R. 1983. "Individual Rationality, Decentralization, and the Rational Expectations Hypothesis." In R.E. Frydman, Jr, and E.S. Phelps, eds, *Individual Forecasting and Aggregate Outcomes: "Rational Expectations" Examined*, 97–122. Cambridge: Cambridge University Press.

Furet, F. 1972. "Quantitative History." In Gilbert and Graubard, eds, 45–61.

Galbraith, J.K. 1967. *The New Industrial State*. Boston: Houghton Mifflin.

– 1969. *The Affluent Society*. 2nd ed. Boston: Houghton Mifflin.

– 1973. *Economics and the Public Purpose*. Boston: Houghton Mifflin.

– 1983. *The Anatomy of Power*. Boston: Houghton Mifflin.

– 1987. *A History of Economics*. London: Hamish Hamilton.

– 1991. "Economics in the Century Ahead." *Economic Journal* 101: 41–6.

– 1992. *The Culture of Contentment*. Boston: Houghton Mifflin.

– 1996. *The Good Society: The Humane Dimension*. Boston: Houghton Mifflin.

Gale, D. 1960. *The Theory of Linear Economic Models*. New York: McGraw-Hill.

Gale, S., and G. Olsson, eds. 1979. *Philosophy in Geography*. Dordrecht: D. Reidel.

Gallay, A. 1983. *L'archéologie demain*. Paris: Pierre Belfond.

Galtung, J. 1984. *There Are Alternatives!* Nottingham, UK: Spokesman.

Gans, H.J. 1995. *The War against the Poor*. New York: Basic Books.

Gardiner, P., ed. 1959. *Theories of History*. Glencoe, IL: Free Press.

Garfinkel, H. 1967. *Studies in Ethnomethodology*. Englewood Cliffs, NJ: Prentice-Hall.

– 1988. "Evidence for Locally Produced, Naturally Accountable Phenomena of Order, Logic, Reason, Meaning, Method, etc." *Sociological Theory* 6: 103–9.

Gauthier, D. 1986. *Morals by Agreement*. Oxford: Clarendon Press.

Geertz, C. 1966. "Religion as a Cultural System." In D. Culter, ed., *The Religious Situation*, 639–88. Boston: Beacon Press.

– 1973. *The Interpretation of Cultures*. New York: Basic Books.

– 1983. *Local Knowledge: Further Essays in Interpretive Anthropology*. New York: Basic Books.

– 1984. "Anti Anti-Relativism." *American Anthropologist* 86: 263–78.

Gellner, E. 1973. *Cause and Meaning in the Social Sciences*. London: Routledge & Kegan Paul.

– 1974. *Legitimation of Belief*. Cambridge: Cambridge University Press.

– 1983. *Nations and Nationalism*. Oxford: Basil Blackwell.

– 1984. "The Social Roots of Modern Egalitarianism." In G. Radnitzky and G. Andersson, eds, *Rationality in Science and Politics*, 111–30. Dordrecht: Reidel.

– 1985. *Relativism and the Social Sciences.* Cambridge: Cambridge University Press.

– 1988. *Plough, Sword and Book.* Chicago: University of Chicago Press.

– 1993. *The Psychoanalytic Movement.* 2nd ed. London: Fontana Press.

– 1996. "Return of a Native." *Political Quarterly* 67: 4–13.

Geoffrin, A.M. 1992. "Forces, Trends, and Opportunities in MS/OR." *Operations Research* 40: 423–45.

Gerken, G. 1994. *Die fraktale Marke.* Düsseldorf: Econ Verlag.

Gibbard, A. 1974. "A Pareto-Consistent Libertarian Claim." *Journal of Economic Theory* 7: 383–410.

Gibbard, A., and H. Varian. 1978. "Economic Models." *Journal of Philosophy* 75: 664–77.

Giddens, A. 1973. *The Class Structure in Advanced Societies.* London: Hutchinson.

– 1984. *The Constitution of Society: Outline of the Theory of Structuration.* Cambridge: Polity Press; Berkeley and Los Angeles: University of California Press.

Giddens, A., and D. Held, eds. 1982. *Classes, Power, and Conflict.* Berkeley and Los Angeles: University of California Press.

Gilbert, F., and S.R. Graubard, eds. 1972. *Historical Studies Today.* New York: W.W. Norton.

Gilovich, G. 1991. *How We Know What Isn't So: The Fallibility of Human Reason in Everyday Life.* New York: Free Press.

Gini, C. 1952. *Patologia economica.* 5th ed. Torino: UTET.

Girard, M., ed. 1994. *Les individus dans la politique internationale.* Paris: Economica.

Givón, T. 1979. *On Understanding Grammar.* New York: Academic Press.

Godelier, M. 1984. *L'idéel et le matériel.* Paris: Fayard.

Goffman, E. 1963. *Behavior in Public Places.* New York: Free Press.

Goldberger, A.S. 1978. "Genetic Determination of Income." *American Economic Review* 68: 960–9.

Goldsmith, A., J.R. Veum, and W. Darity, Jr. 1996. "The Psychological Impact of Unemployment and Joblessness." *Journal of Socio-Economics* 25: 333–58.

Goldsmith, M., and A. Mackay, eds. 1964. *The Science of Science.* London: Souvenir Press.

Goldstein, L.J. 1958. "The Two Theses of Methodological Individualism." *British Journal for the Philosophy of Science* 9: 1–11.

– 1977. "History and the Primacy of Knowing." *History and Theory,* Beiheft 16: 29–52.

Goldstone, J.A. 1991. *Revolution and Rebellion in the Early Modern World.* Berkeley: University of California Press.

– 1994. "Is Revolution Individually Rational?" *Rationality and Society* 6: 139–66.

Good, K., and D. Chanoff. 1991. *Into the Heart: One Man's Pursuit of Love and Knowledge among the Yanomama.* New York: Simon & Schuster.

Gorz, A. 1982. *Farewell to the Working Class*. London: Pluto Press.

Götschl, J., ed. 1995. *Revolutionary Changes in Understanding Man and Society*. Dordrecht: Kluwer.

Gottschalk, L., ed. 1963. *Generalization in the Writing of History*. Chicago: University of Chicago Press.

Gould, R.V. 1993. "Collective Action and Network Structure." *American Sociological Review* 58: 182–96.

Gouldner, A.W. 1960. "The Norm of Reciprocity: A Preliminary Statement." *American Sociological Review* 25: 161–78.

– 1970. *The Coming Crisis in Western Sociology*. New York: Basic Books.

Granovetter, M. 1974. *Getting a Job: A Study of Contacts and Careers*. Cambridge, MA: Harvard University Press.

– 1983. "The Strength of Weak Ties: A Network Theory Revisited." In R. Collins, ed., 201–33.

– 1985. "Economic Action and Social Structure: The Problem of Embeddedness." *American Journal of Sociology* 91: 481–510.

– 1991. "Construction of Economic Institutions." In Etzioni and Lawrence, eds, 75–81.

– 1994. "Business Groups." In Smelser and Swedberg, eds, 453–75.

Green, D.P., and I. Shapiro. 1994. *Pathologies of Rational Choice Theory: A Critique of Applications in Political Science*. New Haven, CT: Yale University Press.

Greenstein, F.I., and N.W. Polsby, eds. 1975. *Handbook of Political Science*. 9 vols. Reading, MA: Addison-Wesley.

Greenwood, E. 1948. *Experimental Sociology*. New York: King's Crown Press.

Greiner, L.E. 1972. "Evolution and Revolution as Organizations Grow." *Harvard Business Review* 50: 37–46.

Gross, M.L. 1978. *The Psychological Society*. New York: Random House.

Gross, P.R., and N. Levitt. 1994. *Higher Superstition: The Academic Left and Its Quarrels with Science*. Baltimore, MD: Johns Hopkins University Press.

Gross, P., N. Levitt, and M.W. Lewis, eds. 1996. *The Flight from Science and Reason, Annals of the New York Academy of Sciences, Vol. 775*. New York: New York Academy of Sciences.

Gurr, T.R., ed. 1980. *Handbook of Political Conflict*. New York: Free Press; London: Collier Macmillan.

Habermas, J. 1968. *Technik und Wissenschaft als Ideologie*. Frankfurt: Suhrkamp.

– 1973. *Theory and Practice*. Boston: Beacon Press.

– 1981. *Theorie des kommunicatives Handelns*. 2 vols. Frankfurt: Suhrkamp.

– 1988 [1967]. *On the Logic of the Social Sciences*. Cambridge, MA: MIT Press.

Hagstrom, W.O. 1965. *The Scientific Community*. New York: Basic Books.

Hahn, F.H. 1981a. *Money and Inflation*. Oxford: Basil Blackwell.

– 1981b. "General Equilibrium Theory." In D. Bell and I. Kristol, eds, 123–38.

– 1983. "Comment." In Frydman and Phelps, eds, 223–31.

Hahn, F., and R. Solow. 1995. *A Critical Essay on Modern Macroeconomic Theory.* Cambridge, MA: MIT Press.

Halal, W.E. 1986. *The New Capitalism.* New York: John Wiley & Sons.

Hall, J.A. 1985. *Powers and Liberties: The Causes and Consequences of the Rise of the West.* London: Penguin.

Halsey, A.H. 1990. "Educational Systems and the Economy." *Current Sociology* 38: 79–101.

Hamel, G., and C.K. Prahalad. 1994. *Competing for the Future.* Boston: Harvard Business School Press.

Hamilton, R.F. 1996. *The Social Misconstruction of Reality: Validity and Verification in the Scholarly Community.* New Haven, CT: Yale University Press.

Hamilton, W.D. 1964. "The Genetical Evolution of Social Behavior." *Journal of Theoretical Biology* 7: 1–52.

Hammond, J.S., III. 1967. "Better Decisions with Preference Theory." *Harvard Business Review* 45: 123–41.

Hammond, T.H. 1994. "Structure, Strategy, and the Agenda of the Firm." In Rumelt et al., eds, 97–154.

Handy, C. 1994. *The Age of Paradox.* Boston: Harvard Business School Press.

Hannan, M.T., and J. Freeman. 1977. "The Population Ecology of Organizations." *American Journal of Sociology* 82: 929–64.

Harcourt, G.C. 1972. *Some Cambridge Controversies in the Theory of Capital.* Cambridge: Cambridge University Press.

Hardin, G. 1968. "The Tragedy of the Commons." *Science* 162: 1243–7.

– 1985. *Filters against Folly.* New York: Viking Penguin.

Hardin, R. 1982. *Collective Action.* Baltimore: Johns Hopkins University Press.

Harding, S. 1986. *The Science Question in Feminism.* Ithaca, NY: Cornell University Press.

– 1991. *Whose Science? Whose Knowledge? Thinking from Women's Lives.* Ithaca, NY: Cornell University Press.

Harris, M. 1968. *The Rise of Anthropological Theory.* New York: Crowell.

– 1976. "History and Significance of the Emic-Etic Distinction." *Annual Reviews of Anthropology* 5: 329–50.

– 1977. *Canibals and Kings: The Origins of Cultures.* New York: Random House.

– 1979. *Cultural Materialism: The Struggle for a Science of Culture.* New York: Random House.

– 1989. *Our Kind.* New York: Harper & Row.

Harris, M., and E. Ross. 1987. *Death, Sex and Fertility: Population Regulation in Pre-Industrial Societies.* New York: Columbia University Press.

Harrison, B., and B. Bluestone. 1988. *The Great U-Turn: Corporate Restructuring and the Polarization of America*. New York: Basic Books.

Hart, H.L.A. 1961. *The Concept of Law*. Oxford: Oxford University Press.

Hausman, D.M., ed. 1984. *The Philosophy of Economics*. Cambridge: Cambridge University Press.

Hausman, J.A., and D.A. Wise. 1985. *Social Experimentation*. Chicago and London: University of Chicago Press.

Hayek, F.A. 1944. *The Road to Serfdom*. Chicago: University of Chicago Press.

– 1949. *Individualism and Economic Order*. London: Routledge & Kegan Paul.

– 1955. *The Counter-Revolution of Science*. Glencoe, IL: Free Press.

– 1979. *Law, Legislation and Liberty*. Vol. 3: *The Political Order of a Free People*. Chicago: University of Chicago Press.

– 1989. "The Pretence of Knowledge." *American Economic Review* 79: 3–7.

Heal, G.M. 1973. *The Theory of Economic Planning*. Amsterdam: North-Holland.

Heal, G.M., and P.S. Dasgupta. 1979. *Economic Theory and Exhaustible Resources*. Cambridge: Cambridge University Press.

Hebb, D.O. 1953. "On Motivation and Thought." In H.A. Buchtel, ed., *The Conceptual Nervous System*, 17–21. Oxford: Pergamon Press, 1982.

– 1966. *A Textbook of Psychology*. 2nd ed. Philadelphia: W.B. Saunders.

– 1980. *Essay on Mind*. Hillsdale, NJ: Lawrence Erlbaum Associates.

Hedström, P., and R. Swedberg, eds. 1997. *Social Mechanisms: An Analytical Approach to Social Theory*. Cambridge: Cambridge University Press.

Heidegger, M. 1953. *Einführung in die Metaphysik*. 5th ed. Tübingen: Max Niemeyer, 1987.

Heilbroner, R.L. 1980. *Marxism: For and Against*. New York: W.W. Norton.

Heinsohn, R., and C. Packer. 1995. "Complex Cooperative Strategies in Group-Territorial African Lions." *Science* 269: 1260–2.

Hempel, C.G. 1942. "The Function of General Laws in History." *Journal of Philosophy* 39: 35–48.

– 1965. *Aspects of Scientific Explanation*. New York: Free Press.

Hendry, D.F. 1980. "Econometrics – Alchemy or Science?" *Economica* 47: 387–406

Hendry, D.F., and N.R. Ericsson. 1983. "Assertion without Empirical Basis." In *Bank of England Panel of Academic Consultants* Paper no. 22, 45–101. London: Bank of England.

Herman, J.L., ed. 1987. *Program Evaluation Kit*. 9 vols. Newbury Park, CA: Sage.

Hernegger, R. 1989. *Anthropologie zwischen Soziobiologie und Kulturwissenschaft*. Bonn: Habelt.

Heskett, J.H., T.O. Jones, G.W. Loveman, W.E. Sasser, Jr, and L.A. Schlesinger. 1994. "Putting the Service-Profit Chain to Work." *Harvard Business Review*, March–April.

Hessen, B. 1971 [1931]. "The Social and Economic Roots of Newton's 'Principia.'" In N. Bukharin et al., *Science at the Cross Roads*, 149–212. London: Cass.

Hicks, A., J. Misra, and T.N. Ng. 1995. "The Programmatic Emergence of the Social Security State." *American Sociological Review* 60: 329–49.

Hicks, J. 1979. *Causality in Economics*. Oxford: Basil Blackwell.

Hilbert, R.A. 1990. "Ethnomethodology and the Micro-Macro Order." *American Sociological Review* 55: 794–808.

Hirschman, A.O. 1958. *The Strategy of Economic Development*. New Haven, CT: Yale University Press.

– 1970. *Exit, Voice, and Loyalty: Responses to Decline in Firms, Organizations, and States*. Cambridge, MA: Harvard University Press.

– 1977. *The Passions and the Interests: Political Arguments for Capitalism Before Its Triumph*. Princeton: Princeton University Press.

– 1981. *Essays in Trespassing: Economics to Politics and Beyond*. Cambridge: Cambridge University Press.

– 1982. *Shifting Involvements: Private Interest and Public Action*. Princeton, NJ: Princeton University Press.

– 1984. "Against Parsimony: Three Easy Ways of Complicating Some Categories of Economic Discourse." *American Economic Review* 74: 89–96.

– 1990. "The Case against 'One Thing at a Time.'" *World Development* 18: 1119–20.

– 1991. *The Rhetoric of Reaction: Perversity, Futility, Jeopardy*. Cambridge, MA: Belknap Press of Harvard University Press.

– 1992. *Rival Views of Market Society*. Cambridge, MA: Harvard University Press.

– 1994. "Social Conflicts as Pillars of Democratic Market Society." *Political Theory* 22: 203–18.

Hirshleifer, J. 1985. "The Expanding Domain of Economics." *American Economic Review* 75: 53–68.

Hirshleifer, J., and J.C. Martínez-Coll. 1988. "What Strategies Can Support the Evolutionary Emergence of Cooperation?" *Journal of Conflict Resolution* 32: 367–98.

Hobsbawm, E.J. 1972. "From Social History to the History of Society." In Gilbert and Graubard, eds, 1–26.

– 1980. "The Revival of Narrative: Some Comments." *Past and Present* 86: 3–8.

– 1995. *Age of Extremes: The Short Twentieth Century*. London: Abacus.

Hobson, J. 1938a [1902]. *Imperialism: A Study*. London: Allen & Unwin.

– 1938b. *Confessions of an Economic Heretic*. London: Allen & Unwin.

Hodder, I. 1992. *Theory and Practice in Archaeology*. London and New York: Routledge.

Hodson, R. 1996. "Dignity in the Workplace under Participative Management: Alienation and Freedom Revisited." *American Sociological Review* 61: 719–38.

Hogarth, R.M., and M.W. Reder, eds. 1986. *Rational Choice. The Contrast between Economics and Psychology.* Chicago: University of Chicago Press.

Holland, S. 1987a. *The Market Economy: From Micro to Mesoconomic.* London: Weidenfeld & Nicholson.

– 1987b. *The Global Economy: From Meso to Macroeconomics.* London: Weidenfeld & Nicholson.

Hollingsworth, J.R., P.C. Schmitter, and W. Streeck, eds. 1994. *Governing Capitalist Economies.* New York and Oxford: Oxford University Press.

Hollis, M., and S. Lukes, eds. 1982. *Rationality and Relativism.* Cambridge, MA: MIT Press.

Hollis, M., and E. Nell. 1975. *Rational Economic Man.* London: Cambridge University Press.

Holton, G. 1992. "How to Think about the 'Anti-Science' Phenomenon." *Public Understanding of Science* 1: 103–28.

Homans, G.C. 1950. *The Human Group.* New York: Harcourt Brace Jovanovich.

– 1974. *Social Behavior: Its Elementary Forms.* Rev. ed. New York: Harcourt Brace Jovanovich.

Horkheimer, M. 1972. *Critical Theory.* New York: Herder & Herder.

Horowitz, I.L. 1972. *Foundations of Political Sociology.* New York: Harper & Row.

Hubbard, H.M. 1991. "The Real Cost of Energy." *Scientific American* 264(4): 36–42.

Hunt, S.D. 1990. "Truth in Marketing Theory and Research." *Journal of Marketing* 54: 1–15.

Huntington, S.P. 1968. *Political Order in Changing Societies.* New Haven, CT: Yale University Press.

– 1991. *The Third Wave: Democratization in the Late Twentieth Century.* Norman: University of Oklahoma Press.

– 1993. "The Clash of Civilizations?" *Foreign Affairs*, Summer 1993: 22–49.

Husserl, E. 1950[1931]. *Cartesianische Meditationen.* In *Husserliana: Gesammelte Werke*, vol. 1. The Hague: Martinus Nijhoff.

Hutchison, T.W. 1964. *"Positive" Economics and Policy Objectives.* London: George Allen & Unwin.

Huth, P., and B. Russett. 1993. "General Deterrence between Enduring Rivals: Testing Three Competing Models." *American Political Science Review* 87: 61–73.

Iannaccone, L.R. 1991. "The Consequences of Religious Market Structure." *Rationality and Society* 3: 156–77.

Iannone, A.P., 1994. *Philosophy as Diplomacy.* Atlantic Highlands, NJ: Humanities Press.

Iannone, A.P., ed. 1987. *Contemporary Moral Controversies in Technology.* New York: Oxford University Press.

– 1989. *Contemporary Moral Controversies in Business.* New York: Oxford University Press.

Ibn Khaldûn. 1967 [1377?]. *The Muqaddimah*. 3 vols, 2nd ed. Trans. F. Rosenthal. London: Routledge & Kegan Paul.

Ingenieros, J. 1923. *Emilio Boutroux y la filosofía universitaria en Francia*. Buenos Aires: Cooperativa Editorial Limitada.

Jackson, J.E. 1992. "The Meaning and Message of Symbolic Sexual Violence in Tukanoan Ritual." *Anthropological Quarterly* 65: 1–18.

Jarvie, I.C. 1984. *Rationality and Relativism*. London: Routledge & Kegan Paul.

Jefferson, T. 1853–4 [1809]. *The Writings of Thomas Jefferson*. Ed. H.A. Washington. Washington: Taylor & Maury.

Jewkes, J., D. Sawers, and J. Stilleman. 1956. *The Sources of Invention*. London: Macmillan.

Jones, E.L. 1981. *The European Miracle: Environments, Economies and Geopolitics in the History of Europe and Asia*. Cambridge: Cambridge University Press.

Jouvenel, B. de. 1993 [1945]. *On Power: The Natural History of Its Growth*. Indianapolis: Liberty Fund.

Joynt, C.B., and N. Rescher. 1961. "The Problem of Uniqueness in History." *History and Theory* 1: 150–62.

Juster, F.T. 1991. "Rethinking Utility Theory." In Etzioni and Lawrence, eds, 85–103.

Kahn, A.E. 1966. "The Tyranny of Small Decisions: Market Failures, Imperfections, and the Limits of Economics." *Kyklos* 19: 23–47.

Kahneman, D., J.L. Knetsch, and R.H. Thaler. 1986. "Fairness as a Constraint on Profit Seeking: Entitlements in the Market." *American Economic Review* 76: 728–41.

– 1990. "Experimental Tests of the Endowment Effect and the Coase Theorem." *Journal of Political Economy* 98: 1325–48.

Kahneman, D., and D. Lovallo. 1993. "Timid Choices and Bold Forecasts: A Cognitive Perspective on Risk Taking." *Management Science* 39: 17–31.

Kahneman, D., P. Slovic, and A. Tversky, eds. 1982. *Judgment under Uncertainty: Heuristics and Biases*. Cambridge: Cambridge University Press.

Kahneman, D., and A. Tversky. 1979. "Prospect Theory: An Analysis of Decision Under Risk." *Econometrica* 47: 263–91.

Kaldor, N. 1972. "The Irrelevance of Equilibrium Economics." *Economic Journal* 82: 1237–55.

Kapp, K.W. 1971 [1950]. *The Social Cost of Private Enterprise*. New York: Schocken Books.

Karni, E., and Z. Safra. 1995. "The Impossibility of Experimental Elicitation of Subjective Probability." *Theory and Decision* 38: 313–20.

Katouzian, H. 1980. *Ideology and Method in Economics*. London: Macmillan.

Katz, J.J. 1981. *Language and Other Abstract Objects*. Totowa, NJ: Rowman & Littlefield.

Kaufman, H. 1985. *Time, Chance, and Organizations: Natural Selection in a Perilous Environment.* Chatham, NJ: Chatham House.

Kelley, J., and M.D.R. Evans. 1995. "Class and Class Conflict in Six Western Nations." *American Sociological Review* 60: 157–78.

Kelsen, H. 1941–2. "The Law as a Specific Social Technique." *University of Chicago Law Review* 9: 75–97.

– 1945. *General Theory of Law and State.* Cambridge, MA: Harvard University Press.

Kennedy, P. 1989. *The Rise and Fall of the Great Powers.* New York: Random House; London: Fontana Press.

Kenny, A. 1964. *Action, Emotion and Will.* London: Routledge & Kegan Paul.

Keyfitz, N. 1977. *Introduction to the Mathematics of Populations.* Reading, MA: Addison-Wesley.

– 1984. "Biology and Demography." In Keyfitz, ed., 1–7.

– 1995. "Between Knowledge and Power: Utilization of Social Science in Public Policy-Making." *Policy Sciences* 28: 79–100.

Keyfitz, N., ed. 1984. *Population and Biology: Bridge between Disciplines.* Liège: Ordina Editions.

Keynes, J.M. 1926. *The End of Laissez-faire.* London: Hogarth Press.

– 1936. *The General Theory of Employment, Interest and Money.* In *Collected Works,* vol. 2. Cambridge: Royal Economic Society, 1973.

Kiel, L.D., and E. Elliott, eds. 1996. *Chaos Theory in the Social Sciences.* Ann Arbor: University of Michigan Press.

Kim, H., and P.S. Bearman. 1997. "The Structure and Dynamics of Movement Participation." *American Sociological Review* 62: 70–93.

Kindleberger, C.P. 1970. *Power and Money.* New York: Basic Books.

Kindleberger, C.P., ed. 1970. *The International Corporation: A Symposium.* Cambridge, MA: MIT Press.

Kirman, A.P. 1992. "Whom or What Does the Representative Individual Represent?" *Journal of Economic Perspectives* 6: 117–36.

Kitcher, P. 1985. *Vaulting Ambition: Sociobiology and the Quest for Human Nature.* Cambridge, MA: MIT Press.

– 1993a. "The Evolution of Human Altruism." *Journal of Philosophy* 90: 497–516.

– 1993b. *The Advancement of Science: Science without Legend, Objectivity without Illusion.* New York: Oxford University Press.

Klibansky, R., and H.J. Paton, eds. 1936. *Philosophy and History.* Oxford: Clarendon Press; Harper Torchbooks, 1963.

Kliksberg, B. 1978. *El pensamiento organizativo: Del taylorismo a la teoría de la organización.* 3rd ed. Barcelona and Buenos Aires: Paidos.

Knetsch, J.L. 1995a. "Asymmetric Evaluation of Gains and Losses and Preference Order Assumptions." *Economic Inquiry* 33: 134–41.

- 1995b. "Assumptions, Behavioral Findings, and Policy Analysis." *Journal of Policy Analysis and Management* 14: 68–78.

Knight, F. 1940. "What is 'Truth' in Economics?" *Journal of Political Economy* 48: 1–32.

Knoke, D. 1988. "Incentives in Collective Action Organizations." *American Sociological Review* 53: 311–29.

Knorr-Cetina, K.D. 1981. *The Manufacture of Knowledge: An Essay on the Constructivist and Contextual Nature of Science.* Oxford: Pergamon.

- 1983. "The Ethnographic Study of Scientific Work: Towards a Constructivist Interpretation of Science." In Knorr-Cetina and Mulkay, eds, 115–40.

Knorr-Cetina, K.D., and A.V. Cicourel, eds. 1981. *Advances in Social Theory and Methodology: Towards an Integration of Micro- and Macrosociology.* London: Routledge & Kegan Paul.

Knorr-Cetina, K.D., and M. Mulkay, eds. 1983. *Science Observed: Perspectives on the Social Study of Science.* London, Beverly Hills, and New Delhi: Sage Publications.

Koblitz, N. 1988. "A Tale of Three Equations; or, the Emperors Have No Clothes." *Mathematical Intelligencer* 10: 4–10.

Koford, K.J., and J.B. Miller. 1991. *Social Norms and Economic Institutions.* Ann Arbor: University of Michigan Press.

Kolko, G. 1994. *Century of War: Politics, Conflict, and Society since 1914.* New York: New Press.

Kolnai, A. 1938. *The War against the West.* London: Gollancz; New York: Viking Press.

Koopmans, T. 1979. "Economics among the Sciences." *American Economic Review* 69: 1–13.

Kosslyn, S.M., and O. Koenig. 1995. *Wet Mind: The New Cognitive Neuroscience.* 2nd ed. New York: Free Press.

Kozicki, H., ed. 1993. *Developments in Modern Historiography.* New York: St Martin's Press.

Kraft, J. 1957 [1934]. *Die Unmöglichkeit der Geisteswissenschaft.* 2nd ed. Frankfurt: Oeffentliches Leben.

Kroeber, A., and C. Kluckhohn. 1952. *Culture: A Critical Review of Concepts and Definitions.* Papers of the Peabody Museum of American Archaeology and Ethnology, vol. 47.

Kropotkin, P. 1902. *Mutual Aid.* Boston: Extending Horizon Books, 1955.

Krugman, P. 1996. *The Self-Organizing Economy.* Cambridge, MA: Blackwell.

Kuhn, A. 1974. *The Logic of Social Systems.* San Francisco: Jossey-Bass.

Kuhn, T.S. 1962. *The Structure of Scientific Revolutions.* Chicago: University of Chicago Press.

Kuklinski, J.H., E. Riggle, V. Ottati, N. Schwartz, and R.S. Wyer. 1991. "The Cognitive and Affective Bases of Political Tolerance Judgments." *American Journal of Political Science* 35: 1–27.

Kuper, A. 1989. "Coming of Age in Anthropology?" *Nature* 338: 453–5.

Kurtz, P., ed. 1989. *Building a World Community*. Buffalo, NY: Prometheus.

Kuttner, R. 1984. *The Economic Illusion: False Choices between Prosperity and Social Justice*. Boston: Houghton Mifflin.

Lacan, J. 1966. *Ecrits*. Paris: Ed. du Seuil.

Lagerspetz, K.M.J. 1981. "Combining Aggression Studies in Infra-Humans and Man." In P.F. Brain and D. Benton, eds, *Multidisciplinary Approaches to Aggression Research*, 389–400. Amsterdam and New York: Elsevier.

Lakatos, I. 1971. "History of Science and Its Rational Reconstruction." In R.S. Cohen and R. Buck, eds, *Boston Studies in the Philosophy of Science* VIII, 91–136. Dordrecht: Reidel.

Lamendella, J.T. 1977. "General Principles of Neurofunctional Organization and Their Manifestations in Primary and Nonprimary Language Acquisition." *Language Learning* 27: 155–96.

Lamont, C. 1982 [1949]. *The Philosophy of Humanism*. 6th ed. New York: Frederick Ungar.

Lancaster, K.J. 1966. "A New Appproach to Consumer Theory." *Journal of Political Economy* 74: 132–57.

Lane, F.C. 1958. "Economic Consequences of Organized Violence." *Journal of Economic History* 18: 401–17.

Lane, R.E. 1981. *The Market Experience*. New York: Cambridge University Press.

Lang, S. 1981. *The File*. New York: Springer-Verlag.

– 1990. "Case Study of Political Opinions Passed off as Science and Mathematics." Videotape. American Mathematical Society and Mathematical Association of America.

Laponce, J.A., and P. Smoker, eds. 1972. *Experimentation and Simulation in Political Science*. Toronto: University of Toronto Press.

Laski, H.J. 1935. *The State in Theory and Practice*. London: George Allen & Unwin.

Lasswell, H. 1958. *Politics: Who Gets What, When, How*. 2nd ed. Cleveland and New York: World Publishing Co.

Lasswell, H., and A. Kaplan. 1952. *Power and Society: A Framework for Political Inquiry*. London: Routledge & Kegan Paul.

Latour, B. 1983. "Give Me a Laboratory and I Will Raise the World." In Knorr-Cetina and Mulkay, eds, 140–70.

– 1987. *Science in Action: How to Follow Scientists and Engineers through Society*. Cambridge, MA: Harvard University Press.

– 1988. "A Relativistic Account of Einstein's Relativity." *Social Studies of Science* 18: 3–44.

Latour, B., and S. Woolgar. 1979. *Laboratory Life: The Social Construction of Scientific Facts*. London and Beverly Hills: Sage.

Latsis, S.J. 1972. "Situational Determinism in Economics." *British Journal for the Philosophy of Science* 23: 207–45.

Lawler, E.J., and J. Yoon. 1996. "Commitment in Exchange Relations: Test of a Theory of Relational Cohesion." *American Sociological Review* 61: 89–108.

Leamer, E.E. 1983. "Let's Take the Con out of Econometrics." *American Economic Review* 73: 31–43.

Lee, R.B. 1992. "Art, Science, or Politics? The Crisis in Hunter-Gatherer Studies." *American Anthropologist* 94: 31–54.

Le Grand, J., and S. Estrin, eds. 1989. *Market Socialism.* Oxford: Clarendon Press.

Lekachman, R. 1976. *Economists at Bay.* New York: McGraw-Hill.

León-Portilla, M. 1980. *Toltecáyotl: Aspectos de la cultura náhuatl.* México: Fondo de Cultura Económica.

Leontief, W. 1966. *Essays in Economics: Theories and Theorizing.* New York: Oxford University Press.

– 1982. "Academic Economics." *Science* 217: 104–7.

– 1983. "Academic Economics Continued." *Science* 219: 902–3.

Levins, R., and R. Lewontin. 1985. *The Dialectical Biologist.* Cambridge, MA: Harvard University Press.

Levinson, S.C., and P. Brown. 1994. "Immanuel Kant among the Tenejapans: Anthropology as Empirical Philosophy." *Ethos* 22: 3–41.

Lévi-Strauss, C. 1953. "Social Structure." In A.L. Kroeber, ed., *Anthropology Today: An Encyclopedic Inventory,* 524–53. Chicago: University of Chicago Press.

Lewis, W.A., 1949. *The Principles of Economic Planning.* London: Dennis Dobson.

– 1955. *The Theory of Economic Growth.* London: George Allen & Unwin.

Lewontin, R.C., 1991. *Biology as Ideology: The Doctrine of DNA.* Concord, Ont.: Anansi.

– 1992. "The Dream of the Human Genome." *New York Review of Books* 39(10): 31–40.

Lichbach, M.I. 1990. "Will Rational People Rebel against Inequality? Samson's Choice." *American Journal of Political Science* 34: 1049–76.

Lieberman, P. 1984. *The Biology and Evolution of Language.* Cambridge, MA: Harvard University Press.

Lincoln, A. 1953 [1854?]. *The Collected Works of Abraham Lincoln.* Ed. R.P. Basler. New Brunswick, NJ: Rutgers University Press.

Lindblom, C.E. 1982. "Another State of Mind." *American Political Science Review* 76: 9–21.

– 1990. *Inquiry and Change.* New Haven and London: Yale University Press and Russell Sage Foundation.

Lippi, M. 1988. "On the Dynamics of Aggregate Macroequations: From Simple Microbehaviors to Complex Macrorelationships." In Dosi et al., ed., 170–96.

Lipset, S.M. 1959. "Political Sociology." In Merton et al., eds, 81–114.
– 1960. *Political Man*. Garden City, NY: Doubleday.
Llewellyn, K.N. 1930. "A Realistic Jurisprudence – the Next Step." *Columbia Law Review* 30: 431–65.
Lloyd, C. 1991. "The Methodologies of Social History: A Critical Survey and Defense of Structurism." *History and Theory* 30: 180–219.
Locke, J. 1993 [1681–9]. *Two Treatises of Government*. London: J.M. Dent.
Loftus, E. 1994. *The Myth of Repressed Memory*. New York: St Martin's Press.
Lomnitz, L. 1977. *Networks and Marginality: Life in a Mexican Shantytown*. San Francisco: Academic Press.
– 1988. "Informal Exchange Networks in Formal Systems: A Theoretical Model." *American Anthropologist* 90: 42–55.
Lovell, M.C. 1986. "Tests of the Rational Expectation Hypothesis." *American Economic Review* 76: 110–24.
Lowe, A. 1965. *On Economic Knowledge: Towards a Science of Political Economics*. New York: Harper & Row.
Lucas, R.E. 1978. "Unemployment Policy." *American Economic Review*, May supplement, 353–7.
Lucas, R.E., and T.J. Sargent, eds. 1981. *Rational Expectations and Econometric Practice*. Minneapolis: University of Minnesota Press.
Luce, R.D., and H. Raiffa. 1957. *Games and Decisions. Introduction and Critical Survey*. New York: John Wiley & Sons.
Luce, R.D., N. Smelser, and D. Gerstein, eds. 1989. *Leading Edges in Social and Behavioral Science*. New York: Russell Sage Foundation.
Ludwig, D., R. Hilborn, and C. Walters. 1993. "Uncertainty, Resource Exploitation, and Conservation: Lessons from History." *Science* 260: 17–36.
Luke, T.W. 1985. "Reason and Rationality in Rational Choice Theory." *Social Research* 52: 65–98.
Lukes, S. 1977. *Essays in Social Theory*. New York: Columbia University Press.
Lundstedt, A.V. 1956. *Legal Thinking Revised: My Views on Law*. Stockholm: Almqvist & Wiksell.
Lynch, M., E. Livingston, and H. Garfinkel. 1983. "Temporal Order in Laboratory Work." In Knorr-Cetina and Mulkay, eds, 205–38.
Lyttelton, A. 1973. "Introduction." In A. Lyttelton, ed., *Italian Fascisms: From Pareto to Gentile*, 11–36. London: Jonathan Cape; New York: Harper & Row.
McAdam, D., J.D. McCarthy, and M.N. Zald. 1988. "Social Movements." In Smelser, ed., 695–737.
McClelland, P.D. 1975. *Causal Explanation and Model Building in History, Economics, and the New Economic History*. Ithaca, NY: Cornell University Press.
McCloskey, D.N. 1985. *The Rhetoric of Economics*. Madison: University of Wisconsin Press.

MacCoun, R.J. 1989. "Experimental Research on Jury Decision-Making." *Science* 244: 1046–50.

McDonald, L. 1993. *The Early Origins of the Social Sciences.* Montréal and Kingston: McGill-Queen's University Press.

McGrew, W.C. 1992. *Chimpanzee Material Culture: Implications for Human Evolution.* Cambridge: Cambridge University Press.

McGuire, W.J. 1973. The Ying and the Yang of Progress in Social Psychology: Seven Koan. *Journal of Personality and Social Psychology* 26: 446–56.

Machiavelli, N. 1940 [1513]. *The Prince and the Discourses.* New York: Modern Library.

Machina, M.J. 1987. "Expected Utility Hypothesis." In Eatwell et al., eds, 2: 232–8.

Machina, M.J., and B. Munier, eds. 1994. *Models and Experiments on Risk and Rationality.* Dordrecht and Boston: Kluwer.

Machlup, F. 1955. "The Problem of Verification in Economic Theory." *Southern Economic Journal* 22: 1–21.

McKeown, T. 1979. *The Role of Medicine.* 2nd ed. Princeton, NJ: Princeton University Press.

MacKinnon, C.A. 1989. *Toward a Feminist Theory of the State.* Cambridge, MA: Harvard University Press.

McPhee, W.N. 1963. *Formal Theories of Mass Behavior.* New York: Free Press.

Macpherson, C.B. 1973. *Democratic Theory: Essays in Retrieval.* Oxford: Clarendon Press.

Macy, M.W., and A. Flache. 1995. "Beyond Rationality in Models of Choice." *Annual Reviews of Sociology* 21: 73–91.

Mahner, M., and M. Bunge. 1997. *Foundations of Biophilosophy.* Berlin, Heidelberg, and New York: Springer.

Majone, G. 1989. *Evidence, Argument and Persuasion in the Policy Processes.* New Haven, CT: Yale University Press.

Makridakis, S.G. 1990. *Forecasting, Planning, and Strategy for the 21st Century.* New York: Free Press; London: Collier Macmillan.

Malinowski, B. 1926. Article. "Anthropology." *Encyclopaedia Britannica.* 13th ed., suppl. I.

Malinvaud, E. 1967. "Decentralized Procedures for Planning." In Malinvaud and Bacharach, eds, 170–208.

– 1984. *Mass Unemployment.* Oxford: Basil Blackwell.

– 1991. *Voies de la recherche macroéconomique.* Paris: Odile Jacob.

Malinvaud, E., and M.O.L. Bacharach, eds. 1967. *Activity Analysis in the Theory of Growth and Planning.* London: Macmillan; New York: St Martin's Press.

Malitza, M. 1971. "A Model of Michael the Brave's Decision in 1595." In F.R. Hodson, D.G. Kendall, and P. Tautu, eds. *Mathematics in the Archaeological and Historical Sciences,* 516–23. Edinburgh: Edinburgh University Press.

Mandel, E. 1968. *Marxist Economic Theory*. Trans. B. Pearce. London: Merlin Press.

Mandelbaum, M. 1955. "Societal Facts." *British Journal of Sociology* 6: 305–17.

Mann, M. 1970. "The Social Consensus of Liberal Democracy." *American Sociological Review* 35: 423–39.

– 1986. *The Sources of Social Power*. Vol. I: *A History of Power from the Beginning to A.D. 1760*. Cambridge: Cambridge University Press.

– 1993. *The Sources of Social Power*. Vol. II: *The Rise of Classes and Nation-States, 1760–1914*. Cambridge: Cambridge University Press.

March, J.G., and Z. Shapira. 1987. "Managerial Perspectives on Risk and Risk Taking." *Management Science* 33: 1404–18.

March, J.G., and H.A. Simon. 1958. *Organizations*. New York: John Wiley.

Marcuse, H. 1964. *One-Dimensional Man*. Boston: Beacon Press.

Marsden, P.V., and N. Lin, eds. 1982. *Social Structure and Network Analysis*. Beverly Hills, CA: Sage.

Marshall, A. 1920 [1890]. *Principles of Economics*. 8th ed. London: Macmillan.

Marshall, G.D., and P.G. Zimbardo. 1979. "Affective Consequences of Inadequately Explained Physiological Arousal." *Journal of Personality and Social Psychology* 37: 970–88.

Martin, A. 1957. "How Economic Theory May Mislead." *British Journal for the Philosophy of Science* 8: 225–36.

Martindale, D. 1975. *Functionalism in the Social Sciences*. Philadelphia: American Academy of Political and Social Sciences.

Martinelli, A., and N.J. Smelser. 1990. "Economic Sociology: Historical Threads and Analytic Issues." *Current Sociology* 38: 1–49.

Marwell, G., and R.E. Ames. 1981. "Economists Free Ride, Does Anyone Else?" *Journal of Public Economics* 15: 295–310.

Marx, K. 1852. *The Eighteenth Brumaire of Louis Bonaparte*. In Marx and Engels, *Selected Works of K. Marx and F. Engels*, 95–180.

– 1859. *A Contribution to the Critique of Political Economy*. In Marx and Engels, *Selected Works*, 181–5.

– 1967 [1867]. *Capital: A Critique of Political Economy*. 3 vols. New York: International Publishers.

– 1973 [1857–8]. *Grundrisse: Foundations of the Critique of Political Economy*. New York: Penguin Books.

– 1975 [1847]. *The Poverty of Philosophy*. Moscow: Progress Publishers.

Marx, K., and F. Engels. 1986. *Selected Works of K. Marx and F. Engels*. New York: International Publishers.

Maslach, C. 1979. "Negative Emotional Biasing of Unexplained Arousal." *Journal of Personality and Social Psychology* 37: 953–69.

Matessi, C. 1984. "Natural Selection for Mortality Patterns." In N. Keyfitz, ed., 269–85.

Mathews, J. 1989. *Age of Democracy: The Politics of Post-Fordism*. Melbourne: Oxford University Press.

Mattessich, R. 1978. *Instrumental Reasoning and Systems Methodology*. Dordrecht and Boston: Reidel.

Mauss, M. 1968 [1901]. *Essais de sociologie*. Paris: Ed. de Minuit.

Max-Neef, M., A. Elizalde, and M. Hopenhayn. 1990. *Human Scale Development*. Uppsala: Dag Hammarskjöld Centre.

May, E.R. 1973. *"Lessons" of the Past: The Use and Misuse of History in American Foreign Policy*. New York: Oxford University Press.

May, K.O. 1954. "Intransitivity, Utility, and the Aggregation of Preference Patterns." *Econometrica* 11: 1–13.

Maynard Smith, J. 1982. *Evolution and the Theory of Games*. Cambridge: Cambridge University Press.

– 1992. *Did Darwin Get It Right?* New York and London: Chapman & Hall.

Mayrl, W.W. 1977. "Ethnomethodology: Sociology without Society?" In Dallmayr and McCarthy, eds, 262–79.

Mead, M. 1928. *Coming of Age in Samoa*. New York: William Morrow.

Medawar, P.B. 1988. *Memoir of a Thinking Radish*. Oxford and New York: Oxford University Press.

Melman, S. 1989. "Some Avoided Topics in Economics." *Journal of Economic Issues* 23: 563–8.

Menger, C. 1883. *Untersuchungen über die Methode der Socialwissenschaften, und der politischen Oekonomie insbesondere*. Leipzig: Dunker and Humblot. Vol. 2 of *Gesammelte Werke*, 2nd ed. Tübingen: J.C.B. Mohr, 1969.

Merton, R.K. 1936. "The Unanticipated Consequences of Purposive Social Action." *American Sociological Review* 1: 894–904.

– 1938a. *Science, Technology and Society in Seventeenth-Century England*. New York: Harper & Row, 1970.

– 1938b. "Science and the Social Order." In Merton 1973, 254–66.

– 1957a. *Social Theory and Social Structure*. Rev. ed. New York: Free Press.

– 1957b. "The Role Set: Problems in Sociological Theory." *British Journal of Sociology* 8: 106–20.

– 1968. "The Matthew Effect in Science." *Science* 159: 56–63.

– 1971 [1946]. *Mass Persuasion: The Social Psychology of a War Bond Drive*. Westport, CT: Greenwood Press.

– 1973. *The Sociology of Science: Theoretical and Empirical Investigations*. Chicago: University of Chicago Press.

– 1987. "Three Fragments from a Sociologist's Notebooks." *Annual Reviews of Sociology* 13: 1–28.

Merton, R.K., L. Broom, and L.S. Cottrell, Jr, eds. 1959. *Sociology Today: Problems and Prospects.* New York: Basic Books.

Messick, D.M., and M.H. Bazerman. 1996. "Ethical Leadership and the Psychology of Decision Making." *Sloan Management Review* 37(2): 9–22.

Meyerhoff, H., ed. 1959. *The Philosophy of History in Our Time.* Garden City, NY: Doubleday.

Midlarsky, M.I. 1982. "Scarcity and Inequality: Prologue to the Onset of Mass Revolution." *Journal of Conflict Resolution* 26: 3–38.

Milinkski, M. 1987. "TIT FOR TAT in Sticklebacks and the Evolution of Cooperation." *Nature* 325: 433–5.

Mill, J.S. 1924 [1873]. *Autobiography.* New York: Columbia University Press.

– 1952 [1875]. *A System of Logic.* 8th ed., repr. London: Longmans, Green.

– 1965 [1871]. *Principles of Political Economy.* 7th ed. In *Collected Works,* vol. 3. Toronto: University of Toronto Press; London: Routledge & Kegan Paul.

– 1977 [1859]. *On Liberty.* In *Collected Works,* vol. 8. Toronto: University of Toronto Press, 1977.

Miller, D. 1977. "Socialism and the Market." *Political Theory* 5: 473–89.

– 1989a. *Market, State and Community.* Oxford: Clarendon Press.

– 1989b. "Why Markets?" In Le Grand and Estrin, eds, 25–49.

Miller, G.R., and J.B. Stiff. 1993. *Deceptive Communication.* London: Sage.

Miller, N.E. 1964. "Physiological and Cultural Determinants of Behavior." *Proceedings of the National Academy of Sciences* [USA] 51: 941–54.

Mills, C.W. 1959. *The Power Elite.* London: Oxford University Press.

Mintzberg, H. 1994. *The Rise and Fall of Strategic Planning.* New York: Free Press.

– 1996a. "Managing Government, Governing Management." *Harvard Business Review,* May–June: 75–83.

– 1996b. "Musings on Management." *Harvard Business Review,* July–August: 61–7.

Mitcham, C. 1994. *Thinking Through Technology.* Chicago: University of Chicago Press.

Moaddel, M. 1994. "Political Conflict in the World Economy: A Cross-National Analysis of Modernization and World-System Theories." *American Sociological Review* 59: 276–303.

Moene, K.O., and M. Wallerstein. 1995. "How Social Democracy Worked: Labor-Market Institutions." *Politics & Society* 23: 185–212.

Moessinger, P. 1988. *La psychologie morale.* Paris: Presses Universitaires de France.

– 1991. *Les fondements de l'organisation.* Paris: Presses Universitaires de France.

– 1996. *Irrationalité individuelle et ordre social.* Geneva: Droz.

Molm, L.D. 1994. "Is Punishment Effective? Coercive Strategies in Social Exchange." *Social Psychology Quarterly* 57: 75–94.

Moore, B. 1967. *Social Origins of Dictatorship and Democracy. Lord and Peasant in the Making of the Modern World.* Boston: Beacon Press.

Moore Lappé, F., and J. Collins. 1988. *World Hunger: 12 Myths*. London: Earthscan Publications.

Moran, M., and M. Wright. 1991. "Conclusion: The Interdependence of Markets and States." In M. Moran and M. Wright, eds, *The Market and the State: Studies in Interdependence*, 239–49. New York: St Martin's Press.

Morgenstern, O. 1963. *On the Accuracy of Economic Observations*. 2nd ed. Princeton NJ: Princeton, University Press.

– 1972a. "Descriptive, Predictive and Normative Theory." *Kyklos* 25: 699–714.

– 1972b. "Thirteen Critical Points in Contemporary Economic Theory: An Interpretation." *Journal of Economic Literature* 10: 1163–89.

Morse, P.M., and H.E. Kimball. 1951. *Methods of Operations Research*. New York: Technology Press of MIT and John Wiley & Sons; London: Chapman & Hall.

Mortimore, G.W. 1976. "Rational Social Choice." In Benn and Mortimore, eds, 384–404.

Mosteller, F. 1981. "Innovation and Evaluation." *Science* 21: 881–6.

Mountcastle, V. 1995. "The Evolution of Ideas Concerning the Function of the Neocortex." *Cerebral Cortex* 5: 289–95.

Mueller-Vollmer, K. 1989. *The Hermeneutics Reader*. New York: Continuum.

Mulkay, M. 1972. "Some Aspects of Cultural Growth in the Natural Sciences." In Barnes, ed., 126–42.

– 1979. *Science and the Sociology of Knowledge*. London: Allen & Unwin.

Müller, R.-A. 1996. "Innateness, Autonomy, Universality? Neurobiological Approaches to Language." *Behavioral and Brain Sciences* 19: 611–31.

Munier, B., ed. 1988. *Risk, Decision and Rationality*. Dordrecht and Boston: Reidel.

Murphey, M.G. 1994. *Philosophical Foundations of Historical Knowledge*. Albany: State University of New York Press.

Myrdal, G. 1942. *An American Dilemma*. Repr. New York: Harper & Row, 1962.

– 1954 [1930]. *The Political Element in the Development of Economic Theory*. New York: Simon & Schuster.

– 1960. *Beyond the Welfare State: Economic Planning and Its International Implications*. New Haven, CT: Yale University Press.

– 1968. *Asian Dream*. New York: Pantheon Books.

– 1969. *Objectivity in Social Research*. New York: Pantheon Books.

Nadel, S.F. 1957. *The Theory of Social Structure*. Glencoe, IL: Free Press.

Nagel, E. 1952. "The Logic of Historical Analysis." *Scientific Monthly* 74: 162–9.

– 1961. *The Structure of Science*. New Yok: Harcourt, Brace & World.

Nahmias, S. 1989. *Production and Operations Analysis*. Homewood, IL, and Boston: Irwin.

Negroponte, N. 1996. *Being Digital*. New York: Vintage Books.

Newmeyer, F.J., ed. 1988. *Linguistics: The Cambridge Survey*. 4 vols. Cambridge: Cambridge University Press.

New York Times. 1996. *The Downsizing of America*. New York: Random House.

Nielsen, F., and A.S. Alderson. 1997. "The Kuznets Curve and the Great U-Turn: Income Inequality in U. S. counties, 1970 to 1990." *American Sociological Review* 62: 12–33.

Noble, W., and I. Davidson. 1991. "The Evolution of Modern Human Behavior: Language and Its Archaeology." *Man*, new series, 26: 223–53.

Nonaka, I. 1991. "The Knowledge-Creating Company." *Harvard Business Review*, November–December.

Nordhaus, W.D. 1992. "An Optimal Transition Path for Controlling Greenhouse Gases." *Science* 258: 1315–19.

Noussair, C.N., C.R. Plott, and R.G. Riezman. 1995. "An Experimental Investigation of the Patterns of International Trade." *American Economic Review* 85: 462–89.

Nove, A. 1983. *The Economics of Feasible Socialism*. London: Allen & Unwin.

– 1989. "Central Planning under Capitalism and Market Socialism." In Elster and Moene, eds, 97–109.

Novick, P. 1988. *That Noble Dream*. Cambridge: Cambridge University Press.

Nowak, M., and K. Sigmund. 1993. "A Strategy of Win-Stay, Lose-Shift That Outperforms Tit-for-Tat in the Prisoner's Dilemma Game." *Nature* 364: 56–8.

Nye, A. 1990. *Words of Power: A Feminist Reading in the History of Logic*. London and New York: Blackwell.

Oakes, G. 1988. *Weber and Rickert: Concept Formation in the Cultural Sciences*. Cambridge, MA: MIT Press.

Oakeshott, M. 1983. *On History and Other Essays*. Oxford: Oxford University Press.

O'Brien, P.K. 1988. "The Costs and Benefits of British Imperialism 1846–1914." *Past and Present*, no. 120: 163–200.

O'Hara, S.L., F.A. Street-Perrott, and T.P. Burt. 1993. "Accelerated Soil Erosion around a Mexican Highland Lake Caused by Prehistoric Agriculture." *Nature* 362: 48–51.

Okun, A.M. 1981. *Prices and Quantities: A Macroeconomic Analysis*. Washington: Brookings Institution.

Oliver, P.E., and G. Marwell. 1988. "The Paradox of Group Size in Collective Action: A Theory of Critical Mass. II." *American Sociological Review* 53: 1–8.

Oliver, P.E., G. Marwell, and R. Teixeira. 1985. "A Theory of Critical Mass." I. Interdependence, Group Heterogeneity, and the Production of Collective Action. *American Journal of Sociology* 94: 502–34.

Olshavsky, R.W., and D.H . Granbois. 1979. "Consumer Decision Making – Fact or Fiction?" *Journal of Consumer Research* 6: 93–100.

Olson, M. 1971. *The Logic of Collective Action. Public Goods and Theory of Groups*. 2nd ed. Cambridge, MA: Harvard University Press.

– 1982. *The Rise and Decline of Nations*. New Haven: Yale University Press.

– 1993. "Dictatorship, Democracy, and Development." *American Political Science Review* 87: 567–76.

Ormerod, P. 1994. *The Death of Economics*. London: Faber & Faber.

Outhwaite, W. 1986. *Understanding Social Life: The Method Called Verstehen*. 2nd ed. Lewes, UK: Jean Stroud.

Papadakis, M. 1994. "Did (or Does) the United States Have a Competitiveness Crisis?" *Journal of Policy Analysis and Management* 13: 1–20.

Pareto V. 1935 [1916]. *A Treatise on General Sociology*. 4 vols. New York: Harcourt, Brace & Co.

– 1974 [1906]. *Mannuale di economia politica*. Padova: Cedam.

Parsons, T. 1940a. "An Analytical Approach to the Theory of Social Stratification." *American Journal of Sociology* 45: 841–62.

– 1940b. "Motivation of Economic Activities." *Canadian Journal of Economics and Political Science* 6: 187–203.

– 1951. *The Social System*. New York: Free Press.

Pasinetti, L.L. 1981. *Structural Change and Economic Growth*. Cambridge: Cambridge University Press.

Pasmore, W.A., and J.J. Sherwood, eds. 1978. *Sociotechnical Systems: A Sourcebook*. La Jolla, CA: University Associates.

Patai, D., and N. Koertge. 1994. *Professing Feminism. Cautionary Tales from the Strange World of Women's Studies*. New York: Basic Books.

Perroux, F. 1973. *Pouvoir et économie*. Paris: Bordas.

– 1975. *Unités actives et mathématiques nouvelles*. Paris: Dunod.

– 1981. *Pour une philosophie du nouveau développement*. Paris: Aubier, Les Presses de l'Unesco.

Persson, T., and G. Tabellini. 1994. "Is Inequality Harmful for Growth?" *American Economic Review* 84: 600–21.

Petroski, H. 1993. *The Evolution of Useful Things*. New York: Alfred A. Knopf.

Pettis, M. 1996. "The Liquidity Trap: Latin American's Free-Market Past." *Foreign Affairs* 75(2): 2–7.

Phelps Brown, H. 1972. "The Underdevelopment of Economics." *Economic Journal*. 82: 1–10.

Piaget, J. 1965. *Etudes sociologiques*. Genève: Librairie Droz.

Pickel, A. 1993. "Authoritarianism or Democracy? Marketization as a Political Problem." *Policy Sciences* 26: 139–63.

– 1997. "The Jump-Started Economy and the Ready-Made State: A Theoretical Reconsideration of the East German Case." *Comparative Political Studies* 30: 211–41.

Pierson, C. 1995. *Socialism after Communism: The New Market Socialism*. University Park: Pennsylvania State University Press.

Pigden, C. 1995. "Popper Revisited, or What is Wrong with Conspiracy Theories?" *Philosophy of the Social Sciences* 25: 3–34.

Pigou, A.C. 1927. *The Economics of Welfare*. London: Macmillan.

Pinch, T.J. 1979. "Normal Explanation of the Paranormal." *Social Studies of Science* 9: 329–48.

Pinch, T.J., and H.M. Collins. 1979. "Is Anti-Science Not-Science?" *Sociology of the Sciences Yearbook* 3: 221–50.

– 1984. "Private Science and Public Knowledge: The Committee for the Scientific Investigation of the Claims of the Paranormal and Its Use of the Literature." *Social Studies of Science* 14: 521–46.

Plott, C.R. 1986. "Laboratory Experiments in Economics: The Implications of Posted-Price Institutions." *Science* 232: 732–8.

Plott, C.R., and G. George. 1992. "Marshallian vs. Walrasian Stability in an Experimental Market." *Economic Journal* 102: 437–60.

Polanyi, K. 1944. *The Great Transformation*. New York: Rinehart.

Polanyi, K., C.M. Arensberg, and H.W. Pearson, eds. 1957. *Trade and Market in the Early Empires: Economies in History and Theory*. New York: Free Press.

Polanyi, M. 1958. *Personal Knowledge*. Chicago: University of Chicago Press.

Politz, A. 1990. *The Politz Papers: Science and Truth in Marketing Research*. Ed. H.H. Hardy. Chicago: American Marketing Association.

Popper, K.R. 1957 [1944–5]. *The Poverty of Historicism*. London: Routledge & Kegan Paul.

– 1959 [1935]. *The Logic of Scientific Discovery*. London: Hutchinson.

– 1961. "Zur Logik der Sozialwissenschaften." In *Auf der Suche einer besseren Welt*. 79–98. München: Piper 1984.

– 1962 [1945]. *The Open Society and Its Enemies*. 2 vols., 4th ed. London: Routledge & Kegan Paul.

– 1967. "The Rationality Principle." In D. Miller, ed., *Popper Selections*, 357–65. Princeton: Princeton University Press, 1985.

– 1972. *Objective Knowledge*. Oxford: Clarendon Press.

Porter, M.E. 1980. *Competitive Strategy*. New York: Free Press.

– 1990. *The Competitive Advantage of Nations*. New York: Free Press.

– 1994. "Toward a Dynamic Theory of Strategy." In Rumelt et al., 423–61.

– 1996. "What Is Strategy?" *Harvard Business Review*, November–December.

Porter, T.M. 1986. *The Rise of Statistical Thinking 1820–1900*. Princeton: Princeton University Press.

Portes, A. 1989. *The Informal Economy*. Baltimore, MD: Johns Hopkins University Press.

Portes, A., and S. Sassen-Koob. 1987. "Making It Underground: Comparative Material on the Informal Sector in Western Market Economies." *American Journal of Sociology* 93: 30–61.

Posner, R. 1990. *The Problems of Jurisprudence*. Cambridge, MA: Harvard University Press.

Pound, R. 1931. "The Call for a Realist Jurisprudence." *Harvard Law Review* 44: 697–711.

– 1954 [1924]. *An Introduction to the Philosophy of Law*. Rev. ed. New Haven CT: Yale University Press.

Prather, M., P. Midgley, F.S. Rowland, and R. Stolarski. 1996. "The Ozone Layer: The Road Not Taken." *Nature* 381: 551–4.

Prebisch, R. 1981a. *Capitalismo periférico*. México: Fondo de Cultura Económica.

– 1981b. "Diálogo acerca de Friedman y Hayek." *Revista de la CEPAL*, no. 15: 161–82.

Przeworski, A. 1991. *Democracy and the Market*. Cambridge: Cambridge University Press.

Putnam, H. 1978. *Meaning and the Moral Sciences*. London: Routledge.

Quintanilla, M.A. 1989. *Tecnología: Un enfoque filosófico*. Madrid: Fundesco.

Radcliffe-Brown, A.R. 1935. "On the Concept of Function in Social Science." *American Anthropologist* 37: 397–402.

Radnitzky, G. 1993. "Private Rights against Public Power: The Contemporary Conflict." In G. Radnitzky and H. Bouillon, eds, 1993. *Governmnent: Servant or Master?*, 23–71. Amsterdam and Atlanta: Rodopi.

Rapoport, A. 1966. *Two-Person Game Theory*. Ann Arbor: University of Michigan Press.

– 1968. "Critiques of Game Theory." In Buckley, ed., 474–89.

– 1980. "Various Meanings of 'Rational Political Decision.'" In L. Lewin and E. Vedung, eds, *Politics as Rational Action*, 39–59. Dordrecht and Boston: Reidel.

– 1989a. *Decision Theory and Decision Behaviour*. Dordrecht Boston: Kluwer.

– 1989b. *The Origins of Violence*. New York: Paragon House.

– 1990. "Comments on Tsebelis." *Rationality and Society* 2: 508–11.

Raup, D.M. 1991. *Extinction: Bad Genes or Bad Luck?* New York: W.W. Norton.

Rawls, J. 1971. *A Theory of Justice*. Cambridge, MA: Belknap Press.

Raz, J. 1970. *The Concept of a Legal System*. Oxford: Clarendon Press.

– 1978. "Introduction." In J. Raz, ed., *Practical Reasoning*. Oxford: Oxford University Press.

Reed, J.H. 1996. "Participation, Power, and Democracy." In S.L. Esquith, ed., *Political Dialogue: Theories and Practices*, 239–61. Amsterdam and Atlanta: Rodopi.

Reich, R.B. 1992. *The Work of Nations*. New York: Vintage Books.

Reich, R.B., ed. 1988. *The Power of Public Ideas*. Cambridge, MA: Harvard University Press.

Renfrew, C. 1988. *Archaeology and Language: The Puzzle of Indo-European Origins*. Cambridge: Cambridge University Press.

Renfrew, C., and E.B.W. Zubrow, eds. 1994. *The Ancient Mind: Elements of Cognitive Archaeology*. Cambridge: Cambridge University Press.

Renner, M. 1997. "Transforming Security." *State of the World 1997*, 115–31. New York.

Rescher, N. 1969. *Introduction to Value Theory*. Englewood Cliffs, NJ: Prentice-Hall.

- 1975. *Unselfishness*. Pittsburgh: University of Pittsburgh Press.

- 1983. *A Philosophical Introduction to the Theory of Risk Evaluation and Management*. Washington: University Press of America.

Restivo, S. 1992. *Mathematics in Society and History*. Dordrecht and Boston: Kluwer.

Riecken, H.W., and R.F. Boruch. 1978. "Social Experiments." *Annual Review of Sociology* 4: 511–32.

Rifkin, J. 1996. *The End of Work*. New York: G.P. Putnam's Sons.

Riley, J. 1985. "On the Possibility of Liberal Democracy." *American Review of Political Science* 79: 1135–51.

Robbins, L. 1935. *An Essay on the Nature and Significance of Economic Science*. 2nd ed. London: Macmillan.

Robinson, J. 1933. *The Economics of Perfect Competition*. London: Macmillan.

- 1953–4. "The Production Function and the Theory of Capital." *Review of Economic Studies* 21: 81–106.

- 1962. *Economic Philosophy*. Hardmondsworth: Penguin, 1964.

Robinson, J., and J. Eatwell. 1974. *An Introduction to Modern Economics*. Rev. ed. London: McGraw-Hill.

Roemer, J.E. 1994. *A Future for Socialism*. Cambridge, MA: Harvard University Press.

Roethslisberger, F.J., and W.J. Dickson. 1943. *Management and the Worker*. Cambridge, MA: Harvard University Press.

Rose, H., and S. Rose. 1974. "'Do Not Adjust Your Mind, There Is a Fault in Reality.'" Ideology in the Neurobiological Sciences." In R. Whitley, ed., *Social Process of Scientific Development*, 148–71. London: Routledge & Kegan Paul.

Rosegger, G. 1990. "Aspects of the Life Cycle in Industry and Trade." In T. Vasko, R. Ayres, and L. Fontvieille, eds, *Life Cycles and Long Waves*, 19–34. New York: Springer-Verlag.

- 1995. "Technical Change without Humans: Innovation in the Neoclassical Economic Theory." In Götschl, ed., 39–51.

- 1996. *The Economics of Production and Innovation*. 3rd ed. Oxford: Butterworth Heinemann.

Rosenau, J.N. 1990. *Turbulence in World Politics: A Theory of Change and Continuity*. Princeton: Princeton University Press.

Rosenberg, A. 1976. *Microeconomic Laws*. Pittsburgh, PA: University of Pittsburgh Press.

- 1980. *Sociobiology and the Preemption of Social Science*. Baltimore: Johns Hopkins University Press.

Rosenberg, N., ed. 1982. *Inside the Black Box: Technology and Economics*. Cambridge: Cambridge University Press.

Ross, A[lf]. 1968. *Directives and Norms*. London: Routledge & Kegan Paul.

Ross, A[ndrew]. 1991. *Strange Weather: Culture, Science, and Technology in the Age of Limits*. London and New York: Verso.

Ross, D. 1991. *The Origins of American Social Science*. Cambridge: Cambridge University Press.

Rostworowski de Díez Canseco, M. 1983. *Estructuras andinas del poder: Ideología religiosa y política*. Lima: Instituto de Estudios Peruanos.

Rowley, R. 1995. "History, Structure and the Wandering Natural Rate of Unemployment." *Economie appliquée* 68(1): 133–55.

Rubinstein, A.Z. 1991. "New World Order or Hollow Victory?" *Foreign Affairs* 70(4): 53–65.

Rueschemeyer, D., E. Huber Stephens, and J.D. Stephens. 1992. *Capitalist Development and Democracy*. Chicago: University of Chicago Press.

Rumelt, R.P., D.E. Schendel, and D.J. Teece, eds. 1994. *Fundamental Issues in Strategy: A Research Agenda*. Boston: Harvard Business School Press.

Russell, B. 1914. *Our Knowledge of the External World*. London: Allen & Unwin 1952.

– 1934. *Freedom versus Organization 1814–1914*. New York: W.W. Norton.

– 1960. *Authority and the Individual*. Boston: Beacon Press.

Russett, B., and H. Starr. 1981. *World Politics: The Menu for Choice*. San Francisco: W.H. Freeman.

Ryan, A. 1991. "When It's Rational to Be Irrational." *New York Review of Books* 38(15): 19–22.

Saari, D.G. 1994. *The Wavering Invisible Hand*. Cambridge, MA: MIT Press.

Sahlins, M. 1977. *The Use and Abuse of Biology: An Anthropological Critique of Sociobiology*. London: Tavistock Publications.

Saikh, A. 1974. "Laws of Production and Laws of Algebra: The Humbug Production Function." *Review of Economics and Statistics* 56: 115–120.

Samuelson, P.A. 1976. *Foundations of Economic Analysis*. New York: Atheneum.

Samuelson, P.A., W.D. Nordhaus, and J. McCallum. 1983. *Economics*. 6th ed. Toronto-New York: McGraw-Hill Ryerson.

– 1988. *Macroeconomics*. 6th ed. Toronto and New York: McGraw-Hill Ryerson.

Sardar, Z., and M. Wyn Davies. 1992. "The Future of Eastern Europe: Lessons from the Third World." *Futures* 24: 150–7.

Sargent, T.J. 1987. *Macroeconomic Theory*. 2nd ed. New York: Academic Press.

Sartori, G. 1987. *The Theory of Democracy Revisited*. Chatham, NJ: Chatham House.

Saussure, F. de. 1916. *Cours de linguistique générale*. Paris: Payot.

Savage, J. 1954. *The Foundations of Statistics*. 2nd ed. Repr.: New York: Dover, 1972.

Savage-Rumbaugh, E., and E. Rubert. 1992. "Language Comprehension in Ape and Child: Evolutionary Implications." In Y. Christen and P. Churchland, eds, *Neuro-

philosophy and Alzheimer's Disease, 30–48. Berlin, Heidelberg, and New York: Springer-Verlag.

Schachter, S., and J.E. Singer, 1962. "Cognitive, Social and Physiological Determinants of Emotional States." *Psychological Review* 69: 379–99.

Schelling, T.C. 1978. *Micromotives and Macrobehavior.* New York: W.W. Norton.

Schotter, A. 1985. *Free Market Economics: A Critical Appraisal.* New York: St Martin's Savage Press.

Schrödinger, E. 1935 [1932]. *Science and the Human Temperament.* London: Allen & Unwin.

Schultz, T.W. 1961. "Investment in Human Capital." *American Economic Review* 51: 1–17.

Schumacher, E.F. 1973. *Small Is Beautiful.* London: Blond & Briggs.

Schuman, H., L. Bobo, and M. Krysan. 1992. "Authoritarianism in the General Population: The Education Interaction Hypothesis." *Social Psychology Quarterly* 55: 379–87.

Schumpeter, J.A. 1934 [1912]. *The Theory of Economic Development,* 2nd ed. Cambridge, MA: Harvard University Press.

– 1950 [1942]. *Capitalism, Socialism and Democracy.* Intro. T. Bottomore. New York: Harper Torchbooks.

– 1954. *History of Economic Analysis.* New York: Oxford University Press.

– 1991. *Joseph A. Schumpeter: The Economics and Sociology of Capitalism.* Ed. R. Swedberg. Princeton, NJ: Princeton University Press.

Schütz, A. 1940. "Phenomenology and the Social Sciences." In M. Farber, ed., *Philosophical Essays in Memory of Edmund Husserl,* 164–86. Cambridge, MA: Harvard University Press.

– 1953. "Common Sense and the Scientific Interpretation of Human Action." *Philosophy and Phenomenological Research* 14: 1–38.

– 1967 [1932] *The Phenomenology of the Social World.* Evanston, IL: Northwestern University Press.

– 1974. *The Structures of the Life-World.* London: Heinemann.

Schwartz, B. 1986. *The Battle for Human Nature.* New York: W.W. Norton.

Scitovsky, T. 1976. *The Joyless Economy.* New York: Oxford University Press.

Scott, J. 1985. *Weapons of the Weak: Everyday Forms of Peasant Resistance.* New Haven, CT: Yale University Press.

Scott, M., and H. Rothman. 1992. *Companies with a Conscience: Intimate Portraits of Twelve Firms That Make a Difference.* New York: Birch Lane Press.

Sears, D.O., and C.L. Funk. 1990. "The Limited Effect of Economic Self-Interest on the Political Attitudes of the Mass Public." *Journal of Behavioral Economics* 19: 247–71.

Sebenius, J.K. 1992. "Negotiation Analysis: A Characterization and Review." *Management Science* 38: 18–38.

Seebass, G., and R. Tuomela, eds. 1985. *Social Action.* Dordrecht and Boston: Reidel.

Seidman, S., ed. 1989. *Jürgen Habermas on Society and Politics: A Reader.* Boston: Beacon Press.

Seldon, A. 1990. *Capitalism.* Oxford: Blackwell.

Selznick, P. 1959. "The Sociology of Law." In Merton et al., eds, 115–27.

Semler, R. 1993. *Maverick: The Success Story behind the Most Unusual Workplace in the World.* New York: Warner Books.

Sen, A.K. 1970a. *Collective Choice and Social Welfare.* San Francisco: Holden-Day; repr. North-Holland, 1984.

– 1970b. "The Impossibiity of a Paretian Liberal." *Journal of Political Economy* 78: 152–7.

– 1979. "Utilitarianism and Welfarism." *Journal of Philosophy* 76: 463–89.

– 1982. *Choice, Welfare and Measurement.* Cambridge, MA: MIT Press.

– 1987. *On Ethics and Economics.* Oxford: Blackwell.

– 1995. "Rational and Social Choice." *American Economic Review* 85: 1–24.

Seni, D.A. 1993. "Elements of a Theory of Plans." Ph.D. dissertation, University of Pennsylvania. Ann Arbor: U.M.I., 1994.

Shankman, P. 1996. "The History of Samoan Sexual Conduct and the Mead-Freeman Controversy." *American Anthropologist* 98: 555–67.

Shanks, M., and C. Tilley. 1987. *Re-Constructing Archaeology: Theory and Practice.* Cambridge: Cambridge University Press.

Shapiro, F., and P. Dawson. 1972. "Social Mobility and Political Radicalism: The Case of the French Revolution of 1789." In Aydelotte et al., eds, 159–91.

Sheldon, E.B., and W.W. Moore. 1968. *Indicators of Social Change.* New York: Russell Sage Foundation.

Sherif, M. 1977. "Crisis in Social Psychology. Some Remarks towards Breaking Through the Crisis." *Personality and Social Psychology Bulletin* 3: 368–82.

Sherman, P.W. 1977. "Nepotism and the Evolution of Alarm Calls." *Science* 197: 1246–53.

Shils, E. 1982. "Knowledge and the Sociology of Knowledge." *Knowledge: Creation, Diffusion, Utilization* 4: 7–32.

Shoemaker, P.J.H. 1992. "Subjective Expected Utility Theory Revisited: A Reduction ad Absurdum Paradox." *Theory and Decision* 33: 1–21.

Short, J.F. Jr, ed. 1986. *The Social Fabric: Dimensions and Issues.* Beverly Hills, CA: Sage Publications.

Shubik, M. 1984. *A Game-Theoretic Approach to Political Economy.* Cambridge, MA: MIT Press.

Silberston, A. 1970. "Surveys of Applied Economics: Price Behavior of Firms." *Economic Journal* 80: 511–82.

Simmel, G. 1923 [1907]. *Die Probleme der Geschichtsphilosophie: Eine erkenntnis-theoretische Studie*. 5th ed. München and Leipzig: Duncker & Humblot.

– 1950 [1908]. *Soziologie: Untersuchungen über die Formen der Vergesellschaftung.* Partial trans. in K.H. Wolff, ed., *The Sociology of Georg Simmel*. Glencoe, IL: Free Press.

Simon, H.A. 1970. *The Sciences of the Artificial*. Cambridge, MA: MIT Press.

– 1977. *The New Science of Management Decision*. Englewood Cliffs, NJ: Prentice-Hall.

– 1979. "Rational Decision Making in Business Organizations." *American Economic Review* 64: 493–513.

– 1987. "Rationality in Psychology and Economics." In Hogarth and Reder, eds, 25–40.

Simpson, M. 1990. "Political Rights and Income Inequality: A Cross-National Test." *American Sociological Review* 55: 682–93.

Sims, C.A. 1980. "Macroeconomics and Reality." *Econometrica* 48: 1–48.

Sioui, G.E. 1989. *Pour une autohistoire amérindienne*. Preface by B.G. Trigger. Québec: Presses de l'Université Laval.

Sivard, R.L. 1987. *World Military and Social Expenditures 1987–88*. Washington: World Priorities.

Skinner, B.F. 1938. *The Behavior of Organisms: An Eperimental Analysis*. New York: Appleton-Century-Crofts.

Skopcol, T. 1985. *Bringing the State Back In*. New York: Cambridge University Press.

Smelser, N.J. 1988. "Social Structure." In Smelser, ed., 103–30.

Smelser, N.J., ed., 1988. *Handbook of Sociology*. Newbury Park, London, and New Delhi: Sage.

Smelser, N.J., and R. Swedbeg, eds. 1994. *Handbook of Economic Sociology*. Princeton, NJ: Princeton University Press; New York: Russell Sage Foundation.

Smith, A. 1976 [1776]. *The Wealth of Nations*. Chicago: University of Chicago Press.

Smith, C.L. 1991. "Measures and Meaning in Comparisons of Wealth Equality." *Social Indicators Research* 24: 367–92.

Smith, E., and B. Winterhalder. 1992. *Evolutionary Ecology and Human Behavior*. New York: Aldine de Gruyter.

Smith, M.R. 1992. *Power, Norms, and Inflation: A Skeptical Treatment*. New York: Aldine de Gruyter.

Smith, P.M., and B. Boyle Torrey. 1996. "The Future of the Behavioral and Social Sciences." *Science* 271: 611–12.

Smith, V.L., 1962. "An Experimental Study of Competitive Market Behavior." *Journal of Political Economy* 70: 111–37.

– 1991. *Papers in Experimental Economics*. Cambridge: Cambridge University Press.

Smithin, J.N. 1990. *Macroeconomics after Thatcher and Reagan: The Conservative Policy Revolution in Retrospect.* Aldershot: Edward Elgar.

Snoyenbos, M., R. Almeder, and J. Humber, eds. 1983. *Business Ethics.* Buffalo, NY: Prometheus Books.

Snyder, G.H. 1971. "'Prisoner's Dilemma' and 'Chicken' Models in International Politics." *International Studies Quarterly* 15: 66–103.

Soderbaum, P. 1987. "Environmental Management: A Non-Traditional Approach." *Journal of Economic Issues* 21: 139–65.

– 1990. "Neoclassical and Institutional Approaches to Environmental Economics." *Journal of Economic Issues* 24: 481–92.

Sokal, A. 1996. "A Physicist Experiments with Cultural Studies." *Lingua Franca* 6(4): 62–4.

Solbrig, O.T. 1994. *So Shall You Reap: Farming and Crops in Human Affairs.* Washington: Island Press.

Solow, R.M. 1986. "What Is a Nice Girl Like You Doing in a Place Like This? Macroeconomics after Fifty Years." *Eastern Economic Journal* 12: 191–8.

Sørensen, A.B. 1979. "Theory and Models of Mobility." *IHS Journal* 3: B79–97.

– 1986. "Social Structure and Mechanisms of Life-Course Processes." In A.B. Sørensen, F.E. Weinert, and L. Sherrod, eds, *Human Development and the Life Course: Multidisciplinary Pespectives,* 177–97. Hillsdale, NJ: Erlbaum.

– 1997. "Theoretical Mechanisms and the Empirical Study of Social Processes." In Hedström and Swedberg, eds, 238–66.

Spaulding, A.C. 1988. "Archaeology and Anthropology." *American Anthropologist* 90: 263–71.

Spiegel, G.M. 1990. "History, Historicism, and the Social Logic of the Text." *Speculum* 65: 59–86.

Stacey, R.D. 1992. *Managing the Unknowable.* San Francisco: Jossey-Bass.

Stanford, C.B. 1996. "The Hunting Ecology of Wild Chimpanzees: Implications for the Evolutionary Ecology of Pliocene Hominids." *American Anthropologist* 98: 96–113.

Steele Commager, H. 1966. *The Study of History.* Columbus, OH: Charles E. Merrill Books.

Steiner, I.D. 1974. "Whatever Happened to the Group in Social Psychology?" *Journal of Experimental Social Psychology* 10: 94–108.

Stern, A. 1967. *Geschichtsphilosophie und Wertproblem.* München: Ernst Reinhardt.

Stevens, G., D. Owens, and E.C. Schaefer. 1990. "Education and Attractiveness in Marriage Choices." *Social Psychology Quarterly* 53: 62–70.

Steward, J. 1993. "Rational Choice Theory, Public Policy and the Liberal State." *Policy Sciences* 26: 317–30.

Stigler, G.J. 1983. "The Process and Progress of Economics." *Journal of Political Economy* 91: 529–45.

Stigler, G.J., and G.S. Becker. 1977. "De gustibus non est disputandum." *American Economic Review* 67: 76–90.

Stinchcombe, A.L. 1968. *Constructing Social Theories*. Chicago: University of Chicago Press.

Stoczkowski, W. 1991. "Anthropologie naïve et visions savantes du milieu naturel des premiers hominidés." *Annales de la Fondation Fyssen*, no. 5/6: 24–34.

Stone, J. 1966. *Social Dimensions of Law and Justice*. Stanford, CA: Stanford University Press.

Stone, L. 1972. *The Causes of the English Revolution 1529–1642*. London: Routledge & Kegan Paul.

– 1979. "The Revival of Narrative: Reflections on a New Old History." *Past and Present*, no. 85: 3–24.

Stromsdorfer, E.W. 1985. "Social Science Analysis and the Formulation of Public Policy: Illustrations of What the President 'Knows' and How He Comes to 'Know' It." In Hausman and Wise, eds, 257–72.

Suppes, P., and J.L. Zinnes. 1963. "Basic Measurement Theory." In R.D. Luce, R.R. Bush, and E. Galanter, eds, *Handbook of Mathematical Psychology*, vol. 1: 1–66. New York: Wiley.

Susskind, H. 1973. *Understanding Technology*. Baltimore: Johns Hopkins University Press.

Swedberg, R.M. 1990. *Economics and Sociology: Redefining Boundaries: Conversations with Economists and Sociologists*. Princeton, NJ: Princeton University Press.

– 1994. "Markets as Social Structures." In Smelser and Swedberg, eds, 255–82.

Szenberg, M., ed. 1992. *Eminent Economists: Their Life Philosophies*. Cambridge: Cambridge University Press.

Taha, H.A. 1992. *Operations Research: An Introduction*. 5th ed. Upper Saddle River, NJ: Prentice Hall.

Taylor, A.J.P. 1961. *The Origins of the Second World War*. London: Hamish Hamilton.

– 1963. *The First World War*. London: Hamish Hamilton.

Tellis, G.J., and P.N. Golder. 1996. "First to Market, First to Fail? Real Causes of Enduring Market Leadership." *Sloan Management Review* 37(2): 65–75.

Temin, P., ed. 1973. *New Economic History*. Hardmondsworth: Penguin Books.

Thomas, D.S. 1925. *Social Aspects of the Business Cycle*. London: George Routledge & Sons; New York: E.P. Dutton.

Thomas, H., and C. Logan. 1982. *Mondragón: An Economic Analysis*. London: Allen & Unwin.

Thomassin, P.J., J.C. Henning, and L. Baker. 1991. "Old Paradigms Revisited and New Directions." *Canadian Journal of Agricultural Economics* 39: 689–98.

Thurow, L.C. 1983. *Dangerous Currents: The State of Economics*. New York: Random House.

Tiger, L., and R. Fox. 1971. *The Imperial Animal*. New York: Holt, Rinehart & Winston.

Tillers, P. 1991. "Decision and Inference." *Cardozo Law Review* 13: 253–56.

Tilley, C.Y., and M. Shanks. 1987. *Re-Constructing Archeology: Theory and Practice*. Cambridge: Cambridge University Press.

Tilly, C. 1984. *Big Structures, Large Processes and Huge Comparisons*. New York: Russell Sage Foundation.

– 1990. *Coercion, Capital, and European States*. Oxford: Blackwell.

– 1996. "The Emergence of Citizenship in France and Elsewhere." *International Review of Social History*, supplement 2: 223–36.

Tinbergen, J. 1986. "Recent Innovations in Economic Science." In Deutsch et al., eds, 105–26.

Titmuss, R.M. 1971. *The Gift Relationship: From Human Blood to Social Policy*. London: Allen & Unwin.

– 1976. *Commitment to Welfare*. 2nd ed. London: Allen & Unwin.

Tobin, J. 1980. *Asset Accumulation and Economic Activity*. Chicago: University of Chicago Press.

Tocqueville, A. de. 1835. *Democracy in America*. 2 vols. New York: Vintage Books, 1945.

– 1945 [1856]. *The Old Regime and the French Revolution*. Oxford: Basil Blackwell, 1949.

– 1985. *Selected Letters on Politics and Society*. Ed. R. Boesche. Berkeley: University of California Press.

Tönnies, F. 1979 [1887]. *Gemeinschaft und Gesellschaft*, 8th ed. Darmstadt: Wissenschaftliche Buchhandlung. Trans.: *Community and Association*. London: Routledge & Kegan Paul, 1955.

Touraine, A. 1994. *Qu'est-ce que la démocratie?* Paris: Fayard.

Trevor-Roper, H.R. 1967. *Religion, the Reformation and Social Change*. London: Macmillan.

Triffin, R. 1980. "The Future of the International Monetary System." *Banca Nazionale del Lavoro Quarterly Review*, no. 132: 29–55.

Trigger, B.G. 1978. *Time and Traditions: Essays in Archeological Interpretation*. Edinburgh: Edinburgh University Press.

– 1989. *A History of Archaeological Thought*. Cambridge: Cambridge University Press.

– 1991. "Constraint and Freedom: A New Synthesis for Archaeological Explanation." *American Anthropologist* 93: 551–69.

– 1993. *Early Civilizations. Ancient Egypt in Context*. Cairo: American University in Cairo Press.

– 1995. "Archaeology and the Integrated Circus." *Critique of Anthropology* 15: 319–35.

Truesdell, C. 1984. *An Idiot's Fugitive Essays on Science*. Berlin, Heidelberg, and New York: Springer-Verlag.

Tsebelis, G. 1990. "Penalty Has No Impact on Crime: A Game-Theoretic Analysis." *Rationality and Society* 2: 255–86.

Tullock, G. 1967. "The General Irrelevance of the General Impossibility Theorem." *Quarterly Journal of Economics* 81: 256–70.

– 1971. "The Paradox of Revolution." *Public Choice* 1: 89–99.

Tversky, A. 1969. "The Intransitivity of Preferences." *Psychological Review* 76: 31–48.

– 1975. "A Critique of Expected Utility Theory: Descriptive and Normative Considerations." *Erkenntnis* 9: 163–73.

Tversky, A., and I. Simonson. 1993. "Context-Dependent Preferences." *Management Science* 39: 1179–89.

Upton, M. 1979. "The Unproductive Production Function." *Journal of Agricultural Economics* 30: 179–91

Uzzi, B. 1996. "The Sources and Consequences of Embededness for the Economic Performance of Organizations: The Network Effect." *American Sociological Review* 61: 674–98.

Vaitsos, C.V. 1974. *Intercountry Income Distribution and Transnational Enterprises.* Oxford: Clarendon Press.

van den Berg, A. 1988. *The Immanent Utopia. From Marxism on the State to the State of Marxism.* Princeton, NJ: Princeton University Press.

– 1997. "Is Sociological Theory Too Grand for Social Mechanisms?" In Hedström and Swedberg, eds, 204–37.

Vanek, J., ed. 1975. *Self-Management: Economic Liberation of Man.* Hardmondsworth: Penguin Books.

Veblen, T. 1961 [1899]. *The Theory of the Leisure Class.* New York: Modern Library.

Verba, S. 1996. "The Citizen as Respondent: Sample Surveys and American Democracy." *American Political Science Review* 90: 1–7.

Vining, D.R. 1986. "Social versus Reproductive Successs: The Central Theoretical Problem of Human Sociobiology." *Behavioral and Brain Sciences* 9: 167–216.

von Mises, L. 1949. *Human Action: A Treatise on Economics.* New Haven: Yale University Press.

– 1962. *The Ultimate Foundations of Economic Science.* Princeton: Princeton University Press.

von Neumann, J., and O. Morgenstern. 1953. *Theory of Games and Economic Behavior.* 3rd ed. Princeton: Princeton University Press.

von Schelting, A. 1934. *Max Webers Wissenschaftslehre.* Tübingen: J.C.B. Mohr.

von Weizsäcker, C.C. 1973. "Modern Capital Theory and the Concept of Exploitation." *Kyklos* 26: 245–81.

Vygotsky, L.S. 1978. *Mind in Society: The Development of Higher Psychological Processes.* Cambridge, MA: Harvard University Press.

Waldo, D. 1975. "Political Science: Tradition, Discipline, Profession, Science, Enterprise." In Greenstein and Polsby, eds, 1–130.

Wallace, M.D. 1979. "Arms Race and Escalation." *Journal of Conflict Resolution* 23: 3–16.

Wallace, W.L. 1984. *Principles of Scientific Sociology.* New York: Aldine.

Wallerstein, I. 1974. *The Modern World-System.* 3 vols. New York: Academic Press.

– 1991. *Unthinking Social Science: The Limits of Nineteenth Century Paradigms.* Cambridge: Polity Press.

Waltz, K.N. 1979. *Theory of International Politics.* Reading, MA: Addison-Wesley.

Walzer, M. 1977. *Just and Unjust Wars.* New York: Basic Books.

– 1983. *Spheres of Justice.* New York: Basic Books.

Wand, Y., and R. Weber. 1990. "Mario Bunge's Ontology as a Formal Foundation for Information Systems Concepts." In Weingartner and Dorn, eds, 123–50.

Wandsnider, L.A., ed. 1992. *Quandaries and Quests: Visions of Archaeology's Future.* Carbondale, IL: Center for Archaeological Investigations.

Warner, W.L. 1960 [1949]. *Social Class in America.* New York: Harper & Brothers.

Weber, M. 1920a [1904–5]. *Die protestantische Ethik und der Geist des Kapitalismus.* In *Gesammelte Aufsätze zur Religionssoziologie* 1: 1–206.

– 1920b. *Gesammelte Aufsätze zur Religionssoziologie.* 2 vols. Tübingen: J.C.B. Mohr.

– 1922. *Wirtschaft und Gesellschaft: Grundriss der Verstehende Soziologie.* 3 vols. 5th ed. Tübingen: J.C.B. Mohr, Paul Siebeck.

– 1988a [1913]. "Ueber einige Kategorien der vestehenden Soziologie." In *Gesammelte Aufsätze zur Wissenschaftslehre*, 427–74. Tübingen: J.C.B. Mohr.

– 1988b [1918]. "Der Sozialismus." In *Gesammelte Aufsätze zur Soziologie und Sozialpolitik*, 492–518. Tübingen: J.C.B. Mohr.

Wedgwood, C.V. 1967. *The Thirty Years' War.* London: Jonathan Cape.

Weinberg, S. 1993. *Dreams of a Final Theory.* New York: Pantheon.

Weinberger, O. 1985. "Freedom, Range for Action, and the Ontology of Norms." *Synthese* 65: 307–24.

Weingartner, P., and G.J.W. Dorn, eds. 1990. *Studies on Mario Bunge's Treatise.* Amsterdam and Atlanta: Rodopi.

Weitzman, M.L. 1984. *The Share Economy: Conquering Stagflation.* Cambridge, MA: Harvard University Press.

Weldon, J.C. 1988. "The Classical Theory of Distribution." In Asimakopulos, ed., 15–47.

Wellman, B. 1983. "Network Analysis: Some Basic Principles." In R. Collins, ed., 155–200.

Wendt, A.E. 1987. "The Agent-Structure Problem in International Relations Theory." *International Organization* 41: 335–70.

West Churchman, C., R.L. Ackoff, and E.L. Arnoff. 1957. *Introduction to Operations Research*. New York: John Wiley & Sons.

White, H[arrison]. 1981. "Where Do Markets Come from?" *American Journal of Sociology* 87: 517–47.

White, H[ayden]. 1978. *Tropics of Discourse*. Baltimore: Johns Hopkins University Press.

White, L[eslie]. 1975. *The Concept of Cultural Systems: A Key to Understanding Tribes and Nations*. New York: Columbia University Press.

Whyte, W.F., and K.K. Whyte. 1988. *Making Mondragón*. Ithaca, NY: ILR Press, Cornell University.

Wiener, N. 1994. *Invention: The Care and Feeding of Ideas*. Cambridge, MA: MIT Press.

Wiles, P. 1973. "Cost Inflation and the State of Economic Theory." *Economic Journal* 83: 377–98.

Wiles, P., and G. Routh, eds. 1984. *Economics in Disarray*. Oxford: Blackwell.

Wilkinson, R.G. 1994. "Divided We Fall: The Poor Pay the Price of Increased Social Inequality with Their Health." *British Medical Journal* 308: 1113–14.

Willer, D. 1987. *Theory and the Experimental Investigation of Social Structures*. New York and London: Gordon & Breach.

Wilson, E.O. 1975. *Sociobiology: The Modern Synthesis*. Cambridge, MA: Belknap Press.

Wilson, I. 1993. "Strategic Planning Isn't Dead – It Changed." *Long Range Planning* 27: 12–24.

Wolff, P. de. 1967. "Macroeconomic Forecasting." In H. Wold et al., *Forecasting on a Scientific Basis*, 191–390. Lisboa: Fundaçao Calouste Gulbenkian.

Woolgar, S. 1986. "On the Alleged Distinction between Discourse and Praxis." *Social Studies of Science* 16: 309–17.

Wootton, B. 1945. *Freedom under Planning*. Chapel Hill, NC: University of North Carolina Press.

World Commission on Environment and Development. 1987. *Our Common Future* [Brundtland Report]. Oxford and New York: Oxford University Press.

Wright, W. 1992. *Wild Knowledge: Science, Language, and Social Life in a Fragile Environment*. Minneapolis: University of Minnesota Press.

Zagorin, P. 1990. "Historiography and Postmodernism: Reconsiderations." *History and Theory* 29:263–74

Zamagni, S. 1987. "Economic Laws." In J. Eatwell et al., eds, 2: 52–4.

Zeitlin, I.M. 1968. *Ideology and the Development of Sociological Theory*. Englewood Cliffs, NJ: Prentice-Hall.

Zelditch, M., Jr, and J. Butler Ford. 1994. "Uncertainty, Potential Power, and Nondecisions." *Social Psychology Quarterly* 57: 64–73.

Zhukow, E. 1983. *Methodology of History.* Moscow: USSR Academy of Sciences.

Zuckerman, H. 1977. *Scientific Elite: Nobel Laureates in the United States.* New York: Free Press.

– 1988. "The Sociology of Science." In Smelser, ed., 511–74.

Zwerdling, D. 1980. *Workplace Democracy.* New York: Harper & Row.

Index of Names

Index of Subjects